DOCUMENTS
RELATING TO THE
COLONIAL HISTORY
OF THE
STATE OF NEW JERSEY,

FIRST SERIES - VOLUME XXXII

CALENDAR OF NEW JERSEY WILLS,
VOLUME III 1751-1760

A. Van Doren Honeyman

HERITAGE BOOKS
2008

HERITAGE BOOKS
AN IMPRINT OF HERITAGE BOOKS, INC.

Books, CDs, and more—Worldwide

For our listing of thousands of titles see our website at

www.HeritageBooks.com

Published 2008 by
HERITAGE BOOKS, INC.
Publishing Division
100 Railroad Ave. #104
Westminster, Maryland 21157

Copyright © 1924 A. Van Doren Honeyman

Other books by A. Van Doren Honeyman:

Documents Relating to the Colonial History of the State of New Jersey, Calendar of New Jersey Wills, Volume II, 1730-1750

Documents Relating to the Colonial History of the State of New Jersey, Calendar of New Jersey Wills, Volume IV: 1761-1770

Documents Relating to the Colonial History of the State of New Jersey, Calendar of New Jersey Wills, Volume V: 1771-1780

The van Doorn Family (Van Doorn, Van Dorn, Van Doren, Etc.) in Holland and America, 1088-1908

CD: Joannes Nevius and His Descendants

CD: The van Doorn Family (Van Doorn, Van Dorn, Van Doren, Etc.) in Holland and America, 1088-1908

All rights reserved. No part of this book may be reproduced or transmitted in any form or by any means, electronic or mechanical, including photocopying, recording or by any information storage and retrieval system without written permission from the author, except for the inclusion of brief quotations in a review.

International Standard Book Numbers
Paperbound: 978-0-7884-0122-0
Clothbound: 978-0-7884-7149-0

Introductory Note

This, the third volume of Abstracts of Wills of New Jersey, includes wills, administrations and guardianships from Jan. 1, 1751, to Dec. 31, 1760, a period of ten years. The matter was mostly prepared many years ago. The Editor has had added by another hand such omissions as were found by comparison with the published "Index of Wills, Inventories," etc., but has not personally made the Abstracts, and is not responsible for their accuracy. He has simply made the text available for the printer, as the Abstracts were not in the necessary technical shape for that purpose. As the Abstracts have been made by different persons employed, they are not always uniform in style, but alike give the necessary facts.

For the information of the curious it may be stated that Bibles, books and looking-glasses of that period, which have come down in families, are now greatly prized by possessors, and it is, doubtless, for that reason that these articles are so often noted in the transcripts made of inventories, and sometimes in wills.

The proper names of persons and places are believed to be given as in the originals. This early period was one, however, when names were spelled so indifferently that, in the case of the surnames of persons in heavy boldface type, arranged alphabetically, the reader may have to consider various ways of spelling in order to discover certain of the various surnames.

The Index does not repeat the surnames of those whose wills, etc., are abstracted, except in the instances where alternative spellings, in parentheses, are so extremely divergent from the alphabetical arrangement that they may not be otherwise discovered. Such alternative spellings, however, are not made by the Editor but by the abstracters and are not always to be considered as correct.

The total number of wills, intestacies, etc., abstracted for this volume is about 2400.

This publication is made possible by a Legislative appropriation of 1923.

EDITOR.

Calendar of New Jersey Wills

NOTE.—The books cited as Libers 1, 2, 3, etc., are of West Jersey wills. Those cited as Libers A, B, C, etc., are of East Jersey wills. Where matters beside recorded wills, such as inventories, accounts, etc., are noted, the originals may be found in the proper envelopes (arranged by counties), reference to which is made in the volumes (three volumes) entitled "Index to Wills," published by the Secretary of State in 1912 and 1913, which should always be consulted in case originals are to be referred to. Where the chief matter is not of record in books the envelope numbers are given herewith, although in Bergen, Essex, Middlesex, and Monmouth counties, the original papers are bound instead of being in envelopes. All original matters herein abstracted are to be found in the Secretary of State's office at Trenton.

1752, ——, ——. Aaronson, John, son of Joseph, dec'd, of Mansfield, Burlington Co. Petitions to have uncle, John Folwell, of same place, yeoman, made guardian.

1752, June 20. Bond of John Folwell as guardian; James Hammell, fellow-bondsman.   Burl. Wills, 4921 B.

1752, Mar. 7. Aaronson, Joseph, Jr., of Mansfield Twsp., Burlington Co., yeoman; will of. Wife, Ann. Children—John, Benjamin, Sarah, Mary, Hannah, all under age. Real and personal estate. Executors—the wife and Joseph Talman. Witnesses—Benjamin Talman, William White, Isaac De Cow. Proved Apr. 7, 1752.

1752, Mar. 28. Inventory, personal, £182.6.3, by David Rockhill and Benjamin Talman.

1758, Nov. 28. Account filed.   Burl. Wills, 4925 C; 5989 C.

1756, Jan. 9. Abbett, Abdon, of Piles Grove, Salem Co. Int. Bond of Martha Abbett as Adm'x, Aldon Abit (Abbett) fellowbondsman; both of said place.

1756, Jan. 13. Inventory, £99.3.3. Incl. a servant man and a right in timber bought, made by George Hildebrand and Samuel Lippincott.   Lib. 9, p. 95.

1751, Feb. 28. Abel, Andres, of "Rocksberg," Morris Co.; will of. Wife, Maria. Sons—Mathias, Paul, Michael and Andreas. Real and personal estate. Executors—Johannes Moelich and Philip Weiss, who also sign as witnesses. Proved April 23, 1751. (In German.)   Lib. 7, p. 60.

1751, Apr. 9. Inventory, £183.9.6, by Baltis Bickel and Jacob Shipman.

1759, Apr. 26. Abit, Martha, of Piles Grove, Salem Co., widow; will of. Children—Martha Orsborn (eldest daughter), Hannah Abit, Mary Orsborn, Kizia Abit, Benjamin Abit (youngest son, under age) and Joseph Abit; latter sole Executor. Personal estate. Legacy to

Elizabeth Thompson. Witnesses—Abdon Abit, Benjamin Abit and Abigail Commines. Proved June 6, 1759.   Lib. 9, p. 361.

1760, May 13. **Ackerman, David,** of Peramus, Bergen Co., yeoman; will of. Wife, Margaret. Children—Abraham (oldest son), Garret, David, Lawrence, Jannetie Ackerman (alias van Voorhis), Altie Ackerman (alias van Blerkum). Real and personal estate, including "a great household Bible." Executors—son David and son-in-law, Jacob van Voorhis. Witnesses—Will. Cairns, Don Cairns and Cornelia Cairns. Proved Nov. 25, 1760.   Lib. G, p. 332.

1760, Aug. 18. Inventory of personal estate, £107.6.9, by Will. Cairns and Johannes Ackerman.

1751, Apr. 9. **Ackerman, Johannes,** of Peramus, Bergen Co., blacksmith; will of. Wife, Rachel. Brothers—Abraham, Garret, David, and Lawrence Ackerman; sisters, Jannite and Altie. Real and personal estate. Executors—father, David Akerman, and uncle, Alebartus Terhune. Witnesses—Jan van Voorhees, Albert C. Zabriski, Will. Cairns. Proved August 20, 1751.   Lib. E, p. 542.

1751, Sept. 23. Inventory of estate—real, £320, personal, £312, incl. a "decriped" negro, £10; made by Roelof Westervelt and Will. Cairns.

1760, Dec. 11. **Ackerman, Johannis,** of Bergen Co., (dec'd June 18, 1760). Inventory of personal estate, £85.17.0, made by Executors, Abraham L. Ackerman and Abraham Abraham, and appraised by Allebartis Ter Huyn and Reynier van Giese.   Bergen Wills, 400 B.

1758, May 26. **Ackerman, Thomas,** of Peramus, Bergen Co., wagen maker; will of. Lot of land on the Plains to brother Abraham Ackerman; also the vest and "bretches," mounted with silver buttons; and bequeath to father a pair of leather "bretches." Other legacies to Cornelius Demarest and his wife, Marttie (sister to testator), to uncle David Abraham Ackerman, to Abraham Storm, and sister Altie. Brother, Abraham, and Cornelius Demereast. Executors. Witnesses—William Hoppe, Antie Hopper and Will. Cairns. Proved March 27, 1759.   Lib. G, p. 53.

1758, June 29. Inventory by Abraham van Boskerk and Will. Cairns, including 28 acres of land, £45; vest and "bretches," with silver buttons, £5; suit of broad cloth, £4; other clothing, £5, and other personal property, £38.9.2.

1752, Dec. 28. **Adams, John,** of Bedminster, Somerset Co.; will of. Wife, Elizabeth. Children—Matthew, William, Margaret, Mackdole, James, Samuel. Legacy to Ephrem Mackdole (McDowell). Real and personal estate. Son, Mathew, sole Executor. Witnesses—Ephrm. Mackdowel, James O'Harah, William Adams. Proved Dec. 24, 1753.
Lib. F, p. 161.

1750, Aug. 1. **Addams, Rebecah,** of Great Egg Harbour, Gloucester Co., widow; will of. Children—Abigail Somers, Isaac, Sarah Covenover, Elizabeth van Gelder, Ester Roberson and Joseph. Grandchildren—Sarah Roberson, and Ester Hickman. Grandson-in-law, David, son of Jeremiah Addams, dec'd; great-grandson, John Hickman. Personal estate. Son, Joseph Addams, sole Executor. Witnesses—Richard Devenny, Sarah Ireland, John Lumley. Proved June 28, 1754.   Lib. 7, p. 473.

CALENDAR OF WILLS—1751-1760 7

1754, Feb. 8. Inventory, £31.15.11, made by Edmund Cordeary and John Lee.
1754, Dec. 28. Account by Executor, Joseph Addams. Amount—£40.15.9.

1755, Jan. 7. Addis, Thomas, of Burlington Co. Int. Bond of widow, Ann Addis, as Adm'x; William English, yeoman, fellowbondsman, both of said Co. Lib. 8, p. 87.
1755, Jan. 18. Inventory, £15.9.9., incl. a violin; made by Jacob Haiys (Hayse) and Walter Vanshiver.

1749, Oct. 12. Afflack, John, of Woodbridge, Middlesex Co., tailor; will of. Brothers—William Afflack, living at Rumford; Paul Afflack, of Rottenton, near White Haven and Robert Afflack. They and Robert's son. (a mason by trade), of the Parish of Cleeter, in the Island of England, made heirs of the personal estate. Executors—brother Robert, William Browon and David Edgar, of Woodbridge. Witnesses—John Rolph, Benjamin Pack, David Inslee. Proved Nov. 8, 1751. Lib. F, p. 5.
1751, Nov. 11. Inventory, £797.8.10¾., incl. bond of Isaac Latorch for £300, equal to £344.6.8. Jersey money; of Henry Patterson, £142.15.8. Jersey. Made by William Jackson and David Inslee. (Afflack died October 6, 1751).

1760, May 29. Agnew, William, of Somerset Co. Int. Sarah, widow, authorizes her brother, Peter Ayers, to administer on late husband's estate.
1760, May 31. Bond of Peter Ayers as Am'r; Levi Ayers fellowbondsman, both of Somerset Co., yeomen.
1760, June 5. Inventory, £36.4 by John Collyer and Abraham Southard. Som. Wills, 237 R.

1754, Nov. 10. Aikman, John, of Morris Co.; will of. Wife, Jean. Children—William, Alexander, and three daughters, names not given. Grandson—William Aikman. Real and personal estate. Executors—Samuel Niblet and Alexander Aikman. Witnesses—William Gamble, Samuel McElrath, Matthew Gillilance. Proved Dec. 9, 1755.
Lib. F, p. 302.

1760, Jan. 8. Aker, William, of Amwell, Hunterdon Co., yeoman; will of. Wife, Anne. Children—Peter (eldest son), and others not named. Executors—his wife and Peter Moor. Witnesses—Joseph Runyon, Philip Yoger, John Opdyck. Proved Feb. 20, 1760.
Lib. 10, p. 121.
1760, Jan. 17. Inventory, £186.2.6, by Joseph Runyon and John Opdyck.

1760, Oct. 17. Albertson, Isaac, of Newton, Gloucester Co., yeoman; will of. Children—Isaac, Enoch, Nehemiah (under age) and Lætitia. Real and personal estate. Executors—son Isaac and brother, Jacob Albertson. Witnesses—Achsach Siddons, Jonathan Albertson, J. Harrison. Proved Nov. 24, 1760. Lib. 10, p. 408.
1760, Oct. 31. Inventory, £948.16.4, incl. bonds and book debts, £278.6.1; gold buttons, silver teaspoons and silver tongs, £2.10; 8 negroes, £235; made by J. Harrison and John Mickle.

1760, June 6. Albertson, Nicholas, of Hunterdon Co. Int. Inventory, £111.12.5., incl. book debts and notes, £45.3.1, made by Chas. Hoff, Jr., and Benjamin Opdyke.

1760, June 6. His widow, Anglechea Albertson, relinquishes administration of estate to her son, Garret Albertson.

1760, June 17. Bond of Garret Albertson of Bethlehem, said Co., as Adm'r; Constantine ONeill of same place, fellowbondsman.
Lib. 10, p. 462.

1754, Mar. 12. Albertson, William, of Newton Township, Gloucester Co., yeoman; will of. Wife, Hannah. Children—William, Sarah, both under age and an expected child. Sisters—Sarah and Ann Albertson. Brother—Nathan Albertson. The last two under age. Home farm on Newton Creek to go to brother Simeon, Thomas Dennis and John Doron (?); other real and also personal property. Executors—the wife and Jacob Albertson. Witnesses—Hugh Jones, Wm. Harrison, Jr., Jos. Harrison. Proved June 18, 1754. Lib. 8, p. 109.

1754, Apr. 18. Inventory, £527.0.11, incl. bonds, book debts and cash, £84.17.1.; a negro woman, £45.; a watch £9.; made by Samuel Harrison and John Mickle.

1758, Sept. 11. Alderman, William, of Salem Co.; will of. Wife, Abigail. Children—William, Joel, Sarah, Mary, Rachel, Elizabeth, all under age, Susanna, Tabitha, and Abigail. Real and personal estate. Executors—the wife and Jacob Elwell. Witnesses—James Arans, Richard Stonebanks, Matt'w Jones. Proved April 24, 1759.
Lib. 9, p. 374.

1759, Apr. 7. Inventory, £222.7.8., incl. books, £3.5.6., by Jacob Du Bois and Thomas Mayhew.

1745, Mar. 13. Alexander, James, of New York City; will of. Real and personal estate in large amounts. Lengthy will. Mentions wife, Mary; son-in-law, John Provost; sons, James, deceased and William; daus., Anne, Elizabeth, Katherine, Susannah, Mary. Executrix—wife, Mary Alexander. Witnesses—Arch'd Kennedy, Mary Kennedy, Evert Bancker.

1748, Feb. 17. Codicil. Dau., Anne, had died since will of 1745. Witnesses—Arch'd Kennedy, John Lewis, Abm. Cool.

1749, Sept. 29. Codicil. Same witnesses as in 1748.

Will and codicils recorded in Essex Co., May 3, 1756.
Lib. F, p. 345.

1756, July 27. Alexander, Mary, of New York City, widow of James Alexander, Esq.; will of. Mentions—eldest son John Provost, merchant, of New York City; late son David; son William Alexander; eldest dau., Mary Livingston, (wife of Peter Van Brugh Livingston, merchant); dau., Elizabeth (wife of John Stevens of New Jersey, merchant); dau., Catherine Parker, and her two ch., Clarinda and Bristoll; youngest dau., Susannah; "my negro wench called Phillis and her son called London; also my negro man called Sharper." Real and personal estate. Executors—son William and four daughters—Mary, Elizabeth, Catherine and Susannah. Witnesses—Corn's C. Wynkoop, Evert Bancker, Jr., John Taylor, Jr., Al. Lodge.

1758, Feb. 27. Codicil (very lengthy, chiefly concerning his son-in-law Peter Van Brugh Livingston). Witnesses—Henry Ludlow, Evert Bancker, jr., John Taylor, Jr.

CALENDAR OF WILLS—1751-1760 9

1760, Feb. 19. Codicil. Witnesses—William Livingston, Evert Bancher, Jr., Jacob De Witt. Will and codicils recorded in Middlesex Co. May 16, 1760. Lib. G, p. 199
    1762, Nov. 3. William Alexander, Esq., Earl of Stirling, qualified as Executor.

1759, Mar. 26. Allen, Benjamin, of Greenwich, Gloucester Co., yeoman; will of. Wife, Patience. Children—Benjamin, Joseph and six others, not named; all but the first under age. Real and personal estate. Executors—the wife, Jacob Spicer and Alexander Randall. Witnesses—Jonathan Borden, Andrew Barnes, Enoch Hains. Proved April 7, 1759. Lib. 9, p. 197.
    1759, Apr. 2. Inventory, £285.5.3., incl. a silver watch, £5., by Edward Hollinshead and Enoch Haines.
    1761, Sept. 15. Account by Patience Allen, who has increased it to £735.5.3, by selling 300 acres of land, and reports on hand balance of £213.15.

1759, July 28. Allen, Benjamin, of Allaways Creek, Salem Co. Int. Inventory, £181.8., incl. a clock and looking glass, £8.10., by Francis Test and Thos. Sayre.
    1759, Aug. 25. Bond of widows, Elizabeth Allen, as Adm'x; John Chandler and James Euenes (Evans), yeomen, fellowbondsmen, all of said Allaways Creek. Lib. 10, p. 449.

1754, Mar. 22. Allen, David, of Manasquan, Town of Shrewsbury, Monmouth Co., yeoman; will of. Wife, Catharine. Children—Mercy, wife of Thomas Jeffery, and Samuel. Brother, Joseph Allen, to be maintained. Real and personal estate. Executors—the son and son-in-law. Witnesses—Joseph Lawrence, Ananiah Gifford, Jr., Anthony Woodward, Jr., and Jacob Dennis. Proved April 18, 1760.
Lib. G, p. 425.
    1760, Mar. 5. Inventory, £817.1.9., incl. a looking glass, 6s, books, £2.4., bills, bonds, book debts, cash and notes £530.3.4.; made by James Irons, David Johnston and Samuel Osborn.

1760, Dec. 15. Allen, David and Elisha, sons of Jedediah, dec'd, petition, that John Dickason of Allaways Creek, said Co., yeoman, be appointed their Guardian.
    1760, Dec. 15. John Dickeson appointed Guardian. Bondsmen—Daniel Smith and Thomas Kelly, of Salem Co. Witnesses—G. Trenchard and G. Trenchard, Jr. Lib. 11, p. 23.

1753, Sept. 6. Allen, Elizabeth, widow of George, of Shrewsbury, Monmouth Co.; will of. Son, George, sole Executor. Grandchildren—Lydia Throckmorton; children of Adam Brewer, Hannah Lafetra, Elizabeth Morris, Rachel Lippincott, Mary Lafetra, Margaret, Deborah, Lazarus, George and William Brewer; Joseph Allen; George, son of George. Real and personal estate. Witnesses—Othniel Rogers, Uriah West and Jacob Dennis. Proved December 13, 1756. Lib. F, p. 416.
    1756, Dec. 17. Inventory, £159.16.3., incl. bonds and cash, £68.11.8., by Rich'd Lawrence, John Lippincott, Jr., and William Scott.

1758, Sept. 25. Allen, George, of Evesham Township, Burlington Co. Int. Inventory, £85.12.5., incl. a clock £2., by James Cattell and Abraham Allen. Lib. 9, p. 77.

1758, Oct. 12. Bond of Mary Allen as Adm'x; John Goldy, fellowbondsman, both of said Co.

1753, Feb. 1. Allen, Henry, of Shrewsbury, Monmouth Co., yeoman; will of. Wife, Sarah. Children—Nathan, John, West, Ryley, Margaret and Elizabeth, all under age. Real and personal estate. Executors—George Allen and Garritt Morford. Witnesses—John Holdsworth, Thos. Eatton, Parscan (Pearson) Halstead. Proved March 13, 1753. Lib. F, p. 124.

1744, Nov. 3. Allen, James, of "Aleways" Creek, Salem Co.; will of. Son, Aaron, under age, sole heir, of real and personal estate; if he dies a minor, land to go to testator's brother, Benjamin Allen, John Steward, sole Executor. Witnesses—Benjamin Bacon, John Denn, Sam'l Abbott. Proved February 21, 1751.
1751, Febr. 4. Inventory, £155.3.6., incl. 50 bush. of wheat, £8.15, by Nathaniel Chamles and Benjamin Allen. Salem Wills, 886 Q.

1751, May 21. Allen, Jedidiah, of Shrewsbury, Monmouth Co., cordwainer; will of. Wife, Phebe. Children—William, Ralph, Miriam and Jedediah. Real and personal estate. Executors—the wife and Joseph Potter. Witnesses—Humphry Wady, Jeremiah Tallman, Elihu Williams. Proved June 17, 1751. Lib. E, p. 539.
1751, June 4. Inventory, £673.19.7., incl. bonds, book debts and notes, £294.9.7; two looking glasses and tea things £1.8.; books £1.3; the time of an apprentice, £6.; made by Joseph Parker and Joseph Corlies.
1760, Aug. 16. Account by Executors, £702.12.3¼. Land sold to Wm. Lippincott, £72.15.0.

1759, Jan. 20. Allen, Jedidiah, of Manenton, Salem Co.; will of. Wife, Mary. Children—Judiah, David, Elisha, Champles, Jonathan, Benjamin, Elizabeth, Rebecah and Mary; Champles, Jonathan and Benjamin under 13 yrs. of age. Real and personal estate. Executors—Preston Carpenter and Charles Fogg. Witnesses—Isaac Sharp, Daniel Huddy and John Beesly. Proved March 3, 1759. Lib. 9, p. 364.

1753, Jan. 30. Allen, John, of Springfield, Burlington Co., yeoman. Int. Bond of widow, Mary, of Springfield as Adm'x; John Butcher and Matthew Allen, both of said Co., yeomen, fellowbondsmen.
Lib. 7, p. 307.

1756, Nov. 26. Allen, Jonah, of Pequanack Township, Morris Co. Int. Sarah, widow, resigns her right to administer to Jacob Ford, principal creditor. Lib. F, p. 433.
1756, Dec. 4. Bond of Jacob Ford as Adm'r; William Gamble, fellowbondsman, both of Morris Co.

1758, Feb. 8. Allen, Jonathan, of the Borough of Elizabeth Town, Essex Co.; will of. Wife, Elizabeth. Children—Matthias, Charles and Mary Michel. Grandson, Joseph, son of Joseph Edwards. Homefarm between Charles Toundley, dec'd., the road and Benjamin Trotter, dec'd; 16 acres adjoining John Chanler and Hanry Broodwell;

personal property, incl. a gold ring. Executors—the wife and son, Matthias. Witnesses—Humphrey Spining, Samuel Smith, Richard Tounley. Proved Febr. 18, 1758. Lib. F, p. 514.

1760, July 26. Allen, Matthew, of Hancock Township, Burlington Co. Int. Robert Allen, Administrator. Lib. 10, p. 43.
1760, Aug. 8. Inventory, £64.6.10½., incl. bonds and book debts, £30.10.3.; a silver watch, £5.10; a Bible, 5s; made by Marmeduke Fort and John Goldy.

1760, July 26. Allen, Robert, of (paper destroyed). Int. Bond of Robert Allen, son of, as Adm'r; Thomas Robinson, fellowbondsman, both of Burlington Co. Burl. Adm'x Bonds.

1756, Nov. 17. Allen, William, of Bethleham, Hunterdon Co.; will of. Wife and children, of whom only son William is named, being appointed Executor with Charles Hoff, Jr. Witnesses—John Cowan, Martha Erwine, Thomas Allen. Proved Dec. 3, 1756. Lib. 8, p. 470.
1756, Dec. 1. Inventory, £93.17.7., incl. 2 Bibles, Alen's Alarm, etc., by Abraham Bonnel and John Cowan.
1758, June 2. Account by acting Executor, William Allen, £95.12.2.

1750, July 13. Allin, Benjamin, of Evesham Township, Burlington Co.; will of. Wife, Rebecca. Children—Agnes, Sarah, Abraham. Granddaughter, Mary Allin, dau. of son Benjamin, deceased. Executors—Son, Abraham Allin, and wife, Rebecca. Witnesses—Jacob Heulings, Jacob Howlings, Jr., Gab. Blond. Proved Mar. 3, 1753.
Burl. Wills, 5125 C.
1753, Feb. 23. Inventory, £364.12.0, by James Cattell and Joshua Ballinger.

1754, May 6. Alling, John, of Newark. Int. Martha, widow, Administratrix. Lib. F, p. 230.

1755, May 6. Allinson, Joseph, of Burlington City, yeoman; will of. Wife, Elizabeth, sole Executrix. Children—Peter, Joseph, Jacob, Samuel. Granddaughters—Elizabeth and Mary, daughters of dec'd son Thomas. Legacy to Mary, wife of James Cloather. Meadowland in said City, bought of Francis Smith; house and lot on Pearl Street, bought of Richard Wheat; ditto in High Street, bought of said Smith; personal property. Witnesses—John Saunders, John Hoskins, William Heulings. Proved July 28, 1756. Lib. 8, p. 311.

1752, Mar. 21. Allinson, Thomas, of Bridgetown, Burlington Co., blacksmith; will of. Wife, Mary; daughter, Elizabeth, under age; and expected child. Brothers—Peter, Jacob, Joseph and Samuel Allinson. Personal property. Executors—the wife and Thomas Atkinson, miller. Witnesses—Henry Paxson, Benj. Bispham, Thos. Lawrence. Proved March 14, 1754.
1754, Feb. 6. Inventory, £217.5.2½., incl. a negro girl, £20.; bills and bonds, £84.17.3½.; made by John Budd and Patrick Reynolds.
Burl. Wills, 5353 C.

1759, May 30. Allison, John, of Oxford Township, Sussex Co. Int. Inventory, £522.2.6., incl. bills, bonds, book debts and cash, £331.3.2.; a negro, £20.; a Bible and other books; made by Edward Hunt and James Stinson. Lib. 9, p. 393.

1759, Sept. 1. Bond of widow, Sarah Allison, as Adm'x; Edward Hunt, fellowbondsman, both of Oxford.
1760, Oct. 10. Account by Adm'x, Sarah Allison, £193.2.6.

1756, Mar. 1. Alston, Benjamin, of Woodbridge, Middlesex Co., shipwright; will of. Mother, Rebecca Jaques, widow; sister, Mary, wife of George Brown. A lot of land, bought of Nathaniel Hubbell, Jr.; other real and personal property. Executors—the mother and brother-in-law, Brown. Witnesses—Daniel Moores, Thomas Brown and Nugient Kelly. Proved Dec. 20, 1760. Lib. G, p. 336.

1752, Sept. 14. Alston, Thomas, of Woodbridge, Middlesex Co., mariner; will of. Wife, Mary; an expected child. Sister, Mary, wife of Noah Bishop. If expected child dies without issue, or under age, estate goes to support of a school at Rahway. Real and personal property. Executors—the wife and brother, David Alston. Witnesses—Richard Wilkson, Jonathan Bishop and Joseph Shotwell. Proved Sept. 11, 1756. Lib. F, p. 377.

1760, May 6. Anderson, Benjamin. Int. Bond of Elizabeth Anderson, of Maidenhead, Hunterdon Co., as Adm'x; John Brailey, of same place, farmer, fellowbondsman. Lib. 10, p. 460.

1758, June 12. Anderson, Derrick, of "Redingtown," Hunterdon Co. Int. Inventory, £65.2., incl. accounts and bonds, £55.0.9., by Jacob v. d. Bilt, Marten Wyckof and Anderis Anderisen.
1758, June 13. Bond of his widow, Hannah Anderson, as Adm'x; Nicolas Wyckoff, of Redingtown fellowbondsman. Lib. 9, p. 175.

1757, Mar. 31. Anderson, Enoch, of Trenton, Hunterdon Co. Int. Bond of William Anderson, of Philadelphia Co., Penna., yeoman, as Adm'r; Benjamin Stevens, of Maidenhead, Hunterdon Co., farmer, fellowbondsman. Lib. 8, p. 398.

1751, Sept. 23. Anderson, Jacob, of Worcester Co., Maryland, but now in Kent Co., upon Delaware, merchant; will of. Brother Isaack and children; sister Catherine and children; Jacob, son of brother Abraham. Robert, son of William Burton, and Joseph Carter, Executors for estate in Maryland; brother Isaack Anderson, Joseph Decoe and Samuel Johnson in the Jersies. Witnesses—Nicholas Powel, Rebecca Powel, Edward Norman, William Hazard. Proved in Kent Co., on Delaware, Sept. 27, 1751; sworn to in Hunterdon Co. by John Farnsworth as a true copy of original will, May 2, 1752. Lib. 7, p. 273.

1750, Sept. 12. Anderson, James, of Newtown, Gloucester Co.; will of. Wife, Mary, sole Executrix. Children—James, Isaac, John (under age), Andrew, Lydia and Ann. Land in New Castle Co., Penna., i. e., 250 acres, adjoining New Castle, and called Swanwick, also personal estate. Witnesses—Judith Brodrick, David Brodrick. Proved May 11, 1751. Lib. 7, p. 81.
1751, Apr. 30. Inventory, £195.4., incl. a looking glass, a Dutch servant man's time, £3; another servant's, £8; made by William Stow and Thomas Parker.

1759, Feb. 10. Anderson, Jonathan, of New Hanover, Burlington Co. Int. Bond of Eleanor Anderson as Adm'x; John Anderson and Benjamin Gibbs, fellowbondsmen. Lib. 9, p. 207.

1759, Mar. 19. Inventory, £114.13.6., incl. a servantman, £5., by Anthony Sykes and Benjamin Gibbs.

1754, Jan. 1. Anderson, Joseph, of "Alleways" Creek, Salem Co.; will of wife, Hannah. Children—Joseph, Isaac, Elizabeth, Mary, Esther, Thomas and Simon. Real and personal estate. Executors—the wife and John Chandler. Witnesses—John Fitzpatrick, John Chandler, Abraham Harris. Proved August 1, 1754.   Lib. 7, p. 532.
1754, Feb. 7. Inventory, £46.5., by John Fitzpatrick and Abraham Harris.
1754, Aug. 5.   John Chandler refuses to serve as Executor.

1759, May 1. Andrews, John, of the Town and County of Salem; will of. Wife, Phebe, to receive one-third of the "clear personal" estate; the other two-thirds to be divided between George Landman, of Queen Ann's Co., Maryland, John and Joseph Antrum, of Burlington Borough, Rebeccah, daughter of Thomas Norris, and his four negro slaves, who are conditionally manumitted. Erasmus Kent, sole Executor. Witnesses—John Paschall, Reese Williams, Joseph Gray and Joseph Kay. Proved May 15, 1759.   Lib. 9, p. 378.
1759, May 7. Inventory, £333.11.8., incl. 4 negroes, £120. by Edward Test and William Tufte.

1755, Mar. 1. Andrews, Peter, of Northampton Township, Burlington Co.; will of. Wife, Esther. Children—Thomas, Benajah, Mary, Temperance, Edward, Hannah, Elizabeth and Peter, apparently all under age. Real and personal estate. Executors—the wife and son, Benajah. Witnesses—Josiah Foster, Josiah White, John Woolman. Proved Dec. 6, 1756.   Lib. 8, p. 345.
1756, Dec. 14. Inventory, £262.15.8, incl. books; a lad's time, £5; cash and credits, £79.15.10; made by Joseph Lippincott and John Woolman.

1759, Nov. 28. Andrews, Samuel, of Deptford Township, Gloucester Co., tanner; will of. Wife, Phebe; son, Jacob (under age). Real and personal estate. Executors—the wife and brother, Thomas Andrews, who is also made guardian of the child or children, "if there be two or more of them." Witnesses—Hannah Andrews, George Warfle, William Wood. Proved Jan. 21, 1760.   Lib. 10, p. 78.
1760, Jan. 16. Inventory, £452.9.9., incl. bills and book accounts, £72.6.10., 245 hides in the yard, 26 dry do. in the tan house and 5 skins, £193.17.6; also books; made by William Wood and David Cooper.

1755, July 17. Andrews, Thomas, of Evesham, Burlington Co., yeoman; will of. Children—Dorcas, Amy, (wife of Ebenezer Borden), Ann (wife of Jacob Taylor, who have children Abram and Lydia). Son-in-law, Philipp Flick. Grandchildren, Andrews Hancock, son of dec'd daughter Patience; Hannah, Phebe, Elizabeth and Bulah, daughters of dec'd son Ebenezer. Real and personal estate. Executors—Francis Dudly, Philipp Flick (son-in-law) both of Evesham and Isaac Lippencut, of Chester Township. Witnesses—Alexander Ferguson, George Mires, James Parson (Pearson). Codicil of Feb. 24, 1757, makes a slight change. Witnesses—Abraham Mireover and Abraham Allen. Proved May 21, 1757.   Lib. 8, p. 379.
1757, May 17. Inventory, £149.14.6., incl. bonds and book debts, £25.3.3., by James Cattell and Silas Crispin.

1760, Mar. 6. Andrews, Thomas, of Deptford Township, Gloucester Co., farmer; will of. Wife, Catherine. Children—Thomas, Peter and Azubah, all under age. Executors—the wife, brother Benajah Andrews, and brother-in-law, Lawrence Webster. Witnesses—Chatfield Brown, Rebekah Wood, Rachel Wilkins. Proved August 1, 1760.
Lib. 10, p. 78.
1760, May 13. Inventory, £258.0.8., incl. books, by William Wilkins and William Wood.

1751, Apr. 15. Andrews, William, of Monmouth Co. Int. Account of the estate, £65.18.10., by John Andrews, as Adm'r. (See Vol. XXX. N. J. Archives, p. 21).

1760, May 18. Antram, Isaac, of Springfield, Burlington Co., yeoman; will of. Wife, Ann. Children—David (eldest son), John, Isaac, Job, Hester, all under age. Real and personal estate. Executors—the wife and brother, Thomas Antram. Witnesses—David Antram, George Herbert, John Burr, Jr. Proved July 7, 1760. Lib. 10, p. 56.
1760, Sept. 15. Inventory, £436.4.6, incl. bonds, £41.9.8., by Nathan Folwell and Jonathan Hough.

1759, Dec. 24. Antram, Thomas, Jr., of Springfield Township, Burlington Co. Int. Inventory, £569.7.6, incl. a silver watch, £5.; silver tea spoons; two servants, £20; notes due, £24.6.6; made by Dan'l Doughty and Jonathan Hough.
1759, Dec. 27. Bond of his widow, Margaret Antram, Adm'x; Abraham Leeds, of Evesham, Burlington Co., yeoman, fellowbondsman.
Lib. 9, p. 395.
1761, Feb. 17. Account by Adm'x, Margaret Antram, £569.7.6.

1752, Feb. 3. Applegate, Benjamin, of Nottingham Twsp., Burlington Co.; will of. Son, Thomas, 5 shillings and demand of 13 pounds; sons, Benjamin, William and Richard, 5 shillings each. Daughter, Johannah, a bed. Real and personal estate. Son Daniel to be put to a trade and, when 21, to have 1-3 of estate. Daughter Alse, when 18 and daughter Jomime, the rest. Executors—Richard Sparkes and Walter Ward. Witnesses—Samuel Redford, Elizabeth Redford, William Miller. Proved May 16, 1753. Burl. Wills, 5137 G.

1759, Mar. 1. Applegate, Joseph, of Windsor, Middlesex Co.; will of. Wife, Mary. Children—John, Alice Limming, William, Joseph and Moses. Personal estate. Money left by son Richard in the hands of John Ely, who is made sole Executor. Witnesses—John Brown, Archbald Silver and George Danser. Proved May 3, 1760. Lib. 10, p. 543.
1760, Apr. 28. Inventory, £75.12.9, by G. Danser and John Chamberlin.

1760, May 17. Appleton, Cornelius, Jr., of Burlington Co. Int. Bond of Joseph Appleton, of Nottingham, Burlington Co., carpenter, as Adm'r; Charles Axford, Jr., of Trenton, Hunterdon Co., fellowbondsman. Lib. 9, p. 455.
1760, May 17. Inventory, £76.9., incl. a silver watch and seal, £8.; silver snuff box and pair of gold sleeve buttons, £2.10; 3 pairs of silver buckles, £2.10., made by Charles Axford and Conrad Kotts.

1759, Dec. 30. Archad, Andrew, of Raccoon Creek, Greenwich Township, Gloucester Co., yeoman; will of. Brother, Israel Archad, heir

of real and personal estate, with Andrew, son of Peter and Elizabeth Matson as remainderman, and a legacy to Sarah Adams, daughter of sister Magdalene. Executors—cousin Jacob Orchad and John Derrickson. Witnesses—John Abra. Lidenius (Liedenes), Lawrance Lock, Christian Sarrin. Proved October 6, 1760. Lib. 10, p. 401.
1760, Sept. 20. Inventory, £106.10.11, by Thos. Denny and Lawrance Lock.

1759, Nov. 15. Archer, Amos, of Gloucester Co. Int. Inventory, £35.10.6., incl. "book debts," £17.16.6, by John Maxwell and Daniel Fortiner. Glou. Wills, 640 H.
1759, Nov. 17. Bond of Benjamin Archer as Adm'r; John Maxwell fellowbondsman, both of Haddonfield, said Co., gents.
Glou. Wills, 640 H.

1760, Feb. 15. Archer, Benjamin, of Tewksbury, Hunterdon Co.; will of. Wife, Meleson. Children—Jeremiah, Elizabeth, Hannah, Austen, Meleson (wife of Geresham Silver), John and Benjamin, the last two made Executors. Mentions John, son of eldest son Ananias, dec'd. Witnesses—Ralph Smith, Thomas Smith and Henry Smith. Proved May 20, 1760. Lib. 10, p. 584.
1760, ———, ———. Inventory of the estate; real (the plantation), £300; personal, £202.3.4., incl. a negro boy, £25.; 180 bush. of wheat, £54., made by William Harris and Thomas Smith.

1760, Nov. 9. Archer, Israel, of Greenwich Township, Gloucester Co.; will of. Makes cousin, Andrew Matson, son of sister Elizabeth Matson, heir of land and meadow, bought by brother Andrew Archer of John Ladd, and of other real property, dividing personal estate between sister Magdalen Morice's (?) children, Jacob, John, Mathias, and her eldest daughter (all children of Peter Morise), and children of sister Elizabeth, wife of Peter Matson, viz., Marcy, Judey and Ellenor. Executors—John Derexson and Thomas Denny. Witnesses—John Denny, Daniel Strang, Henry Hendrickson. Proved December 29, 1760. Lib. 10, p. 404.
1760, Nov. 19. Inventory, £210.10.1., incl. bills, bonds, book debts and cash, £183.9.3.; made by Jacob Archord and Lawrance Lock.

1760, Sept. 2. Archer, John, of Deptford Township, Gloucester Co., labourer. Int. Bond of widow, Sarah Archer, as Adm'x; Nixon Chattin, yeoman, fellowbondsman, both of said Township.
Lib. 10, p. 292.
1760, ———. Inventory, £15.18.6., incl. a Bible, by George Kemble and Samuel Ladd.

1756, Aug. 20. Arison, Mary, of Waterford, Gloucester Co.; will of. Daughter, Elizabeth Gibbs. Other beneficiaries are Sarah Atkinson, Mary, John, Hannah and Benjamin (children of Joseph Arison), William Atkinson, sister Rebecca Hutchin and Aaron Arison's three children, names not given. Personal estate. Executors—John Burroughs, Sr., and Isaac Burroughs. Witnesses—John McComb, Katherine Fennin, Robert Gilmore. Proved October 21, 1756. Lib. 8, p. 336.
1756, Oct. 4. Inventory, £224.14.11., incl. bonds, £122.19.10; a negro boy, £32; a negro girl, £25; made by Charles Farguison and John Burroughs, Jr.

1754, Jan. 29. Arnold, Stephen, of Morris Co., Int. Inventory, £149.15.7, incl. bond of Samuel Ludlom, of Mendom, £100; other debts, £19.13.6; 20 bush. of corn, £2.10; made by Samuel Day and Samuel Roberts.

1754, Feb. 16. Bond of Rachel, widow, as Adm'x; Samuel Arnold and Benjamin Freeman, fellowbondsmen, both of Morris Town.
Lib. F, p. 157.

1754, May 15. Account by Rachel Arnold, who has paid out £22.19.11.

1758, Nov. 17. Aronson, Benjamin, and Hannah, children of Joseph, of Burlington Co., deceased, petition for the appointment of James Atkinson, of Northampton, as their Guardian.

1758, Nov. 27. Bond of James Atkinson as such Guardian, Jonathan Jesse, fellowbondsman, both of said Co., yeoman.
Burl. Wills, 597 C, 6229 C.

1758, Nov. 28. Aronson, Joseph, of Mansfield, Burlington Co. Account of the estate, £182.6.3., by David Rockhill and his wife Anne, late Anne Aronson, Executrix of Joseph's last will; sold land for £230.

1751, Mar. 25. Arthur, Rev. Thomas, of New Brunswick, Middlesex Co. Int. Bond of Thaddeus Burr, of Fairfield, Conn., "grandfather by the mother to the son of," as Adm'r; Rev. Aaron Burr, of Newark, N. J., fellowbondsman.
Lib. E, p. 503.

1751, Sept. 21. Inventory, £23.11.6., incl. a tabby gown, £5; a black, a brown, a lutstring ditto, £2.10; a velvet rochet and hood, 15s.; cambrick, linen and muslin aprons, 56s.; made by James Smedly, Benjamin Wynkoop and Benjamin Darling.

1757, Dec. 8. Aten, Adrian, of Reading Township, Hunterdon Co.; will of. Wife, Jacobtie. Children—Ann, Derick, Hendrick, Mary, Cateline, John, Garret, Judah and Adrian. Real and personal estate. Executors—son Hendrick and brother-in-law, Peter Middagh. Witnesses—George Andreas Vierselius, Lowrens Lou (Low) and Jacob Mattison. Proved February 28, 1758.
Lib. 8, p. 526.

1758, Jan. 18. Inventory, £1042.0.11., incl. bills, bonds and book debts, £638.5.5; books £5.10; a negro boy, £40; made by Thomas Atkinson and Cornelius Wyckoff.

1760, Mar. 28. Atkinson, Joseph, of Springfield, Burlington Co.; will of. Wife, Sarah, sole Executrix. Children—William, Aaron, John, Mary, Sary, Elizabeth and Levina, the daughters all under age. Real and personal estate. Witnesses—Richard Gibbs, Samuel Atkinson, Jon. Fenimore. Proved April 23, 1760.
Lib. 10, p. 25.

1760, Apr. 23. Inventory, £708.2.3., incl. bills and bonds, £337.17.6; made by Jon. Fenimore and Samuel Atkinson.

1758, June 10. Atkinson, Rachel, of Chester Township, Burlington Co., widow; will of. Children—Lidia, Susannah, Abigail and John, all under age. Personal estate, incl. a gold ring, six silver teaspoons. Executors—brother Thomas Wallace and John Cox. Witnesses—Thomas Morton, James Toy. Proved June 22, 1758.
Lib. 8, p. 535.

1758, June 19. Inventory, £147.2.10, by Elias and James Toy.

CALENDAR OF WILLS—1751-1760 17

1754, July 26. Atkinson, Sarah, of Burlington Co. Int. Bond of Christian Willson as Adm'x; Richard Harrison, fellowbondsman, both of said Co. Lib. 7, p. 447.

1757, Oct. 15. Atkinson, Thomas, Sr., of Northampton, Burlington Co., miller; will of. Wife, Hannah. Children—Thomas, Rebekah, Hester and Hannah. Gristmill and land in Bridgetown, other real and personal estate incl. negroes. Executors—Henry Cooper and Edward Tonkin. Witnesses—Zachariah Rossell, Jr., Thos. Reynolds, Thos. Lawrance. Proved December 10, 1757. Lib. 8, p. 497.
    1757, Dec. 7. Inventory, of £204.1.3., incl. three negroes, £32; made by Joseph Mullen and Nicholas Toy.
    1760, Apr. 17. Account by Edward Tonkin, one of the Executors, who has sold the goods for £21.4.10. more than valued; adds book debts, £262.13, and has disposed of the real property, viz., house and lot in Bridgetown, £250.; three others ditto, £122; ditto, in Burlington, £135.5; share in the gristmill, £630, and other land, £132.12.

1754, Aug. 22. Atkinson, William, of Northampton, Burlington Co.; will of. Wife, Mary; daughters, Anne Scot, Elizabeth and Hope, the last two under age; an expected child. Real and personal estate. Executors—the wife and brother, Francis Shinn. Witnesses—Francis Venicombe, Lydia Lamb, John Woolman. Proved September 7, 1754. Lib. 7, p. 491.
    1754, Sept. 3. Inventory, £520.24, incl., bills, bonds and book debts, £255.12.2; made by Thomas Budd and George Briggs.

1752, ——— ——. Austen, Esther, daughter of Cornelius Austen, of "Fairefield" Township, Cumberland Co., blacksmith. Petition of, that Joseph Ogden, of the same place, yeoman, be appointed her Guardian. Lib. 7, p. 337.
    1752, Sept. 25. Bond of Joseph Ogden as Guardian; Thomas Ogden, fellowbondsman, both of Fairfield Township, yeomen.

1754, Janr. 24.—Axford, Elizabeth, of Salem Co. Int. Bond of Daniel Huddy, of Salem, merchant, as Adm'r; no fellowbondsman.
Lib. 9, p. 94.

1754, Nov. 26. Axtell, Henry, of Mendum, Morris Co.; will of. Wife, Jemima. Children—Henry (under age), Phebie, Hannah, Jemima, Bethanah, Calvin and Luther. Real and personal estate. Executors—Ebenezer Byram, John Cary, Isaac Babbit and Thomas Briggs of Mendum. Witnesses—Caleb Baldwin, Isaac Babbit, Jacob Cooke. Proved January 28, 1755. Lib. F, p. 247.

1755, June 12. Ayars, James, of Deerfield Township, Cumberland Co. Int. Hannah, widow of, refuses the administration, recommending Matthew Parvin, of said Twsp. as Adm'r. Same date, bond of Matthew Parvin, yeoman, as Adm'r; Silas Parvin, tavernkeeper, and Jonathan Sayre, shoemaker, fellowbondsmen, all of said Co.
    1755, June 18. Inventory, £194.5.9., incl. rent of the mill, £30.; made by John Miller and Hugh Dunn. Cumb. Wills, 109 F.

1759, Feb. 2. Ayars, John, of Hopewell Township, Cumberland Co.; will of. Divides real and personal estate between brother, Halbridge Ayars (sole Executor), sisters Sarah, Rebekah and Tabitha

2

(under age), cousins John and Abiiah, sons of Benjamin Ayars, (both under age), Hambilton and Rachel, children of Aaron Ayars, and Thomas, son of Joseph Bivins. House and 48 acres of land, adjoining Stephan Ayars; 38 a. bought of said Benjamin Ayars; 10 acres between William Ayars and John Jarmon; also personal estate. Witnesses—Joseph Bowen, Elias Robins, Elnathan Davis (4th). Proved March 13, 1759. Lib. 9, p. 252.

1759, ——, —. Inventory of personalty, £53.4.6., incl. a Bible, by Jacob More and John Carll.

1759, May 2. Ayars, Joshua, of Fairfield, Cumberland Co.; will of. Wife, Anne. Children—Seth (under age), Philipp, Esther Davis, Heziah and Deborah (last two under age), an expected child. Real and personal estate, incl. a silver tankard. Executors—the wife and son, Philipp. Witnesses—Joseph Swinney, Hannah Titsworth, Jonathan Davis. Proved May 24, 1759. Lib. 9, p. 256.

1759, May 23. Inventory, £422.11., incl. plate, £39., books £4; made by Abraham Smith and Jacob More.

1759, May 27. Ayers, Caleb, of Hopewell Township, Cumberland Co.; will of. Wife, Rebecca, sole executrix. Children—Aaron, Stephan, Halbridge, William, Sarah, Rebekah, Tabitha and Benjamin. Real and personal estate. Witnesses—Hugh Dunn, Jr., William Russell, Elnathan Davis (4th). Proved February 5, 1760. Lib. 10, p. 54.

1760, Febr. 4. Inventory, £200.11.2, by Richard Richardson and Howel Powel.

1760, Apr. 7. Ayers, Frazee, of Woodbridge, Middlesex Co.; will of. Wife, Phebe. Children—Elelus (son); daughters, Hume, Sarah, Phebe and Mary. Real and personal estate. Executors—the wife, Jonathan Frazee and Ruben Ayers. Witnesses—John Smith, Robert Ayers and James Clarkson. Proved May 5, 1760, when Jonathan Frazee refuses to act as executor. Lib. G, p. 216.

1754, Apr. 17. Ayers, Obadiah, of Woodbridge, Middlesex Co., carpenter; will of. First wife, a sister of Ezekiel Bloomfield; present wife, Mary, to be sole Executrix. Children—Susannah, Johannah, (both under age), and Daniel. Real and personal estate. Witnesses —William Bloodgood, Geach Bloodgood and William Kent. Proved February 1, 1760, when the widow, Mary Ayers refuses to act as Executrix, and Mary, wife of George Harriot, Daniel Ayers and Joanna Ayers, all children of Obadiah, agree, that George Herriot shall administer on the estate. Lib. G, p. 123.

1774, Dec. 31. Account, by George Harriat, Adm'r.

1758, July 11. Aynsley, William. Int. Adm'x., Elizabeth Aynsley, widow; bondsman, Platt Cramwell. Witnesses—Jas. Neilson and Anthony White. Essex Wills, 15437 G.

1754, May 9. Ayrest, Gunsley John. Int. Bond of Francis Hollinshead of Somerset Co., as Adm'r; John Warrell, Esq., of Trenton, Hunterdon Co., fellowbondsman. Hunt. Wills, 339 J.

1744, Jan. 8. Bacon, John, of Cumberland Co.; will of. Wife, Elizabeth. Sons—Thomas, John, David and Job, the last two under

age. Home farm, adjoining Joseph Bacon and Charles Davis; a lot, called Hazelwoode Neck; marsh adjoining Joseph Bacon and John Ware; another marsh between Joseph Bacon and uncle William Bacon; personal property. Executors—the wife, with sons Thomas and John. Witnesses—Peter Randol and Rich'd Wood, Junior. Proved March 1, 1755. Lib. 8, p. 122.
1755, Feb. 20. Inventory, £185,14.9, by Charles Davis and Philipp Dennis.

1758, Mar. 17. Bacon, Joseph, of Greenwich Township, Cumberland Co. Int. Inventory, £304.9.3, by Philipp Dennis and Charles Davis.
1758, Mar. 22. Bond of his widow, Margaret Bacon, as Adm'x; Philipp Dennis and Charles Davis, both of said Township, fellow-bondsmen. Cumb. Wills, 146 F.

1753, Sept. 2. Badcock, Joseph, Sr., of Cape May Co., yeoman; will of. Wife, Mary. Children—Joseph, Rachel, Hannah, Naomi, Sarah and Mary. Real and personal estate. Executors—the wife and Jeremiah Hand. Witnesses—William Evans, Daniel Gerretsen, Job Garretson. Proved June 3, 1755. Lib. 8, p. 172.
1755, June 28. Inventory, £186.18.1., by Richard Smith and Jacob Spicer.
1759, Apr. 5. Account by Executors, who have increased estate by £40. for land sold, and £18. for sundries.

1759, Sept. 19. Badgley, George, Sr., of Elizabeth Town. Int. George, son, Adm'r, widow, Rachel, having renounced.
Lib. G, p. 129.
1759, Sept. 22. Inventory, £76.4.10, by Matthias Hetfield and William Winans.

1759, Sept. 7. Badgley, John, Sr., of the Borough of Elizabeth, Essex Co., yeoman; will of. Wife, Uphamey. Children—Anthony, William, John, Sarah, Mary, Phebe, Elisabeth, Katherine, Hannah and Uphaney. Grandsons—Moses and John Badgley. Granddaughter, Jean. Real and personal estate. Executors—son Anthoney and son-in-law Abraham Clarke (3d). Witnesses—Anthony Badgley, Jr., Robert Badgley, Henry Clarke, Jr. Proved October 16, 1759.
Lib. G, p. 102.
1759, Oct. 17. Inventory, £195.15.5, by Samuel Miller and John Cory, Jr.

1758, Aug. 2. Bailey, Daniel, of Bethlehem, Hunterdon Co. Int. Bond of Ralph Johnson, of Bethlehem, farmer, as Adm'r; James Thatcher, of Amwell, said Co., fellowbondsman.
1758, Aug. 23. Inventory, £49.3.9, incl. bonds and book accounts, £32.4.9., by John Dusinberry and William Everitt.
Hunt. Wills, 433 J.

1760, Jan. 29. Baker, Henry, of Woodbridge Township, Middlesex Co., cordwainer; will of. Wife, Mary. Sons—Henry, Jacob, Cornelius, Matthius and William, the last two under age. Real and personal estate. Executors—son, Henry, Cornelius Hetfield, of Elizabeth Town, and Jonathan Fraze, of Woodbridge. Witnesses—Jonathan, Jaques, Joseph Thorn and Edward Wilkes Jr. Proved April 7, 1760. Lib. G, p. 164.

1751, Aug. 12. Baker, John, of Burlington Co. Int. Inventory, £158.2, incl. a servant boy and girl, £26., by Thomas Moore and Thomas Budd.

1751, Aug. 31. Bond of widow, Barbara Baker, as Adm'x; Thomas Moore and Thomas Budd, cooper, fellowbondsman, all of Northampton. Lib. 7, p. 298.

1755, Dec. 25. Baker, Thomas, of the Borough of Elizabeth, Essex Co., yeoman; will of. Wife, Martha. Children—Thomas, Daniel, Martha (wife of Jeremah Muford), Phebe, Mercy and Patience. Granddaughter, Elizabeth, daughter of Elizabeth Brooks, dec'd. Real and personal estate. Executors—son Daniel and Timothy Whitehead, Esq. Witnesses—Thomas Baly, Samuel Headley, Benjamin Bonnel. Proved January 9, 1756. Lib. F, p. 310.

1756, Jan. 13. Inventory, £221.16.9 by Moses Thompson and Samuel Thompson.

1755, Apr. 9. Baldwin, Caleb, of Morris Co., yeoman; will of. Wife, Hannah. Children—Jabesh, Caleb, Mary and Phebie, all under age, and an expected child. Real and personal estate. Executors—the wife and brother-in-law, Capt. Joseph Beech. Witnesses—Samuel Baldwin, Daniel Cary, Beriah Cary. Proved January 6, 1758.
Lib. F, p. 507.

1758, Jan. 6. The widow, signing herself "Hannah Riky," declines to serve as executrix.

1758, Apr. 29. Inventory, £439.5.5, by Samuel Alling and John Crane.

1758, May 19. 2nd Inventory at New York, £72.17.8, by Abraham Bockee and Samuel Rogers.

1758, May —. At Stratford, 3rd Inventory, £365.0.1, by Theops, Nichols and Ezra Hawley; Joseph Forman, Adm'r.

Articles in Connecticut not inventoried, £18.18.9; deed for 16 acres in Litchfield Co., value unknown.

1758, Mar. 22. Baldwin, Caleb, of Newark, Essex Co., yeoman, now at Derby, New Haven Co., Conn.; will of. Wife, Jemime. Children—Jemime (under age), Jonathan, Noah and Eleazer. Real and personal estate. Executors—the wife and brother, Moses Baldwin. Witnesses—Samuel Ward, James Baldwin, Stephen Ward. Proved at Derby, Conn., April 10, 1758; probated by Thomas Fitch, Governor of Connecticut, May 18, 1758. Lib. F, p. 529.

1757, Dec. 1. Baldwin, James, of Waterford, Gloucester Co., yeoman. Int. Inventory, £89, by William Stone and Henry Wood.

1757, Dec. 12. Bond of Catherine Baldwin as Adm'x; William Stone and Henry Wood fellowbondsmen, all of Waterford. Lib. 8, p. 518.

1758, June 14. Baldwin, John, of Newark, Essex Co., yeoman; will of. Wife, Elisabeth. Children—Joseph, Dorcas, Johana, Mary and Elisabeth. Real and personal estate. Executors—the wife, Nathaniel Dod and David Harrison. Witnesses—Gershom Williams, Mary Baldwin, Joseph Dod. Proved September 23, 1758. Lib. F, p. 561.

1759, June 28. Baldwin, Matthias, of Elizabeth Town, Essex Co., tailor; Will of. Wife, sons and daughters; names not given; the children all under age. Real and personal estate. Executors—Caleb Halstead, Doctor Moses Blomfield, Job Stockton, Robert Ogden, Esq.,

CALENDAR OF WILLS—1751-1760   21

John Ross and Andrew Ross. Witnesses—Phebe Ross, Phebe Nuttman, George Einott. Proved September 5, 1759.
1759, July 26. Inventory, £126.11.9, by Matthias Hetfield and William Winans.

1752, Sept. 2. Ball, Aaron, of Newark, Essex Co., blacksmith; will of. Wife, Hannah. Children—Silas, Joseph, Aaron, Kezia, Margaret, Deborah and Hannah, all under age. Real and personal estate. Executors—the wife, brother Timothy Ball and Moses Baldwin. Witnesses—John Tichenor, Jonas Ball, David Campbell. Proved Dec. 30, 1752.   Lib. F, p. 82.
1752, Dec. 28. Inventory, £182.18.2, by Moses Baldwin, Samuel Crowell, Jonas Ball.

1755, Nov. 1. Ball, Jonathan, of Newark, Essex Co.; will of. Wife, Jemima. Children—Daniel, Sarah, Hannah, Rebecka, Catherine and Jemima, all under age. Real and personal estate. Executors—the wife and Stephen Baldwin. Witnesses—Samuel Crane, John Crane, Jr., Jonathan Sergeant. Proved July 15, 1757.   Lib. F, p. 455.

1752, June 1. Ball, Timothy, of Newark, Essex Co.; will of. Wife, Esther. Children—John, Uzal, Sarah, Charity and Rachel. Real and personal estate. Executors—the wife, brother Aaron Ball, Nathaniel Ball. Witnesses—Jonathan Tompkins, Jedidiah Hedden, William Green. Proved February 3, 1758.   Lib. F, p. 487.
1758, Feb. 7. Inventory, £414.12.5, by Timothy Whitehead and Josiah Crane.

1758, Jan. 3. Ballinger, Amariah, of Debtford Township, Gloucester Co., yeoman; will of. Wife, Mary. Children—Samuel, Ameriah (both under age), Elizabeth, Mary, Sarah and an expected child. Son and daughter-in-law (stepchildren?) Susannah and Thomas Ashbrook. Real and personal estate. Executors and guardians of the two sons—brother, Joshua, and Thomas Ballinger. Witnesses—George Kemble, Isaac Ballinger, Jos. Goldy. Proved April 2, 1760.
Lib. 9, p. 441.
1760, Mar. 24. Inventory, £273.3, by Wm. Davis and Sam. Ladd.

1751, Mar. 21. Baly, Samuel, of Elizabeth Borough, Essex Co., shop keeper; will of. Wife, Abigail; father, Thomas Baly. Children—Phebe, Henry, Jonathan. Real and personal estate, incl. a Palatine servant girl; sawmill on West branch of Rahaway River; homefarm, adjoining Thomas Garner. Executors—the wife, brother, Thomas Baly and Isaac Lyon. Witnesses—Nathaniel Potter, David Horton, Benjamin Bonnel. Proved April 4, 1751.   Lib. E, p. 508.

1759, Oct. 3. Barber, Aquilla, Jr., of Pilesgrove, Salem Co.; will of. Wife, Hannah. Children—Aquilla, James, both under age; daughters' names not given. Real and personal estate. Executors—the wife and George Lawrance. Witnesses—Daniel White, Malachi Herner and Edward Draper. Proved January 24, 1760.   Lib. 10, p. 513.
1760, Jan. 1. Inventory, £166.15.6, by Edward Draper and Daniel Bassett.

1750, Dec. 11. Barber, Samuel, of Amwell, Hunterdon Co.; will of. Wife, Alledee. Children—John, Cornelius, Susannah, Mary, Elizabeth, Rachel and an expected child. Real and personal estate. Executors—the wife and son John. Witnesses—Joseph Bell, George Huston, J. Graham. Proved May 18, 1751. Lib. 7, p. 76.

1751, May 15. Inventory, £140.4.2, incl. silver clasps and vest buttons; Dutch books, £1.; 4 bush. of wheat; by Peter Prall and Derick Hogeland.

1753, Jan. 16. **Barber, William,** of Lebanon, Hunterdon Co. Int. Inventory, £52.19, by Nathaniel Foster and Andrew Bray.

1753, Jan. 18. Jemima Barber declines administration in favour of her father, John Burroughs.

1753, Febr. 1. Bond of John Burroughs (Burrows) of Trenton Township, Hunterdon Co., tanner, as Adm'r; Samuel Henry, of Trenton, merchant, fellowbondsman. Lib. 7, p. 418.

1754, Mar. 18. **Bard, John,** Int. Inventory, £15.10.7., by James Shreve and Israel Butler.

1754, Mar. 19. Bond of James White, carpenter, as Adm'r; James Shreve, yeoman, fellowbondsman, both of said County.
Burl. Wills, 5365 C.

1755, Feb. 19. Account of the estate by the administrator, James White.

1754, Feb. 19. **Barkelow, Conrod,** of Middlesex Co. Citation to Margaret, widow, and Daniel, son of, as surviving executors of his will, to prove the same. Lib. F, p. 157.

1754, Mar. 14. Letter from Daniel Barcolowe at New Brunswick, pleading his mother's illness for not having come in obedience to the citation.

1754, Mar. 28. Letter from Daniel Barricklo, at Ten Mile Run, reporting, that his house had been broken into and his father's will stolen, with other papers.

1755, Apr. 21. **Barker, William,** of Salem Town and Co. Int. Bond of Richard Barker, of Cumberland Co., next of kin, Adm'r; Samuel Wood, of Salem Co., fellowbondsman. Lib. 9, p. 86.

1757, Feb. 25. **Barnes, Samuel,** of Fairfield, Cumberland Co.; will of. Sons—Jonathan, Abraham, (sole executor), John. Grandson, Thomas Barns. Real and personal estate. Witnesses—Richard Townsend, Phebe Bowen, Enuch Bowen. Proved January 30, 1758.
Lib. 8, p. 522.

1758, Jan. 12. Inventory, £164.14.5, by Joseph Daton and Jeremiah Buck.

1752, Apr. 11. **Barracliff, William.** Int. Bond of Josiah Furman as Adm'r; Richard Furman fellowbondsman, both of Trenton, Hunterdon Co., yeoman. Hunt. Wills, 305 J.

1757, Aug. 19. **Barratt, Caleb,** of Hopewell, Cumberland Co., yeoman; will of. Wife, Abigail. Children—Caleb, (under age), Joshua, James, Elizabeth Mulford, Hannah Hall, Abigail Shepard, Rebekah and Sarah. Real and personal estate. Executors—the wife and son Caleb. Witnesses—Caleb Ayars, Patience Bonham, Jonathan Davis. Proved January 12, 1758. Lib. 8, p. 505.

1758, Jan. 15. Inventory of the personal estate, £150.19., made by Caleb Ayars and Jonathan Davis.

CALENDAR OF WILLS—1751-1760   23

1751, Dec. 6. Barratt, James, of Manington, Salem Co. Int. Inventory, £124.15.1., incl. bills, bonds and book debts, £33.5.8; 60 bush. of Indian corn, £5.8.4.; made by Andrew Peterson and Francis Dunlap.
1751, Dec. 13. Bond of Catherine Barrott as Adm'x; Andrew Peterson, fellowbondsman; both of Maninton.   Lib. 9, p. 94.

1758, May 1. Barratt, Thomas, of Mannington, Salem Co., yeoman; will of. Sisters—Rachel, Gwin and Elizabeth Barratt; brothers spoken of, but not by name. Real and personal estate. Sister, Gwin Barratt, sole Executrix. Witnesses—Whitten Cripps, Jonathan Wright and Joseph Wilkinson. Proved August 16, 1758. Lib. 9, p. 103.
1753, Aug. 8. Inventory, £332.4.2., incl. bills, bonds, book debts and notes £316.7.11., made by Edmd Wetherby and Richard Woodnutt.
1764, Mar. 19. Account filed by Stephen Mulford, Ex'r of Gwin Barratt.

1753, Mar. 9. Barrett, Catherine, of Manington, Salem Co.; will of. Daughters—Catherine Taylor and Catherine Grimes (unmarried and under age). Personal property. Nicholas Philpott, sole Executor. Witnesses—John Roberts, Jeremiah Gellvin, Oliver Webb. Proved March 23, 1753.   Lib. 7, p. 542.
1753, Mar. 21. Inventory, £171.18.10, incl. accounts, bills, bonds and cash £130.19.1., by Jeremiah Baker and Jos. Wright.

1759, July 7. Bartleson, Sara, daughter of William of Manington, Salem Co., petitions that Peter Peterson, of Penn's Neck, said Co., be appointed her guardian. Bond of Peter Peterson as such guardian, Henry Jeanes and Gabriel Danielson fellowbondsmen, all of Penns Neck, yeomen.   Lib. 11, p. 24.

1759, Aug. 24. Barton, Edward, of Deptford Township, Gloucester Co.; will of. Wife, Elizabeth, sole Executrix. Children—Thomas, Sarah, John and William. Mother, Ann Barton. Personal property. Witnesses—John Engle, Jacob Evens, Isaac Ballinger. Proved October 15, 1759.   Lib. 9, p. 341.
1759, Sept. 11. Inventory, £251.13, by Isaac Ballinger and Wm. Davis.

1753, Dec. 31. Barton, John. Int. Inventory, £55.8.6, by James Mason and James Cattell.
1754, Jan. 18. Ann, widow, declines to administer on his estate in favour of their son, Edward Barton. Bond of Edward Barton as Adm'r; James Cattell, fellowbondsman, both of Evesham Township.
Lib. 8, p. 38.

1703, April 28. Bartram, Joseph, of Saddle River, Bergen Co.; will of. Wife, Ann. Children—John (only son), Mary (only daughter). Real and personal estate. Executors—son John and friend, James Board. Witnesses—Domini Conily, Thomas Hall, David Board.
1754, Oct. 21. Codicil. Names grandson, Henry Devenport and "oldest son of my daughter Mary" (not of age). Witnesses—Philip Tissa, Ephraim Beach, Joseph Woolcox. Will and codicil probated Oct. 11, 1760.   Lib. G, p. 325.

1759, Aug. 3. Bassnit, Sarah, of Burlington Co. Int. Bond of Daniel Ellis as Adm'r of estate left unadministered by Nathaniel

Thomas, dec'd., who became administrator after the death of Isaac Pearson, Executor of her last will. [See N. J. Archives, Vol. XXX, p. 38, for will]. Lib. 9, p. 450.

1751, Feb. 12. Bate, Mary, daughter of William, of Gloucester Co., 14 years old and upwards. Bond of Jonathan Zane, of Gloucester Co., merchant, as guardian; no fellowbondsman named. Lib. 6, p. 375.

1759, Dec. 24. Bateman, Job, of Fairfield, Cumberland Co.; will of. Wife, Martha; son Aaron. Bequests to James (? Jane) and Louina Bateman, Real and personal estate. Executors—the wife and David Sayre. Witnesses—Joseph Ogden, Joseph Bateman, Timothy Bateman. Proved January 21, 1760. Lib. 10, p. 53.
 1760, Janr. 15. Inventory, £200.19.3; incl. books, £3.5.6; book debts, £29.17.4; made by Joseph Ogden and David Westcote.
 1761, Nov. 14. Account filed by Executors.

1759, May 15. Bateman, Nathan, of Deerfield Township, Cumberland Co., yeoman; will of. Wife, Abigail, sole executrix; son, Manoah, under age; son-in-law (stepson?), Dan Robinson. Real and personal estate. Witnesses—Abner Smith, Eliezer Smith, John McGallerd. Proved August 28, 1759. Lib. 9, p. 297.
 1759, June 25. Inventory £67.14.10., by Daniel Ogden and Abner Smith.

1759, May 8. Bateman, Peter, of Deerfield Township, Cumberland Co., yeoman; will of. Wife, Elizabeth. Children—Nathan, Peter, Moses, Hannah Gentry, Nemiah, Aaron and William, the last three under age. Real and personal estate. Executors—sons Nathan and Moses. Witnesses—John McGallird, John Dare, Samuel Lupton. Proved June 16, 1759. Lib. 9, p. 295.
 1759, June 15. Inventory, £80.11.3, by John Dare and Thomas Joslin.
 1760, June 23. Account by Moses Bateman, one of the executors, who by the sale and collecting debts has raised estate to £92.18.10.

1759, Jan. 31. Bateman, Thomas, of Cohansey, Cumberland Co.; will of. Wife, Mary, sole executrix. Children—Thomas (under age), Sarah, (wife of John Bereman), Rebecca and Phebe. Speaks of "five youngest children," but names only above. Real and personal estate. Witnesses—David Ogden, Joseph Bateman, Joseph Lummis. Proved March 10, 1759. Lib. G, p. 221.
 1759, Mar. 7. Inventory, £229.16.6, incl. a watch, £4; a Bible and other books, £2.12; bills, bonds and book debts £35.8.2; made by Thomas Ogden and Joseph Ogden.

1755, Feb. 27. Bates, Daniel, of Hanover, Morris Co.; will of. Wife (not named, but Elizabeth). Children—Martain, Abigail, Pamal and Lidda, all under age. Real and personal estate. Executors—the wife and Joseph Kitchel. Witnesses—Samuel Parritt, Abner Beach, Mary Allen. Proved March 24, 1755. Lib. F, p. 270.
 1755, Mar. 31. Inventory, £86.1.6., by Daniel Lum and Benjamin Howell and by Joseph Kitchel and Elizabeth Bates executors.

1755, Oct. 24. Bates, Jeremiah, of Mansfield Township, Burlington Co., yeoman; will of. Father, John Bates; sisters, Sarah and Han-

CALENDAR OF WILLS—1751-1760   25

nah Bates; brother, Job and John Bates. Real and personal estate. Executors—the father and the two sisters. Witnesses—William Potts, Thomas Biddle, Wm. Pancoast. Proved Dec. 20, 1755.
Lib. 8, p. 236.
 1755, Dec. 19. Inventory, £38.13.6., by George Folwell and Thomas Biddle.

1756, May 5. Bates, John, of Mansfield Township, Burlington Co. Int. Inventory, £55.7.1; by George Folwell and Thomas Biddle.
 1756, May 8. Bond of Sarah Bates as Adm'x; Thomas Biddle and George Folwell fellowbondsmen, all of said Co. Lib. 8, p. 306.

1752, Jan. 20. Bayley, Simon, of Twsp. and Co. of Gloucester; will of. Bequests to Barzillai Hugg, Jacob Hugg. To son-in-law, Francis Lewis, rest of estate when 21. Executor—said Jacob Hugg. Witnesses—Hannah Wills, Hope Hugg, Joseph Goldy. Proved March 4, 1752. Lib. 7, p. 197.
 1752, March 3. Inventory, by J. Goldy and Isaac Kay, £24.10.0.
 1759, Oct. 27. Account, £28.15.9.

1759, Oct. 9. Beach, David, of Newark, Essex Co.; will of. Wife, Susannah. Children—Phebe, Hannah, William and Junia, all under age, and an expected child. Real and personal estate. Executors— the wife and Joseph Riggs, Jr. Witnesses—Uzal Ogden, Sarah Beach, Lewis Ogden. Proved October 30, 1759. Lib G, p. 116.
 1759, Nov. 2. Inventory, £334.8.10, by Samuel Crowell and Josiah Crane.

1754, May 13. Beal, Alexander, of Deptford Township, Gloucester Co., husbandman. Int. Bond of Thomas Rambo, yeoman, as Adm'r; John Whitall, yeoman, fellowbondsman, both of said Twsp.
Lib. 8, p. 120.

1757, Jan. 11. Beck, Godfrey, of Chesterfield, Burlington Co., innholder. Int. Inventory, £287.15.5., incl. bills, bonds and book debts, £174.4.8; a servant lad's time, £5.; made by Abraham Brown, Jr. and Samuel Farnsworth.
 1757, Jan. 17. Bond of Roweth Beck and Samuel Taylor, Jr., as Adm'rs; John Taylor, fellowbondsman, all of said Co. Lib. 8, p. 357.

1757, Jan. 17. Beck, Mary, of Burlington Co. Int. Bond of Samuel Taylor, Jr., as Adm'r; John Taylor, fellowbondsman, both of said Co.
Lib. 8, p. 357.

1758, Aug. 19. Bedell, John, of "Turkie," Elizabeth Borough, Essex Co., yeoman; will of. Wife, Ann. Children—John, Jacob, Henry (absent), Mary Cannan, Sarah Lee and Phebe Tomkins. Grandchildren—John (son of Henry), and Catherine Bedle. Undivided lands on Long Island, N. Y., and in N. J.; homefarm on Passaic River, between Capt. Jonathan Mulford and Mr. Maxwell; personal property, incl. money in hands of Peter Runion and Peter Layten, and becoming due by "old Peter Runion's will"; also becoming due at death of wife's mother, "old Mrs. Runion." Executors—the wife, with sons John and Jacob. Witnesses—Jonathan Mulford, William Maxfel, William Parsons, Jr. Proved May 31, 1759. Lib. G, p. 63.

1759, July 9. Bedell, John, of Morris Co., yeoman. Int. Bond of Susanna, widow, as Adm'x; Thomas Baker and William Gray, both of Essex Co., yeomen, fellowbondsmen. Lib. G, p. 43.
1759, July 28. Inventory, £111.7.8, by Jacob Bedell (3d) and William Macfell.
1760, July 7. Account by the Administratrix.

1755, Dec. 5. Bedford, Stephen, of Essex Co. Int. Zophar Bedford, son, Adm'r, Sarah Bedford, wife, renouncing. Lib. F, p. 303.
1755, Nov. 22. Inventory, £14.1.9, by Noadiah Potter and Nathaniel Wade.

1760, Apr. 10. Bedgood, Richard, of Bucks Co., Penna. Int. Bond of Jacob Burrough as Adm'r; Joseph Harrison fellowbondsman, both of Gloucester Co. Lib. 9, p. 415.

1750-1, Mar. 1. Beech, Samuel, of Newark, Essex Co.; will of. Wife, Sarah. Children—David, Waldron, John, Samuel, Moses, Stephen, Hannah and Martha; all but David and John under age. Home-farm, of about 100 acres; meadow on Black Stake Creek; personal property. Executors—sons David and John. Witnesses—Timothy Ward, Uzal Ogden, Gabriel Ogden. Proved September 18, 1753.
Lib. F, p. 213.
1753, Sept. 19. Inventory, £132.18.7, by Isaac Lyon and Samuel Crowell.

1760, Dec. 25. Beesley, Benjamin, of Pilesgrove, Salem Co., yeoman, deceased. Int. Adm'r—John Beesley, and John Loyd fellowbondsman.
1760, Dec. 17. Inventory, £57.19.0, by Bateman Lloyd and John Loyd.

1751, May 27. Beesley, John, of Salem Co., yeoman. Int. Bond of Mary Beesley as Adm'x; Jeremiah Wood fellowbondsman, both of said Co. Salem Wills, 879 Q.

1755, July 14. Belcher, Jonathan, Governor of New Jersey, at Elizabeth Town, "far advanced in years;" will of. Mentions wife, Louisa; eldest son, Andrew; Jonathan (Chief Justice of Nova Scotia); daughter, Sarah (wife of Byfield Lyde, Esq.); gr. dau., Mary Belcher Lyde; daughter-in-law, Elizabeth Belcher (wife of my son Andrew). Executor—son, Andrew. Request made that "my worthy friends, Samuel Woodruff and Robert Ogden, Esq., stand as Executors in trust for my aforementioned Executor." Witnesses—Matthias Hetfield, Cornelius Hetfield, John Radley. Probated Oct. 1, 1757.
Lib. F, p. 456.

1758, July 29. Belyeu (Billue) John, of Morris Co. Will of. Wife, Ruth; brothers, Peter, Daniel and Isaac Billue; Isaac, son of brother, Jacob Billue. Personalty. Witnesses—Samuel Matex, Elizabeth Gragou, Edward Pigot. A "Schedule" (Codicil) of same date annexed disposes of right and title in the Purchase of Elizabeth Town "by promise of a gift from Stephen Crane and the rest of the Committee," and gives a legacy to Elizabeth Tomson; appoints the wife and brother Isaac executors. Same witnesses. Proved October 7, 1758.
Lib. F, p. 553.

CALENDAR OF WILLS—1751-1760   27

1755, July 16. Beng, Jacob, of the Corporation of New Brunswick, Middlesex Co., farmer; will of. Wife, Frances. Children—Mary, Elizabeth, William (the last two under age). Real and personal estate. Executors—the wife and daughter, Mary. Witnesses—Gerret Voorhees, James Perrine, Ernestus van Harlingen. Proved Nov. 28, 1755. Lib. F, p. 299.
1755, Nov. 26. Inventory, £341.8.6, incl. a negro man, £25.; a negro girl, £40; another, £30; 6 silver spoons, £6; made by Folckert van Roordstrant and Gerret Voorhees.

1746, Apr. 14. Bennet, Gertruy, of Freehold, Monmouth Co., spinster; will of. Sister, Oryonetia, wife of Wm. Covenhoven; brothers, William, Hendrick and Johannes Bennet; niece, Gertruy, dau. of Wm. Covenhoven, and cousin, Oryonche, dau. of brother Johannes. Personal property, incl. a Dutch Testament. Executor—brother Johannes and brother-in-law Covenhoven. Witnesses—Willem C. Kouenhoven, Samll Thompson, John Nathan Hutchins. Proved April 12, 1751.
Lib. E, p. 513.
1751, Mar. 1. Inventory, £154.0.2, incl. 3 gold rings, £1.8; silver sleeve buttons, 1s.6p.; bond and a note, £133.10; made by Johannes Luyster and John Bowne.

1755, Apr. 29. Bennet, Michael, of Fairfield, Cumberland Co. Int. Bond of Hezekiel Bennet as Adm'r; Isaac Garrison, fellowbondsman, both of Deerfield, said Co. Cumb. Wills, 111 F.

1752, May 11. Bennet, Thomas, of Bridgetown, Burlington Co., saddler. Int. Susannah, widow, resigns her right of administering to Henry Paxson, Esq., of said place.
1752, May 13. Bond of Henry Paxson, of Northampton, as Adm'r; Patrick Reynolds, of same place, yeoman, fellowbondsman.
Lib. 7, p. 303.
1752, July 11. Inventory, £65.6.2., incl. 91 lbs. of bacon, £1.17.11, by Patrick Reynolds and Thos. Atkinson, miller.

1751, Nov. 12. Bennett, James, (otherwise called James Valentine), of Gloucester Township and County, yeoman. Int. Bond of widow, Ann Bennett, as Adm'x; Edward Williams, yeoman, fellowbondsman, both of said township. Glouc. Wills, 478 H.

1752, Nov. 7. Berrien, Peter, yeoman, of Newtown, Queen's Co., Nassau Island, New York; will of. Real and personal estate. Wife, Elizabeth. Children—Cornelius (eldest), Samuel, John, Petrus, Janetie, Nicholas, Jacob and Benjamin. Executors—brother, Nicholas Berrien, and brother-in-law, Samuel Fish. Witnesses—James Hazard, Thomas Hazard, Thomas Fish. Proved Nov. 5, 1752.
Lib. F, p. 74.

1760, Dec. 4. Berry, James, of Allaways Creek, Salem Co., schoolmaster. Int. Inventory, £27.1.4, incl. book debts, £4.5.10; "waigers" for teaching school, £7.7.6; made by John Holme and William Oakford.
1760, Dec. 13. Bond of Nehemiah Hogbin as Adm'r, John Holme, fellowbondsman; both of Allaways Creek yeomen. Lib. 10, p. 443.
1764, June 18. Account by Administrator.

1758, Sept. 20. Berry, John, of Bedminster, Somerset Co.; will of. Wife, Ezabell. Children—Thomas, David, John (under age), Mary Lockhart, Ezebell, Sidney, Elizabeth and Ebenezer, the three last under age. Real and personal estate. The wife, sole Executrix, with son Thomas and son-in-law, James Lockhart, as overseers. Witnesses—Ralph Smith, William Colwell and John Henry. Proved Jan. 29, 1759.
Lib. G, p. 24.

1757, Sept. 7. Bescher, Jacob, of Roxbury Township, Morris Co.; will of. Divides real and personal estate between brothers and sisters, John, Abraham, Margret, Elizebeth, Mary and Catherine Bescher. Executors—Benjamin Maning and Nathaniel Drake. Witnesses—Henry Crosley, Thomas Grigson, Elizabeth Ogden. Proved Oct. 15, 1757.
Lib. F, p. 459.

1751, Nov. 24. Bescherer, Jacob, of Roxbury, Morris Co., yeoman; will of. Wife, Barbra. Children—John, Jacob, Abraham and Margret, the last two under age. Real and personal estate. Executors —the wife, Joseph Hinds of Mendom, said Co., and Brice Riky, of Somerset Co. Witnesses—David Budd, Francs Blackly, Barbra Miller. Proved Dec. 13, 1751.
Lib. F, p. 13.

1751, Dec. 11. Joseph Hinds, one of the executors named, declines to serve.

1728, Aug. 16. Beswick, Aaron, of Burlington, tinker; will of. John Buffin, of Burlington Co., sole heir and Executor of real and personal estate. Witnesses—Jacob Worell, Samuel Jorden, Nathaniel Walton, Jr. Proved April 4, 1751.
Burl. Wills, 4785 C.

1757, Oct. 7. Bevis, Thomas, of Chesterfield Township, Burlington Co., brushmaker; will of. Wife, Elisabeth. Children—Esecor (Isachar), sole Executor, Margret and three other sons, names not given; all but the first under age. Real and personal estate. Witnesses—John Holloway, Joseph Woodward, Joseph Reckless. Proved Nov. 14, 1757.
Lib. 8, p. 545.

1757, Oct. 26. Inventory, £196.15.8, by John Steward and Joseph Reckless.

1752, June 4. Bickham, Thomas Sr., of Greenwich Township, Gloucester Co.; will of. Wife, Elisabeth. Children—Thomas, Joshua, Patience, Caleb, Margret and Elizabeth. Real and personal estate. Executors—sons Thomas and Joshua. Witnesses—Thomas Wilkins, Francis Wood, David Loyd. Proved July 19, 1754.
Lib. 8, p. 115.

1754, June 17. Inventory, £688.3.4., incl. a clock and case, £8; bills, bonds and book debts, £540.6.1., made by Wm. Wilkins and James Wood.

1754, Nov. 30. Bickham, Thomas, Jr., of Greenwich Township, Gloucester Co. yeoman; will of. Mother (not named); brothers and sisters, Joshua, Patience, Caleb, Margret and Elisabeth. Real and personal estate. Executor—James Hinchman. Witnesses—Abram Chattin, Joseph Lord, Nixon Chattin. Proved Dec. 12, 1754.
Lib. 8, p. 105.

1755, June 5. Inventory, £121.4.11, by Thos. Wilkins and William Key.

CALENDAR OF WILLS—1751-1760   29

1756, May 23. Bigger, James, of Bethlehem, Hunterdon Co., yeoman; will of. Wife, Martha; sons, Joseph, Robert and James. Real and personal estate. Executors—the wife and John Hackett. Witnesses—Thomas Little, Thomas Little, Jr., John Rockhill. Proved Nov. 1, 1760, the executrix signing "Martha Bigars."   Lib. 10, p. 467.
1760, Oct. 8. Inventory, £256.0.6., incl. 100 bush. of wheat, £25; 30 do. of rye, £5.5; 50 do. of oats, £3.15; made by Robert Shields and Joseph Gordon.

1752, Nov. 24. Bilderback, Daniel, of "Pen's Neck," Salem Co. Int. Inventory, £220.11.8., incl. bills, bonds and book debts, £28.17.4., by Jos. Wright and Francis Miles.
1752, Nov. 27. Bond of Catherin Bilderback as Adm'x; Francis Miles and Martin Skeer fellowbondsmen, all of Pen's Neck.
Lib. 7, p. 449.

1755, Mar. 11. Bills, Nathaniel, of Shrewsbury, Monmouth Co., farmer. Int. Bond of widow, Mary Bills, and Richard Bills, blacksmith, as Admr's; Timothy Akin, yeoman, fellowbondsman, all of Shrewsbury.   Lib. F, p. 252.
1755, Mar. 13. Inventory, £197.3.6., incl. bills, bonds and book debts, £124.9.4, by Gersham Bills and Samuel Osborn.
1757, Apr. 2. Account by the administrators, Mary Bills, the widow of dec'd., and Richard Bills. (Mary had been married before and had a child by first husband).

1753, Apr. 7. Bills, William, of Shrewsbury, Monmouth Co. Int. Silvanus Bills declines administering on the estate. Bond of Thomas Bills as Adm'r; Josiah Halstead fellowbondsman, both of Shrewsbury, yeomen.   Lib. F, p. 117.
1753, Apr. 13. Inventory, £520.13.11, incl. bills, bonds and book debts, £322.1.5; 3 years' use of a house and lot, £33; a negro boy, £50; made by George Allen, Joseph Eatton and John Wardell.

1760, Mar. 3. Bird, John, of Elizabeth. Int. Sarah, widow, Adm'x, renounces in favor of brother-in-law, Capt. Ephraim Terrill.
Lib. G, p. 130.
1760, Mar. 10. Inventory, £33.6.8, by Abraham Clark and Joseph Tooker.
1769, Nov. 22. Account by Ephraim Taylor, Adm'r.

1756, Mar. 10. Birdsell, Nathan, of Monmouth Co. Int. Inventory, £200.16.10, incl. books, 10s; bonds and debts, £33.2.2; made by Ben. Randolph and John Conklin.
1756, Mar. 31. Bond of Abigail, widow, and Levi Cramer, yeoman, as Adm'rs; Timothy Willets, Jr., fellowbondsman. Dedimus potestatem to John Nevill and Timothy Ridgway, or either of them, to administer to said Abigail Birdsell the oath to be taken by administrators, she being unable to travel.   Lib. F, p. 358.

1752, Mar. 2. Bishop, Abigail, daughter of Daniel Bishop, of Cumberland Co., yeoman, 12 years old and upwards. Bond of Ananias Sayre, Esq., Greenwich Township, said Co., as guardian; Joseph Bishop of Hopewell Township, same Co., yeoman, fellowbondsman.
Cumb. Wills, 75 F.

1753, ——— ———. Bishop, Daniel, son of Daniel, of Cumberland Co. Petition of, that Ananias Sayer, Esq., of Greenwich Township, said Co., be appointed his guardian.
 1753, Oct. 24. Certificate of Elias Cotting, that Daniel made the foregoing choice of his own free will.
 1754, Jan. 26. Bond of Ananias Sayre, Esqre., as guardian of Daniel Bishop, Thomas Harris fellowbondsman, both of Cumberland Co.   Cumb. Wills, 94 F.

1758, May 26. Bishop, Esther, of Hopewell Township, Cumberland Co., widow. Int. Bond of Mary, oldest daughter, and her husband, Adam Valentine, as Adm'rs; Jonathan Bowen and Othniel Johnson, both of Hopewell, yeoman, fellowbondsmen.   Lib. 8, p. 528.
 1758, June 1. Inventory, £35.14.7, by Jonathan Bowen and Othniel Johnson.

1757, Jan. 10. Bishop, Joseph, of Cumberland Co. Int. Adm'r— Joseph Bishop.   Lib. 8, p. 350.

1752, Aug. 12. Bishop, Joshua, of Northampton Township, Burlington Co., yeoman; will of. Wife, Martha. Children, all under age, names not given. Real and personal estate. Executors—the wife and Francis Vinecomb. Witnesses—Samuel Cripps, William Attkinson, John Woolman. Proved Dec. 1, 1758.   Lib. 9, p. 144.
 1758, Nov. 18. Inventory, £232.17.8, incl. bonds and debts, £76.6.9; a servant's time, £10.; made by Thomas Budd and George Briggs.
 1762, May 25. Account by Edward Stiles and wife, Martha, (late Martha Bishop, the executrix named above), who add to the inventory, £15.13.11, but make the estate their debtor for £126.12.3.

1759, Mar. 25. Bishop, Mary, of Evesham Township, Burlington Co., widow; will of. Children—Mary Bozorth, Hannah, Daniel, Thomas, Jonathan and Robert. Grandchildren—John (son of Daniel), Barzillai Bozorth, (son of Mary). Personal estate. Executors —son Robert and Joseph Stokes, Jr. Witnesses—Bethsheba Evans, Atlantica Stokes, Isaac Evens. Proved May 31, 1759.
                              Lib. 9, p. 274.
 1759, Mar. 30. Inventory, £88.3, incl. bonds and book debts, £44.16., by Jacob Prickit and James Allen.

1756, Aug. 31. Bishop, Moses, of Hopewell, Cumberland Co. Int. Bond of Levi Bishop as Adm'r; Othaniel Johnson fellowbondsman, both of said place.   Cumb. Wills, 135 F.

1760, Feb. 14. Bishop, Moses, of Woodbridge, Middlesex Co.; will of. Children—David, Beniamen, Moses, (all three Executors), and Rachel. Son-in-law, Joseph Moore; grandson, John Bishop. Real and personal estate. Witnesses—Richard Wilkson, Joseph Williams and William Edgar. Proved March 18, 1760.   Lib. G, p. 149.

1759, Sept. 5. Bishop, Noah, of Woodbridge. Int. Widow, Mary, renounces. Jonathan Alston and James Balen, creditors of deceased, Administrators.   Lib. G, p. 95.

1753, Dec. 15. Bishop, Robert, of Evesham, Burlington Co. Int. Bond of Mary, widow, and Robert, son of, as Adm'rs; Jacob Pricket

and James Allen, both of Northampton Township, fellowbondsmen.
Lib. 8, p. 15.

1753, ———— ——. Inventory £288.1.0, by James Allen, Jr., and Jacob Pricket.

1757, Apr. 25. Account by administrators, Robert and Mary Bishop.

1759, May 24. Bishop, William, of Woodbridge, Middlesex Co.; will of. Wife, Mary; daughter, Mary, by former wife. Real and personal estate. Executors—brothers James and Aaron Bishop, with William Edgar. Witnesses—Hannah Skinner, John Blanchard and Joseph Moore. Proved June 15, 1759.   Lib. G, p. 68.

1753, Feb. 27. Bispham, Benjamin, Esq., of Bridgetown in Northampton, Burlington Co.; will of. Friend, Elizabeth White, £100. Sons—Joseph, Thomas and John, residue. Executors—brother Joshua and my eldest son, Joseph. Witnesses—Wm. Harrison, Samuel Kemble, John Burr, Jr. Proved July 16, 1753.

1753, July 10. Inventory, £3907,14.6, by Henry Paxson and Patrick Reynolds.   Burl. Wills, 5149 C.

1753, July 18. Bispham, Joseph, of Bridgetown, Burlington Co., sadler; will of. Wife, Elizabeth, all real and personal, and she to give my infant son tender care. Executors—wife, Elizabeth, brother-in-law, John Hinchman, and uncle Joshua Bispham. Witnesses—Nicholas Toy, Thos. Atkinson, Thos. Lawrence. Proved Aug. 8, 1753.

1753, Aug. 8. Inventory, £500.10.8, by Thos. Atkinson and Nicholas Toy.   Burl. Wills, 5149 C.

1754, Sept. 26. Black, John, of Burlington Co. Int. Bond of Amy Black as Adm'x; William Black fellowbondsman, both of said Co.   Lib. 7, p. 498.

1755, Jan. 9. Inventory, £128.14.2., incl. pictures, 40s; silver spoons and creampot, £10; 2 looking glasses, £6.5; made by Thomas Folkes and Thomas Watson.

1751, Sept. 11. Black, Thomas, of Springfield, Burlington Co., yeoman; will of. Mother, Sarah Black; wife Mary; an expected child; sisters, Ann Wright and Sarah Gantt, who has daughters Hannah and Sarah; brothers Edward, William and Samuel Black; son-in-law (stepson?) Jonathan Barton (under age). Real and personal estate. Executors—brothers William and Samuel. Witnesses—Henry Wayman, Elizabeth Fenton, John Grimes. Proved Sept. 30. 1751.

1751, Oct. 7. Inventory, £1129.17.11, incl. bills, bonds and book debts, £274.7.2; a servant girl, £14.; made by David Rockhill, Daniel Doughty and Anthony Sykes.   Burl. Wills, 4779 C.

1759, Dec. 31. Black, William, of Chesterfield, Burlington Co., yeoman; will of. Wife, Mary. Children—Achsah (under age), Edward, Ezra, Ann, John, William (last three also under age). Farm in Mansfield and Springfield Township, partly inherited, partly bought, and now occupied by Benjamin Gibbs; home-farm; a lot of 100 acres on York Great Road, bought of brother Edward Black; personal estate. Executors—brother Samuel Black and brother-in-law, Amos Wright. Witnesses—Joseph Archer, Abigail Ivins, John Grimes. Proved Jan. 30, 1760.   Lib. 9, p. 400.

1760, Feb. 5. Inventory, £534.10.3½., by Benjamin Field, Joseph English and Samuel Taylor.

1766, Oct. 21. Account by Samuel Black and Amos Wright, Executors, £1421.13.10½. Paid Sarah Black for her right of Dower, £30; to maintenance of Sarah Black, mother to dec'd, 2 years, boarding of Edward Black, his son, 13 months while at school; schooling of Edward and John. Legacy paid to Achsah Black.

1783, May 2. Account of Edward Black, Acting Exec'r of Samuel Black, dec'd, who was Executor of William Black, £604.15.7½. Paid keeping Billy and Nancy, 4 mos. and 3 weeks; cash due uncle Edward Black from estate, till deceased son, William is of age.

1751, May 6. Blackall, Robert, of Hopewell, Hunterdon Co.; will of. Children—Robert, (eldest son), Anne, Francis, Thomas, Jacob, Mary and Elizabeth. Homefarm, 50 acres, between Isaac Herrin and John Titus; another farm of 166 a; personal property. Executors—sons Francis and Jacob. Witnesses—Joseph Moore, Vinson Runyon, Reuben Armitage. Proved April 11, 1757.

Lib. 8, p. 401.

1757, Apr. 8. Inventory, £186., incl. bills and bonds, £89.18, by Reuben Armitage and Jonathan Furman.

1751, May 6. Blackwell, Robert, of Hopewell, Hunterdon Co.; will of. Eldest son, Robert, unmarried. Daughter, Anne (single). Second son, Francis, 105 acres where he lives. Third son, Thomas, 166 acres where he lives. Youngest son, Jacob, rest of plantation. Son, Robert, plantation. Daughters, Mary, Anne and Elizabeth, money from sale of movables. Executors—Sons, Francis & Jacob. Witnesses—Joseph Moore, Vinson Runyan, Reuben Armitage. Proved April 11, 1757.

1757, April 8. Inventory, £186.0.0, by Reuben Armitage and Jon Furman.

1768, Aug. 24. Account, £206.10.6. Paid James Yates and his wife, legatee, £48.11.2; Zacariah Drake and wife, legatee, £48.11.2; Ann Blackwell, legacy; Ephraim Manning and wife.

Lib. 8, p. 401; 13, p. 439.

1757, July 21. Blake, John, of Newton, Gloucester Co., husbandman; will of. Wife, Sarah, sole Executrix, with the assistance of "relation," Isaac Mickle. Children, apparently all under age, but names not given. Real and personal estate. Witnesses—Archibald Mickle, John Eastlack, William Hill. Proved Nov. 10. 1757.

Lib. 9, p. 64.

1757, Aug. 25. Inventory, £224.2.3, incl. bills, bond, book debts and cash, £163.12.3; by Robert Stephens and Joseph Ellis.

1757, Jan. 21. Blanchard, Peter, of New York City, seafaring man; will of. Mother, Mrs. Mary Giffard, of N. Y. City, sole heiress and Executrix of real and personal estate, with remainder to her daughter, Mary Giffard. Attached power of attorney. Witnesses—Thomas Fox, Gerard Walton, Frederick Willson. Proved June 22, 1759.

Lib. G, p. 84.

1753, Jan. 7. Blanchfield, John, of Burlington Co. Int. Inventory, incl. bond of Philipp Wallis, of Burlington Co., for £62.15.3 3-4," now in suit," in the hands of Richard Farmar.

CALENDAR OF WILLS—1751-1760   33

1753, Jan. 5. Bond of Richard Farmar, of Philadelphia, "practioner in physick," as Adm'r; David James Dove, of Gloucester Town and County, gentleman, fellowbondsman. Lib. 8, p. 182.

1753, Dec. 20. Bland, Robert, of Springfield, Burlington Co. Int. Bond of Caleb Shreve, of Springfield, yeoman, as Adm'r; no fellowbondsman. Lib. 8, p. 15.

1756, Sept. 1. Blaw, John, Sr., of Somerset Co., yeoman; will of. Children—John (eldest son), Antje, (widow of Abraham Ouke), Janetje, (wife of John Doxey) and Frederick, son-in-law (stepson?) Henry Sartor, who has son John. Personal property, incl. a silver "drink beker," 6 silver spoons, and silver quart punch bowl. Executors—son John, son-in-law Henry Sartor and John Berrien. Witnesses—James Sutfin, Anthony Denton and Caleb Haviland. Proved Oct. 17, 1757. Lib. 8, p. 480.
1757, Oct. 11. Inventory, £947.10.8., incl. bills, bonds, cash and notes, £775.6.2; a plate tankard and 5 spoons, £14.18; a negroman and woman, £30; made by Arter Sutven and Zebulon Stout.

1760, Mar. 17. Blinckerhoff, Hendryck, of "Hackingsack," Bergen Co.; will of. Children—Jacobus, Neckasie, Joris, Hendrick and Antie. Real and personal estate. Executors—brothers Jacob, George and Albert L. van Voorhesen. Witnesses—Isaac Boogert, Cornelia Bantow and Guilliam Bertholf. Proved May 27, 1760.
Lib. G, p. 281.
1760, May 22. Inventory, £457.16.0, incl. 6 slaves, £210; a Dutch clasped Bible, £3; a pocket Bible; two New Testaments, 19sh.; 15 old Dutch books, 4 sh.; made by George Brinkerhof, Jacob Bryckhof and Albert van Voorhesen, the Executors, and appraised by Jacob Titsort and Guilliam Bertholf.

1752, Feb. 3. Bloodgood, William, of Woodbridge, Middlesex Co., tanner; will of. Wife, Mary. Sons—Gach, Moses, Aaron and Joshua; Homefarm, land on Eastside of road from Woodbridge to Amboy, bought of George Lessle; saltmeadow, bought of Ephraim Anderson; lot bought of Nathaniel Harned; lot bought of Obediah Ayres; lot bought of Elizabeth, widow of Jeremiah Reader, and of Isaac Dye; lot bought of Zebulon Pike, Ex'r of Timothy Pike, of Woodbridge; house and lot in Perth Amboy, next to Presbyterian graveyard, formerly belonging to father-in-law, James Savage; freehold and associate rights to lands in common; also personal property. Executors—the wife and Thomas Gach, Esq. Witnesses—Nathaniel Pike, Martha Bloodgood and William Kent. Proved March 22, 1756.
Lib. F, p. 330.

1759, July 10. Bloomfield, Catherine, dau. of Jeremiah, of Woodbridge, deceased. Guardian appointed. Jonathan Brooks. Bondsman, Justus Walker. Lib. G, p. 90.

1757, Janr. 9. Bloomfield, Ezekiel, of Woodbridge Township, Middlesex Co., gent.; will of. Wife, Elizabeth; son, Ruben, under age. Real and personal estate. Executors—father-in-law, Wright Skinner, and brother, Jonathan Brooks. Witnesses—Jonathan Brooks, Hannah Brooks, Mary Hinds and Daniel Price. Proved Jan. 21, 1758. Lib. F, p. 486.

3

1757, Jan. 14. Bloomfield, Jeremiah, of Elizabeth, weaver, Int. Hannah Brooks, Ursula Bloomfield and Mary Bloomfield renounce and desire that their brother-in-law, Jonathan Brooks, may administer on their brother's estate. Same day Jonathan Brooks of Woodbridge yeoman. Adm'r. Bondsman—John Deare, Esq., of Perth Amboy.

1757, Jan. 12. Inventory, £50.3.4, by Jane Marshall and Stephen Burrowes. Lib. F, p. 394.

1760, Apr. 18. Bloomfield, John, of Woodbridge, Middlesex Co.; will of. Children—Nathaniel, Samuel and Reuth. A lot of 12 acres on the Northside of the road to Mattutchen, bought of Ebbenezer Williams, adjoining Nathaniel Heard; homefarm. Executors—Alexander Edgar and Nathaniel Heard. Witnesses—John Conway, Dennis Combes and William Kent. Proved December 8, 1760. Endorsed: "The exrs decline qualifying as the legatees are all of age who propose to divide the estate immediately according to the will. Fees so far are 8/8 procl." Lib. G, p. 321.

1758, May 2. Bloomfield, Richard, of Woodbridge, Middlesex Co.; will of. Wife, Sarah. Children—Richard and Pheby, wife of Frasey Ayres. Real and personal estate. Executors—the wife, Samuel Barns and Frasey Ayres. Witnesses—Jonathan Thickstun and Samuel Preston. Proved May 19, 1758. Lib. F, p. 524.

1758, Mar. 31. Bloomfield, Sarah, of Woodbridge. Int. Benjamin Bloomfield, Sr., husband. Administrator. Lib. F, p. 517.

1752, Aug. 4. Bodine, Isaac, of Bridgewater, Somerset Co. Int. Angtetic (Annetie) Bodine, widow, renounces her right of administering to their son Frederick. Lib. F, p. 61.

1752, Aug. 4. Bond of Frederick Bodine, eldest son of Isaac, as Adm'r; Abraham Bodine fellowbondsman, both of Bridgewater, yeomen.

1757, Sept. 9. Bodine, John, of Lebanon, Hunterdon Co. Int. Inventory of the personal estate of, £40.5.8., made by John Hall and John Hinderhit.

1759, Sept. 19. Bond of Cornelius Bodine as administrator of the estate, John Hall fellowbondsman, both of Lebanon.
Lib. 8, p. 515.

1758, Aug. 25. Account by Cornelius Bodine, Adm'r.

1760, Nov. 19. Inventory, by Abraham Westervelt and Nickasie Kep, £457.10.8., incl. 2 slaves, £145, and a bond for £70.

1760, Oct. 22. Boggs, James, of Elizabethtown. Int. Nathaniel Rusco, Adm'r. Lib. G, p. 344.

1760, Aug. 16. Boice, George, of Piscataway, Middlesex Co., yeoman; will of. Wife, Lena. Children—John, Lena, Mary and Siche, and an expected child. Real and personal estate. Executors—brother, John Boyse, and brother-in-law, Charles Sudam, both of said Co. Witnesses—Leonard Boice, Benjamin Morgan and Cornelius Sujdam. Proved Oct. 18, 1760. Lib. G, p. 316.

1760, Oct. 21. Inventory of the personal estate of, £306.9., incl. a negro boy £65., made by William Williamson and Reune Runyon; John Boice and Charles Suidam executors.

CALENDAR OF WILLS—1751-1760   35

1754, Dec. 30. Bolmer, Robert, of Bridgewater, Somerset Co., farmer; will of. Wife, Mary. Children—John, Allabortes, Abraham, Robert, Marcy, Ann Fasey, Rosena, Magdalen, Elizabeth and Jenney. Lands adjoining Donies Tuneson and John Sebring; personal estate. Executors—Jacob Eoff and David Sutton. Witnesses—Tobias Lauer, Henry Patmor and Jacob Eoff, Jr. Proved March 14, 1755.   Lib. F, p. 252.

1755, Febr. 13. Inventory, £140.8.3, by Luc. Bilyeu and Abraham van Tuyl.

1758, July 28. Boltinghouse, Elisabeth, of Upper Freehold, Monmouth Co. Int. Bond of Joseph Boltinghouse as Adm'r; Joseph Wright fellowbondsman, both of said place, yeoman. Lib. 9, p. 22.
1758, July 28. Inventory, £177.17.4, by Tobias Polemus and Jonathan Thomas.

1759, May 26. Bond, Benjamin, of the Borough of Elizabeth, Essex Co.; will of. Wife, Susana (apparently dead); children—Robert, Rebackah, (wife of Daniel Sayrs), and Benjamin. Grandsons—Benjamin and Jacob Bond and John Sayrs. Legacies to Charles Allen, Phebe Sturges and Hannah Edwards. Real and personal estate. Executors—son Robert, John Ogden and Amos Day. Witnesses—Caleb Camp, Moses Price, Nathaniel Woodruff. Proved June 10, 1760.   Lib. G, p. 252.

1760, Mar. 7. Bond, Robbart, of Essex Co.; will of. Wife, Mary. Children—Stephen, Robert, Elihu, Sarah, Mary and Phebe, all under age. Real and personal estate. Executors—John Ogden and Joseph Lyon. Witnesses—Alexander Simpson, John Porterfield, Josiah Broadwell. Proved April 16, 1760.   Lib. G, p. 247.

1760, Nov. 26. Booth, Richard, of "Allaway" Creek Township, Salem Co., yeoman; will of. Daughters—Elizabeth, Jane, Ruth and Sarah, all under age. Legacy for the Poor of Allaway Creek Preparative Meeting, to be paid to Salem Monthly Meeting of Quakers. Real and personal estate. Nephew, Nathaniel Hancock sole Executor, and, in case of his death, Salem Monthly Meeting. Witnesses—William Bradway, Sarah Bradway, and John Barber. Proved Dec. 22, 1760.   Lib. 10, p. 487.
1760, Dec. 3. Inventory, £106.17.9, by John Stewart and William Bradway.

1758, June 14. Borden, Benjamin, of Evesham, Burlington Co. Int. Inventory, £119.12.6, incl. 20 bush. of clean rye, by Samuel Stokes and John Cox.
1758, June 17. Bond of Joseph Borden, of Salem Co., yeoman, as Adm'r; John Cox, of Chester Township, Burlington Co., fellowbondsman.   Lib. 8, p. 534.

1753, Feb. 3. Borden, Francis, of Shrewsbury, Monmouth Co.; will of. Wife, Mary. Children—Francis, Thomas, John, Elizabeth, Jean and Amy. Granddaughter, Mary Bills. Real and personal estate. Executors—the wife and son, Francis. Witnesses—Richard Borden, Joseph Borden and Benjamin Borden. Proved April 6, 1759.
Lib. G, p. 105.

1759, Apr. 5. Inventory, £169.2.6, by Isaac Hance and Josiah Parker.

1754, July 26. Borden, Jeremiah, of Shrewsbury, Monmouth Co.; will of. Wife, Easter, sole heiress and, with Robert Hartshorne. Executors. Real and personal estate. Witnesses—John Corlis, Lucy Hartshorne, John Hartshorne. Proved August 28, 1754.
Lib. F, p. 215.

1751, Apr. 5. Borden, Richard, of Evesham, Burlington Co., yeoman; will of. Wife, Mary. Children—Joseph, Jonathan, James, Benjamin, Hannah Coxe, Amey Tindal, Mary Toy and Anne. Brother, Samuel Borden, to be maintained during his life. Real and personal estate. Executors—the wife, son James, and son-in-law, James Toy. Witnesses—John Huestis, Joseph Huestis, John Green. Proved May 4, 1751. Burl. Wills, 4787 C.

1753, July 5. Born, John, of Hanover Twsp., Burlington Co., yeoman; will of. To Rev. Collen Campbell, £5; to friend Abraham Kelley, £5; to friend, widow Hope Atkinson, £3; to Jonathan Budd, son of William and Susanna Budd, £6, when of age; to Mary, daughter of William Budd, £4; to Samuel Budd, son of William Budd, Bible; to friend, Thomas Budd, residue. Executor—said Thomas Budd. Witnesses—Jacob Sulavan, Gab. Blond. Proved July 18, 1753.
 1753, July 16. Inventory, £93.12.7, by James Wills, George Briggs.
Burl. Wills, 5155 C.

1760, May 9. Borradaill, Arthur, of Chester, Burlington Co., yeoman; will of. Wife, Margery. Children—Hannah Elton, Rebecca Shute, Ester Venable, Elizabeth Brown, Mary Venable, William, John, Sarah and Ruth, the last four under age. Real and personal estate. Executors—the wife and son-in-law, Samuel Shute. Witnesses—Thomas Morton, Mary Wallace, John Cox. Proved June 30, 1760.
Lib. 10, p. 44.

1759, Apr. 11. Borton, John, Jr., of Waterford, Gloucester Co., sawyer. Int. Elizabeth, widow of, declines to administer on his estate.
 1759, Apr. 11. Inventory, £228.4, incl. a servant's time, £10, by James Cattell and John Woolman.
 1759, Apr. 13. Bond of Abraham Borton, of Gloucester Co., as Adm'r; William Borton and James Cattell, both of Evesham, Burlington Co., yeomen, fellowbondsmen. Lib. 9, p. 207.
 1760, Apr. 8. Account by Abraham Barton, Administrator.

1752, Feb. 6. Borton, William, of Evesham Township, Burlington Co.; will of. Kinsman, Samuel Garwood, principal heir and Executor of real and personal estate. Legacy to tenant, Samuel Parker. Witnesses—Richard Willets, Sarah Middleton, Cathrine Hawk. Proved Jan. 10, 1755, when Sarah Middleton testifies as "Sarah Ewar."
Lib. 8, p. 77.
 1755, Jan. 10. Inventory, £38.16, by Richard Willets, Jr., and Benjamin Haines.

1758, Apr. 18. Boss, Joseph, Sr., of Amwell Township, Hunterdon Co., yeoman; will of. Wife, Catrin. Children—Joseph, Nicholas, John and Elisabeth Ties. Granddaughter, Ann Moore. Real and personal estate, incl. a negro wench. Executors—the three sons. Witnesses John Boss, Johann Petter Hammer and Garrard Williamson. Proved May 23, 1758.   Lib. 9, p. 155.

1755, Nov. 29. Boudinot, Marie Catherine, of Elizabeth Town, N. J.; will of. Children—Mary (wife of John Emott), Elias and Susanna Vergerau. Bequests to Jane (wife of Thomas Bradbury Chandler) and Mary, both daughters of John and Mary Emott, and to Elizabeth (wife of William Rickets). Real and personal estate. Executors—William Rickets, Thomas Bradbury Chandler and Susanna Vergerau. Witnesses—Richard Jaques, Joseph Morse, Jr., George Ross (3d). Proved July 16, 1757.   Lib. H, p. 103.

1760, Aug. 4. Bougaert, John, of "Pearemis," Bergen Co.; will of. Wife, Antie. Oldest son, Jacobus, who gets the Bible. Other children—Abram, Cobes, Steven, Willimptie, Angenietie, Nitie; "daughter's child, Cornelia Hoppe." Executors—Roelof Westervelt and Luykes Bougaert. Real and personal estate. Witnesses—Allebartis Terhuijn, William S. Van Emburgh, Abraham Terhuijn. Probated Nov. 25, 1760.   Lib. G, p. 329.

1753, Aug. 18. Boulton, Isaac, of Mansfield Twsp, Burlington Co., yeoman; will of. Wife, Sarah. Daughters, Mary and Elizabeth. Son, Isaac. Children not of age. Plantation and moveables to be sold. Executors—George Folwell and Caleb Scattergood. Witnesses—John Lamb, Richard Watson, Edward Boulton. Proved Sept. 6, 1753.
1753, Sept. 4. Inventory, £171.10.6, by Thomas Biddle and Joseph Curtis.   Burl. Wills, 5161 C.

1755, Apr. 4. Bouman, Thomas, of "Riding" Township, Hunterdon Co., yeoman; will of. Wife (not named). Children—Cornelis (eldest son), Elisabeth (wife of Andries Johnson), Neeltie (wife of Jaques Vontine). Mentions children of son, Thomas Bouman, and of daughter, Jannetie, wife of Andries Johnson, the son of Minderd. Land bought of Wynand van Deventer; other real and personal property, incl. a Dutch Bible. Executors—son Cornelis and son-in-law, Andries Johnson. Witnesses—Wynant van Deventer, Samuel Wyckoff, Jacob v. d. Bilt. Proved August 15, 1755.   Lib. 8, p. 330.
1755, June 17. Inventory, £456.19.7, incl. bonds and cash, £421.2.1, by Jacob v. d. Bilt and Peter Perine.

1760, Nov. 7. Bowman, Providence, of Somerset Co. Int. Bond of John Bowman as Adm'r; Daniel Pearse fellowbondsman, both of said Co.   Lib. G, p. 320.

1756, Mar. 8. Bown, Samuel, of Middletown, Monmouth Co., yeoman. Int. Bond of Esther, widow, as Adm'x; Capt. James Grover of the same place fellowbondsman.   Lib. F, p. 403.

1749, Sept. 25. Bozorth, Simon, of Evesham Twsp., Burlington Co.; will of. Sons Thomas, John, Samuel; latter to have that part of farm over the road. Wife, Mary, use of rest of lands. Daughter, Experience, being in the house while single. Son, Andrew, rest of farm. Other daughters, Elizabeth Springer, Mary Longman and

Experience. Executors—wife, Mary, and son Andrew. Witnesses—Hannah Foster, Amos Haines, Wm. Foster. Proved March 17, 1753. 1753, Feb. 19. Inventory, £94.11.4, by James Allen and Wm. Foster.
Burl. Wills, 5169 C.

1760, May 10. Bradford, William, of Fairfield, Cumberland Co.; Int. Inventory, £52.14, by Joseph Daten and John Bateman. Bond of Thomas Ogden as Adm'r; Joseph Daten, fellowbondsman, both of Fairfield. Lib. 10, p. 31.

1759, Apr. 3. Bradway, Abigal, of Fairfield, Cumberland Co.; will of. Children—Jeremiah Harris, Abigal Harris and Reuben Harris, all under age. Legacy of de'd. husband's wearing apparel and silver watch to James Wigings and wife, Hanah, if they will discharge the remainder of the (personal) estate. Thomas Ogden, sole executor. Witnesses—David Wescote, David Bower, Jeremiah Buck. Proved April 16, 1759. Lib. 9, p. 215.
1759, Apr. 6. Inventory, £173.8.3, incl. a silver watch, £5.10, by David Wescote and Jonathan Lorance.
1760, Dec. 19. Account by the Executor, who has increased estate by £90.1, not appraised, and reports on hand £177.19.8.

1759, Sept. 7. Brairley, Elizabeth, of Maidenhead Township, Hunterdon Co., widow; will of. Children—Benjamin, Rachel, Sarah and Elizabeth. Real and personal estate. Executor—brother-in-law, George Rozel. Witnesses—Abraham Skirm and John Rozel. Proved Sept. 12, 1759. Lib. 11, p. 416.
1759, Sept. 15. Inventory, £150.16.10. incl. 4 Testaments, made by John van Cleave and Henry Mershon.

1759, Sept. 1. Braman, Benjamin, son of Robert, of Gloucester Co., petitions, that William Mickle of said Co. be appointed his Guardian.
Glou. Wills, 686 H.

1756, May 7. Braman, Martha, of Greenwich Twsp., Gloucester Co., widow; will of. Children—Benjamin and Sarah, both under age. Their shares of the personal estate to be kept for them, until of age, by testatrix' sisters, Marcy Pall and Sarah Wilkinson. Daughter, Sarah, to live with cousin Sarah Lippincott. Executor and guardian of son, Benjamin William Mickle. Witnesses—Thomas Bright and Joshua Lord. Proved June 14, 1756. Lib. 8, p. 376.
1756, May 11. Inventory, £97.19.8, incl. two Testaments, a "salter," a "Young Man's Companion" and a spelling book; made by Gerret Vanaman and Andrew Long.

1754, Jan. 7. Braman, Robert, of Gloucester Co., yeoman; will of. Wife, Martha, sole executrix. Children—Benjamin (under age) and Sarah. Sons-in-law (stepsons?) Thomas and John Bright. Brother, Thomas Brayman. Real and personal estate. Witnesses—John Brayman, Jonathan Burt, Alexander Randall. Proved Feb. 22, 1754.
Lib. 7, p. 450.
1754, Mar. 4. Inventory, £164.18.9, by Jacob Cozens and Garit Vanaman.

1760, May 14. Brandreth, Daniel, of Lower Pen's Neck, Salem Co.; will of. Wife, Catherine, who has sons Jacob, Judah and Daniel, and

CALENDAR OF WILLS—1751-1760 39

daughters Catherine, Millicent and Sarrah Townsend. Daughters, Mary Edwards and Elizabeth. Grandsons—John and Titus Ireland. Real and personal estate, incl. marriage outfit, bought for daughter Elizabeth in Philadelphia and at Lewis Owens in Salem. Executors— the wife, daughter Elizabeth and Sarah Townsend. Witnesses—Alexander Hill, Moses Hill and John Marshall. Proved June 21, 1760.
Lib. 10, p. 488.

1760, June 18. Inventory, £1146.5, incl. a silver tankard; other silver and china, £36.14; clock; Bible and other books; a negro man, £60; negro woman, £15; bonds, book debts and cash, £626.7.6; made by Andrew Sinnickson and Joseph Wright.

1754, Apr. 2. Branson, Elizabeth, of Springfield, Burlington Co. Int. Bond of John Fenimore, of Burlington Co., yeoman, as Adm'r; Thomas Atkinson, of Burlington City, innholder, fellowbondsman.
Lib. 7, p. 467.

1754, June 27. Brant, William, of Hanover, Morris Co. Int. Inventory £133.5.8., incl. bonds and bookdebts, £97.0.9.; made by Ezekiel Halsey and David Ludlam.

1754, Sept. 27. Bond of Phebe, widow, as Adm'x; Barnabas Brant, of the same Co., fellowbondsman.
Morris Wills, 58 N.

1759, June 19. Brass, Ryker, of Bergen Co. Int. Bond of Lucas Brass, father of, as Adm'r; Henry Brass, of Perth Amboy, fellowbondsman.
Bergen Wills, 3170 B.

1758, March 22. Bray, James, Sr., of Kingwood, Hunterdon Co. will of. Wife, Elizabeth. Children to live on place four years. Eldest son, James, land on south side of creek, part of which I bought of William Fowler, formerly his father's, deceased; he to pay to his sisters, Susanna and Anne Bray, £10 each. At end of 4 years plantation to be sold and money divided among my wife and children, except James. Sons, Daniel, John, and daughter, Hannah Bray named. Executors—brother, Andrew Bray, of Lebanon, & friend Isaac Leet, of Kingwood. Witnesses—Thomas Herbert, Daniel Everitt, James Warford. Proved May 1, 1758.
Lib. 9, p. 160.

1759, Feb. 6. Inventory, £337.4.4, by Daniel Lake and Jeremiah Thatcher.

1760, Sept. 20. Brayman, Jonathan, of Winsor, Middlesex Co. Int. Inventory, £180.12.3, incl. bills and bonds, £52.12.9, by John Cubberley and Amos Rogers; sworn to by Sarah Brayman as administratrix.

1760, Oct. 2. Bond of Sarah Brayman as Adm'x; Amos Rogers and Robert Rogers fellowbondsmen, all of said Co.
Midd. Wills, 3403 L.

1760, May 10. Brea, Thomas, of Middlesex Co. Int. Samuel Neilson, principal creditor, Adm'r, widow, Jean Brea, having renounced.
Lib. G, p. 192.

1756, June 8. Brearley, Benjamin, of Maidenhead, Hunterdon Co., yeoman; will of. Wife, Elizabeth. Children—Benjamin (under age), Rachel, Sarah, Rebekah and Elizabeth. Homefarm, 60 acres, adjoining Alexander Boyles and Jesper Smith; land on Five Miles Run, between David Braily and Alexander Boyles, bought of Thomas Green; 5 a. of meadow on Assunpink Creek; 375 a. in Morris Co.; personal property, incl. a mulatto boy and girl. Executors—brother, John

Braily (signs Brearley), and brother-in-law, George Rossell. Witnesses—Rachel Woolsey, John Brearley, Abram Shirm. Proved March 17, 1757. Lib. 8, p. 413.

1757, Mar. 19. Inventory, £510.8.10, incl. bonds, £321.0.10; made by John van Cleave and Henry Mershon.

1754, Octbr. 1. Breckenridge, Joseph, of Sussex Co. Int. Bond of widow, Esther Breckenridge, as Adm'x; James Hanna fellowbondsman, both of said Co. Lib. 7, p. 499.

1755, Mar. 19. Inventory, £841.16.2, by John Anderson and John Vannatta.

1755, May 8. Account by Adm'x, Esther Breckenridge.

1759, Febr. 1. Bretten (Brittain), William, of Mannington, Salem Co.; will of. Divides personal estate between Samuel Mason, cousin Arthur Simpson, Richard, son of Jonathan Woodnutt, Archibald, Charles and William Hamilton, Charles Elliot and William Parker, making said Samuel Mason sole Executor. Witnesses—Isabeel Parker, John Baird and Bowes Wray. Proved Feb. 21, 1759.
Lib. 9, p. 365.

1759, Feb. 19. Inventory, £67.7.7, incl. books, 15s, bonds and notes, £57.17; made by William Hall and Charles Fogg.

1759, Sept. 22. Brewer, Peter, of Shrewsbury, Monmouth Co. Int. Bond of widow, Anne, James Hankinson and Thunis Amack as Admr's; John Hans, Jr., fellowbondsman, all of said Co.
Lib. G, p. 99.

1758, July 24. Brian, Haran, of Mountholly, Burlington Co.; will of. Wife, Joannah, sole Executrix. Children—Haran, Susannah, Esther, Samuel and Joseph. Witnesses—Thomas Lawrance, John Woolman. Proved Oct. 26, 1759. Lib. 9, p. 306.

1759, Oct. 25. Joannah Brian, Executrix, refuses to act and wishes administration granted to her son-in-law (stepson?), Haran Brian.

1759, Oct. 25. Inventory, £61.1, by John Woolman and John Atkinson.

1759, Oct. 26. Bond of Haran Brian, the son, as Adm'r; Earl Shinn fellowbondsman. both of said Co.

1761, June 2. Account by the Administrator.

1755, June 10. Brian, William, of Bridgetown, Northampton Township, Burlington Co., blacksmith; will of. Mother, Mary Brian, sole executrix. Brothers—Abraham, Uriah and Thomas, the last two under age. Sister, Rebecca. Land in Bridgetown near the Stone Bridge, 22½ acres near Saml. Crips, bought of brother Abraham. Personal property. Witnesses—Josiah White, James McElhage, John Fenimore. Proved Jan. 12, 1756. Lib. 8, p. 235.

1756, Jan. 9. Inventory, £27.11.1, by Samuel Kemble and James McElhage.

1737, Aug. 29. Brick, John, Esq., of Cohansie, Salem Co.; will of. Wife, Hannah. Children—William, Elizabeth Donlap, Hannah Hancock, Joshua, Joseph, John. Grandsons—John and Ephraim Worthington. Home farm; land on and near Tindall's Island; land on Stoke Creek, bought of Anthony Woodhouse; farm bought of Leonard Gibbon; 300 acres at Carle Town, said Co., bought of Clement Plumsted

CALENDAR OF WILLS—1751-1760   41

and Israel Pemberton; personal estate, incl. 6 negroslaves. Executors—the wife and sons John and Joseph. Witnesses—Thomas Bright, Isaiah Harrison, John Podmore. Proved April 26, 1753.
Lib. 6, p. 453.

1757, Dec. 6. Brick, John, of Hopewell Township, Cumberland Co.; will of. Wife, Ann. Children—John, Joseph, Mary Hall, Elizabeth Reeve, Ann, Hannah, Ruth and Jane. Real and personal estate. Executors—the wife, sons John and Joseph, with friend and relation, Charles Davis, as assistant. Witnesses—Ebenezer Miller, Isaac Wheaten, Ebenezer Miller, Jr. Proved March 1, 1758. Lib. 8, p. 512.
1758, Febr. 7-13. Inventory, £2270.4.8., incl. bills, bonds and book-debts, £1041.14.9.; 3 servants, £12.12.6.; made by Philipp Dennis and Ebenezer Miller.

1757, Jan. 12. Bridge, Thomas, of Morris Town, Morris Co., yeoman; will of. Wife, Mary. Children—David, John, Ralph, Thomas, Benjamin, Elizabeth, Sarah and Pamela, all under age. Real and personal estate. Executors—the wife, Benjamin Pierson and Abraham Pierson, both of said Co. Witnesses—John Pierson, Abraham Pierson, Jr., Isaac Pierson. Proved Jan. 16, 1760. Lib. G, p. 140.
1759, Oct. 10. Inventory, £205.11.4, by Benjamin Pierson and Abraham Pierson.

1752, March 10. Briggs, John, of Northampton Twsp., Burlington Co., yeoman; will of. Son George, land in Salem Co. on Stow Creek, of 800 acres, out of which 400 acres has been sold to my son Francis, and 100 more. Daughter, Rachel Cowgill, £100. Grandson, George Cowgill, "my riding creature." Daughter, Hannah Borton. Grandson David Davis £12 when of age. Grandson, John Cowgill, residue. Executors—son George and son-in-law Isaac Cowgill. Witnesses—George Allen, Mary Allen, Gab Blond. Proved Jan. 27, 1753.
1753, Jan. 20. Inventory, £209.15.2, by appraisers James Wills and Thomas Budd.
Burl. Wills, 5177 C.

1755, Jan. 16. Brittin, Joseph, of Trenton, Hunterdon Co.; will of. Wife, Charity. Children—Isaac and Joseph, both under age. House and lots in Trenton and other land and personal property. Executors—the wife and Moore Furman of Trenton. Witnesses—James Cumine, Joseph De Cow, Mary De Cow. Proved April 23, 1756.
Lib. 8, p. 546.
1781, Nov. 20. Account of the estate, £323.9., by Charity Britton, Executrix, who makes it her debtor for £12.5.7.

1754, Mar. 26. Britton, John, of Middletown, Monmouth Co. Int. Rachil, widow, "informs Mr. Barto," that neither she nor her son will administer on his estate and desires administration granted to Isaac van Dorn.
1754, Apr. 20. Bond of Isaac van Dorn, of Freehold, principal creditor, as Adm'r; James Newell, of Perth Amboy, fellowbondsman.
Lib. F, p. 171.
1754, ———. Inventory, £5.12, by William Nickel and Thomas Petty.
1755, Mar. 20. Account by Isaac van Dorn, who has received £9.15.2, and has paid out £12.17.3.

1758, Jan. 14. Brokaw, Peter, of Somerset Co., farmer; will of. Wife, Jude. Children—Margret (wife of Peter Wortman), Catrine,

(wife of Peter Sutfin), Jude, (wife of George Davis). Grandchildren—Peter, John, and a daughter, children of Margaret Wortman; Margaret, daughter of Catrine Sutfin; Isaac, Peter, Janetje (wife of Folkert Fisher); Jude (wife of Abr. Brokaw); Cathrine (wife of Peter van Nest); Margaret, Hannah and Mary, children of Jude Davis. Homefarm; farm on west side of the North branch of Raritan River; personal property, incl. (a negro man and wench). Executors—brothers-in-law, Jeronemus van Nest and John van Nest, with cousin, John Brokaw. Witnesses—Edmund Arrosmith, Isaac Brokaw and Joseph Arrosmith. Proved March 30, 1758.
Lib. F, p. 519.

1758, Feb. 22. Inventory: Real estate—a farm of 229 acres on the South side of Raritan River, £1030.10; a farm of 300 acres on the West side of the North branch of said river, £1080. Personal, £912.12.7, incl. bills, bonds and cash, £393.17.6; jewels, £3; a silver tankard, £14.10; silver buckles and spoons, £3.8.6; grain; four negroslaves, £175; books, £3.3; made by Coanrod Teneick, Jr., and Burgon Hoff.

1751, July 2. Brookfield, William, of Burlington Co. Int. Bond of widow, Catharine Brookfield, of Little Eggharbour, Burlington Co., as Adm'x; John Inskeep and Charles Brookfield, both of said Co., yeoman, fellowbondsmen.
Burl. Wills, 4931 C.

1751, Aug. 8. Inventory, £379.4.1; incl. bills, bonds and book debts, £148.19.1; a negro man, £50; made by Stephen Cramer and John Dearnal.

1754, ———— ————, Brooks, Henry, son of Henry Brooks, of Fairfield Township, Cumberland Co., Petitions that Jonathan Lawrence of said Co., yeoman, be appointed his guardian.

1754, Apr. 27. Certificate of Surrogate Elias Cotting, that Henry Brooks selected his guardian of his own free will. Bond of Jonathan Lawrence as such guardian; Daniel Elmer, Jr., fellowbondsman, both of Fairfield Township, yeomen.
Cumb. Wills, 95 F.

1754, ———— ————, Brooks, Mehetable, daughter of Henry Brooks, of Fairfield Township, Cumberland Co., petitions that Jonathan Lawrence of said Co., yeoman, be appointed her Guardian.

1754, May 28. Bond of Jonathan Lawrence as such Guardian; Daniel Elmer, Jr., fellowbondsman, both of Fairfield Township, yeoman.
Cumb. Wills, 96 F.

1759, May 25. Brown, Andrew, of Woodbridge, Middlesex Co.; will of. Wife, Sarah. Children—Joseph, Eunice Thorp, Greer, William and George. Grandson, Andrew Thorp. Real and personal estate. Executors—the wife, son Joseph and friend George Brown. Witnesses—Thomas Thorp, Thomas Brown and John Brown. Proved June 21, 1759.
Lib. G, p. 83.

1759, June 13. Inventory, £120.2.8 by George Brown and Thomas Brown.

1759, June 15. Brown, Anthony, of Newark. Int. Martha, his widow, Adm'x, Peter DeGarmo, fellowbondsman.
Lib. G, p. 76.

1757, Mar. 13. Brown, Arthur, of Monmouth Co.; will of. Wife [not named]. Children—Cabes, Jane, Mary and Isabel, all under age.

CALENDAR OF WILLS—1751-1760   43

Real and personal estate. Executors—Capt. John Anderson and Peter Bowne. Witnesses—Zacharias Sickles, Margaret Brown and Robert Savage. Proved April 27, 1757. Lib. F, p. 419.
1757, Apr. 29. Inventory, £658.15.10., incl. 10 books, 3 maps and 5 pictures; a boat and long boat, £80.; 2 negromen £90.; bonds £370.9.7.; made by John Burrowes and Duncan Robertson.

1751, May 20. Brown, Caleb, of Greenwich Township, Gloucester Co., sawyer. Int. Mary, widow, asks that Benjamin Lodge be appointed administrator of her husband's estate.
1751, May 21. Bond of Benjamin Lodge, shopkeeper, as Adm'r, Jonathan Fisher, yeoman, fellowbondsman, both of Greenwich Township.
1751, May 22. Inventory, £35.1.9, by Jonathan Fisher and Isaac Stephens. Glou. Wills, 479 H.

1760, Sept. 18. Brown, Chatfield, of Deptford Township, Gloucester Co., yeoman; will of. Divides personal estate between friend, Hannah Andrews, brothers John, James and David Brown, children of brother Thomas Brown, viz., John, David, James and Mary, and children of sister Mary Davice, names not given. Brother, John Brown, sole Executor. Witnesses—Lawrence Webster and David Cooper. Proved Dec. 9, 1760. Lib. 10, p. 394.
1760, Dec. 1. Inventory. Real estate—a house on Henry Wood's land, £2.10; a meadow leased of Henry Wood, £40. Also personal, £472.2.11, incl. bookaccounts, cash and notes, £115.15.11, and books; made by James Hinchman and Joshua Lord.

1759, May 21. Brown, Esther, of Woodbridge, Middlesex Co.; will of. Son, Carlile Brown. Daughter, Hume. Grandchildren—William and James Brown. Mentions also Thomas ———— and cousin Phebe Baremore. Legacy to Rev. Aaron Richards. Personal property. Cousin, David Edgar, Executor. Witnesses—John Lee, Robert Lee and Benjamin Elston, Jr. Proved Nov. 12, 1759. Lib. G, p. 111.

1745-6, Jan. 24. Brown, Hendrick, Sr., of Second River, Essex Co., blacksmith; "being aged," will of. Wife, Margret. Children—Hendrick, John, Elizabeth Codmus, Lao Manderfield, Saiche Kerstead, Sauke Woutesse and Alche Sip. Grandchildren, Jacobes Brown and Margaret King. Real and personal estate. Executors—sons Hendrick and John. Witnesses—Jonathan Sergeant, Jacobus van Dicke, Abraham Peir. Proved March 14, 1757. Lib. F, p. 453.

1760, Nov. 4. Brown, James. Int. Bond of Lyndon Brown as Adm'x; John Hutchin fellowbondsman, both of Burlington Co.
Lib. 10, p. 168.
1760, Nov. 8. Inventory, £35.3.8., incl. books 5s.; 3,000 staves, £7.10.; made by Joseph Talman and Thomas Smith.
1761, Nov. 12. Account by Adm'r, who makes estate his debtor for £6.2.9.

1755, Nov. 18. Brown, John, of Morris Co., miner. Int. Bond of Jacob Ford of said Co., principal creditor, as Adm'r; John Deare, Esq., of Perth Amboy, fellowbondsman. Lib. F, p. 294.

1752, Jany. 29. Brown, Preserve, of Burlington Co., account of the estate, £68.0.3., by the Adm'x, Mary Brown, who has spent £82.8.7;

in paying for the funeral, £5.0.10, and debts due to Wm. Folwell, Marcus Hedding, Daniel Stockden, Richard Bowker, John Monrow, Joseph Scattergood, Josiah White, George Briggs, Jacob Gaskell, Wm. Sorsby, Susannah Tool and Exrs. of Benjamin Jones.
[See N. J. Archives, Vol. XXX, p. 69].

1759, June 13. Brown, Preserve, of Nottingham, Burlington Co., shop keeper; will of. Wife, Mary. Children—Abia, Richard, William, Mary Jones, Sarah Scholy. Land in Nottingham Township, bought of William Morris, on S. E. side of the Millpond and Doctor's Creek; also adjoining William Murfin on the road from Crosswicks to Trenton; three houses and lot on Vine Str., next to Second Str., Philadelphia; another house and lot next to the preceding; houses and lots in Chesterfield, said Co.; also personal property. Executors—sons Richard and William, and son-in-law, John Jones. Witnesses—Samuel Redford, James White, John Brown, Peter Dahlman. Proved Dec. 11, 1760. Lib. 10, p. 209.

1760, June 2. Inventory of personal estate, £5.835.10.1, incl. a bookcase and books, £2.5; a clock, £2.15; 4 maps, £1.7.6; 6 large silver table spoons, £6; 6 teaspoons; 2 pr. of teatongs; shopgoods, £667.8.11; bills and bonds, £1,351.10.2; book debts, £2,795.12.5; made by William Murfin and Samuel Stevenson.

1759. Aug. 13. Brown, Sarah, dau. of Stephen Brown, Jr., deceased, an orphan "of upwards of 15 years." Daniel Wade, her uncle, appointed guardian. Lib. G, p. 94.

1758, Oct. 18. Brown, Stephen, Jr., of Newark. Int. Sarah, his widow, Administratrix. Lib. G, p. 18.
1758, Oct. 21. Inventory, £151.14.1, by Joseph Riggs and Josiah Crane.

1758, Dec. 26. Brown, Thomas, of Woodbridge, Middlesex Co. Int. William Smith, Adm'r, per request of widow. Lib. G, p. 13.
1758, Dec. 28. Inventory, £337.18.5, incl. bonds and cash, £111.17.3; a silk bed quilt, £3; 3 silver spoons and ½ doz. teaspoons, £3.15; a negro wench and child, £60; pair of silver sugar tongs, 3s.6d.; made by David Edgar and Samuel Force.

1759, Mar. 1. Brown, William, of Woodbridge, Middlesex Co.; will of. Wife, Esther. Children—Carlile and Hume (under age). Grandsons—William, James and Thomas Brown. Homestead; land bought of Benjamin Gray; 10 acres of Raway Meadows, bought of Isaac Thorn; a lot called Turkis Hill; 5 ac., bought of Robert Lee; 5 ac. of Raway Meadows, bought of Widow Rolph; also personal estate incl. three negroslaves. Executors—the wife, son Carlile, and cousin David Edgar. Witnesses—William Smith, Samuel Cutter and James Crowell. Proved May 28, 1759. Lib. G, p. 59.

1758, May 8. Brown, Zebulon, of Mansfield Township, Burlington Co., yeoman. Will of. Wife, Martha. Children—Jonathan, Leah, Alice, Zebulon, Martha, and Samuel. Grandson, Zebulon, son of Jonathan. Real and personal estate. Executors—the wife and son Samuel. Witnesses—Edward Boulton, William Boulton, John Watkinson. Proved August 1, 1758.

CALENDAR OF WILLS—1751-1760 45

1758, Aug. 15. Inventory, £222.3.1, by William White and Arent Schuyler.

1764, Aug. 25. Account by Martha Brown and Sam'l Brown, Executors, includes payments to Jonathan Tuly, husband of Martha Tuly; Francis Ellis, husband of Sarah Ellis; Alice Garwood; Jonathan Brown, and Zebulon Brown, legatees. Burl. Wills, 6023 C.

1754, June 5. Browne, Elizabeth, of Upper Freehold, Monmouth Co., widow of Dr. John Brown of Burlington Co.; will of. Daughter, Elizabeth (wife of Elisha Lawrence), sole Executrix. Grandchildren —John Browne, John Lawrence, Elizabeth Lawrence (now Newell), Elisha Lawrence, Jr., Lucy Lawrence, Anne Lawrence. Personal property, incl. a silver pint cup and silver spoons). Witnesses— James Magee, Peter Imlay, Jr., and William Dunterfield. Proved June 5, 1759. Lib. 9, p. 219.

1759, Jan. 16. Bruen, John, Jr., of Newark. Int. Uzal Ogden, Esq., principal creditor, appointed Adm'r, widow having renounced.
Lib. G, p. 24.

1760, Oct. 4. Brundage, Nathan, of Newton Township, Gloucester Co., carpenter; will of. Wife, May (Mary), sole heiress and executrix of real and personal estate. Witnesses—Alexander Patterson, Benjamin Willson, Alexander Ferguson. Proved Oct. 20, 1760.
Lib. 10, p. 375.

1760, Oct. 17. Inventory, £238.7.6, incl. a bond and interest, £200., by Isaac Andrews and Robert Frd. Price.

1759, Oct. 26. Brunson, Mary, widow of Barefoot Brunson, Esq., of Somerset Co.; will of. Children—John, Cathrine Cull, Susannah Wiggins, Thomas, Samuel, Barefoot, Frances Mount, Rachel Smith, Mary Bateman and Anna Davison. Personal property, incl. a negro man. Executors—son Samuel Brunson and Thomas Wiggins. Witnesses—Samuel Baxtor, William Kouenhoven and Thomas Craven. Proved Dec. 31, 1760. Lib. 10, p. 573.

1760, Dec. 27. Inventory, £211.18, incl. a Bible, £1.5, and bond payable in four years £200; made by Dirreck Longstreet and Henry Sillcock.

1750, Aug. 20. Bryan, Elizabeth, widow of Samuel, of Bridgetown, Northampton Township, Burlington Co.; will of. Daughter, Elizabeth (wife of Jonathan Hough). Son, Jacob. Grandson, Thomas, son of son Solomon Curtis. Legacy to Elders and Churchwardens of the Church at Bridgetown. Real and personal estate. Executor— brother William Heulings. Witnesses—Nicholas Toy, Mary Morris, John Burr, Jr. Proved Nov. 28, 1751. Burl. Wills, 4791 C.

1751, Nov. 28. William Heulings, Executor named in the will refuses to serve. Bond of Jonathan Hough, of Springfield, said Co., yeoman, as Adm'r with the will annexed; Nicholas Toy, of Bridgetown, and Abraham Hewlings, of Burlington City, merchant, fellow-bondsmen.

1756, May 28. Bryan, John, of "Gloster" Township and Co., yeoman; will of. Wife, Mary. Children—Robert, Benjamin, John, Abraham, the last three under age, Ellinor Smallwood, Ann (under age)

and Thomas. The Blue Anchor land; land along the road near Hinckston's; 5 acres of cedar swamp; also personal estate. Executors —the wife and son, Thomas. Witnesses—Daniel O'neall, Thomas Magee, Stephen Morris. Proved March 8, 1757. Lib. 8, p. 391.
1757, Sept. 20. Inventory, £163.12.6., incl. bookdebts, £102.7.6; by John Hillman and Richard Cheesman.

1759, Dec. 11. Buck, Jeremiah, Esq., of Fairfield, Cumberland Co. Int. Bond of Mary Buck, daughter, and Nathan Leek, of Deerfield, said Co., as Adm'rs; Jonathan Lorance (Lawrence) and John Whitecar (Whitaker), both of Fairfield, fellowbondsman. Lib. 10, p. 108.
1760, May 29. Inventory, £298.7, by Charles Clark and William Monigle.
1762, Mar. 16. Account by Nathan Leek, Adm'r, inc. nursing for smallpox; Ephraim Sayre, for keeping one child six months, and, ditto, to John Buck.

1760, Nov. 13.—Buck, Temperance, of Fairfield, Cumberland Co., widow of. Jeremiah Buck. Int. Bond of David Fithian as Adm'r; Henry Pearson and Theophi Elmer fellowbondsmen, all of Fairfield.
Lib. 10, p. 178.

1753, Oct. 22. Buckelew, Frederick, Sr., of Perth Amboy, Middlesex Co., yeoman. Will of. Children—Phredrick, George, John, Peter, Thomas, Ann. Grandchildren—Phredrick, Abram, Susannah. Ann, Rebecka and Pressilla. Children of deceased, eldest son, William; two daughters of daughter Ann; John, son of Peter, and said John's wife, Mary, who has daughter Jeane Jones. Real and personal estate. Executors—sons Phredrick and Thomas. Witnesses—Joseph Hall, William Melvin, Nicholas Everson. Proved Oct. 31, 1754.
Lib. F, p. 224.
1754, Dec. 20. Inventory, £118.12.1. by Thomas Bockelew, Ex'r.

1760, June 3. Budd, David, of Northampton Township, Burlington Co., yeoman; will of. Wife, Catherine. Children—William, Joseph, Henry, Daniel (all under age), and Elizabeth Reynolds. Farm, now occupied by Henry Bolton, between Samuel Jones, Daniel Doughty and Marmoduke Fort; other real and personal estate, incl. 3 negroes. Executors—the wife, son William and brother, Thomas Budd—Witnesses—Francis Briggs, Levi Briggs, Joseph Goldy. Proved June 19, 1760. Lib. 10, p. 46.
1760, June 16. Inventory, £1034.4.9½, incl. bills, bonds and mortgage, £276.0.10; 5 negroes, £147; a servant man's time, £15; made by George Briggs and John Goldy.

1753, Feb. 26. Budden, William, of Chester Twsp., Burlington Co., husbandman; will of. Daughters Haney and Mary Budden, £5 each, when of age. Wife, Elizabeth, and the child which she now bears to be maintained, and if a boy he to have all that is left. Executrix—wife. Witnesses—John Eyanson, William Ward, Ruth Ward. Proved Sept. 24, 1753.
1753, Sept. 17. Inventory, £111.9.1, by Mathew Allen and John Cox.
Lib. 7, p. 384.

1757, Sept. 13. Bulock, Susannah, of New Hanover, Burlington Co., widow; will of. Children—Sarah Harison, Mary Branson, Rebecca

CALENDAR OF WILLS—1751-1760

Warick, John Bulock, William Bulock, Elizabeth Craig. Grandchildren—Mary (daughter of son William), Ann Burtis, Sarah Burtis, Ruth Persons. Daughters-in-law—Elliner Dennis and Elizabeth Fowlwell. Real and personal estate. Executor—son, Joseph Bulock. Witnesses—John Glover, Gasper Smith, Richard Weeks. Proved Oct. 8, 1757, the name being written "Bullock." Lib. 8, p. 461.

1750, June 15. Bunn, Garret, of the South Branch of "Rarinton," Somerset Co., yeoman; will of. Wife, Mary. Sons—Edward and Lawrence (underage). Legacy to nephew and godson, Garret Bunne. Real and personal estate. Executors—Rem van der Beck and Gerret v. Wagenen. Witnesses—John Mathews, Harpert Hoose, John Bready. Proved June 20, 1752. Lib. F, p. 58.

1752, July 31. Inventory, £225.16.6, incl. a negro boy.

1752, July 31. Rem van der Beeck and Gerrit van Wagenen, named as executors in the will, decline to act.

1752, Aug. 7. Bond of Mary, widow of Garret Bunn, and Edward Stoneman, alias Bunn, both of Somerset Co., as Adm'rs., with the will annexed.

1760, Dec. 29. Bunn, James, of Woodbridge Middlesex Co. Int. Matthew Bunn, the father, Adm'r. Lib. G, p. 339.

1759, Mar. 4. Burch, Jeremiah, of Deptford Township, Gloucester Co., sawyer. Int. Bond of John Ladd as Adm'r; Thomas Kimsey fellowbondsman, both of said Township, yeoman. Lib. 9, p. 186.

1759, Apr. 17. Inventory, £21.12.8, by Isaac Dilkes and Thomas Kimsey.

1760, Sept. 1. Burdge, David, of Middletown, Monmouth Co. Int. Bond of Patience, widow of, as Adm'x; Capt. James Grover fellowbondsman. Lib. G, p. 370.

1760, Apr. 5. Burgess, Moses, Jr., of Piscataway, Middlesex Co. Int. Moses Burgess, Sr., the father, Adm'r. Lib. G, p. 151.

1759, Oct. 2. Burling, Jane, of Burlington City, widow; will of. Daughters—Mary Burling, Jane Large Burling and Hannah Burling, all under age. Cousin, Elizabeth Smith. Personal estate. Executors and guardians of daughters, father, Ebenezer Large, and nephew, Thomas Pryor, Jr. In case of father's death, relations, Samuel, John and Elisabeth Smith are to act with Thomas Pryor. Witnesses—Hannah Woolston, Hannah Kirkbride, Richard Smith. Proved March 18, 1760. Lib. G, p. 429.

1759, Nov. 20. Inventory, £175.2.3, by Joseph Noble and Edward Cathrallu (?).

1759, Jan. 16. Burns, Peter, of Burlington Co. Int. Bond of Patrick Larking as Adm'r; John Saunders fellowbondsman.
Burl. Adm. Bonds, 187.

1757, Sept. 28. Burr, Rev. Aaron, of Princeton, President of the College of N. J.; will of. Mother, Elizabeth Burr. Wife, Esther. Children—Aaron and Sarah. The College of N. J. to inherit children's share, if they die in their nonage. Legacy to brother, Peter

Burr, and his son Aaron; Trustees of said College residuary legatees. Executors—the wife, William Peartree Smith of New York, and Jonathan Sergeant of Newark. Witnesses—William Symonds, William Shippen, Richard Stockton. Proved September 28, 1757.
Lib. 8, p. 476.

1757, Sept. 29. Inventory, £1916.17.10., incl. maps, 25s.; clock, £12; silver coffee pot and tankard, £14; silver spoons, £5.5, silver can and pepperbox, £6.10; bonds, book debts and notes, £1,107.6.6; three negroes, £150; library of books as per catalogue (not extant) £136.3; made by Thomas Watson and Samuel Horner.

1758, Apr. 4. Burr, Esther, of Princeton, Middlesex Co.; will of. Children—Sarah and Aaron, Sister, Elizabeth Edwards. Mentions also Sarah, daughter of Rev. Mr. Prince in Boston; Doctor William Shippen of Philadelphia, and Jonathan Sergeant of Newark, Trustees of College of New Jersey (to have clock and terrestrial globes). Mother, Sarah Edwards, residuary legatee. Rev. Alexander Cumming, of New Brunswick, to preach the funeral sermon. Real and personal estate. Executors—Dr. Shippen and Mr. Sergeant. Witnesses—Robert Smith, Samuel Hornor and Lucy Edwards. Proved July 28, 1758.
Lib. 10, p. 60.

1760, Mar. 22. Burr, Sarah and Aaron, daus. of Rev. Aaron Burr of Princetown, deceased, both under 14. Guardian appointed—Timothy Edwards, "nearest relation by the mother's side."
Lib. G, p. 143.

1756, Jan'y 21. Burrough, Enoch, of "Watterford" Township, Gloucester Co., yeoman; will of. Wife, Deborah. Children—Thomas and Phebe, both under age. Father, John Burrough, remainderman of real estate. Executors—the father and the wife. Witnesses—Samuel Burrough, Jr., William Fowler, Josiah Burrough. Proved June 7, 1756.
Lib. 8, p. 288.

1756, Feb. 20. Inventory, £163.5.11, incl. books, by Charles Farguison and Joseph Morgan.

1756, Mar. 12. Burrowes, Thomas, Jr., of Hopewell, Hunterdon Co.; will of. Wife, Mary. Children—Forster, Rachel, (wife of Jonathan Stout), Rebecca, Charity, Job and Stephen. Executors—brother, Stephen Burrows, and Jeremiah Woolsey. Witnesses—Thomas Baldwin, Joseph Baldwin, John Guild. Proved April 26, 1756.
Lib. 8, p. 468.

1752, Oct. 9. Burrows, Thomas, of Salem Co. Int. Bond of Thomas Hancock, Esq., of Elsinburough, Salem Co., as Adm'r; no fellowbondsman.
Lib. 8, p. 90.

1758, Mar. 30. Burt, Mary, of Hopewell, Hunterdon Co., widow; will of. Children—Richard, Deborah, Sarah, Margreat Howell, Elisabeth Whitson and Mary, all under age. Personal estate. Executors —Jacob Reader and Moses Baldwin. Witnesses—Nickles Stillwill and Andrew Smith, Jr. Proved Sep. 11, 1759.
Lib. 10, p. 16.

1759, Sept. 7. Inventory, £202.0.8, incl. bills, bonds and book debts, £82.0.7; books and bees, £1.6; made by Nickles Stillwill and Andrew Smith, Jr.

1759, June 23. Burton, William, of Burlington Co. Int. Bond of John Burton as Adm'r; William Vanse fellowbondsman, both of said Co.
Burl. Adm'n Bonds, 199.

CALENDAR OF WILLS—1751-1760   49

1754, Feb. 9. Butcher, James, of "Stoe" Creek, Cumberland Co., yeoman; will of, Wife, Mary. Daughter, Hannah, under age. Cousin, Thomas, son of Richard Butcher, remainderman. Legacy to brother, Thomas Platts. Real and personal estate. Executor—uncle, Richard Butcher. Witnesses—Dan Simkins, Abigill Shepherd, Peter Long. Proved May 10, 1754. Cumb. Wills, 97 F.
1754, April 2. Inventory, £209.2.6, by Peter Long and Dan Simkins.

1760, May 25. Butcher, Joseph, of "Willingboroug" Township, Burlington Co.; will of. Wife, Prudence. Children—Samuel, Joseph, Anne, Easter and Patience, all under age. Executors—the wife, brother-in-law, William Rogers, and Abraham Perkins. Witnesses—Henry Nordike and Samuel Allinson. Proved June 14, 1760.
Lib. 10, p. 33.
1760, June 13. Inventory, £264.10.10., incl. 50 bush. of Indian corn, £6.5; a negro girl, £28; made by Joshua Ballinger and Wilm. Heulings.
1765, Aug. 5. Account of by Prudence Butcher and William Rogers, the surviving executors, who report on hand £114.15.3.

1759, Dec. 25. Butcher, Mary, widow of James, of Stow Creek, Cumberland Co. Int. Bond of Richard Butcher, of Stow Creek Township, yeoman, as Adm'r; Josiah Miller, of Cohansey Bridge, said Co., surveyor, fellowbondsman. Lib. 10, p. 109.
1760, Jan. 31. Inventory, £54,12.3, by Philipp Dennis and John Barracliff.

1760, Febr. 5. Butcher, Thomas, of Springfield Township, Burlington Co., yeoman; will of. Wife, Elizabeth. Brother, Samuel Butcher. Executors—the wife and Benjamin Jones. Witnesses—John Butcher, Daniel Haines, John Watkinson. Proved March 10, 1760.
Lib. 9, p. 433.
1760, Mar. 8. Inventory, £98.14.9, incl. bonds, £56.12.8, by Jon, Fenimore and James Childs.
1760, Mar. 10. Elizabeth Butcher, the widow, being "antient," refuses to act as executrix, leaving all the duties to Benjamin Jones.

1757, —— ——. Butler, James, of Hanover, Burlington Co., shoe maker. Int. Elizabeth, widow, refuses to administer on his estate, recommending Peter Boynsette.
1757, Oct. 24. Inventory, £15.7.1., by Samuel Wright, Jr., and Jonathan Branson, attested by "Peter Pintset,"
1757, Nov. 1. Bond of Peter Poyntsett, as Adm'r; Samuel Wright., Jr., fellowbondsman, both of New Hanover Township, said Co.
Lib. 8, p. 517.
1758, Oct. 27. Account by Peter Poyntsett, Adm'r, £18.9.4.

1756, Nov. 16. Butterworth, Caleb, of Deptford Township, Gloucester Co., labourer. Int. Bond of John Young, of Deptford Township, husbandman, as Adm'r; John Sparks, of Greenwich Township, said Co., farmer, fellowbondsman. Lib. 8, p. 395.

1755, Oct. 19. Busby, Benjamin, of "Wellingborow" Township, Burlington Co.; will of. Cousins—Joseph Busby (sole Executor), Thomas, Amos, Isaac and Daniel Busby, to inherit personal estate, incl. money due from brother, **William Busby.** Witnesses—George Bass, Mary Hollinshead, Robert Farrell. Proved Feb. 9, 1756.

1755, Nov. 19. Inventory, £37.1.7, by Obadiah Ireton and Barzillia Rossell. Burl. Wills, 5675 C.

1754, Jan. 7. Busby, John, of "Willingburrough," Burlington Co., yeoman; will of. Late wife, Hannah. Children—John, Samuel, Jabiz, Anne, Grace and Hannah. Homefarm; land on North side of Mill Creek in Burlington Townbounds, received from father-in-law, Nathaniel Cripps; also personal property. Executors—brother, William Busby, and Samuel Stokes. Witnesses—Samuel Cripps, Samuel Beesly, John Burr, Jr. Codicil of January 9, 1754, disposes of 40 acres of cedar swamp on Mechepotuxing, between John Dawes and Jacob Webber. Witnesses—Samuel Cripps, Thomas Buzby, John Burr, Jr. Proved Feb. 2, 1754. Lib. 12, p. 369.

1754, Feb. 23. Inventory, £944.12.3, incl. a clock, credits on books and notes, £694.7; made by John Deacon and Hugh Hollinshead.

1756, June 5. Account by Wm. Buzby, Acting Executor, £341.12.2.

1759, Sept. 3. Busby, William, of "Wellingburrow," Burlington Co., yeoman; will of. Wife, Mary. Children—Elizabeth and William, both under age. Real and personal estate. Executors—the wife, Joshua Raper and Joseph Buzby. Witnesses—Thomas Buzby, Jonathan Wills, Asher Woolman. Proved Sept. 21, 1759. Lib. 9, p. 265.

1759, Sept. 20. Inventory, £367.4.6, incl. bills and book debts, £73.2; made by John Deacon and George Elkinton.

1749-'50, Mar. 20. Byram, Ebenezer, of "Mendum," Morris Co.; will of. Wife, Hannah. Children—Ebenezer, Eliab, Mary, Abigail, and Japheth. Grandchildren—Hannah (dau. of son Naphtily, dec'd), Zenus and Leaha Bauldwin; children of daughter, Hannah. Real and personal estate in New England; homefarm, bought of Isaac Johnson; 28 acres bought of Ezekell Lyon; 7 acres of meadow, bought of John Booline. Other real and personal property. Executors—sons Ebenezer and Eliab. Witnesses—Ezra Cary, Phebe Cary, Caleb Lenard. Proved Oct. 18, 1753. Lib. F, p. 139.

On the same sheet is a former will, made by Ebenezer Byram, November 2, 1738, in which he calls himself of Bridgewater, Plymouth Co., New England.

1754, Mar. 16. Byram, Eliab, of Amwell Township, Hunterdon Co.; will of. Wife, Sarah. Children—Eliab, Sarah, Perkin and Martha. Real and personal estate. Brother, Ebenezer Byram, sole Executor. Witnesses—Jacob Gray, Gershom Lee, Jacob Mattison. Proved May 1, 1754. Lib. 7, p. 511.

1754, Apr. 9. Inventory, £197.10.11, incl. books, £11.9.1; a watch, bond and other things, £75.18.9; his wench, bookcase and other things, £57.11.5; made by Jacob Gray and Gershom Lee.

1760, Nov. 29. Cain (Kain), William, of Burlington Co. Int. Bond of Catharine Cain (called in body of bond Charity Cain) as Adm'x; James Budd, fellowbondsman, both of said Co. Witness—S. Blackwood. Lib. 10, p. 169.

1759, May 31. Caine, James, of Sussex Co. Int. Adm'x—Catherine Caine. Lib. 9, p. 393.

CALENDAR OF WILLS—1751-1760   51

1759, April 18. Caldwell, Allen, of Greenwich Township, Gloucester County, blacksmith. Int. Adm'x—Rebecca Caldwell. Bondsman—William Sharp, of Greenwish Twsp., yeoman. Witness—Samuel Parker. Lib. 9, p. 233.
1759, April 7. Inventory, £11.3.11, by Gabriel Rambo and Samuel Parker.
1760. Account by Rebecca Caldwell, Adm'x.

1753, Oct. 15. Camble, William, of Gloucester Co. Int. Bond of Mary Cambel, of Tuckaho, as Adm'x of estate; Jacob Garitson, of same place, fellowbondsman. Cape May Wills, 163 E.
1753, Oct. 16. Inventory, £57.19, incl. a negro man, £40.; made by James Hathorn and Ephraim Sayre.

1759, June 19. Camfield, Ephraim, of Newark. Int. Adm'x—Sarah Camfield, his widow. Witness—Thomas Barton. Lib. G, p. 83.

1751, Feb. 15. Camp, John, of Tuckaho, Cumberland Co. Int. Inventory, £38.9.4, made by Peter Scull and Nathan Goldin.
1751, Apr. 1. Bond of Joseph Camp of Tuckaho as Adm'r.
Cape May Wills, 149 E.

1760, Apr. 6. Campbell, David, of Woodbridge, Middlesex Co., weaver; will of. Wife, Sarah. Children—Jesse (under age), Sarah, Phebe, Ehster and Mary, the last two under age. Real and personal estate. Executors—the wife and George Brown. Witnesses—Samuel Pangburn, William Martin and Israel Thurston. Proved April 24, 1760. Lib. G, p. 178.
1760, Apr. 19. Inventory, £110.4.9, incl. a Bible and other books, by Thomas Brown and John Brown. Mem: "Be it Remembred that the Inventory on the other Side was taken at the request of Sarah Cambell, one of the Executors of David Cambell, decd, the other not yet qualified. She did soon after expose sundry of goods and chattells to publick sale, but on May 12th, 1760, She dec'd. The Care of the whole estate came into the hands of George Brown, the other Executor, who, then qualifying, did on June 2, 1760, proceed as is common & does here give in a true account." The same appraisers made a return of £154.3.8, for the estate.

1760, Mar. 7. Campbell, James, of Stow Creek, Cumberland Co. Int. Bond of Charles Campbell, of Stow Creek, as Adm'r; Thomas Richardson, of Fairfield, and David Mills, of Hopewell, both of said Co., fellowbondsman. Witnesses—Daniel Briant and Daniel Elmer.
Lib. 9, p. 451.
1760, Mar. 11. Inventory, £30, by Isaac Mills, Jr., and David Mills.

1760, Feb. 13. Campbell, John, of Piscataway, Middlesex Co.; will of. Wife, Mary. Sons—Robert, James, John, Alexander, Obediah and Eneas; and an expected child. Executors—son James and Capt. William MacDaniel. Witnesses—Robert Ross, Elisha Smalley, Jr., and Reune Runyon. Proved June 26, 1760. Lib. G, p. 239.
1760, June 16. William McDaniel, one of the Executors named above, declines.
1760, Apr. 15. Inventory, £161.15.2, incl. bonds, £122.0.1; 4 bush. of Indian corn; a Bible, 7s.; made by Richard Taylor and Alexander Thomson; James Campbell, Executor.

1758, Dec. 19. Campbell, Robert, of Somerset Co. Int. Bond of Mary Campbell, of Prince Town, Somerset Co., as Adm'x; James Cumine (Cummins) of Trenton, Hunterdon Co., fellowbondsman.
Hunt. Wills, 436 J.

1760, June 12. Campbell, William, of Orange Co., N. Y. Int. Bond of Hendrick Kipp, of Bergen Co, as Adm'r; Reynier van Giesen fellowbondsman.
Bergen Wills, 441 B.

1759, Oct. 24. Campton, John, of Hopewell, Hunterdon Co.; will of. Wife, Mary, one third part of my estate. Sons—Moses, John, William and Jeams, to have rest of estate. Executors—wife, Mary, and friend, Zebulon Stout, of Somerset Co. Witnesses—Stephen Barton, John Stout, Robert Cowan. Proved Nov. 2, 1759.
Lib. 10, p. 456.

1755, June 14. Cane (Cain), John, of Burlington Co., inventory, £33.13.7½, by Thomas Budd and James Dobbin; affirmed by Joseph Burr, Jr., as administrator.
Burl. Wills, 5597 C.
1758, Jan. 16. Account, by Joseph Burr, Jr., Adm'r.
Burl. Wills, 6039 C.

1756, Aug. 23. Canfield, David, of Newark, Essex Co. Int. Jemimah Canfield, widow, renounced and released to Thomas Canfield, her right. Thomas Canfield, Adm'r, gave bond, with Nathaniel Johnson, Esq., of Newark, as fellowbondsman. Witness—Uzal Ogden.
Lib. F, p. 404.

1753, Oct. 4. Cannon, William, of Burlington City, clockmaker. Int. Bond of Joseph Hollinshead, Esq., as Adm'x; Daniel Ellis, Gent., fellowbondsman, both of said City.
Lib. 7, p. 422.

1760, June 5. Carl, Abraham, late a soldier in the New Jersey Regiment. Int. Bond of William Carl, of Essex Co., as Adm'r; Isaac Jones, of Morris Co., fellowbondsman.
Morris Wills, 91 N.
1760, July 3. Inventory, £23.12.8., being cash found in hands of the Commissary of the Government.

1759, Mar. 5. Carll, Eliakem, of Alloways Creek, Salem Co., yeoman; will of. Wife, Elizabeth. Children—Phinehas, Henry, Elizabeth Brick, Rachel Moore, Martha Padgett, William, Jeremiah and Jesse. Real and personal estate. Executors—the wife and son Phinehas. Witnesses—John Barber, Jane Norbury and William Stretch. Proved April 9, 1759.
Lib. 9, p. 353.
1759, Apr. 16. Inventory, £179.1, by Thomas Sayre and Benjamin Allen.

1752, Febr. 25. Carll, Elikam, Jr., of Salem Co. Int. Inventory, £128.18.3, incl. half a shallop, £50; made by David Platts and Jonathan Bradway.
1752, Mar. 7. Eliakim Carll, of Cumberland Co., father of Elicam Carle abovesaid, resigned his right to administer on the estate, to Ephraim Mills, who gives bond as Adm'r, with Eliakim Carll (father), as fellowbondsman.
Salem Wills, 1008 Q.

1759, Mar. 12. Carll, Elisabeth, of "Alloos" Creek Township, Salem Co., widow; will of. Children—Elesabeth Brick, Jeremy, Henry,

William, Jessey, Phineas, Rachel More and Martha Padgett. Personal estate. Executors—sons Henry and William. Witnesses—John Barber, Jane Norbury and David Padgett. Proved April 9, 1759.
Lib. 9, p. 288.

1760, Dec. 5. Carll, Elisabeth, late Elisabeth Hancock, daughter of Thomas Hancock. Int. Bond of Phinehas Carll, of Greenwich, Cumberland Co., as Adm'r; Zachariah Shaw and John Hall, both of Hopewell, said Co., fellowbondsmen. Lib. 10, p. 178.

1759, Apr. 10. Carman, Jasper, of Amwell, Hunterdon Co,. weaver; will of. Wife, Hannah, sole heiress and Executrix of real and personal estate, with legacy of 5sh. to Hezekiah, son of John Carman. Witnesses—John Rouze, Thomas Searle and William Fleming. Proved Oct. 9, 1759. Lib. 10, p. 20.
1759, Oct. 3. Inventory, £238.2.6, incl. bonds, book debts and notes, £128.12.2; a servant girl, £3.10; made by Thomas Kitchin and Samuel Furman, Jr.

1754, July 12. Carmick, Peter, of Philadelphia, but late of Salem Town and Co., merchant; will of. Children—Stephen, Elizabeth Campbell and Sarah Farmar, Dec'd son John mentioned. House and lot of 16 acres in Salem Town; two lots of marsh and 12 a. of land in said Town, next to the Meeting House; sawmill on the West side of Morris River in Cumberland Co.; land on either side of said river; 1,000 acres in Piles Grove, Salem Co.; personal property. Executors—the son and daughters. Witnesses—John Hatkinson, Daniel Dupuy, John Reily. Codicil of July 5, 1755, makes unimportant changes. Witnesses—William Savery Branson van Leer, John Reily. Proved Feb. 20, 1759. Burl. Wills, 6273 C.

1753, Oct. 9. Carpenter, Edward, of Turkey, in the "Boorrough" of Elizabethtown, Essex Co.; will of. Wife, Phebe. Daughters—Phebe and Elizabeth. Farm in Turkey; land over the brook; personal estate. Executors, brothers Samuel Ross and William Jones. Witnesses—Henry Broadwell, Ezekiell Mulford, Jonathan Mulford. Proved Nov. 9, 1753. Lib. F, p. 151.
1753, Oct. 27. Inventory, £56.8.10, by Benjamin Pettit and Samuel Ross.

1760, March 4. Carpenter, Jacob, late a soldier of the New Jersey Regiment. Int. Elizabeth Carpenter, his widow, renounced in favor of her son, John Carpenter. Witness—Elizabeth Denman.
1760, March 14. John Carpenter, of Elizabeth Town, gave bond as Adm'r; Abraham Clark, Jr., of same place, fellowbondsman. Witness—John Smyth. Lib. G, p. 136.

1760, May 23. Carpenter, John, of Deptford, Gloucester Co., weaver; will of. Wife, Sarah. Children—boys and girls, all under age, names not given. Real and personal estate. Executors—the wife and Joshua Lord, Jr. Witnesses—Richard Clarke, Stephen Clark, Jonathan Kimsey. Proved July 15, 1760. Lib. 10, p. 88.
1760, —— ——. Inventory, £142.5.6, incl. books, £1.10; book debts, £28.4; made by Richard Clarke and Jonathan Kimsey.

1755, June 4. Carr, Sarah, of Piles Grove, Salem Co., widow. Int. Bond of William Summeril as Adm'r; James Dunlap fellowbondsman, both of Penn's Neck, said Co. Lib. 8, p. 235.

1755, July 3. Inventory, £49.8.4, incl. an old Bible and a sermon book; bonds and notes, £26.2.10; made at the house of William Summeral by Garret Vanemam and John Helms.

1751, May 15. Carroll, Thomas, of Northampton, or of Bridgetown, Burlington Co. Int. Ann, widow of, resigns her right of administration on his estate to Peter Bard of Philadelphia, or John Abraham de Normandie, of Bristol, both merchants.

1751, June 3. Bond of Peter Bard as Adm'r; John Abraham de Normandie fellowbondsman.

1751, June 6. Inventory, £32.11., incl. a Dutch servant boy, £20.
Burl. Wills, 4807 C.

1753, June 16. Carter, Benjamin, of Morris Town and County. Int. Inventory, £118.9.9, incl. books, £1, by Jeremiah Genung and John Looker.

1753, June 19. Bond of Sarah, his widow, as Adm'x; Barnabas Carter, of said Co., fellowbondsman. Lib. F, p. 136.

1758, June 16. Inventory, £116.4.9, by Jeremiah Genung and John Looker.

1758, May 18. Carter, Benjamin, of the Borough of Elizabeth, Essex Co.; will of. Wife, Hannah. Children—Abegil (wife of Samuel Day), Sarah, Hannah, Rhodey, Unice, Elener, Nance, David and Stephen. Real and personal estate. Executors—Benjamin Bonnel and Stephen Morehouse. Witnesses—James Carter, Seth Crowell, William Badcock. Proved June 16, 1759. Lib. G, p. 80.

1759, Dec. 26. Inventory, £232.19.0, by Josiah Broadwell and Richard Minthorn. "The plantation and mills sold for £1,000; a Townright for land, £8,15.0."

1759, Aug. 6. Carter, Daniel, of Essex Co. Int. Adm'r—Nathaniel Rusco, to whom John Carter, father of Daniel Carter, resigned his right of administration. Bondsman—Abraham Cadmus. Witnesses —Thomas Bartow. Lib. G, p. 92.

1760, Dec. 26. Carter, Joseph, of Newtown, Sussex Co. Int. Bond of widow, Mary Carter, as Adm'r; John Hayes fellowbondsman, both of said Co. Lib. 10, p. 463.

1760, Dec. 26. Inventory, £3.12.6, by Ephraim Darby and John Willson, Jr.

1759, Sept. 20. Carter, Luke, of Hanover, Morris Co., gentleman; will of. Wife, Martha. Children—Bate, Luke, Martha, Phebe, George and Thomas, the last three under age. Real and personal estate. Executors—the wife, son Luke and Josiah Miller. Witnesses—Thomas Genung, James Woodruff, John Post. Proved Jan. 22, 1760.
Lib. G, p. 142.

1757, Feb. 16. Carter, Nathaniel, of Springfield, Burlington Co., weaver. Int. Inventory, £9.16.2, by James Budd and Samuel Lippincott.

CALENDAR OF WILLS—1751-1760 55

1757, Feb. 19. Bond of **Mary Carter** as Adm'x; Anthony Morris and James Budd fellowbondsmen, all of Burlington Co. Lib. 8, p. 357.
1757, Aug. 22. Account by the administratrix, Mary Carter.

1758, Mar. 20. Cary, Elizabeth, of Penn's Neck, Salem Co. Int. Bond of James Dunlap as Adm'r; John Creag and Richard Moore fellowbondsmen, all of said Co. Lib. 8, p. 529.
1758, Mar. 20. Inventory, £94.17.7, incl. books, by John Creag and Richard Moore for the use of Mary Ann Dunlap, daughter of the dec'd.

Case, (see Kaes).

1754, Mar. 11. Cashow, Jaromes, of Somerset Co. Int. Jane Blaw, late widow of, and her present husband, Fredrik Blaw, refuse to administer on the estate of said Cashow, recommending Peter Nevius as administrator.
1754, Mar. 18. Bond of Peter Nevius as Adm'r, David Nevius fellowbondsman, both of said Co., yeoman. Lib. F, p. 161.

1754, Nov. 29. Castner, John, of Raritan Landing, in Middlesex Co., Shopkeeper. Int. Adm'x—Helena Castner. Bondsmen—Albert Bolmer, of Somerset Co., and William French, of Middlesex Co. Witnesses—Phebe Blomfield and George Hagawout. Lib. F, p. 229.
1755, Febr. 20. Inventory, £519.2.2, incl. 2 English Bibles, a Dutch Testament and Psalm book, £1.10; a silver watch, £7; book debts, £211.2.11; made by William Williamson, Daniel Bray and Edward Antill.

1756, Sept. 14. Castner, Peter, Sr., of Somerset Co., farmer; will of. Wife, Mary. Children—Peter, Jacob and Juliana, Home farm; another farm in said Co., adjoining Aaron Boylon's; personal property. Executors—Franciss Corsart and James Castner. Witnesses—Daniel Castner, Sarah Castner and Thomas Layten. Proved Dec. 1, 1756. Lib. F, p. 391.
1756, Dec. 3. Inventory, £275.17.11, incl. bond, book debts and notes, £49.4; a clock, 8s.; a Bible and other books, £2; a negro man, £50; a negro wench and child, £40; made by William McClelian, John Remer and David Castner.

1760, Dec. 17. Cathcart, Robert, of Upper Freehold, Monmouth Co. Int. Bond of Joseph Cathcart, of Upper Freehold, son of, as Adm'r; Obadiah Lippincott, of Shrewsbury, yeoman, fellowbondsman.
Lib. G, p. 369.
1760, Dec. 3. Inventory, £194.14.0, by Samuel Preston, Ezekiel Mount, Daniel Clark.

1760, Dec. 29. Chamberlain, Benjamin, of Newtown. Sussex Co. Int. Bond of widow, Mary Chamberlain, as Adm'x; Japheth Byram, Esq., fellowbondsman, both of Newtown. Lib. 10, p. 463.
1761, Jan. 1. Inventory, £110.13.5, by William Marsh and Isaac Harlow, the administratrix signing as "Mary, wife of Japheth Byram."

1759, Dec. 15. Chamberlen, William, of Monmouth Co.; will of. Wife, Caty, sole heiress and Executrix of real and personal estate. Witnesses—John Coates, Jane Chamberlin and Margret Dillon. Proved July 7, 1760. Lib. G, p. 379.

——, —— ——. Inventory, £161.1, incl. 12 books; bonds and notes, £51.12; made by Francis Jeffery, John Jeffery and James Lippencoot. (Filed June 16, 1761).

1757, Nov. 29. Chanders, John, of Hope, "Summerset" (Hunterdon?) Co., mariner, supposed to be lost at sea. Int. Bond of John Stout, of Summerset Co., as Adm'r; George Tucker, of New Jersey, fellowbondsman. Lib. 9, p. 174.
1758, Feb. 6. Inventory, £9.7.8., by David Stout and Edward Cooper.

1758, Oct. 31. Chandler, Abigal, of Manington, Salem Co., widow; will of. Divides personal estate between Richard, James Mason and Sarah (children of Jonathan Woodnut of Manington); sister, Sarah Smith, of Burlington, and her son Samuel Smith; Henry Woodnut; son, Samuel Mason and said Jonathan Woodnut, making the last named sole Executor. Witnesses—Willim Britten, John Kain and Josiah Kay. Proved June 5, 1759. Lib. 9, p. 371.
1759, June 5. Inventory, £335.17.5, incl. apparel, bonds, book debts, cash and notes, £251.4.11; made by Richard Woodnut and Whitten Cripps.

1750, Mar. 10. Chandler, John, of Elizabeth Town, Essex Co., cordwainer; will of. Wife, Mary; nephews—John and Moses, sons of brother Joseph Chandler, dec'd; Samuel, son of brother Samuel Chandler; John, son of brother Nathaniel Chandler. Sisters—Mary and Hannah Chandler. Real and personal estate. Executors—the wife and brother, Nathaniel Chandler. Witnesses—Stephen Crane, John Charlton, Robert Ogden. Proved June 16, 1759. Lib. G, p. 77.
1759, Mar. 26. Nathaniel Chandler, one of the executors named above, refuses to qualify, "because I suppose and conclude that there is no real occation for the same."
1759, Apr. 10. Inventory, £490.12.10, by Jonathan Crane and Caleb Crane.

1754, Nov. 9. Chandler, William, of Manington, Salem Co., yeoman; will of. Wife, Abigail, to receive for life the farm, now occupied by Seth Smith. The other real and personal estate to be divided between Edmund Kent, Erasmus Kent, Richard Vickory, brother John Chandler, sister Hannah Huse, and to cousins Hannah Hacket, Mary Evens, Moses Padget, children of cousin Mary Holts, to be paid to their father, Lawrence Holts, and brother, Samuel Chandler. Land bought of John Acton, 200 acres, adjoining William Willis and Jeremiah Smith, taken up by a right from Clement Hall; land bought by testator and Samuel Nicholson of William Hall and, Exr's of Clement Hall; lands bought of Simon Warner; 12 ac., part of Salem Town marsh, bought of Thomas Hill. Executors—the wife and Benjamin Cripps. Witnesses—Charles Fogg, Thomas Curry, Josiah Kay. Proved Jan. 21, 1755. Lib. 8, p. 237.
1755, Jan. 31. Inventory, £969.12.8, incl. cash in the house, £62.15; a large Bible; silver spoons, a servant man, £15; bonds, book accounts and notes, £485.3.11; made by William Hall and Jedidiah Allen.

1760, Aug. 23. Chapman, Abraham, son of Edward, of Burlington Co., deceased, asks, that John Chapman, of Chesterfield, said Co., yeoman, be appointed his guardian. Bond of John Chapman as such

CALENDAR OF WILLS—1751-1760   57

guardian; Isaac Heulings, of Burlington Co., merchant, fellowbondsman. Lib. G, p. 455.

1754, Mar. 14. Chapman, Edward, of Burlington Co. Int. Bond of Samuel Rogers, merchant, as administrator of the estate; Elisha Lawrence, gentleman, fellowbondsman, both of Allinstown, Monmouth Co. Bur. Adm'ns, 129.

1758, May 30. Chapman, John, of Burlington Co. Int. Inventory, £21.8.7, incl. a black walnut tea table, £1; a large Bible, £1; made by Jacob Brian and Joseph Peace.

1758, June 6. Bond of Joseph Reckless as Adm'r; Abraham Hewlings, Esq., fellowbondsman, both of said Co. Lib. 8, p. 533.

1758, Aug. 2. Account by the Adm'r, Joseph Reckless, of said Co., who makes it his debtor for £2.4.5.

1760, Sept. 13. Charney, John, of Upper Freehold Township, Monmouth Co., laborer; will of. To the Baptist Society £5. To my friend, Abiel Cook, Jr, £10. To Friend Nathaniel Cook, £10. To Friends William Tapscott and John Coward the overplus. Executors—Thomas Farr and Abel Cooke, Jr. Witnesses—John Leming, Abiel Cook, Joseph Strickland. Proved Nov. 4, 1760. Lib. 10, p. 420.

1755, Mar. 3. Cheesman, Benjamin, of Greenwich, Gloucester Co., yeoman; will of. Wife, Azubeth. Children—Mary Cupper, Hannah Cuzens, Jane Matlock, Benjamin and Martha, the last two under age. Real and personal estate. Executors—the wife and Francis Batten. Witnesses—Henrich Fabre, Francis Batten, Ann Batten. Proved August 28, 1755. Lib. 8, p. 278.

1755, July 17. Inventory, £241.7.5, incl. bonds and notes, £73.18.6, by Benjamin Liddon and Levi Shinn.

1757, Oct. 7. Cheesman, John, of Gloucester Township and Co. Int. Bond of widow, Bersheba Cheesman, as Adm'x; Edward Williams fellowbondsman, both of said County. Lib. 9, p. 61.

1757, Dec. 12. Inventory, £82, incl. wearing apparel, book debts and notes, £50.19; a Bible, 7sh.; made by John Carpenter and George Morgan.

1757, Feb. 4. Cheesman, Jotham, of Gloucester Co. Int. Inventory, £237.13.5, incl. two servantmen's time £27; a tame deer, £1; made by Thomas Bate and Robert Frd. Price.

1757, Feb. 8. Bond of Esther Cheesman as Adm'x; William Cheesman fellowbondsman, both of said Co. Lib. 8, p. 357.

1755, Aug. 14. Cheesman, Richard, of Newtown Township, Gloucester Co., yeoman; will of. Wife, Hannah, Jotham Cheesman and Robert Friend Price. Executors of real and personal estate. Children, apparently all under age, spoken of, but names not given. Witnesses—George Weed, William Harry, Mary Harry. Proved Sept. 18, 1755. Lib. 8, p. 371.

1755, Sept. 4. Inventory, £213.14.3, incl. book debts and cash, £49.18.3, by Joseph Ellis and Samuel Clement.

1761, Nov. 2. Account by Robert Friend Price and Tatum Williams and wife Hannah, late Hannah Cheesman, Executors, who have increased it to £270.18, and report a balance on hand of £141.4.10.

1753, Dec. 3. Cheesman, William, Sr., of New Brunswick Corporation, Middlesex Co.; will of. Wife, Martha. Children—Mary, Martha, Catherine, William, John, Joseph, Benjamin and Samuel. Grandchildren—Mary and Martha, daughters of daughter Charity (? dec'd.), and grandson, Safety Borden. Real and personal estate. Executors—Rev. James Carman and Jonathan Combs. Witnesses—William Ouke, Jacob Ouke and Isaac Hagewout. Proved Jan. 30, 1759.
Lib. G, p. 57.

1759, Jan. 29. Inventory, £225.2.2, incl. a negro man, £35; Indian corn, £14.14; a bond of Daniel Grandine, £27.10; due by Samuel Cheesman, 5sh.10d.; made by Fredrick Outgilt and Daniel Coler (Carter).

1759, Jan. 8. Cheesman, William, Jr., of the South Ward of Perth Amboy; will of. Wife, Mary. Daughters—Lydia and Martha, both under 21. Real and personal estate. Executors—brother, Joseph Cheasman, and Andrew Smyth. Witnesses—Thomas Combs, John Cosman and Benjamin Ward. Proved Jan. 24, 1759. Lib. G, p. 17.

1759, Jan. 16. Inventory: Real estate—a tract of 130 acres, £100; a farm of 10a., £250; a house and one acre, £50. Personal estate—£560.4.6, incl. 2 looking glasses, £1.11; a silver watch, £5; a map of Amsterdam, 4 sh.; 5 negroes (one a child), £125; bills, bonds and cash, £263.15.8; made by William Crawford and John Disbrow.

1751, July 15. Chetwood, William, of Essex Co. Int. Adm'x Margaret Chetwood, widow, of Elizabeth Town. Bondsman—Mathias Williamson, of same place. Witness—Uzal Ogden.

1751, July 31. Inventory, £58.16.6, by John Halstead and John Ross.
Lib. E, p. 538.

1753, Nov. 29. Chew, Joseph, of Deptford Township, (Gloucester Co.), West Jresey, but now in Philadelphia; will of. Wife, Elanor, sole heiress and Executrix of real and personal estate, directed to pay bond of £50. (due with Michael Fisher) to Hannah Cooper. Children spoken of, but not by name. Witnesses—Thomas Chew, Richard Chew, Michaell Fisher. Proved Dec. 26, 1753.
Lib. 8, p. 13.

1759, Oct. 19. Chew, Richard, of Gloucester Township and Co., yeoman; will of. Wife, Abigail, sole Executrix. Children—Constantine, Nathaniel, William, Alice Hampton, Massey Davis and Abigail. Real and personal estate. Witnesses—Mary Smallwood, Jane Penquite, William Wood. Proved Oct. 27, 1759.
Lib. 9, p. 344.

1759, Oct. 31. Inventory, £168.7.2., by Richard Cheesman and Benjamin Collines (Collins).

1760, Jan. 26. Christie, Dr. John, of Middlesex Co. Int. Letter praying grant of Letters of Administration of goods of John Christie to James Murray, of New York, druggist, principal creditor, there being no relation known to reside in America, and no person appearing to oppose the same; from Fra. Bernard to Thomas Bartow, Esq., who appointed as Adm'r. James Murray, of New York, principal creditor. Bondsman—Courtland Skinner, Esq., of Perth Amboy.
Lib. G, p. 123.

1760, Sept. 15. Churney, John, of Upper Freehold Township, Monmouth Co., laborer; will of. Divides estate between the Baptist

CALENDAR OF WILLS—1751-1760 59

Society, Thomas Farr, Abial Cook, Jr., Nathaniel Cook, William Tapscot and John Coward. Executors—Thomas Farr and Abial Cook, Jr. Witnesses—John Liming. Abiel Cook and Joseph Stricklan. Proved Nov. 4, 1760. Lib. 10, p. 420.
1760, Oct. 15. Inventory, £73.6.6, incl. bills, bonds and book debts, £65.10.6; made by John Liming and Moses Robins.

1756, May 6. Cile, Ann, of Burlington City. Int. Bond of John Ferguson, boatman, as Adm'r; Jonathan Thomas and Elias Hughes fellowbondsmen, all of said City. Lib. 8, p. 306.

1754, Nov. 28. Cipres Elizabeth, of Burlington Co. Int. Bond of Johann Adam Johe (signs in German script) as Adm'r; John Goldy fellowbondsman, both of said Co. Lib. 8, p. 65.
1754, Nov. 28. Inventory, £64.19.5, by Robert Hill and John Goldy.
Lib. 8, p. 65.

———, ——— ———. Clark, Daniel, of the "Burrough" of Elisabeth, Somerset (?) Co.; will of, "signed with the consent of Abigail Clark, his wife." Children—John, Daniel, Stephanus, Jabesh, Sarah, Deborah and Keturah, all under age; an expected child. Home farm; saltmeadow, given by father, John Clark, to testator and brother Jotham; town rights; personal estate. Executors—the wife, brother Jotham Clark and William Parrot. Witnesses—Nathaniel Rogers, Sarah Bebout, Timothy Allen. Proved April 21, 1756. Lib. F, p. 443.
1756, Apr. 12. Inventory, £74.7.10, by Josiah Broadwell and Thomas Baker.

1758, Dec. 29. Clark, Daniel, of Elizabeth Town, Essex Co. Int. Adm'x—Rebecka Clark, widow. Bondsman—Daniel Clark, son of Daniel Clark, dec'd. Witness—Thos. Bartow.
1759, Jan. 3. Inventory, £99.9.9, by John Cory and John Miller.
Lib. G, p. 13.

1760, Oct. 8. Clark, Elizabeth, of Greenwich, Cumberland Co., widow; will of. Daughters—Susannah Stathem and Elizabeth Penton. Personal estate. Executor—nephew, John Reves. Witnesses—Thomas Ewing, Elizabeth Leek, Maskell Ewing. Proved Dec. 2, 1760.
Lib. 10, p. 182.
1760, Nov. 1. Inventory, £51.3.4, by Thomas Parke and Thomas Ewing.

1752, Dec. 19. Clark, James, Sr., of the "Burro" of Elizabeth, Essex Co., yeoman; will of. Wife, Anne. Children—Jeremiah, Elias, James (all under age), Rachel and Mary Ann. Real and personal estate, incl. money due by brother Samuel. Executors—the wife and Recompense Stanbery. Witnesses—Sarah Craig, Robert More, John Joline. Proved Feb. 24, 1753. Lib. F, p. 101.
1753, Jan. 15. Inventory, £211.5.4, by Thomas Clark and Eliphalet Frazey.

1751, Nov. 18. Clark, Joseph, Jr., of Elizabeth Town, yeoman. Int. Adm'x—Mary Clark, widow. Bondsman—Andrew Craig of same Town, yeoman. Witness—Thos. Bartow. Lib. F, p. 3.

1758, June 27. Clark, Joshua, of the Borough of Elizabeth, Essex Co., yeoman; will of. Wife, Mary. Children—Robert (sole Executor), Keziah, Abigail, Jane, Sarah, Elizabeth, Joannah and Phebe. Real and personal estate. Witnesses—Lewis Mulford, Joseph Conkling, Abraham Clark, Jr. Proved March 12, 1759. Lib. G, p. 39.

1752, Dec. 29. Clark, Samuel, of Elizabeth Borough, Essex Co., yeoman; will of. Mother, Hannah Clark; cousin, Richard Clark. Real and personal estate. Executor—Thomas Clark, Esq. Witnesses —James Still Coberly, Lambert Robson, Abraham Clark, Jr. Proved Oct. 2, 1753. Lib. F, p. 138.

1752, July 16. Clark, Thomas, of Egg Harbour, Burlington Co. Int., Inventory of his personalty and of his three sons, Thomas, David and Elijah Clark, £207.19, incl. a Bible, and bonds due by Richard Fitz Randolph, Paul Miller and Simon Nichols, £65; made by Nehemiah Beebe and Robert Morss.
1752, July 20. Bond of David Clark, of Little Eggharbour, Burlington Co., yeoman, as Adm'r; Robert Morss (Morse), of Great Eggharbour, Gloucester Co., fellowbondsman. Lib. 7, p. 304.
1753, Oct. 5. Account of Adm'r.

1756, Aug. 14. Clarke, Benjamin, Jr., of Middlesex Co., son of Benjamin, dec'd, petitions that John Robins be appointed his guardian. Bond of John Robins of Monmouth Co., blacksmith, as such guardian, George Eyre of Burlington City fellowbondsman.
Mon. Wills, 2131 M.

1759, May 24. Clarke, John, of Fairfield Township, Cumberland Co. Int. Inventory, £50.11.11, incl. books, blacksmith's tools, iron and "cole," £15.14.9; 10 yds. of flannel cloth at the mill, £1.15; made by Joseph Ogden and Theophi Elmer.
1759, June 16. Bond of his widow, Esther Clarck, as Adm'x of the estate; Joseph Ogden and Theophi Elmer, both of Fairfield, fellowbondsmen. Lib. 10, p. 109.

1755, June 24. Clarke, Samuel, of Cumberland Co. Int. Inventory £174.3.7, incl. a negroman, £40, by Hugh Dunn and Benjamin Garrison.
1755, June 30. Bond of his widow, Esther Clark, as Adm'x; Reuben Jarman, yeoman, fellowbondsman, both of said Co.
1762, Mar. 25. Account by Azel Peirson, representative of the deceased Administratrix, Esther Clark, who charges for supporting three small children of dec'd., the youngest 4 months old, for 4 years and 9 months, £42.5, and reports on hand £24.18.5.
Cumb. Wills, 264 F.

1757, Oct. 25. Clarkson, John, of Woodbridge, Middlesex Co.; Will of. Children—James, Robert, Christian Stelle, Susannah Dunham, Experience Edgar. Grandsons—John, Isaac and Clarkson Manning, children of daughter Cathrine and Isaac Manning. Real estate—A lot of 5 acres in Rariton meadows; other land in Woodbridge; a freehold right in the Township. Personal property—Tool's Annotations on the New Testament; a large house Bible; Bunyon's books; a sermon book of "Mr. Flavel's Seting Out;" a volume of English history; negro slaves. Executors—son James, William McDaniel and John Heburn. Witnesses—Jeremiah Wright, John Shotwell and William Jennings. Proved Nov. 19, 1757, when John Hepburn refuses to serve as Executor. Lib. F, p. 467.

CALENDAR OF WILLS—1751-1760   61

1758, Aug. 18. Clawson, Cornelious, Sr., of Piscataway, Middlesex Co.; will of. Wife, Mary. Children—Cornelious, William, Zachariah, Mary Shaver, Sarah Potter, Jane Sutton, Catharine Campbell and Hanna Long. Grandchildren—Benjamin ———, Susannah Drake and Elizebeth Potter. Real and personal estate. Executors—son, Cornelious, and son-in-law, Joseph Campbell. Witnesses—Elisha Whitehead, John Campbell and Daniel Barto. Proved Sept. 11, 1758
Lib. F, p. 551.
1758, Aug. 29. Inventory, £429.6.1, incl. bills, bonds, book debts and cash, £192.12.8; made by John Hepburn and Reune Runyon.

1759, June 19. Clayter, Edgecomb, of Essex Co. Int. "A Soldier in the New Jersey Regiment." Adm'x—Alice Clayter, his widow. Bondsman—Peter Selove, yeoman. Witness—Thomas Bartow.
Lib. G, p. 83.

1760, Apr. 28. Cleverly, Jonathan, of Gloucester Township and Co., husbandman. Int. Inventory, £20.1.10, by Thomas Parker and John Porck.
1760, May 2. Bond of John Connilly, husbandman, as Adm'r; Luke Gibson, yeoman, fellowbondsman, both of Deptford Township, said Co.
Lib. 10, p. 80.

1757, Nov. 8. Clifford, George, of Bethlehem, Hunterdon Co.; will of. Wife, Mary, sole Executrix. Children—John, James, Mary, Margaret, Sarah and Anne, who has son George. Witnesses—Daniel McKintash and Joseph Beavers. Codicil of November 9 makes slight changes. Witnesses—Garrett Albertson and Joseph Beavers. Proved Dec. 12, 1757.
Lib. G, p. 169.
1757, Dec. 8. Inventory, £462.3.1., incl. bills, bonds and notes, £274.3.7; books; John Tolberd's time for 6 years, £10; Jacob Sroy's time for 3 months, £2.10; made by Charles Hoff, Jr.; and Samuel Everitt.

1751, Nov. 21. Clifton, Thomas, of Waterford, Gloucester Co., yeoman; will of. Wife, Amey. Children—Simon, Rachel and Mary, all under age. Real and personal estate. Executors—the wife and Henry Wood of said Co. Witnesses—John Daniel, John Jones, Samuel Spicer. Proved Dec. 12, 1751.
Lib. 7, p. 159.
———, ——— —. Inventory, £64.16.6, by Samuel Davis and James Lecouy.

1753, Nov. 10. Clothier, Anne, of Chesterfield, Burlington Co., widow of Henry Clothier; will of. Mother, Mary Rockhill. Son-in-law, James Clothier. Daughter-in-law, Mary Allen. Sister, Sarah Black. Cousins—Sarah Borradaill, Mary Done, Bridget Rockhill, Sarah English, William Black, Achsah Black, Ezra Black; also John Black and Edward Black, the sons of William Black. Cousins—Richard Rockhill, Ann Trout. Sister-in-laws—Mary Rockhill, Sarah Rockhill, Anne Rockhill. Cousins—Mary Godley, Anne Robinson. Achsah Rockhill, Mercy Curtis, Margaret Rockhill, Hannah Rockhill, Abigail Rockhill and Sarah Rockhill. To brothers, $2 each. Executors—Cousins, William Black and Samuel Black. Witnesses—Henry Wayman, Sarah Taylor. Proved Dec. 5, 1753.
Lib. 6, p. 5.
1753, Dec. 8. Inventory, £144.3.1, by Joseph Curtis and Samuel Taylor, Jr.

1743, Dec. 20. Clowes, Joseph, of Burlington City, yeoman; Will of. Wife, Patience, sole heiress and Executrix of real and personal estate. Witnesses—Joseph Allinson, Martha DeCow, Isaac DeCow. Proved Oct. 4, 1752. Burl. Wills, 4941 C.

1752, June 18. Clowes, Patience, of Burlington City, widow; Will of. Gives reality (a house and lot in High Str.) and personal estate to sister, Abigail Barker, and Elizabeth, daughter of Joshua Barker, of Burlington, tanner, dec'd. Executors—Joshua Raper and Samuel Smith, both of Burlington. Witness—Rowland Ellis, who wrote the instrument and testifies, testatrix intended to call other witnesses, but failed to do so. Proved Sept. 11, 1759. Lib. 9, p. 299.

1751, May 5. Coate, John, of Kingwood Township, Hunterdon Co., tavern keeper; Will of. Wife, Esther. Children spoken of, but not by name, except son, Henry, who, and his mother are made Executors. Witnesses—Nathaniel Leforge, James Brooks, John Simcock, Sr. Proved Sept. 10, 1751. Lib. 7, p. 222.

1751, Sept. 3. Inventory, £368.16.3, incl. books; a silver spoon; bonds and book debts, £320; made by John Mullinner and Nathaniel Leforge.

1760, Sept. 3. Cobb, Samuel, of Greenwich Township, Gloucester Co., husbandman. Int. Inventory, £20.16.7, incl. book debts and notes, £7.13.2, by Mathew Gill and Nathan Boys.

1760, Sept. 13. Bond of widow, Rachael Cobb, as Adm'x; Nathan Boys, yeoman, fellowbondsman, both of said Township.
Lib. 10, p. 292.

1758, Apr. 29. Cock, John, of Somerset Co. (South Branch of the Raritan); will of. Children—John, Samuel, Henry, Jacob, Thomas, Maudlen Middagh, Elenor Hall, Catharine (wife of Edward Hall), and Margaret, wife of Dumenicus van Dicke. Grandchildren, i. e., children of son William, names not given. Real and personal estate including 3 negroes. (Elenor Hall and Maudlen Middagh are apparently residents of Esopus, N. Y.). Executors—the five sons, first above named. Witnesses—Cornelius Low in Somerset, Fradrick van Fleet and Gerades Aten. Proved July 31, 1758. Lib. F, p. 542.

1758, July 5. Inventory, £88.18.4, incl. notes, £43.3.2, by Cornelius vaen Kaempen and Cornelius Low.

1751, Apr. 30. Cock, Thomas, of Kingwood, Hunterdon Co. Int. Inventory, £530.6.3, incl. 5 negro slaves, £194, by Lawrence Haff (Hoff) and James Thatcher.

1751, Sept. 26. Bond of his widow, Elleanor Cock, Adm'x; Lawrence Haff of Kingwood, fellowbondsman. Lib. 6, p. 456.

1758, Nov. 2, Cock, William, of Bridgewater, Somerset Co., yeoman. Int. Bond of Cornelia, widow, as Adm'x; Yan van Neste, of said Co., yeoman, fellowbondsman. Lib. F, p. 560.

1758, Nov. 14. Inventory, £199.11.11, incl. books, wheat, rye, corn, bonds and cash, £47.4.7, by Cornelius vaen Kaempen and Edward Hall.

1760, Oct. 18. Account by Adm'x, Cornelia Cock.

1757, Nov. 11. Coddington, John, of Woodbridge Township, Middlesex Co.; Will of Wife, Margret. Children—Abigail, Sarah, (both under age), James, Robert, John, Daniel and David (the last four un-

CALENDAR OF WILLS—1751-1760   63

der age). Home farm, 41 acres on Cedar Cove, bought of Jacob Fitzrandolph; 3½ ac. in Sunken Marsh, bought of Samuel Fitzrandolph; personal property, incl. a negro wench. Executors—the wife and William Edgar. Witnesses—Job Pack, Isaac Fitz Randolph and David Donham. Proved Jan. 5, 1758. Lib. F, p. 482.

1757, Aug. 1. Coddington, Samuel, of Woodbridge, Middlesex Co. Int. Admr's—Mary Coddington, his widow, and David Coddington, of Woodbridge, his brother. Bondsman—John Coddington. Witness—Thomas Bartow. Lib. F, p. 441.
1757, July 29. Inventory, £67.12.6, by William Edgar and Jacob Fitzrandolph.

1746, Dec. 1. Codemus, Thomas, of Newark, Essex Co., yeoman; will of. Wife, Sarah. Children—Malechi, Anne, Frances, Sarah, Jane, Rachel, Katherine, Margeret. Three children of dec'd. daughter, Mary. Real and personal estate. Executors—son Malechi, and nephew, Abraham Codemus. Witnesses—Israel Bauldwin, Henderek Spier, Daniel Taylor. Proved Sept. 11, 1753. Lib. F, p. 231.
1753, Sept. 12. Inventory, £37.9.3, by Daniel Pierson and William Dow.

1750, May 26. Codington, Benjamin, Sr., of Woodbridge, Middlesex Co., yeoman; will of. Wife, Mary. Children—Margaret (wife of Abner Wright), Sarah (wife of William Oliver), Mary (wife of William Pangburn), Martha (wife of Jonathan Frazee), Elizabeth (wife of Solomon Bycount), Lydia (wife of Job Couger, Jr.), Zillah (wife of Enoch Couger), Rebecca, Mary (called Mary Codington), Sabrah, Elizabeth Codington, Benjamin, Thomas, Isaac, John, Ashur, Uzziah, Joatham and Reuben. Real and personal estate. Exectuors—the wife, with sons Benjamin and Isaac. Witnesses—Francis Everitt, William Messenger, Thomas Chapman. Proved May 19, 1753.
Lib. F 2, p. 120.
1753, Apr. 30. Inventory, £171.5, by Isaac Prall and William Moore.

1759, Oct. 27. Codmus, Abraham, of Second River, Essex Co., merchant; Will of. Wife, Chertey. Children—Thomas, Peter, John Speere, Abraham Speere and Mary King. Homestead of 14 acres, bought of Simeon Vrelandt and wife, Marretye; small lot adjoining, bought of Franscoys Wouterse; lot of 25 a., 49 rods, on the Third River, Newark, bought of Malicut Codmus, and wife, Elizabeth; also personal property. Executors—sons John Speere and Thomas Codmus. Witnesses—Thomas Codmus, Corneleya Caddemus, William Hawhey. Proved Feb. 20, 1760. Lib. G, p. 162.
1760, Mar. 11. Inventory, £139.6.0, by Samuel Whittemore and William Dow.

1751, Nov. 18. Cohlan, Patrick, of Bridgetown, Burlington Co., labourer. Int. Bond of John Justice, tailor, as Adm'r; Nathan Watson and Zachariah Rossell, yeoman, fellowbondsmen, all of Bridgetown.
Lib. 7, p. 299.

1759, Apr. 7.. Coldwell (Caldwell), Allen, of Greenwich Township, Gloucester Co., blacksmith. Int. Inventory, £11.3.11, by Gabriel Rambo and Samuel Parker.

1759, Apr. 18. Bond of **Rebecca Caldwell** as Adm'x; William Sharp, yeoman, fellowbondsman, both of Greenwich Township.
Lib. 9, p. 233.

1759, Jan. 14. **Cole, Elias,** of Gloucester Co., Int. Bond of Johanna Cole as Adm'x; Samuel Hugg fellowbondsman, both of said Co.
Lib. 9, p. 177.

1754, Jan. 31. **Cole, James,** of Morris Town, Morris Co. Int. Bond of Phebe, widow, as Adm'x; Jacob Ford and Joseph Prudden, both of said Co., fellowbondsmen. Lib. F, p. 157.
1754, Mar. 17. Inventory, £48,16, by Caleb Osborn and Samuel Hudson, Jr.

1759, Sept. 20. **Cole, Tunis, Jr.,** of Readingstown, Hunterdon Co. Int. Bond of Teunis Cole of Readingstown as Adm'r; Isaac Yard, of Trenton, said Co., fellowbondsman. Lib. G, p. 455.
1760, May 1. Account by the Adm'r.

1760, May 6. **Cole, Tunis,** of Hunterdon Co.; will of. Wife, Sarah. Children—John, Benjamin, David, Ezekiel, Isaiah (under age), Sarah. Daughter of dec'd son, Tunis, whose widow, expecting another child, is also provided for. Real and personal estate. Executors—Marten Ryerson and George Reading. Witnesses—George Bigges (Biggs), Benjamin Alleger and Edward Wilmot. Proved June 2, 1760.
Lib. 10, p. 598.
1760, May 24. Inventory, £307.14.3, incl. a negro wench, £60., by George Biggs and Benjamin Alliger.

1752, Febr. 17. **Cole, William, Jr.,** "Elisabette," (Elizabeth), yeoman; will of. Wife, Elisabeth. Children—William, Dennis, Elisabeth, Mary, James, Phebe, the sons all under age. Real and personal estate. Executors—brother, Joseph Cole, and John Shotwell. Witnesses—Robert Willis, Robert Crosley, Mary Crosley. Proved Nov. 20, 1754. Lib. F, p. 226.

1752, Oct. 26. **Cole, William Clayland,** of Bridgetown, Burlington Co. Int. Bond of Peter Allinson, of Bridgetown, joiner, as Adm'x; Joseph Allinson, of Burlington, yeoman, fellowbondsman.
Lib. 7, p. 306.

1756, Dec. 23. **Coleman, Nathaniel,** of Hunterdon Co. Int. Inventory, £140.5.6, by Daniel Vliet and William Scholey.
1756, Dec. 28. Bond of Anne Coleman, as Adm'x; Daniel Vliet fellowbondsman, both of Bethleham, said Co. Lib. 8, p. 397.

1754, July —. **Colkitt, Robert,** son of James Colket of Philadelphia, petitions that Robert Powel, of Burlington Co., be appointed his guardian.
1754, July 6. Bond of Robert Powell as such guardian; Benjamin Brown fellowbondsman; both of Burlington Co., yeoman.
Burl. Wills, 5401 C.

1755, July 9. **Collard, William,** of Freehold, Monmouth Co., cordwainer. Int. Bond of Elijah Collard, of Sussex Co., yeoman, as Adm'r; George Eggers, of Morris Co., yeoman, fellowbondsman.
Lib. F, p. 265.

CALENDAR OF WILLS—1751-1760   65

1755, July 12. Inventory, £154.10.8, incl. a bond and cash, £139.1.6, by Timothy Lloyd and Gerrit Wyckoff.

1757, June 27. Collings, Joseph, of Middletown, Monmouth Co., cooper. Int. Mary, widow, consents that Joseph Dorsett and John Collings should administer on his estate. Bond of Joseph Dorsett and John Collings as Adm'rs; John Dennis fellowbondsman, all of Middletown, yeomen.   Lib. F, p. 437.
1757, June 29. Inventory, £317.10.7, incl. bonds, book debts and notes £267.7.7, by James Mott and Jonathan Peairs.

1760, Mar. 29. Collins, Abijah, of Burlington Co. Int. Bond of Samuel Jones as Adm'r; Daniel Ellis Fellowbondsman, both of said Co.   Lib. 9, p. 415.

1756, June 10. Collins, Benjamin, of Newton Township, Gloucester Co., carpenter. Int. Bond of Priscilla Collins as Adm'x; Ebenezer Hopkins and Joseph Hedger fellowbondsmen, all of said Co.
   Lib. 8, p. 395.
1756, June 11. Inventory, £407.9.8, incl. bonds, book debts and notes, £294.8.2, and a clock made by Thomas Hinchman and Robert Frd. Price.

1758, Apr. 18. Collins, Joseph, Jr., son of Benjamin, of Gloucester Co., petitions that Samuel Clement, Jr., be appointed his guardian.
1753, May —. Bond of Samuel Clement, Jr., as such guardian; Joseph Harrison, Esqr., fellowbondsman; both of Gloucester Co.
   Lib. 8, p. 544.

1755, Mar. 4. Collum, Mary, of Burlington City and Co.; Will of. Children—Elizabeth (wife of Joseph Woodard) and James. Real and personal estate. Executors—son, James, and Abraham Heulings. Witnesses—John Shaw, Elias Hughes, William Heulings. Proved March 17, 1755.   Lib. 8, p. 130.
1755, Mar. 19. Inventory, £110,6.6, incl. an 8-day clock, £10; a gilt-framed looking glass, £2.5; a large do., £4; a negro woman, £1; made by Jonathan Smith and John Bacon.
1762, Jan. 29. Account by the above named Executors, who add to the inventory the value of an old negro woman, £1 and the price of the house and lot in Burlington, £110.

1758, Jan. 22. Colson, George, of Piles Grove Township, Salem Co., yeoman; will of. Wife (not named). Children—George, Jonathan, David, William, Hannah and Sarah, all but George under age. Real and personal estate. Executors—the wife, son George and Samuel Lippincott. Witnesses—Thomas Davis, John Duell, Jr., and Abraham Lord. Proved March 23, 1758.   Lib. 9, p. 5.
1758, Mar. 15. Inventory, £137.2, by Elisha Bassett and Joseph Champneys.
1758, Mar. 20. Samuel Lippincott, one of the Executors named above, declines to act.
1766, Apr. 25. Account by George Colson, Acting Executor.

1752, Oct. 5. Combs, Francis, of Upper Freehold, Monmouth Co. Int. Bond of John Warrick (Warwick), of Upper Freehold, wool-

5

comber, as Adm'r; William Bunting, of Chesterfield, Burlington Co., yeoman, fellowbondsman. Lib. 7, p. 305.
1752, Oct. 4. Inventory, £4.4, incl. books, 2 sh., by Thomas Harbut and William Bunting.

1757, June 7. Combs, Thomas, of Upper Freehold Township, Monmouth Co., yeoman; will of. Wife, Kesiah. Children—John, James, Lydia and Dinah. Real and personal estate. Executors—the wife and son John. Witnesses—Wm. Liming, Joseph Robins and William Lawrence. Proved Dec. 22, 1757. Lib. 9, p. 166.

1758, Jan. 14. Compton, Cornelius, Jr., of Middletown, Monmouth Co., carpenter. Int. Bond of William Compton, father, as Adm'r; Samuel Tilton fellowbondsman, both of Middletown, yeomen.
Lib. F, p. 486.
1758, Jan. 19. Inventory, £16.3, by George Taylor and Jonathan Stout.

1754, May 16. Compton, William, of Woodbridge, Middlesex Co.; will of. Brother, John. Children of brothers David and Samuel Compton. Sister, Sarah Kelly, and her children, viz., Daniel Alward and Anne White, heirs of real and personal estate. Executors—brothers John and David Compton. Witnesses—Jonathan Thickstun, William McCreery, Samuel Preston. Proved June 4, 1754.
Lib. F, p. 183.
1754, June 14. Inventory, £110.11.4, incl. bills and bonds, £65.0.1, by Charles Ford and Henry Sutton.

1756, Apr. 10. Conckling, Jonathan, of Morris Town, Morris Co., yeoman; will of. Wife, Abegael. Children—John, Matthew, Josiah and Abegael, all under age. Real and personal estate. Executors—the wife, Gideon Hedges of South Hanover, and nephew, Stephen Conckling. Witnesses—Benjamin Baylis, Samuel Baylis, Richard Kemble. Proved Nov. 4, 1756. Lib. F, p. 387.

1760, June 9. Conet, Elizabeth, of the Borough of Elizabeth, Essex Co.; will of. Children—Elezebeth, Ruth, Sarah and Samuel. Legacies to Henry Wells and John Conet. Personal estate. Executor—Garnier (Gardner) Conet. Witnesses—Ruth and Anthoney Badgley, Abraham Clarke (3), Thomas Woodruff. Proved June 19, 1760.
Lib. G, p. 338.

1749, Jan. 30. Conger, Job, Sr., of Woodbridge—Raway Neck, Middlesex Co., yeoman; will of. Wife, Kezia. Children—Job, Enoch, Moses, Ruth (wife of Nathaniel Price), Sarah (wife of Daniel Codington), Elizabeth (wife of Reuben Hierd), Esther and Bathia, the last two under age. Real and personal estate. Executors—the wife, son Enoch and William Moore. Witnesses—Job Pack, Benjamin Tharp and Thomas Chapman. Proved Feb. 17, 1758. Lib. F, p. 497.

1751, July 1. Conine (Konyn), Dierck, of Pacatio—(Piscataway), Middlesex Co., "gantalman"; will of. Wife, Catlinty. Sons—Fillip, Andris (to have the home). Dirrick, David, John, Jacob. Real and personal estate. Executors—the wife and son Andries. Witnesses—Michael Field, Cornelius Dalley, Daniel McKinney. Proved Nov. 21, 1751. Lib. F, p. 9.

CALENDAR OF WILLS—1751-1760

1751, Nov. 14. Inventory, £266.10.6, apparently incomplete, but incl. 5 negro slaves, £145, made by Jeremiah Field and William Olden.

1752, Nov. 24. Conine, Phillip, of Freehold, Monmouth Co., miller; will of. Wife, Elisabeth. Children—Richard and Rachel, both under age. Real and personal estate. Executors—Joseph Rue and William Laird. Witnesses—Michell Eickson (Erickson), David English, Jr., Robert English Smith. Proved Dec. 11, 1752. Lib. F, p. 79.
1752, Dec. 6. Inventory of the estate. Reality, a small farm at Panalapan, £120; personal, £1,807.19; incl. "desperit" debts (Indians and negroes among the debtors), £56.11.5½; 17 books, 10s.; made by James Day, Thomas Lauree (?) and William Cowenhoven.
1753, Oct. 1. Statement, by the Executors at Bound Brook, Brigewater Township, of what the widow carried away, valued at £6.16.7.; do. by Thomas ——— and Samuel Coryell of goods in her possession, £4.13.
1753, Dec. 3. Additional Inventory, £221.14, by the Executors.
1758, Dec. 21. Account of the estate by the Executors.

1757, May 25. Coningham, Alexander, late of Cumberland Co. Int. Adm'x—Elizabeth Bourten, spinster. Bondsmen—Alexander Smith and Eleanah Dare, husbandmen. Witnesses—Elizabeth Mulford and Elias Cotting. Cumb. Wills, 144 F.

1752, June 1. Conly, John, of Deerfield Township, Cumberland Co. Int. Adm'r—Thomas Ogden, yeoman, of Fairfield Township. Bondsman—Silas Parvin, of Hopewell Township. Cumb. Wills, 85 F.

1751, Apr. 20. Conner, Charles, of Salem Co. Int. Bond of Attwood Shule, of Philadelphia, merchant, as Adm'r; no fellowbondsmen. Salem Wills, 876 Q.

1760, Feb. 14. Connet, Matthew, Sr., of the Borough of Elizabeth, Essex Co.; will of. Children—James, Benjamin, Matthew, Rebekah, Mary, Hester and Anna. Real and personal estate. Executors—John Meeker and Samuel Hicks. Witnesses—Samuel Willis, Jonathan Marsh, Jr., Jonathan Danells. Proved March 11, 1760. Lib. G, p. 148.

1760, June 19. Connet, Samuel, of Essex Co. Int. Adm'r—Gardner Connet, of said Co. Bondsman—Thomas Woodruff of said Co. Witness—John Smyth. Lib. G, p. 232.

1759, Dec. 21. Connoway, Robert, of Pen's Neck, Salem Co., yeoman; will of. Wife, Margret, sole Executrix of real and personal estate. Daughters—Rebecca Pauling, Margret Philpot, Ann and Mary. Witnesses—Sarah Vickery, Esther Smith and Peter Litsinger. Proved Jan. 25, 1760. Lib. 10, p. 530.
1760, Jan. 28. Inventory, £274.16.1, by John Dunn and Joseph Wright.

1752, Aug. 1. Conrow (Conoro), Jacob, of Eggharbour. Int. Grace, widow, signing "Grace Stockham," certifies, with Israel Stoakham, that they have delivered all of the goods and chattels of the dec'd. to James Pharo.
1752, Aug. 5. Bond of James Pharo, of Little Eggharbour, as Adm'r; Jeremiah Baker, of Burlington Co., yeoman, fellowbondsman. Lib. 7, p. 304.

1752, Apr. 15. Inventory £9.18.3, by Jeremiah Baker, Jr., and John Perkin (Purkins, Parker?) at New Stafford, and sworn to by them before Timothy Ridgway, J. P., for Monmouth Co.

1760, Febr. 19. Cook, Ebenezer, of Shrewsbury Township, Monmouth Co.; will of. Wife, Sarah. Children—Thomas, William, Hannah, Faith and Mary, all under age. Real and personal estate. Executors—Joseph Cook and Thomas Tilton, Jr. Witnesses—David Johnston, Danel Mitchel, John Morris and Isaac Mitchel. Proved March 15, 1760. Lib. G, p. 230.

1763, Mar. 20. Inventory, £253.18.9, by David Johnston and Joseph Potter.

1756, Mar. 11. Cook, Ellis, of Hanover, Morris Co., yeoman; will of. Sons—William, Ellis (both named Executors), Jonathan, Epaphras and John. Real and personal estate. Witnesses—Jonathan Squier, Thomas Biglow and William Dixon. Proved Aug. 31, 1756.
Lib. F, p. 404.

1752, Apr. 22. Cook, Richard, of Essex Co. Int. Adm'r—George Harris, principal creditor; Joseph Johnson, fellowbondsman.

1752, May 4. Inventory, £14.8.6, by Henry Brockholls and George Vreland. Additional inventory, made by George Harris, the Administrator, Nov. 4, 1752, adds £2.10.3. Bergen Wills, 338 B.

1754, Jan. 24. Cooke, Jacob, of Mendum, Morris Co. Int. Rebeckah, widow, resigns her right to administer on his estate to his son, Asa Cooke.

1754, Feb. 5. Bond of Asa Cooke as Adm'r; Ebenezer Byram fellowbondsman, both of Mendum. Lib. F, p. 156.

1760, Aug. 20. Cooke, William, of Chesterfield Township, Burlington Co. Int. Bond of Mary, the widow, and William Cleayton, of Trenton, as Admr's; Richard Saltar, of Nottingham, and Michael Newbold, of Chesterfield, fellowbondsmen.

1760, Sept. 1. Inventory, £3772.17, incl. plate, £18; bonds, £2411.15; bonds supposed to be insolvent, or little worth, £827.14.2; books; book debts, £114.12.10; a negro man (no value given, as he is to be set free); made by Anthony Sykes and John Steward.
Burl. Wills, 6613 C.

1757, Febr. 18. Cooley, James, of Bethlehem, Hunterdon Co. Int. Bond of Mary Cooley and James Dickey as Admr's; Robert Shields fellowbondsman, all of Bethlehem. Lib. 8, p. 397.

1757, — —. Inventory, £127.4.6, by Robert Shields and Benjamin Smyth.

1757, Nov. 14. Account by the Administrators.

1755, May 17. Cooper, Benjamin, of Middletown, Monmouth Co., yeoman; will of. Wife, Hester. Children—Benjamin, Obadiah, David, Josiah, Elizabeth, Phebey and Ellenor. Real and personal estate. Executors—Edward Taylor and Joseph Stilwell, both of Middletown. Witnesses—William Applegate, Nathaniel Leonard and Hester Bowne. Proved June 24, 1755. Lib. F, p. 315.

CALENDAR OF WILLS—1751-1760   69

1760, April 29. Cooper, Benjamin, of Middlesex Co. Int. Adm'r—Benjamin Haviland, of Monmouth Co., Catherine Cooper renouncing. Bondsman—William Rose, of Middlesex Co. Witness—John Smyth.
Lib. G, p. 169.
1760, Apr. 29. Inventory, £68, by John and Richard Ball.

1760, Apr. 26. Cooper, Daniel, of Greenwich Township, Gloucester Co., yeoman. Int. Inventory, £105.7.2, by William Nickle and Daniel Hillman.
1760, May 5. Bond of widow, Esther Cooper, as Adm'x; Andrew Lock, yeoman, fellowbondsman, both of said Township. Lib. 10, p. 80.

1753, Dec. 27. Cooper, Hannah, widow of Joseph, of Newton, Gloucester Co.; will of. Grandchildren—Mary Howel, Hannah Howel and Lydia Howel. Cousin—Hannah Spence. Brother—Robert Dent and his wife. Brother-in-law—William Gott and his wife. Personal estate. Executors—Israel Pemberton, Jr., and William Mood both of Philadelphia merchants, and granddaughter, Mary Howel. Witnesses—Daniel Fortiner, Thomas Cooper, Samuel Spicer. Proved Sept. 3, 1754.
Lib. 8, p. 102.
1754, Feb. 15. Inventory, £762.5, incl. a watch and chain, £7; silver buckles and other trinkets, £4; bonds and notes, £299.1.3; a clock, £12; a looking glass, £3; a Bible and other books, £5.17; 187 oz. of plate, including tankards and spoons, £79.9.6; a negro man, £30; a white servant boy, Mattias Koen, who has 7½ years to serve yet, £18; made by Richard Matlack and Thomas Bate.

1756, Dec. 6. Cooper, Hannah, of Newark, Essex Co., "being aged"; will of. Children—Thomas Sergeant, Jonathan (sole Executor), Hannah Day and Mary Peirson. Grandchildren, i. e., children of dec'd. sons Daniel and John Sergeant, and of dec'd. daughter Martha Harrison, viz., Hannah Williams, Dorcas Harrison and Martha Quimby. Personal estate. Witnesses—Hannah Sergeant, Sarah Sergeant. Proved Feb. 23, 1758.
Lib. F, p. 516.

1758, Oct. 25. Cooper, Henry, of Northampton, Burlington Co., yeoman; will of. Wife, Elizabeth, to have £30 yeary. Elizabeth Hunt, living in Sherburn, in Wiltshire, Great Britain, £5 yearly. Kinsman, Thomas Cooper and Elizabeth, his wife, my plantation where I live. Thomas Cooper and my wife may sell the estate, if they have a desire to return to England. Executor—said Thomas Cooper. Witnesses—T. Shinn, Daniel Jones, Jr., Thomas Lawrance. Proved Dec. 26, 1760.
Inventory made by Thomas Shinn and Daniel Jones, Jr., same date as above.
Burl. Wills, 6955 C.

1759, Dec. 20. Cooper, Ichabod, of Hanover, Morris Co., yeoman; will of. Children—Henry, George, Constant, Jerusha, Ichabod and John, the last two under age. Real and personal estate. Executors—Deacon John Ball and John Kitchel. Witnesses—Peter Beach, John Ball, Jr., William Dixon. Proved Jan. 29, 1760. Lib. G, p. 160.

1758, ——— ———. Cooper, James, son of Benjamin, and legatee of Joseph Cooper, all of Gloucester Co., petitions, that Benjamin Cooper, Jr., be appointed his guardian.
1760, Oct. 3. Bond of Benjamin Cooper, Jr., as such guardian; Joseph Cooper fellowbondsman, both of said Co. Lib. 10, p. 439.

1753, Jan. 30. Cooper, John, of Elisabeth Borough, Essex Co., tailor; will of. Wife, Mary. Children—William, Caleb (both under age) and Martha. Real and personal estate. Executors—the wife, brother-in-law, Rev. Caleb Smith, and Timothy Whitehead, Esq. Witnesses—John Lamb, Temperance Odell, Daniel Talmage. Proved March 29, 1753. Lib. F, p. 193.
 1753, Apr. 11. Inventory, £441.12.10, by Jeremiah Mulford and Thomas Thompson. Mentions "legacy from his sister Jane."

1751, May 3. Cooper, Joseph, of Middletown, Monmouth Co., yeoman. Int. Bond of Deborah, his widow, as Adm'x; John Shepherd, of Shrewsbury, yeoman, fellowbondsman. Lib. E, p. 528.

1760, ———— ——. Cooper, Samuel and William, sons of Benjamin Cooper, of Gloucester Co. and legatees of Joseph Cooper of said Co., petition that their brother, Joseph Cooper, and friend, Enoch Roberts, be appointed their guardians.
 1760, Oct. 3. Bond of Joseph Cooper and Enoch Roberts as such guardian; Benjamin Cooper, Jr., fellowbondsman, all of Gloucester Co. Lib. 10, p. 439.

1760, Dec. 16. Cooper, William Southerby, of Haddonfield, Newton Township, Gloucester Co., carpenter. Int. Inventory, £139.0.4, incl. book debts, £63.7.4; a bond, "a desperate debt," £35; made by James Davis and Samuel Clement, Jr.
 1760, Dec. 20. Bond of widow, Mary Cooper, of Newton Township, as Adm'x; Joseph Harrison, Esq., of Gloucester Township, fellowbondsman. Lib. 10, p. 291.

1755, May 19. Copner, Samuel, of Penn's Neck, Salem Co., yeoman; will of. Wife, Sarah, sole heiress of "whole estate," and, with Thomas Vickry, Executors. Children, Joseph, Isaac and a daughter (name not given). Witnesses—Jeremiah Baker, Peter Bilderback and Hinrey Gilliohnson. Proved May 8, 1758. Lib. 9, p. 43.
 1758, Apr. 26. Inventory, £202.9.8, by Francis Miles and Alen Congelton.
 1762, Jan. 11. Account by the surviving Executrix, Sarah Lambson, late Sarah Copner, and her husband, Matthias Lambson, who report as due to the estate, £179.18.1.

1755, Jan. 1. Corbitt (Corbet), John, of Bethlehem Township, Hunterdon Co.; will of. Wife, Mary. Children—William and Ann. Executors—the wife and brother, William Corbet, who are also to take care of the children. Witnesses—John Thomas, Jr., James Richey. Proved March 17, 1755. Lib. 8, p. 165.
 1755, Mar. 15. Inventory, £125.9.1, incl. 2 Bibles; bonds and notes, £47.5.1; made by John Parke and James Richey.

1757, June 8. Cordeary, Clement, of Great Egg Harbour Township, Gloucester Co. Int. Inventory, £228.14.2, incl. bills and bonds, £131.10; a silver watch, £7; made by Joseph Addams and Edward Doughty, Jr.
 1757, June 14. Bond of Edmund Cordeary as Adm'r; Joseph Addams fellowbondsman. Lib. 8, p. 442.
 1759, Mar. 6. Account by the Administrator.

CALENDAR OF WILLS—1751-1760   71

1760, Feb. 12. Corlis, John, of Shrewsbury, Monmouth Co., yeoman; will of. Wife, Zilpha. Sons—Samuel and John (under age). Real and personal estate. Executors—the wife, son Samuel and uncle, Joseph Corleis. Witnesses—Britain White, Benjamin Borden, Joseph Morris and Jacob Dennis. Proved August 18, 1760.
Lib. G, p. 300.
1760, Aug. 27: Inventory, £855.6. incl. books, £12.5.11; apparel, cash and plate, £26; a repeating clock, £18; a looking glass, £3.10; a barrel of metheglene, £2; the unexpired term of a lease from James Corleis, £12; six negroes, £220; made by Joseph Parker, John Borden and Josiah Parker.

1754, Apr. 10. Corlis, William, of Burlington Co. Int. Inventory, £221.8.6½, incl. a looking glass, 20s.; two Bibles, £3; six silverspoons, £4.10; bonds and notes, £198.17.9; made by Job Lippincott and Caleb Shreve.
1754, Apr. 19. Bond of William Corlis as Adm'r; Job Lippincott fellowbondsman. Burl. Wills, 5405 C.

1740-1, Feb. 18. Cornel, Cornelis, Sr., of Three Mile Run, Middlesex Co., yeoman; will of. Wife, Jannetje, sole Executrix of real and personal estate. Children—William, Joseph, Cornelius. (who are to be Executors in case of wife's re-marriage or death), Jacobus, Adrian and Jannetje. Witnesses—Jacobus Schuurman, Leffert Waldron, John Michael Sperling. Proved Sept. 9, 1756, when Cornelius Cornel is sworn in as one of the executors, Joseph Cornel being sworn September 18. Lib. F, p. 379.
1756, Sept. 27. Inventory, £684.5, incl. 5 negroes, £213; books, £1.10; bonds and cash, £379.18.6; a silver cup; made by Chrisstoffel Probasco and Leffert Waldron.

1753, Apr. 30. Cornelienson, Cornelius, of Penn's Neck, Salem Co., yeoman. Int. George Cornelienson, of Penn's Neck, labourer, his son, refuses to administer on his father's estate. Bond of George Trenchard as Adm'r; Daniel Mestayer fellowbondsman, both of Salem Co. Lib. 8, p. 88.

1756, July 19. Cornelinson, Jacob, of Penn's Neck, Salem Co., husbandman; will of. Wife, Catharine. Children—Michael, Judith and Catharine, all under age. Tobias Casperson to inherit the land, if children die without issue. Real and personal estate. Executors—the wife and Peter Boon. Witnesses—James Dunlap, Jans Jrh. Hirmesen (signs in German script, and is written "Heremise" in proof), and Samuel Whitehorne. Proved March 8, 1758. Lib. 8. p. 531.
1757, Jan. 11. Inventory, £116.15.4, incl. books—by Alen Congelton and Samuel Whitehorne.

1759, May 8. Cornelinson, John, of Penn's Neck, Salem Co. Int. Bond of Peter Bilderback as Adm'r; Andrew Standly, and Thomas Jones fellowbondsmen, all of Penn's Neck, yeomen. Lib. 10, p. 449.

1760, June 20. Cornelison, Andrew, son of Charles, late of Penn's Neck, Salem Co., ward. Guardian—Peter Brynbery, blacksmith, of same place; Andrew Standley fellowbondsman. Witness—G. Trenchard. Lib. 11, p. 23.

1757, Apr. 15. Cornell, Job, of "Lettell Eggharbur," Burlington Co. Int. Inventory, £12.11.9, incl. a Bible, by David Woodmansee and Gabriel Woodmansee.
1757, June 26. Bond of his widow, Sarah Cornell, as Adm'x; Gabriel Woodmansee, of Barnegatt, yeoman, fellowbondsman.
Lib. A, p. 432.
1757, Nov. 15. Account by the Administrator.

1756, Mar. 12. Corsen, Jacob, of Reading Township, Hunterdon Co., turner; will of. Wife, Arianty. Children—John, Margaret Smock, Geertry Cole, Yannetie, Matte Coursen and Tunis Coursen. Granddaughter, Ida, daughter of Yannetie, by David Kinny. Real and personal estate. Executors—sons-in-law, Jacobus Smock and Benjamin Cole. Witnesses—John Reading, Abraham Zutphan, John Aller. Proved August 20, 1756. Lib. 8, p. 399.
1756, July 3. Inventory of the estate: Real, a house and lot, £18; personal, £28.4.4. incl. a Dutch book, 2/6; made by Abr. Zutphan and John Aller.
1756, July 17. The executors, named in the will, refuse to serve.
1756, Aug. 20. Bond of John Corssen (Carson) of Rocksbury, Morris Co., as Adm'r; Daniel McKinney, of Readingtown, Hunterdon Co., fellowbondsman.

1759, Jan. 29. Corson, Jacob, son of Benjamin, of Reading, Hunterdon Co., 19 years old, having chosen Major Ralph Smith of said Co. as his guardian, Governor Bernard approves and said Smith gives bond as such guardian. Hunt. Wills, 457 J.

1753, Dec. 3. Cortrecht, Hendrick Janse, of Manissink, in Orange Co., New York, yeoman; will of. Cousin—Hendrick Williamse Cortrecht, son of William Cortrecht, dec'd, to have my land on Great and Little Manissink Island, with my homestead, except to my wife, Gerritje Cortrecht, the southermost-room of my house. Hendrick Williamse Cortrecht is to provide for his sister, Gerritje Cortrecht, Jr., and to allow her the girl which she brought up, till she is 21. My cousin, Jurrian Westvael, son of Johannis Westvail, ½ of 64¼ acres, which was bought of Richard Gardiner. Executors—wife, Gerritje, and Johannis Westvail, my brother in law. Witnesses—Johannis Rosekrans, Benjamin Westbrook, William Ennes. Proved June 26, 1760 (in Essex Co.). Lib. 10, p. 424.
1760, June 9. Inventory, £177.2.4, by William Ennes and Tereck VanKeuren Westbroock.

1758, Sept. 26. Coryell, Abraham and Sarah; wards. Children of Emanuel Corriell, of Amwell, Hunterdon Co. Guardian—their brother Cornelius Coryell, of said Co.; Joseph Higbee, of Trenton, fellowbondsman. Witnesses—John Coryell and Theodore Severns.
Hunt. Wills, 437 J.

1757, Nov. 1. Coryell, Emanuel, of Amwell, Hunterdon Co. Account of the estate of, £854.12.8., by the executors Sarah Coryell and John Coryell, who have added to it as not in the inventory £6., receive from John Miles, and part payment for the house and lot in Bound Brook sold by the Sheriff, £42.17.1., reporting as on hand a balance of £7.9.1. [See N. J. Archives, Vol. XXX, p. 114].
Hunt. Wills, 210 J.

CALENDAR OF WILLS—1751-1760 73

1760, Jan. 17. Coryell, Samuel, of Bridgewater, Somerset Co., tavernkeeper; will of. Devises "worldly estate" to children, names not given, who are to be brought up by the Executors, brother David Coryell and cousin Elias van Court. Witnesses—William Riddel, Asa Kelly and William Kelly. Proved Feb. 25, 1760. Lib. G, p. 128.

1757, Jan. 13.—Cosart, Johannes, of Bridgewater, "Summerset" Co., yeoman; will of. Wife (not named), sole heiress of real and personal estate, for use and maintenance and bringing up of my small children, sons Anthony, Derick, Benjamin, John and Jacob (the last four under age), and daughters Elizabeth and Jane. Executors—Peter Williamson and Abraham Van Tuyl, of Somerset Co. Witnesses—Joseph Ross, Jr., James MacElrath and Sarah Macelrath. Proved May 19, 1757. Lib. E, p. 426.
1757, May 16. Inventory, £182.4.8, incl. books, 16s.; a bond, £53; made by David Sutton and Folkert Sebring; signed also by Abraham van Tuyl and Peter Williamson.

1747, Apr. 25. Coul, Court, of Somerset Co., yeoman; will of. Wife, Coartrout (?). Daughters—Ann (wife of Mical Miers) and Margret (wife of Peter Laffnard). Land in Somerset and in Hunterdon Co's, bought of John Chambers and Joseph Cirdrite (?). Personal property. Executors—the two sons-in-law and John Garrison. Witnesses—Harbart Hummer, Tunis Young and John Garrison. Proved August 7, 1755. Lib. 8, p. 267.
1755, Apr. 3. Inventory, £76, incl. 15 bush. of rye, £2.5, by Lucas Neaffey, John Garrison and Tomas Pietersen. Peter Laffnard, one of the executors, signs as "Peter Lafler."

1759, Jan. 19. Courtney, Thomas, of Penns Neck, Salem Co., innkeeper; will of. Wife, Jane. Children—Sarah, Benjamin and Thomas, all under age. Legacy to brother John Courtney, "if he comes into this country within a year." The "pailing around the Sweed's Churchyard" at Penns Neck to be repaired. Personal estate. Executors—the wife and Robert, son of George Clark, of Piles Grove. Witnesses—Samuel Whitehorne, Christianna Whitehorne and John Scott. Proved April 3, 1759. Lib. 10, p. 505.
1759, Mar. 21. Inventory, £184.0.8., incl. credits and desperate debts, £33.17.6, by John Proctor and Samll Whitehorne.

1743, Mar. 15. Couwenhoven, Pieter, of Freehold, Monmouth Co., yeoman; will of. Wife, Patience. Children—Peter, William, Elias, Hannah Antonides, Jane Williamson, Mary Schenck, Aeltje Williamson and Anne Longstreet. Real and personal estate. Executors—the three sons. Witnesses—Robert Cumming, Andrew McGallird and John Henderson. Proved April 23, 1755. Lib. F, p. 259.
1755, Sept. 16. Inventory, £35.19.01, incl. a negro wench, £3; a negro man, £1; made by Isaac Voorhees, Dirick Zutphen, Jr., and Isaac Sutphen.

1751, Febr. 7. Covenhoven, Elias, of Middletown, Monmouth Co. Inventory, £447.11, incl. a negro man, £60; a negro woman, £50; a negro boy, £10; a Bible and other books, £2.5; 200 bush. of wheat, £30; made by Nicholas Johnson, Garrett Schanck and Elias Golden. [For will, see Vol. XXX, N. J. Archives, p. 115]. Mon. Wills, 1877 M.

1753, Nov. 30. Covenover, Isaiah, of Egg Harbour, Gloucester Co. Int. Bond of widow, Mary Covenover, of Egg Harbour as Adm'x; Joseph Adams, of the same place, yeoman, fellowbondsman.   Lib. 8, p. 15.
1753, Nov. 26. Inventory, £54.9.0, by Joseph Addams and William Read.

1756, Apr. 3. Covert, Margret, of Freehold, Monmouth Co.; widow; will of. Children—Uriah Conseljey, Francis Covert, Ann Johnston, Elenor van Dyke, Jean Reid and Margeret Cooper. Personal property. Executors—son Francis, Thomas Cooper and Thomas van Dyke, Jr. Witnesses—Job Throckmorton, Stephen Havelon (Haviland) and Mary Cooper. Proved May 8, 1756.   Lib. F, p. 354.

1760, June 12. Coward, John, of Upper Freehold Township, Monmouth Co., yeoman; will of. Wife, Alice. Children—John, Joseph, Jonathan, Thomas, Alice Brown, Deliverence Fitz Randolph, Patience, Rebeckah and Elizabeth. Farm, now occupied by son, John, bought of Jeremiah Stilwell; home farm on North side of Burlington Path. Personal property. Executors—sons John and Joseph with James Holmes. Witnesses—Richard Herbert, Content Hornor and Anthony Woodward, Jr. Proved Sept. 12, 1760.   Lib. G, p. 295.

1757, Jan. 7. Cowgill, Esther, of Gloucester Township and County, widow. Int. Inventory, £21.19.6; incl. a pine table and swinging glass, 25s., by Samuel Harrison and Joseph Harrison.
1757, Jan. 17. Bond of William Harrison as Adm'r; Wm. Harrison, Jr., fellowbondsman, both of said Co.   Lib. 8, p. 384.

1760, Mar. 10. Cox, David, of Mt. Holly, Burlington Co. Int. Bond of John Cox, of Mores Town, as Adm'r; Zachariah Rossell, of Mt. Holly, fellowbondsman.   Lib. 10, p. 30.

1759, Mar. 18. Cox, Gornor, of Gloucester Co., gentleman; will of. Wife, Magdalen, sole heiress and she and John Reynolds to be Executors. Witnesses—Andrew Cox, Lawrance Lock. Proved May 25, 1759.   Lib. 9, p. 273.
1759, May 12. Inventory, £103.17.3, incl. book debts and notes, £81.19.11; silverspoons; books; made by Matthew Gill and Lawrence Lock.

1756, Feb. 14. Cox, James, of Monmouth Co. Account of John Cox and Joseph Cox, Executors. Balance to be distributed according to the will into 6 equal parts, viz., to Dorothy, Elizabeth, Else, Rachell; the 4 daughters of Ann, daughter of testator; the children of Rebecca, daughter of testator. [For will, see N. J. Archives, Vol. XXX, p. 117].   Mon. Wills, 2145 M.

1753, Mar. 13. Cox, James, Jr., of Upper Freehold, Monmouth Co.; will of. Wife, Elizabeth. Children—Nathaniel and John, both by first wife; Thomas, Isaac, Elisha; daughters spoken of but names not given; all the last under age. Real and personal estate. Executors—the wife and brother-in-law, Thomas Fenton, Jr. Witnesses—William Kinnan, John Cox, Joseph Robins. Proved May 7, 1753. Lib. 7, p. 336.
1753, Apr. 28. Inventory, £152.11, incl. a "Palentine" boy, £11; made by Joseph Robins.

1756, Apr. 12. Cox, Jonas, of Deptford Township, Gloucester Co., yeoman. Int. Inventory, £24.9.11, by William Wilkins and Isaac Stephens.
 1756, Apr. 19. Sarah, the widow of Jonas, renounces her right of administration on the estate in favour of her son, Moses Cox.
 1756, Apr. 21. Bond of Moses Cox as Adm'r; John Rambo fellowbondsman, both of Deptford Township, yeomen. Lib. 8, p. 308.

1757, Aug. 6. Cox, Mary, widow of Thomas, of Upper Freehold, Monmouth Co., 86 years of age; will of. Son, Thomas. Grandchildren—William Cheesman, son of daughter Lydia; Richard, Thomas, Elizabeth and Rebecca Cox. Names Thomas van Horne; Joseph and Mary Lawrence; Elizabeth Hutchinson. Legacy to Baptist Ch. in Upper Freehold. Personal estate. Executors—grandson, Richard Cox, and John Coward, Jr. Witnesses—David Gorden, William Liming and William Lawrence. Proved Sept. 12, 1760. Lib. G, p. 294.
 1760, July 29. Inventory, £1472.15.3, incl. bills, bonds, book debts and mortgages, £1345.5; made by James Holmes, Richard Duglass and Joseph Robins.

1757, Jan. 15. Cox, Sarah, of Gloucester Co., spinster. Int. Bond of Moses Cox as Adm'r; John Rambo fellowbondsman, both of said Co. yeomen. Lib. 8, p. 394.
 1757, Jan. 15. Inventory, £24.12.3, of which £20.2.3, are bills, bonds and book accounts; made by William Wilkins and John Rambo.

1750-'51, Jan. 3. Cox, William, of Shrewsbury, Monmouth Co.; will of. Wife, Catherine. Children—William, Thomas, John, Longfield, Samuel, Cornelius, Mary, and Sarah (wife of Christopher Beekman). Legacies to grandson, William (son of Christopher Beekman) and to William, (son of John Wiley, of N. Y., distiller). Homefarm, bought of Capt. Leonard's relict's estate, left by kinsman, Walter Cox, of Cheltenham, Gloucestershire; personal estate. Executors—the wife, with sons William and Thomas. Witnesses—Jonathan Holmes, Minister, Archelaus Lewis, John Wiley Proved May 5, 1752.
Lib. F, p. 96.

1753, Sept. 9. Cox, William, of Willinbrough Township, Burlington Co., yeoman; will of. Wife, Hannah. Children—Hannah Wright, Rane, Elisabeth, Parthena, William, Jonathan, Joseph, Samuel and Abram. Speaks of "five" daughters, but mentions only the four above, and calls them under age. Real and personal estate. Executors—the wife, Hugh Hollinshead and kinsman, John Cox. Witnesses—William West, Owen Murphy, Gabriel Blond. Proved Oct. 27, 1759. Burl. Wills, 6281 C.
 1759, Oct. 2. Inventory, £216.0.2, by Thomas Buzby and George Elkinton.

1753, Aug. 18. Coxe, Daniel, of Trenton, Joseph Murray and James Alexander, the surviving executors, resign their trust. [See, for will, Vol. XXX, N. J. Archives, p. 118].
 1753, Aug. 21. Bond of William Coxe, as Adm'r with the will annexed; Daniel Cox fellowbondsman. Lib. K, p. 346.

1757, Jan. 25. Coxe, Daniel, of Trenton, Hunterdon Co.; will of. Wife, Abigail. Children—Grace and Daniel. Farm at Hopewell, called Belmont; undivided share of the tract in Hunterdon Co., called Mount Carmel; land on Long Island, called Crab Meadow; 385 acres, being lot No. 2 of the last Indian purchase in Morris or Sussex Co.; 222 ac. in Sussex Co.; 1,000 ac. at the Great Pond, or Ponds, in Sussex or Essex Co.; 500 ac. near Cohansey, Salem Co.; 1-3 of the tract of 7,540 ac. near Millstone River, patented to the grandfather; two lots in Burlington City; 884 ac. on Tohocouchung, or lot A of the equivalent Tract; other real and personal estate. Executors—the wife, the daughter, brother William Coxe and William Pidgeon. Witnesses—Michael Houdin, Pontius Stelle and Thomas Kennedy. Codicil of December 28, 1757, refers to bequests made to the wife, and to the marriage settlement, in which brother William Coxe and William Pidgeon are made her trustees. Witnesses—Mary Ashfield, William Clayton, George Davies. Proved Jan. 21, 1758. Lib. 8, p. 536.

1762, Jan. 1. Account of the estate, i. e., of goods, chattels, bonds and cash, £3516.9.1, of which £2690.4.3 are to be divided among the three heirs and legatees.

1753, Apr. 8. Coxe, John, of Trenton, Hunterdon Co.; will of. Devises real and personal estate to brother, William Coxe, and to Daniel and Grace, children of brother, Daniel Coxe. Legacy to Charles, commonly called Charles Coxe, and to Daniel Coxe Lockheart, and to any public donation in the Province the Executors shall think most proper. Executors—brother William Coxe, and Robert Lettice Hooper. If Joseph Murray and James Alexander should decline the execution of father's will, brothers Daniel and William Coxe are to be the substitutes for testator. Witnesses—David Cowell, Joseph Reed, Moore Furman. Proved August 28, 1753. Lib. 7, p. 343.

1753, June 25. Inventory, £425.14.7, incl. 6 pictures (one Hogarth's Harlot's Progress), 18s.; a clock and case, £8; a looking-glass, £2; 12 pictures (Philosophers' heads), £3; 5 maps, £1.5; Princess Louise picture, 4s.; china ware, £11.12; silver plate, 135 oz. 2 pwt., 18 gr., at 8s.6p., £57.8.7; a silver watch, £6; gold sleeve buttons, 14s.; silver spurs, £1; a negro man, 80 yrs. old, no value; three other slaves, £80; made by William Clayton and Moore Furman.

1753, July 31. List of law books (191 titles, 302 volumes), not included in the inventory, appraised at £225.16.9, by Charles Read and Francis Costigan.

1753, Sept. 25. List of additional books, 97 vols, 77 titles, £37; made by David Cowell and Moore Furman.

1759, Feb. 16. Cozens, George, of Greenwich Township, Gloucester Co., yeoman; will of. Wife, Elener. Children—William, Samuel, Sarah, Amy, John and George, the last three under age. Farm of 150 acres and other land, bought of William Chester; land in Deptford Township, said Co., bought of John Chester; 13 acres of meadow near Homan's Creek in Greenwich Township. Personal property. Executors—the wife, with sons William and Samuel. Witnesses—Elizabeth Cozens, Elizabeth Nelinger, Joshua Cozens. Proved Nov. 26, 1759.
Lib. 9, p. 417.

1768, Mar. 26. Inventory, £91.6.6½, by John Rambo and Samuel Paul.

1760, Jan. 27. Cozens, Jacob, of Greenwich, Gloucester Co.; will of. Wife, Elizabeth. Children, of whom only son Samuel is named. Said

Samuel, and Solomon Lippincott are made Executors of the real and personal estate. Witnesses—Ansell Long, John Chester, Rachel Mawfelt. Proved April 2, 1760. Lib. 9, p. 425.
1760, Mar. 12. Inventory, £488.1.5, incl. a silver watch and chain, £8; the "revercion" of a servant lad's time, £2; bonds and book debts, £182.16.9; books, £1.10; made by William Wood and Joshua Lord, Jr.

1748, Oct. 29. Craft, James, of Mansfield, Burlington Co., yeoman; will of. Children—James, Elizabeth, Margret, Sarrah and Ann. Grandchildren—James (son of Gershom Craft dec'd) and Joseph Bates. Real and personal estate. Executor—Joseph Curtis. Witnesses—John Tillton, Benjamin Owen, William Pancoast. Proved April 17, 1752. Burl. Wills, 4945 C.
1752, Apr. 16. Inventory, £172.17.2, incl. due on bonds, £145.6.8; made by Thomas Potts and William Pancoast.

1757, Oct. 21. Craft, Margrit, of Mansfield, Burlington Co., widow; will of. Son, Thomas Craft, who has children, viz., George, Samuel, Sarah and Hannah. Granddaughter, Margret Rockhill. Farm bought of Doctor John Brown. Personal estate. Executor—Samuel Rockhill. Witnesses—William Ricketts, Thomas Shreve. Proved March 14, 1759. Burl. Wills, 6289 C.
1759, Mar. 14. Inventory, £62.15.8, incl. a bond, £42.9; rent of her place, £6.4.8; made by Thomas Shreve and Thomas Hall.
1760, Aug. 26. Account by Executor.

1750-'51, Feb. 25. Craig, Archibald, Esq., of Freehold, Monmouth Co.; will of. Wife, Mary. Children—John, William, widow Ursula Forman, Sarah (wife of John Anderson), Hannah (wife of William Crawford), Mary (wife of Peter Gordon). Catherine (wife of John Loyd), and Elizabeth (wife of John Gordon). Grandchildren—Walter and Margaret Ker (both under age); John, Elizabeth, Ursula and Mary (last three under 21), children of dec'd son Samuel. Land on North side of Spotswoods North Brook, granted by father, John Craig, April 2, 1702; 2 lots at Middletown Point, where the landing is; land bought of father September 2, 1717, and of Jacob Sutvan, April 24, 1733. Personal property. Executors—the wife, son John and son-in-law, John Anderson. Witnesses—John van Schaiack, Robert van Skiack, Alexander Tomson. Proved April 24, 1751.
Lib. E, p. 515.
1751, Apr. 27. Inventory, £358.5, incl. books and pamphlets, £3.; a lookingglass, 35s.; 2 negroes, £56; made by Samuel Ker, Joseph Ker and William Hamton.

1753, May 9. Craig, John, of Somerset Co.; will of. Wife, Ann, sole Executrix. Children—Samuel, John, Alexander Chambers, William Linn, Margrat, James. Personal estate. Witnesses—John Belyeu, Wm. McQuown, Robert Craig. Proved June 6, 1753.
Lib. F, p. 175.
1753, June 11. Inventory, £397.10, incl. books, 10s.; 2 bush. of buckwheat; a negro man, £55; the improvement, £30; made by Moses Craig and Thomas Holms.

1758, Aug. 22. Craig, John, of the Borough of Elizabeth, Essex Co., yeoman; will of. Children—Timothy, Andrew, John, Sarah Por-

ter, Phebe King and Catherine Kelley. Grandsons—David Craig and Andrew Craig. Homefarm; part of Raway meadows, bequeathed by father, Andrew Craig, to testator and his brother, Andrew Craig. Personal estate. Executors—sons Andrew and John. Witnesses—Joseph Clark, John Hunt, Abraham Clark, Jr. Proved August 25, 1758.
Lib. F, p. 547.

1758, Aug. 24. John Craig, one of the Executors named above, leaves the duties solely to his brother, Andrew.

1758, Aug. 29. Craig, John, ward. Guardian—his brother, Andrew Craig, Jr., of Elizabeth, yeoman. Bondsman—Timothy Craig, yeoman, of same place. Witness—Thomas Bartow. Lib. F, p. 549.

1759, May 18. Cramer, David, of Middlesex Co. Int. "I, John Rowlison and my wife, do impower Phenes Ayrs to receive the hul of David Cramer's weigers that was due to him when he dide, from Cornal Peter Schyler." Signed, John Rowlison, Mary Rowlison.

1760, March 11. Phineas Ayers, principal creditor, appointed Adm'r of David Cramer, late a Soldier in the N. Jersey Regiment. Bondsman—Henry Day. Witness—Thomas Bartow. Lib. G, p. 136.

1760, Apr. 14. Cramer, John, of Northampton, Burlington Co. Int. Bond of Amariah Foster as Adm'r; Thomas Budd and George Briggs fellowbondsmen, all of said Co. Lib. 9, p. 416.

1760, Apr. 14. Inventory, £114.2, by Thomas Budd and George Briggs.

1761, Feb. 26. Account by the Adm'r, who reports the value as only £104.2, and has paid to the widow of dec'd. the balance on hand of £35.10.3.

1752, Nov. 8. Crane, Azariah, Jr., of Newark, Essex Co., weaver; will of. Wife, Phebe. Children—Sarah, Rebecca, Silas, Daniel and Caleb. Real and personal estate. Executors—brother Job Crane and friend Noah Crane. Witnesses—William Crain, Gamaliel Crane and Daniel Lamson. Proved Nov. 21, 1752. Lib. F, p. 97.

1760, Jan. 12. Crane, Christopher, of Essex Co., cordwainer; will of. Wife, Lydia, and son, Nathaniel, heirs and Executors of real and personal estate. Sons of brother, Caleb Crane, viz., Nehemiah, or Jacob, remaindermen. Legacies to their brother, Caleb, and cousins David and Demaris Crane. Witnesses—Joshua Marsh, Mary Price, Ebenezer Price. Proved April 7, 1760. Lib. G, p. 167.

1760, Apr. 5. Inventory, £122.10.9, by Thomas Woodruff and Daniel Perrine.

1760, Apr. 7. Jonathan Crane, of Essex Co., made Adm'r, with will annexed.

1754, May 1. Crane, Daniel, of Newark, Essex Co. Int. Adm'rs—Jeremiah Crane and Phinehas Crane, principal creditors. Bondsman—Samuel Huntington, of Newark. Witness—Uzal Ogden.
Lib. F, p. 230.

1759, June 19. Crane, Ezekiel, of Newark, Essex Co. Soldier. Int. Adm'x—his widow, Elizabeth Crane. Bondsman—Joseph Mun, of Newark. Witness—Thomas Bartow. Lib. G, p. 83.

1759, June 23. Inventory, £24.12.7, by Samuel Peirson and Samuel Williams.

CALENDAR OF WILLS—1751-1760

1750-'51, Feb. 22. Crane, James, of Newark, Essex Co., blacksmith; will of. Divides real and personal estate between brothers, Jeremiah Crane and Phineas Crane, who are named Executors, and sisters, Johanna Young, Lydia Comes and Patience Crane; and also Temperence Turner, sister to Dr. William Turner. Witnesses—Thomas Sargeant, Thomas Price, David Ogden. Proved April 1, 1751.
Lib. F, p. 507.

1753, Oct. 25. Crane, Moses, of Essex Co., blacksmith. Int. Adm'x—his widow, Joanna Crane. Bondsman—Samuel Miller, Jr., of Essex Co. Witness—Thomas Bartow. Lib. F, p. 141.
1753, Oct. 30. Inventory, £153.19.4, by Samuel Hinds and Daniel Ross, Jr. Witness—John Ross.

1758, July 15. Crane, Nathaniel, of Elizabeth Town, Essex Co.; will of. Wife, Mary. Son, David (under age). Son-in-law (stepson?) Stephen Pasallo (Paslo). Homefarm; grist and sawmill; a lot between brother Caleb and Benjamin Trotter; another lot between brother Jonathan Crain and John Potter; a lot over Rahway River, between brothers Jonathan and Christopher Crain; a lot between brother Caleb and Con'll Richets, formerly belonging to the Schuylers; meadow in the Town Creek; meadow in the Grait Meadow, on the Southside of Slooping Creek; meadow in the Grait Meadow, formerly Capt. Daniel Price's. Personal estate. Executors—the wife, the son and Jonathan Thompson. Witnesses—Caleb Crane, Stephen Hindesjun, Elijah Davis. Proved June 16, 1759.
1759, May 3. Inventory, £307.9.6, by Henry Garthwait and Elijah Davis. Includes "cash for the mill, £150." Lib. G, p. 81..

1760, Apr. 7. Crane, Nathaniel, son of Christopher, of Essex Co., in 10th year; Jonathan Crane made Guardian. Lib. G, p. 123.

1760, Nov. 25. Crane, Nathaniel, of Newark, Essex Co., yeoman; will of. Wife, Elisabeth. Children—William, Noah, Nathaniel, Elisabeth Young and Jene Smith. Granddaughter, Abigail Richards. Real and personal estate. Executors—sons Noah and William, with Stephen Morris. Witnesses—John Dod (3d), Timothy Crane, Sary Baldwin. Proved Dec. 17, 1760. Lib. G, p. 386.

1752, Dec. 16. Crane, Nehemiah, of Essex Co. Int. Adm'x—his widow, Lydia Crane. Bondsman—David Rogers, of Newark. Witness—Uzal Ogden. Lib. F, p. 94.

1760, Jan. 15. Crane, Phineas, of Newark, Essex Co. Int. Adm'r—Jeremiah Crane, heir-at-law. Bondsman—Samuel Huntington, of Newark. Lib. G, p. 100.
———, ——— —. Inventory, £105.9.0, by Samuel Huntington and Thomas Sargent.

1755, June 30.—Crane, Robert, of Newark, Essex Co.; will of. Wife, Phebe. Children—Timothy, Isaac, Josiah, Mary, Phebe and Lydia. Real and personal estate. Executors—the wife, with sons Timothy and Isaac. Witnesses—Humphrey Nichols, Nathaniel Anderson, Nehemiah Baldwin. Proved Feb. 10. 1757. Lib. F, p. 407.

1753, Nov. 18.—Crane, Samuel, Sr., of Elizabeth "Borrough," Essex Co., yeoman; will of. Wife (not named). Children—Nathaniel, Sam-

uel and Jane, all under age. Brothers—Mathias and Benjamin Crane, remaindermen. Land inherited from brother Joseph Crane; 4 acres in the Great Meadows; personal estate. Executors—father-in-law, Nathaniel Bonnel and brother, Benjamin Crane. Witnesses—James Meeker, Jacob Dehart, Abigail de Hart. Proved December 11, 1753.
Lib. F, p. 152.

1751, June 16. Crawford, Richard, of Cape May Co; will of. Wife, Rachel. Sons—Issachar and Benjamin (under age). Real and personal estate, incl. plantation, cedar swamp and 40 acres adjoining Eleazer Hand. Executors—the wife and James Whilldin. Witnesses—James Hedges, Loes Crowel, Peter Toullard. Proved August 6, 1751. Lib. 14, p. 536; 15, p. 517.

1751, Oct. 17. Inventory, £206.18.9, inc. an old negro, £21, by Elisha Hand and Ebenezer Johnson.

1752, July 16. Crawford, Samuel, of Freehold, Monmouth Co., yeoman. Int. Bond of Naomi Craford (Crawford) and John van Brakle, both of said Co., as Admr's. Lib. F, p. 59.

1752, Oct. 1. Inventory, £58.3, by Cornelius van der Hovefman and Isaac Hance.

1760, Mar. 16. Crawford, William, of Middlesex Co.; will of. Children—William Redford, Lewis, Margaret (is to receive her share, when 30 years old or at marriage), Gertruyd and Lydia, all under age. Tract near the Meeting House in Monmouth Co., owned in partnership with Andrew Johnston. Personal property. Executor—Andrew Smyth. Witnesses—James Johnston, Samuel Neilson and Whitehead Leonard. Proved April 22, 1760. Lib. G, p. 186.

1760, Mar. 26. Inventory, £1,117.19; incl. 7 silver teaspoons, £1.10; a volume of Jersey Laws, 15s.; cash, £307.18.8; bills, bonds and mortgages, £729.12.1; made by John Disbrow and Daniel Sperling.

1755, Oct. 23. Cresse, David, of Cape May Co. Int. Inventory, £92.5.5, by James Cresse and John Shaw.

1755, Oct. 28. Bond of Lewis Cresse as Adm'r; James Cresse fellowbondsman, both of Cape May Co. Cape May Wills, 170 E.

1758, May 15. Cresse, Josiah, of Cape May Co., yeoman; will of. Wife, Mary. Children—Aaron, Salathiel, Israel, Unis and Ruth, the last two under age. Real and personal estate. Executors—the wife and son Israel. Witnesses—William Goff, John Smith, Nathaniel Jenkins. Proved August 3, 1758. Cape May Wills, 185 E.

1758, July 31. Inventory, £51.7.6, by William Goff and Nathaniel Jenkins.

1758, Apr. 18. Cripps, Benjamin, of Manington, Salem Co., yeoman; will of. Wife, Mary. Sons—Whitten and John, both under age. Daughter—Hannah Mason. Home farm with meadows on the other side of the creek; farm bought of Thomas Barret; land in Mount Holley, Burlington Co. Personal property. Executors—the wife and son Whitten. Witnesses—John Paschall, Josiah Kay and Jost Meller. Codicil of same day directs the son, Whiten, to give title for lands sold to Thomas Clark and Elijah Lummes upon receipt of payment. Same witnesses. Proved June 8, 1758. Lib. 9, p. 40.

1758, Dec. 30. Inventory, £905.2.5, incl. a riding horse, saddle, bridle, wearing apparel and cash, £220.7.6; bills, bonds and book debts, £263.6.5; 2 negroes, £50; John Graies' time, £15; made by Preston Carpenter and Jost Meller.

1753, May 29. Crishan, Adolphus, of Amwell, Hunterdon Co. Int. Inventory of the estate: Real (189 acres of land), £230. Personal, £278.7.5, incl. book debts and bonds, £145.15; made by Joseph King, Mansfield Hunt and Andrew Johnson.
  1753, May 31. Bond of widow, Sarah Crishan, of Amwell, and Cornelius Quick, of Kingwood, said Co., farmer, as Admr's; Andrew Johnson, of Amwell, farmer, fellowbondsman. Lib. 8, p. 14.

1753, Dec. 20. Crispin, Benjamin, yeoman, of Northampton, Burlington Co. Int. Inventory, £272.4, made by Caleb Haines and Joshua Ballinger.
  1754, Jan. 1. Bond of Silas Crispin as Adm'r, Caleb Haines, of Burlington City, fellowbondsman. Lib. 8, p. 16.
  1755, June 10. Account by the Administrator, Silas Crispin, who reports balance on hand, £119.7.4.

1759, Aug. 7. Critser, Leonard, of Lebanon Township, Hunterdon Co. Int. Adm'r—Thomas Armstrong of said Co., farmer. Bondsman—William Cline of said Co., farmer. Witnesses—Charles Hoff, Jr., and Theodore Severns. Lib. 10, p. 69.
  1759, Aug. 3. Inventory, £315.19.0, by David Fetter and William Cline.

1753, Dec. 4. Croker, John, of Essex Co. Int. Adm'x—Elizabeth Croker, the widow. Bondsman—Nathaniel Kingsland, of Newark. Witness—Uzal Ogden. Lib. F, p. 229.

1760, Dec. 26. Crosby, John, of Wellingborough, Burlington Co. Int. Inventory, £67.14.11, incl. bonds, book debts and notes, £33.15; made by Wm. Heulings.
  1761, Jan. 8. Bond of John Crosby and Patrick Kelly as Admr's; Samuel Newton fellowbondsman, all of said Co. Lib. 10. p. 170.

1751, Nov. 6. Crosby, Nathan, of Wellingborough, Burlington Co., yeoman. Int. Inventory, £116.4.9, incl. bills, bonds and notes, £91.11.8; made by William Cox and Daniel Stockton.
  1751, Nov. 30. Bond of widow, Elizabeth Crosby, and Samuel Garwood, yeoman, as Admr's; William Cox and Daniel Stockton fellowbondsmen, all of Burlington Co. Burl. Wills, 4809 C.

1759, Apr. 30. Crosley, Moses, of Fairfield Township, Cumberland Co.; will of. Wife, Sarah. Children—Bethnia (wife of Jacob Golder), Hannah, Rachel Harris, Abraham. Grandsons—Moses, Aaron and George Crosley, Son-in-law, Jacob Harris. Real and personal estate. Executors—daughter, Hannah Crosley, and son-in-law, Jacob Harris, with John Ogden and Jonadab Shepherd as trustees for son Abraham. The executors are charged to make grandson, Moses Crosley, an apprentice of Henry Shaw, to learn the tailor's trade, and to sell apprentice, Elisha Hall, and servant boy, Melchus, to his father. Witnesses—Thomas Cheesman, Joseph Page, Silas Church. Proved May 21, 1759. Lib. 9, p. 381.

1759, May 21. Inventory, £164.19.5., by Joseph Page and Silas Church.

1759, Apr. 10. Crosman, Nathan, of Morris Co., soldier. Int. Phebe Crosman, widow, resigns her right of administering on his estate to Joseph Geren, the principal creditor.

1759, July 13. Bond of Joseph Geren as Adm'r; John Logan fellowbondsman, both of Morris Co.   Lib. G, p. 90.

1758, —— ——. Crow, William, of Salem Town and Co. Int. Susanah, widow, resigns her right to administer on his estate to brother George Crow and Samuel Tylor.

1758, June 30. Bond of George Crow, of Wilmington, New Castle Co. upon Delaware, and Samuel Tyler, of Salem, tanner, as Admr's; William Tust, of Salem, fellowbondsman.   Lib. 9, p. 97.

1755, Nov. 28. Crowell, Edward, Sr., Esq., of Woodbridge, Middlesex Co.; will of. Children—John, Samuel, Edward, Thomas, James, Elizabeth Addleton, Mary Alston, Sarah Morris, Kathrine Evens, Annable and Agnes. Real and personal estate. Executors—William Brown and Thomas Gauch. Witnesses—James Brown, Thomas Hadden and Nugient Kelly. Proved Oct. 17, 1756.   Lib. F, p. 382.

1751, Oct. 18. Crowell, Mathew, of Cape May Co. Int. Inventory, £68.15.10, by Elisha Hand and Ebenezer Johnson.

1751, Oct. 28. Bond of Loes Crowell as Adm'r; James Godfrey, fellowbondsman, both of said Co.   Cape May Wills, 151 E.

1754, Mar. 20. Cubberley, James, of Nottingham Township, Burlington Co., yeoman; will of. Wife, Mary. Children—William, Isaac, James, John, Mary. Grandchildren—William, son, and three daughters of dec'd. son, Thomas; John, son of James; two sons of son Isaac; two sons of daughter Mary. Home farm, 237 acres, bought of son Thomas, being part of lot No. 3 in Winsor Township, Middlesex Co. Personal property, incl. 4 negro slaves. Executors—the wife and son John. Witnesses—Robert Chambers, John Nilson, John Morlaw. Proved July 3, 1754.   Lib. 7, p. 513.

1754, June 22. Inventory, £1,131.10.3, incl. bills, bonds and book debts, £947.6.7; made by William Murfin and John Abbott.

1753, Apr. 16. Cuberley, Thomas, of Middlesex Co. Int. Inventory, £137.0.6; incl. bills and book debts, £15.5.6; made by William Murfies and John Abbott.

1753, May 18. Bond of Anne Cuberly as Adm'x; John Tindall and Thomas Tindall fellowbondsmen, all of Middlesex Co.   Lib. 7, p. 413.

1755, Feb. 15. Account by Adm'x.

1753, May 13. Cumin, James, of Bethleham Township, Hunterdon Co.; will of. Wife, Mary. Children—Mary, Marget, Sarah and James. Legacy to brother, Thomas Cumin. Real and personal estate. Executors—Samuel Lowden and Joseph Culwell. Witnesses—Joseph Coldwell, Samuel Lowden, Thomas Cumin, Henry Cotten. Proved May 30, 1753.   Lib. 8, p. 7.

1753, May 26. Inventory of the estate: Real, the plantation, £50; personal, £85.9.11; made by Thomas Cumins, Francis Mason and John Kelly.

1763, Nov. 7. Cummins, Thomas, of Bedminster Township, Somerset Co.; will of. Wife, Rosey, sole Executrix and to have 1-3 of land. Children—William (under age), Robert, Jane, Margret and Martha. Real and personal estate. Witnesses—John Hanna, Peter McDowel and John McDowel. Proved Dec. 1, 1757. Lib. F, p. 473.

1752, July 31. Cundit, Jotham, of Newark. Int. Adm'r Samuel Cundit, of Newark. Bondsman—Daniel Pierson, of Newark. Rebekah Cundit, widow, renounced. Lib. F, p. 70.
1753, Feb. 10. Inventory, £172.12.0, by Joseph Harrison and John Cundit.

1760, Oct. 3. Cunningham, Elisha, of Monmouth Co. Int. Bond of Isaac Rogers, of Monmouth Co., as Adm'r; Peter Tallman, of Burlington Co., fellowbondsman. Lib. 10, p. 103.

1756, Dec. 2. Currie, James, of Greenwich, Gloucester Co., yeoman. Inventory, £270.11.8, incl. book debts and cash, £74.16.1; shopgoods, £14.15.2; books of divinity, £1.6.; made by Alexander Randall and Nicholas Justice.
1756, Dec. 6. Bond of widow Mary Currie (Curry) and John Sparks, yeoman, both of Greenwich, as Admr's; John Marshall of Deptford Township, said Co., blacksmith, fellowbondsman. Lib. 8, p. 396.

1760, May 13. Curtis, Harbort, of Mannesquan, Shrewsbury, Monmouth Co.; will of. Wife, Liddea. Sons—William and Thomas. Real and personal estate. Executors—brother, John Curtis, and brother-in-law, Thomas Tilton, Jr. Witnesses—James Lawrence, David Curtis, Jr., and Peter Curtis. Proved June 2, 1760. Lib. G, p. 232.
1760, May 30. Inventory, £192.14.7, by James Lawrence and David Johnston.

1752, Mar. 9. Cushman, Isaac, of Northampton, Burlington Co. Int. Bond of John Dennis of Northampton, as Adm'r; Nathaniel Thomas, Esq., of Burlington City, fellowbondsman. Lib. 7, p. 301.
1752, Apr. 23. Inventory, £4.12.3, incl. 3 books, 4s.; made by Edward Mullin and Thos. Atkinson.
1752, Oct. 30. Account by the administrator, John Dennis, who has increased it to £45.8.6¼, by collection of debts due by the Mount Holly Company, Joseph Prat, John Cain and James Sturdevent. After deducting administration fees and paying debts due to Dr. Fanning, Dr. Denormandie, Martin Clyme, Richard Jones, John Fury, John Budd, John Ewan, Edw. Mullen, Francis Briggs, Alex. Bennet, Jane Louder, Thomas Atkinson, he reports £22.5.1¾. on hand.

1759, June 19. Cushman, Oliver, a soldier. Int. Adm'r his father, Thomas Cushman, of Elizabeth, yeoman. Bondsman—Jacob Clarke, of Elizabeth, yeoman. Lib. G, p. 83.
1759, Aug. 15. Inventory, £42.1.6, by Joshua Pettit and Thomas Baker.

1752, May 29. Cutler, William, of Amwell, Hunterdon Co., cordwainer; will of. House and lot where I live and 200 acres in Morris Co. to be sold, as also my movable estate, and, after debts are paid, remainder to my wife, Jane. Executors—my wife and my friends,

Peter Lott, Sr., and Peter Lott, Jr. Witnesses—Samuel Henry, Noah Gates, Elizabeth Stevenson. Proved June 12, 1752. Lib. 7, p. 277.

1752, June 6. Inventory, £17.5.6, by Gershom Mott and Samuel Henry.

1756, Oct. 21. Account by Executors.

1757, Nov. 23. Cutten (Cotting), Elias, of Hopewell Township, Cumberland Co.; will of. Wife, Elisabath. Daughters—Elisabeth James and Mary Bower (Bowen?). Real and personal estate. Executors—the wife and Benjamin Mulford. Witnesses—Jeams Johnson, Solomon Hall, James Reed. Proved Jan. 7, 1758. Lib. 8, p. 507.

1758, Oct. 5. Cutter, John, of Woodbridge, Middlesex Co.; will of. Wife, Christian. Children—James, Agness and Mary, all under age. Real and personal estate. Executors—Samuel Cutter and George Brown. Witnesses—Mary Baker and Thomas Brown (who was dead when the will was proved, January 15, 1759). Lib. G, p. 15.

1759, May 18. Cutter, Keziah, of Woodbridge, Middlesex Co., widow of Samuel; will of. Son, Richard, under age. Sisters—Phebe Frazee, Mary (wife of John Moore) and Humes Frazee, all daughters of Shiphat Frazee. Executors—uncle Thomas Scudder and cousin Jonathan Frazee. Witnesses—Edward Frazee, George Frazee and David Edgar. Proved Oct. 29, 1759. Lib. G, p. 108.

1759, Nov. 13. Cutter, Mercy, of Woodbridge, Middlesex Co.; will of. Children—William, Rebeccah Frazee, Mary (wife of Jacob Baker), and Ebbenezer. Grandchildren—Kilsey Cutter, Mary Cutter, John and Mercy Baker. Personal property. Executors—son, Ebbenezar, and daughter, Rebeccah. Witnesses—Francis Campyon, Joseph Thorne and Benjamin Jackson. Proved May 28, 1760. Lib. H, p. 74.

1756, Sept. 20. Cutter, Richard, of Woodbridge, Middlesex Co.; will of. Wife. Mercy. Children—William, Richard, Joseph, Ebenezer, Samuel, John, Ephraim, Sarah Jaquesh, Hannah Dennis, Esther Marsh, Rebecka Cutter and Mary Baker. Land, 22 acres & 10 acres, on the Eastside of the road to Metuchin, between Isaac Tappen and David Evans; 6a. of saltmeadow on the Westside of the road from the upland to the bridge over the Houselot Creek in Raraton meadows; old homefarm on the North side of the road from Cornfield Landing to the Amboy road, between Zebulon Pike on the North, the Great Creek and son William on the East, an island of meadow on the Northside of Bradly's Creek, bought of Col. Elisha Parker; lot on Strawbury Hill, bought of Richard Dole; 10 a. on Southside of Pike's Brook; 27 a. near Lockheart's Hill; 60 a. of woodland near the Pumpkin Patch in Woodbridge; 20 a. of woodland on Northside of Piscataway Road; other real and personal estate. Executors—sons William, Richard and Joseph. Witnesses—Willian Kent, Richard Jaques, Joseph Heveland (Haviland) and David Donham. Proved Jan. 22, 1757. Lib. F, p. 397.

1758, Aug. 12. Cutter, Samuel, of Woodbridge, Middlesex Co.; will of. Wife, Keziah. Son, Richard, under age. Brothers—John, Ephraim, William, Richard, Joseph and Ebenezer Cutter. Sisters—Rebeckah Frazee and Mary Baker, who are to be remaindermen of real and personal estate. Executors—brothers John and Ephraim

CALENDAR OF WILLS—1751-1760   85

Cutter. Witnesses—Christian Cutter, Henry Frazee and David Edgar. Proved June 12, 1759. Lib. G, p. 65.

1759, May 11.—Cyder, Christopher, of Morrice's River, Cumberland Co. Int. Inventory, £58.14.8, incl. 9,000 feet of board, £16.17.6; debts due, £29.7.1.; made by Phillip Grace and William Jones.
   1759, May 14. Bond of Abraham Jones, of Morrice's River Township, as Adm'r; William Cobb and Daniel Peterson, both of Fairfield, said Co., fellowbondsmen. Lib. 9, p. 256.
   1763, Mar. 24. Account by Administrator.

1756, Aug. 27. Dagworthy, John, of Maidenhead, Hunterdon Co., yeoman; will of. Wife, Sarah. Children—John, Mary, Ely, Elisabeth Clayton, Sarah. Grandchildren—four sons and a daughter, names not given, of daughter Margaret and James Mitchel; John Clayton. Legacies to Ann, wife of Joseph Yard, Mrs. Andrew Reed, Rebekah Anderson and her eldest daughter, Rev. David Cowel, Joseph Hidgby and Benj. Stevens. Cornerhouse fronting on Lower Street and garden running East to Duther Street. Personal property, incl. gold chains, silver cups, a negro boy and negro girl. Executors—said Joseph Yard and Andrew Reed, both of Trentown. Witnesses—Mary Ellett, Thomas Walters, Benjamin Stevens. Proved Sept. 6, 1756. Lib. 8, p. 407.

1758, Nov. 2. Daniels, Ebenezer, of Piscataway, Middlesex Co.; will of. Wife, Mary. Children—Sterlin, Uriah, Edward, John, Benjamin, Jerimiah, Abigail and Mary. Real and personal estate. Executors—the wife, son Uriah and Aaron Bishop. Witnesses—Peter Haris (Harris), Leah Harper and Daniel Barto. Proved Nov. 21, 1758. Lib. G, p. 7.
   1758, Nov. 22. Inventory, £97.6.9, by Samuel Drake and Daniel Barto.

1755, July 25. Dare, Elizabeth, of Fairfield, Cumberland Co., widow; will of. Children—Jonathan and Nathan Lorance, Violetta Harris, Abigail Elmer, Elizabeth Shepherd and Rhoda Johnson. Personal estate. Executor—son, Jonathan Lorance. Witnesses—Jonathan Stratton, Abigail Stratton, Jonathan Lorance, Abigail Lorance. Proved at Cohansie Bridge, Jan. 30, 1756.
   1756, Jan. 29. Inventory, £130.10.6, incl. plate, £5.18; a great Bible; bonds and specialties, £52.4.1; made by Jeremiah Buck and Henry Wescote. Cumb. Wills, 136 F.

1759, Mar. 17. Dare, Elkana, of Cohansey, Cumberland Co.; will of. Wife, Elisabeth. Children—Benoni, Elkana and six daughters, names not given, all under age. Homefarm; land bought of John Rementon; marsh on Stow Creek, adjoining Stephen Mulford; land in Hell Neck, bought of Joseph Brick, of which part is already sold to, but not yet paid for by John Plummer. Personal estate. Executors—the wife and son Benoni. Witnesses—John Rementon, Noah Wheaton, Ezekel Bennett. Proved April 28, 1759. Lib. 9, p. 228.
   1759, Apr. 28. Inventory, £74.6.6, by John Rementon and Ezekel Bennett.

1759, Dec. 12. Dare, William, of Deerfield, Cumberland Co., yeoman; will of. Wife, Hannah (apparently second and not mother of

children). Children—William, Levi, Jonathan (under age), Mary Bowen, Abigail, Freelove, Rachel and Amey. Real and personal estate. Executors—the wife and Joseph Ogden. Witnesses—Benoni Dare, Daniel Ogden, Charles Clark. Proved March 7, 1760.
Lib. 10, p. 180.

1760, Feb. 28. Inventory, £139.14.4, by Thomas Joslin (Joslane) and David Ogden.

1763, May 11. Account of the estate by Joseph Ogden, one of the Executors, who has increased it to £163.18.11 by the collection of debts not inventoried, and reports on hand. £114.16.4.

1748-'49, Feb. 1. Darkin, John, of "Elsinburrough" Township, Salem Co., yeoman; will of. Daughters—Hannah, Ann (both under age) and Jale Fitzrandolph, who has daughters Sarah and Jane Fitzrandolph. Real and personal estate. Executors—brother-in-law, Richard Butcher, and daughters Hannah and Ann Darkin. Witnesses—Joshua Thompson, John Smith, George Trenchard. Proved Oct. 21, 1751.
Lib. 7, p. 256.

1751, Oct. 17. Inventory, £582.15.10½, incl. cash and plate, £82.3.1; bills, bonds and book debts, £353.14.7½; books and lookingglasses, £1.13; an old clock, £4; a negroman, £55; made by Nathan Smart and Joshua Thompson.

1760, Dec. 22. Daten (Dayton), Ephraim, of Fairfield Township, Cumberland Co. Int. Inventory, £411.12.11, incl. a negro man, £70; a negro woman, £35; a servant man, £10; made by Thomas Ogden and Philipp Shepherd.

1760, Dec. 23. Bond of Joseph Daten (Dayton) as Adm'r; Thomas Ogden and Philipp Shepherd fellowbondsmen, all of Fairfield Township.
Lib. 10, p. 177.

1760, Jan. 24. Daten (Dayton) Henry, late of Long Island, since of Eggharbour. Inventory, £177.6, incl. 3 old books; 3 large silver spoons @ 18s. and 3 small do. @ 3s., £3.3; a negro man, £55; a negro boy, £35; a negro child, £10; a note, £10; made by John Smith and Robert Morss.
Glou. Wills, 700 H.

1757, Nov. 5. Davenport, Rev. James, of Hopewell, Hunterdon Co.; will of. Wife, Parnel. Children—John (is at College), and Elizabeth, both under age. Nephews—Ebenezar, son of brother John Davenport of Stanford, and John, son of brother Abraham Davenport of Stanford, remaindermen. Land in Stanford County; other real and personal property, incl. a negro slave, a library, a silver cup, and silver watch. Executors—the wife and said brother, Abraham. Witnesses—John Ballard, Nathan Moore, John Guild. Proved February 20, 1758.
Lib. 9, p. 46.

1758, Feb. 17. Inventory, £987.15.1, incl. a watch, £10; debts due, £739.10.3; a negro wench and child, £50; 14 silver spoons, £7; a silver cup, £2.5; a looking glass, £1.5; 2 pictures, 7/6; another looking glass, £1.15; 245 books and pamphlets, £39.12.6; made by Henry Woolsey and Nathan Moore.

1755, Dec. 19. Davice, (Davis), Thomas, of Menington "Present" Salem Co.; will of. Wife, Mary, and son, John MacKoun, sole heirs and Executors of real and personal estate, with remainder to Sarah Ryan. Apprentices—John Aherrin, Daniel Fretch and James Right,

CALENDAR OF WILLS—1751-1760 87

all under 17, to "be sent to a trade." Witnesses—Isaac Johnson, William Harvey and James Kelly. Proved Jan. 28, 1756.
Lib. 8, p. 300.
1756, Feb. 16. Inventory, £117.17.5, by Hans Bilderback and William Peterson.

1750, ——— ———. Davis, David, of Philadelphia, mariner. Int. Account (Burlington Co.) of the estate, £171.7.11, by the Adm'x, Lydia Davis, who charges against it £206.2. for payment of a debt due to James Murgatroyd. [See N. J. Archives, Vol. XXX, p. 133].
Burl. Wills 4641 C.

1753, Feb. 7. Davis, David, Esq., Piles Grove Township, Salem Co.; will of. Wife, Dorothy. Children—David, Jacob, Hannah, Sarah, Griscom, Mercy Redman and Amy Gill, Three tracts of land on Oaldman's Creek, bought of David Jess, Aaron Silver and Joshua Bispham; home farm, with 55 acres, bought of brother, Isaac Davis; a lot bought of Samuel Ladd; land bought of Samuel Wright; meadow, leased to Lewis Mulford. Personal property. Executors—the wife and sons, David and Jacob. Witnesses—William Brick, John Kee, Joseph Pauline (Pawling). Proved Oct. 31, 1754.
Lib. 8, p. 45.
1754, Oct. 20. Inventory, £596.15.5, incl. bills, bonds, book debts and cash, £218.10.11; a servantman, £14; 33 "chears," a couch and 3 lookingglasses, £6.0.6; made by Isaac Sharp and Samuel Lippincott.
1759, Sept. 27. Account by Jacob Davis and David Davis.

1760, Feb. 20. Davis, John, Jr., of Essex Co., yeoman; will of. Wife, Sarah. Children—John, Jacob and Anna. Real and personal estate. Executors—the wife and John Crane, Jr. Witnesses—Samuel Roberson, Isaac Crane, Rebekah Clark. Proved August 4, 1760.
Lib. 9, p. 273.

1760, Nov. 27. Davis, Joseph, of the "Borrough" of Elizabeth, Essex Co.; will of. Wife, Sarah. Children—Caleb, John, Joseph, and Phebe, all under age. "Two children the wife had when I married her." Real and personal estate. Executors—the wife, Caleb Brown and Amos Day. Witnesses—Moses Rolfe, Joseph Whitehead, Samuel Rolfe. Proved Dec. 13, 1760.
Lib. G, p. 389.
1760, Dec. 18. Inventory, £171.13.0, by John Ogden and Josiah Crane.

1754, Apr. 27. Davis, Samuel, of Greenwich Township, Gloucester Co., farmer; will of. Wife, Anne, sole heiress and Executrix of real and personal estate, with legacies to brothers Benjamin and William Davis, and sister Elizabeth Jones. Witnesses—Mary Taylor, Benjamin Barns, John Rumford. Proved May 28, 1754.
Lib. 8, p. 111.
1754, June 8. Inventory, £250.13.2, incl. dues, debts and specialties, £55; silver buckles; made by John Rumford and Thomas Denny.

1756, Aug. 30. Davis, William, of Gloucester Township and County, yeoman; will of. Children—John, Gabriel, William, Ezekiel, Samuel and James. Granddaughter, Hannah Dukemaneer. Personal property. Executors—sons John and Samuel. Witnesses—Thomas Robson, Mary Fordam, Michael Fisher. Proved July 29, 1757.
Lib. 8, p. 437.

1757, July 26. Inventory, £397.0.3, incl. bills, bonds and bookdebts, £368.9.11; made by Michaell Fisher and John Hillman.

1760, Oct. 17. **Davis, William,** of Monmouth Co. Int. Bond of Isaac Rogers, of Allen Town, Monmouth Co., as Adm'r; John Lawrence, of Burlington City, fellowbondsman. Lib. 10, p. 103.
1760, Nov. 29. Inventory, £17.7.0, by Thomas Tyrer and Nathaniel Warner.
1761, Oct. 17. Account by Administrator, Isaac Rogers.

1749, June 6. **Davison, John,** of New Brunswick, yeoman; will of. Wife, Ann. Mother, Sarah Davison. Children—Agnes and George. Personal estate, incl. debt due by Vincent Dye. Executors—the wife, father-in-law Daniel Baker and Jonathan Combs. Witnesses—Duncan Campbell, John Devison, John Ireland. Proved June 19, 1751.
Lib. E, p. 535.
1751, June 8. Inventory, £264.12.11, incl. bonds and book debts, £206.19.5; made by John Wogelom and Duncan Campbell. The estate is indebted £22.17.1, to Mathew Collins, Tice Johnston, James Brown, Samuel Rogers, Jean Davison and Folkert van Nordstrant.

1757, Aug. 13. **Davison, Josiah, Esq.,** of Middlesex Co.; will of. Wife, Mary. Children—John, Andrew, Amaziah, Nathaniel (absent on an expedition), Annias and Mary (wife of Joseph Skelton). Grandson, Josiah Davison. Homefarm; another of 202 acres, bought of James Alexander of New York; 120 ac. adjoining the last on the South side; a lot on Divel's Brook; meadow adjoining James Davison; a farm near the Great Bridge and the milldam; a lot on the new road and Stony Brook, adjoining Cornelius Covenhoven; meadow above the Falls' Dam; houses and lots in Princeton. Personal estate. Executors—son John, son-in-law Joseph Skelton and Jacob Scudder. Witnesses—Albert Schenck, Jacob Schenck and Nathaniel Scudder. Proved Nov. 24, 1759. Lib. 10, p. 62.
1759, Nov. 15. Inventory, £129.14.6, incl. a book (Conductor Generalis), 7/6; made by Joseph Hornor and Robert Priest; 8 bonds called unsettled and no value given.

1760, Apr. 12. **Day, Daniel,** of "Mendum," Morris Co.; will of. Wife, Marey. Children—Benjamin, Samuel, Desire, Timothy, Daniel, Zekiel, Artemas, Nehemiah, Jeremiah and Marcy, the last five under age. Real and personal estate. Executors—sons Benjamin and Samuel. Witnesses—William Minthorn, John Daniel, Brice Riky. Proved June 10, 1760. Lib. G, p. 254.

1754, June 4. **Day, David,** of the Parish of New Providence, "Burrough" of Elizabeth, Essex Co.; will of. Daughters—Abigail (wife of William Maxfell), Sarah, Mary, Jemima and Susanna. Land on and near Long Hill, bought of Joseph Jagger and Timothy Harrison; home farm. Personal property (money at 8s. per oz.). Executors—brother Samuel Day of Morris and Josiah Broadwell of New Providence. Witnesses—Jonathan Mulford, John Hall, Timothy Allen. Proved July 2, 1754. Lib. F, p. 195.
1754, Aug. 21. Inventory, £250.7.2½, by Samuel Rolph and Elnathan Cory.

1758, Sept. 16. **Day, Humphrey,** of Waterford, Gloucester Co., yeoman; will of. Wife, Jane. Children—Charles and Rebecca

CALENDAR OF WILLS—1751-1760   89

Spicer. Granddaughter, Abigail Rudderow. Real and personal estate. Sole executor—Henry Wood, of Waterford, yeoman. Witnesses—William Hepard, Ephraim Stiles, Samuel Spicer. Proved Jan. 31, 1760. Lib. 9, p. 401.
 1760, Jan. 24. Inventory, £222.0.6; incl. books, £1.10; 2 lookingglasses and maps, £2; made by William Stowe (Stone?) and Samuell Spicer.

1760, Mar. 19. Day, Jane, widow of Humphrey, of Waterford, Gloucester Co.; will of. Children—Rebekah, Spicer and Charles, the latter sole executor. Granddaughter, Abigail Rudderow. Personal property. Witneses—John Holmes, Samuell Spicer. Proved April 4, 1760. Lib. 10, p. 36.
 1760, Apr. 3. Inventory, £199.16.6, incl. books, £1.10; a bond of Charles Day, £168.19.10; made by Henry Wood and Samuel Spicer.

1760, Dec. 3. Deacon, John, of Burlington City. Int. Inventory, £306.12, incl. books, £1.18.6; a goldring; made by William Heulings and John Antram. Sworn to by George Antram as Adm'r.
 1760, Dec. 9. Bond of George Deacon as Adm'r; John Antram fellowbondsman, both of said City. Lib. 10, p. 170.

1757, Aug. 28. Deal, Samuel, of Hunterdon Co., yeoman; will of. Wife, Mary. Daughters—Mary and Sarah. Legacies to Edmond Beeks and William Clayton, both of Trenton. Executors—William Clayton and Nathan Beeks, also of Trenton. Witnesses—James Cumine, John Chapman, Will Ball. Proved Sept. 6, 1757.
 Lib. 9, p. 350.

1752, Dec. 13. Dean, Samuel, of Amwell, Hunterdon Co., schoolmaster. Int. Bond of William Gano as Adm'r; Joakim Griggs fellowbondsman, both of said Amwell, farmers. Hunt. Wills, 307 J.
 1752, Dec. 27. Inventory, £22.14.4, incl. a library of books, 19/4; made by David Oliphant and Richard Holcombe.
 1753, Nov. 13. Account by Adm'r.

1759, Jan. 4. Deare, John, of Perth Amboy. Int. Margaret Deare renounced her right to administer on her husband's, John Deare's, estate, in favor of James Newell and Jonathan Deare. Witness—William Deare.
 1759, Jan. 18. Adm'rs—James Newell and Jonathan Deare, both of Perth Amboy. Bondsmen—Thomas Johnson and David Gosling. Witness—Thomas Bartow. Lib. G, p. 17.
 1759, Feb. 2. Inventory, £270.0.8, incl. bills, bonds and bookdebts, no amount given; a clock, £7; spoons and other silverware, £10.11.6; a Bible, 10s.; a negro man, £60; a negro woman, £20; made by Thomas Skinner and Robert Sproull.
 1760, Jan. 3. Account by Jonathan Deare as surviving administrator, who gives its value as £325.16.3.

1759, Sept. 15. Deare, William, of Monmouth Co. Int. Bond of Joseph Forman as Adm'r; Ezekiel Forman fellowbondsman.
 Lib. G, p. 98.

1759, Mar. 29. Dearnal, John, of Evesham Township, Burlington Co.; will of. Wife, Hannah. Children—Lewis, Edward and Jemima (under age). Farm of 600 acres at Eggharbour, between Mullikons River and Waiding River; homefarm adjoining Abram Borton and James Mayson (formerly Richard Boyes). Personal estate. Executors—the wife and son, Lewis. Witnesses—William Foster, Hannah Foster, Jr., Josiah Foster. Codicil of same date describes two pieces of cedar swamp, one of 4½ acres in Telpahakin woods; the other of 2 ac. at the head of Homan's Neck on a branch of Waiding River. Same witnesses. Proved Oct. 11, 1759. Lib. 9, p. 301.

1759, May 12. Inventory, £191.18.10, incl. a servant lad's time, £7; made by John Woolman and James Cattell.

1756, Mar. 10. Deboogh, Frederick, of Freehold, Monmouth Co., yeoman; will of. Wife, Hannah. Children—van Hook (?) Debogh, Hannah, Mary van Hook, Francis, Sarah and Solomon. Grandson, Frederick Brown. Real and personal estate. Executors—the wife, the son and son-in-law, Laurance Debogh and Mathias Mount. Witnesses—James Romine, Robert Cumming, James Romine, Jr. Proved Feb. 8, 1758. Lib. G, p. 9.

1759, April 17. Decamp, Benjamin, of Woodbridge, Middlesex Co., yeoman. Int. Adm'x—Elizabeth DeCamp, widow. Bondsman—John Lee, of Woodbridge. Witness—Thomas Bartow. Lib. G, p. 56.

1750, Oct. 7. De Cow, Isaac, Sr., of Burlington City, yeoman; will of. Wife, Martha. Children—Isaac, Anne Fenemer, and Joseph. Granddaughter, Frances De Cow. Daughter-in-law, Sarah De Cow. Legacies to Mary Sands and Elizabeth Blundon. Meadow and upland, 6-7 acres, in townbounds; 2 ac. of meadow next London Bridge on the Island of Burlington; farm of 400 ac., called Rehoboth, in New Hanover, house and lot on Second Str., Burlington, next to Joshua Raper's orchard; another on said street, now occupied by John Henry; homestead in High Str.; 500 ac. in Morris Co., now occupied by Henry Dill; land at the Marble Mountain. Personal estate, incl. a large Bible and rents due by John Clauinger. Executors—the two sons: witnesses Edw. Rads Price, Nathl Thomas, Rebecca Trapnell. Proved July 29, 1755, by John Trapnell, widower of said Rebecca, and Joseph Hollingshead as acquainted with the signatures of the witnesses, who are all dead. Lib. 8, p. 209.

1755, Jan. 29. De Cow, Isaac, of Burlington, joiner; will of. Wife, Hannah, sole Executrix. Daughters—Hannah and Anne, both under age. Real and personal estate. Witnesses—Alice Read, Lewis Ogden, Ara. Read. Proved Sept. 8, 1755. Lib. 8, p. 203.

1759, June 25. Degamo, John, of Newark. Int. Adm'x Lucretia Degamo, his widow. Bondsman—Thomas Gould, of Newark. Witness—Uzal Ogden. Lib. G, p. 92.

1750, Feb. 10. Dehart, Daniel, Sr., of Elizabethtown, Essex Co., yeoman; will of. Children—Margret, Anne, Elizabeth, Catherine, Daniel, Baltus, Mathias and Samuel. Children of dec'd. daughter, Sarah, viz., Catherine, Mary and Sarah. Real and personal estate. Executors—the four sons. Witnesses—Robert Ogden, David Ogden, Andrew Hay. Proved Dec. 14, 1753. Lib. F, p. 153.

CALENDAR OF WILLS—1751-1760 91

1759, Dec. 17. Dehart, Jacob, Jr., of Elizabeth Town, Essex Co. Int. Adm'x—Elizabeth Dehart, the widow. Bondsman—Jacob Dehart, Esq., of Elizabeth Town. Witness—Lewis Ogden.
Lib. G, p. 120.

1737, July 12. DeHart, Mathias, of Elizabeth Town, Essex Co., mariner; will of. Daughter—Margaret Williamson, a widow, to have land in said town. Executrix—said Margaret. Witnesses—James Keen, Margaret Van Pelt, George Emott. Proved Aug. 17, 1758.
Lib. F, p. 538.

1760, May 3. Dels (Debs?), Peter, of Amwell Township, Hunterdon Co., yeoman; will of. Wife, Mary. Children—Ann, Sarah and Peter (under age). Executors—father Peter Debs and brother John Dels, both of said Township. Witnesses—Dennes Habbich (Hopaugh, later, Hoppock), Henrich Delsz (both signing in German script) and John Opdyke. Proved August 25, 1760. Lib. 10, p. 591.
1760, Aug. 26. Inventory, £125.9, by John Opdyck and Daniel Carroll.

1758, Nov. 8. Demarest, David, of Hackinsack, Bergen Co., yeoman; will of. Children—David, Rachel, Mary, Elisabeth, Sara, Anna, Martintie, William (dec'd?) who has left a son David, a minor. Grandchildren—David and Jacobus Demarest; Sara, daughter of Elisabeth. Land near the Church at Schraalingburgh, bought of Lucas van Horn. Personal property. Executors not appointed. Witnesses—Johannes Demarest, Peter Demarest and Lourens Torse. Proved March 4, 1760.
Lib. G, p. 130.
1760, Mar. 4. Bond of David Demarest, his son, as Adm'r with will annexed (will missing); Johannes Demarest fellow-bondsman.

1755, Jan. 29. de Money, Henry, of the Boro' of Elizabeth, Essex Co., tailor; will of. Children—Henery Demoney, Augustus Demoney, An Wood, Easter Freeman, Marey Frasey and Suzanah Demoney. Real and personal estate. Executor son (son-in-law.) Joseph Frasey of said Boro'. Witnesses—Moses Frazee, Samuel Willis, John Stits. Proved Feb. 5, 1755. Lib. F, p. 248.
1755, Feb. 6. Inventory, £186.8.8½ by Joseph Frazee and Benjamin Littell.

1755, Dec. 30. DeMott, Maties, of Township and Co. of Bergen. Gentleman; will of. Son, Michael, to have blacksmith tools as his birthright. Sons, Michael and Joris, to have house and lands where I live. Son, Hendrick, the plantation where he lives in Morris Co. Son, Jacob, the plantation where he lives. Daughter, Clasie, £160. Daughter, Ontie, £160. Daughter, Maritie, £200. Sons, Michael and Joris, and daughter, Maritie, to have outset as other children had. Executors—sons Mickel, Hendrick, Joris and Jacob. Witnesses—Reynier van Griess, Jacob Van Winckel, Daniel Van Winckel. Proved June 8, 1756. Lib. F, p. 368.
1757, Nov. 9. Inventory (much of it eaten away) of the personal estate, incl. a gold doubloon, £5.12; a gold St. Johannis, £24; 6 small pieces of gold, £9; 6 negro slaves (young and old), £108.10; a silver cup, £4; many bonds; made by Machyel de Moedt (De Mott), Henderyck de Moedt and Yocob de Mot, Executors; appraised by Reynier van Giesen and Zacharias Sickels.

1760, Feb. 24. Denham, James, of the South Ward of Perth Amboy; will of. Wife, Abigail. Children—James, John, William, Obadiah and Margaret, all under age. Real and personal estate. Executors—Samuel Throckmorton and Andrew Smyth. Witnesses—William Crawford, John Brown and John Abraham. Proved April 23, 1760.
Lib. G, p. 187.

1751, April 19. Denman, William, of Essex Co. Int. Adm'x—Lydia Denman, widow. Bondsman—John Denman, of Essex Co. Witness—Uzal Ogden.
1751, March 23. Inventory, £40.3.3, by Jonathan Allen and John Potter.
Lib. E, p. 528.

1758, Feb. 20. Denn, John, of Alleways Creek, Salem Co., yeoman; will of. Wife, Elizabeth. Children—James, David, John (the last two under age), Rachel and Elizabeth. Brother, Paul Denn, remainderman. Real and personal estate. Executors—the wife and Joseph Stretch. Witnesses—John Bacon, Benjamin Tyler and Philipp Dennis, Jr. Proved Feb. 8, 1760.
Lib. 10, p. 524.
1759, Nov. 16. Inventory, £249.8.9, by Solomon Ware and John Stewart.

1752, Oct. 16. Denn, Joseph, of Stoe Creek Precinct, Cumberland Co., yeoman; will of. Wife, Rebeckah. An expected child. Cousins—Amos and Joseph (sons of Daniel and Mary Bacon), remaindermen. Farm bought of John Padgett. Personal property. Executor—John Barrowclif. Witnesses—Moses Padgeg (Padgett), Aaron Daniel, Peter Long. Proved Dec. 4, 1752.
1752, —— ——. Inventory, £145.13.4, by Peter Long and Richard Butcher.
1756, Sept. 18. Account by the Executor. Cumb. Wills, 76 F.

1759, July 24. Denn, Paul, of Allaways Creek, Salem Co., labourer. Inventory, £101.6.9, by Jonathan Bradway and John Stewart.
1760, Feb. 20. Bond of Lydia Denn as Adm'x; John Stewart and Samuel Hancock fellowbondsmen, all of Allaways Creek.
Lib. 10, p. 448.

1760, Dec. 30. Dennis, Jacob, of Goodluchin, Monmouth Co. Int. Bond of Joseph Bullock as Adm'r; Joseph Reckless fellowbondsman, both of Burlington Co., gents.
Lib. 10, p. 293.

1756, May 8. Dennis, John, of "Shrosbury" Township, Monmouth Co.; will of. Wife, Ellinor. Children—James, John, Jacob, Philipp, Sarah Platt, Susannah Platt, Rebecca Platt, Anna Jonson, Rachel and Hannah. Land on North and South side of "Seader" Creek, on the Bay. Personal property. Executors—sons Jacob and Philipp. Witnesses—William Worth, Elizabeth Ogley and Samuel Emily. Proved August 2, 1756.
Lib. 8, p. 313.
1756, July 22. Inventory, £96, by David Lippincott and Samuel Emley.

1756, Sept. 9. Dennis, John, of Piles Grove, Salem Co.; will of. Wife, Elizabeth. Children—George William and Anne, all under age. Home farm; 2 lots of land on Cedar Creek, Shrewsberry, Monmouth Co. Personal property. Executors—Jacob Dennis and Philip Dennis,

CALENDAR OF WILLS—1751-1760   93

both of Shrewsberry. Witnesses—Robert Clark, Jonathan Fowller, Andrew Sinnickson and Bowes Wray. Proved Oct. 6, 1756.
Lib. 8, p. 446.
1756, Sept. 30. Inventory, £108.12.5, by Robert Clark and John Beesly.

1759, Sept. 8. Dennis, Jonathan, of Somerset Co., yeoman; will of. Wife, Agness. Son, Robert. Real and personal estate. Executors—the son and Abraham van Tuyl of said Co. Witnesses—Jonas Greenway, Benoni Coshow and Elias v. Court. Proved September 24, 1759.
Lib. G, p. 98.
1759, Sept. 26. Inventory, £379.19.6, incl. bonds, £127; Flavel's Works, £2; Hall's Works, 18s.; a Commentary upon the Revelations, 7s.; a Bible and other books, 7s.; made by Folkert Sebring and Thomas Coon, Jr.; Abraham van Tuyl and Robert Dennes, Executors.

1754, Sept. 11. Dennis, Joseph, of Piles Grove, Salem Co.; will of. Brothers—Joseph (sole Executor) and James. Sisters, Sarah Plats, Rebeckea Plats, Susannah Plats, Ann Jonson, Rachel Dennis and Hannah Dennis, to inherit the estates. Witnesses—Robert Clark, William Cattell, Thomas Roberts. Proved Oct. 28, 1754.
Lib. 8, p. 121.
1754, Oct. 16. Inventory, £60.4.7, incl. bills and bonds, £48.11.7; made by Jacob Andrews and Samuel Emiley.

1752, Mar. 3. Denton, William, of Cumberland Co., yeoman; will of. Wife, Ann, sole heiress and Executrix of real and personal estate. Legacies to William Tullis, husband of eldest daughter Ellena Denton, and to daughter, Mary Denton. Witnesses—Henry Stevens, Dan Bowen, Samuel Woodruff. Proved August 4, 1752.
1752, July 12. Inventory, £53.2.2, incl. books, by Joseph Lord and Andrew Erickson.
Cumb. Wills, 77 F.

1751, Sept. 22. Derickson, Manoah, of Greenwich, Gloucester Co.; will of. Wife, Christian. Children—John, Deborah, Elenor Matton and Erick. Real and personal estate. Executors—son John and John Jones. Witnesses—William Cobb, Peter Cox, John Jones. Proved Jan. 8, 1754.
Lib. 7, p. 433.
1754, Dec. 27. Inventory, £42.15, incl. books, £1.10; made by Lawrence Lock and Andrew Archard.
1754, Janr. 8. John Jones, one of the Executors, named in the preceding will, refuses to serve.

1753, Dec. 28. Derrickson, Peter, of Penn's Neck, Salem Co. Int. Inventory, £132.18.2, incl. credits and "desparate" debts, £95.13.2; made by Alen Congelton and John Vanneman.
1754, Feb. 7. Bond of William Derickson as Adm'r; John Vanneman fellowbondsman, both of Pen's Neck.
Lib. 9, p. 93.

1759, Sept. 4. Devansue, John, of Essex Co. Int. Adm'x—Easter Devansue, widow. Bondsman—Michael Vrelandt, of Acquacknong, in Essex Co. Witness—Lewis Ogden.
Lib. G, p. 289.

1749-'50, Feb. 19. Devenny, William, of Freehold, Monmouth Co., yeoman; will of. Wife, Mary. Children—George, William (both under age) and Leah. Real and personal estate. Executors—the

wife and Hendrick Vorehis. Witnesses—Timothy Lloyd, John Johnson, John Anderson. Proved Oct. 16, 1751. Lib. E, p. 550.
1750, Nov. 16. Inventory, £93.9, incl. old books 12s., made by Timothy Lloyd and Richard Pettinger.

1757, June 25. Dickenson, Mark, of Alloways Creek, Salem Co. Int. Bond of Margreat Dickenson (Dickerson) as Adm'x; John Holme fellowbondsman, both of said Co. Lib. 9, p. 89.
1757, June 25. Inventory, £290.11.7, by John Holme and William Oakford.

1756, Mar. 2. Dickey, Robert, of Manington, Salem Co. Int. Inventory, £57.10.6, by Hans Bilderback and William Moore.
1756, Mar. 19. Bond of Deborah Dickey, widow of Robert, as Adm'x; William Moore, of Manington, fellowbondsman.
Lib. 9, p. 93.

1747, Oct. 14. Dickinson, Rev. Jonathan of Elizabeth. Inventory, £703.5.11. made by Edward Sale and John Ross. (Inventory filed March 21, 1752). [See N. J. Archives, Vol. XXX, p. 143, for will].
Essex Wills, 1435 G.

1751, May 11. Dilkes, James, of Deptford, Gloucester Co., yeoman; will of. Wife, Ann. Children—Isaac, Abraham, John, Joseph, James, Thomas, Rachel Moore and Sarah Nightingale. Real and personal estate. Executors—the wife and son Isaac. Witnesses—Peter Marriage, John Irwen, David Scram. Proved Feb. 22, 1759. Lib. 9, p. 190.
1759, Jan. 29. Inventory, £103.15, by George Flaningam and James Cattell.

1751, Feb. 26. Dingee, Judith, of Great Egg Harbour, Gloucester Co.; will of. Children—Susannah Steelman, Mary, Judith, John Steelman, Peter Steelman. Son-in-law, Noah Smith. The last two named made Executors of personal estate. Legacy to apprentice girl, Mary Plunket. Witnesses—Pheby Hackney, Hanah Denis. Proved May 24, 1751.
1751, May 16. Inventory, £59.10.6, by Gideon Scull and James Somers.
Glou. Wills, 481 H.

1748-'49, Jan. 27. Disbrow, Griffin, of Perth Amboy, Middlesex Co., yeoman; will of. Wife, Hannah. Children; of whom son, Benjamin, only is named. Legacy to mother, Mary Disbrow. Real and personal estate, incl. a negroman. Executors—Richard (?) Eserson, Esq., and Richard Fitz Randolph, joiner. Witnesses—John Disbrow, James Willson, Thomas Fox. Proved March 11, 1754.
Lib. F, p. 158.

1760, Nov. 10. Ditrich, Peter, of Burlington Co. Int. Adm'r—Henry Paxson. Bondsman—Thomas Shinn. Witnesses—S. Blackwood and Gabriel Blond. Lib. 10, p. 169.
1760, Dec. 30. Inventory, £17.1.11, incl. silver buttons and buckles, £1.11.8; made by Daniel Jones, Jr., and John West. Lib. 10, p. 169.

1751, May 2. Dod, Timothy, of Newark. Int. Adm'rs—Samuel Farand and John Dod, Jr., of Newark. Bondsman—Joseph Ball, of Newark. Witnesses—Uzal Ogden and John Dehart. Lib. E, p. 528.

CALENDAR OF WILLS—1751-1760   95

1756, Jan. 17. Dolan, Charles, of Sussex Co. Int. Bond of John Allison, of Sussex Co., as Adm'r; Moore Furman, of Trenton, Hunterdon Co., fellowbondsman. Attached to the bond a letter from Charles Hoff, Jr., to Johanna, widow of William Hendrickson, Nov. 1, 1754, asking for payment of her late husband's debts. She replies, that she refuses to administer on the estate. Lib. 8, p. 79.

1756, —— ——. Inventory, £14.8.4, by William Juell and John Cornelison.

1758, June 5. Donham (Dunham), David; of Woodbridge, Middlesex Co., yeoman. Int.. Adm'x—Mary Dunham, widow. Bondsman—Isaac Freeman, of Woodbridge, yeoman. Witness—Thomas Bartow. Lib. F, p. 526.

1758, June 13. Inventory, £303.12.6, incl. 3 Bibles and other Books, 18s.; 2 silver spoons, 16s.; made by Samuel Barron and Nathaniel Fitz Randolph. Lib. F, p. 526.

1761, June 23. Account, by the Adm'x, Mary Dunham, who charges against it £43.15.3. as the widow's third, and £30. as "a legacy left me by my mother," in all £253.10.7.

1756, Apr. 13. Donham (Dunham), Denness, of Middlesex Co.; will of. Gives personal estate to brother, Robart Donham, and sisters, Mary and Sarah. No executor named. Witnesses—Samuel Kelly, and Elisebeth Kelly. Proved June 2, 1756, when administration, with the will annexed, is granted to Robert Donham. Lib. F, p. 359.

1759, Mar. 14. Doody, Richard, of Elsinburrough, Salem Co. Int. Inventory, £328.17.11, incl. a servant boy, £8; a set of musquito nets; outstanding debts, £41.7.5; made by William Goodwin and Aaron Bradway.

1759, May 15. Bond of Elinor Doody as Adm'x; John Mason fellowbondsman, both of Elsinburrough. Lib. 9, p. 353.

1757, Nov. 2. Doolhagen, Frederick, of New Brunswick, Middlesex Co. Int. Inventory, £682.5.2, incl. bills and bonds, £242.9.1; 6 negroes, £195; made by Mathias van Dike and Joseph Skelton.

1757, Nov. 22. Bond of Martha Doolhagen, of Middlesex Co., as Adm'x; Benjamin Stout, Jr., of Hopewell, Hunterdon Co., fellowbondsman. Lib. 8, p. 515.

1755, Nov. 1. Dooren (Dorne), Cornelius, of Middletown, Monmouth Co.; will of. Wife (not named). Children—Cornelius, Nicholas, Catharine, Joseph, Deatluf, Elinor and Anne. Grandson—James Wilson. Real and personal estate. Executors—sons Deatluf, Cornelius and Nicholas. Witnesses—John Wall, Jr., Cornelious van der Belt and John Bowne. Proved Dec. 16, 1755. Lib. F, p. 304.

1754, June 27. Dorlandt, Jan. of Somerset Co., yeoman; will of. Wife, Aeltje. Friend, Hendrick Pettinger. Youngest sister, Antje. Another sister, Gertje. Three brothers. Executors—Leffert Lefferson and Isaac Lot, of Long Island, N. Y., and Hendrick Pettinger, of Somerset Co. Witnesses—Samuel Tilton, Richard Pittenger, Teunis Middagh. Proved August 8, 1754. Lib. F, p. 204.

1754, Aug. 10. Inventory, £275.2, incl. 4 negroes, £170; taken by his Executors, Leffert Leffertse and Isack Lott; appraised by Richard Parsell and Abraham Voorhees.

1754, July 5. Dormeus, John, of Bergen Co., yeoman; will of. Wife, Elizabeth, to have all real and personal estate she may want during life; then son, Cornelius, to have the real estate. Oldest son, John; daughters, Jannetje (wife of Michel Hertie) and Elizabeth. Children of daughter, Aeltje, viz., Jacob, Elizabeth and Annatje. Children of son Abraham, viz., John and Cathreen. Executors—son, Cornelius, and son-in-law, Michel Hertie. Witnesses—Deyrck Dey, Nicholas Kip, Phillip Schuyler. Proved Feb. 7, 1758. Lib. F, p. 513.

1759, June 30. Doty, Moses, Jr., yeoman, of Somerset Co. Int. Inventory, £81.11.6, by Joseph Pound and Nathaniel Ayers.
1759, Oct. 9. Bond of Rachel, his widow, as Adm'x; William Worth and Nathaniel Ayers, both of said Co., fellowbondsmen.
Lib. G, p. 100.

1757, Oct. 14. Douglas, George, of Chesterfield Township, Burlington Co.; will of. Wife, Elkalannah (Althalannah). Children—John, Mary Teay, Demuras Till, and William. Grandchildren—Ellick-Sander (Alexander) Douglass, George Douglass, John and Ann Ginkins (children of John Ginkins), William ———, daughter Mary's children, and other grandchildren, (names not given). Land in Nottingham Township, said Co.; also on the seashore. Personal property. Executors—the wife and son William. Witnesses—Marmaduke Watson, Peter Dopson, Hugh Newell. Proved Nov. 12, 1757.
Lib. 8, p. 466.
1757, Nov. 7. Inventory, £745.10.8, incl. bills, bonds and bookdebts, £517.4.4; made by Joseph Thorn and Samuel Farnsworth.

1752, Mar. 24. Douglass, William, of Burlington Co. Int. Bond of Neil Levingston as Adm'r; Charles Axford fellowbondsman, both of Trenton. Burl. Wills, 4949 C.

1758, Feb. 17. Dowdney (Downey), John, of Hopewell Township, Cumberland Co., mason; will of. Wife, Tabitha. Children—Nicholas, Nathaniel, John, Burrows, George and Mary. Homefarm and other land. Personal property, incl. books. Executors—the wife and son Nicholas. Witnesses—William Dowdney, Nicholas Johnson, Robert Kelsay. Proved March 22, 1758. Lib. 9, p. 89.
1758, Mar. 15. Inventory, £523.14.10, incl. bills, bonds, etc., $221.7.6, made by Samuel Fithian and Robert Ewing.

1756, Jan. 16. Down, Jemima, widow of Robert, of Deptford Township, Gloucester Co.; will of. Children—Aquila, John (both married), William, Jemima, (wife of William Smallwood). Granddaughters—Mary (wife of James Hilman), Sarah Down and Jemima Smallwood. Sister, Hannah (wife of John Kentin). Mentions, also, Mary, wife of brother, Anthony Sharp. Personal estate. Executor—son William. Witnesses—Thomas Andrews and Jos'a Lord. Proved Feb. 23, 1756.
Lib. 8, p. 295.

1760, May 8, Down, Mary, of Gloucester Co. Int. Bond of John Down as Adm'x; Thomas Cox fellowbondsman, both of Deptford Township, Gloucester Co., yeoman. Lib. 9, p. 420.

1752, Sept. 14. Down, Robert, of Newtown, Gloucester Co., yeoman. Int. Inventory, £258.7.6, incl. bonds, book debts, cash and notes,

CALENDAR OF WILLS—1751-1760   97

£166.2.6; a watch, silver spoons, etc., £8; made by Robert Stephens and Joseph Ellis.

1752, Nov. 5. Bond of widow, Ann Down, of Newton Township, as Adm'x; John Down, of Deptford Township, yeoman, fellowbondsman.
Lib. 8, p. 182.

1756, Jan. 6. Account, by John Eastlack, husband of Ann Down, the widow and administratrix of Robert.

1757, Jan. 25. Doyle, Robert, of Newton, Gloucester Co., yeoman. Int. Inventory, £97.11, incl. bills and bonds, £87.2, made by James Powell and Isaac Mickle.

1757, Apr. 7. Bond of Isaac Stephens as Adm'r; Robert Stephens fellowbondsman, both of Gloucester Co., yeomen.   Lib. 8, p. 384.

1753, Feb. 7. Drake, Francis, of Hopewell Township, Hunterdon Co.; will of. Divides personal estate between Baptist Society in Hopewell, (the interest of the bond against brother-in-law Richard Evans to be paid for the use of said Society to Zebulon Stout and Capt. David Stout), the father, brother Zachariah Drake, and half sister Hannah Drake (under age). Executors—brothers Edmond and Daniel Drake. Witnesses—Thomas Drake, Joseph Newton, Zachariah Drake. Proved April 17, 1753.   Lib. 7, p. 401.

1750, Apr. 13. Inventory, £91.0.9, incl. bills, bonds and book debts, £62.11.9; made by Azariah Hunt and Andrew Vannoy.

1754, May 7. Drake, Henry, of New Brunswick. Int. Adm'x—Kezia Drake, widow. Bondsman—James Mathis, of New Brunswick.
Lib. F, p. 174.

1756, Jan. 3. Drake, Isaac, of the Borough of Elizabeth, Essex Co.; will of. Children—Samuel, Daniel, Nathaniel and Hannah (wife of George Lang). Grandchildren—Martha (daughter of Samuel), Isaac, Nathaniel and Sarah (children of dec'd. son, Isaac). Legacies to Thomas Johnson and to the Baptist Church in Piscataway. Real and personal estate, incl. negro slaves. Executors—sons Samuel and Daniel. Witnesses—Jeremiah Manning, James Manning, Reune Runyon. Proved Jan. 29, 1759.   Lib. G, p. 27.

1759, Jan. 25. Inventory, £456.8.10, by James Manning and John Blackford.

1757, Dec. 9. Drake, James, of Woodbridge, blacksmith. Int. Adm'rs—Isaac Stelle and Joseph Fitz Randolph, both of Piscataway. Witness—Thomas Bartow. Easther Drake, the widow, renounced.
Lib. F, p. 477.

1759, Jan. 19. Drake, Jeremiah, of Piscataway, Middlesex Co.; will of. Wife (not named). Children—Andrew, Jeremiah, Hugh, Ruth Dunham and Martha, all under age. Real and personal estate. Executors—brother Fitz Randolph Drake and brother-in-law David Dunham. Witnesses—Trustrum Manning, Thomas Holtom and Reune Runyon. Proved February 5, 1759.   Lib. G, p. 29.

1759, Feb. 6. Inventory, £264.10.9, incl. a large Bible 14s.; other books 7s.; 2 deerskins, £1.10; made by David Fitzrandolph and Reune Runyon.

1744, Dec. 12. Drake, John, of Piscataway, Middlesex Co.; will of. Wife, Ann, sole heiress. Brother-in-law, Joseph Fitzrandolph

7

and cousin, Joseph Fitzrandolph, Jr., Executors. Witnesses—Jeremiah Drake, Joseph Fitz Randolph, Jr., Marey Dannis. Proved May 30, 1751. Lib. E, p. 526.
1751, May 29. Inventory, £69.11.6, incl. books, 5s.; made by John Hepburn and George Marlett.

1754, Feb. 8. Drake, Joseph, of Piscataway, Middlesex Co., yeoman; will of. Wife. Sarah. Sons—Ephraim, Ruben, Simmeon, Imle and Joseph. Real and personal estate. Executors—the wife and brother-in-law, James Matthes. Witnesses—Isaac Stelle, Benjamin Dunn and Mary Kip. Proved Feb. 7, 1758. Lib. F, p. 488.
1758, Mar. 21. Inventory, £223.5.10, incl. a Bible and other books 7s.; a negro man, £25; made by Reune Runyon and Isaac Stelle.

1752, Feb. 27. Drake, Rachel, of Hopewell, Hunterdon Co. Int. Inventory, £152.18.3, incl. a goldring with silver buckle and girdle, 19/6; Indian corn and flaxseed; made by Henry van Kirk and Reuben Armitage.
1752, Mar. 2. Bond of Francis Drake and Thomas Drake as Adm'rs; Henry van Kirk fellowbondsman, all of Hopewell, yeomen.
Hunt. Wills, 308 J.
1756, Mar. 23. Account by Thomas Drake, acting Executor.

1752, Mar. 14. Drake, William, of Hopewell Township, Hunterdon Co., labourer; will of. Wife, Susannah. Son, William, under age. Real and personal estate. Executors—the wife and brother, Richard Evins. Witnesses—Benjamin Drake, Daniel Drake, Edward Cooper. Proved April 6, 1752.
1752, Apr. 4. Inventory of the estate: Real, 88 acres of land, £120; personal, £57.4.6; made by Henry van Kirk and Edmund Drake. Hunt. Wills, 209 J.

1760, Feb. 12. Dubois, Jamentie (Jemima), of Piles Grove, Salem Co.; will of. Refers to "children," but names only sons Abraham and Jacob, the latter being named sole Executor. Witnesses—Louis Dubois, Elizabeth Rose and Rebecah Elwell. Proved March 3, 1760.
Lib. 10, p. 509.
1760, Feb. 25. Inventory, £203.7.6, incl. a negro girl, £25; a negro child, £1; a silver cup, 20s.; bonds, cash, "intrust" and money as yet "unsarten," £160.15.6; made by Isaac and Benjamin Burroughs.

1759, Oct. 15. Dubois, Samuel, late of Staten Island, N. Y., now of Perth Amboy, Middlesex Co.; will of, John Thomson, husband of sister. Margaret Dubois, sole heir and Executor. Witnesses—Abraham Webb, Jonathan Deare and William Fondrill. Proved Nov. 12, 1759.
Lib. G, p. 109.

———, ———, —. **Dubois, Solomon,** of Piles Grove Township, Salem Co., yeoman; will of. Brother, Garret Dubois, sole heir of personal estate and part of father's plantation, if brother Abraham keeps his part. Executors—said brother Garret and Dr. Patrick Gray. Witnesses—Thomas Hatter, William Lewis and Patrick Gray. Proved Jan. 21, 1756. Lib. 8, p. 294.
1755, Dec. 20. Inventory, £63.2.10, incl. bonds and notes, £26.5; made by Joshua Garrison and Abraham Nilukirk.

1756, Jan. 21. Patrick Gray, of Piles Grove, one of the Executors named above, refuses to serve.

1755, Jan. 22. Duboys, Abraham, of Somerset Co.; will of. Children—Abraham, Francyntje (wife of Bragon Hoff), Marytje (wife of George Ryerse), Cathrine (wife of David Gano), Elizabeth (wife of Stephen Gano), Rebecca (wife of Frederick Van Vliet). Grandchildren—Mary and Susannah Jubert and Abraham Duboys. Land in said Co., 2,200 acres, divided into 6 lots. Personal estate. Executors—Sons-in-law Hoff and Reyerse. Witnesses—William Ouke, Hendrick Staats and Minnie V. Voorhies. Codicil of Jan. 26, 1755, disposes of shares given to the grandchildren, in case they should die under age and without issue. Same witnesses. Proved April 4, 1758.
Lib. F, p. 522.

1757, Aug. 5. Duckmenere, John, of Gloucester Co., having been "absent out of the Province five years," not having been heard of since and having left a daughter, Hannah Duckmenere, under 14 years of age, to whom her grandfather, William Davis, left a legacy, likely to be wasted by the executors of said Davis' will, her uncles, John, James and Azekil Davis, petition that their brother, William Davis be appointed her guardian.

1758, Apr. 18. Petition of Hannah Dukemanear to the same effect.
1758, Apr. 19. Bond of William Davis as such guardian, John Hinchman, fellowbondsman, both of Gloucester Town and County, yeoman.
Lib. 8, p. 543-4.

1755, Nov. 13. Duell, Thomas, of Pen's Neck, Salem Co.; will of. Wife, Gain. Brother, John Duel. Cousin, John Duel (receives son Thomas' wearing apparel). Farm of 200 acres. Personal property. Executors—brother John Duel and Isaac Sharp. Witnesses—Joseph Applin, Obadiah Loyd and Mary Aplin. Proved Dec. 20, 1755.
Lib. 8, p. 297.

1755, Dec. 18. Inventory, £1,482.2.2, incl. a clock; merchant's goods, £113.4.1; bills, bonds, book debts and notes, £1,127.7; a servant man, £16; made by Mathew Gill and Samuel Lippincotte.

1755, Dec. 18. Isaac Sharp, named as one of the Executors, refuses to serve.

1760, July 19. Dukeminer, Thomas, of Newton, Gloucester Co., husbandman. Int. Bond of widow, Lydia Dukeminner, of Waterford Township, Adm'x. Jacob Stokes, of Newton, yeoman, fellowbondsman.
Lib. 10, p. 81.

1761, Nov. 30. Account, £50, by the Adm'x, who has increased it by £2, and reports on hand a balance of £6.6.7.

1759, Jan. 1. Dumont, John, of Somerset Co.; will of. Wife, Annatje. Children—John, Peter, Dirck, Abraham, and Femmetje. Real and personal estate. Executors—brother Abraham Dumon and cousin John Brokaw. Witnesses—William Lane, John Davis and Joseph McKenzie. Proved June 6, 1759.
Lib. G, p. 120.

1759, Febr. 28. Inventory: Real—home farm of 615 acres, @ £3.10. per acre, £2,152.10; two lots at Rariton Landing, Middlesex Co., £50; a right laid out on the Northbranch, £3.5.4. Personal—£1,073.-13.4, incl, bonds, cash and notes, £63.4; 9 negroes, £265; 3 looking-glasses, £4.2; 5 silver spoons and a silver cup, £5.10; 400 bush. of wheat, @ 5s., £100; 50 bush. of Indian corn, @ 2/6, £6.5; book debts, £149.0.6; appraised by Peter Wortman and Matheus ten Eick.

1759, Dec. 27. Abraham Dumon, one of the Executors named above, refuses to serve.

1756, Mar. 6. Dunahu (Donoho), Patrick, of Morris Co.; will of. Friend, Daniel Cooper, Jr., sole heir and Executor of personal estate. Witnesses—John Bowman, Peter Layten, Jacob McCollum. Proved Sept. 20, 1757.   Lib. F, p. 450.

1757, Dec. 8. Inventory, £107.5, by Peter Layton and John Carl.

1752, May 9. Dunbarr, David, of Trenton, Hunterdon Co. Int. Inventory, £74.9.6, incl. 2 looking glasses, 19s.; 4 maps and 6 pictures, 6s.; 6 silver spoons and a silver child's spoon, 17s.; 3 Bibles; Tillotson's Works and other books; made by Joseph Yard and Alexander Chambers.

1752, June 1. Bond of widow, Sarah Dunbar, as Adm'r; John Yard and Benjamin Yard fellowbondsmen, all of Trenton.

Hunt. Wills, 310 J.

1752, Aug. 5. Dunham, Jonathan, Jr., of Piscataway, Middlesex Co. Int. Inventory, £411.1.4, incl. 122 sides of leather, at 9s, £54.18; 239 do. and 8 skins, supposed to be in the tan vats, £85.13; Peter King's servant man's time, £20; bills and book debts, £60.7.9, of which £8.1.3. are called bad debts; made by David Fitzrandolph and John Gilinan.

1752, Aug. 6. Bond of Keziah, widow, and Malachi Fitz-Randolph of Woodbridge, as Adm'rs; Jonathan Fitzrandolph, of Piscataway, fellowbondsman.   Lib. F, p. 60.

———, ——— ———. **Dunham, Mary,** of Woodbridge, Middlesex Co., Inventory, £74.18.8, by Timothy Blomfield and Benjamin Allword, (Filed Sept. 12, 1760).

1761, Feb. 23. Account, by Jonathan Dennis dec'd, the administrator; signed by Robert Dennes, who charges £26. for the support of Rachael Donham during 2 years, 3 months, attendance and funeral; £60. for support of Lewis Donham, 3 yrs. 9 m. old, when his mother died; 12s. for Jonathan's schooling 2 quarters, and nothing for Phebe Donham.   Mid. Wills, 1409 L.

(For administration, see Vol. XXX, p. 155, N. J. Archives).

1758, July 22. Dunkin, John, of Salem, Salem Co., yeoman. Int. Bond of widow. Elizabeth Dunkin, of Salem, as Adm'x; Daniel Dorwill (Dorrell) of Elsinburough, said Co., yeoman, fellowbondsman.

Lib. 9, p. 97.

1758, Mar. 4. Dunlap, Capt. James, of Penn's Neck, Salem Co., yeoman; will of. Wife (not named; apparently second, who has daughter Mary Anne). Sons—John, James and Thomas. Real and personal estate. Executors—son James and Isaac Sharp. Witnesses —Alen Congelton, William Dallbow and Robert Howard. Proved March 20, 1758.   Lib. 8, p. 529.

1758, Mar. 20. Isaac Sharp, one of the Executors named above, refuses to act.

1758, Mar. 20. Inventory, £398.10.4, of which the share of Mary Anne and her mother is £91.17.7; incl. a looking glass and 7 silver spoons;—, books;—. John is to receive £7; James, gold buttons and a sword, £6; Thomas, £271.11.3; and £22.1.6. not bequeathed in the will; made by John Creag and Richard Moore.

1753, Dec. 11. Dunn, Ebenezer, of Penn's Neck, Salem Co. Int. Inventory, £259.15, incl. a servant man; accounts and bonds, £38.5.7; made by Martin Skeer and Samuel Copner.

1753, Dec. 17. Bond of Esther Dunn and Samuel Copner as Adm'rs; John Dunn fellowbondsman, all of Penn's Neck. Lib. 8, p. 92.

1754, Sept. 30. Account by the above named Administrators, who report £211.7.11 on hand for distribution.

1759, June 1. Dunn, Hugh, of Stow Creek, Cumberland Co.; will of. Wife, Amey. Children—Hugh, Amey Dunham, Samuel, Zurviah Barratt, Keziah Ayars (eldest daughter), Mary Riyel (?) and Sarah Davis. Real and personal estate. Executors—the wife and son Hugh. Witnesses—Joseph Ayars, William, Russell, Jr., Jonathan Davis. Proved July 10, 1759. Lib. 9, p. 261.

1759, June 27. Inventory, £208.4, by Jonathan Davis and Josiah Parvin.

1755, Apr. 14. Dunn, Zachariah, of Piscataway, Middlesex Co., carpenter. Int. Inventory, £26.17.9, incl. 2 books; made by Nehemiah Dunham and Azariah Dunham. Lib. F, p. 319.

1756, Jan. 29.—Bond of widow, Rachel, as Adm'x. Bondsman—Phinehas Dunn, of Piscataway, yeoman. Witnesses—David Dunham and Thomas Bartow. Lib. F, p. 319.

1754, Feb. 5. Dye, Isaac, of Piscataway, Middlesex Co., yeoman; will of. Wife (not named). Children—Isaac (under age), Catharine, Hannah, Sarah, Ussallar. An expected child. Real and personal estate. Executors—William Williamson, Jeremiah Field, both of said Co., and Peter Williamson of Somerset Co. Witnesses—William Olden, William Wortman, Elias v. Court. Proved August 24, 1754.
Lib. F, p. 206.

1754, Aug. 28. Inventory, £189.15.10, by Elias v. Court and Andrew Conine.

1752, Oct. 25. Eakin, James, of Philadelphia, merchant; will of. To William McHenry, minister in Bucks Co., Pa., £15 in trust to pay it to my nephew, John Eakin, the son of my brother, Thomas Eakin, and, if he dies. then his sister, Mary, to have it. To brother, Thomas, clothing. My land in Hanover township, Morris Co. N. J., which I bought of John Scott and wife Sarah, to be sold. To my father, John Eakin, of County of Tyrone in Ireland, and my two sisters, Margaret and Mary, the rest. Executor—my friend, George Orr, of Philadelphia, coppersmith. Witnesses—Mathias Nider, Joseph Yeates, John Reily. Lib. F, p. 189.

1754, May 25. The Executor died before probate and administration with will annexed was granted to Sarah Orr, widow of George Orr. Signed, William Plumsted, Register General of Penna.

1754, June 4. Adm'r—Elijah Gillett, of Morris Co., a creditor of James Eakin; appointed with will annexed. Bondsman—John Scott, of Morris Co. Morris Wills, 56 N.

1751, Nov. 2. Earl, Thomas, of New Hanover, Burlington Co. Schoolmaster. Int. Inventory, £181.11.4, by John Steward and John Bullock.

1752, Jan. 2. Bond of widow, Judith Earl, of New Hanover, Adm'x; Joseph Steward and Thomas Emley, of the same place, yeoman, Samuel Woodward, Esq., of Burlington City, and Abraham Brown, Jr., of Chesterfield, yeoman, fellowbondsmen. Burl. Wills, 4813 C.

1758, Oct. 13. Earl, William, of New Hanover Township, Burlington Co. Int. Inventory, £233.0.1, incl. a silverwatch, £8.10; made by John Croshaw, William Stockton, and Samuell Wright, Jr.
1758, Oct. 24. Bond of Mary Earl as Adm'x; Thomas Earl fellowbondsman, both of New Hanover. Lib. 9, p. 93.

1750, Oct. 18. Earle, Edward, of Seacacoss, Bergen Co., gentleman, will of. Children—Edward, John, Philipp, Antlebee, Robert, Mary (wife of John Nelson), Elizabeth, Hester. Granddaughters—Elizabeth Daves, Elizabeth Nelson. House and lot; plantation adjoining Reyneer van Gezen on Hackensack River. Personal property. Executors—son, John Earle, brother, William Earle, and kinsman, Daniel Smith. Witnesses—William Earle, Morris Earle and James McKinley. Proved May 12, 1755. Lib. F, p. 273.
1755, May 8. Inventory, (very worm eaten) made by Philipp Smith and John Smith.

1756, Apr. 23. Earle, Henry, of Gloucester Co. Int. Bond of Thomas Redman (Rodman) as Adm'r; Charles Farguison fellowbondsman, both of said Co., yeoman. Lib. 8, p. 305.
1756, Apr. 24. Inventory, £26.19.9; incl. book debts, £14.5.3; made by Robert Frd. Price and Richard Weeks.

1753, Apr. 30. Earle, Joseph, of Burlington Co. Int. Inventory, £20.12, incl. silver buckles, £1.10; made by John Dearnale (Darnal) and John Leek.
1753, May 14. Bond of Mathias Johnson as Adm'r; John Leek fellowbondsman, both of said place. Lib. 7, p. 421.

1757, June 8. Eastlack, Elizabeth, of Gloucester Co. Int. Inventory, £17.13.6, by Abel Janny and Henry Hill, schoolmaster.
1757, June 15. Bond of William Alexander, husbandman, as Adm'r; Abel Janney, yeoman, fellowbondsman, both of Newton Township, Gloucester Co. Witnesses—John Lawrence and John Ladd.
Lib. 8, p. 437.

1751, Oct. 22. Easton, Richard, Jr., of Morristown, Morris Co., yeoman; will of. Wife, Sarah, sole heiress of real and personal estate. Land in Hanover Township. Executors—Hirrick Benjamin and Joseph Lacey, of Morris Town, yeoman. Witnesses—David Brant, Dorcas Easton, Ezekiel Cheever. Proved July 2, 1753. Lib. F, p. 126.
1753, June 28. Inventory, £73.7.9, incl. 2 inkstands; a Bible and other books, 14s.; made by Jeremiah Genung and John Looker.

1758, June 12. Eastwood, John, of Piscataway, yeoman. Int. Adm'r—Cortland Skinner; Mary Eastwood, the widow, having renounced, in favor of Cortland Skinner, on June 5th. Lib. F, p. 526.

1747, Nov. 14. Eayre, Elizabeth, widow of Richard Eayre, late of Evesham Twsp., Burlington Co., gent.; will of. Advanced in age. Son, Ralf Brock, to have the rent due me in Yorkshire, Great Britain;

CALENDAR OF WILLS—1751-1760   103

and my land in Wistow, Yorkshire, to go to my grandson, Ralf Brock, the son of my son Ralf. Granddaughters—Jane, daughter of John and Jane Miers, of Lewis Town, on Delaware; Tabitha Brock, Elizabeth Brock, Susanna Brock and Elizabeth Pierce, daughters of Richard Brock; Charity, the wife of John Garwood. Richard Eayre was Ex'r of my deceased husband. Daughter, Margaret Wills. Children of my daughter, Mary Clarke (not named). Granddaughter, Elizabeth Wright. Grand-children living in Penn'a. Executors—son-in-law, Thomas Eayre, and grandson, John Garwood. Witnesses—Richard Eayre, Sarah Eayre, Gabriel Blond. Proved June 22, 1753.

1753, June 22. Inventory, £106.3.6, by John Hiller and Henry Burr.
Burl. Wills, 5269 C.

[See Eyres].

1759, Sept. 4. Eddy, John, of Morris Co.; will of. Wife, Hannah. Children spoken of, but names not given. Executors—the wife, brother Garvin Eddy, of Middlesex Co., and Seth Crowell, of Morris Co. Witnesses—Stephen Morehouse, Thomas Darling, Edward Crowell. Proved Sept. 29, 1759. Lib. G, p. 298.
1759, Sept. 26. Inventory, £146.8.6; signed by Nathaniel Bonnel, Richard Minthorn, Hanah Eddey, Seth Crowell, Sr., and Gawen Eddey.

1751, Apr. 13. Edwards, John, 14 years old, son of Owen Edwards of Burlington Co. Petition of, asking for the appointment of Joseph Curtis as his guardian, to take care of the land inherited from grandfather Daniel Farnsworth.
1751, Apr. 13. Bond of Joseph Curtis as such guardian, Thomas Folkes fellowbondsman, both of Burlington Co. Burl. Wills, 4815 C.

1757, June 15. Edwards, Richard, of Philadelphia, merchant. Int. Bond of William Wishart and Jemima Edwards, both of Philadelphia, merchants, as Adm'rs; bond filed in Burlington Co.; no fellowbondsman. Lib. A, p. 442.

1760, May 20. Eglington, Timothy, of Greenwich Township, Gloucester Co., yeoman. Int. Inventory, £27.11.9, by Benja Lodge and Moses Butterworth.
1760, Oct. 3. Bond of John Eglington as Adm'r; Benjamin Lodge fellowbondsman, both of said Township, yeoman. Lib. 10, p. 293.

1755, Dec. 8. Eiler, George, of Salem Co.; will of. Wife, Mary. Children—John, Henry, George, Jacob, Margreta, Leonards, Cathrina Calz, Mary and Susannah. Homefarm; place by Oldman's Creek; messuage in Piles Grove. Personal property, incl. slaves. Executors—the wife and son John. Witnesses—Rev. Erick Unander, George Clark and Matthias Keiger. Proved Feb. 6, 1756. (The instrument begins as the will of John Ejler, but is signed by the mark of George Ejler). Lib. 9, p. 112.
1756, Jan. 10. Inventory, £59.3.1, by Adam Leberger and George Clark.

1759, Aug. 15. Eldredge, Daniel, of Cape May Co. Int. Inventory, £110.15.2, incl. half a vessel, £21; book debts, £32.3.8; made by John Leonard and Zebulon Swain.
1759, Aug. 18. Bond of Thomas Eldredge as Adm'r; Zebulon Swain, gentleman, fellowbondsman, both of Cape May Co. Lib. 9, p. 313.

1756, Sept. 18. Eldredge, Elihu, of Cape May Co. Int. Bond of Daniel Eldredge as Adm'r; David Smith fellowbondsman, both of said Co. Lib. 8, p. 334.
    1756, Sept. 20. Inventory, £45.5.5, incl. book debts and cash notes, £21.0.5; books, made by Zebulon Swain and David Smith.

1758, May 27. Eldredge, Elisha, of Cape May Co. Int. Inventory, £41.4, by John Eldredge and Ebenezer Johnson.
    1759, Aug. 20. Bond of Persilah Eldredge as Adm'x; Daniel Hand fellowbondsman, both of Cape May Co. Lib. 9, p. 313.

1758, Feb. 14. Eldredge, Levi, only son and heir of Levi Eldredge of Cape May, petitions, that Mr. Lemuel Swaine, of Cape May, be appointed his guardian.
    1758, Mar. 18. Bond of Lemuel Swain, of Cape May Co., yeoman, as such guardian; Henry Young, Esq., of the same Co., fellowbondsman. Cape May Wills, 186 E.

1760, June 7. Eldridge, James, of Evesham Township, Burlington Co., yeoman; will of. Wife, Esther. Children—Abigail, Enoch, William, Isaac, Abram (Abraham), Levi and James. Lot in White Street, Mount Holly, bought of George Shinn; homefarm; land on Rackoon Creek in Gloucester Co., bought of John Gosling. Personal estate. Executors—the wife, with sons Abraham and Levi. Witnesses—Sarah Woodoth, Thomas Ballinger, Joshua Ballinger. Proved June 26, 1760. Lib. 10, p. 36.
    1760, June 30. Inventory, £520.5, incl. bills, bonds and book debts, £13.13; 5 negroes, £175; made by William Foter, Silas Crispin and Joshua Ballinger.
    1763, May 27. Account by Abraham and Levi Eldridge, two of the Executors, who report on hand, £219.1.2.

1754, Apr. 21. Ellis, Jonathan, of Waterford, Gloucester Co., yeoman; will of. Wife, Mary. Children—Joseph, Rebekah and Mary, all under age. Home farm; another farm, bought of Richard Hains. Personal property. Executors—the wife and brother Joseph Ellis. Witnesses—John Holme, Benjamin Holme, Joseph Hanes (Haines). Proved August 17, 1754. Lib. 7, p. 484.
    1754, Aug. 12. Inventory, £1,240.18.1, incl. bills, bonds and book debts, £577.18.7; a clock and case, £12; books, 15s.; a negrowoman, £45; 3 'pentices time, £31; a servant man's time, £10; made by Samuel Cole and Benjamin Holme.

1757, Dec. 26-28. Ellis, Joseph, of Newtown, Gloucester Co. Int. Inventory, £1,275.15.8, incl. a silver watch, £8; a clock, £16; a large looking glass, £3; books, £2; two negro men, £105; bonds, £628.4.8; made by George Kemble and Samuel Harrison, Jr.
    1757, Dec. 30. Bond of Jacob Stokes, of Newtown, as Adm'r; Isaac Mickle, of the same place, and Jacob Albertson, of Gloster Township, fellowbondsman, all yeomen. Lib. 9, p. 38.
    1759, Aug. 11. Inventory of goods belonging to said Joseph Ellis, in the possession of Caleb Hewes of Philadelphia, hatter, £25.12.3; incl. a looking glass, £2.5; made by the same appraisers as above.

1759, Apr. 18. Ellis, William, of Waterford Township, Gloucester Co. Int. Inventory, £634.17.2, incl. a looking glass in the parlor, 15s.;

CALDENDAR OF WILLS—1751-1760   105

books, 20s.; 6 silver spoons, £1; three negro men, £75; one negro girl, £35; made by Samuel Coles, Kendal Coles and Josiah Shivers.
  1759, Apr. 25. Bond of Catherine Ellis, of Waterford, Gloucester Co., and John Cox, of Chester, Burlington Co., as Adm'rs; Samuel Coles, of Waterford, fellowbondsman.   Lib. 9, p. 213.

1753, June 30. Elmer, Daniel, of Cumberland Co., clerk; will of. Wife, Susanna. Children—Theophilus, Theodorus, Silvanus, Margaret Loomis, Samuel, Elisabeth and Ramolla. Children of daughter Mary, viz., Jason and Elmer Ogden. Child of daughter Ruhamaleo (?), viz. Ephraim Daten. Real and personal estate. Executors—the wife, with sons Theophilus and Theodorus. Witnesses—Thomas Harris, Ephraim Harris, Ruth Harris. Proved Jan. 21, 1755.
Lib. 8, p. 95.
  1755, Jan. 28. Inventory, £428.4.6, incl. books, £17.9; 2 watches, £13; Doctor's drugs, £10; silver spoons, £2.17; book debts, £123.12.6; made by John Ogden and Thomas Harris.

1751, Jan. 1. Elston, Abraham, of Woodbridge, Middlesex Co.; will of. Children—Samuel, Agness, Anna and John, all under age. Land in Woodbridge; 3 acres in Rarantain meadows. Personal property, incl. a negro girl, inherited by daughters from their grandmother Spencer. Executors—brother Spencer Elston, Willum Brown and David Edgurs. Witnesses—Henry Demoney, Jr., William Collins, John Rowlison. Proved May 14, 1751.   Lib. E, p. 521.

1750, Sept. 22. Elston, Benjamin, of Woodbridge, Middlesex Co., yeomen; will of. Wife, Margaret. Children—Isaack, Enoch, Abraham and John (all under age). Son-in-law (stepson?). Lowrance van Camp (also under age). Sister, Hannah. Real and personal estate. Executors—son Isaack, James Clarkson and Daniel Shotwell. Witnesses—Joseph Shotwell, Abraham Shotwell and Josiah Davis. Proved May 15, 1760.   Lib. G, p. 211.
  1760, May 3. James Clarkson and Daniel Shotwell, two of the Executors named above, refuse to act.
  1760, May 12. Margaret Elstone, the widow, declines the administration of the estate in favour of son-in-law (stepson?) Abraham Elstone.
  1760, May 20. Inventory, £201.15.11, incl. 3 Bibles and other books, 6s.; 9 bush. of wheat, £3.3; 20 bush. of rye, £2.5.6; 3 do. of oats; 2 do. of Indian corn; made by Jonathan Frazee and Ebenezer Foster.
  1760, June 27. Account by the Administrator, Abraham Elston, who charges against it £127.17.1.

1755, Mar. 11. Elston, Spencer, of Woodbridge, Middlesex Co., weaver; will of. Wife, Mary. Children—Rhoda, Elisa and Jonathan, all under age. Land bought of Samuel Pangborn; land bought of Abraham Lee. Personal estate. Executors—David Alston and Jonathan Bishop. Witnesses—Phebe Watkins, Thomas Alston, William Jennings. Proved April 15, 1755.   Lib. F, p. 257.

1758, Apr. 15. Elwel, John, of Piles Grove, Salem Co., carpenter; will of. Wife, Rachel. Children—John (sole Executor), Elizabeth Holten, Rachel Newman, Rebecca Chandler and Ester. Grandson, Andrew Lock. Real and personal estate. Witnesses—Isaac Sharp, John Plummer and Jehiel Dearwin. Proved May 2, 1758. Lib. 8, p. 106.

1758, May 1. Inventory, £153.5.7, by Elisha Bassett and Samuel Lippincott.

1760, Feb. 4. Elwell, John, of Pilesgrove, Salem Co., yeoman; will of. Mother, Rachel Elwell. Sisters—Elisabeth Hatton, Esther Elwell, Rachel Newman and Rebecca Chandler. Legacy for the Poor of Pilesgrove Precinct. Home farm of 300 acres. Personal estate. Executors—Joseph Chamblis and Daniel Bassett. Witnesses—Edward Draper, Joseph Champneys and Bateman Lloyd. Proved March 13, 1760. Lib. 10, p. 511.

1760, Mar. 12. Inventory, £119.2.6, incl. books, £1.12; rent due by Redolph Shophner, £5.10; made by Elisha Bassett and Samuel Lippincott.

1758, Oct. 28. Elwell, Joseph, of Penns Neck Township, Salem Co., husbandman, also called yeoman. Int. Inventory, £97.2.9, by Allen Congelton and Samuel Whitehorne.

1758, Nov. 18. Bond of his widow, Mary Elwell, as Adm'x; Hance Jaquett, of Penn's Neck, yeoman, fellowbondsman. Lib. 9, p. 352.

1753, Dec. 28. Elwell, Thomas, of Pen's Neck, Salem Co. Int. Inventory, £139.17.2½, by Thomas Penington and Francis Miles.

1754, Jan. 19. Bond of Mary Elwell as Adm'x; Mathias Lambstone and Thomas Penington fellowbondsmen, all of Pen's Neck.
Lib. 8, p. 80.

1759, Oct. 13. Elwell, Thomas, of Pen's Neck, Salem Co. Int. Inventory, £40.10.5, incl. half of a shallop, £30; made by Michael Pedrick and John Park.

1759, Nov. 2. Bond of Joseph and Samuel Elwell as Adm'rs; John Marshall and Earick Gill Johnson, fellowbondsmen, all of Pen's Neck.
Lib. 10, p. 447.

1760, Mar. 12. Ely, Joshua, of Maidenhead, Hunterdon Co. Int. Jacob Ely, brother of, relinqushes the right of administering on his estate to cousin, George Ely.

1760, Mar. 14. Bond of George Ely, of Bucks Co., Penna., as Adm'r; Thomas Tindall, of Maidenhead, fellowbondsman. Lib. 10, p. 463.

1760, May 22. Inventory, £154.9.3, incl. bonds, book debts and purse, £153.8.3; made by Thomas Tindall and William Ely.

1769, Feb. 20. John Pownal, claiming in right of his wife, one third of the estate, accuses George Ely of neglect in the administration of it and refusing an account, therefore he asks for a copy of his bond with leave to prosecute. Granted by Governor Franklin.

1752, Jan. 24. Ely, Noah, of Elizabeth "Borrough," Essex Co., "Studiant in physick;" will of. Wife, Puah, sole heiress and, with father-in-law, Major John Merry, Executors. Witnesses—Simon Searing, John Merrey, Jr., Benjamin Bonnel. Proved May 5, 1752.
Lib. F, p. 53.

1752, May 2. Inventory, £264.9.10½, by John Stite, Esq., and Simon Sering.

1767, May 23. Account by Puah Ely, Executrix.

1756, Dec. 12. Emans, Andries, Adm'r—Benjamin Emans, of Somerset Co., one of the legatees of Andries Emans. Bondsmen—Sam-

CALDENDAR OF WILLS—1751-1760   107

uel Stockton and Thomas Leonard, Jr., of said Co. Witness—Richard Stockton. 'Andries Emans, father of said Benjamin, about Sept. 1, 1728, made a will and gave legacies to his son, and appointed Hendrick Emans one of the Executors. The other Executors have died, and Hendrick has refused to pay Benjamin his legacies.'
Somerset Wills, 1253 Q.

[In documents in the New Jersey Supreme Court, filed in 1758 and 1759, it appears that Andries Emans was of New Utrecht, L. I.; that according to his will his executors were Hendrick, Rebecca and Johannes Emans, John Vankirk and Teunis Polhemus; that his estate was to have been divided, after the death of Rebecca, his widow, among his children, Hendrick, Johannes, Andries, Benjamin, Jacobus, Ann, Sarah—another child, Rebecca, died before a settlement, Benjamin was single when his father died, but married later. Rebecca, testator's widow, died about Nov. 15, 1755. Johannes and Sarah had children, but were also deceased before 1759. Ann's husband was Jaques Denys; perhaps she was also deceased in 1759, when the Court in New Jersey directed a settlement of the estate of legacies, which Hendrick, as surviving Executor, still had in hand. An execution followed against Hendrick, who, like Benjamin, plaintiff in the suit, resided at Six-Mile Run, Somerset Co., N. J.]

1752, Mar. 3. **Emans, John,** of the Township of "Ridingtown," Hunterdon Co.; will of. Wife, Teuntje. Children—Andris, John, Jacobus, Abraham, Jacob, the last four under age, Rebecca, Annaa, Catreanna and Sarah. Farm of 210 acres, formerly belonging to Mr. Buskerk; farm of 300 ac., bought of Adrian Lane; farm of 310 ac. Personal property. Money bequests at 8s. per oz. Executors—sons Andris and John, and Dyrk Low. Witnesses—Gisbert Crom, Cornelius Lane, Harmen Lane. Proved May 18, 1752.   Hunt. Wills, 311 J.

1752, May. 11. Inventory, £583.6.9, incl. 2 looking glasses, £1.13; 500 bush. of wheat, £100; books, 15s.; 4 negro wenches and 2 children, £80; bills, bonds and book debts, £44.3.9; made by Gysbert Krom and Dirck Marlet.

1758, Oct. 9. Account, £743.0.6, by Edward Robeson and wife, Ellinor, late Ellinor Emans, Executrix of John's will; they make the estate their debtor for £131.9.9, charging £60. for maintaining and schooling three children of testator, viz., Rachell, Ellinor and Cathrine, the eldest being 6 years of age, and £18. paid to Nicholas Emans, one of the legatees. Testator then said to have been "of Gravesend, Hunterdon Co."

1760, Apr. 25. **Embry, Nicholas,** of Northampton Township, Burlington Co.; will of. Divides personal estate between Nicholas Whoman, Mary (widow of Thomas Wills) and Leonard Yearling. Bonds due by Benjamin Brown, Christian Eselow and Jacob Wills. Executors—Thomas Budd and Nicholas Whoman. Witnesses—Zilpah Uenecomb, John Goldy. Proved May 3, 1760.   Lib. 10. p. 43.

1760, May 3. Inventory includes purse and apparel, £4.17.9; bonds and book debts, £38.2.11; made by George Briggs and John Goldy. (Nicholas Whoman, one of the Executors, signs as Nicolaus Wuchman, in German script).

1751, Mar. 28. **Emley, William,** of Kingwood Township, Hunterdon Co., tanner; will of. Father, John Emley. Daughter, Sarah, under age. Sisters, Rachel Schooley and Mary. Father-in-law, Samuel

Wright. Brothers—Elisha, John and Robert Emley. Legacies to children of Phobe Hartshorn, to two apprentices, to apprentice girl and John Pincock, Sr. Real and personal estate. Executors—father, John Emley, Sr.; brother, Elisha Emley and John Emley, Jr. Witnesses—Samuel Large, Robert Large, James Willson, Danniel Pegg. Proved June 20, 1751. Lib. 7, p. 66.

1751, May 17. Inventory, £293.16.10, incl. bills and book debts, £61.10.7; an old watch, £3; made by Abraham Bonnel and Charles Hoff, Jr.

1759, July 13. Emmans, Nicholas, of Reading Township, Hunterdon Co., yeoman; will of. Wife, Sycha, to be maintained for life by sons Abraham and Jerome, who are made heirs and Executors of real and personal estate. Witnesses—John Atkinson, George Ryerson and William van Vliedt, Jr. Proved Oct. 3, 1759, when Abraham Emmans, one of the Executors named, refuses to serve.
Lib. 10, p. 450.

1752, Feb. 22. Empson, Charles, of Penn's Neck, Salem Co., husbandman. Int. Inventory, £302.15, incl. credits and desperate debts, £150; made by Thomas Carney and Sa.nuel Whitehorne.

1752, Mar. 4. Bond of Ebenezer and James Empson as Adm'rs; Thomas Carney and Samuel Whitehorne, fellowbondsmen, all of Penn's Neck. Salem Wills, 923 Q.

1758, Sept. 13. Engel, William, of "Sum mar Set" Co.; will of. Children—Nicolaas (sole Executor), Antye Winterstine, Cornelia Beem. Children of daughter Elsye Trimmer, dec'd, i. e., William, Johanis, Nicolaas, Antye, Christian and Yudik Trimmer. Real and personal estate. Witnesses—Jan Everse, Bout Woortman, and John Woertman. Proved Nov. 1, 1758. Lib. F, p. 559.

1759, Apr. 17. Enloes, Anthony, of Pen's Neck, Salem Co., labourer; will of. Divides personal estate between uncle, John Richman, brother, Peter Enloes; both named as Executors. Brother, Joseph Enloes. Sister, Tenah Enloes. Cousin, Daniel Richman (under age). Witnesses—John Phillpott, John Pennington and Matthias Bilderback. Proved May 10, 1759. Lib. 10, p. 532.

1759, May 10. Inventory, £64.5.10, incl. wearing apparel and sundries, £7; accounts and bonds, £52.3.7; 2 pistols, £2.14; more cash, £2.8.3; made by Thomas Jones and Alen Congelton.

1753, March 1. Enloes, Peter, of Salem Co. Int. Adm'rs—Peter Enloes and Joseph Enloes. Bondsmen—Allen Congleton and Nicholas Phillpott, both of Salem Co. Witnesses—Grant Gibbon and Nicholas Gibbon. Salem Wills, 875 Q.

1752, Feb. 24. Erwin, James, of Newton, Gloucester Co., yeoman. Int. Inventory, £146.4, incl. a negro boy, £35; made by Thomas Spicer and Thomas Atmore.

1752, Feb. 26. Bond of widow, Sarah Erwin, of Gloucester Co., as Adm'x; William Lecony, of Burlington Co., yeoman, fellowbondsman. Lib. 7, p. 300.

1759, Aug. 22. Estell, Joseph, Jr., of Somerset Co. Int. Late a soldier. Bond of Joseph Estell, father, as Adm'r; Henry Davis fellowbondsman, both of Somerset Co., yeoman. Lib. G, p. 96.

1756, May 25. Estlack, William, of Gloucester Co., William, son of, petitions, that Joshua Lord be appointed his guardian. Bond of Joshua Lord as such guardian; Francis Eastlack, fellowbondsman; both of Gloucester Co. Lib. 8, p. 360.

1760, March 4. Evangame, Joseph, of Monmouth Co. Int. Adm'x —Mary Evangame. Bondsman—Hugh McCullum, of said Co. Witnesses—Gabriel Blond and Jasper Smith.
1760, March 1. Inventory, £26.18.3, by John Stevens and Hugh Mc Cullum.
1760, May 31. Account by the Adm'x. Lib. 9, p. 409.

1755, Nov. 14. Evans, David, of Cape May Co.; Will of. Cousin Nicholas Stillwell, of said Co., merchant, sole heir and Executor. Witnesses—Isaiah Hand and John Leek. Proved Feb. 5, 1760.
Lib. 9, p. 406.
1759, Nov. 20. Inventory, £152.1.3, incl. cash and debts due, £53.8.3; one third of a sloop, £50; made by John Willets and James Hathorn, who add a list of things, apparently given away by said Evans before his death and valued at £10.7.6, i. e., a silver watch, £5.10; a pair of gold buttons, £1; a quadrant and books, £1.17.6, and shoebuckles, £2.

1756, Mar. 4. Evans, John, of Alloways Creek, Salem Co., tailor. Int. Bond of Benjamin Allen as Adm'r; John Stewart fellowbondsman, both of said Co. Lib. 9, p. 80.
———, ——— ———. Inventory, £28.14, by John Stewart and John Denn.

1751, Oct. 8. Evans, Richard, of Monmouth Co., labourer. Int. Bond of Robert Savage, the principal creditor as Adm'r; Duncan Robertson fellowbondsman, both of said Co., merchants.
Lib. E, p. 550.

1759, June 11. Evans, Richard, of Hopewell Township, Hunterdon Co.; will of. Wife, Elisabeth. Children—Jerusha (by present wife), Mary, William, David, Benjamin, Hannah and Sarah, all under age. Executors—Henry van Kirk and Azariah Hunt. Witnesses—Daniel Hart, Jacob Stout and Daniel Drake. Codicil of September 14, 1759, makes Capt. David Stout and William Bryant, Trustees. (Codicil not executed). Lib. 10, p. 99.
1760, Jan. 14. Inventory: Real, 100¼ acres, £280; personal, £97.4.9, by William Bryant and Daniel Hart.

1759, Apr. 25. Evelman, Mary, of Monmouth Co. Inventory, of estate left her by the last will of her husband, William Evilman, £131.5.3, incl. cash, £70; 9 months' service of a negro man, £13.10; made by Moses Robins and James Hepburn.
1759, May 25. Bond of Daniel and Moses Robins as Admrs; John Bruce fellowbondsman, all of Allentown, Monmouth Co.
Lib. 9, p. 315.

1757, June 25. Evelman, William, of Upper Freehold, Monmouth Co., yeoman, "arrived to an age above three score and ten years;" will of. Wife, Mary. Children—John, William, Mary Hankins, Anne Coulton (who has son John Cox and dau. Sara Cox), and Sarah Brown. Real and personal estate, incl. two negroslaves. Executors

—sons-in-law, William Hankins, Robert Brown and John Cox. Witnesses—Stephen Warne, Cornelis Wyckoff and Corneles van Artsdalen. Proved April 11, 1759. Lib. 9, p. 323.
 1759, Apr. 7. Inventory, £416.6.8, incl. bills and bonds, £211.0.8; a negro boy, £50; made by James Hepburn and Moses Robins.
 1759, Apr. 25. Additional inventory, £95.0.7, incl. a negrowoman, £40; Thomas Lawrie's receipt for 177½ bush. of wheat, £42.3.1; made by James Hepburn and Moses Robins.

1758, Oct. 5. Evens, Thomas, of Evesham, Burlington Co.; will of. Wife, Hannah. Children—Sarah, Even, Mary, Isaac and Martha, all under age. Real and personal estate. Executor—John Roberts. Witnesses—Alexander Crawford, Enoch Roberts, George Weed. Proved November 4, 1758.
 1758, Nov. 3. Inventory, £136.15.6, by Kendal Cole and Enoch Roberts.
 1766, Mar. 7. Account by Ex'r, John Roberts. Burl. Wills, 6055 C.

1752, Feb. 5. Eves, Mary, wife of Thomas Eves, Jr., of Evesham Township, Burlington Co., yeoman; will of. Testatrix makes the will as sole Executrix of her former husband, John Ashead, of Waterford Township, Gloucester Co., and with the consent of the present husband who also signs it. Mentions as children, John Ashead and Elizabeth Ashead and gives legacy to Amos Ashead's widow. Estate includes a farm. Personal estate includes money due by Joseph Hollinshead, George Matlock, Thomas Gill and Thomas Parker; a looking glass received from daughter Elizabeth's grandmother Eves. Executors—father, Thomas Middletown, and Samuel Stokes. Witnesses—Mary Standly, Thomas Wallis, Hope Wallis. Proved April 3, 1752.
 1752, Mar. 24. Inventory, £96.9, incl. bills, bonds and other debts, £57.9; made by Freedom Lippincot and Thomas Wallis.
Burl. Wills, 495 7 C.

1753, Mar. 7. Eves, Samuel, of Evesham Township, Burlington Co.; will of. Wife (not named). Children—John, Ann (wife of Jonathan Lippincott), Mary Campion and Joseph. Grandsons—James and Lewis Lippincott. Real and personal estate. Executors—sons John and Joseph. Witnesses—John Inskeep, John Hooton, Gabriel Blond. Proved Feb. 26, 1759. Lib. G, p. 178.
 1759, Feb. 23. Inventory, £122.14.4, by Isaac Buzby and Joshua Ballinger.

1757, Mar. 9. Eves, Thomas, of Evesham Township, Burlington Co., yeoman; will of. Children—Thomas (unmarried), Mary De Cow, Annah Hollinshead, Sarah De Cow and Abigail More. Grandson, Thomas Hollinshead. Homefarm of 450 acres; 50 ac. adjoining Freedom Lippincott, bought of brother John Eves. Personal property. Executors—sons-in-law, Hugh Hollinshead and Samuel Moore. Witnesses—Joseph Hackney, Joshua Humphris, John Cox. Proved April 16, 1757. Lib. 8, p. 377.
 1757, April 2. Inventory, £340.19.5½, incl. bills, bonds and book debts, £296.4.4.; real estates, 50 ac., ordered to be sold, £100; made by Joshua Bispham and Samuel Stokes.

CALENDAR OF WILLS—1751-1760

1754, Aug. 3. Exceen, William, of Hunterdon Co. Int. Bond of John Manners, Jr., of Amwell, Hunterdon Co., as Adm'r; John Manners, Sr., fellowbondsman. Lib. 7, p. 64.
1754, Sept. 12. Inventory, £24.15.6, incl. a Bible; made by John Garrison and Samuel Gulick.

1755, Apr. 13. Exceen, William, of "Kingswood," Hunterdon Co., innholder; will of. Wife, Nuell. Son, John, of New York, to have 20 s. Son, Job, is "under the wants of natural understanding." Real and personal estate. Executors—the wife and Bairfoot Brunson. Witnesses—Nathaniel Fostor, Nathaniel Farnsworth, Jonathan Robeson. Proved Jan. 2, 1756. Lib. 8, p. 276.
1755, Dec. 27. Inventory of the estate: Real, being house and lot £150. Personal, £59.10.4, incl. bills and book debts, £23.15.4; made by John Emley, Abraham Bonnel and Mansfield Hunt.

1754, Nov. 28. Eyres, Elizabeth, of Burlington Co. Int. Adm'r—Adam Yohe. Inventory, £64.19.5. Lib. 8, p. 65.

1754, Sept. 27. Fairchild, Abraham, of Morris Co. Int. Bond of Hannah, widow of, as Adm'x; Daniel Bates, of said Co., fellowbondsman. Lib. F, p. 231.

1752, June 10. Farmer, Colonel Thomas, of New Brunswick, Middlsex Co. Int. Bond of Jacob Ouke as Adm'r; William Ouke fellowbondsman, both of said place, gentlemen. Lib. F, p. 57.

1751, July 29. Farnsworth, Damaris, widow of Samuel, of Chesterfield Township, Burlington Co.; will of. Children—Mary Corlis, Hannah Ashton, Susanah Warrin, Samuel Farnsworth, Ann Griggs. Grandsons—Samuel UppDike and Amariah Farnsworth. Personal estate. Executors—daughters Susanah and her husband John Warin, and Ann, with husband Thomas Griggs. Witnesses—George Douglass, Elizabeth Cooke, Thomas Folkes. Proved August 24, 1751.
1751, Aug. 23. Inventory, £124.5.3, incl. debts due by Samuel Farnsworth, John Thorn, Anthony Bunting, Owen Edwards' estate and John Clayton, £45.6.10; made by Jonathan Collings and Samuel Farnsworth. Burl. Wills, 4819 C.

1758, Oct. 9. Farnsworth, Henry, of Kingwood Township, Hunterdon Co.; will of. Children—John, Henry, Ruth (wife of John Hull), Mary (wife of Cornelius Anderson), Daniel and Thomas. Real and personal estate. Executors—sons Henry and Daniel. Witnesses—Samuel Layton, Jeremiah King and Elijha Emley. Proved April 30, 1759. Lib. 9, p. 330.
1759, Apr. 25. Inventory, £200.16.5, incl. bills, bonds and book debts, £140.12.4; made by John Mullinner and Elijha Emley.

1757, Oct. 24. Farnsworth, Nathaniel, of Kingwood Township, Hunterdon Co. Int. Inventory, £49.7.10, by Robert Laning and John Hull.
1757, Nov. 14. Bond of Hannah Farnsworth, of Kingwood, as Adm'x; Robert Laning (Lanning) of Bethleham said Co., fellowbondsman. Lib. 8, p. 516.
1758. Dec. 20. Account by Executrix.

1760, July 18. Farrand, Joseph, of Newark, Essex Co.; will of. Wife, Sarah. Children—Hannah, Margaret, Lydia, Stephen, James and Enos, all under age. Legacies to John, Catharine and Hannah, children of brother, Daniel Farrand. Real and personal estate. Executors—the wife and brothers Nathaniel and Daniel Farrand. Witnesses—John Low, Gilbert Taylor, Joseph Ball. Proved Sept. 2, 1760.
Lib. G, p. 323.

1756, May 21. Farrington, Abraham, of Northampton Twsp., Burlington Co.; will of. My lands near Egg Habor, bought of John Smith, and the lands I lately took up, to go to my son Samuel, and he is to clear his brother, Joseph, from all debts to John Smith. Son Samuel also to have my plantation, now in the tenure of Matthias Boatman. Son Joseph to have my land joining Oddey Brock and John Butchier, of 4 acres and 12 of meadow. My daughter, Mary, Farrington to have £100; my granddaughter, Phebe Delaplain, £50, when 18. Executors—sons Samuel and Joseph. Witnesses—James Southwick, David Jess, Rachel Southwick. Proved June 1, 1758.
Lib. 9, p. 78.
1758, June 1. Inventory, £47.7.3, by David Cox and Josiah White.

1760, Aug. 21. Farrington, Mary, of Perth Amboy, Middlesex Co.; will of. Divides real and personal estate between nieces, Sarah Billop, Rachal Sarjant and Elizabeth (wife of Francis Goelet), the Springhill meetinghouse and John Bown. Executors—John Berrien and Samuel Sarjant. Witnesses David Gosling, James Reed and Miles Weeks. Proved Dec. 19, 1760.
Lib. G, p. 334.

1760, March 25. Farrot, David, of Middlesex Co. Int. Adm'r—Henry Farrot (the eldest son), of Woodbridge. Bondsman—Neil Campbell, of Woodbridge. Witness—John Smyth. Lib. G, p. 146.

1758, Jan. 4. Fawcet, Walter, of Greenwich Township, Gloucester Co.; will of. Wife, Margeret. Children—Nathan, Hannah, Jonathan and John, the last two under age. Mother, Greace Fawcet. Real and personal estate. Executor—James Hinchman. Witnesses—Robert Rusel (Russell), Isaac Wright, Cornelius Bryen. Proved Feb. 20, 1758.
Lib. 9, p. 115.
1758, Feb. 17. Inventory, £47.5., incl. a "caw fee pot;" made by Abel Scull and Abel Scull, Jr.

1758, Dec. 11. Feiler, David, of Deerfield Township, Cumberland Co. Int. Inventory, £16.1, by Jeremiah Parvin and Noah Harris.
1758, Dec. 16. Bond of John Filer (Fyler), as Adm'r; Jeremiah Parvin and Noah Harris fellowbondsmen, all of Deerfield Township.
Lib. 9, p. 178.

1752, July 22. Fenimore, Henry, of Northampton, in Burlington Co., yeoman. Int. Adm'r—Benjamin Bispham, of Northampton. Bondsman—Patrick Reynolds, of same place. Witnesses—Jonathan, Thomas and Joseph Scattergood.
1752, July 18. Mary Fenimore, the widow, renounced in favor of Benjamin Bispham, the principal creditor. Witnesses—Nathan Watson and Richard Fenimore.
Burl. Wills, 4961 C.

1756, Jan. 12. Fenimore, Joseph, Jr., of "Wellingborrow" Township, Burlington Co., yeoman; will of. Wife, Sarah. Sons—Joseph (oldest),

John, James. Daughters, but names not given. All under age. Farm of 30 acres, where Rebecca Clark lately lived; homefarm; land near John Crosby's, bought of brother Richard; marsh on Rancocus Creek Point, received from father, Joseph Fenimore. Personal property. Executors—brother, Richard Fenimore, and brother-in-law Joshua Humphries. Witnesses—William Heulings, John Wills, Daniel Ellis. Proved May 29, 1756. Lib. 8, p. 286.
   1756, May 28. Inventory, £171.14.10, by William Smith and William Heulings.
   1772, Jan. 11. Account by Richard Fenimore, surviving Executor.

1759, Dec. 13. Fennimore, Joseph, of Wellingborough, Burlington Co., yeoman; will of. Wife, Elizabeth. Children—William, Jonathan, Richard. Daughter-in-law, Sarah Fennimore. Bequest to son Jonathan lapses, if he does not return home in five years after testator's death. Farm at the mouth of Rancocas Creek; 100 acres adjoining farm of son, William; 50 ac. between Joshua Fennimore, Abraham Perkins, James Pearson and Seth Lucas. Executors—sons Joshua (not named before as son) and Richard. Witnesses—William Heulings, Peter Banckson, S. Blackwood. Proved Dec. 24, 1759.
Lib. 9, p. 293.
   1759, Dec. 24. Inventory, £29.11, incl. a Bible; made by Abraham Perkins and Seth Lucas.

1755, Mar. 8. Fenton, Enoch, of Springfield Twsp., Burlington Co., blacksmith. Int. Bond of Robert Fenton as Adm'r; Jonathan Taylor fellowbondsman, both of said Co, yeoman. Lib. 8, p. 304.
   1756, Apr. 10. Inventory, £33.1.6, by George Briggs and John Budd.
   1757, Mar. 8. Account by the executor, Robert Fenton, who charges £2.7.11. as due him after settling the estate.

1756, Mar. 16. Fetters, Erasmus, of Salem Co.; will of. Divides real and personal estate between the following: late wife's children, Rebeckah, Mary and Sarah Chamness; the two children of his sister Mary by Henry van Meter; William, son of John Whitall; Roger Sherron; Griffin Sherron; John., son and Susanna, daughter of John Goodwin; Lewis Goodwin; Samuel Nicholson; Sarah, wife of Thomas Goodwin; Mary, wife of William Goodwin; Jale, wife of William Shipley; Ann, wife of Samuel Bassett; Sarah and Hannah, daughters of William Goodwin. Executors—John Whitall and William Goodwin. Witnesses—Thomas Hancock, John Ambler, Jr., and Jacob Ambler. Proved May 18, 1756. Lib. 9, p. 4.
   1756, May 19. Inventory, £1,671.11.2, incl. plate and old gold, £9.10; bonds and book debts, £1,474.2.2; a negro boy, £35; a negro girl, £25; made by Josiah Kay and James Wiggins.
   1758, Dec. 6. Account. by the Executors, who add to it £10. for rent due and not inventoried, and report on hand £1,119.18.5.

1759, Oct. 8. Fidler, John, Sr., of Hopewell, Hunterdon Co., yeoman; will of. Wife, Sarah. Children—Sarah (youngest daughter), Thomas, John, Mary Rose, Elizabeth Stillwell, Timothy, Nathan, the last two under age. Real and personal estate. Executors—son, John, and son-in-law, Ezekil Rose. Witnesses—Andrew Smith, Jr., Richard Reed, John Titus, Jr. Proved Oct. 25, 1759. Lib. 10, p. 115.
   1759, Oct. 22. Inventory, £154.10.11, incl. a library round table; made by Timothy Smith and John Titus, Jr.

8

1754, Feb. 1. Field, Robert, of Mansfield Township, Burlington Co.; will of. Children—Robert, Samuel, Mary Yardly and Sarah; Samuel and Sarah under age. Grandson—Robert, not yet 11 years old, son of dec'd daughter Susannah, and William Lawrence. Farm at Whitekill on the N. E. side of the road from the Landing to Curtis' Mill; meadow on "Croseweeks" Creek in Nottingham Township; a lot between Front, Ferry and Second Streets in (?); another lot between Front and Ferry Streets and the lot sold to Preserve Brown; another lot between Front, Lawrell and Second streets; a house and lot at the head of the hollow, "As Clodworth Read now lives in." Personal estate, incl. a negro girl. Executors—son Robert, William Pancost of "Bordin Town,' and William Black, of Chesterfield Township, said Co. Witnesses—Thomas Watson, Mary Swain, Jacob Swain. Codicil of January 26, 1757, deducts from the sum, bequeathed to son Samuel, £100 Jamaica Currency, given him in Jamaica by his brother Robert. Witnesses—Richard Potts, Rebecca Potts, Ann Boyd. Proved Aug. 12, 1758. Lib. 9, p. 29.

1758, Aug. 12. Bond of Thomas Yardley of Bucks Co., Penn'a, as Adm'r, with will annexed; John Imlay and Joseph Borden, Jr., Esqs., both of Burlington Co., fellowbondsmen.

1755, Jan. 2. Fight, John, of Deptford Township, Gloucester Co., yeoman; will of. (Drawn by James Cooper, but not executed). Wife (not named). Daughters—Catharin and Elizabeth, both under age. Servant lad, Adam Vince, to be set free. Personal estate. Executors—the wife and Joshua Lord. Lib. 8, p. 120.

1755, Feb. 12. Inventory, £245.13.10., incl. bonds, £106.0.11; time of the servant lad, George Tigger, £10; a Dutch Bible and other books 10s.; made by William Wilkins and James Cooper.

1755, Feb. 14. Bond of widow, Susanna Fight, and Joshua Lord, Jr., as Adm'rs; Thomas Reves, yeoman, fellowbondsman, all of Deptford Township. Lib. 8, p. 120.

1759, Feb. 24. Fine (Fein), John, of "Greenwitch," Sussex Co. Int. Inventory, £8.5.6., by William Scholey (Schooley) and Peter Seiler.

1759, May 2. Bond of Elisabeth Fain (signed in German script) as Adm'x; Jonathan Pettit, Esq., fellowbondsman, both of "Grinwich." Lib. 9, p. 394.

1757, Mar. 20. Finlaw, John, of Stow Creek Township, Cumberland Co.; will of. Wife, Rebeckah. Children—James, David (under age), William, Margaret Long, John, Nathan, Elisabeth, Jane and Sarah. Real and personal estate. Executors—the wife and son William. Witnesses—Ananias Sayre, James Campbel, David Long. Proved June 17, 1757. Lib. 8, p. 430.

1757, June 16. Inventory, £138.12.10, by Maskell Ewing and Thomas Ewing.

1760, Dec. 27. Fish, Michael, of Gloucester Co. Bond of Isaac Fish as Adm'r of the estate left unadministered by John Fish, the brother and Executor of Michael, said John having died intestate; Henry Wood fellowbondsman, both of said Co. [See N. J. Archives, Vol. XXX, p. 176, for Will]. Lib. 10, p. 440.

1759, Sept. 12. Fish, Nathaniel, of Newtown, Sussex Co., yeoman. Int. Bond of widow, Bersheba, as Adm'x; William Southworth fellowbondsman, both of Newtown. Lib. 10, p. 111.

CALENDAR OF WILLS—1751-1760   115

1757, Sept. 12. Inventory, £5.8.10, incl. an old Bible, 2s.; made by Elkanah Fuller and Constant Hart.
1759, Sept. 20. Account by the Administratrix.

1759, Jan. 30. Fishall, Andrew, of Cumberland Co. Int. Bond of Jonathan Stratton as Adm'r; Jonathan Holmes, Esq., and Thomas Brown fellowbondsmen, all of said Co.   Lib. 9, p. 181.

1753, Sept. 5. Fisher, Jonathan, of Greenwich Township, Gloucester Co., sawyer. Int. Bond of Jonathan Fisher, yeoman, as Adm'r; Benjamin Lodge, yeoman, fellowbondsman; both of said Township.
Lib. 7, p. 466.
1753, Sept. 16. Inventory, £361.6.4, by Benjamin Lodge and George Flaningam.
1755, July 14. Account by the Administrator.

1759, Jan. 13. Fishorne, Andrew, of Cumberland Co. Int. Inventory, £33.3.4, incl. cash and debts, £22.5.10; made by Peter Moslander and Joseph Savage.
1761, Feb. 14. Account by the Administrator, Jonathan Stratton, who reports on hand £27.0.4.   Cumb. Wills, 178 F.

1754, Feb. 15. Fithian, David, of Fairfield Precinct, Cumberland Co.; will of. Wife, Temperance. Children—David, Ephraim, Lot, Jonathan, Aaron, Joseph, Temperance and Sarah; all under age. Land in Dearfield Precinct and elsewhere. Personal property. Executors—the wife and son David. Witnesses—Jeremiah Buck, Thomas Bateman, Henry Wescote. Proved April 29, 1754.
1754, Apr. 25. Inventory, £264.16.3, incl. book; shoemaker's tools, leather and hides, £18.10.8; book debts, £49.10.3; made by Jeremiah Buck and Thomas Bateman.
1762, Mar. 15. Account by the surviving Executor, David Fithian, who reports estate increased by £14.18.9., debts not inventoried; and has paid out £241.12.10 to Theophilus Elmer, Thomas Harris, Martha Mills, Isaac Mills, Daniel Johnston, Job and Timothy Bateman, Nathan Leeks, Benjamin Parvins, Edward Lummus, Samuel Barns, Silas Newcomb, Benjamin Sayer, William Sarjant, Zaruiah Fithian, James Abbot, Abram Sayre, Henry Westcoat, Thomas Whittiker, Daniel Rice, Enoch Bowen, Mary and Sarah Fithian (for nursing one of the young children in the small pox).   Cumb. Wills, 98 F.

1751, May 10. Fithian, Samuel, of Greenwich, Cumberland Co., yeoman; will of. Wife, Abigail. Cousins—Lot Fithian, Samuel Fithian and John Fithian. Brother, Isaac Fithian. Home farm; 100 acres of land on "Stooe" Creek, adjoining John Cook and Peter Long, bought of John Alexander; 2 ac. adjoining Benjamin Tyler and Watson, bought of Edward Harden and wife Hannah, land bought of brother Josiah Fithian, formerly Henry Joyce's, adjoining John Pledger; 16 ac. formerly John Pleger's; 8 ac. formerly Joshua Barkestead's, adjoining Thomas Walling. Personal property. Executors—brother Isaac and the three cousins named above. Witnesses—Joseph Fithian, John Butler, Jr., Sarah Jones. Proved April 6, 1752.
Cumb. Wills, 99 F.
1752, Apr. 1. Inventory, £541.3.2¾, incl. a clock, silver tankard and other goods, £53.13; bills, bonds and book debts; £234; made by Philipp Dennis and Ananias Sayre.

1754, June 7. Account by Samuel Fithian, Executor, who reports goods (sold for £25.8.4 more than appraised and has paid out £284.14.0¼, to Elias Cotting in fees), Abram Murry, Daniel and Elijah Bowen, Richard Wood, Francis Brewster, James Alexander, Abram Reeves, Jacob Ware, Joseph Bacon, John Scott, John Dun, Samuel Clark, Isaac, Joseph and Noah Whiton, Thomas Ewing, Thomas Fruhen, Enos Woodruff, Ebenezer Miller, Jr., Job Shephard, Jeremiah Fithian, David Gillman, Sarah Dixon. He deducts from the inventory as not collectable debts due by Samuel Lummas, John Richardson, Cornelius Cornelison, John Crowell, John Bacon (baker), Uriah Whiten, David Edwards, Anne Wright, Rachel Ball, Richard Brick and Nicholas Gibbins.

1759, Apr. 14. Fithian, Sarah, the 5 years old daughter of Sammuel of Greenwich, Cumberland Co. Enoch Moore, of Greenwich, petitions to be appointed her guardian. Bond of said Enoch Moore, brother of the halfblood to said Sarah Fithian, as her guardian; Jonathan Stathem, of Greenwich Township, and David Padgett, of Stow Creek, said Co., fellowbondsmen. *Cumb. Wills 176 F.*

1759, Sept. 4. Fitz Randolph, Edward, of Woodbridge, Middlesex Co.; will of. Children—Robert, Nathaniel, Eseck, Hartshorne, Mary Jackson and Mary Coddington. Grandchildren—Edward (son of Hartshorne), George, Catherine, Thomas, Mary and Edward, (children of dec'd. son Richard). Eight children, names not given, of daughter Mary Jackson. Legacy to the Friends' Meeting in Woodbridge. Freehold right in Woodbridge Commons. Personal property. Executors—son Nathaniel and Samuel Marsh. Witnesses—James Parker, Abraham Tappen and William Kent. Proved March 26, 1760. *Lib. G, p. 151.*

1754, Aug. 31. Fitz Randolph, Isabell, widow of Joseph, of Woodbridge, Middlesex Co.; will of. Daughter, Margaret, wife of Thomas Hadden. Grandchildren—Elizabeth, Mary, Nathaniel, Joseph, Thomas, Margarett, Martha, Isabel (all daughters of Margaret Hadden). Real and personal estate, incl. 3 negroes, 6 silver spoons, gold sleeve buttons, a great Bible with silver clasps. Executors—son-in-law, Thomas Hadden, and Jacob Fitz Randolph, of Woodbridge. Witnesses—Samuel Moffat, Anne Moffat, Nugient Kelly. Proved Jan. 18, 1755. *Lib. F, p. 242.*

1759, May 2. Fitz Randolph, Jeremiah, of Woodbridge, Middlesex Co.; will of. Wife, Rachel. Children—Thomas and Jenett, both under age; an expected child. Brothers—Nathaniel and Joseph Fitz Randolph. Real and personal estate. Executors—said brother Nathaniel and brother David Edgar. Witnesses—Job Tharp, James Clarkson and David de Bonrepos. Proved May 28, 1759. *Lib. G, p. 61.*

1752, Feb. 18. Fitzrandolph, Moses, of Piscataway, Middlesex Co.; will of. Children—Benjamin, Rubin, Hull (under age), Joseph, Moses, Rachel (wife of Thomas Holton), Ann and Sarah (under age). Granddaughter—Rachel Bolsbe. Real and personal estate. Executors—Jeremiah Dunn and Azariah Dunham. Witnesses—James Thomson, Jonathan Fitchrandolph and Benjamin Stelle. Proved April 7, 1759, when the Executors named above refused to act, recom-

mending Benjamin and Reuben Fitzrandolph as Administrators, to whom letters were issued. Lib. G, p. 54.
1759, Apr. 14. Inventory, £170.17.6, by James Thomson and Isaac Stelle.

1754, Nov. 20. Fitz Randolph, Richard, of Amboy, Middlesex Co., carpenter; will of. Wife, Elizabeth. Children—George, Thomas, Katherine, Richard, Mary and Edward; all under age. Real and personal estate, incl. a negro woman, a silver tankard, a silver cup, 4 silver tablespoons. Executors—brother Nathaniel Fitz Randolph and Jonathan Hornett. Witnesses—Thomas Fox, Miles Weekes, Crawley Borrowe. Proved Nov. 25, 1754. Lib. F, p. 228.

1750, May 22. Fitzrandolph, Samuel, Sr., of Woodbridge, Middlesex Co.; will of. Wife, Mary. Children—Samuel, Prudence Smith, Jacob. Granddaughter—Susanah Copland. Personal estate. Executors—son Jacob and Richard Carman. Witnesses—Jeremiah Fitz Randolph, Job Pack, John Coddington. Proved August 5, 1754.
Lib. F, p. 198.
1754, July 4. Inventory, £82.19.10, incl. 3 large and 2 tea silver spoons, £2.5; a large Bible, £1.10; 2 old negroes, £3.10; a clock, £4.10; made by Jonathan Kinsey and William Gilman.
1759, Oct. 8. Account by Jacob Fitz Randolph, the Executor, who charges for his mother's board for four years (to August 23, 1758), £55.8, and for her clothing, £3.2.8.

1757, Jan. 24. Flatt, John, of Lebanon, Hunterdon Co., Bond of Benjamin Archer as Adm'r; Robert Austin and Nicholas Fleming fellowbondsmen, both of Lebanon. Lib. 8, p. 398.
1757, Feb. 25. Inventory, £57.7.5, by Henry Smith and Cornelius van Sickle.
1758, Apr. 3. Account by the Administrator (shows wife of testator was dead).

1755. Jan. 8. Flemman (Fleming), Stephen, of Manasquan, Town of Shrewsbury, Monmouth Co., yeoman; will of. Son, Joseph, and daughter, Jane (Jeane), sole heirs and Executors of real and personal estate. Witnesses—Thomas Bell, William Newbrey and Henry Herbert. Proved Feb. 19, 1759, when Jane, the daughter and Executrix, qualifies as wife of Daniel Havens of Shrewsbury. Proved Feb. 19, 1755. Lib. F, p. 320.
1755, Jan. 16. Inventory, £799.2.2, incl. 38 bush. of "Endon" corn, £4.15; a great Bible and other books, 18s.; bills, bonds, book debts, cash and cash notes £675.5.10; made by Henry Herbert, William Davis and Thomas Bell.

1756, Apr. 20. Flintham, John, of Chesterfield, Burlington Co. Int. Inventory, £45.14.7, by Samuel Farnsworth and John Butler, Jr.
1756, May 2. Bond of Sarah Flintham as Adm'x; Samuel Shourds (Shores) fellowbondsman, both of Chesterfield Township.
Lib. 8, p. 305.
1757, Apr. 25. Account by Administratrix, who makes estate her debtor.

1758, Oct. 10. Flower, John, of Shrewsbury, Monmouth Co., yeoman. Int. Bond of Joseph Potter as Adm'r; Josiah Halstead fellowbondsman, both of said Shrewsbury, yeomen. Lib. G, p. 44.

1760, Nov. 24. Fogg, David, of "Allaways" Creek, Salem Co. Int. Bond of Joseph Fogg as Adm'r; Daniel Fogg fellowbondsman, both of Allaways Creek, yeoman.   Lib. 10, p. 433.

———, ——— ———. Inventory, £34.3.7, incl. a silver watch, by Matthew Morrison and Daniel Fogg.

1758, July 22. Fogg, Samuel, of "Alleways" Creek, Salem Co. Int. Inventory, £90.19.11, by Joseph Stretch and Thomas Sayre.

1758, July 25. Bond of widow, Sarah Fogg, as Adm'x; Joseph Stretch and Thomas Sayre fellowbondsmen, all of Allaways Creek.
Lib. 9, p. 96.

1760, Dec. 1. Folwell, Elizabeth, of Burlington Co.; will of. Children—Mary (wife of Samuel Newton), John, Sarah, Nathan, Thomas and Elizabeth. Grandchildren—Elizabeth, Susannah and Mary Newton; Ann, daughter of son Nathan; Jean Atkinson and George Folwell. Personal property. Executors—son Thomas. Witnesses—Solomon Shinn, Jonathan Fenimore. Proved Dec. 13, 1760.
Lib. 10, p. 137.

1760, Jan. 3. Folwell, Nathan, of Springfield, Burlington Co., yeoman; will of. Wife, Elizabeth, sole Executrix. Children—Nathan, John, Mary (wife of Samuel Newton), Thomas, Elizabeth and Sary (wife of John Atkinson). Real and personal estate. Witnesses—Joseph Atkinson, Daniel Zely, Jonathan Fenimore. Proved April 23, 1760.   Lib. 9, p. 437.

1760, Feb. 25. Fontine, John, of Middlesex Co., yeoman. Int. Adm'r—Charles Fontine, his brother. Bondsman—Elias Van Court, of Somerset Co., "taylor." Witness—Thomas Bartow. Lida "Fontin," the widow, renounced in favor of Charles Fontine. Witnesses—Cornelius Bice (Boice) and Jacob Boice.   Lib. G, p. 129.

1760, Feb. 28. Inventory, £83.3.7., incl. bonds and book debts, £18.10.7; 74 lasts, £1.4; made by John Boorom and Jacob Boice.

1752, Apr. 14. Fontine (Van Tine), Rinear, of Pasetay (Piscataway), Middlesex Co.; will of. Gives to Nicholas Leforge that part of the estate which he had given to his daughter, (testator's wife). The rest divided between brothers Charles, John and Abraham Funtine, and sisters (names not given). Executor—brother John. Witnesses—William French and William Horn. Proved Feb. 18, 1760, when the Executor, named above, being dead, Charles Fontine was sworn in as Administrator of the estate.   Lib. G, p. 127.

1760, Feb. 29. Inventory, £92.5.5, by Jacob Boice and John Boorom.

1748, Sept. 27. Fontyn, Jacques, of Somerset Co., yeoman; will of. Wife, Anna. Son, Charles. Son-in-law, Hendrick van der Bilt. Daughter (niece?) Anna, of sister Lena. Grandchildren—Yacus, John and Charles Fontine. Real and personal estate. Executors—son Charles, cousin Charles Fontine and Hendrick Fisher. Witnesses—Cornelius Suydam, Hendrick van der Bieldt, Charles Fountayn. Proved Feb. 8, 1752.   Lib. F, p. 20.

1752, May 14. Inventory, £152.10, incl. a negro woman about 40 yrs old, £20; a negro boy, £25; a bond, £30; a silver cup, £6; another

CALENDAR OF WILLS—1751-1760   119

silver cup, spoons and tankard, £18; books, £3; made by John Fountayn and Albart Voorhes.

1759, Feb. 9. Forbes, Robert, of Perth Amboy, Middlesex Co. Cordwainer. Int. Adm'r—Joseph Forman, of New York, merchant principal creditor. Bondsman—Ezekiel Forman, of Monmouth Co., yeoman. Witnesses—David Knott and William Deare. Mary Forbes, widow of Robert Forbes, renounced in favor of Joseph Forman.
Lib. G, p. 31.

1759, Feb. 19. Inventory, £65.16.6, taken at Perth Amboy by James Reed and Thomas Inglis; Jos. Forman Administrator.

1752, Aug. 5. Ford, Samuel, of Hanover, Morris Co., yeoman; will of. Wife, Sarah. Children—Samuel, Jonathan, Demas, James, Charity, Hanah and Eunis. Real and personal estate. Executors—the wife, only brother Jacob Ford and Daniel Lindsly. Witnesses—Nathaniel Stilvel, Jean Wick, Jacob Ford. Proved Nov. 23, 1752, when Jacob Ford, one of the Executors named, refuses to act. Lib. F, p. 76.

1760, Feb. 9. Forgeson, Benjamin, of Sussex Co. Int. Inventory, £143.18.5; real estate, £50; made by Richard Gardiner and Joseph Barton.
1760, Mar. 31. Inventory of goods, left by dec'd. in Morris Co., £75.18.8; principally bonds and notes, £65.19; made by Samuel Hudson and Samuel Loree.
1760, Apr. 1. Bond of his widow, Hannah Forgerson, as Adm'x; Samuel Loree, of Morris Co., fellowbondsman. Lib. G, p. 146.

1754, Feb. 19. Foreman, Jonathan, of Cape May Co. Int. Adm'x—Patience Foreman.
Lib. 5, p. 463.

1758, Sept. 26. Forman, Isaac, Jr., of New Hanover, Burlington Co., yeoman; will of. Parents, Isaac and Elizabeth Forman. Brother, Thomas Forman. Sister, Susanna Woodrow. Home farm, now in the tenure of James Cassaday. Personal estate. Executors—the father and the brother. Witnesses—Thomas Parent, Joseph Arney, Jr., Thomas Ensley. Proved Nov. 14, 1758. Burl. Wills, 6189 C.
1758, ——— ———. Inventory of the estate: the farm £600., personal £181.19.4., mostly dry goods and groceries, made by Henry Woodrow and Thomas Emley.

1758, June 20. Forman, Jonathan, Jr., of Upper Freehold, Monmouth Co., yeoman. Int. Inventory, £407.0.10, incl. a negro man and negro boy, £80; made by James Holmes and James Lawrence.
1758, June 21. Bond of Sarah Forman, James Throckmorton and Peter Forman as Adm'rs; Job Throckmorton fellowbondsman, all of Monmouth Co. Lib. 9, p. 454.

1760, May 13. Fortner, Daniel, of Newton, Gloucester Co. Int. Bond of Barsheba Fortner as Adm'x; John Gill fellowbondsman, both of said Co. Lib. 9, p. 416.
1760, May 10. Inventory, £90.0.6, by Isaac Kay and John Gill.

1759, Aug. 6. Foster, Moses, of Essex Co. Int. Adm'r—Nathaniel Rusco, at the request of William Foster, the father of Moses.
Lib. G, p. 92.

1751, Aug. 13. Foster, Richard, of Cape May Co. Int. Bond of Christopher Lupton as Adm'r; Cornelius Schalbank (Skilleager) fellowbondsman, both of said Co., yeomen. Cape May Wills, 152 E.

1754, Mar. 19. Fowler, Isaac, of Greenwich Township, Gloucester Co. Int. Inventory, £115.5.10, incl. bonds and book debts, £40.0.7, by Alexander Randall and John Sparks.
1754, Apr. 19. Bond of widow, Grace Fowler, as Adm'x; Jonathan Fowller, yeoman, fellowbondsman, both of said Township.
Lib. 7, p. 467.

1760, Oct. 30. Fowler, Jonathan, Sr., of Greenwich Township, Gloucester Co., yeoman; will of. Wife, Marcy. Children (names not given). Executor—Thomas Denny. Witnesses—John Denny, Ledeya Chester, Andrea (or Ann) Vanneman. Proved Dec. 29, 1760.
Lib. 10, p. 404.
1760, Dec. 18. Inventory, £41.15.5, by John Jurin and Elias Boys.

1747, Sept. 23. Fowler, William, of Bethlehem Township, Hunterdon Co., yeoman; will of. Wife, Rebecca. Children—William, Rebecca, Rettenhouse, Elizabeth Everet, Susannah, Abigail, Lydia, Deborah and Hannah. Legacy to Baptist Church in said township. Home farm, adjoining John Worford. Personal estate. Executors—the wife, William Fowler and William Emley. Witnesses—Jonathan Burdge, James Warford, Isaac Rittinghousen. Proved Oct. 15, 1751. Lib. 7, p. 217.
1751, Aug. 2. Inventory, £103.13.3, by Jonathan Burdge, James Warford and John Emley.

1756, Jan. 31. Fox, Charles, of Cumberland Co., farmer; will of. Wife, Mary. Children—William, James, John (under age), Mary, Easter, Gatte, Ephraim and Charles. Real and personal estate. Executors—sons William and James. Witnesses—John Bragg, Nathan Shaw, Patiance Shaw. Proved March 20, 1758. Lib. G, p. 86.
1758, Mar. 15. Inventory, £93.11, incl. books; made by John Bragg and Richard Robbens.

1754, Apr. 27. Fox, George, of Kingwood, Hunterdon Co., yeoman; will of. Wife, Mary. Sons—George, Ambros, Absolem, Amos, Gabriel; all under age. Daughters spoken of, but not by names. Real and personal estate. Executors—sons George and Gabriel. Witnesses—Malakiah Bonham, Nehemiah Bonham, William Lock. Proved June 24, 1754. Lib. 7, p. 515.
1754, June 21. Inventory, £165.18, by Malakiah Bonham and Richard Green.

1760, June 7. Fox, George, of Kingwood, Hunterdon Co., cooper; will of. Wife, Rachel, sole Executrix. Children—Charles and George, sons, and daughters, but names not given; all under age; an expected child. Real and personal estate. Witnesses—Malakiah Bonham, Joshua Waterhouse, John Johnson and Gabriel Fox. Proved June 25, 1760. Lib. 10, p. 578.
1760, June 23. Inventory, £151.9.6, by Joshua Waterhouse, Malakiah Bonham and Richard Green.

1760, Feb. 19. Fox, William, of Dividing "Creks," Cumberland Co., farmer; will of. Wife, Deborah (sole heiress) and Gabrell Glan

(Glenn), Executors. Real and personal estate. Witnesses—John Bragg, Benjamin Blizard, John Blizard. Proved March 31, 1760.
Lib. G, p. 452.

1760, Mar. 5. Inventory, £29.19.9, by John Bragg and William Pepper, both of Dividing "Creks."

1754, Sept. 27. Francis, Jane, of Burlington City. Int. Bond of John Tylee as Adm'r; James Smith fellowbondsman, both of said City.
Lib. 7, p. 499.

1754, Sept. 27. Inventory, £1.4., by Daniel Ellis and John Hoskins.
1755, May 2. Account by the Adm'r, Overseer of Burlington City, who, by the Mayor's orders has given some of the clothing of the dec'd. to Margaret Moon and Thomas Dunphy, and has spent £2.6.8. more than the inventory.

1758, Dec. 13. Franks, Henry Benjamin, of Bridgetown, Burlington Co.; will of. Devises all estate to Jacob Franks, of New York and David Franks of Philadelphia, "to dispose of it between my mother, my brothers and sisters as they shall think proper." Executor—said David Franks. Witnesses—Phineas Bond, Daniel Hopewell, Moses Mordecai. Proved Jan. 10, 1759. Lib. 9, p. 312.

1758, Dec. 20. Inventory, £795.0.8, incl. his purse, £165.12.6; shop goods, £413.6.8; a negro wench, £20; bonds, book debts and notes, £140.9.6; made by Zachariah Rossell, Jr., and Daniel Jones, Jr.

1758, June 29. Frazee, Abraham, of Elizabeth Town, Essex Co. Int. Adm'x—Esther Frazee, widow, and Timothy Frazee. Bondsman—Abraham Pain. Witness—Thomas Bartow. Lib. F, p. 531.

1758, Aug. 7. Frazee, Eliphelet, of Borough of Elizabeth, Essex Co. Int. Phebe Frazee renounced in favor of Thomas Scudder and Abraham Clark, Jr., who were appointed Adm'rs by Thomas Bartow, Surrogate. [See Frazee, James, infra].
1758, Aug. 8. Inventory, £763.17.6, by Abraham Clarke and Ephraim Terrill, Jr.
1760, Nov. 22. Account of Adm'rs filed.
Essex Wills, 2427 G; 2505 G.

1759, June 19. Frazee, Ephraim, Jr., of Borough of Elizabeth, Essex Co., Soldier; Int. Adm'r—Jacob Bebout, of said place, yeoman. Bondsman—William Lines, of Elizabeth, yeoman. Witness—Thomas Bartow. Lib. G, p. 82.
1759, Sept. 1. Inventory, £48.18.10, by Recom. Stanbery and William Line. Somerset Wills, 241 R.

1754, Feb. 11. Frazee, Gershom, of Elizabeth Borough, Essex Co., yeoman; will of. Wife, Abigail. Sons—Moses, Abraham, Gershom and Mathias. Real and personal estate. Executors—the wife and son Abraham. Witnesses—Richard Scuder, Stephen Frazee, John Lee. Proved Feb. 28, 1754. Lib. F, p. 157.
1754, Feb. 28. Abigail Frazee, the widow and Executrix, refuses to act.
1754, Feb. 27. Inventory, £91.16.10, by Richard Scudder and David Miller.

1759, July 7. Frazee, James, of Elizabeth. Petition of several relatives of Eliphalet Frazee, late of Elizabeth Town, dec'd, stating that the said Eliphalet died seized of a valuable tract of land in Elizabeth Town, and leaving but one son, James, and, dying intestate, the land descended on the said son, now about 11 years of age. The widow, living on the said plantation and enjoying the profits thereof, has lately married; therefore it prays that a Guardian may be appointed for said child. Signed by Thomas Scudder, Robert Ogden, Stephen Crane, Samuel Woodruff, Jonathan Hampton.

1759, July 9. Abraham Clark, Jr., appointed Guardian of James Frazee. Bondsman—Thomas Scudder, of Elizabeth Town.

1764, Feb. 11. Letter from Abraham Clark, Jr., stating that "James Frazee did not behave well at school and is not at my house, and I will have no more care of him or his plantation; and he must sign a petition to have some other person appointed."

1764, Feb. 14. Petition of James Frazee, stating his Guardian requests to be released and he makes choice of George Brown.

1764, Feb. 21. George Brown made Guardian of James Frazee, aged 16 years. Bondsman—John Moore, of Middlesex Co.
Essex Wills, 3363 G.

1757, May 10. Frazee, Jeremiah, late one of the "Battol men" under Captain William Lynes. Int. Adm'r—Joseph Frazee, of Elizabeth, yeoman. Bondsman—Ephraim Frazee, of same place, yeoman. Witness—Thomas Bartow. (Joseph Frazee states that his son, Jeremiah, died without a will). Lib. F, p. 425.

1755, April 3. Frazee, William, of Woodbridge, turner. Int. Adm'rs —Rebeckah Frazee, widow, and Jonathan Frazee, Esq., of Woodbridge. Bondsman—Michael Moore, of same place, yeoman. Witness—Thomas Bartow. Lib. F, p. 257.

1755, Apr. 26. Inventory, £282.3.3, incl. 2 Bibles and other books, 15s.; bills, bond and book debts, £138.0.11; made by David Donham and Samuel Barron.

1758, March 24. Account by Administrators, who report on hand £177.13.

1760, May 7. Frazer, Hannah, of Fairfield, Cumberland Co., spinster; will of. Sisters—Ann Dollas and Phebe Lore. Cousins—Ann Lore, Hannah Eldreg and Elizabeth Dollas, youngest child and Hannah, daughter of sister Abigail Westcot, dec'd. Personal estate. Executors—brother Seth Lore and Mark Reeve. Witnesses—Dorcas Dennis, Milysent Reeve, Mary Doubleday. Proved Oct. 28, 1760.
Lib. 10, p. 199.

1760, Oct. 11. Inventory, £118.16.10, incl. bonds, cash and debts, £60.9.10; made by Daniel Lore and John Bragg.

1759, Dec. 17. Frazer, William, Esq., of Salem Town and Co.; will of Daughters—Elizabeth Frazer (sole Executrix) and Hannah, wife of John Rolfe. Witnesses—Roger Sherron, Jos: Gray and Grant Gibbon. Proved March 1, 1760. Lib. 10, p. 101.

1760, Jan. 31. Inventory, £95.19, incl. 17 pictures; draft of Middle British Colonies; a silver tankard and other silver, £35; book debts, £33.15.3; made by Jonathan Hart and Branson van Leer.

1760, Dec. 17. Freeman, Henry, late of Woodbridge, Middlesex Co. Int. Adm'x—Mary Freeman, widow. Lib. G, p. 334.

CALENDAR OF WILLS—1751-1760   123

1755, Apr. 1. Freeman, John, of Cumberland Co. Int. Adm'r—Jonathan Bowen; Timothy Brooks fellowbondsman.   Lib. 8, p. 144.

1755, Mar. 1. Freeman, Morris, of Mountholly, Burlington Co., yeoman; will of. Wife, Mary Freeman, alias Mary Sill, sole heiress and Executrix of real and personal estate. Witnesses—John Woolman, Samuel Andrews, John Allen. Proved April 1, 1755.
Lib. 8, p. 132.
1754, Mar. 24. Inventory, £33.18.4, by John Woolman and Samuel Andrews.

1760, Jan. 21. Freeman, Sarah, late of Woodbridge, widow. Int. Adm'r—Frazee Ayers, of Woodbridge, Middlesex Co., principal creditor. Bondsman—John Magee, of Woodbridge. Witness—Thomas Bartow.
Lib. G, p. 123.

1756, Oct. 20. Freeman, William, of Woodbridge, yeoman. Int. Adm'x—Sarah Freeman, of Woodbridge, widow. Bondsman—Frazee Ayers, of Woodbridge, yeoman. Witness—Thomas Bartow.
Lib. F, p. 383.

1756, Apr. 29. Frilinghuysen, Rev. Johannis, of Somerset Co. Int. Inventory, £555.11.3., incl. a library of Dutch English, Greek and Latin books, £68.17; silver spoons and forks, £24; a silver coffee pot, £18; a silver tea canister and other silver ware, £7; 3 gold buttons, £1.10; an old silver watch, £2.10; a negro, man, woman and child, £100; made by Dirck van Veghten, Jeronimus van Neste and Hendrick Fisher.
1758, Oct. 2. Bond of Jacob Rutson Hardenbergh and wife, Dina, late Dina Frelinghuysen, as Adm'rs; Peter Williamson and Teunis Post fellowbondsmen.   Lib. 9, p. 553.
1759, Oct. 5. Account by Adm'rs, who report, they have received £566.11.3, and paid out £199.7.

1752, July 8. French, Joseph, of Shrewsbury, Monmouth Co., yeoman. Int. Bond of James Farrill as Adm'r; William Laird fellowbondsman, both of Freehold, said Co., yeomen.   Lib. F, p. 84.
1752, July 17. Sales list of the personal estate, £35.10.8, signed by James Farrill as Adm'r, and John Redford and Willim Laird as appraisers.

1760, Aug. 3. French, Robert, of Chester, Burlington Co., yeoman; will of. Wife, Hannah. Children—Jonas, Mary, Hannah, Thomas, Elizabeth, Robert, James, Kiziah and Anne. Real and personal estate. Executors—the wife, son Jonas and brother-in-law James Cattell. Witnesses—Thomas Morton, John Matlack, Samuel Gaskill, John Cox. Proved October 1, 1760.   Lib. 10, p. 132.
1760, Sept. 24. Inventory, £233.12.1., incl. 8,000 shingles still in the cedar swamps, £16; made by John Cox and Enoch Roberts.

1757, May 5. French, Thomas, of Chester Twsp., Burlington Co. Int. Inventory, £262.12.11, incl. book debts, £16.13; an old watch, 20s.; 15 bush. of Indian corn, 3 3/9; 20 do. of oats £1.11.8; made by Joshua Humphris and John Cox.
1757, May 6. Bond of widow, Jemima French, and Robert French,

yeoman, as Adm'rs; John Cox, blacksmith, fellowbondsman, all of said Township. Lib. 8, p. 385.
    1761, Aug. 25. Account by the Administratrix.

    1758, Aug. 4. French, Uriah, of Newton Township, Gloucester Co., bricklayer. Inventory, £202.4.5, incl. 6 silver spoons; the time of two 'prentice boys, £20; made by Jacob Clement and John Gill.
    1758, Aug. 7. Bond of widow, Mary French, of Newton Township, as Adm'x; Charles French, of Waterford Township, said Co., fellowbondsman. Lib. 9, p. 456.
    1764, Apr. 2. Account by Hugh Creighton and wife Mary, late Mary French, Administratrix of said Uriah, who report £20.9.1 on hand.

    1754, Apr. 6. Friend, Lawrence, of Gloucester Co. Int. Bond of Samuel Shivers, of Gloucester Co., yeoman, as Adm'r; Joseph Hollinshead, of Burlington City, gentleman, fellowbondsman.
Glou. Wills, 537 F.

    1755, Dec. 15. Frost, John, of Morristown, Morris Co., gentleman; will of. Wife, Susannah, sole heiress and Executrix of real and personal estate. Witnesses—Samuel Frost, Hannah Frost, Ephraim Price. Proved Jan. 26, 1758. Lib. F, p. 511.

    1759, Dec. 5. Fullerton, James (19 years old) and Jane (15 yrs), children of James Fullerton, of Bedminster, Somerset Co. Bond of William McClellan (McClelan), of said Co., as Guardian.
Lib. G, p. 113.

    1753, Nov. 2. Fulse, Jacob, of Marple Township, Chester Co., Penna., yeoman; will of. Mother, Mary Fulse and brother, Frederick Fulse, receive three-quarters of the proceeds of the farm on Racoon Creek, Greenwich Twsp., Gloucester Co., to be sold by the Executors, Bernard van Leer of said Marple Township and Ephram Pea, of Greenwich Township, who are to have the fourth-quarter. Witnesses—Thomas Cross, George van Leer, William Dougherty. Proved Nov. 26, 1753, (in Gloucester Co.). Lib. 7, p. 430.
    1754, Apr. 3. Inventory, £12.8.7, incl. a Bible and books; made by Matthew Gill and Thomas Roberts.
    1756, Sept. 15. Account by Bernhard von Leer, one of the Executors, who has sold the plantation for £95, and has paid debts to the amount of £97.6.1.

    1752, Feb. 13. Furman, Richard, of Trenton Township, Hunterdon Co.; will of. Wife, Sarah. Children—Jonathan, Josiah, Francis, Sarah Closon, Mary Clark and Elizabeth Kitchen. Real and personal estate. Executors—sons Jonathan and Josiah, with Joseph De Cow. Witnesses—Samuel Tucker, Jr., Elijah Bond, Hezekiah Howell. Proved Nov. 8, 1757. Lib. 8, p. 473.
    1758, Jan. 6. Inventory, £224.18.11, incl. a servant girl's time; bonds and book debts, £72.4.9; made by Capt. Joseph Tindall and Joseph Green.

    1755, Apr. 25. Galaspy, Gloud, of Penn's Neck, Salem Co. Int. Bond of Joseph Wright, of the same place, as Adm'r; no fellowbondsman. Lib. 8, p. 236.

1755, Apr. 25. Inventory, £32.18.3, by Jeremiah Baker and Andrew Sinnickson.
1755, May 16. Additional inventory, £3.5, by the same.

1754, Dec. 27. Galleher, John, of "Allaways" Creek, Salem Co., yeoman; will of. Brother, Charles Galleher. Sisters—Susanna Galleher and Ezebel Gilmer. Cousin—Alexander, son of David Gilmer. Real and personal estate. Uncle, John Walker, sole Executor. Witnesses—Bulbe (Bilby) Shepherd, William Walker, Job Shepherd. Proved March 7, 1755. Lib. 8, p. 148.
1755, Mar. 7. Inventory, £36.15.6, by Job Shepherd and Samuel Oakford.

1754, Jan. 29. Gambel, Samuel, of Northampton Township, Burlington Co., mason; will of. Wife, Rebecca. Children—Olive, Samuel and Burgess, all under age. Real and personal estate. Thomas Atkinson, miller, sole Executor. Witnesses—Sarah Fenimore, Joseph Baker, Patrick Byrne. Proved Feb. 22, 1754. Burl. Wills, 5419 C.
1754, Feb. 21. Inventory, £39.18.10, by John Budd and Patrick Byrne.

1757, Nov. 29. Gandy, David, of Cape May Co. Int. Inventory, £245.14.4, incl. bonds and book debts, £101.1.9; made by Joseph Goldin and Joseph Edward.
1757, Dec. 13. Bond of Rebecca Gandy as Adm'x; Joseph Goldin fellowbondsman, both of Cape May Co. Lib. 8, p. 497.

1760, Mar. 13. Gano, Stephan, of "Somasset" Co. Int. Inventory, £115.13, incl. a negroman, £50; made by Tomas Pietersen and Joshua Cosahn.
1760, Mar. 19. Bond of Elisabeth, widow, Adm'x; "Joshuha Coshan" (Kishan) of said Co., fellowbondsman. Lib. G, p. 142.

1752, Apr. 1. Gard, William, of Evesham, Burlington Co. Int. Inventory, £161.13.3, by Freedom Lippincott and Joshua Ballinger.
1752, Apr. 2. Bond of widow, Sarah Gard, as Adm'x, Freedom Lippincott fellowbondsman, both of Burlington Co. Burl. Wills, 4965 C.

1759, Aug. 18. Gardiner, Lion, of Roxbury, Morris Co.; will of. Wife, Mary, sole heiress of estate, with remainder to daughter, Hannah. Executors—David Luce, Esq. and Daniel Dickerson, both of Roxbury. Witnesses—Isaiah Younglove, Barnabas Curtice, Ebenezer Blachlye. Proved Sept. 3, 1759. Lib. G, p. 94.
1759, Aug. 29. Inventory, of real and personal: Real—houses and lands, £49; iron works, £150; sawmill, £12. Personal, £138.16.5. Made by David Luse and Daniel Dickerson.

1751, May 21. Garner, Samuel, of Hanover, Morris Co. Bond of Zeruah Garner, widow, as Adm'x; Joseph Wood and William Bates, both of Hanover, fellowbondsmen. Lib. E, p. 529.

1753, Oct. 20. Garrison, Abraham, of Monmouth Co.; will of. Wife, Mary. Children—John, Catherine, Elizabeth and Hartshorn. Real and personal estate. Executors—the wife and James Mott. Witnesses—Jarratt Wall, James Dorsett and Thomas Bullman. Proved May 17, 1756. Lib. F, p. 357.

1753, Dec. 24. Inventory, £226.6.3, incl. silver buckles and gold buttons, £1.10; silver spoons, £5.3; a bond, £30; a negro woman, £45; made by Jarratt Wall and James Dorsett.

1750, July 15. Garrison, Jacob, of Deerfield Township, Cumberland Co., yeoman; will of. Wife, Elizabeth. Children—Benjamin Christain Joeling, Rachel Plates (?), Samuel, Sarah Reves, Jacob, Mary Steavens, Elizabeth, Daniel, Ephraim, William, Cornelius, Anna, Phebe, Alphaias, the last seven under age. Real and personal estate. Executors—the wife and Ephraim Seely. Witnesses—Samuel Woodruff, Dan Bowen, Elias Cotting. Proved April 30, 1751. Cumb. Wills, 67 F.
1751, Apr. 18. Inventory, £90.1.2½., by Samuel Woodruff and Dan Bowen.

1752, Apr. 8. Garrison, Jacob, Inventory, £99.14, incl. bonds from Samuel Tilton and Peter Bastedo, £28.15; made by Samuel Rogers and Isaac Parr.
1752, Apr. 9. Bond of John and Jacob Garrison, of Middlesex Co., yeoman, as Adm'rs; Samuel Rogers, of Monmouth Co., merchant, fellowbondsman. Lib. 7, p. 302.

1750, Mar. 2. Garrison, Jeremiah, of Salem Co., yeoman; will of. Wife, Mary, sole Executrix. Children—Jeremiah, Gamaliel, Joel, John, Mary, Abigill, Phebe and Hannah. Land in "Engin and Island neck, which is the forth peart of 1010 Eacors." Personal estate. Witnesses—John van Meter and Elisabeth Dubois. Proved May 1, 1751.
 Lib. 7, p. 242.
1751, —— ——. Inventory, £154.3.11, incl. books, 19s.; book debts, £29.13.1; made by Jacob Dubois and John Creag.

1752, Feb. 22. Garwood, John, of Evesham Township, Burlington Co.; will of. Wife, Charity, sole Executrix. Children—Hope, Presilla, and Israel. Homefarm; pineland, bought of Richard Parke and Daniel Parke; pineland taken up on a Proprietary's right. Personal estate. Witnesses—John Goldy, Thomas Ballinger, William Foster. Proved April 8, 1752. Burl. Wills, 4969 C.
1752, Apr. 8. Inventory, £266.10.1, incl. a negro man, £30; made by William Foster and Thomas Ballinger.

1752, Apr. 13. Garwood, Solomon, of Evesham, Burlington Co. Int. Bond of William Garwood as Adm'r; Daniel Garwood fellowbondsman, both of Evesham, yeoman. Lib. 7, p. 302.
1752, Apr. 24. Inventory, £28.15.6., incl. debts due by William Haise, Joshua Beverly, John Garwood, dec'd, Zebulon Rawsel, Anthony Alcott and John Stratton; made by Robert Bradock and Joshua Ballinger.
1752, Aug. 8. Account by the Adm'r, who charges for nursing, doctor's fees and funeral, £10.6.2, and has paid debts due to Richard Condon (crier at the vendue), Robert Powell, Frettwell Wright, Robert Hartshorne, Joshua Ballinger and Robert Braddock, reporting £4.5.5 on hand.

1754, Sept. 4. Gaskill, Jonathan, of Springfield Township, Burlington Co.; will of. Wife, Jane. Children—Joshua, Josiah (under age), Livina, Mary, Hope, Rachel, Patience and Charity. Real and personal estate. Executors—the wife and brother-in-law, Jacob Shinn. Wit-

nesses—Absalom Ewan, Hanah Ewan, Gabriel Blond. Proved Dec. 9, 1754. Lib. 7, p. 528.
1754, Dec. 6. Inventory, £205.2.4, by Aaron Robbins and Samuel Lippincott.

1759, Nov. 19. Gaskill, Joshua, of Newtown, Gloucester Co., husbandman. Int. Inventory, £74.9, by Josiah Shivers and John Barton.
1759, Dec. 10. Bond of his widow, Ann Gaskill, as Adm'x; Thomas Hinchman fellowbondsman. Lib. 9, p. 341.

1752, May 15. Gaskill, Zorobable, of Northampton, Burlington Co., yeoman; will of. Sons—Nathan, Moses, Joseph and Zorobable. Land on the Burlington road (north side); homefarm on southside of said road. Personal estate. Executors—brother, Joseph Gaskill, and Samuel Cripps, and they to take care that son Joseph duly gives to Meeting. Son, Zorobable, to have a year's schooling and learn "the art and mystery of a carpenter," at son Nathan's. Witnesses—James Southwick, Caleb Ogborn, Thomas Lawrence. Proved June 10, 1752.
Lib. 7, p. 232.
1752, May 29. Inventory, £117.17.1, incl. book debts and cash notes, £59.19.10½; made by James and Josiah Southwick.

1753, July 20. Gaskill, Zorobabal, Jr., of Northampton, Burlington Co. Int. Bond of Adam Farquhar as Adm'r; Peter Allinson fellowbondsman, both of said place. Lib. 7, p. 421.
1753, July 21. Nathan Gaskill, the brother, refuses the administration in favour of brother-in-law, Adam Farquhar.
1753, July 21. Inventory, £66.16.5, by John Burr, Jr., and Peter Allinson.

1759, Aug. 28. Geiger, Mathias, of Piles Grove, Salem Co., yeoman; will of. Children—Adam, Henry, Simon and Susannah (under age). Real and personal estate. Executors—son Adam and Hans Martin Holder (who signs jurat of executors in German script as Martin Halter). Witnesses—John Abram Lidenius, Joseph Wood and Michael Bauer (signs in German script). Proved Sept. 27, 1759.
Lib. 10, p. 520.
1759, Sept. 25. Inventory, £338.10.2, incl. son William's clothes, £2.12.6; indenture of a servant man, £10; 2 leases, £7.15; made by Bateman Lloyd and Joseph Wood.

1749-'50, Feb. 21. Gerrard, Margret, of "Greenwitch" Township, Gloucester Co., widow; will of. Children—Miles, William, Thomas, and seven daughters, of whom only Hacels (?) is mentioned by name. Granddaughter, Sarah Paull. Lot in Philadelphia. Personal estate. Executors—brother-in-law, Gabriel Rambo, and Joshua Lord, of Deptford Township. Witnesses—John Haines, Ann Cooper, Thomas Robson. Codicil of February 25, ———, tells daughter Hackels (?) being still in her infancy; daughter Elizabeth, wife of John Chew, is to have bed and furniture, and, with her sister Tamzin, are to be placed in the charge of brother-in-law Gabriel Rambo. Witnesses—Ann Erwen, Joanna Wilkins. Proved Jan. 12, 1754. Lib. 8, p. 16.
1754, Jan. 12. Joshua Lord and Gabriel Rambo decline to act as Executors. Same date bond of William Gerrard as Adm'r of the estate with the will annexed; Thomas Gerrard fellowbondsman, both of Greenwich Township, yeomen.

1754, Jan. 12. Inventory, £479.12.3½., principally bills and bonds; also a silver watch, £5; a servantlad's time, £15; silver spoons, £6.13; 2 looking glasses; made by William Wilkins and Jacob Cozens. Endorsed: "Margaret Gerrard's Inventory. This Inventory caveated by John Sparks, Mathias Nathermuch (?), James Wood and Simon Sparks."

1754, Nov. 19. Gerrard, Miles, of the Town and County of Gloucester, yeoman; will of. Sisters—Sarah, Elizabeth, Margarett, Gwin, Jane, Heckles and Tammazin. Brothers-in-law—Simon Sparks and Isaac Camron. Mentions also Robert, son of brother William Gerrard. Lot in Philadelphia. Personal estate, incl. bond due by brother William; two hhds. of molasses sent to sea by brother-in-law Isaac Camron. Executors—John Mickle and Joseph Harrison of said Co., yeoman. Witnesses—Samuel Harrison, Jr., Jacob Clement, Jr., Joseph Hugg, Jr. Codicil of Nov. 25, 1754, directs legacy to sister Gwin Sparks out of the bond due by brother William. Witnesses—Mary Cole, Mary Rambo, Samuel Paul. Proved Dec. 30, 1754, when the Executors above named decline to act. Lib. 8, p. 104.

1754, Dec. 30. Inventory, £161.12.5., incl. bonds and notes, £138.5; made by Samuel Harrison and Samuel Harrison, Jr.

1754, Dec. 30. Bond of Simon Sparks, innholder, as Adm'r, with will annexed; Joseph Harrison, yeoman, fellowbondsman, both of Gloucester Town. Glou. Wills, 538 H.

1754, Nov. 29. Gerrard, Thomas, of Greenwich Twsp., Gloucester Co. Int. Inventory, £409.11.3, incl. a servant boy's time, £5; a negro boy, £35; bonds and accounts, "all desperate," £121.4.10; made by Alexander Randall and Richard West.

1754, Nov. 18. Bond of William Gerrard as Adm'r; Isaac Stephens, of Deptford Township, fellowbondsman. Lib. 8, p. 72.

1743, Sept. 9. Gerretse, Hendrick, of Acquacknong Precinct, Essex Co., yeoman; will of. Wife, Margeriet. Children—Garret, John, Cornelius, Henry, Abraham, Gesie (wife of Marinus van Winkell), Antie (wife of Jurie Pieterse), Janetie (wife of Adrian Post), Margret and Lena (wife of Thomas Jurianse or Thomas van Ripe). Real and personal estate. Executors—the wife and the five sons. Witnesses—John Low, Abraham Low, Cornelius Low, minor. Proved Nov. 20, 1758. Lib. G, p. 19.

1758, June 29. Gerretson, John, of Weesel, Essex Co. Int. Adm'x—Marrete Gerretson, widow. Bondsman—Cornelius Gerretson, of Wessel. Witnesses—Uzal Ogden. Lib. F, p. 541.

1758, June 30. Inventory, £178.6.0, by Cornelius Gerritson and Hendrick Gerrits.

1758, June 9. Gerritsen, Gerrit, of "Middilbus" (Middlebush), Somerset Co., yeoman; will of. Wife and children; son Samuel only mentioned by name. Real and personal estate. Executors—brothers Samuel and Johannis Gerritsen, and son Samuel. Witnesses—John Kroesen, Peeteres Wycof, Abraham Metseler. Proved Dec. 1, 1752.
Lib. F, p. 78.

1752, Dec. 1. Inventory, £300.6.9. by Abraham Voorhees and Petrus Wyckoff.

1753, May 26. Account by Ex'rs, incl. sale of real estate, 198½ acres, for £794.

CALENDAR OF WILLS—1751-1760   129

1745'6, Feb. 4. Gerritsen, Wilhelmus, of Somerset Co., yeoman; will of. Wife, Mary. Children—John, Eyda, Anna and Samuel (under 12 years). Personal estate. Executors—brothers Rem and John Gerritsen. Witnesses—Samuel Gerritsen, Petrus Wyckoff, Derrick Kroesen. Proved March 22, 1755. Lib. F, p. 255.

1756, Apr. 1. Gibbins, Benjamin, of Middletown, Monmouth Co., yeoman; will of. Wife, Mary. Brother, Richard Gibbins. Mentions also Jonathan Gibbins, Robert Patterson, sister Rachel (wife of John Vaughan) and Joseph ———. Real and personal estate. Executors—Robert Lawrence and John Williams, both of said Co. Witnesses—Thomas Mount, George Mount and John Taylor. Proved March 7, 1757. Lib. F, p. 408.

1758, Mar. 24. Gibbon, Nicholas, Esq., of Salem Town and Co. Int. Bond of Grant Gibbon, son, as Adm'r; Benjamin Cripps and Edward Keasbey, fellowbondsmen, all of said Co. Lib. 8, p. 529.
  1758, Apr. 28. Inventory, £1370.14.5, incl. a watch, £10; cash in the escritoire, £97.11.6; plate in the "beaufet," £21.10; bonds, book debts, notes, rents and other debts, £848.17.6; a looking glass, £3.10; another do., £1.10; a third do., £2; 5 maps and 5 small pictures, £2.11.6; books, £13; 3 negroes, £110; made by Edward Test and Edward Keasbey.

1750, April 3. Gibbs, Francis, of Mansfield Twp., Burlington Co., yeoman; will of. Plantation to be sold. All estate to be divided between my wife, Elizabeth, and my sons, Richard and Francis Gibbs, and my daughters, Elizabeth and Mary Gibbs. Executors—friend Benjamin Talman and Joseph Talman. Witnesses—Caleb Scattergood, Thomas Thompson, Job Talman. Proved May 9, 1750.
  1750, May 8. Inventory, £319.3.4½, by Job Talman and John Antrum.
  1752, Oct. 23. Mem. taken from the papers of Joseph and Benjamin Talman in presence of legatees. Plantation sold for £576. Received from Isaac Gibbs' estate, £119.17.10. Burl. Wills, 4667 C.

1753, July 23. Gibbs, John, of Chesterfield, Burlington Co. Int. Bond of Benjamin Gibbs, of Chesterfield, farmer, as Adm'r; Jonathan Thomas, of Burlington City, innholder, fellowbondsman.
Lib. 7, p. 421.

1754, ——. Gibson, Isaac, of Burlington Co. Int. Ann Carter, widow, declines the administration in favour of Lott Ridgaway.
  1754, Oct. 31. Bond of Lott Ridgaway as Adm'r; Benjamin Jones, fellowbondsman, both of said Co., yeoman. Lib. 8, p. 64.
  1754, Dec. 9. Inventory, £102.3., incl. a bond for £100; made by Abraham Marit (Marrot) and William West.
  1755, Feb. 4. Account by the Adm'r, who balances the value of the inventory with his expenditures.

1752, Feb. 24. Gibson, John, of Springfield, Burlington Co., yeoman; will of. Wife, Sarah. Mother, Sarah Levinor. Daughters, Mary and Levina, both under age. Farm at Eggharbour, sold to Nehemiah Nicholson, for which the Executors are to give deed. Personal property. Executors—father-in-law, John Levinor, and Joseph Lamb. Witnesses—Zachariah Rossell, Jr., Samuel Clark, John Burr, Jr. Proved May 11, 1752.

9

1752, Apr. 6. Inventory of the estate: Real—home farm in Springfield, £148; do. at Great Eggharbour, £170. Personal, £100.5.10. Appraised by William Budd and David Budd.

1762, May 22. Account by the Executors, who charge for the funeral £2.17.7, and for administration £33.3.11, and have paid debts due to Nehemiah Nicholson, Michael Newbold as Executor of Benjamin Shreve, Daniel Smith, Benjamin Bispham, George Rennie, Daniel Wills, Jr., John Ewan, Henry Paxson, Samuel Lippincott, Absalom Ewan, Joseph Scattergood, William Budd, Samuel Clark, Samuel Thorn for John Hutchin, Patrick Field, Doctor Ross, Briggs Rossell, John West, Thomas Atkinson, Ebenezer Dotey, Ezekiel Eldridge, John Burr, Jr., Sarah Reeves, Jonathan Taylor, George Collings, Aaron Gaskill, William Harris, Benjamin Morton, James Atkinson, Jonathan and John Shreve, Edward Mullen, Robert Farrell, Elizabeth Cowgill, George Briggs, Lott Ridgway, William Shinn, John Budd, Henry Jones, John Gillaim, John Lavennor, Joseph Ridgway, Isaac De Cow, Jr., Jonathan Thomas, Jacob Shinn, Amos Shreve, William Skeeles, Thomas Price, Abram Marriott, James Southwick, Joseph Arney, Stephen Gaskill, John Adams and John Eacrit (in full of a legacy given to his wife, testator's widow).

Burl. Wills, 4989 C.

1750, July 18. Gibson, William, of Deptford, Gloucester Co., yeoman; will of. Brother, Luke Gibson, to have the 117½ acres, adjacent to his plantation, it being one-half of the farm, left to testator by his father, Luke Gibson; the other half to go to sister, Mary Gibson. Sisters, Hannah and Rebacah Gibson, to have personal property. Brother Luke, sole Executor. Witnesses—Richard Clarke, James Neill, Benjamin Lodge. Proved June 4, 1751. Lib. 7, p. 144.

1750, Sept. 19. Inventory, £24.12, by Richard Clarke and George Flaningam.

1749, Dec. 13. Giffing, Francis, of Trenton, Hunterdon Co., blacksmith; will of. Wife, Margaret. Children—Martha, Rebeckah and John, all under age. Real and personal estate. Executors—the wife and Joseph Yard. Witnesses—Edward Stevenson, Annah Pidall (Findall), Elizabeth Tucker. Proved Jan. 15, 1756. Lib. 8, p. 271.

1753, Mar. 25. Gifford, Ananiah, Jr., of Shrewsbury, Monmouth Co.; will of. Children—Stephen, John, Zilphia, Hannah and Phebe, all under age. Real and personal estate. Executors—Thomas Tilton, David Allen and Guisebert Longstreet. Witnesses—William Lawrence, Peter Parker, Joshua Gifford and John Morris. Proved Jan. 19, 1758. Thomas Tilton refuses to serve.

Lib. F, p. 510.

1758, Jan. 9. Inventory, £281.3.5, incl. bills, book debts and notes, £51.1.6; 134 bush. of corn, £15.6.6; made by James Irons, David Curtis and David Johnston.

1755, Sept. 30. Gilbert, John, of Hanover, Morris Co., yeoman; will of. Wife, Pashanc (Patience). Children—Pashanc, Sary, Mary, (all made Executrixes). Annah (wife of Zacharyah Blackman). Grandchildren—Abraham (son of son Thomas Gilbert); children of daughter Marcy (wife of Jesyah Cain). Real and personal estate. Witnesses—Isaac van Duyn, David Harriman, Job Allen. Proved Oct. 4, 1756. Lib. F, p. 381.

CALENDAR OF WILLS—1751-1760   131

1757, Oct. 10. Gilman, William, of Rahway, Middlesex Co. Int. Adm'x—Sarah Gilman, widow. Bondsman—Joseph Gilman, of Essex Co. Witness—Thomas Bartow.   Lib. F, p. 459.
    1757, Nov. 18. Inventory, £48.19, incl. a large Bible, 15s.; made by Charles Marsh and Joseph Moore.

1760, Jan. 2. Ginn, Thomas, of Monmouth Co., labourer. Int. Bond of Edward Bonnell, principal creditor, as Adm'r; William McKnight fellowbondsman, both of said Co.   Lib. G, p. 120.

1756, Nov. 24. Gittings, John, of Salem Co. Int. Bond of Robert Patterson, of Piles Grove, Salem Co., shopkeeper, as Adm'r.
    Lib. 8, p. 445.
    1756, ——— —. Inventory, £14.17.10, by John Richman and Hugh Giboney.

1751, Apr. 27. Glaspy, William, of Somerset Co., brewer. Int. Bond of William Layton, of Somerset Co., principal creditor, as Adm'r; Richard Fitz Randolph, of Perth Amboy, carpenter, fellowbondsman.
    Lib. E, p. 520.
    1751, July 23. Inventory, £6.4.1, by John Grant and Aaron Boylan.

1759, Mar. 15. Goith, Elizabeth, of Perth Amboy, Middlesex Co. Int. Adm'r—Thomas Inglis, of Perth Amboy. Bondsman—Edward Higgins, of same place.   Lib. G, p. 40.

1759, Aug. 24. Goldin, Joseph, of Cape May Co.; will of. Children—Jacob, "addicted to the excessive use of spirituous liquors," John, Deborah Nicolson (widow), Mary Daniels, Eleazer (now in the service of the Crown). Grandchildren—Dorcas Goldin, Abiah Goldin, Ezekiel Hand, all three under age. Home farm of 200 acres in said Co. on Great Egg Harbour River; upland and marsh at Tuckahoe, bought of James Hubbert. Personal property. Executors—son John and Jeremiah Leaming. Witnesses—Jacob Garretson, Jeremiah Hand, David Evans, Jacob Spicer. Proved Feb. 11, 1760, when Jeremiah Leaming refuses to act as Executor.   Lib. 9, p. 404.
    1760, Feb. 15. Inventory, £277.0.3, incl. books, 15s., made by Joseph Corson and Joseph Edwards.

1751, Apr. 6. Goldy, William, of Evesham Township, Burlington Co. Int. Inventory, £463.7.2, incl. bills, bonds and book debts, £371.1.8; a silver spoon and other silver, £1.4; a little Bible and another book, 6s.; 2 bush. of Indian corn, 5s.; made by John Hiller and Jacob Prickitt.
    1751, Apr. 8. Bond of Joseph and John Gooldy, of Gloucester Co., husbandmen, as Adm'rs; Jacob Pricket, of Northampton Township, Burlington Co., and Jonathan Thomas, of Burlington City, fellowbondsmen. Witness—John Hiller.   Burl. Wills, 4823 C.

1755, Dec. 23. Goodden, David, of Middlesex Co.; will of. Wife, Cosiah. Eldest son, Samuel. Other children, names not given. Real and personal estate. No executor named. Witnesses—Moses Bishop, Richard Skiner (Skinner) and John Spencer. Proved Jan. 26, 1756.
    Lib. F, p. 319.

1752, Sept. 2. Goodfellow, Hezekiah, of Woodbridge, Middlesex Co., cordwainer; will of. Wife, Elizabeth. Son, Thomas. Executors—

John Robards, of Elizabeth, and David Inslee, of Woodbridge. Witnesses—David Edgar, Samuel Freeman. Proved May 18, 1754.
Lib. F, p. 173.

1759, Feb. 10. Gordon, John, of Pen's Neck, Salem Co. Inventory, £129.7, incl. book debts and cash, £27.8.7; made by Francis Miles and Andrew Sinnickson.

1759, Feb. 12. Bond of Jane Gordon as Adm'x; John Mecum and Samuel Swanson fellowbondsmen, all of Pen's Neck. Lib. 9, p. 352.

1756, Oct. 28. Gosling, John, Esq., of Evesham, Burlington Co. Int. Sarah, widow, renounces her right of administering.

1756, Nov. 2. Bond of John Gosling, of Salem Co., as Adm'r; Joseph Hollinshead, Esq., of Burlington City, fellowbondsman.
Lib. 8, p. 340.

1756, Nov. 24. Inventory, £488.7, incl. bonds, £390; books, £23; made by Joshua Ballinger and Isaac Evens.

1754, May 7. Gould, James, Esq., of Hunterdon Co. Int. Bond of George Tuker (Tucker), of Hunterdon Co., blacksmith, as Adm'r of estate left unadministered by Anne Gould at her death; Samuel Tucker, Jr., of said Co., merchant, and Joseph Hollinshead, of Burlington City, fellowbondsmen. Hunt. Wills, 163 J.

1755, Mar. 26. Graden, Dorothy, of Stow Creek, Cumberland Co., spinster; will of. Granddaughter, Lucy Daten, daughter of Peter Daten, dec'd., sole heiress of personal estate, which, if she dies before coming of age, is to go to the Presbyterian Congregation of Greenwich for the support of the Ministry. Thomas Ewings, of Greenwich, sole Executor. Witnesses—Ephraim Loyd, James Lister, David Padgett. Proved April 3, 1755. Lib. Z, p. 136.

1755, Apr. 3. Inventory, £45.19.6, incl. bonds, £26.2.11; made by Thomas Sayre and David Padgett.

1754, Jan. 16. Graham, James, of Bedminster, Somerset Co.; will of. Lands to be sold. Wife, Mary, £100. Oldest son's, John's, children, viz., James, John, Mary, Ann and Sarah, all under age. Daughter's, Mary's, children, viz., John, William, James, Samuel, Stephen, Mary and Jean, all under age. Mentions sons William (and children, viz., Peter and John), James, Ann, Sarah. Executors—wife, friends Daniel McEowen and Jacob Vanderveer, and son James. Witnesses—Moses Craig, George Forman, Joseph Vanderveer. Proved June 13, 1757.
Lib. F, p. 430.

1753, Sept. 18. Grant, John, of Westfield in the Borough of Elizabeth, Essex Co., minister. Int. Phebe Grant, the widow, renounced and prayed for Jonathan Crane, Esq., and John Crane, Jr., to be appointed adm'rs in her place, they being the persons Mr. Grant desired to act just before he died. Witness—Daniel Ross, Jr.

1753, Sept. 20. Jonathan Crane and John Crane, Jr., appointed Adm'rs; Daniel Ross, Jr., fellowbondsman. Lib. F, p. 135.

1753, Sept. 25. Inventory, £209.15, by Timothy Whitehead and Joseph Cory.

1756, June 28. Account filed by Adm'rs, mentions minor children, John and Phebe Grant, and Increase Grant, Guardian.

CALENDAR OF WILLS—1751-1760

1754, Jan. 21. Graves, Richard, of Manington, Salem Co., yeoman; will of. Children—Sarah Acret, John, Thomas, Eady and Prudence. Personal estate. Executor—Edmund Wetherby. Witnesses—Sarah Austin, Francis Biggs and Edmund Wetherby, Jr. Proved Jan. 17, 1757. Lib. 9, p. 9.
1757, Jan. 19. Inventory, £94.11.6, incl. books, by Benjamin Cripps and Richard Woodnutt.

1760, July 3. Gray, Andrew, of Woodbridge, Middlesex Co. Int. Mary Gray and Benjamin Gray renounced; one the widow and the other brother and largest creditor, of said Andrew. Andrew Bloomfield and Ephraim Cutter, both of Woodbridge, appointed Adm'rs. Witness—John Smyth. Lib. G, p. 242.

1753, Mar. 6. Gray, Ebenezer, of Woodbridge, Middlesex Co. Int. Bond of Benjamin Gray, brother, as Adm'r; Benjamin Rolph, of Perth Amboy, cooper, fellowbondsman. Lib. F, p. 92.

1760, April 21. Gray, Eunice, of Essex Co., widow. Int. George Badglly made oath, that he heard James Bailey, of Elizabethtown, ask Daniel Tremble, son-in-law to Eunice Gray, to join him in settling the estate, but he would have nothing to do with it.
1760, Feb. 26. Adm'r—James Baily, son-in-law to Eunice Gray. Bondsman—Jonathan Bishop, of Woodbridge, yeoman. Witness—Thomas Bartow. Lib. G, p. 166.

1754, Mar. 2. Gray, Jonathan, of Hopewell, Hunterdon Co., yeoman; will of. Children—Jonathan, Benjamin, both under age, Sarah and Martha. Real and personal estate. Executors—Richard Hart, of Hopewell, and John Burt, of Trenton. Witnesses—John Moore, Amos Hart, Samuell Moore. Proved March 14, 1754.
1754, Mar. 8. Inventory, £210.10.7, incl. 2 servantmen's time, £25; made by Samuel Fitch. Hunt. Wills, 343 J.

1754, Feb. 21. Gray, Joseph, of Hopewell, Hunterdon Co., yeoman; will of. Wife, Sarah. Children—Sarah, Mary and Ann Gray (now Rozzel), and Jonathan. Grandson, Stephen Rozzel. Real and personal estate, latter incl. negroes. Executors—the wife and son Jonathan. Witnesses—Sarah Hart, Margaret Hart, Thomas Craven. Proved March 14, 1754. [In a footnote to the will it is said, that Rozzel was now the name of all three daughters].
1754, Mar. 6. Inventory, £216.12.6, incl. a negro man, £40; a negro wench and child, £55; made by Jeremiah Woolsey and James Adames.
1755, June 23. Bond of Thomas Roszell (Rozell), of Philadelphia Co., Pa., as Adm'r; Peter Rosell, of Sussex Co., N. J., fellowbondsman, the Executors named in the will having both died.
Hunt. Wills, 344 J.

1759, Apr. 29. Gready, Daniel, of Allentown, Monmouth Co.; will of. Directs, that proceeds of estate be sent, through Father Hardin of Philadelphia, to brothers John and James Gready in Thurlos, Barony of Eliogerty, County of "Tiprary" [Ireland], and substitutes his own Executor, John Bruce, as Executor of the last will of Cornelius Murphy. Witnesses—Daniel Robins, Moses Robins and Peter Bruere. Proved May 25, 1759; when John Bruce adds, that testator gave his "cloathing" to Nicholas Dun. Lib. 9, p. 328.

1759, May 9. Inventory, £73.6.9, incl. bonds, book debts and notes, £67.11.3; made by Peter Bruere and Daniel Robins.

1760, Sept. 3. Green, Samuel, of Hardwick, Sussex Co., yeoman; will of. Wife, Hannah, sole Executrix. "First" children—Sarah Severns, Samuel, Margaret Opdike, Richard and Ann Opdike. "Last" children—Adam, John, William, Daniel, George, Rebeckah and Mary, these last seven under age. Home-farm of 50 acres on the East side of Mill Creek, adjoining Jonathan Pettit; a mill and lot of 20 acres let to Charles Murry; 300 ac., formerly the home farm; 300 ac., incl. said mill, adjoining George Allen; 300 ac. next to the last, adjoining Anthony Morrice; 300 ac. more, and land in and about the Great Meadows. Personal property. Witnesses—Solomon Willits, Jr., Jonathan Willits, John Goodin. Proved Nov. 22, 1760.
Lib. 10, p. 471.

1760, —— ——. Inventory, of the personal estate, £226.13, incl. a large looking glass, £2; a silver cup and 7 silver spoons, £5; made by Thomas Robinson and Solomon Willits, Jr.

1754, Nov. 8. Green, Thomas, of "Willingboruh" Township, Burlington Co., yeoman; will of. Wife, Hannah. Children—two sons and three daughters, names not given. Real and personal estate. Executors—brothers Joseph Green and John Clark. Witnesses—Asher Woolman, Daniel Wills, John Green. Proved Dec. 7, 1754.
Lib. 7, p. 526.

1754, Nov. 22. Inventory, £171.13, by Asher Woolman and Thomas Buzby.

1754, Dec. 11. Michael Nutbold's account of the estate of Thomas Green. "This account compared with the Vouchers in presence of Edward Pennington, attorney to John Green and Ann Tree, both of Great Britain, and allowed of by Charles Read, Surrogate."

1754, Oct. 24. Green, William, Jr., of Trenton, Hunterdon Co., yeoman; will of. Mother, Mary Green. Brothers—Richard and George (under age). Children of eldest sister, Rebecka, viz., Richard More, William Moore and Eliza More, all under age. Children of youngest sister, Christian, viz., Ely Moses and Ephram Moore, all under age. Mentions Hezekiah, son of Benjamin Green, of Trenton. Real and personal estate. Executors—the mother and brother Richard. Witnesses—Charles Clark, Benjamin Clark, John Moore. Proved Dec. 19, 1754.
Lib. 8, p. 82.

1754, Dec. 24. Inventory, £275.13.7, incl. bills and bonds, £178.17.7; made by Charles Clark and John Moore.

1754, Aug. 17. Griffe, Edward, of the Borough of Elizabeth, Essex Co., cordwainer. Int. Susanna Griffe renounced and gave her right to John Ross. Witness—George Ross. Adm'r—John Ross, Jr., of Elizabeth, yeoman. Bondsman—George Ross, Jr., of same place.
Lib. F, p. 202.

1754, Aug. 18. Inventory, £45.18.1, by John Scudder and Daniel Perrine.

1755, March 4. Account by Adm'r. House and land sold for £138.11.

1752, Oct. 9. Griffith, Mary, of Burlington. Int. Bond of John Raworth, glover, as Adm'r; John van de Grift, cooper, fellow-bondsman, both of Burlington City.
Lib. 7, p. 306.

CALENDAR OF WILLS—1751-1760   135

1757, Aug. 22. Griggs, Daniel, of Amwell Township, Hunterdon Co.; will of. Wife, Jacomincha. Children—John, Joacham, Daniel, Samuel, Catline, Mary and Margaret. Home farm; land on Mount Carmel, bought of Charles Cox. Personal estate. Executors—the four sons. Witnesses—Samuel Hulluck (Hulick), Martin Schuffels (?), (signs in German script), Jacob Mattison. Proved Nov. 4, 1759.
Lib. 10, p. 124.

1758, Jan. 20. Griggs, John, of Tom's River, Monmouth Co., farmer. Int. Bond of Nicholas Veghte, of Somerset Co., principal creditor, as Adm'r; Barnt Griggs, of Middlesex Co., fellowbondsman.
Lib. F, p. 486.

1758, Mar. 27. Grimes, William, of Piles Grove, Salem Co., yeoman. Int. Inventory, £132.7.3, by John Murphy and Peter Johnson.
1758, June 6. Bond of Judith Grimes as Adm'x; Jacob Dubois, blacksmith, and John Murphy, weaver, fellowbondsmen, all of Piles Grove.
Lib. 9, p. 97.

1755, June 14. Gross, Benjamin, of Borough of Elizabeth, Essex Co. Int. Adm'r—Mica Howell, one of the principal creditors. Bondsman—William Harriman, cooper. Witnesses—Samuel Woodruff and Robert Ogden.
1755, July 4. Inventory, £6.13.9, by Thomas Pound and Micajah Dunn.
Lib. F, p. 265.

1749, July 19. Grover, James, of Middletown Township, Monmouth Co.; will of. Wife (not named). Children—James, Silvanus, Hannah and Rebecca. Homefarm on Fulling Brook; two lots near Jumping Brook; two cedar swamps, called the Round and Asher Cleayton's Swamp. Personal property, incl. a negro man. Executors—the two sons. Witnesses—John Eatton, William Lawrence, Jr., John Lippincott, Jr. Proved Jan. 1, 1753.
Lib. F, p. 90.
1753, Jan. 5. Inventory, £1176.16.7, incl., 4 doubloons, £24.5; 5 white servants' "time yet to come," £58; a negro man, £20; bonds, book debts, cash and mortgages, £629.17.1; made by Jacob Dennis, Josiah Holmes and Hugh Hartshorne.

1747, Dec. 9. Guest, John, of Middlesex Co.; will of. Wife (not named), and son, William, Executors. Other children spoken of. "Intres" (interests) in Bergen Co. Personal property. Witnesses—Peter Stryker, Gerret Stothoff. Proved March 3, 1755. Lib. F, p. 251.
1755, Mar. 19. Inventory; no values given; made by Derrick Ven Horsdol [Van Arsdale] and John Guest, father of dec'd., at New Brunswick. Note at bottom says: "This is an account taken of my brother John's estate, and I can find no other account among my father's papers. It was taken by the directions of my father, who was Ex'r to my brother John." Signed by "William Guest, Executor of John Guest, the Elder."

1757, Feb. 11. Guiberson, James, of Middlesex Co. Elizabeth Guiberson desires that letters be not given on the estate of her husband, unless he brings a note from her, or Isaac Rogers, of Allentown, who is principal creditor. Witness—George Danser.
1757, Feb. 24. "I quit my claim to administer on my father, James Giberson's, estate, and desire that letters be given to Isaac Rogers." Signed, "John Giberson." Witness—James Silver, Jr.

1757, March 21. "I give all my right to administer to John Tomson." Signed, "Isaac Rogers."
1757, Feb. 23. Inventory, £44.11, by G. Danser, John Height, Isaiah Shaw and Matthew Collins.
1762, Mar. 17. Account by the Adm'r, John Tomson, who has sold the estate for £58.3.2, all of which he has paid out.
Mid. Wills, 2973 L.

1747, Oct. 1. Gulick, Hendrick, of Somerset Co., farmer; will of. Children—Jocham, Derrick, Yocomyntie de Hart, Samuel, Catrin, Mary, Gerrebradi (a daughter), Hendrick, Peter and Autye. Children of daughter Alche. Real and personal estate. Executors—sons Jocham, Derrick and Samuel. Witnesses—Benjamin Emens, John Fine and Peter Berrien. Proved Jan. 6, 1758.   Lib. F, p. 484.

1731, Mar. 24. Gulick, Johannes, of "Rockehill," Somerset Co., farmer; will of. Wife, Rantsha. Children—Jocham, Jochamyntia, Fernandus, John and Minnah, all under age. Real and personal estate. Executors—his brothers, Hendrick, Jocham and Peter Guilick. Witnesses—Daniel Griggs, Thomas Stilwill, Lodewych Metseler. Proved July 23, 1755. (Proved in Hunterdon Co.).   Hunt. Wills, 365 J.

1757, Dec. 16. Hackney, Thomas, of Chester Township, Burlington Co., yeoman; will of. Children—Thomas, Elizabeth, Joseph and Rebecca (wife of George Matlack). Real and personal estate. Executors—the two sons. Witnesses—Samuel Atkinson, Jr., Anne Atkinson, Samuel Atkinson. Proved August 25, 1758.   Burl. Wills, 6667 C.
1758, Aug. 21. Inventory, £280.7, incl. bills, bonds and book debts, £22.14; an 8 day clock, £12; made by Samuel Stokes and Hugh Hollinshead.
1761, June 29. Account by the Executors.

1760, July 16. Hadden, Margaret, of Middlesex Co. Int. Adm'r—Thomas Hadden, of same Co., husband. Witness—John Smyth.
Lib. G, p. 257.

1754, Mar. 30. Haddock, Francis, of the Town and County of Gloucester; will of. Children—Margaret, and sons, but only John mentioned by name. Executors—son John Haddock and John Mickle. Witnesses—James Talman, David Brodrick, Thomas Cowgill. Proved May 16, 1754.   Lib. 8, p. 118.

1758, May 12. Haines, Abraham, now in Evesham Township, Burlington Co.; will of. Son, Thomas, to have my part of a tract devised to me and brother Isaac by my father in Virginia, in Frederick Co., on Back Creek, when Thomas is 21. Son, Benjamin, land I bought of Thomas Chinoph and land I bought of Charles Adams, all on the said Back Creek, when he is 21. Son, Nathan, my land on Bullskin in said Frederick Co., when he is 21. Sons Abraham and Simeon land when 21. Wife, Sarah, to have profits of lands. Son, Benjamin, all my right in the old Cedar swamp above Haines' Mills, which my father devised to me. Daughter, Sarah, £100. Executors—brothers Benjamin and Noah Haines, and my two friends James Cattle (Cattell), and Samuel Pearson, living in Frederick Co., Va. Witnesses—Abram Allen, Thomas Eves, Edmund Haines. Proved Oct. 1, 1760.
Lib. 10, p. 126.

CALENDAR OF WILLS—1751-1760 137

1757, Aug. 10. Haines, Abram, of Evesham Township, Burlington Co.; will of. Wife, Grace. Children—Abram, Isaac, Benjamin, Noah, Edmond, Isajah, Semeon (the last two under age), Mary (wife of William Sharp), and Agnis (wife of Joseph Hackney). Land, 900 acres, in Virginia; 55 ac. bought of brother, Richard Haines; 130 ac. upon Muskoneckon; 380 ac. bought of Elizabeth Sharp; 42 ac. bought of Thomas Sharp; 18 ac. adjoining, and 14 ac. bought of David Wills; 10 ac. of meadow, bought of Thomas Sharp; home-farm; 320 ac. bought of Hugh Sharp. Personal estate, incl. 6 negroes. Executors—sons Noah and Edmond. Witnesses—James Eldridge, Sarah Sharp, William Foster. Proved Feb. 1, 1758.
Lib. 8, p. 502.
1758, Jan. 5. Inventory, £1525.1.4, incl. bonds and mortgages, £688.5.1.; uncertain debts, £100.13.6; 4 negroes, £110; made by John Dearnal and James Cattell.
1763, May 24. Account by executors.

1746, Sept. 26. Haines, Amos, of Evesham Township, Burlington Co.; will of. Wife, Rebecca, sole Executrix. Daughters—Rebecca and Elisabeth, both under age. Real and personal estate. Witnesses—John Prickitt, Jacob Prickitt, Gabriel Blond. Proved Nov. 26, 1756.
Burl. Wills, 5687 C.
1756, Nov. 20. Inventory, £608.16, incl. a clock and books; a Dutch lad, £18; negroes, £100; made by Isaac Buzby and Micajah Wills.
1758, Nov. 20. Account by the Executrix.

1756, Dec. 4. Haines, Caleb, of Burlington, yeoman; will of. Children—Josiah (under age), Esther (wife of Amos Austin, who has sons Seth and Amos Austin), Mary (wife of Tanton Earle), Elizabeth (wife of Samuel Wright) and Patience (wife of Silas Crispen). Legacy to negroservants, already set free. Real and personal estate. Executors—sons-in-law, Samuel Wright and Silas Crispen. Witnesses—Joseph Burr, Hannah Burrough, John Woolman. Proved Jan. 3, 1757.
Lib. 8, p. 347.
1757, Dec. 23. Inventory, £624.3.8½, incl. bonds and book debts, £163.9.2; silver teaspoons and watch; made by Joseph Burr and John Deacon.
1760, Feb. 9. Account by the Executors.

1760, Apr. 4. Haines, George, Sr., of Northampton, Burlington Co., yeoman; will of. Wife, Margrett. Children—Isaac, George, Thomas, Mary, Elizabeth, Margrett, Ann and Levina. Real and personal estate. Executors—son, Isaac and son-in-law, Hezekiah Jones. Witnesses—John Bishop, Caleb Ogborn, Daniel Jones, Jr. Proved April 12, 1760.
Lib. 10, p. 27.
1760, Apr. 11. Inventory, £891.6.7, incl. cash and apparel, £137.6; bonds and book debts, £274.0.7; silver spoons and tea table, £3.17.6; a negro man, £5; a folio Bible, £2; made by Thomas Budd and George Briggs.

1760, June 4. Haines, George, Jr., of Burlington Co., yeoman. Son of George, petitions that Hezekiah Jones, of Northampton, said Co., be appointed his guardian. Bond of said Jones as such guardian; Isaac Hines (Haines) of said Co., fellowbondsman.
Burl. Wills, 6661 C; 6685 C.

1751, June 24. Haines, Nathan, Sr., of Evesham Township, Burlington Co., yeoman; will of. Wife, Sarah. Children—William, Amos, John, Nathan, Sarah and Mary. Legacy to sister's daughter, Prudence Brown. Homefarm; land between Daniel Hopewell and Philipp Wallis. Personal estate. Executors—sons William and Amos. Witnesses—Samuel Coles, Freedom Lippincott, Charles French, Peter Bryan. Proved Sept. 4, 1751. Burl. Wills, 4825 C.
  1751, Sept. 3. Inventory, £431.10, incl. (estimated) 250 bush. of wheat and rye, £31.5; 450 bush. of Indian corn standing, £33.15; a neagro woman, £5; made by Samuel Coles and Joshua Ballinger.

1748, Jan. 17. Haines, Thomas, of Northampton, in Burlington Co., yeoman; will of. Sons—Daniel and Thomas, 5 shillings each; George, plantation where I live; Amos, £10. Six children named, viz., Daniel, Thomas, George, Amos, Anne (wife of William Hooten) and Margaret (wife of Thomas Busby). Executor—son George. Witnesses—Abel Shinn, Walker Atkinson, John Burr, Jr. Proved Aug. 30, 1753.
  1753, Sept. 1. Inventory, £340.8.10, by Samuel Woolston and James Wills. Burl. Wills, 5197 C.

1752, Mar. 24. Haines, William, of Northampton, Burlington Co., yeoman; will of. Sons—Nathaniel and Jeremiah, latter sole Executor. Granddaughter, Prudence Brown, Cedar swamp at Wesickamaning in said Co.; other real and personal estate. Witnesses—Mary Erwin, Samuel Reeve, John Woolman. Proved April 29, 1754.
Lib. 8, p. 99.

1757, Nov. 28. Haines, William, of Greenwich Township, Gloucester Co., yeoman; will of. Wife, Sarah. Children—Elizabeth, Mary, Sarah, John and William, the last two under age. Land on Woodberry Creek; home farm, in which the mother still has an interest; personal property, Executors—the wife and brother, Jacob Spicer. Witnesses—John Brown, Thomas Rambo, John Walker. Proved May 23, 1758. Lib. 9, p. 70.
  1758, May 3. Inventory, £351.8.10, incl. bills, bonds, book debts and cash, £73.4.3; a watch; made by Joshua Lord, Jr., and John Brown.

1759, May 21. Haines, William, of Piles Grove Township, Salem Co., yeoman; will of. Wife, Elizabeth. Sons and daughters, names not given. Real and personal estate. Executors—the wife and Samuel Lippincott. Witnesses—George Mackniccol, Michael Richman and Jacob Richman. Proved June 13, 1759. Lib. 9, p. 377.
  1759, June 12. Inventory, £240.16.1, incl. books, £1.2; made by Elisha Bassett and George McNichol.

1760, June 6. Hains, Abraham, Jr., of Evesham Township, Burlington Co. Inventory, £750.9, incl. purse and apparel, £512.3, made by Joshua Ballinger and Enoch Roberts, affirmed by Benjamin Haines and James Cattell, the executors of his will. (No will at Trenton).
Book 10, p. 126.
  1765, July 3. Account by the Executors.

1754, Jan. 12. Hains, John, of Greenwich Township, Gloucester Co., yeoman; will of. Wife, Jane. Sons—William and David. Grandson, John, son of David. Land in Goshen Township, Penna.; homestead. Personal estate. Executors—the wife and son William. Witnesses

—William Gerrard, Thomas Robson, Joshua Lord. Proved March 16, 1754. Glouc. Wills, 542 H.
1754, Mar. 2. Inventory, £193.17, incl. bonds, £89.5.9; books £1; made by Jacob Cozens and James Cooper.

1752, Mar. 23. Hains, Joseph, of Evesham, Burlington Co. Int. Inventory, £293.8.9, incl. apparel, cash, bills, bonds and book debts, £186.7.4; made by William Foster and William Sharp.
1752, Apr. 1. Bond of Patience, his widow, as Adm'x; William Sharp, yeoman, of Evesham, fellowbondsman. Lib. 7, p. 301.
1763, Apr. 11. Account by Thomas Smith, husband of Patience Hains, late Adm'x of Joseph Hains. The accountant charges £336.-13.3. against the estate for debts paid to John Enoch, Emanuel Stratton, William Sharp, Daniel Garwood, Daniel Park, William Cooper, Henry Cooper, John Tanner, Robert Howe, Thomas Guinnot, Jacob Prickett, Robert Hill, Amos Sharp. Zeb. Rossell, Mathias Brooks, William Austin, Jonathan Haines, Richard Perry, Joseph Lewis, D. Hale's widow, Mary West, William Pettitt, William Garwood, Thomas Atkinson, John Burr, Charles Brookfield, Enoch Strattan, Francis Austin, Zach. Rossell, Absalom Thomas, John Endicott, Henry Paxson, Hab. Eayre, John Small, George Munroe, Thomas Rodman, Rece Price, Rebecca Hains, G. Mifflin, John Engle, Zacheria Prickett, Jonathan Austin, John Goldy, Elizabeth DeGuele (?), William Wilkins, George Hains, Thomas Bechinhead (?), John Sharp, James Dobbin, John Simons, Amos Haines, D. Jonathan Smith, Benjamin, Carline, Enoch Hains, Joshua Bispham, Charity Garwood, Hudson Middleton, Jacob Lamb, Abram Haines, Richard Cameron, George Marple, Samuel Moore, Thomas Joyce, Daniel Lippincott, Job Hains, Benjamin Springer and William Foster.

1756, Mar. 27. Hall, Ann, of Alloways Creek, Salem Co. Int. Bond of Peter Smith as Adm'r; John Fitz Patrick fellowbondsman, both of Alloway Creek, yeoman. Lib. 9, p. 85.
1756, ———. Inventory, £50.5.2, by John Fitz Patrick and Francis Test.

1760, Mar. 4. Hall, Bartholomew, of Mansfield, Burlington Co., yeoman; will of. Gives real estate, derived from dec'd. brother Thomas Hall, of Mansfield, cordwainer and personal property to father, Henry Hall, and sisters, Elizabeth Hutch, Martha Gibbs, Nancy Thomas, Lydia Wells, Polly Hall and Hannah Hall. Executor—Thomas Biddle. Witnesses—William Thompson, Dinnis O Nale (O'Neal), John Grimes. Proved May 5, 1760. Lib. 10, p. 23.
1760, Apr. 30. Inventory, £10.5.6, incl. a book, £1.13; made by William Potts and Gilbert Smith.

1751, Novbr. 20. Hall, Burgess, of Burlington Co. Account of the estate by the Adm'x, Abigail Hall, who has increased it to £242.3.8., by overplus house was sold for, "more than paid Henry Woodro." Debts paid to Uriah Kerll, Robert Hartshorn, Joseph Scattergood, widow Shaw, John Thorn, Israell Buttler, John Flinton, Doctor Hevil, Joseph Bordin, Moses English, Beasy Lovel, Anthony Sykes, Joseph Richards, Isaac Gibbs, Benoney Grigorey, Philipp Merriott, John Hatch, John Imley, William Lawrence, John Horner, John Cox, Ambros Field, John Beck, Robert Field, Preston Vanlaw, Robert Ashton, Charles Taylor, Joseph Field, Thomas Folkes, Jacob Taylor, Joseph Wright, John Sikes, Robert Wills and Benett & Murell as surviving partners of the firm of Benett, Murell & Hall. (For Will, etc., see Vol. XXX, N. J. Archives, p. 211).

1759, Feb. 22.—Hall, Edward, of Pilesgrove Township, Salem Co., labourer; will of. Brother, Elisha Hall, under age. Sisters—Elizabeth Highter and Mary Hall. Personal estate. John van Meter, sole Executor. Witnesses—Ephraim van Meter, Jeremiah Garrison and Joseph van Meter. Proved June 5, 1759. Lib. 9, p. 355.

1759, May 30. Inventory, £21.3.8, by Ephraim and Joseph van Meter.

1748, Sept. 24. Hall, George, Sr., of the South Branch of Rariton River, Somerset Co., yeoman; will of. Children—George, Thomas, Edward, Angletie (wife of Dirck Middagh), Elizabeth (wife of Frederick Morris), Mary (wife of Thomas Rock). Grandchildren, i. e., children of son Henry, dec'd, and his wife Nelltia, still living, viz., Ootie, Mary, George, John, Henry and Thomas. Real and personal estate, incl. slaves. Executors—sons George, Thomas and Edward. Witnesses—Bernardus Ver Bryck, William Dealy, James Lyne. Codicil of Jan. 15, 1752, repeats, that "the wife of son Thomas had owned and confessed that her child, Thomas, who was born within two or three months after Marriage Celebrated between her and my said Son Thomas, was not his Child, but the Child of another Man," and directed that this child is not to share in what is given to son Thomas. Witnesses Dirck Schuyler, Ann Lyne, James Lyne. Proved April 20, 1752. Lib. F, p. 43.

1752, Apr. 23. Inventory, £757.4.4, by Henry Stevens and B. Bryte.

1758, May 5. Hall, George, Jr., of the South Branch, Raritan River, Somerset Co.; will of. Wife, Blandina. Children—George, Anne (who has daughter Sarah) and Mary. Real and personal estate. Executors—brothers, Edward Hall and Thomas Hall, with Henry Stevens and Johannis Pettinger. Witnesses—Richard Persell, John Cock, Jr., and Lawrance Demott. Proved August 16, 1758.

Lib. F, p. 545.

1758, Aug. 1. Inventory, £188.4.6, incl. books, £1.6; 8 bush. of wheat, £1.12; made by Teunis Middagh and R. V. Bryck.

1759, Aug. 6. Hall, Jedidia, of Essex Co. Int. Adm'r—Nathaniel Rusco, of Essex Co. Bondsman—Abraham Cadmus, of said Co. Witness—Thomas Bartow. Lib. G, p. 92.

1759, Nov. 6. Hall, John, of Essex Co. Int. Adm'r—Nathaniel Rusco of Essex Co. Bondsman—Abraham Cadmus, of said Co. Witness—Thomas Bartow. Lib. G, p. 92.

1755, July 12. Hall, Joseph, of Elsinborough, Salem Co. Int.. Bond of Ann, widow, as Adm'x; John Fitzpatrick and Peter Brynbery, both of said Co., fellowbondsmen. Lib. 8, p. 235.

1755, ——— ——. Inventory, £63.17.5, incl. books; made by John Fitzpatrick.

1752, June 19. Hall, Richard, of Somerset Co., yeoman; will of. Wife, Elizabeth. Children—Richard, Tobias, Thomas, Rebackah and Elizabeth. Real and personal estate. Executors—the wife and

CALENDAR OF WILLS—1751-1760 141

Tobias Denyck. Witnesses—John Bready, Cornelius vaen Kaemepen (van Kempen), Andris Pouelson, John Cavelier. Proved Nov. 27, 1752. Lib. H, 2, p. 116.
1752, Dec. 7. Inventory, £1478.17.9¾, by Henry Stevens and George Hall.

1752, Feb. 28. Hall, Samuel, of Mountholly, in Northampton, Burlington Co., "Doctor of Phisic;" will of. Wife, Elizabeth, sole Executrix, Daughter, Mary. Children of sisters Elizabeth and Mary. Daughters of testator's father, Charles Hall, of Westerleigh Parish, Co. of Gloucester, England. Legacy of 1s. to Mary, daughter of Moses Carter of Walten Parish, Co. of Somerset, England, "to whom I was once married, who wickedly broke her marriage covenants with me and frequented the company of another man." Witnesses—Josiah White, Rebeca White, Thomas Stowe, John Woolman. Proved April 6, 1752. Burl. Wills, 5011 C.
1752, Mar. 25. Inventory, £478.12.4, incl. bills, bonds and book debts, £234.2.7; a clock; made by James Lippincott and John Woolman.

1759, July 13. Hall, Theodoras, of Amwell, Hunterdon Co. Int. Inventory, £10.3.6, by William Hogeland and David Cuming.
1759, Sept. 23. Bond of Gartrude Hall, of Amwell, as Adm'x; Joseph Howell, of Kingwood, said Co., fellowbondsman. Lib. 9, p. 454.

1760, Mar. 6. Hall, Thomas, of Mansfield, Burlington Co. Int. Bond of widow, Mabel Hall, of Burlington City, as Adm'x; William Hammell and James Craft, both of said Co., yeomen, fellowbondsmen.
Lib. 9, p. 409.
1760, Apr. 30. Inventory, £167.2.7, incl. bills, bonds and book debts, £110.16.2; an apprentice's time; made by William Potts, Joseph Archer and Gilbert Smith.

1756, Mar. 23. Hall, William, of Somerset Co.; will of. Nephews—John, George, Edward and Thomas Hall and Frederick Mourise, heirs and, with exception of John, Executors of real and personal estate. Witnesses—Benjamin Low, Garrit van Zandt, Are van Note and Madalena van Zandt. Proved April 7, 1758. Lib. F, p. 537.
1758, Apr. 19. Inventory, £224.9, incl. 9 bush. of wheat, £2.0.6; 3 negroes, £65; made by Martynus Hoagelant and Henry Stevens.

1757, Nov. 13. Hammit, John, of Waterford, Gloucester Co., yeoman; will of. Wife, Sarah. Children—John, Aaron, Prudance, Hannah, Ann and Sarah, all under age. Executors—brother, George Hammitt, and Joshua Stokes. Witnesses—Benjamin Pine and Abraham Allen. Proved Dec. 17, 1757. Lib. 9, p. 67.
1757, Dec. 5. Inventory, £199.4.9, incl. 2 white servants' time, £20; "remainder of the time in the plantation, £15; made by Isaac Buzby and Benjamin Pine.

1752, Aug. 19. Hampton, Edward, of Gloucester, Gloucester Co., yeoman. Int. Inventory, £132.16, incl. a servant, £15; "Hutanchels belonging to Husbendre Business," £8.17; made by Richard Cheesman Gabriel Daveis (Davis).
1752, Sept. 29. Bond of William Hampton as Adm'x; Henry Sparks, fellowbondsman, both of Gloucester Co., yeomen. Lib. 8, p. 164.
1755, May 28. Account by the Administrator.

1756, Oct. 24. Hampton, William, of Gloucester Twsp. and County, yeoman; will of. Children—John, Mary Zane, Rossanna Albertson, Sarah Baggs, Judeth Anderson and William, the last sole Executor of real and personal estate. Witnesses—Judath Anderson, Matthias Albertson, Joseph Harrison. Proved Feb. 11, 1757. Lib. 8, p. 386.
    1756, Dec. 10. Inventory, £136.9.11, incl. bills and bonds, £84.19.11; made by John Chew and Gabreil Daveis.

1758, Oct. 21. Hance, Samuel, of Burlington Co., labourer; will of. Mother, Elizabeth Hance and friend, Priscilla Page, heiresses. John Newbold to be Executor of personal estate. Witnesses—Mary Holloway, Isaac De Cow, Josach Sitter (?). Proved Nov. 4, 1758.
Lib. 9, p. 118.
    1758, Nov. 3. Inventory, £74.5.7; incl. deed bills, bonds and other debts, £43.18; made by Samuel Satterthwait and Isaac DeCow.

1757, Nov. 24. Hancock, Edward, of Burlington City. Int. Rebekah, widow, declines the administration in favour of Joseph Hancock, of said City.
    1757, Dec. 3. Bond of Joseph Hancock as Adm'r; Daniel Ellis fellowbondsman, both of Burlington. Lib. 8, p. 518.

1756, Dec. 15. Hancock, Thomas, of Salem, Salem Co. Int. Inventory, £539.5, incl. cash, bonds, notes and book debts, £95.13; a clock, desk, looking glass and oval table, £17.10; a silver "creme" jug. spoons and tea tongs; books and maps, a negro man and negro girl, £90; made by Joshua Thompson and Aaron Bradway.
    1757, Feb. 23. Bond of his widow, Susannah Hancock, as Adm'x; William Hancock, Jr., and Aaron Bradway fellowsbondmen, all of Salem Co. Lib. 9, p. 14.
    1758, July 28. Account by the Administratrix.

1759, May 11. Hand, Abraham, of Fairfield, Cumberland Co., yeoman; will of. Wife, Hannah, sole heiress of real and personal estate, but if she should have a child within ten months "after my decease," then said child is to have all the real property. Executors —the wife and father, Benjamin Chard. Witnesses—Josiah Ogden, Jeriel Bowen, Jeremiah Buck. Proved June 21, 1759. Lib. 9, p. 333.
    1759, May 24. Inventory, £69.16.1, by Joseph Newcomb and William Newcomb.

1749, June 5. Hand, Elisha, of Cape May Co; will of. Wife, Lydia. Daughter, Experience. Brothers Silas and Elihu Hand to be remaindermen. Homefarm, 500 acres of upland and marsh at Nummies, personal estate. Executors—the wife and brother-in-law, John Eldredge, Trustees, brother Silas Hand and brother-in-law, Jacob Spicer. Witnesses—Nathaniel Foster, Thomas Bancroft, Ebenezer Johnson. Proved August 8, 1753. Cape May Wills, 164 E.
    1753, July 20. Inventory, £470.11.6, incl. cash and debts, £117.9.3; a silver watch; books, £5.13.6; household goods, plantation utensils, shoemakers' tools, £142.8.3¾; a negro man, £45; a negro woman, £35; made by Elijah Hughes and Jacob Spicer.
    1755, Jan. 22. Experience, the daughter named above, petitions that Jacob Spicer be confirmed as her guardian.
    1755, Jan. 29. Bond of Jacob Spicer, of Cape May Co., as such guardian; Gabriel Blond fellowbondsman.

1758, June 21. Hand, George, Sr., of Cape May Co., yeoman; will of. Children—Thomas, Jeremiah, Daniel and Sarah Stillwill. Grandchildren—Thomas, son of Jeremiah; issue of daughter Eunice Norton, to-wit: Hannah (wife of David Smith) George and Mary (wife of Job Young); children of dec'd son George, viz., Elias, George, Sarah, Rhoda and Lois; children of dec'd son, Nathan, viz., Japhet, Nathan, Stephen and Hannah. Legacy to Presbyterian Meeting House at Cold Spring. Homefarm at Cape Island; land at the Thicket; land called the Five Mile Beach. Personal estate. Executors—the three sons. Witnesses——James Whilldin, John Foster, John Coulon. Proved August 1, 1758. Lib. 9, p. 18.

1758, July 29. Inventory, £397.5.10, incl. bonds, book debts, cash and notes, £292.15.4; made by John Eldredge and James Whilldin.

1759, Dec. 26. Hand, Jeremiah, of the Lower Precinct, Cape May Co.; will of. Wife, Rachel, sole Executrix. Children—David, Sarah, Jane, Deborah, Rachel, Douesalah (?) and Emily (testator speaks of the last five as five daughters). Real and personal estate. Witnesses—Daniel Lawrence, Thomas Hand. Proved Feb. 5, 1760.
Lib. 9, p. 407.

1760, Jan. 25. Inventory, £188.10.11, by Richard Stites and Isaiah Hand.

1756, Nov. 18. Hand, Levi, of Cape May Co. Int. Inventory, £80.13.10, by Edward Church and Jacob Richardson.

1756, Dec. 1. Bond of Mary Hand as Adm'x; Jacob Richardson and Edward Church fellowbondsmen, all of Cape May, said Co.
Cape May Wills, 177 E.

1754, Nov. 19. Hand, Lydia, of Cape May Co.; will of. Daughter, Experience, sole heiress, under guardianship of Jacob Spicer, and, in case of her death without issue, the estate is to be divided between Hannah, (daughter of William Eldredge), Elisha Hughes, Lydia, (daughter of John Eldredge), Hannah (daughter of Nathan Hand), Jeremiah (son of Ezekiel Eldredge, dec'd), Nancy, (daughter of Rev. Daniel Lawrence). Legacy to Presbyterian Meetinghouse, "now erecting in the Lower Prescinct of this County." Executor—Jacob Spicer. Witnesses—Samuel Eldredge, Mary Eldredge, Isaac Whildin. Proved March 31, 1755. Lib. 8, p. 153.

———, ——— —. Inventory, £227.5.10, by Elijah Hughes and James Whilldin in December, 1754, January, 1755, and February, 1756. Exceptions taken to the Inventory before Henry Young, Surrogate for Cape May Co., by Jacob Spicer. The appraisers include a turkey, 22s.6d.; the apparel for John Hughes and Judith Brooks, apprentices; open accounts against Thomas Johnson, Edward Saunders and Josena Schillinks, (all absconded), James Taylor, Elizabeth Nicoles and Richard Forster (all insolvent), and a pair of family spoon moulds belonging to John Hand, father-in-law of deceased.

1759, ——— —. Account by the Executor, Jacob Spicer, who reports the estate as £536.15., incl. the inventory of £227.5.10; rents of the plantations at Coxe Hall, £26.18.6, and at "Nummies," £22.5.10, left by her husband, Elisha Hand, in his will, £208.13.5.

1755, Apr. 30. Hand, Nathan, of Cape May Co; will of. Wife, Lydia. Children—Japheth, Nathan, Stephen and Hannah, all under age. Real and personal estate. Executors—the wife, Ezekiel Mulford and Isaiah

Hand. Witnesses—John Eldridge, John Leek, Jacob Crowell. Proved Oct. 31, 1755. Lib. 8, p. 226.
1756, May 11. Inventory, £167.12.9, incl. a servant man, £8; made by John Eldredge and James Whilldin.

1758, Oct. 17. Hand, Nathan, of Cape May, gentleman; will of. Wife, Rachel. Children—Nathan, Johannah and Rachel. Real and personal estate. Executors—the wife and son-in-law, Elijah Hand. Witnesses—Thomas Smith, Elihu Smith, Edward Foster. Proved Nov. 13, 1758. Lib. 9, p. 151.
1758, Nov. 16-18. Inventory, £542.14.1, incl. cash, apparel and negroes, £207.9.3; cattle, horses, sheep, hogs and geese, £212.4; made by Jeremiah Hand and Thomas Smith.
1762, May 18. Account of the Adm'rs, showing balance of £402.15.1.

1752, Jan. 4. Hand, Nathaniel, of Cape May Co., weaver; will of. Wife, Hannah. Sons—Timothy, Ezekiel, Eleazer and Henry. Home farm; another farm of 120 acres; 52 ac. bought of Isaac Whildine, Bud's Island, and 26 ac. bought of Joseph Whildine. Personal estate. Executors—son Ezekiel and Elijah Hughes. Witnesses—Eleazar Crawford, Joseph Fencher (Fancher), John Leek. Proved May 19, 1752. Cape May Wills, 159 E.
1752, June 24. Inventory, £163.9.4., incl. bonds, book debts and cash, £57.17.11; made by Elisha Hand and Ebenezer Johnson.
1754, May 30. Account by the Executors.

1758, Oct. 3. Hand, Thomas, of Middle Precinct, Cape May Co., yeoman; will of. Wife, Elisabeth. Children—Gidion, Neri, David Thomas, some of them under age, or other children, names not given, for whose "bringing up" the wife is given the use of the personal estate. Land at Mores on the Bayside of said Co., between brother Nathan Hand, Pond Creek and the Bay; land, at Tuckahoe; land at Gravity Run on the seaside. Personal property. Executors—the wife, with sons Gideon and David. Witnesses—Thomas Hewet, Thomas Stites, Nathaniel Jenkins. Proved Nov. 25, 1760. Lib. 10, p. 224.
1760, Nov. 21. Inventory, £358.6.2, by Lewis Cresse and Nathaniel Jenkins.

1751, May 7. Hanley, Thomas, of Salem Co. Int. Bond of Christopher Hanley as Adm'r; John Andrews and William Taft, both of Salem Co., and Peter Rambo, of Gloucester Co., fellowbondsmen.
Lib. 7, p. 104.

1753, Jan. 12. Hanly, Christopher, of Salem Co., butchers. Int. Edward Test, Daniel, Es. Kent, Samuel Tyler, John Whittall, William Taft and James Smith, creditors, request, that John Stow be made Adm'r.
1753, Jan. 20. Bond of John Stow, of Salem Co., practicioner in physics, as Adm'r; John Gosling, Jr., and James Smith, both of said Co., yeoman, fellowbondsmen. Lib. 7, p. 307.

1759, May 14. Hanson, John, of Burlington Co. Int. Bond of Thomas Shinn, as Adm'r; Zachariah Rossell fellowbondsman, both of Northampton, said Co. Burl. Adm'ns, 193.

1750-'51 Feb. 17. Harbert, Walter, of Springfield Township, Burlington Co., yeoman; will of. Wife, Deborah. Children—George

(eldest son) and four others, names not given. Real and personal estate. Executors—the wife and Edward Tonkin. Witnesses—Eleazar Fenton, Enoch Fenton, John Betts. Proved ———, 1751.
1751, ——— ———. Inventory, £169.0.10, by James Lippincott and John West. Burl. Wills, 4835 C.

1755, Jan. 20. Harbert, Dr. Walter, of Shrewsbury, Monmouth Co.; will of. Wife, Pheby. Daughters—Meriby Curtis, Sarah Worth, Lydia Brewer and Deborah Herbert. Children of son Walter, viz., George, John, Timothy, Isaac and Deborah. Children of son Paul (?), viz., John, Peter and Rebecca. Children of son Timothy, viz., Jemime, Levina, Peter, Timothy and Edward. Real and personal estate. Executors—David Curtis, Sr., and James Irons, Sr. Witnesses—Gersham Bills, William Morton and John Morris, Jr. Proved Jan. 27, 1755. Lib. F, p. 250.
1755, Jan. 28. Inventory, £298.14.6, incl. "Docktor's Medisons, instruments, vyols, pots, book and chest," £4.1; a Bible, 20s.; bills and book debts, £56.12.4; a silver spoon and watch, £6; made by Gisbert Longstreet, Samuel Osborn and Gersham Bills.

1755, Apr. 8. Hardin, Thomas, of Amwell Township, Hunterdon Co., tailor; will of. Divides estate between father, mother, brothers Samuel and Martin, and sisters Susannah and Ann. Executors—brother Samuel and Garrard Williamson. Witnesses—Martin Hardin and George Thomson. Proved April 21, 1755. Lib. 8, p. 168.
1755, Apr. 19. Inventory, £113.5.6, incl. bonds and book debts, £93.5; made by Ichabod Leigh and John Jewell.

1752, ——— ———. Harker, James, of Morris Co. Int. Rachell, widow, refuses to administer on his estate in favour of son, Daniel Harker.
1752, Apr. 10. Bond of Daniel Harker as Adm'r; John Anderson and Thomas Scott fellowbondsmen, all of Morris Co.
1752, Apr. 10. Inventory, £794.16.10, incl. bills, bonds and book debts, £332.10; 41 horses, mares and colts, £150; made by John Anderson and Thomas Scott. Sussex Wills, 312 J.
1755, Mar. 26. Account by the Administrator.

1750, Nov. 9. Harman, Susanna, of Penn's Neck, Salem Co., widow; will of. Children—David and John Straughan, Ann Danielson and Samuel Straughan. Executors—son John and son-in-law, Gabriel Danielson. Witnesses—David Price, George Trenchard. Proved April 5, 1751.
1751, April 6. Inventory, £65.7.0, by Andrew Sinnickson and Jeremiah Baker. Lib. 7, p. 255.

1758, May 12. Harmon, Thomas, of Pequanac, Morris Co., soldier; will of. Wife, Mary, sole Executrix. Sons—William, Lemuel, Thomas and Jonathan (under age). Real and personal estate. Witnesses—David Hambelton, Daniel Jerolman, Philip Price. Proved Dec. 28, 1758. Lib. G, p. 23.

1758, Mar. 28. Harriman, Joseph, of Morris Co., yeoman. Int. Bond of John Harriman as Adm'r; Lemuel Bowers fellowbondsman, both of said Co. Lib. F, p. 517.

1758, Feb. 13. Inventory, £135.0.5, by Daniel Tuttle and Ephraim Price, Jr.
1759, Mar. 23. Account by the Administrator.

1759, Nov. 6. Harris, Elijah, of Piscataway, Middlesex Co., yeoman; will of. Wife, Emme. Children—all under age, of whom only son William is mentioned by name; an expected child. Brothers—Benjamin, Samuel, Isaac and Jacob, remaindermen. Real and personal estate. Executors—Reune Runyon, Esq., and Jeremiah Field, both of Piscataway. Witnesses—Andrew Conine, Stynche Cussaar and Elias v. Court. Proved May 19, 1760. Lib. G, p. 219.
1760, June 2. Inventory, £163.16.7, incl. a Bible and other books, 10s., made by Joseph Ross and Benjamin Field.

1754, Mar. 21. Harris, George, of Bergen Co., yeoman; will of. Wife, Elen. Children—David, John, Daniel, Ezeghiel, Mary. Land held in partnership with John Bardan and Johannes Cadmus. Home farm. Personal property. Executors—the wife and son John. Witnesses—Philipp Schuyler, Daniel Hennion, Johannes Hennion. Proved Sept. 17, 1754. Lib. F, p. 234.

1755, Mar. 12. Harris, Jeremiah, of Fairfield, Cumberland Co. Int. Inventory, £297.16, incl. books; book debts, £55.4.3; made by David Wescott and Jeremiah Buck.
1755, Apr. 5. Bond of his widow, Abigail Harris, as Adm'x; Jonathan Stratton fellowbondsman, both of Fairfield. Lib. 8, p. 150.

1759, Oct. 29. Harris, Mercy, widow, of Piscataway, Middlesex Co. Int. Adm'r—Benjamin Harris, of Somerset Co., yeoman. Bondsmen—Elijah Harris and Michael Schooley. Lib. G, p. 106.
1759, Oct. 29. Inventory, £104.0.4, by Michael Schooley and John Miller.

1759, Mar. 6. Harris, Thomas, Jr., of Fairfield, Cumberland Co. Int. Inventory, £343.19.1, incl. books; bills, bonds and book debts, £121.3.10; made by David Wescote and Joseph Ogden.
1759, Mar. 9. Bond of his widow, Violetta Harris, as Adm'x; Jonathan Lorance and Nathan Lorance both of Fairfield, fellowbondsmen. Lib. 9, p. 210.

1754, Aug. 20. Harris, William, Sr., of Piscataqua Township, Middlesex Co., yeoman; will of. Wife, Mersey (second one). Children—John, James, Sarah, Elizabeth, Mary, Rachel, Mersey, Benjamin, William, Samuel, Thomas, Isaac, Jacob, Peter and Elijah. Grandchildren, i. e., Sarah's first two daughters, Mersey and Sarah. Legacy to the Presbyterian Congregation of Bound Brook, Bridgewater Township, Somerset Co. Homefarm, 50 acres adjoining Johanes Sebring and William Olden; farm on Raritan Road between Daniel Hendricks and John Anderson in Bridgewater Township, Somerset Co. Personal property, incl. negroes. Executors—the wife, son, John and son-in-law, Nathaniel Maning. Witnesses—Hesther Miller, John Miller, Elias van Court. Proved Nov. 21, 1757. Lib. F, p. 469.
1757, Nov. 23. Inventory, £652.1.1, incl. bills, bonds and book debts, £390.4.7; a large Bible, £1; other books 12s.; a looking glass 8s.; made by David Fitzrandolph and Reune Runyon.

CALENDAR OF WILLS—1751-1760   147

1757, Mar. 22. Harris, William, of Lebanon Township, Hunterdon Co. Int. Inventory, £47.19, incl. 67 bush, of rye, 43 do. of wheat, 8 do. of oats, 9 do. of "Ingian" corn; made by John Bowlby and Joseph Hegaman, Jr.
    1757, July 2. Hunterdon Co., Bond of David Parke, of Sussex Co., as Adm'r; Cornelius Anderson, of Bathlehem, farmer, fellowbondsman.   Lib. 8, p. 500.

1756, Nov. 24. Harrison, Ganatta, of Perth Amboy; will of. Children—Mary Lyell, Ganennetta Harrison and William Harrison. Nephew, Campbell Stevens. Granddaughter—Ganennetta Harrison. Mrs. Mary Forster and Mary Moore, sister of dec'd. husband. Land and share of mines at Rockyhill, house and lot in Amboy. Personal estate, incl. £1,200, N. Y. currency, due from David Ogden, of Newark, and William Cox, of Philadelphia; a negro wench and negro boy. Executors—the three children. Witnesses—Elizabeth Leslie, John Smyth and Jonathan Deare. Proved Sept. 6, 1758.   Lib. F, p. 550.

1753, Jan. 10. Harrison, George, of Newark, Essex Co.; will of. Wife, Azubah. Children—Caleb and Phebe Camp. Real and personal estate. Executors—the wife and son, Caleb. Witnesses—John Cranstone, Robert Sandford, David Ogden. Proved March 8, 1753.
    Lib. F, p. 104.

1758, May 27. Harrison, Ouke, of Bridgewater Township, Somerset Co., blacksmith; will of. Wife (not named). Children spoken of as small, but names not given. Real and personal estate. Executors—brother, Matthew Harrison, and Isaac Powel of said Co. Witnesses—Tobias van Norden, William Riddel and Elias V. Court. Proved June 26, 1758.   Lib. F, p. 528.

1760, Aug. 10. Harrison, Rachell, of Middlesex Co.; will of. Divides personal property between son, John Harrison (absent), niece, Jehannah Randolph, friends Mather Bloodgood, Mary Rattoon, Catrin Lets, Mary and Hanah Johnston, nurse Mrs. Colins and Sarah Higgins; Edward Higgins to manage affairs (Executor?), till son, John, comes home. Witnesses—Marsh Noe and Elisabeth Letts. Proved [no date of proof; probably 1760].   Mid. Wills, 3511 L.

1752, July 27. Hart, Edward, of Hopewell, Hunterdon Co. Int. Bond of John Hart as Adm'r; Daniel Hart, fellowbondsman, both of Hopewell.   Hunt. Wills, 313 J.
    1752, July 28. Inventory, £73.4.9., incl. 2 Bibles and a dictionary £1.10; 5 silver spoons and 6 tea spoons, £6; book debts, £13.3.9; made by Joseph Tindall and Benjamin Temple.

1752, Sept. 28. Hart, John, Sr., of Hopewell, Hunterdon Co.; will of. Wife, Sarah. Children—John, Richard, Mary, Elizabeth and Joanna. Real and personal estate, incl. money in hands of William Welling. Executors—the wife and son Richard. Witnesses—Joseph Hart, Benjamin Temple, John Guild. Proved March 17, 1753.   Lib. 7, p. 403.

1751, Hart, Joseph, son of Robert, merchant, of Salem, petitions that his uncle, James Bayard, of Cecil Co., Maryland, merchant, be appointed his Guardian.

1751, Apr. 13. Bond of James Bayard as such Guardian; Robert Hartshorne, of Burlington City, attorney-at-law, fellowbondsman.
Salem Wills, 918 Q.

1752, June 27. Hartshorne, Robert, of Burlington, attorney-at-law. Int. Bond of widow, Hannah Hartshorne, as Adm'x; Samuel Smith, merchant, fellowbondsman, both of Burlington.
Lib. 7, p. 424; Lib. 16, p. 473.

1752, Aug. 14. Inventory, £5,605.11, incl. a gold watch and diamond seal, £25; a gold stockbuckle, 11 pwt., 6 grs., £3; a pair of silver shoe buckles, 10s.; 246 oz., 6 pwt., 8 grs., of wrought plate, at 8/6, £104.10.8; 13 maps, £1.5; 40 ells of Ozinbriggs, at 1/5, £2.16.8; a large looking glass, £6.10; 6 New England chairs, with leather bottoms, £2.14; five negro slaves, £173; a chaise, £20; another, £25; 60 bush. of Indian corn, £4.10; books, £123.5; debts due by Benjamin Jones, Lot Ridgway, Henry Worthington, Joseph Pearson, John Lawrence, John Poole, John and Peter Covenhover, Thomas Duell, John Bacon, Michael Newbold, Daniel Smith, Daniel Huddy, Mathew Allen, Thomas Shinn, Ebenezer Tomlinson, Osten Hicks, James Talman, Abigail Hall, Salomon Burr and John Buzby, £2,082.7.11; doubtful and unsettled debts due by Thomas Clayton, Thomas Lenord, Charles Reed, William Hugg, Joseph Worrell, Nathan Watson, Henry Paxton, William Freinen, Philo Leeds, Benett Bard, Richard Bowlby, Joseph Ballenger, Peter Marriage, Thomas Hampton, Samuel Maffet, Francis Haddock, Casper Smith, Benjamin Lodge, William Wallice, Henry Row, William Hampton, Jr., Thomas Clement, Lucy Hubbs, James Borden, William Brookfield, William Skeels, John Scholey, Caleb Shinn, Jonathan Wright, David Gale, Andrew King, Nathan Starkey, George Eyre, George Palmer, William Sorsby, Samuel Wickward (?), John Hancock, Jonathan Lovell, Jonathan Shreve, Thomas Foster, Obadiah Ireton, Thomas Staples, Jr., Joseph Richards, John Nickelson, Joseph Loyd, William Barker, James Dunbar, Thomas Atkinson, Roger Fort. The following are called book debts "Doubtful:" Letitia Aubray v. Elisa Bass, John Penn v. James Steel, Adm'r of Haize, Samuel Hazell v. Francis Gervis, Thomas Morgan v. William Sheppard, William Branson v. Ex'rs of Carree, Daniel Corbit v. Thomas Rossell, William Mountgomery v. Richard Jones, John Green ex dem. Cornelius Mason v. Josiah Parvin, Adm'r of Leeds v. Will Norcross, Samuel Parr v. William Rawsor, Peter Le Count v. John Brittain, Peter Turner v. Benjamin Eaton, Samuel Nicholson v. John Hall, Edward Moon ads. John Buttler, Mathias Aspden v. Edward Noble, Rebecca Reeve, John Kimble ads. Mathew McCarthy, Jacob Hooker ads, of Thomas Caskie, Harmanus King ads, James Johnson, William Hooper v. Julius Ewan, Ex'rs of Andrew Tompson v. Daniel Mestayer, Joseph Richards ads. John Terry, William Coate v. Martha Milnor, Hannah Sawyer v. Isaac Hutchinson, John Ord v. Thomas Leonard, Robert Maffet v. John Prickett, John Imlay v. Nathaniel Starkey, Ex'rs of Vanculin v. John Tompson, John Conner ex dem. Thomas Devereux v. John Turnout, Morris Conner v. Stewart, Andrew Lycans v. Caleb Shinn, Thomas Thorn v. Thomas Kendall, Alexander Moore v. Joseph Seeley, Jacob Hall v. John Betts, John Ervin v. Peter Bryan, Job Lippencott v. Joseph Rivers, George Gray v. John Irannell, John Erwin v. Reuben Jackaway, Archibald Campbell v. Reuben Eldridge, David Erwin v. Peter Bryan, William Hampton v. John Prosser, John Bryan v. Jonas Jones, Morris Morgan v. Morgan Conner, William Smallwood ads. of John Price; Ex'rs of John Powell, Joseph Zanes,

CALENDAR OF WILLS—1751-1760   149

Mary Champion and Samuel Shivers v. Mary Easley, Ex'x of Robert Champion, William Gerrard ads. Abram Perkins, Ann Gray v. Peter Rambo, Henry Sparks v. Abigail Kaighain, John Sparks Farmer v. John Patterson and wife Ann, Peter Longacre and wife Sarah v. John Fleming and wife Rachel, John Bryan v. Robert Noble, John Bryon v. Daniel O'Neil, Samuel Raris v. Evan Morgan, Henry Roe ads. Israel Williams, Henry Roe v. James Russell, John Smallwood v. Maim Southwick, John Smallwood v. David Ward, John Bond v. Elias Gandy, Peter Cheesman v. Samuel Ward, Rowland Rice v. John Proser, Samuel Maffett v. John Woodward; in all £1,192.5.4; made by Joseph Noble and Robert Smith, who say of this last sum: "The sums mentioned from page the 7th to page the 12th [of the Inventory] amounting to £1,192.5.4., stands charged in the books of said Robert to the several persons whose names to their respective sums are affixed as unsettled amounts which may perhaps hereafter be settled and adjusted between the Administratrix and the several parties therein concerned.":

1773, Jan. 30. Account by the Adm'x, showing payments of £577.4.5 to daughter, Catherine and her husband, Benjamin Fordham, and £497.6.9 to Hannah, the other daughter.

1754, Jan. 30. Harvey, John, of Mansfield Township, Burlington Co., yeoman, advanced in years; will of. Wife, Elizabeth. Son, Peter, to have 10 acres of meadow. Son, Job, £3. Daughter, Sarah, the goods she brought when she removed from her brother, Peter and also £40. Daughter, Mary Haines, £25, to Robert Hunt, son of Samuel Hunt, £10, when 21. Son, John, the rest of my plantation. Executor—son John, "and, if he die intestate, and not married, before the completion of this my will, then I appoint my son Job." My daughter, Mary, is the wife of Nathaniel Haines. Witness—George Taylor, John Hutchin, Isaac De Cow. Proved Aug. 31, 1754.

1754, Aug. 23. Inventory, £501.5.10, by George Folwell and John Fenimore.   Burl. Wills, 5449 C.

1756, June 14. Harvey, Josiah, of Newton Township, Gloucester Co.; will of. Divides personal estate between kinswoman, Rebecca Harvey of Philadelphia (who is sole Executrix), John Steel's wife, apprentice James Wooden, brother Job Harvy, Mary Harvy, Peter Still and Sarah Kelly. Witnesses—George Weed, John Maxwell, James Mulock. Proved Nov. 8, 1756.   Lib. 8, p. 367.

1756, Nov. 8. Inventory, £80.14.4, incl. books, 5s.; book debts, £40.0.10; made by Samuel Hugg and Isaac Kay.

1760, Mar. 6. Haselton, Hannah, of Mansfield, Burlington Co. Int. Bond of Thomas Baker as Adm'r; Joseph Imlay, Esq., fellowbondsman, both of said Co.   Lib. 9, p. 409.

1760, May 23. Haselton, Jarvis, of Monmouth Co. Int. Ann Hazleton desires, that administration on his estate be granted to Benjamin Fitz Randolph and James Haywood.

1760, May 27. Bond of James Haywood (Heywood) and Benjamin Randolph, both of said Co., as Adm'rs.   Lib. G, p. 215.

1760, Jan. 6. Hathaway, Jonathan, of Morris Town, Morris Co. Int. Adm'r—Abel Hathaway, of said Town, the eldest brother. Bondsman—Henry Primrose, of same place. Witness—Lewis Ogden.
Lib. G, p. 270.

1754, Feb. 9. Hatheway, Shadrach, of Morris Town, Morris Co., bloomer; will of. Wife, Phebe. Children—Abner and Elizabeth. Mother, Sarah Hatheway. Brothers—Abraham, Jonathan and Benjamin Hatheway. Nephew, Philip Hatheway. Real and personal estate. Executors—brothers Abraham and Jonathan. Witnesses—Henry Primrose, Samuel Arnold, Samuel Tuthill. Proved Jan. 6, 1756. Lib. F, p. 309.

1754, June 28. Hatheway, Simeon, of Morris Co. Int. Bond of Meriam, widow, as Adm'x; Job Allen (Alling) of said Co., fellowbondsman. Lib. F, p. 230.

1756, Feb. 1. Hauck, Jacob, of "Oxforth" Township, Essex Co., farmer; will of; also signed by his wife, Ana Maria, both signing in German script. Children—Davith, Johanes, Johan Philipp, Johan Jacob, Johan George, Catharina, Ana Barbara, Anna Margretha and Elisabetha. Executors—Philipp Drumm (Tromm) and Phil. Will. Blim (?). Witnesses—Conrad Lorsbach and George Schneider. Proved (in Hunterdon Co.) March 14, 1757. Lib. 8, p. 406.
1757, May 28. Inventory, £65.11.6, incl. a Bible; made by William Scholey and Peter Lance of "Greenwitch."

1754, June 20. Havens, Joseph, of Shrewsbury, Monmouth Co., yeoman. will of. Brothers—William Havens, who has son John; Edward Havens. Sister—Dinah Rodgers, who has daughters Mary, Elisabeth and Sarah. Son of sister Elisabeth, i. e., Lewis Mitchell. Personal property. Executor—brother Edward. Witnesses—David Allen, Latham Clark, James Irons, Jr. Proved June 25, 1754.
Lib. F, p. 197.
1754, July 1. Inventory, £70.12, by David Allen and Luke Johnston.

1752, Nov. 1. Hay, Doctor Adam, of Woodbridge, Middlesex Co. Int. John Watson, a principal creditor, declines the administration in favour of Courtland Skinner. [For Will, proved 1741, see N. J. Archives, Vol. XXX, p. 226].
1752, Nov. 1. Bond of Courtland Skinner, Esq., of Perth Amboy, as Adm'r of the estate, left unadministered by David Martin, Executor of the will; William Skinner, of the same place, clerk, fellowbondsman. Lib. F, p. 73.

1756, Oct. 25. Hay, David, of New Brunswick, Middlesex Co. Int. The widow, Jane, renounced. Adm'r—Gilbert Barton, of Cranberry, blacksmith. Bondsman—Daniel Carson, of Cranberry, waggoner.
Lib. F, p. 384.
1757, Feb. 25. Inventory, £33.14.6, by Matthew Collins and David Williamson.
1759, Jan. 1. Account filed by administrator.

1752, Apr. 4. Haynes, Thomas, of Manington, Salem Co.; will of. Wife [not named]. Children—Jonathan, Jane (under age), Mary and Rebecca. Real and personal estate, subject to a bond given to Peter Popeloe. Son, Jonathan, sole Executor. Witnesses—John Armor, Anthony Sanderson, John Gosling, Jr. Proved April 30, 1752.
Lib. F, p. 260.
1752, Apr. 29. Inventory, £69.12.1, by John Rose and James Mason.

CALENDAR OF WILLS—1751-1760   151

1759, Feb. 2. Hays, William, of Burlington City; will of. Wife [not named]. Children—William, Isaac (under age), Henry, John, Abraham (under age), Jacob, Mary (wife of James Inglish), Hannah (wife of Lewis Stannerd), Ann (wife of John Reynolds). Grandson, John Hayes. Farm, bought of Richard Ridgway; land bought of Lemuel Oldale; land bought of William Cutler; house, lot and stone quarry in "Pensilvania," bought of Isaac Connero; farm in Willingborough Township, bought of Timothy Thomas. Personal estate. Executors—son, Jacob, and Arent Schuyler, both of said city. Witnesses—Solomon Oldale, Ann Oldale, Fridrick Ham. Proved Feb. 26, 1759. Lib. 9, p. 188.
    1759, — —. Inventory, £355.15.7, inc. bonds, £193.14.4; an old negro man, £2; 40 bush. of wheat, £9.10; 40 do. of buckwheat, £3.10; 16 do. of Indian corn, £1.12; 18 do. of rye, £2.5; made by William Smith and William Miller.
    1761, Apr. 6. Account by the Executors.

1759, July 23. Hayse, Robert, of Newark, Essex Co.; will of. Wife, Hannah. Nephews—David, Thomas and Daniel Hayse. Brother—Joseph Hayse, who has children, viz., Samuel, David, Joseph and Martha. Children of brother Thomas Hayse and of sister Freman. Real and personal estate. Executors—Joseph Hayse, Samuel Hayse and David Hayse. Witnesses—Obadiah Bruen, Solomon Davis, John Ogden. Proved Nov. 6, 1759. Lib. G, p. 117.
    1759, July 23. Inventory, £63.3.9. Second Inventory, 1765, £395.16.3, by Obadiah Bruen, Solomon Davis and John Ogden.

1750, June 25. Hayward, Ebenezer. Inventory of personal estate, £155.15.1, incl. books 8s.; book debts, £62.16.2; made by Peter Gordon and Frederick Buckelow. [not filed until Sept. 11, 1758. For will, see N. J. Archives, Vol. XXX, p. 228]. Mid. Wills, 2305 L.

1758, Aug. 3. Hazard, Samuel. Int. Letter from Philadelphia: "Dear Brother, I beg you to take the administration of my husband's affairs, both in New York & New Jersey, as well as you have done in Pennsylvania as I renounce. I am affectionately, Catherine Hazard."
    1759, June 21. Adm'r—Nathaniel Hazard, of New York City, merchant. Bondsman—Ephraim Terrill, of Elizabeth. Witnesses—Robert Ogden and Thomas Bartow. Lib. G, p. 129.

1760, May 23. Hazleton, Jarvis, of Monmouth Co. Intestate. Ann Hazleton renounced in favor of James Haywood and Benjamin Fitz Randolph, in presence of William Haywood.
    1760, May 27. Adm'rs—James Haywood and Benjamin Randolph, both of said Co. Witness—John Smyth. Lib. G, p. 215.

1756, Feb. 23. Heard, John Esq., of Woodbridge, Middlesex Co.; will of. Wife, Mary. Children—Nathaniel (sole Executor), Sarah (wife of James Smith), Phebe (wife of John Taylor), and Mary. Real and personal estate. Witnesses—Samuel Crow, Elnathan Holly and David Donham. Proved April 16, 1757. Lib. F, p. 418.
    1757, Apr. 22. Inventory, £1089.6.2, incl. gold sleeve buttons, £1.15; silver shoe buckles, 21s.; clock, £7; looking glass, £2; silverware, £24.9.6; an old, large Bible and a small book 4s.; a looking glass 18s.; 14 negroes (incl. 2 children), £505; 91 gall. of wine, £40.1.8; 101 gallons of rum, £20.10.4; cash, £160; made by Alexander Edgar and James Pike.

1756, Apr. 16. Heard, William, Esq., of Woodbridge, Middlesex Co. Int. Inventory, £984.10.11, incl. a gold watch, £28; pair of gold buttons, 45s.; silverware, £29.2; clock, £13; large looking glass, £3.10; another, 20s.; a large Bible, 14s.; 8 books, £3.9; books of "navigations, with 1 Seale Quadron and Divideors," £3; 10 negroes, males and females, £400; made by Alexander Edgar and James Pike.

1756, Aug. 25. Bond by Agnes Heard and John Taylor as Adm'rs; Nathaniel Heard and Alexander Edgar fellowbondsmen. Witness— Thomas Bartow. Lib. F, p. 373.

1760, Dec. 11. Heart, Michael, of Piscataway, Middlesex Co. Int. Adm'x—Elizabeth Runyon, principal creditor. Bondsman—Peter Runyon, of Piscataway. Witness—John Smyth. Lib. G, p. 323.

1760, Jan. 26. Inventory, £11.4.3, by George Marlett and Elijah Pound.

1759, June 21. Hedge, Samuel, of Salem Town and Co. Int. Inventory, £217.6.1, incl. apparel, cash and plate, £46.13; made by Josiah Kay and Thomas Goodwin.

1759, June 29. Bond of widow, Hannah Hedge, of Salem, as Adm'x; Richard Woodnutt and Elisha Bassett, Jr., both of Manington, said Co., yeoman, fellowbondsmen. Lib. 9, p. 350.

1757, Jan. 2. Hedger, Joseph, of Gloucester Township and Co.; will of. Wife, Martha. Children—John, Deborah and Meribah, all under age. Real and personal estate. Executors—the wife and Michael Fisher, of Deptford Township, said Co. Witnesses—Richard Cheesman, David Roe, Samuel Blackwood. Proved Jan. 28, 1757.
Lib. 8, p. 372.

1757, Jan. 24. Inventory, £215.15.9, incl. bills, bonds and book debts, £74.14.3; made by David Roe and Richard Chew.

1757, Jan. 29. Michael Fisher, named as one of the Executors, refuses to act.

1759, July 12. Hegeman, Dolleus, Esq., of Middlesex Co.; will of. Children—Dennis, Syche Corle, Grace (wife of Andris Anderson), Barnt, Dolleus, Anne Dobbins, Jacobus, Charity Funk and Adrian. Real and personal estate. Executors—sons Dennis, Dolleus, Adrian and Jacobus. Witnesses—Nehemiah Smith, William Jones and Andrew Brown. Proved May 20, 1760. Lib. G, p. 222.

1760, Apr. 22. Inventory, Real estate: Plantation of 200 acres, value not stated. Personal estate, £231.1.6, incl. a clock, £4; 3 negroes, £190. Made by Daniel Barcolowe, Jacobus Lake and Nehemiah Smith.

1755, Jan. 15. Helms, Andrew, of Greenwich, Gloucester Co.; will of. Wife, Allice. Daughters—Jael and Elizabeth, both under age. Real and personal property. Executors—the wife and Thomas Wilkins. Witnesses—Ereck Reynolds, Thomas Wilkins, Jr., David Loyd. Proved Dec. 11, 1758. Lib. 9, p. 267.

1758, Oct. 4. Inventory, £123.12.7, incl. a silver watch; book debts and notes, £23.15.1; made by Thomas Denny and Abel Scull.

1760, Dec. 29. Helms, Susannah, of Greenwich, Gloucester Co., widow. Bond of James Steelman as Adm'r; Thomas Clark, fellow-

CALDENDAR OF WILLS—1751-1760   153

bondsman, both of Greenwich Township, yeoman. Witnesses—Charles Lock and John Ladd. Lib. 10, p. 291.

1760, ——— ———. Inventory, £135.17, incl. a clock, £7; books, 15s.; "cash just received for rent," £22.10; made by Thomas Thomson and Thomas Clark.

1762, ——— ———. Account by the Administrator.

1760, July 21. Hendricks, John, Jr. of Middlesex Co., yeoman; will of. Wife, Phebe, sole heiress and, with brother-in-law, John van der Belt, and wife's cousin, Thomas Hunn, Executors of personal estate. Witnesses—John Hendricks, Andrew Forman and Lewis Forman. Codicil, of same date, makes bequests to brother-in-law, John van der Belt, and brothers, William and Gilbert Hendricks. Same witnesses. Proved July 26, 1760. Lib. G, p. 258.

1755, July 4. Hendrickson, Andrew, of Greenwich Township, Gloucester Co.; will of. Wife, Elizabeth. Sons—David, Okenus and Jonas (eldest son). Home farm on Kopopow Creek; cedar swamp on Timber Creek; land adjoining Hance Vrian, at Kopopow; meadow on said creek, bought with brother Henry Hendrickson. Personal property. Executors—the wife and brother-in-law, John Denny. Witnesses—John Reynalds, Peter Homan, Jester Lock. Proved Dec. 29, 1760. Lib. 10, p. 406.

1760, Nov. 12. Inventory, £150.12.3, incl. reading books, made by John Reynalds and Charles Lock.

1753, Mar. 24. Hendrickson, Hendrick, of Middletown, (Monmouth Co.), yeoman. Int. Neelle, widow, refuses to administer, in favour of son, Daniel Hendrickson, William Hendrickson and Garet Scanck.

1753, Mar. 28. Bond of Daniel Hendrickson, Jr., William Hendrickson and Garret Schanck as Adm'rs; Daniel Hendrickson fellowbondsman. Lib. F, p. 107.

1754, Nov. 11. Hendrickson, William, of Morris Co. Int. Bond of Charles Hoff, Jr., of Kingwood, Hunterdon Co., as Adm'r; Moore Furman, of Trenton, said Co., fellowbondsman. Lib. 8, p. 79.

1754, Nov. 13. Inventory, £22.17.2, in bonds, and £1.10 in apparel; made by John Reeder and Samuel Bonham.

1751, Sept. 23. Hendry, Thomas, of Burlington City, merchant. Int. Bond of widow, Dinah Bard, as Adm'x; Joseph Reckless and Bennet Bard, yeomen, fellowbondsmen, all of Burlington.
Burl. Adm'n, 77.

1756, Sept. 30. Henerie (Henry) William, of Greenwich, Sussex Co., yeoman; will of. Wife, Hannah. Children—Arthur, Micah, Nathaniel, Jane, Elizabeth and Sarah, all under age. Home farm between Muskonetcong and Pohatcong Creeks. Personal estate. Executors—the wife, father Michael Henry and William Bishop. Witnesses—Philipp Chapman, Alexander White, George Andrew Viesselius. Proved Nov. 9, 1756. Lib. 8, p. 404.

1756, Nov. 1. Inventory, £339.5, incl. law books, £2; divinity books, £2.10; 4, 8-mo. vols., £1.15; a negro man and wench, £90; made by William Scholey and Alexander White.

1759, May 23. Account by Benjamin McCollogh and wife, Hannah, late Hannah Henerie, and William Bishop, the Executors, who report £161.12.7 on hand.

154   NEW JERSEY COLONIAL DOCUMENTS

1767, May 21. Additional account by McCollogh and wife, who have reduced the balance on hand to $137.7.

1751, May 14. Henley (Hanley), Thomas, of Salem, shopkeeper. Int. Inventory, £1159.14.10, mostly merchandize, but also bonds and book debts, £553.16.1; made by Peter Rambo and Thomas Hancock; sworn to by Christopher Hanley.
1752, July 13. Bond of Peter Rambo and John Andrews as Adm'rs; Amos Penton fellowbondsman, all of Salem Co. Lib. 7, p. 104.
1752, Aug. 22. Inventory of the unadministered estate, £415.17.6, Edward Test and Willm. Maxfield.

1758, Jan. 28. Henry, Robert, of Salem Co. Int. Isebel Henry refuses to administer, leaving it to Isaac Barber.
1758, Feb. 7. Inventory, £95.13, by David Davis and Edward Draper.
1758, Feb. 10. Bond of Isaac Barber as Adm'r; David Davis and Edward Draper fellowbondsmen, all of Salem Co., yeomen.
Salem Wills, 1064 Q.

1759, Nov. 15. Hepard, William, of Waterford, Gloucester Co., ferryman; will of. Children—Sarah Knight, Thomas, Hannah, William, Mary, Deborah, Amey and Joseph. Executors—brothers-in-law, Thomas Hinchman, of Newton, and Joshua Stokes, of Waterford. Witnesses—Thomas Spicer, Samuel Spicer. Proved Dec. 10, 1759.
Lib. G, p. 344.

1759, Nov. 30. Inventory, £326.8.4, incl. books, 18s.; bills, book debts and notes, £48.13.10; made by Henry Wood and Josiah Shivers.
1759, Dec. 8. Joshua Stokes, one of the Executors named, refuses to act.
1760, July 14. Thomas Hinchman, acting Executor, having died, Thomas Hepard appointed Adm'r of goods unadministered on. Bondsman—Charles Day; both of Gloucester Co.

1757, May 5. Herbert, Obadiah, of Perth Amboy, Middlesex Co.; will of. Wife, Hannah. Children—Obediah, John, William, Francis, Richard, Felix, Hannah and Routh, all under age. Land in said Co.; a right of propriety, bought of cousin Hew Hartshorne; land in Monmouth Co. Personal property, incl. surveyor's instruments. Executors—the wife and eldest son, Obediah. Witnesses—Cornelies Lamberson (Lambertson), William Morgan and N's Everson. Proved June 18, 1759. Lib. G, p. 69.

1754, Mar. 7. Herd, Thomas, of Chesterfield Township, Burlington Co., yeoman; will of. Wife, Elce. Children—Samuel, John (both under age), and a daughter, name not given. Real and personal estate. Executors—the wife and Isaac Ivins. Witnesses—James Brown, Andrew Ware, Edith Ware. Proved May 29, 1756.
Lib. 8, p. 290.
1756, May 22. Inventory, £23.17, by Samuel Satterthwaite and John Forsyth.

1756, Feb. 17. Heritage, Joseph, of Chester, Burlington Co., yeoman; will of. Children—Richard, John, Mary Thorn, Hannah Roberts, Benjamin (sole Executor). Grandchildren—Ephraim, Joseph and

CALENDAR OF WILLS—1751-1760   155

Rachel, children of dec'd son Joseph, all three under age, and Keziah Roberts, dec'd. Daughter, Elizabeth, mentioned. Homefarm; share of Proprietary rights in West Jersey. Personal property. Witnesses —Joshua Bisham, John Cox, Samuel Atkinson. Proved Nov. 27, 1756.
Lib. 8, p. 358.

1756, April 7. Herrin, Isaac, of Hopewell Twsp., Hunterdon Co.; will of. Son, Edmund, to have south side of my plantation. Rest of plantation to be sold and money to be paid to my wife, Penelope, to Isaac my grandson, the son of Edmund, and to my daughters Anne, Martha, Mary, Rebecca and Rachel, each one-seventh. To Isaac Woolverton's three children "that were born of the body of my daughter Abigail," £10 each, when of age. Executors—William Hoagland and John Jewell. Witnesses—Reuben Armitage, Azariah Hunt, Nathan Hunt. Proved May 17, 1756.   Lib. 8, p. 291.

1756, Apr. 20. Inventory, £503.10.8, incl. bills, bonds and book debts, £65.8.1; 7 negroes, a man, a woman and child, 4 girls and a boy, £211.10; a great Bible and other books, £1.15; made by Reuben Armitage and Wilson Hunt.

1756, Apr. 20. Herriott, David, of Bedminster, Somerset Co.; will of. Wife, Ursulla. Sons and daughters, but only Ephraim and the "two youngest sons," Andrew and John Forman Herriott, spoken of by name. Real and personal estate. Executors—the wife, son Ephraim, and Ephraim Lockhart. Witnesses—Andrew Lake, Nathan Ker and Thomas Tyson. Proved June 1, 1756.   Lib. F, p. 261.

1756, May 29. Inventory, £343.13, incl. 40 bush. of wheat, £10; 5 do. of rye, 15s.; 2 do. of salt 6s.; a looking glass, 12s.; books, £1.10; a negroman, £60; made by John Berry and William Ker.

1759, Jan. 15. Herritage, Ephraim, of Deptford Township, Gloucester Co., tailor. Int. Bond of George Morgan, Jr., as Adm'r; George Morgan fellowbondsman, both of said Township.   Lib. 9, p. 178.

1759, Feb. 1. Inventory, £29,14.6, by Michaell Fisher and John Carpenter.

1759, Nov. 6. Hetfield, Abraham, of the Borough of Elizabeth, Essex Co., cordwainer; will of. Wife, Helena, sole heiress of real and personal estate. Orchard adjoining David Man's homelot; share of a tanyard and barkmill by the creekside; salt-meadow near Ben's Point, adjoining John Ogden and William Winants. Executors—brother Samuel Hetfield and William Winants. Witnesses—Willumpe Blackledge, John Jones, Josiah Phillips. Proved Dec. 10, 1759.
Lib. G, p. 114.

1759, Dec. 11. Inventory, £34.12.6, by John Ogden, Jr., and Josiah Wynants.

1752, Jan. 3. Hetfield William, of Essex Co.; ward. Guardian—Samuel Hetfield, of Elizabeth, yeoman. Bondsman—Jacob Hetfield, of same place, yeoman. Witness—Thomas Bartow. Essex Wills, 1955 G.

1758, Apr. 21. Heulings, Dorothy, of Evesham, Burlington Co., widow; will of. Children—Joseph, William, Abraham, Theodosia Vause and Rebecca Wills. Grandchildren—Theodosia, Sarah and Agnes (daughters of dec'd. son Jacob Heulings) Abigail, Rebecca and Dorothy (daughters of Joseph). Bequest to Theodosia Vause conditional

upon her return to and living in West Jersey. Personal estate. Executors—the three sons and son-in-law, Micajah Wills. Witnesses —Joshua Ballinger, Sarah Stratton, Elizabeth Buckman. Proved May 6, 1758. Lib. 9, p. 451.
 1758, Apr. 29. Inventory, £588.18, incl. a clock, bonds and debts, £88.19; negroes, £62.10; silverware; made by Joshua Ballinger and James Cattell.

1757, Dec. 26. Heulings, Jacob, Sr., Esq., of Evesham Township, Burlington Co.; will of. Wife, Dorothy. Children—Jacob, Joseph, William, Abraham, Theodosia Vause and Rebecca Wills. Grandson, Samuel Heulings. Real and personal estate, incl. books relating to "mathematicks" and surveying and a negro boy. Executors—the wife and son Abraham. Witnesses—John Dearnale, George Weed, Abram Allen. Proved Feb. 4, 1758. Lib. 8, p. 500.
 1758, Jan. 26. Inventory, £722.19.4, incl. apparel and cash in the house, £201.5.10; 4 negroes, £100; made by James Cattell and Joshua Ballinger.

1758, Mar. 31. Heulings, Jacob, Jr., of Evesham, Burlington Co.; will of. Wife, Agnes. Children—Jacob, Theodosia, Sarah and Agnes (all under age). Real and personal estate. Executors—the wife, brother William Heulings and brother-in-law, Micajah Wills. Witnesses—Hannah Thorne, Abraham Heulings, Elizabeth Buckman. Proved May 30, 1758. Lib. 9, p. 49.
 1758, Apr. 28. Inventory, £273.12.3, incl. a negroman, £40; made by Joshua Ballinger and James Cattell.

1753, Jan. 31. Hewes, Aaron, of Somerset Co., mason; will of. Wife, Providence. Children—Sarah Allen, Joseph, Josiah, Daniel, Aaron, Mary; the sons all under age. Legacy to kinswoman, Mary Hewes, brought up by testator. Mansion House and plantation, personal estate. Executors—brothers-in-law, Samuel and William Worth. Witnesses—Joseph Stockton, Barefoot Brunson, Robert Holinshead. Proved at Trenton August 21, 1753. Lib. 8, p. 11.
 1753, Aug. 8. Inventory, £422.15.8, incl. bills and notes, £56.3.2; 2 looking glasses; a clock; a servant man's time, £20; made by John Clarke and Joseph Skelton.

1758, Sept. 25. Hewes, Abigail, heretofore Abigail Ellis, of Newton, Gloucester Co. Int. Bond of Caleb Hewes as Adm'r; Hugh Forbes fellowbondsman, both of Philadelphia, Pa. Lib. 9, p. 77.

1753, Nov. 8. Hewes, Joseph, of "Peen's Neck," Salem Co., shoemaker; will of. Wife, Rachel, sole heiress and, with Thomas Pedrick, weaver. Executors of real and personal estate. Apprentice, Hugh Pedrick, to be placed with Richard Carson, of Wilmington, for the rest of his time. Land inherited from his father. Witnesses— James Hewes, George Lawrence, William Pedrick. Proved Dec. 1, 1753. Lib. 8, p. 52.
 1753, Nov. 30. Inventory, £112.0.2, by James Hewes and William Pedrick.

1759, Apr. 17. Hewett, Moses, of Greenwich, Gloucester Co. Int. Inventory, £121.14.9, by Enoch Haines and John Holton.
 1759, July 14. Bond of widow, Rebekah Hewett, as Adm'x; Joshua Hewett fellowbondsman, both of said Township. Lib. 9, p. 422.

CALDENDAR OF WILLS—1751-1760   157

1741, July 17. Hewett, William, of Greenwich, Gloucester Co., yeoman; will of. Wife [not named]. Children—William, Moses, Sarah, Susannah, Amy. Real and personal estate. Executors—the wife and son William. Witnesses—Susana Glaesick (Glasset), Charles Rylie (Reily) and Allex'r Randall. Proved September 26, 1752.
Lib. 7, p. 392.
1752, Sept. 19. Inventory, £127.13.1½, by Peter Long and Alexander Randall.

1760, Jan. 1. Hewit, Joshua, of Gloucester Co. Int. Inventory, £87.9, by Mathew Tomlins and Ezekel Gooding.
1760, Apr. 2. Bond of Ann Hewit as Adm'x; Aaron Dilkes (Dilks), fellowbondsman, both of said Co. Lib. 9, p. 421.

1751, Sept. 14. Higgins, Gershom, of Elizabeth Town, Essex Co., blacksmith; will of. Wife, Mary. Children—Nathaniel, Mary, Hannah and Abigail. Grandchildren—Michael and William, sons of dec'd son William. Lot in said town between Mat. Baldwin, Daniel Jewet, Robert Little and the highway; 7 acres of meadow near Oyster Creek; homestead; land adjoining the late Rev. Mr. Dickinson, Cornelius Hetfield and the highway. Personal property. Executors—the wife and Joseph Ogden. Witnesses—Elias Grazeillier, Joseph Hetfield, John Ross. Proved Feb. 18, 1758. Lib. F, p. 517.
1758, Apr. 6. Inventory, £86.7.0, by Matthias Baldwin and Benjamin Spinning.

1750, Feb. 21. Hill, Aaron, of Salem Co.; will of. Land to my four sons, and they to pay to William Robertson £10. Wife, Jean to have personal estate. Executors—wife and son, Alexander. Witnesses—Noah Harris, Garret Vanmeter, James Dunlop. Proved April 20, 1751.
1751, April 1. Inventory, £353.16.11, by Garret Vanemen and William Vanneman. Lib. 7, p. 254.

1751, Mar. 30. Hill, Joseph, of Amwell, Hunterdon Co. Int. Bond of Samuel Hill, of the same place, as Adm'r; John Smith, of Maidenhead, said Co., fellowbondsman. Lib. 7, p. 70.
1751, Apr. 11. Inventory, £105.8.8, by Abraham Larew and Thomas Hunt.

1760, July 22. Hill, Robert, of Northampton Township, Burlington Co.; will of. Wife, Ann. Daughter, Ann, to inherit the estate. Executors—the wife, James Dobbins and John Goldy. Witnesses—William Venicombe, Thomas Bichinsha (Bechinshea), Joseph Goldy. Proved Aug. 20, 1760. Lib. 10, p. 81.
1760, Aug. 7. Inventory, £76.4.10, incl. looking glasses; a legacy from John Endecote, £20; made by Francis Venicombe and Isaac Marriott.

1757, Sept. 11. Hiller, John, of Northampton, Burlington Co., yeoman; will of. Children—John, Rebecca Burden and Massy Brock. Grandson, John Hiller (under age). Real and personal estate. Executors—Revell Elton, Esq., and Henry Cooper, yeoman. Witnesses—Zachariah Rosell, Zachariah Rossell, Jr., David Jones, Jr. Proved Sept. 26, 1757. Lib. 8, p. 443.
1757, Sept. 19. Inventory, £256.8, incl. bills and bonds, £136.5; made by Thomas Moore and James Allen.
1758, Jan. 20. Account by the executors; balance on hand, £219.9.5.

1753, Nov. 1. Hilliard, Joseph, of Watterford Township, Gloucester Co., yeoman; will of. Wife, Ann, sole Executrix. Children—Sarah Hammet, Ann, Hannah, Joseph, Abraham, the last three under age. Real and personal estate. Witnesses—Richard Matlack, Phineas Bond, George Weed, William Sorsby. Proved Nov. 23, 1753.
Lib. 8, p. 1.
1753, Nov. 17. Inventory, £144.6, by Richard Matlack and Thomas Bate.

1754, Oct. 14. Hillman, Daniel, of Gloucester Township and County, yeoman; will of. Wife, Elizabeth. Sons—Joseph (under age), John, Daniel and James, Homefarm; land (100 acres) on Great Timber Creek, 98 ac., adjoining William Clarke, bought of John Ashbrook; dec'd; 50 ac. near Thomas Cheesman, bought of Francis Austin; house and lots in Haddonfield Town; 12 ac. of woodland between John Hindeman, Isaac Andrews and Uriah Frenche, bought of James Hinchman; farm of 175 ac. on Great Timber Creek adjoining Richard Arrell; a stone quarry. Personal estate. Executors—the wife, with sons John and Daniel. Witnesses—William Clark, Cornelius Clark, Joseph Harrison. Proved May 6, 1755. Lib. 8, p. 367.
1755, Apr. 19. Inventory, £422.11, incl. books, 27s.; a clock, £14; book debts, £141.8.9; a looking glass, 17s.; the time of two servant boys, £21; made by William Clark and Josiah Albertson.

1756, June 1. Himmrich, (Himry), Conrad, of Lebanon, Hunterdon Co.; will of. Wife, Margreth. Children—Jacob, Petter, John, Henry, Catharina, William and two married daughters, names not given. Real and personal estate. Executors—Herman Cline and Zachary Flamenfeld. Witnesses—Nicholas Luneberg, Mathias Mart and David Fetter. Proved June 13, 1757. Lib. 8, p. 485.
1757, May 4. Inventory, £381.15.2, incl. books £3; bills, bonds and cash, £96.6; made by David Fetter and James White.

1754, Aug. 15. Hinchman, John, of Gloucester Township and County, yeoman. Int. Inventory, £760.9.11, incl. bills, bonds and book debts, £140.16.3; a large looking glass, £10; a smaller do., £3; a clock, £6; old plate, £8.12; a negro woman, 3 negro young men and 2 negro boys, £280; made by Samuel Clement and Joseph Ellis.
1754, Aug. 17. Bond of John Hinchman as Adm'r; Joseph Ellis fellowbondsman, both of said Co. Lib. 7, p. 497.

1751, Oct. 12. Hinchman, Kesiah, of Gloucester, W. J., widow; will of. Son-in-law, James Talman, and wife Kesiah, heirs and executors of real and personal estate. Legacies to Hinchman Talman, James Talman, Jr., and Mary Cooper, wife of William Southerby Cooper. Witnesses—Hannah Hicks, David Brodrick. Proved Nov. 12, 1751.
Lib. 7, p. 161.

1760, Apr. 30. Hinchman, Thomas, of Newton, Gloucester Co., yeoman; will of. Son, Joseph (under age). Legacies to sisters, Mary Zane, Amey Stokes and Hannah Gill, children of William Hepperd. Real and personal estate. Executor and guardian of son, Robert Friend Price. Witnesses—Margarett Buxton, James Lawrence, J. Harrison. Proved June 12, 1760. Lib. 10, p. 86.
1760, May 23, 24. Inventory, £547.11.9., incl. a looking glass, 40s.; Sewell's History, 20s.; bonds and book debts, £250.5.11; made by Samuel Clement and J. Harrison.

CALENDAR OF WILLS—1751-1760   159

1758, Dec. 14. Hindes, James, of the Borough of Elizabeth Town, Essex Co.; will of. Wife, Mary. Children—Jonathan, John, James and Macy. Grandchildren—Jacob, Abraham, Mary and Macy, children of dec'd. daughter Anna Osborn; Jaems and Daniel, sons of daughter Mary Jones. Real and personal estate. Executors—Daniel Potter and Timothy Whitehead. Witnesses—John Ogden, John Ogden, Jr., Ezekiel Ogden. Proved Feb. 12, 1759. Lib. G, p. 49.

1755, Feb. 18. Hinds, John, of the Borough of Elizabeth, Newark Co.; will of. Wife, Joan (Jeane). Children—Benjahman, Sarah Knihoof and Mary Baker. Grandchildren—John Knihoof and David Baker. Sons (sons-in-law?)—Paul Knihoof and Jacob Baker. Daughters-in-law (stepdaughters?)—Jean Brodwill and Ann Brodwill (under age). Nephew, Benjahman, son of brother, Jonathan Hinds. Farm, formerly belonging to wife's first husband; home farm; other real and personal property. Executors—son Benjahman, Jonathan Dayton and John Ogden. Witnesses—John Jewel, John Ogden, Jr., Richard Townley, John Megie. Proved April 19, 1755. Lib. F, p. 363.

1754, March 30. Hingston, Daniel, of Gloucester Co. Int. Adm'r—Joseph Sims, of Philadelphia, merchant. Bondsman—John Bacon, of Burlington, merchant. Witnesses—Samuel Peart and Charles Read, Jr.
1765, April 9. Account of the Administrator.
Gloucester Wills, 545 H.
1754, Apr. 11. Inventory, £234.13, incl. 50 acres of green corn, £12.10; 6½ negroes, men, women and children, £177.10; made by John Hider and Richard Cheesman.
1754, Apr. 13. Appraised in Philadelphia by Joseph Richardson and Nehemiah Allen, two negromen, £60 (one of them blind at £15).

1758, July 26. Hinman, Jonah, of Newark, Essex Co., mason; will of. Wife, Elizebeth. Children—Sarah Lyon, Elizebeth, Samuel (under age), John, Jemima, Hannah Wade, Naomi, Rebecca, Experience, and Mary. Real and personal estate. Executors—son Samuel, Israel Crane and Caleb Camp. Witnesses—Samuel Camp, Moses Robarts, John Ogden. Proved Sept. 25, 1758. Lib. F, p. 561.

1752, Feb. 10. Hodgskins, Thomas, of Pens Neck, Salem Co. Int. Bond of Hugh Davis as Adm'r; Edward Keasbey and Abner Sims fellowbondsmen, all of said Co. Lib. 10, p. 602.
1752, Feb. 13. Inventory, £211.7.9, incl. bonds, book debts and notes, £124.19.8; a watch and pocket compass, £2.10; made by Samuel Linch and Othniel Tomlinson.
1752, Dec. 13. Account by the Administrator.

1760, July 28. Hoffman, John, of Morris River, Cumberland Co., yeoman; will of. Wife, Elizabeth. Sons—Frederick, David and John. Brothers Jonas and Frederick Hoffman mentioned. Real and personal estate. Executors—the wife, Hezekiah Lore and Gabriel Vaneman. Witnesses—Larance Peterson, Samuel Vaneman, John Hovey. Proved Sept. 3, 1760. Lib. 10, p. 187.
1760, Aug. 22. Inventory, £139.7.9, incl. a Bible and other books; bonds and book debts, £69.13; made by William Cobb and David Vanneman.

1754, May 6. Hoffmire, Samuel, of Middletown, Monmouth Co., yeoman. Int. Bond of Mary, widow, as Adm'x; Isaac Hoffmire, of the same place, yeoman, fellowbondsman. Lib. F, p. 174.

1760, Apr. 5. Hoffmire, William, of Middletown, Monmouth Co.; will of. Wife, Elizabeth. Children—Josiah, two daughters (names not given). Real and personal estate. Executors—the wife, William Crawford and Isaac Hoffmire, all of Middletown. Witnesses—John Caffarity, Patrick Lynch and John Taylor. Proved June 16, 1760.
Lib. G, p. 228.

1754, Aug. 21. Hohenschilt (Hosiel), Adam, of Stow Creek, Cumberland Co.; will of. Children—George, Justin, Michael, Adam, Mary Welden, Christiana Ranshart, Louise, Mary. Grandchildren—Henry Hossiel, George Hosiel, Elizabeth, Mary. Real and personal estate. Sister-in-law, Chatharana, to live in house during life. Executors—sons Michael and Adam. Witnesses—Josep Long, John Dall, Robert Nicholls. Proved Sept. 10, 1754. [The testator signs in German handwriting; likewise one of the sons and executors, i. e., Johan Michel Hohenschilt; the other making his mark as Adam Howsell].
Cumb. Wills, 100 F.
1754, Septbr. 9. Inventory, £250.17.11, incl. books, £1.10; made by Hugh Dunn and Fill (Philip) Sauter.

1759, Aug. 27. Holden, Daniel, of "Morrices River," Cumberland Co. Int. Inventory, £105.8.8, incl. books, £2.10; debts due, £28.10.2; made by Randol Daniels and Gabrel Wanneman (Vanneman).
1759, Sept. 1. Bond of his widow, Hannah Holden, as Adm'x; Gabrel Wanneman, of Morrices River, fellowbondsman. Lib. 9, p. 340.
1762, Dec. 9. Account by said administratrix, who makes it her debtor for £13.11.6½.

1755, Dec. 10. Holden, Sarah, of Cape May Co.; will of. Children—Reeves Iszard, John Iszard, Simeon Iszard (under age), whose father, Michael Iszard, is named. Real and personal estate. Executor—Jacob Spicer. Witnesses—Deborah Spicer, Christopher Leamyng, Sylvia Spicer, Sarah Spicer. Proved Jan. 2, 1758. Lib. 8, p. 520.

1757, June 3. Holder, John, of Trenton, Hunterdon Co. Int. Bond of John Marsellis (Marselius) as Adm'r; Iden (Eden) Marselis and Charles Oxford fellowbondsmen, all of Trenton. Lib. 8, p. 401.

1757, Mar. 4. Holdsworth, John, of Shrewsbury, N. J., weaver; will of. Brother, William Holdsworth, heir of his estate (real and personal), with legacy to Richard Lawrence, who is made sole Executor. Witnesses—Benjamin Borden, Joseph Borden and Esther Borden. Proved March 24, 1757. Lib. F, p. 417.
1757, Mar. 25. Inventory, £16.0.11., George Allen and Othniel Rogers.

1758, Sept. 13. Holgloaser, James, of Salem Co., tinker. Int. Adm'r—John Andrews. Lib. 9, p. 98.

———, ——— ———. Hollings, (Hulings) Lorance, of Waterford, Gloucester Co., yeoman; will of. Wife, Abigail. Children—Jacob, Lorance, Abigail and Sarah, all under age. Real and personal estate.

CALENDAR OF WILLS—1751-1760 161

Executors—the wife and brother-in-law, John Wallace. Witnesses—Thomas Spicer, Jr., Isaac Fish, Moses Marshel. Proved Oct. 21, 1758. Lib. 9, p. 114.
    1758, Oct. 11. Inventory, £239.11.6, incl. purse and apparel, £77.2.6; a looking glass, £1.10; a boat and sail, £5; made by Henry Wood and Henry Daniel, Jr.

    1754, Apr. 28. Hollingshead, Anthony, son of William, of Chester Township, Burlington Co., petitions that Thomas Gill, of said Co. be appointed his Guardian.
    1754, May 9. Bond of Thomas Gill, of Chester Township, as such Guardian; Thomas Brooks, of Evesham Township, said Co., fellow-bondsman. Burl. Wills, 5453 C.

    1755, Dec. 19. Hollinshead, George, of "Morrises River," Cumberland Co., yeoman; will of. Wife, Anne. Children—James (made sole Executor, and charged with care of his father's father, William Hollinshead), Samuel, George, Mary Low, Grace Mosslander, Adorithey Crandol and Anne Regain. Real and personal estate. Witnesses—Joseph Savage, Benjamin Hancock, Martha Savage. Proved Jan. 31, 1756. Lib. 8, p. 282.
    1756, Jan. 14. Inventory, £194.11.2, by Joseph Savage and Benjamin Hancock.

    1759, Mar. 1. Holman, William, 18 years old, son of Elias Holman of Freehold, Monmouth Co., farmer, chooses William Cole, of Freehold, farmer, as his Guardian.
    1759, Mar. 1. Bond of said William Cole as such Guardian.
Lib. G, p. 36.

    1754, Sept. 13. Holme, Benjamin, of Waterford, Gloucester Co., yeoman; will of. Wife, Hannah, sole Executrix. Children—Martha, Benjamin, Hannah, Phebe, Agnes, Hoppe and Jacob; all but Martha under age. Real and personal estate. Witnesses—Isaac Matlack, Daniel Fortimer, Thomas Roberts. Proved July 22, 1758.
Lib. 9, p. 13.
    1758, ——— ———. Inventory, £111.4, by Isaac Matlack and Thomas Roberts.

    1743, Aug. 13. Holme, Samuel, of Waterford, Gloucester Co., yeoman; will of. Children—John, William, Phebe Ward, Benjamin (sole Executor, who is also to take care for life of son Samuel). Grandchildren—Martha Holme, Benjamin Holme and Hannah Holme. Real and personal estate. Witnesses—Rowland Owen, Robert Powell, Daniel Saint. Proved August 17, 1754. Lib. 7, p. 482.
    1754, June 10. Inventory, £72.3; by Rowland Owen and Richard Price.

    1758, Sept. 18. Holmes, John, of Monmouth Co. Int. Bond of James Holmes and James Mott as Adm'rs; Obadiah Holmes, fellowbondsman, all of said Co., yeomen; the widow, Mary Holmes desiring them to act. Lib. F, p. 553.
    1759, Sept. 12. Account by the Administrators.

    1759, Aug. 28. Holmes, John, of Gloucester Co., yeoman; will of. Wife, Susannah. Children—James, John, Haunce, Sarah, Eleanor and

11

Sussannah, all under age. Real and personal estate. Executors and Guardians of the children—the wife, William Mickle and Alexander Randall. Witnesses—Israel Helms, Okee Halms (Helms), Charles Steelman. Proved Sept. 21, 1759. Lib. 9, p. 347.
 1759, Sept. 7. Inventory, £331.12.9, by Thomas Thompson and Joseph Wilkinson.

 1752, Oct. 17. Holmes, Obadiah, Jr., of Freehold, (Monmouth Co.), yeoman. Int. Bond of Joseph Holmes, brother, as Adm'r; William Holmes fellowbondsman, both of said Co., yeoman. Lib. F, p. 69.
 1753, Jany 15. Inventory, £609.17.2, incl. silver clasps, 3s.; a Dutch Testament and another book, 4s.; 3.000 feet of oak plank, £15; 3,000 do. of inch pine boards, £6; 2,400 do. of pine plank, £12; a negro man, £55; a year's rent for the mill house, 15s.; do. for another house, £10; book debts, £407.7.10; made by Matteys Pitersen (Pietersen) and James van Brakal.

 1759, Apr. 5. Holmes, Samuel, of Freehold, Monmouth Co., yeoman; will of. Wife, Huldah. Real and personal estate. Executors— brother, James Holmes, and brother-in-law, James Mott. Witnesses —John McConnell, John Niellson and Lydia Hanlon. Proved March 7, 1760. Lib. G, p. 133.
 1760, Mar. 14. Inventory, £1664.9.11, incl. 12 large and 6 small silver spoons, £10.10; a silver tankard, can and 4 candlesticks, £18.6; 2 negro wenches, £50; 2 looking glasses, and books; bills, bonds, book debts, cash and notes. £716.9.5; made by Richard Crawford and William Crawford.

 1728, Jan. 24. Holton, Gunloe, of Pen's Neck, Salem Co., widow; will of. Children—John Bartleson, Mary Holton, Cristian Holton and Andrew Bartleson. Home farm of 75 acres on Delaware River, between Lause Peterson and Robert Pittman. Personal property. Executors—the two sons. Witnesses—Ann Simpson, Alexander Simpson. Proved August 6, 1755 (when Ann Simpson testifies as Ann Kent, wife of Erasmus Kent). Lib. 8, p. 243.
 1755, July 19. Inventory, £74.4.4., by Garret Vaneman and Robert Howard.
 1755, Aug. 6. Bond of Andrew Vanneman as Adm'r with the will annexed; Larance Holton fellowbondsman, both of Pile's Grove, said Co., yeoman.

 1755, Oct. 10. Holton, John, of Greenwich Township, Gloucester Co., yeoman. Int. Inventory, £366.11, incl. bills, bonds and book debts, £119.17.8; "Sweed" books, 15s.; a large "Inglish" Bible and small books, £1.4; made by William Key and Isaac Tatum.
 1755, Oct. 15. Bond of widow, Bretta Holton, as Adm'x; Thomas Wilkins fellowbondsman, both of Greenwich Township. Lib. 8, p. 394.

 1759, May 11. Homan, Andrew, of Greenwich, Gloucester Co., farmer; will of. Sisters—Christian Mullican, Ellenner Hendrickson and Mary (wife of John Cook), who has daughter Catherine. Real and personal estate. Executor—John Rumford. Witnesses—Isaiah Davenport, John Reynalds, Isaac Davenport. Proved May 25, 1759.
Lib. 9, p. 270.
 1759, May 18. Inventory, £110.8.1, incl. book debts and cash in Penrose's hand, £65.5.11, to which is added the money received for the farm sold, £161; made by Matthew Gill and John Reynalds.

CALENDAR OF WILLS—1751-1760

1760, Sept. 25. Bond of **Elias Thomas** as Adm'r; Nathan Boys (Boyce) fellowbondsman, both of said Township, yeomen.

1760, Sept. 27. Bond of Jonathan Rumford as Administrator of as much of the estate, as John Rumford, the Executor named in the will, dec'd, left unadministered at his death; Thomas Roberts fellowbondsman, both of Gloucester Co.

1762, ———— ——. Account by Jonathan Rumford, one of the Executors of John Rumford, who had been named Executor in the preceding will. The estate is a debtor to the accountant for £2.11.6.

1752, Sept. 23. Honeywell, John, of Greenwich, Morris Co. Int. Mary, widow, resigns her right to administer on his estate to her son John Hunnywell.

1752, Oct. 9. Bond of John Hunnywell (Honeywell) of Greenwich, husbandman, as Adm'r; Samuel Jaques, of Woodbridge, blacksmith, fellowbondsman. Lib. F, p. 69.

1752, Nov. 8. Inventory, £96.17., incl. a bond for £44; made by Jonathan Hopkins and Edward Megrey, who separately appraise a lot of land, belonging to the estate, at £35. (Filed January 9, 1753).

1758, Oct. 20. Account by the Administrator.

1756, June 4. Hooks, William, of Piscataway, Middlesex Co., yeoman; will of. Wife, Mary, sole heiress of real and personal estate, with remainder to Margaret, Mary, William, Elizabeth, Joseph and Patience, the children of John Standfast. Executors—the wife, Nathaniel Manning and John Gilman, all of Piscataway. Witnesses—Thomas Pyatt, Joseph Dunn and John Dunn. Codicil of July 22, 1756, includes a list of personal property, given to the wife, among it a "great" Bible and two other books. Witnesses—John Dunn. Joseph Dunn and Josiah Davis. Proved Sept. 1, 1756. Lib. F, p. 375.

1756, Aug. 25. Inventory, £121.0.2, of which goods, appraised at £34.17.8, were left by the will of dec'd. to his widow; Made by Benjamin Stelle junior and Isaac Fourat.

1759, Aug. 25. Hooper, William, of Northampton, Burlington Co. Int. Inventory, £24.11.10, by John Budd and Thomas Lawrance.

1759, Aug. 25. Margret Hooper, widow, renounces her right of administration in favour of Thomas Budd.

1759, Aug. 26. Bond of Thomas Budd as Administrator; John Budd fellowbondsman, both of said Co.

1760, May 9. Account by the Administrator. Lib. 9, p. 312.

1755, Jan. 18. Hoose, Harbert, of Somerset Co., weaver; will of. Wife, Janitye. Daughter, Cornelia. Real and personal estate. Executors—the wife, John van Neste and Hendrick van Stay. Witnesses—Frederick Bodine, Abraham Bodin, Peter van Neste. Proved Dec. 1, 1755. Lib. F, p. 300.

1757, May 27. Hooton, Thomas, of Hunterdon Co., yeoman; will of. Wife, Rachel. Children—all under age, names not given. Executors—the wife, Thomas Barnes, Sr., and Nathan Beakes. Witnesses—John Barnes, Jr., Asher Mott, Theodore Severns. Proved March 14, 1758. Lib. 9, p. 155.

1757, July 14. Inventory, £566.16.7, by John Allen and Theophilus Severns.

1758, Apr. 18. Hopewell, John, of Evesham Township, Burlington Co. Int. Bond of Daniel Hopewell as Adm'r; James Cattell fellowbondsman, both of said Co., yeomen.

1754, Mar. 31. Hopewell, Joseph, of Evesham Township, Burlington Co., blacksmith; will of. Divides personal estate between cousin, Elizabeth Smith, brother-in-law, Samuel Murrel, and cousin, Nathaniel (son of Hudson Middleton). Brother, Daniel Hopewell, mentioned. Cousin, Thomas Smith, sole Executor. Witnesses—Hudson Middleton, Daniel Hopewell, Joshua Ballinger. Proved May 21, 1754.
1754, ——— ———. Inventory, £34.18.8, by Hudson Middleton and Nathan Haines. Burl. Wills, 5457 C; 10689 C.

1757, Nov. 7 & 8. Hopkins, Ebenezer, of Newton, Gloucester Co., yeoman. Int. Inventory, £945.11.9, incl. books, £28.2.6; purse and apparel, £136.13.1; bills, bonds and book debts, £125.9.6; a clock; silver mug; silver spoons and sugar tongs, £24.8; mathematical instruments, £10.8.6; watchmaker's, saddler's and carpenter's tools, £11.15; a servant lad's time, £12; made by Samuel Clement and Robert Frd. Price.
1757, Dec. 30. Bond of his widow, Sarah Hopkins, as Adm'x; Thomas Redman, shop keeper, and William Griscom (Griscomb), saddler, fellowbondsmen, all of Newton. Lib. 9, p. 38.

1758, June 5. Hopkins, John, of Newark, Essex Co.; will of. Josiah Crane, of Newark, gunsmith, sole heir and Executor of personal estate prize money due from the Captain of the privateer, called the Columbine. Witnesses—Nathaniel Anderss, Matthias Crane. Proved Dec. 22, 1758. Lib. G, p. 22.

1750, June 17. Hopkins, William, of Chesterfield, Burlington Co., labourer; will of. Legacy to Isabell Ware, and remainder of the estate for the maintenance of the mother at the discretion of Joseph Reckless, Jr., who is named Executor. Witnesses—Joseph Reckless, Roweth Beck, Benjamin Busson. Proved June 20, 1752.
1752, Oct. 24. Inventory, £185.17.5, incl. debts due by George Hopkins, William French, William Chapman, Marmeduke Noland, William Taylor, Joseph Reckless and John Ansley, £156.0.8; made by Thomas Duglass and Roweth Beck. Burl. Wills, 5027 C.

1760, Apr. 14. Horn, Simon, of the South Ward of Perth Amboy, Middlesex Co., carpenter; will of. Wife, Elinor. Three children spoken of, but only sons William and Stephen, both under age, mentioned by name. Home farm, bought of Gilbert Barton; other real and personal property. Executors—the wife, "brother" Stephen van Voorhees, and Lucas Schenck. Witnesses—Stephen Warne, Martha Kar and Henry Swinter. Proved May 14, 1760. Lib. G, p. 218.
1760, May 8. Inventory, £145.6.6, incl. silver buckles and a gold ring, £1.12; a Bible and other books; a looking glass, 2s.; cash, £55; made by Gilbert Bartow and Henry Swinter.

1754, Aug. 27. Hornbeck, Evert, blacksmith, of Sussex Co., yeoman. Int. Lenah, widow, resigns her right of administration to their son, Jacobus Hornbeck.
1754, Aug. 28. Bond of Jacobus Hornbeck as Adm'r; Pieter Kuykendal and Jurian Westfall fellowbondsmen, all of Sussex Co., yeoman. Lib. F, p. 215.

1754, Oct. 7. Inventory, £151.19.10½, incl. 163 lbs. of new iron, £2.16.10½; 561 lbs. old do., £2.6; a looking glass, 3s.; a Dutch Psalm book, 8s.; a Dutch Bible; made by Mathewes Brinck and William Ennes. Morris Wills, 63 N.

1750, Aug. 9. Horner, Frances, of Prince Town, Somerset Co., widow; will of. Son-in-law, Joseph Stout, sole Executor. Daughter, Ruth Stout. Grandsons—John and Jonathan Stout, John and Thomas Brunson. Daughter, Mary Farnsworth. Granddaughters—Frances Peat and Ruth Leonard (daughter of Joseph Stout). Witnesses—Joseph Hedger, Edward Avery and Nathaniel Fitz Randolph. Proved March 1, 1756. Lib. 8, p. 265.

1757, Feb. 14. Inventory, £777.13.1, incl. 240 oz. of silver plate, £108; 6 gold rings and a pair of gold sleeve buttons, £4.10; 6 negroes (a man, two women, a girl and two boys), £240; 2 looking glasses; a Bible and 6 other books, £2.5; doubtful bonds, bills, book debts and notes, £274.3.1; made by John Hart and William Bryant.
Hunt. Wills, 408 J.

1758, May 3. Horner, Job, of Wellingboro, Burlington Co. Int. Bond of Jonathan Borden and Joshua Horner as Adm'rs; George Eyre (Eayre) fellowbondsman, all of said Co. Lib. 8, p. 533.

1758, June 5. Inventory, £73.10.8, by Jehu Claypoole and Thomas Buzby.

1759, Sept. 21. Hornor, Isaac, of Mansfield Township, Burlington Co., yeoman; will of. Son, Samuel, has had his share. Son, Joseph to have my plantation, he paying my son, Benjamin, £50, and my daughter, Amy, £50. Daughter, Rachel Taylor, to have use of a room while widow. Son, Isaac, had his share. Son, Benjamin, to have my house and lot in Bordentown. Daughter, Elizabeth Watson, £10, which her husband stands charged with in my book. Daughter, Amy Hornor, to have my negro, Fanny. Sons Joseph and Benjamin to have my meadow land in Nottingham Township. Rest of personal estate given to four daughters, Rachel Taylor, Mary Field, Elizabeth Watson and Amy Hornor. Executors—sons Samuel and Joseph Hornor. Witnesses—Richard Potts, Samuel Field, John Bliss. Proved Dec. 5, 1760. Lib. 10, p. 558.

1760, Dec. 5. Inventory, £210.11.6, by Aaron Watson and Richard Potts.

1750, Oct. 25. Hornor, John, of Windsor, Middlesex Co.; will of. Divides real and personal estate between sisters, Rachel Taylor, Mary, (wife of John Field who seems to have left her), Elizabeth (wife of Thomas Watson), Amy Hornor (under age); brothers, Isaac and Benjamin Hornor, both under age; nephews Joseph Taylor, John Field and niece, Sarah Field. Right to land in Chesterfield, Burlington Co.; homefarm in Middlesex Co., part of which is leased to William Mountor (?) of Prince Town. Residuary legatees, brothers Samuel and Joseph Hornor, who, with John Clark are Executors. Witnesses—John Hull, Henry Sillcock, Major Scott. Proved May 30, 1753. Lib. 8, p. 9.

1753, May 24. Inventory, £649.3., incl. bills and bonds, £358; servants £35; made by William Worth and Joseph Skelton.

1752, Sept. 2. Horsfull, Richard, of Upper Freehold Township, Monmouth Co., yeoman; will of. Children—John, Sarah (wife of William Harcourt), and Mary (wife of Amer Jackson). Real and personal estate, incl. a negro woman. Executors—son John and John Wetherill. Witnesses—John Wetherill, William Imlay, Thomas Lawrie. Proved Oct. 23, 1752. Lib. 7, p. 280.

1760, Jan. 21. Hose, George, of Piles Grove, Salem Co.; will of. Wife, Catharine. Sons—Michael, (sole Executor) and Jacob. Real and personal estate. Witnesses—Conrath ——— (signed in German script and in jurat of proof called Gauger), John Murphy and Jacob Richman. Proved June 3, 1760. Lib. 10, p. 500.
1760, May 14. Inventory of the personal estate, £70.9.6., incl. 10½ bush. of Indian corn, £1.6.3., a Bible and 17 small Dutch books £1.5., made by John Murphy and Georg Gauger.

1759, Apr. 4. Host, Michael, of Greenwich Township, Gloucester Co., labourer. Int. Bond of Elias Boys (Boyce) as Adm'r; John Boys (Boyce) fellowbondsman, both of said Township, yeoman.
Lib. 9, p. 197.
1759, Sept. 1. Inventory, outstanding debts, £6.4.10, and a handgun, 15s.; made by Jacob Spicer and Thomas Denny.

1760, Apr. 2. Houghton, Richard, of Gloucester Co. Int. Bond of Mary Houghton as Adm'x; Aaron Dilks fellowbondsman, both of said Co. Lib. 9, p. 421.
1760, —— ——. Inventory, £17.3.4, by Mathew Tomlins and Samuel Huitt (Hewitt).
1761, Mar. 25. Account by the Administratrix.

1758, Nov. 8. Howard, Joseph, of Morris Town, Morris Co. Int. Bond of Marah (Mary), widow, as Adm'x; Peter Condict, of same place, blacksmith, fellowbondsman. Lib. G, p. 12.

1755, Mar. 5. Howard, Thomas, of Perth Amboy, laborer. Int. Inventory, £10.9.8, by John Jones and Thomas Smith.
1755, May 2. Margaret Howard renounced and desired Daniel Morgan to be appointed Administrator.
1755, May 3. Daniel Morgan, of Perth Amboy, appointed Adm'r; Thomas Skinner, of same city, baker, fellowbondsman. Lib. F, p. 261.
1756, May 3. Account by the Administrator.

1753, Oct. 6. Howel, George, of Greenwich Township, Gloucester Co., yeoman; will of. Wife, Lucey, sole Executrix. Children—Jacob, Benjamin, Ann, Rachel, George, Moses, Aron, Mary and Isaac. Real and personal estate. Witnesses—Isaiah Davenportt, Peter Dalbo, Elinor Lord. Proved May 29, 1755. Lib. 8, p. 263.
1755, Mar. 14. Inventory, £239.3.1, incl. a canoe and paddles, 5s.; made by Isaiah Davenportt and Gilbert Ranels.

1758, Apr. 28. Howell, Charles, of Fairfield, Cumberland Co. Son of Charles, petitions that his grandfather, Israel Petty, of Fairfield, be appointed his guardian.
1758, Apr. 28. Bond of Israel Petty as such Guardian; James Johnson (Johnston) of Hopewell, said Co., Doctor of Physics, fellowbondsman. Lib. 9, p. 77.

1759, June 18. Howell, Charles, of Morris Town, Morris Co., will of. Wife, Deborah. Sons—Abraham, Silas, Henry, Caleb, John and Samuel, all under age; an expected child. Real and personal estate. Executors—the wife and Timothy Mills, of Morris Town. Witnesses—Samuel Bayles, Daniel Losee, Timothy Johnes. Proved August 9. 1759. Lib. G, p. 242.

1759, June 25. Inventory, £443.10.5, incl. 4 silver teaspoons, 17s.4d.; a looking glass, 15s.; an hour glass 1s.; a new Bible and other books, 28s.; 14 bush. of wheat, 77s.; a negro wench, £60; bonds and book debts, £47.12.5; made by Matthew Lum and John Lindsly.

1756, ——— ———, Howsell, Adam, Jr., of Cumberland Co., son of Adam, petitions, that Jonathan Davis and Azell Pearson, both of said Co., be appointed his Guardians.

1756, Apr. 2. Bond of Jonathan Davis, clerk, and Azel Peirson (Pearson), yeoman, both of Stow Creek, Cumberland Co., as such Guardians; Hugh Dunn, Esq., of the same place, and Silas Parvin, of Hopewell, said Co., innkeeper, fellowbondsmen.

Cumb. Wills, 138 F.

1760, May 5. Huckings, Thomas, of Salem Co. Int. Inventory, £138.9.9, by Elisha Bassett and Edward Draper.

1760, July 25. Bond of Mercy Huckings as Adm'x; Edward Draper and John White fellowbondsmen, all of Pilesgrove, Salem Co.

Lib. 10, p. 443.

1753, Feb. 24. Hudson, Isaac, of Alleways Creek, Salem Co.; will of. Wife, Rachel. Children—Elizabeth, Joseph, Obed and Rachel (the two sons under age). Land in Cumberland Co.; 14 acres of cedar swamp at "Morrish" River; land on Alleways Creek. Personal property, incl. a Bible. Executors—the two sons and Edward Kasby (Keasbey). Witnesses—Mary Whitefield, Abigail Lestorgen, John Fitzpatrick. Proved March 10, 1753. Lib. 7, p. 535.

1753, Mar. 6-7. Inventory, £237.15.1, by John Fitzpatrick and Jost Miller.

1750, Apr. 24. Hudson, John, of Evesham Township, Burlington Co., yeoman; will of. Nephew, Hudson Middleton, who has son Nathaniel. Children of sister Mary, wife of Thomas Middleton. Mother of Hudson aforesaid. Legacies to Benjamin Crispin and John Lippincott. Land on Rancocus, or Northampton River. Personal estate, incl. 23 plate buttons and timber bought of Micajah Wills and John Lippincott. Executors—brother-in-law, Thomas Middleton, and nephew, Hudson Middleton. Witnesses—John Campion, Dennis Mulloy, Isaac Wilcockson. Proved May 25, 1751.

1751, May 22. Inventory, £80.11.3, incl. bonds in hands of Joseph Hollinshead in Burlington, £50.15; made by Joseph Belcher and Isaac Wilcockson.

1752, Jan. 15. Account by the Executors, have paid out £98.1, in discharging debts due to John Flintham, Joseph Hollinshead, Thomas Shinn, John Hillman, Benjamin Bispham, Samuel Hall, Joshua Humphris, Daniel and Samuel Lippincott, Nathan Watson, Arthur Borradail, Joseph Belcher, John and Mary Pimm, Thos. Moore, Thomas Rodman, Jonathan Austin, John Engle, Peter Bryan, Benjamin Allen, William Pricket and Abraham Wilson (nursing deceased and his mother), and John Pimm's negro woman.

Burl. Wills, 4841 C; 4689 C; 5032 C.

1754, July 12. Huestis, Jonathan, of Evesham, Burlington Co., tailor; will of. Wife, Dorrety, sole Executrix. Real and personal estate. Daughter, Mary, under age. Witnesses—John Green, John Huestis, John Cox. Proved August 23, 1754.

1754, Aug. 20. Inventory, £175.5, incl. books, 15s.; made by John Cox and John Green.   Burl. Wills, 5461 C.

1754, Aug. 29. Huestis, Joseph, of Evesham, Burlington Co., yeoman; will of. Wife, Sarah. Children—Moses, Joseph (both under age) and Hannah. Home farm of 100 acres. Personal estate. Executors—the wife and James "Cattle" (Cattell). Witnesses—John Green, Joshua Bispham, John Cox. Proved Nov. 5, 1754.   Lib. 7, p. 504.

1754, Oct. 14. Inventory, £116.19, by Isaac Evens and Francis Dudley.

1755, Nov. 1. Huff, Joseph, of Hardwick Township, Sussex Co., farmer; will of. Daughter, Easter, sole heiress. Executors—father, William Horn, and brother, Gueshim (Gershom) Huff. Witnesses—John van Tuyl, Daniel Landon. Proved Oct. 30, 1756.
     Sussex Wills, 3 S.

1739, Jan. 26. Hugg, Elias, of Gloucester Township and County; will of. Divides real and personal estate between Jacob, Isaac and Samuel Hugg. Farm on Great Timber Creek. Executors—brother, Jacob Hugg, and Joseph Thackra, of Newton, said Co. Witnesses—Elizabeth Tylee, Hannah Thackra, William Harrison. Proved March 4, 1752 (Elizabeth Tylee, one of the witnesses, then being called "Elizabeth Clement, late Tylee").   Lib. 7, p. 195.

1759, Nov. 24. Hugg, Jacob, of Gloucester Township and Co., yeoman; will of. Wife, Hannah. Sons—Barzellai, Samuel, John and Jacob, all under age; an expected child. Home farm on Great Timber Creek between William Harrison and the Beaver Branch; other real and personal property. Executors—the wife and brother Samuel Hugg. Witnesses—John Greeffyth, William Davis, Joseph Harrison. Proved Dec. 18, 1759.   Lib. 9, p. 306.

1759, Dec. 4. Inventory, £541.19.6, incl. 2 looking glasses; a Bible; 2 servant boys' time, £30; book debts, £89.10; made by Robert Frd. Price and John Greefyth.

1765, June 17. Account, by Lawrence Webster with wife Hannah, late Hannah Hugg, Executrix, and Leze Hugg, Adm'x of Samuel Hugg, dec'd. Executor. The estate made debtor of accountants for £45.13.10.

1757, Oct. 30. Hugg, Joseph, of Newton Township, Gloucester Co., joiner; will of. Wife, Sarah. Sons—Samuel and Joseph, both under age. Personal estate. Executors—the wife, Joseph Lownes, Jr., of Philadelphia, joiner, and John Mickle, of Gloucester Co. Witnesses—Robert Frd. Price, Jonathan French, Edward Gibbs. Proved Nov. 19, 1757.   Lib. 9, p. 66.

1757, Nov. 15. Inventory, £312.4, incl. bonds and book debts, £200.6; a looking glass; pictures; a silver watch; made by Rich'd Weekes and William Hinchman.

1759, May 21. Account by Sarah Hugg, Executrix.

1751, May 9. Hughes, Ellis, of Cape May Co.; will of. Wife, Hannah. Sons Memucan, Jesse, Ellis, Constant and David, the last three under age. Home farm, bought of John Page and lying near New England in the Lower Precinct of said Co.; 40 acres of wood land, adjoining George Hand, James Hedges, Samuel Crowell and others in the same Precinct; 40 ac. of upland, bought at auction out of the estate of Levi Eldredge, adjoining James Whillden. Personal property. Executors—the wife and Richard Crawford. Witnesses—Marcy Ross, Elihu Hand, Jacob Spicer, Nathan Eldredge. Proved Febr. 4, 1752.

1752, July 30. Inventory, £149.11.5, incl. book debts and cash, £47.15.3; made by John Eldredge and James Whillden.
Cape May Wills, 160 E.

1755, May 29. Hughes, Humphrey (3rd), of Cape May Co. Int. Adm'r—Zebulon Swain, of said Co., gent. Bondsman—Joseph Corson of same place, gent. Witnesses—Henry Young and Elizabeth Mackey.
Lib. 8, p. 198.

1757, July 23. Inventory, £39.7.8, incl. rents received and accounted for by Elijah Hughes, £33.14.8; made by John Townsend and Jacob Spicer.

1759, Oct. 15. Hughes, Jesse, son of Ellis Hughes of Cape May Co., between 14 and 21 years old, declares, that he had chosen James Whilldin of said Co. as his Guardian.

1759, Nov. 2. Bond of James Whilldin as such Guardian; Jacob Spicer fellowbondsman.
Lib. 10, p. 602.

1755, Aug. 21. Hughes, John, son of Humphrey Hughes of Cape May. Bond of Elijah Hughes as Guardian; Jacob Spicer fellowbondsman, both of Cape May Co.
Cape May Wills, 173 E.

1750, July 2. Hulett, George, of Shrewsbury, Monmouth Co., yeoman; will of. Wife, Margaret. Children—Michael (youngest son), George, (eldest), Timothy, Thomas, Amy, Mary, Elizabeth, Hannah and Sarah. Homefarm between Merriman's Hole, or Bog. Richard Runders, dec'd, the highway and Peter White's millpond; land and meadow on Little Silver Neck; same at Assinpinck. Personal estate. Executors—sons George and Timothy. Witnesses—William West, Obadiah Lippincott, Jacob Dennis. Proved May 8, 1751.
Lib. E, p. 524.

1759, June 13. Hull, Benjamin, of Newtown, Sussex Co. Int. Bond of Joseph and Isaac Hull as Adm'rs; Ephraim Darby fellowbondsman, all of said Co.
Lib. 9, p. 393.

1759, June 13. Inventory, £60.3.10. by Henry Crosley and Joseph Willits.

1755, Jan. 4. Hull, Hopewell, of New Brunswick, Middlesex Co.; Will of, being aged. Sons—John (who has son John), Joseph and Hopewell, latter being sole Executor. Homefarm and 55 acres of the Great Meadows on Southside of Raritan River near the "Round." Personal estate. Witnesses—John Tomson, Moses Hull, and Stephen Warne. Proved April 4, 1760.
Lib. G, p. 158.

1761, —— ——. Inventory, £36.18.2, incl. real estate of 5 acres of salt meadow near the "Round-a-Bout" on Raritan River, £15; made by Nicholas Britton and James Fitch.

1757, Jan. 12. Humphries, Hannah, of Salem, Salem Co.; noncupative will of. Children—Richard and Mary, both under age. Sister, Mary Siddons. Friends, Ann Gillingham, William Siddons and Joshua Jones. Personal estate, incl. a Bible, silver buckles, silver spoons and a looking glass. Henry Stubbines sole Executor. Witnesses—John Firth, Mary Siddons and Hannah Johns, who testify that the will was read to and approved by testatrix, who died before she could sign it. Proved Jan. 26, 1757. Lib. 9, p. 81.

1757, Oct. 28. Hunt, Edward, of Maidenhead, Hunterdon Co.; will of. Children—James, Sarah, Anna, Anglica and Elenor. Grandchildren—Benjamin, Daniel, Nathaniel, and Elizabeth (sons and daughter of dec'd. eldest son, Edward), legacy to the old or first Presbyterian Congregation in Hopewell and Maidenhead. Real and personal estate. Executors—son-in-law, Isaac Lanning, and nephew, Edward, son of brother Ralph Hunt. Witnesses—Joseph Scudder, Joseph Reed and John Guild. Proved Dec. 13, 1759. (On the will are endorsed receipts for legacies of Henry Cook for wife Eleanor, and Ebenezer Earle, for wife Anglica.

1759, Dec. 12. Inventory, £198.4.9, incl. a negro man, £50; a negro girl, £50; a looking glass, £1.5; made by Joseph Scudder and Nathan Moore. Lib. 11, p. 415.

1757, May 23. Hunt, Jacob, of Somerset Co., carpenter. Int. Bond of Caleb Farley, weaver, as Adm'r; Abraham Couwenhoven, yeoman, fellowbondsman, both of said Co. Lib. F, p. 428.

1757, May 31. Inventory, £31.8.1, incl. book debts and notes, £26.0.1.; made by Abraham Couwenhoven and Rem Ditmars.

1754, Sept. 30. Hunt, Jasper, of Bethlehem, Hunterdon Co., husbandman. Int. Inventory, £162.14.10, incl. bonds and book debts, £100.14.10; made by Thomas Hunt and William McElhenney.

1754, Oct. 28. Bond of Johanna Hunt, of Bethlehem, Hunterdon Co., as Adm'x; Thomas Hunt, of said Co., fellowbondsman. Lib. 8, p. 87.

1759, June 21. Account, by Hugh McAllister and wife Joanna, late Joanna Hunt, the Administratrix, who charges for "schooling children."

1758, Sept. 6. Hunt, John, of Maidenhead, Hunterdon Co.; will of. Mother, Abigal Hunt. Brothers—Ralph (under age), Samuel, Richard and Thomas ("if he returns from his captivity"). Land in Hardwick Township, Sussex Co., inherited from father, Samuel Hunt. Personal property, incl. a negro boy. Executors—Abigail and Samuel Hunt. Witnesses—Abigail Phillips, Sarah Phillips and John Bainbridge. Proved Oct. 28, 1758. Lib. 10, p. 453.

1752, Mar. 13. Hunt, Samuel Sr., of Hardwick Township, Morris Co., yeoman; will of. Wife, Abigael. Children—Samuel, Ralph (youngest son and under age), Sarah Price, Martha, Abigael, Richard, John and Thomas. Farm in Maidenhead. Land in Hardwick Township, bought of heirs of Daniel Coxe, 444 acres; farm of 650 ac. in said Township bought of John Banbridge. Personal property, incl. 7 negroes. Executors—sons Samuel and Richard. Witnesses—George Pettit, Isaac Pettit, Samuel Green. Proved Dec. 28, 1752.
Lib. 7, p. 410.

1752, ——— ———. Inventory, £66, by Philipp Phillips, George Pettit and Isaac Pettit.
1770, Mar. 3. Account by the Executors. Lib. 15, p. 14.

1759, Oct. 10. Hunt, Thomas, Jr., of Greenwich Township, W. J., yeoman. Int. Inventory, £82.3.6, by Jonathan Robins and John Martin.
1759, Oct. 24. Bond of widow, Jeane Hunt, of Sussex Co. (Thomas Hunt is here also called "of Sussex Co.") as Adm'x; Jonathan Robins, of Bethleham, Hunterdon Co., fellowbondsman. Lib. 9, p. 454.

1756, Oct. 18. Husk, Nicholas, of Morris Town. Int. Bond of Thomas Husk, bloomer, as Adm'r; Abraham Baldwin and Samuel Riggs, both carpenters, fellowbondsmen, all of said Co.
Lib. F, p. 384.
1756, Nov. 6. Bond of Jean, widow of Nicholas, as Adm'x; Simon Van Winkle, of Morris Co., fellowbondsman. Lib. F, p. 405.
1765, Oct. 1. Account of Jane Husk, Adm'x. Paid for supporting Rachel, one of the children while under 7 years of age, and supporting Jane, one of the children, four years while under 7 years of age, and for supporting John, the other child, 7 years while under 7 years. Signed by "Jane Husk, alias Vanderhoof."

1753, June 23. Hutchison, Robert, of Newry, Ireland, merchant. Int. Bond of son, John Hutcheson of New York, merchant, as Adm'r; James Newell, of Perth Amboy, tailor, fellowbondsman.
Lib. F, p. 125.

1758, July 24. Hutchinson, Robert, of Penn's Neck, Salem Co., yeoman. Int. Inventory, £62.13.9, by Mounce Keen, Jr., and John Beesly.
1758, Aug. 9. Bond of Joseph Sharp as Adm'r; John Beesly fellowbondsman, both of Piles Grove, said Co., yeomen. Lib. 9, p. 96.

1755, Oct. 20. Hyer, Styntie, of Middlesex Co. Int. Adm'r—Abraham Hyer, her late husband, of New Brunswick. Bondsman—Abraham Hyer, Jr. Witness—Thomas Bartow. Lib. F, p. 285.

1755, Nov. 5. Hyers, Garret, of Elsinborough, Salem Co. Int. Bond of Catharine, widow, as Adm'x; Aaron Bradway, of same place, fellowbondsmen. Lib. 9, p. 85.

1756, May 20. Ilslee, Benjamin, of the Borough of Elizabeth, Essex Co.; will of. Wife, Jean. Children—John, Benjamin (under age), Rabaca and Rachill. Land in Woodbridge, bought of brother, John Ilslee. Other real and personal property. Executors—the wife and brother-in-law, James Marshall, who are directed to pass quit claims for lands sold to cousin, Jonathan Ilslee, and the children of cousin, Elisha Ilslee, dec'd, both of Woodbridge. Witnesses—Jonathan Brooks, John Vail, Jr., Andrew Bloomfield. Proved Aug. 20, 1756.
Lib. F, p. 374.

1754, June 12. Imlay, Robert, of Upper Freehold Township, Monmouth Co.; will of. Wife, Alice. Children—Peter, John, William, Elizabeth and Margaret. Real and personal estate. Executor—

son, Peter, and son-in-law, Peter Tilton. Witnesses—Alexander Moore, Mary Wheiler, John Lawrence. Proved Dec. 10, 1754.
Lib. 7, p. 525.
1754, Dec. 9. Inventory. Real estate, (425 acres of land) £1749.7.6; personal, £311.19.2, incl. a negro wench and child, £40; made by Tobias Polemus and John Polhemus.

1749, Nov. 25. Ingersul, Daniel, of Great Egg Harbour, Gloucester Co., yeoman; will of. Wife, Elizabeth. Children—Daniel, Benjamin, Poseph, Ebenezer, John. Son-in-law, Nicholas Soey, to receive cattle, called "my daughter Jean's." Home farm of 200 acres; land near Maple Swamp; land at Raged Point near Great Eggharbour River; cedar swamp at Absecon; 325 ac. of land on Northside of Absecon; 50 ac. of marsh on S. E. side of Gail's Bay. Personal property. Executors—the wife and son Joseph. Witnesses—James Robison, Hannah Addams, Ester Robison. Proved April 11, 1760.
Lib. 9, p. 434.
1760, Feb. 5. Inventory, £300.18.8, incl. book debts, £36.13.4; 2 old books, 2s.; five negroes, £115; made by Edward Doughty and James Robison.

1753, June 23 (?). Ingham, Jonas, of Kingwood, Hunterdon Co., fuller; will of. Children—Jonathan Ingham, of Solebury, Bucks Co., fuller; Mary (wife of Hezekiah Bye, of Solebury, yeoman); Elizabeth (wife of Joshua Waterhouse, of Kingwood). Grandchildren—John, Jonathan and Jonas Ingham. Personal estate incl. a great Bible and other books. Executor and residuary legatee—Son-in-law, Joshua Waterhouse. Witnesses George Fox, Gabriel Fox, Ambros Fox. Proved December 24, 1754. Lib. 8, p. 84.
1754, Dec. 20. Inventory, £294.0.9, incl. a clock; bond, £263.12.5; made by Malakiah Bonham and Gabriel Fox.

1753, Mar. 1. Inloes, Peter, of Salem Co. Int. Bond of Peter and Joseph Enloes (Inloes) as Adm'rs; Allen Congleton and Nicholas Phillpott, fellowbondsmen, all of Pen's Neck, said Co.
Salem Wills, 875 Q.

1756, Oct. 23. Inskeep, John, of Evesham Township, Burlington Co.; will of. Wife, Sarah. Children—John, William, Isaac, James, Joseph, Ann English, Sarah Leeds, Mary, Benjamin and David. Home farm between Micajah Wills and Freedom Lippincott; land on Goshen Neck, Gloucester Co.; other real and personal property. Executors—sons John, William, Isaac and James. Witnesses—Thomas Evans, Richard Comron, Isaac Evens. Proved March 4, 1757.
Lib. 8, p. 362.
1757, ——— ——. Inventory, £798.14.5, incl. bonds and notes, £321.13.4; a servant man, £3; books and sundries, £1.7.6; made by William Heulings and William Evens.

1751, Oct. 29. Inskip, Catharine, of Big Timber Creek, Gloucester Township and County; will of. Commits child, name not given, to John McCollock and wife, Sarah, who are also to receive all debts owing to testatrix. Father, James Inskip, sole Executor. Witnesses—David Langlee, John Blackwood, Samuel Blackwood. Proved April 13, 1752.
Lib. 8, p. 117.
1752, ——— ——. Inventory, £115.4.6, incl. a bond, £100; small debts, £4.12.6; made by Thomas Chew and John Perce (Peirce).

CALENDAR OF WILLS—1751-1760   173

1750, Dec. 16. Inslee, (Ilsley), Elisha, of Woodbridge, Middlesex Co., shipwright; will of. Wife, Elizabeth. Sons—Elisha, John and Zach, all under age. Real and personal estate. Executors—the wife, brother, Jonathan Ilsley and father-in-law, Thomas Gade. Witnesses —John Pike, William Stone, David Donham. Proved Feb. 26, 1751.
Lib. E, p. 487.

1751, Dec. 3. Ireland, Jacob, of Hopewell, Cumberland Co., carpenter, will of. Wife, Mary. Sons—Jacob, Ananias, Amos, Silas and Isaac. Real and personal estate. Executors—the wife and Joseph Goulden. Witnesses William Russell, Thomas Reeves, Patrick Mitchell. Proved January 21, 1752. Cumb. Wills, 78 F.
1752, Jan. 14. Inventory of the personal estate, £109.5.8., made by Jonathan Bowen and Richard Terry.

1751, Apr. 22. Ireland, John, of Middlesex Co. Int. Bond of Isabella Ireland and James Brown, carpenter, as Adm'rs. (Jurat not executed). Lib. E, p. 515.
1751, Apr. 23. Inventory, £34.1.6, by Jonathan Combs and Duncan Campbell.

1760, Apr. 28. Ireland, John, of Cape May Co. Int. Inventory, £117.1.8, by James Hathorn and John van Gelder.
1760, May 3. Bond of Mary Ireland as Adm'x; John Corson fellowbondsman, both of Cape May Co. Lib. 9, p. 422.

1754, May 4. Ireland, Mary, of Hopewell Township, Cumberland Co., widow. Int. Bond of Timothy Brooks as Adm'r; Jonathan Bowen fellowbondsman, both of said township, yeomen.
Cumb. Wills, 101 F.
1754, —— ——. Inventory, £87.9, by Jonathan Bowen and Daniel Biggs.

1758, Apr. 17. Ireland, Silas, Jr., of Cohansey, Fairfield Township, Cumberland Co. Int. Inventory, £71.12.5, by David Sayres and Philipp Shepherd.
1758, May 19. Bond of his widow, Mary Ireland, as Adm'x; Jonathan Sheppard (Shepherd) and David Sayre, both of Fairfield, yeomen, fellowbondsmen. Lib. 9, p. 15.

1759, Apr. 12. Isard (Izard), Gabrill, of the Township of "Prince Morris River," Cumberland Co., yeoman; will of. Wife, Martha, sole Executrix. Children—Nicholas, Michael, Henry, Catharine, Prissilla, Sarah, Prudance and Martha. Home farm on said river and the upper side of Monantico Creek; farm bought of Peter Hofman on said river and the lower side of said creek. Personal property. Witnesses—Friederick Fuchso (in German script), Jechonias Wood, Jonas Hofman, George Miers, William Jones. Proved May 19, 1759.
Lib. 9, p. 258.
1759, May 8. Inventory, £132.16.6, by William Cobb and William Jones.

1760, Jan. 28. Iselton, Mathias, of Perth Amboy, mason; will of. Children—Robberd, Mathias, Samuel, and Deborah (wife of William van Drill). Grandson, Mathias, son of dec'd son Jacob. Lot in North Ward of the city between Jeams Fulford, shipwright, and Richard

Fits Randolph; homestead; a lot near it; a farm in the South Ward on the river; right of land in said Ward, bought with John Lurting of Richard Ashfield; house and lot on High and Water streets, North Ward; a lot on High street. Personal property. Executors—Nicholas Everson and William Kint (Kent). Witnesses—George Herriot, Robert Ayers and Thomas Combs. Proved Feb. 7, 1760. Lib. G, p. 126.

1754, Aug. 1. Iszard, James, of Cape May Co. Int. Inventory, £82.3, by William Mathews and William Stites.
1754, Aug. 7. Bond of Jane Isard as Adm'x; Ephraim Edwards fellowbondsman, both of Cape May Co. Lib. 8, p. 66.

1757, Jan. 15. Iszard, Michael, of Cape May Co. Account of the estate, £133.13.6.; by Daniel Holding in behalf of his wife, Sarah, late Sarah Issard, Adm'x Michael. After payment of debts due to David Corson, Nathan Corson, Zebulon Swain, Richard Smith, William Eldridge, Henry Young, Daniel Lawrence, Ephraim Selie, Benjamin Ingram, Abram Reeves and Daniel Nickle, balance on hand of £99.5.5. reported, of which 1-3 goes to the widow and the remainder "to be divided among 8." Cape May Wills, 182 E.

1758, Feb. 17. Ivins, Thomas, of Chesterfield, Burlington Co. Int. Inventory, £215.10.6, incl. book debts, £41.0.10; made by William Black and Samuel Farnsworth.
1758, Feb. 27. Bond of Abigail Ivins as Adm'x; Isaac Ivins, Jr., fellowbondsman, both of said Co. Lib. 8, p. 520.
1760, May 21. Account by Stacy Fenton and wife Abigail, late Abigail Ivins, the Adm'x, who adds £300. for a plantation, sold by the Sheriff, and report on hand for distribution £70.7.3½.

1760, Apr. 16. Jackson, Hugh, of Shrewsbury Township, Monmouth Co.; will of. Wife, Mary. Children—Benjamin, Isaac, William, Hue, Peter (under age), Marcy and Mary; an expected child. Real and personal estate. Executors—brother William Jackson and Benjamin Willcot (Wolcutt). Witnesses—Joshua Gifford, Robert Lippincott and John Morris, Jr. Proved May 21, 1760. Lib. G, p. 460.
1760, May 30. Inventory, £122.19.3, by Remembrance Lippencott and Joshua Gifferd.

1756, Jan. 20. Jackson, John, of "Mansfield," Burlington Co., yeoman; will of. Divides real and personal estate between sister, Mary Sutten, (apparently a widow) and her children, Daniel Jackson Sutten, John Jackson Sutten; Mary, Elizabeth and Jane, cousins; the children of Thomas Wallin, viz., Elias and John; cousin Mary, wife of William Smith; cousin Thomas Wallis (under age). Executors—sister, Mary Sutten, with cousins Mary and Daniel Jackson Sutten as assistants. Witnesses—William Folwell, Elizabeth Folwell, John Fenimore. Proved Oct. 4, 1758, when the Executrix is called in the body of the jurat Mary Folwell, signing however, as "Mary Sutten." Lib. 9, p. 55.
1758, Oct. 4. Inventory, £488.8.2, incl. books; ——, bonds and book debts, £343.2.8; made by John Fenimore and William Folwell.

1757, June 21. Jackson, Joseph, of Woodbridge, Middlesex Co., mariner. Int. Adm'rs—Abraham Shotwell and Abraham Smith, both of Woodbridge. Bondsman—Joseph Shotwell, of same place. Witness—Thomas Bartow. Lib. F, p. 433.

CALENDAR OF WILLS—1751-1760   175

1752, Mar. 21. James, John, of Burlington Co. Int. Inventory, £9.3.11, by Thomas Gill and Samuel Atkinson, of Chester Township, Burlington Co., yeoman.
    1752, Mar. 29. Bond of Mary Hollinshead as Adm'x; Samuel Atkinson fellowbondsman, both of said Co.   Lib. 7, p. 301.

1760, Jan. 10. Janeway, Sarah, of Somerset Co., widow. Int. Bond of John Hagewoudt, principal creditor, as Adm'r; William Stewart and Daniel Hendricks fellowbondsmen, all of said County.
                                                                                            Lib. G, p. 122.
    1760, Feb. 9. Inventory, £29.1.7, by Elias van Court and Adrian Hoagland. Shows wages of son, George, in hands of Tobias Van Norden, £7.10.0.

1758, June 27. Jansen, Isaac, of Middletown, Monmouth Co.; will of. Wife, Jannatie. Children—Elizabeth, Johannes, Garret, Sarah, Albertie, Isaac, Jan and Jannatie. Real and personal estate incl. negro woman and her four children manumitted and provided for. Executors—Safety Bown and James Davis. Witnesses—Richard Tilden, John Goodberlet and Cary Ludlow. Proved July 24, 1760.
                                                                                             Lib. G, p. 266.

1756, Mar. 9. Jaquat, Paul, of Penn's Neck, Salem Co., yeoman; will of. Wife, Rebecca. Daughters—Hannah, Sarah and Rebecca, all under age. Real and personal estate. Executors—the wife and Edmund Wetherby, who are directed to give deeds for land sold to Joseph Hawks and Michael Miller. Witnesses—Hance Jaquat, Mary Elwell and Samuel Whitehorne. Proved Oct. 5, 1756, when Edmund Wetherby refuses to serve as Executor.   Lib. 8, p. 454.
    1756, Apr. 22. Inventory, £49.17.10, incl. bonds and book debts, £39.10.10; made by Allen Congelton and Samuel Whitehorne.

1760, Sept. 29. Jarvis, Francis, of Monmouth Co. Int. Catharine, widow, refuses the administration in favour of Isaac Rogers.
    1760, Oct. 3. Bond of Isaac Rogers, of Monmouth Co., as Adm'r; Peter Tallman fellowbondsman.   Lib. 10, p. 103.
    1760, Oct. 11. Inventory, £64.3.9, by Thomas Kirby and William Stevenson.

1755, Mar. 25. Jeffery, Joseph, of Shrewsbury, Monmouth Co.; will of. Gives real and personal estate to sisters, Jemima and Elesebeth, and brothers, Jeremiah, Thomas and John, the last two being named Executors. Witnesses—David Allen, Samuel Weston and Timothy Colver. Proved April 15, 1755.   Lib. F, p. 321.
    1755, Apr. 26. Inventory, £210.3, of which amount £200 is in land; made by David Allen, David Johnston and Ananiah Gifford.

1757, May 1. Jeffery, William, of Shrewsbury, Monmouth Co., yeoman; will of. Brother, Daniel Jeffery, and his children, Richard, Marey, Leady, Margreat, Mary and Zilpah, heirs of real and personal estate. Executors—Job Cook and Joseph Jackson. Witnesses—Benjamin Woolley, Daniel Woolley and William Woolley. Proved May 19, 1757.   Lib. F, p. 439.
    1757, May 27. Inventory, £461.19.6, incl. bonds and book debts, £343; made by Benjamin Woolley and John Tucker.

1758, Oct. 28. Jenings, Isaac, of Gloucester Township and Co., yeoman; will of. Wife, Judeth, sole Executrix. Children—Jacob, Sarah Flaningam and Deborah Burrough. Real and personal estate, incl. 2 negro slaves. Witnesses—Josiah Albertson, John Gill, John Hindman. Proved Jan. 29, 1759. Lib. 9, p. 157.

1754, Mar. 5. Jenkins, Rev. Nathaniel, of Cohansey, Cumberland Co.; will of. Wife, Ruth, who has children of her own. Son, Abindab, sole Executor. Daughter, Ester. Legacies to John Brick and Samuel Fithian. Land, bought of Banbury and of Helby, agent. Personal property. Witnesses—Stephen Mulford, Enoch Shepherd, Ephraim Shepard. Proved June 20, 1754.

1754, —— ——. Inventory, £151, incl. books, £14.6; made by John Rementon and Isaac Wheaten. Cumb. Wills, 102 F.

1759, Aug. 6. Jennings, Benjamin, Jr., of Essex Co. Int. Adm'r—Benjamin Jennings, of Elizabeth Town, yeoman, the father. Bondsman—William Lyne, of said Town, yeoman. Witness—Thomas Bartow.
1759, Aug. 7. Account of Administrator.
1760, Aug. 26. Account of Adm'r for costs on the above account.
Lib. G, p. 92.

1760, May 31. Jess, Jonathan, of Burlington Co. Int. Bond of David Jess as Adm'r; Benjamin Gaskill fellowbondsman, both of said Co. Lib. 9, p. 417.

1758, Jan. 10. Jessep, John, son of John, of Gloucester Co., petitions, that John Brown be appointed his Guardian. Same date, bond of John Brown as Guardian; James Cooper fellowbondsman, both of Gloucester Co., yeomen. Lib. 8, p. 544.

1760, Feb. 23. Jewell, Isaac, of the Borough of Elisabeth, Essex Co.; will of. Wife, Elisabeth. Children—George (under age), Elisabeth, Abigal, Sarah and Mary. Real and personal estate. Executors—the wife, with son-in-law, Joseph Hinds the 3d, as Overseer. Witnesses—Corbett Scudder, Samuel Hand, Thomas Scudder. Proved March 28, 1760. Lib. G, p. 153.

1752, June 13. Jewell, James, of Perth Amboy. Int. Inventory of personal estate, £77.14.0, by Luycas Schenck, Barent Hageman, James Peairs.
1752, July 1. Bond of Martha, widow, as Adm'x; Richard Jewell, of the same place, yeoman, fellowbondsman. Lib. F, p. 59.

1756, Dec. 12. Jewell, Richard, Sr., of "Crambery," Middlesex Co., yeoman; will of. Children—William, Jean, Ellse, Richard, Cornealious, Sarah, Althey, John, Mary and George, some of them under age. Real and personal estate. Executors—Johanes van der Ver, of Rariton, and Lewcus Scanck of Crambery. Witnesses—James Patton and Stephen V. Voorhes. Proved March 24, 1757. Lib. F, p. 437.
1757, Feb. 3. Inventory, £124.11.6, by Luykus Scanck, Barent Hegeman, Stephen van Vorhes.
1757, Mar. 10. Bond of William Jewell, of Crambery, Middlesex Co., promising to stand and abide by his father's last will.

CALENDAR OF WILLS—1751-1760   177

1758, May 13. Jewell, Richard, Jr., of the South Ward of Perth Amboy, Middlesex Co., blacksmith; will of, "being legally called in a defencieve War against our cruell enemies, the French and Indians." Brothers—William and George (under age). Real and personal estate. Daniell Disbrow, sole Executor. Witnesses—Stephen Warne, Cornelius Carhart and Henry Disbrow. Proved March 10, 1760.
Lib. G, p. 134.

1760, Mar. 7. Inventory: Real (house and lot), £12; personal, £11.6; made by Arthur van Kirk, Barent Hegeman and Philip Folkarson.

1754, July 30. Jobs, Samuel, of Mansfield, Burlington Co. Int. Inventory, £45.2.5, by Joseph English and Benjamin Smith.

1754, Aug. 21. Bond of widow, Amy Jobs, Adm'x; George Jobs fellowbondsman, both of said Co. Lib. 7, p. 498.

1756, May 28. Account by the administratrix, who reports it £10.10.2 in debt to her.

1759, Mar. 10. Johnsen, Willemtie. Int. Bond of John Johnsen, of Monmouth Co., turner, husband, as Adm'r; John Jolly, of Middlesex Co., yeoman, fellowbondsman. Lib. G, p. 38.

1757, July 13. Johnson, Benjamin, of Cape May Co., yeoman; will of. Wife (not named). Children—Amos, Milicent, Lydiah Hildreth and Temperance Mathews. Grandchildren—Hannah Newton, Mary Mathews, Phebe and Priscilla Hildreth. Real and personal estate. Executors—son Amos and daughter Milicent. Witnesses—Robert Cress, Jonathan Cresse, Nathaniel Jenkins. Proved Oct. 19, 1757.
Lib. 8, p. 494.

1757, Oct. 18. Inventory, £235.6.10, incl. bills, bonds, book debts and cash, £127.3.1; made by Silas Swain and Nathaniel Jenkins.

1752, June 16. Johnson, Catharine, of Somerset Co. Int. A Citation to William Johnson, Ouke Johnson, Barbara Billieu and Amiantie Bodine, children of Ouke Johnson and Catherine his wife, both deceased, who died Intestate, to show cause why letters should not be granted to Thomas Aten, a creditor.

1752, July 20. Adm'r—Ouke Johnson, of Morris Co.

1752, Aug. 1. Inventory, £31.13.6, by James Calwall and John Bedeel, Jr.

1753, May 7. Account filed by Administrator. Lib. F, pp. 58, 59.

1757, Aug. 16. Johnson, Daniel; will of. Children—Moses, Benjamin, Ebenezer, Daniel, John, Martin and Hanah. Real and personal estate. Executor—son Benjamin. Witnesses—Enuch Bowen, Martha Bradford, Mary Mills. Proved at Fairfield, Cumberland Co., August 22, 1759, when the executor, named in the will, refusing, James Ray is sworn in as administrator.

1759, Aug. 22. Bond of James Ray of Fairfield, Cumberland Co., as administrator of the estate cum testamento annexo, Thomas Harris and Joseph Daton (Daiton), both of same place, fellowbondsmen.
Cumb. Wills, 183 F.

1760, Oct. 16. Johnson, Eliphalet, Esq.; will of. Wife, Margaret Buckingham, sole Executrix. Mentions wife's sister's sons, Samuel Cocker and William Cocker; brother, Samuel Johnson; sister Phebe

12

———; nephew, Jabez Johnson; Margaret Sigler; Sarey Johnson; John, son of brother John; daughters of brother John Johnson. Homestead; land by the Boiling Spring, adjoining James Neisbet and David Ward; wood land on the Long Hill by John Sidmond's, dec'd, and John Sandford; meadow adjoining John Ogden and brother Samuel Johnson; do. on Beef Point, bought of Timothy Davis and Thomas Sergant; a lot at the Sand Banks, adjoining Joseph Rogers, James Neisbet and Elezer Bruen; meadow by the Two Mile Brook. Personal property. Witnesses—Abner Ward, Mathias Ward, Robert Boyd. Proved Nov. 21, 1760. (Proved in Essex Co.). Lib. G, p. 327.

1752, July 18. Johnson, Jacob, of Amwell Township, Hunterdon Co., yeoman; will of. Wife, Sarah. Children—Cornelius, Joseph, Benjamin, Winchy Newman, Hannah (wife of James Stout), Mary (wife of John Hoff), and Jacobus. Real and personal estate. Executors—the four sons. Witnesses—Daniel Keane, Sarah Steel, Thomas Humpriss. Proved April 4, 1753. Lib. 7, p. 399.

1759, May 22. Johnson, James, of Hopewell Township, Cumberland Co., physician; will of. Wife, Eunice. Daughter, Mabel (wife of John Reeves). Grandchildren—Eunice Duvall, Johnson Reeves, Lemuel Reeves and Joel Duvall. Real and personal estate. Executors—the wife and son-in-law, John Reeves. Witnesses—Silas Parvin, Jr., Peter Hopman, Robert Kelsey. Proved June 8, 1759.
Lib. 9, p. 385.
1759, June 1. Inventory, £515.13.9¼, incl. drugs and surgical instruments, £33.12.7½; bonds, book debts and notes, £359.18.2; made by Abraham Reeves and Samuel Fithian.

1752, Mar. 7. Johnson, John, of Newark, Essex Co., cordwainer; will of. Wife, Elizabeth. Children—Eliphelet, Uzal, John, David (under age and at College), Abigail, Elizabeth Crane, Phebe, Comfort, Kezia, Martha and Sarah. Legacy to be paid to John Crane or Jonathan Sergeant for the maintenance of a Presbyterian minister for the first congregation at Newark. Real and personal estate. Executors—the wife and son, Eliphalet. Witnesses—Daniel Farrand, John Ogden, Jr., Silvanus Baldwin. Proved March 13, 1752.
Lib. F, p. 30.

1752, Apr. 2. Johnson, John, Sr., of Maidenhead, Hunterdon Co., yeoman; will of. Wife, Mary. Children—John, Andrew (under age), Catherine, Anna, Rebeakah, Jemima and Mary. Farm, received from father; home farm; land bought by father of "old Richard Stockton," farm bought of Martin Hardin; 50 ac. bought of Capt. John Anderson; farm bought of Malakiah Bonham. Personal estate, incl. a negroman, and a servant named Mathies Smith. Executors—the wife and John Scank. Witnesses—William Updike, Ann Updike. Proved May 23, 1752. Lib. 7, p. 238.
1752, May 21. Inventory, £1063.19.3, incl. bills, bonds and book debts, £611.0.5; a servant man, £12; made by Nathaniel Fitz Randolph and William Worth.

1752, Dec. 19. Johnson, John, of Newark, Essex Co. Int. Adm'x—Mary Johnson, his widow. Lib. F, p. 94.
1756, May 17. Johnson, John, of Amwell Township, Hunterdon Co., yeoman. Int. Inventory, £118.13.6, by Richard Green and Abraham Deremer.

CALDENDAR OF WILLS—1751-1760   179

1756, May 24. Bond of widow, Rachel, as Adm'x; Abraham Deremer, farmer, fellowbondsman, both of Amwell. Lib. 8, p. 331.

1757, Jan. 8. Johnson, Margaret, late Margaret Clark, of New Winsor, Middlesex Co. Int. Bond of James Johnson, of Newwinsor, as Adm'r; John Yard, of Trenton, Hunterdon Co., fellowbondsman. (A footnote says she was the wife of said James Johonson).
Lib. A, p. 396.

1752, Nov. 13. Johnson, Mathias, of Winsor Township, Middlesex Co. Int. Inventory, £40.10, incl. a looking glass, 5s.; made by Joseph Schenck and Joseph Skelton.
1752, Nov. 28. Bond of widow, Elanor, and John Lake, of Middlesex Co., farmer, as Adm'rs; John Schenck, of said Co., fellowbondsman.   Lib. 7, p. 419.

1760, Nov. 21. Johnson (Johnston), Nathaniel, of Hopewell Township, Cumberland Co. Int. Inventory, £183.19.9, by Samuel Fithian and Samuel Miller.
1760, Dec. 2. Bond of widow, Elizabeth Johnston, as Adm'x; Samuel Miller and Preston Bishop, both of Hopewell, fellowbondsmen.
Lib. 10, p. 178.

1759, Dec. 22. Johnson, Othniel, of Hopewell Township, Cumberland Co., yeoman; will of. Wife and children, names not given; children all under age. Real and personal property. Executors—the wife and brother, Samuel Fithian. Witnesses—John Albright, John McKasson (McKearson), Rebecka Sayres. Proved February 26, 1760.   Lib. 10, p. 92.
1760, Jan. 1. Inventory, £149.0.3, by Abraham Reeves and Nicholas Johnson.

1752, Sept. 2. Johnson, Ouke, Sr., of Morris township and Co., gentleman; will of. Wife, Hannatche, sole heiress of personal estate. Legacies (money due from brother William Johnson) to William and Ouke, sons of said William, and to Sarah Rutan. Executors—the wife, John Bedell and Peter Rutan, Jr., both of Morris Co. Witnesses—John Calwall, James Totten, John Hall. Proved Dec. 18, 1752.
Lib. F, p. 81.
1752, July 20. Bond of Ouke, son, as Administrator of Ouke's and Catherine's estates, John Bedell, Jr., and Peter Ratan (Rutan), Jr., fellowbondsmen, all of Morris Town and County.
1752, Dec. 21. Inventory of the personal estate of Ouke, £201.6.1., incl. a bible and other books 10s., cash and credits £140.6.10., made by James Calwall and William Parrat in the presence of Hannacha Johnson, John Bedell, Jr., and Peter Ratan (Rutan, Jr.), Executors.

1759, Apr. 18. Johnson, Penelope, widow of Benjamin; will of. Children—Lidia Eldreth, Milicent Young, Amos and Temperance. Grandchildren—Mary (daughter of Samuel Mathues), Hanah Nuton, Prisaler Keldreth. Personal property. Executor—Samuel Mathues. Witnesses—Robert Cresse, Mary Cresse, Jeremiah Hand. Proved April 21, 1759 (in Cape May Co).   Lib. 9, p. 314.
1759, Apr. 25. Inventory, £64.16.6, by Richard Smith and Jeremiah Hand.

1751, Oct. 2. Johnson, Peter, of Winsor, Middlesex Co. Int. Bond of John Johnson and Jacob Jansen (Johnson) of Philadelphia Co., Penna., weavers, as Adm'rs; John Schenck, of Middlesex Co., farmer, fellowbondsman. Lib. 7, p. 425.
    1751, Oct. 4. Inventory, £133.6.9¾, all notes of hand in light money; made by Thomas van Dyck and Albert Schenck.

1755, Apr. 9. Johnson, William, of Mannington, Salem Co., yeoman; will of. Wife, Kathrine. Children—John, Samuel, Joseph and Hannah, the last two under age. Real and personal estate. Executors—the wife and son John. Witnesses—Job Shepherd, Matthew Morrison, John Dun. Proved May 10, 1755. Lib. 8, p. 245.
    1755, May 3. Inventory, £157.0.3., incl. 56 bush. of wheat, £11.4; 20 do. of corn, £2; 10 acres of upland over the Run, £25; made by Richard Willets and William Dickinson.

1754, Jan. 23. Johnston, Hugh, of Fairefield Township, Cumberland Co. Int. Bond of Daniel Lummas, of said township, chief creditor, as Adm'r; Hance Woolson, of Deerfield Township, tavernkeeper, fellowbondsman. Cumb. Wills, 103 F.

1759, Aug. 2. Johnston, John. Int. Bond of John de Normandie, of Bristol, Penna., as Adm'r; Joseph Hollinshead, of Burlington, fellowbondsman. Lib. 9, p. 243.

1759, Aug. 6. Jolliff, Richard, of Essex Co. Int. Adm'r—Nathaniel Rusco. Lib. G, p 92.

1754, Apr. 29. Jolly, Archibald, of Gloucester Township and County, yeoman. Int. Inventory, £98.8.6, by John Hillman and Joseph Hedger.
    1754, May 6. Bond of widow, Deborah, as Adm'x; Peter Cheesman fellowbondsman, both of Gloucester Township. Lib. 8, p. 111.

1759, May 18. Jolly, James, of Bordentown, Burlington Co., gent.; will of. Sisters—Ann, Mary (both under age) and Elizabeth. Real and personal estate. Executors—father, Charles Jolly, and Joseph Borden, Jr., Esq., of Bordentown. Witnesses—John Edwards, Edward Williams, Lewis Gordon. Proved May 24, 1759. Lib. 9, p 279.

1752, Apr. 29. Jolly, John, of Burlington City. Int. Dinah, widow, declines administration in favour of widow Sarah Thomas.
    1752, Apr. 29. Bond of widow Sarah Thomas as Adm'x; Samuel Jones, cordwainer, fellowbondsman, both of Burlington City.
Lib. 7, p. 302.

1760, Febr. 16. Jones, Benjamin, of Woodbridge, Middlesex Co.; will of. Wife, Sarah. Children—James, Ambros and Ruth. Real and personal estate. Executors—brother, Richard Jones, and Jonathan Inslee. Witnesses—John Dodsworth, Nathan Harned and David Herriot. Proved March 7, 1760. Lib. G, p. 132.

1753, Sept. 3. Jones, Daniel, of Basking Ridge, Somerset Co. Int. Rachel, widow, relinquishes right of administration to their son, Samuel.
    1753, Sept. 5. Bond of Samuel Jones, of Middlesex Co., as Adm'r;

Thomas Pound and Elijah Pound, both of said Co., yeomen, fellowbondsmen. Lib. F, p. 132.
1753, Sept. 6. Inventory, £88.4.8, incl. a Bible and other books, 4s.; made by Samuel Dunn and Nathaniel Ayers.

1752, Aug. 18. Jones, Jane, of New Hanover, Burlington Co., widow. Int. Bond of Joseph Arney, of New Hanover, yeoman, as Adm'r; Samuel Woodward, Esq., of Burlington City, fellowbondsman.
Lib. 7, p. 305.

1755, Apr. 24. Jones, John, of Penn's Neck, Salem Co. Int. Bond of Mary Jons (Jones) as Adm'x; Garret Vaneman fellowbondsman, both of said Co. Lib. 8, p. 235.
1755, ——— —. Inventory, £155.17.6, incl. bonds and book debts £60; made by Samuel Linch and William Dallbow.

1759, May 4. Jones, John, of "Greenwhich," Gloucester Co., yeoman; will of. Wife, Mary. Children—Mathew, Joseph, Alexander, Christina, Mary and Rachel, all under age. Home farm of 65 acres. Personal estate. Mentions estate of brother Mathew. Executors—the wife and Benjamin Lodge. Witnesses—Richard Houghton, Mary Houghton, Benjamin Lodge. Proved Sept. 27, 1759. Lib. 9, p. 345.
1759, June 6. Inventory, £44.10.10, by Edward Hollinshead and Michel Herp (Harp).

1756, Mar. 30. Jones, Mary, of Salem Co., widow. Int. Bond of Thomas Goodwin as Adm'r; Edward Test fellowbondsman, both of said Co. Lib. 8, p. 303.
1756, Mar. 31. Inventory, £96.4.10, incl. 2 looking glasses; a negro man, £3; made by Edward Test and Josiah Kay.

1759, Aug. 13. Jones, Matthew, of Pilesgrove, Salem Co. Int. Bond of John Gray, practitioner of physic, as Adm'r; Michael Richman, yeoman, and William Stonebanks, saddler, fellowbondsmen, all of Piles Grove. Lib. 9, p. 351.
1759, Aug. 15. Inventory, £47.5.7, incl. bonds and book debts, £29.19.8; a large Bible, 18s.; books, 7s.6d.; made by John Nelson and Burgin Ayres.

1760, Jan. 2. Jones, Patrick, of Chester Township, Burlington Co. Int. Inventory, £57.5, by Jeremiah Matlack and Richard Comron.
1760, Jan. 7. Bond of widow, Ann Jones, as Adm'x; Richard Comron (Cameron) of Waterford, Gloucester Co., tailor, fellowbondsman.
Lib. 9, p. 387.

1755, Apr. 22. Jones, Reese, of Christain Bridge, New Castle Co., Pennsylvania. Int. Bond of John Watson and Evan Morgan, both of Pennsylvania, as Adm'rs; George Trenchard, Esq., of Salem Co., fellowbondsman. Lib. 8, p. 303.

1760, Mar. 21. Jones, Samuel, of Piscataway, Midldesex Co.; will of. Wife, Lydia. Children—Sofia, Rachell and Lydia, all under age. Land received by last will of brother-in-law, John Smalley; home farm. Personal property. Executors—the wife and Elijah Pound. Witnesses—Isaac Stelle, John van Bueren and Henry Moor. Proved May 3, 1760. Lib. G, p. 190.

1760, May 7. Jones William, of Scotch Plains, Essex Co. Int. Elizabeth Jones, the widow, renounced, and desired that letters be given to Nathaniel Ball and Jonathan Osborn. Witness—David Ball.
Lib. G, p. 192.

1760, May 9. Adm'rs—Nathaniel Ball and Jonathan Osborn. Witness—John Smyth.

1760, May 12. Inventory, £48.14.5, by David Ball and Joseph Sering.

1757, Nov. 5. Joralemon, Clas (Nicholas), of Second River, Essex Co., blacksmith; will of. Wife, Peterje. Children, all under age, names not given. Real and personal estate. Executors—Mercelius Garrabrantse, of New York, carpenter, Dirick Joralemon, of Second River, and Teunis Joralemon, of Agquecknunk. Witnesses—Thomas Codmus, Isaac van Reype, John Joralemon, Jr. Proved May 18, 1758.
Lib. F, p. 540.

1757, Mar. 26. Joralemon, Jacobus, of Second River, Essex Co., carpenter and wheelwright; will of. Children—Derrick (sole Executor), Hans, Claus, Cornelius, Hannah, Ariantje, Cornelia and Elizabeth. Mentions Phoebe, daughter of dec'd. son Hendrick. Real and personal estate. Witnesses—Mark Dempsy, Thomas Harrison, Edmund Kingsland. Proved Dec. 20, 1760. Lib. G, p. 337.

1752, May 4. Jouet, Mary, of Elizabeth Town, Essex Co., widow; will of. Grandchildren—John Cavalier Trotter, Katharine, Sarah and Elizabeth Trotter, Cavalier Jouet and William Trotter. Real and personal estate in the Parish of St. Andrew's, Island of Jamaica, inherited from brother, Col. John Cavalier of the Parish of St. Andrew's, Holborn. Executors—son-in-law, Benjamin Trotter, of Elizabeth Town, and John Troup, of New York City, merchant. Witnesses—John Keyt, William Barker, George Emott. Proved June 10, 1754. Lib. F, p. 187.

1753, May 3. Jurianse, John, of New Barbados Neck, Bergen Co., farmer; will of. Wife, Neltie. Children—Juria, Gerrebrant; Maritie (wife of Jacob Freeland). Children of daughter, Mollie Freeland. Land on the East side of the Neck; woodland on the Westside; a cedar swamp and meadows. Personal property. Executors —the wife and the two sons. Witnesses—Harme Yuriansen, Jacob van Noorstrandt and Richard Bradberry. Proved May 10, 1759.
Lib. G, p. 74.

1759, May 3. Inventory, £149.19.6, incl. 100 bu. of wheat; one negroman £20; made by Hendrick Kip and Reynier v. Giese, Esq.

1754, Mar. 12. Justeson, Nicholas, of Greenwich Township, Gloucester Co.; will of. Sons, Juster and Nicholas, heirs and Executors of real and personal estate. Witnesses—John Denny, Samuel Cobb, Thomas Denny. Proved March 1, 1759. Lib. 9, p. 187.

1760, Mar. 5. Justeson, Nicholas, Sr., of Greenwich Township, Gloucester Co., yeoman; will of. Wife, Catheren. Sons—John, Nicholas and Andrew. Real and personal estate. Executors—son Nicholas and Thomas Denny. Witnesses—Juster Justeson, Elizabeth Justeson, Isaac Justeson. Proved April 2, 1760. Lib. 9, p. 431.

1760, Mar. 22. Inventory, £192.2.6, incl. a clock, £8; book debts, £26.7.6; a canoe, £3; a looking glass, 2s.; "Sweed" books, 15s.; made by Alexander Randall and John Lord.

CALENDAR OF WILLS—1751-1760   183

1754, Nov. 27. Kaes, Johan Pilipus (Philipp), of Amwell Township, Hunterdon Co., yeoman, will of. Former wife, Ann Elizabeth. Present wife Rachele. Children—William, Eva Marya (wife of Paul Koul), Frona Catharina (wife of Henry Winter), Elizabeth (wife of Peter Aller), Ann (dec'd, who left children Philipp and Hendrick Dilts). Children by present wife—Hendrick, Peter, Philipp and Catherine, all four under age. Real and personal estate. Executors—brother, Peter Young, and son-in-law, Peter Aller, both of said Co., yeomen, and William Poppelsdorph, of New York City, baker. Witnesses—Dirck Schuyler, Theodorus van Wyck, Adolph Bras, Jr. Proved Feb. 12, 1756. (The testator signs in German).
Lib. 8, p. 426.

1756, Febr. 16. Inventory, £256.4, incl. 3 servantmen and one "garl," £38.19; made by James Stout, Benjamin Stout and John Garrison.

1772, Oct. 20. Inventory, "of the money arrising of the sale of the land of Philip Case desc'd," £464.8; made by James Stout and Samuel Furman.

1755, Mar. 25. Kaighn (Cain), John, of Burlington Co., labourer. Int. Bond of Joseph Burr, Jr. ,as Adm'r; George Eyre and Nicholas Toy fellowbondsmen, all of said Co. Lib. 8, p. 161.
1758, Jan. 16. Inventory, £33.13.7½, by the Administrator.

1754, May 6. Kay, Isaac, of Waterford, Gloucester Co., yeoman; will of. Wife, Mariann. Children—John, Isaac, Joseph (all three under age), Elizabeth and Sarah. Homefarm on east side of South Branch of Cooper's Creek; fulling and grist mills in Newton Township, said Co.; farms in Waterford, now occupied by John Collins and Richard Price. Personal property. Executors—the wife, with cousins Josiah and Francis Kay. Witnesses—George Weed, John Maxell, Samuel Spicer. Codicil of November 1, 1756, provides for an expected child. Witnesses—George Wood, Mary Matlack, James Mulock. Proved Jan. 28, 1757. Lib. 8, p. 347.

1757, Jan. 25. Inventory, £422.4.10, incl. bonds, book debts and notes, £179.9.4; a negroman, £25; 2 looking glasses; made by Richard Matlack and Thomas Bate.

1758, May 11. Keich, Philipp, of Amwell, Hunterdon Co. Int. Inventory, £98.14.3, incl. a Bible and other books, 5s.; made by Ichabod Leigh and John Jewell.

1758, May 19. Bond of widow, Elizabeth, as Adm'x; Paul Coole, of Amwell, fellowbondsman.

1752, Apr. 24. Kelcy (Kelsey), Joseph, of the Borough of Elisabeth, Essex Co., yeoman; will of. Brothers—Benjamin Kelsey and Daniel Kelsey, who has daughters Maney and Ruth, both under 18. Mentions cousin, Lowrance Decamp, Hannah and Mary, daughters of sister Mary Oliver, dec'd.; children of sister Ruth, dec'd., wife of Benjamin Elstone; children of dec'd. sister, Phebe Wood; children of sister, Elydia Winans; also sisters Marcey Cutter and Hannah Badgle. Real and personal property. Executors—Joseph Wood, of Middlesex Co., and James Badley, of "Elisabeth Borrow." Witnesses—Daniel Cargel, Jeremiah Oliver, Abraham Clark. Proved Nov. 27, 1753.
Lib. F, p. 147.

1759, Nov. 4. Kelly, Elisha, of Essex Co., mariner; will of. Wife, Catherine. Sons—Crage and William, both under age. An expected child. Real and personal estate. Executors—Ephriam Terrell and Andrew Crage. Witnesses—David Olliver, John Wood, Francis Frazee. Proved Jan. 8, 1760. Lib. G, p. 121.

———, ——— ———. **Kelly (Killey), John,** of Alloways Creek, Salem Co.; will of. Wife, Margeret, sole heiress of personal property and Executrix. Real estate to go, after wife's death, to cousin John, son of brother Thomas Killey, or cousin John, son of sister Martha Wallis, and to brother James Killey. Home farm of 100 acres, with reversion of 500 ac., formerly John Abbott's; 150 ac. on Southside of the main branch of Alloway Creek, bought of Robert Walker and Caspar Wistar and now let to Robert Sneathen. Witnesses—John Dickeson, Elizabeth Thompson, Benjamin Thompson. Proved April 23, 1754.
Lib. 8, p. 55.

1754,- ———. Inventory, £293.13, by John Dickeson and Benjamin Thompson.

1758, Mar. 4. Kelly, John, Jr., of Woodbridge, Middlesex Co.; will of. Children—Asa, William, John, Jesse, Elisebeth, Susannah and Mary, all under age. Executors—Joseph Dunham and Thomas Gage. Witnesses—Nathaniel Whitaker, Elisebeth Kelly and George Kelly. Proved March 15, 1758. Lib. F, p. 501.

1760, Jan. 12. Kelly, Nugent, of Woodbridge, Middlesex Co. Int. Adm'r—Richard Kelly, son of Nugent, who was a schoolmaster.
Lib. G, p. 123.

1758, July 7. Kelly (Killey), William, of Greenwich, Cumberland Co., hatter; will of. Wife, Mary. Children—John, Elizabeth and Mary. Real and personal estate. Executors—the wife and Thomas Ewings, of Greenwich, blacksmith. Witnesses—Samuel Dennis, Phebe Fithian, James Mulock. Proved Oct. 5, 1758. Lib. 9, p. 159.

1758, Oct. 3. Inventory, £80.3.2, by James Mulock and Samuel Dennis.

1759, Jan. 22. Kelsy, Daniel, Sr., of Elizabethtown, Essex Co.; will of. Wife, Jemima. Daughters—Massa, Ruth, Rachel. Sons—Benjamin, Daniel and John. All six children under age. Real and personal estate. Executors—brother, Benjamin Kelsey, of Staten Island, and Stephen Borous of Elizabeth Borough; Abraham Clark, Sr. and Jr., appointed to divide the land between the sons. Witnesses—Reuben Bird, Joseph Bird, Abraham Clark. Proved Feb. 17, 1759.
Lib. G, p. 51.

1759, Oct. 24. Kempter, (Kempton), John, of "Hopwill," Hunterdon Co.; will of. Wife, Mary. Sons—Moses, John, William and Jeams. Executors—the wife and Zebulon Stout of Somerset Co. Witnesses—Stephen Barton, John Stout and Robert Cowan. Proved Nov. 2, 1759. Lib. 10, p. 456.

1756, June 24. Keney, John, Jr., of Morris Co. Int. Bond of Samuel Tuthill and wife, Sarah (late Sarah Keney) widow, as Adm'x; John Ford, of said Co., fellowbondsman. Lib. F, p. 362.

1756, Sept. 20. Inventory, £36.12.4, incl. 4 silver spoons; 2 looking glasses; 2 Bibles; a negro wench "of no value;" a negro boy, £11.12; made by Samuel Palmer and Henry Primrose. [On the same sheet and under same date is an additional inventory of goods, said to be in the hands of John Kiney, Sr., and valued at £133.5.1; signed as before].

1753, Mar. 13. Kennedy, Daniel, of Burlington Co. Int. Katherine, widow, declines the administration in favor of Charles Tonkin, of Burlington City.

1753, Mar. 14. Bond of Charles Tonkin as Adm'r; Ralph Smith, carpenter, fellowbondsman, both of Burlington City. Lib. 7, p. 420.

1753, Mar 13. Inventory, £10.9.0, by Ralph Smith and Peteraris Hodgkinson.

1749, Dec. 21. Kenney, Adrian, of Amwell Township, Hunterdon Co., yeoman; will of. Wife, Charity. Children—Simon, Kathrine, Elizabeth, Agnes Debow, Willempe Quick, Charity Hull. Brother John to be maintained by the Executors. Real and personal estate. Executors—daughters Cathrine, Elizabeth and Agnes. Witnesses—John Opdycke, Garret Lake, John Sutphen. Proved Oct. 28, 1755.
Lib. 8, p. 269.

1755, Oct. 25. Inventory: Real estate, (lands and improvements), £170; personal property, £95.9; made by John Opdycke and Garret Lake.

1755, Mar. 1. Kent, Edmund, of Salem Co. Int. Bond of Sophia Kent as Adm'x; Edward Keasbey and Samuel Tylor fellowbondsmen, all of said Co. Lib. 8, p. 142.

1755, —— —. Inventory, £160.15.6, incl. a servantman's time, £10; made by James Tyler and Seth Smith.

1759, June 20. Kester, Peter, of Amwell, Hunterdon Co., (deceased May 14th). Int. Inventory, £19.12.6, by Jacob Swallow and William Williamson.

1759, June 22. Bond of Anne Keter (Kester), of Amwell, as Adm'x; Squier Lewis, of Burlington Co., fellowbondsman. Lib. G, p. 316.

1759, Sept. 12. Ketcham, Samuel, of Hunterdon Co., Bond of Robert Akers of Hopewell, Hunterdon Co., as Adm'r; Benjamin Ketcham of the same place, fellowbondsman. Lib. 9, p. 455.

1759, —— —. Inventory of the personal estate, £69.4, made by Thomas Reeder and Thomas Lake.

1757, July 20. Kiersteed, Luke, of Saddle River Precinct, Bergen Co. Int. Jane, widow, refuses to act as Adm'x of her late husband and recommends Cobus and Lambart Laroo as Administrators.

1757, July 25. Bond of Jacobus and Lambert Laroo, principal creditors, as Adm'rs; Aurey Laroo fellowbondsman, all of Bergen Co.
Bergen Wills, 365 B.

1754, Feb. 21. Killey, Patrick, of "Allins Town," West Jersey, schoolmaster. Int. Elizabeth, widow, declines to administer on his estate.

1754, Feb. 21. Bond of Patrick Hanlon, of Bristol, Bucks Co., Pa., innholder, as Adm'r; William Borradaill, of Burlington City, carpenter, fellowbondsman. Lib. 8, p. 39.

1754, Sept. 12. Kilpatrick, Andrew, of Baskinridge, Somerset Co., blacksmith. Int. Bond of Mary Minary, late Mary Killpatrick,

widow, as Adm'x; John Roy, of the same place, and Robart Huie, of Morris Co., fellowbondsmen. Lib. F, p. 210.
Dec. 4, 1754. Inventory, £148.17, incl. 2 Bibles and 2 other books, 15s.; made by John Roy and Joseph Gaston, and receipted for with an addition of £7.14.9, by Mary Minary.

1756, Jan. 21. Killpatrick, Thomas, Sr., of Middlesex Co., labourer; will of. Wife, Anne, sole Executrix of real and personal estate, with Robert Savage as adviser. Sons—Thomas and Francis, both under age. Witnesses—John Scoby, John Joan and Robert Savage. Proved Feb. 13, 1756. Lib. F, p. 327.
1756, Apr. 6. Inventory, £80.17.6, by John Joan and James Pattan.

1753, Dec. 20. King, Alexander, of Penn's Neck, Salem Co.; will of. Wife, Bridget. Children—Christian Veneman, Elizabeth and Frederick. Home farm of 150 acres; 150 ac. adjoining; 200 ac. in Sippock's Neck, Piles Grove. Personal estate. William Veneman of Piles Grove, sole Executor. Witnesses—Mary Hodge, Alexander Lynmire, Samuel Rain. Proved May 22, 1754. Lib. 7, p. 537.
1754, May 22. Inventory, £142.7.1, incl. a Bible and other books, 13s.; bonds and book debts, £78.2.3; made by Samuel Linde and Samuel Rain.

1758, Mar. 31. King, Stephen, of Monmouth Co. Int. Bond of Obed Garwood as Adm'r; Samuel Garwood, fellowbondsman, both of Evesham Township, Burlington Co. Lib. 8, p. 520.

1757, Dec. 8. Kinney, William, Sr., of Readingtown, Amwell Township, Hunterdon Co.; will of. Wife, Eve. Children—Peter, Michael, Adrian, David, William, Lydia and Elizabeth. Real and personal estate, incl. a large Dutch Bible. Executors—son Peter and John Shurts. Witnesses—George Reading, Henry Graff, John Arrison. Proved Nov. 10, 1760. Lib. 10, p. 555.
1760, Oct. 17. Inventory, £289.7.9., incl. 4 books 4s.; made by Edward Wilmot and Benjamin Cole.

1760, Dec. 31. Kinney, Zepheniah, of Newtown, Sussex Co. Int. Bond of Ebenezer Byram as Adm'r; Amos Pettit fellowbondsman, both of said Co. Lib. 10, p. 465.
1760, Dec. 31. Inventory, £15.7.6., by Perkins Louell and John Lafoliet.

1758, June 3. Kirkpatrick, Alexander, of Somerset Co.; will of. Wife, Elizabeth. Children—Andrew, David, Alexander (under age) and Mary (unmarried). Mentions son-in-law, Duncan McEwen; grandsons, Alexander Kirkpatrick and Alexander McEwen. Real and personal estate, incl. a great Bible. Executors—sons David and Andrew. Witnesses—Alexander McEwen, John Logan and John Roy. Proved June 12, 1758. [Will entered as Killpatrick, but certainly Kirkpatrick. Signed by mark]. Lib. F, p. 526.
1758, June 7. Inventory, £140.11, by Hugh Campbell and William McClelian.

1753, Sept. 26. Kirkpatrick, (Killpatrick), John, of Baskingridge, Somerset Co.; will of. Children—James, Thomas, Mary and Elizabeth. Real and personal estate. Executors—son James and Joseph

Reed, of "Trentown." Witnesses—Aaron Boylan, David Helm. Proved Nov. 12, 1753. [Will entered Killpatrick, but perhaps Kirkpatrick. Signed by mark]. Lib. F, p. 144.

1753, Nov. 27. Kitchel, David, of Hanover, Morris Co.; will of. Wife, Ruth. Children—Uzal, Stephen, Zenas and Abigail, all under age. Real and personal estate. Executors—the wife, brother Joseph Kitchel and Joseph Tuttle, Jr. Witnesses—Jacob Green, Samuel Tuttle, David Tuttle. Proved Sept. 27, 1754. Lib. F, p. 236.

1758, Apr. 28. Knox, James; will of. Wife, Mary, sole heiress and Executrix of real and personal estate. Witnesses—Ebenezer Foster, Jeremiah Wright and Mary Foster. Proved April 22, 1760, (in Middlesex Co.). Lib. G, p. 177.

1751, Apr. 8. Koehler, (Keeler), George Friedrich, living on Leslie's Land, Hunterdon Co.; will of, gives "all belonging unto me" to wife, Elizabeth. Witnesses—William Tremper, Christian Klin (Kline), Adam Shmit. Proved March 30, 1752.
1752, Mar. 30. Bond of widow, Elizabeth Keeler as Adm'x with the will annexed; William Tremper, cordwainer, fellowbondsman, both of "Redingtown," Hunterdon Co. Hunt. Wills, 315 J.
1752, Apr. 11. Inventory, £132.3, incl. bills, bonds and debts, £122.10; made by William Tremper and Adam Shmit.

1758, Sept. 13. Kolgloaser, Jacob, of Salem, Salem Co., tinker. Int. Bond of John Andrews as Adm'r; William Smith fellowbondsman, both of said place. Lib. 9, p. 48.

1756, Nov. 23. Kouwenhoven, Jan, of Freehold, Monmouth Co., yeoman; will of. Sons—William, Garret, Cornelius, Peter, John, Jacob and Dominicus. Personal estate. Executors—son Garrat, cousin Ruluff Schenck and cousin Garrat Schenck, son of Court. Witnesses—David Williamson, Cornelius Covenhoven and Elbert Williamson. Proved Dec. 29, 1756. Lib. F, p. 392.
1757, Mar. 8. Inventory, £479.7.6., incl. 4 negroes, £195.; 5 pictures; a looking glass; a "salm" book; bonds, £229.11.; made by Cornelius Covenhoven and Elbert Williamson.
(see Covenhoven).

1755, Sept. 29. Kowenhoven, William, of Corroway, Middletown, Monmouth Co.; will of. Wife (not named). Children—Cornelius, Williamtie and Catherine, all under age. Real and personal estate. Owes a bond to father-in-law, Peter Wicoff. Executors—brother, Roleph Cownover and son-in-law (stepson?), Mathias Cownover, both of said Co. Witnesses—William Hendrickson, Garret Schanck, Johannis Bennet and John Bowne. Proved Dec. 22, 1755.
Lib. F, p. 305.
1755, Dec. 10. Inventory, £916.11.4, incl. apparel and purse, £204.1.8; bills and bonds, £199.10.2; Bibles and books, £3.10; 5 negroes (one a child), £121; made by Johannis Bennet, John Schenck and Daniel van Mater.

1760, April 17. Kreager, Christian, of Kingwood Township, Hunterdon Co., soldier; will of. Children—Peter and Katherine, to be bound out. Personal estate to be sold and put out to use till daughter,

Katherine, comes of age, and then the whole to be shared by my children, William, Peth and Katherine. Executor—Isaac Kline. Witnesses—John Eberharett Benz and John Forrester. Proved Dec. 23, 1760.

1760, Dec. 12. Inventory, £26.6.6, by John Forrester and Johnson Emily. Lib. 10, p. 546.

1759, Aug. 3. Kreutzer (Critser), Leonhard, of Lebanon Township, Hunterdon Co. Int. Inventory, £315.19, incl. bills, bonds and notes, £95; made by David Fetter and Willem Klein (who signs in German script).

1759, Aug. 7. Bond of Thomas Armstrong as Adm'r; Willem Klein fellowbondsman, both of Hunterdon Co., farmers. Lib. 10, p. 69.

1758, Mar. 13. Kroesen, Adraiana, only daughter of Cornelius Kroesen of Burlington City, asks that Arent Schuyler, of said City, be made her Guardian.

1758, Mar. 16. Bond of Arent Schuyler as such Guardian; Abraham Hewlings fellowbondsman, both of said City. Burl. Wills, 6147 C.

1758, Jan. 26. Krom, Isaac, of "Ridingtown," Hunterdon Co.; will of. Wife, Mary, sole Executrix. Daughter, Mary. Real and personal estate. Witnesses—Cornelius Lane, Georg Andreas Vierselius and Dirck van Vliet. Proved May 1, 1758. Lib. 9, p. 172.

1758, Apr. 26. Inventory, £170.14.6, by Cornelius Lane and Dirck Marlatt.

1758, May 26. Krozen (Kroesen), Cornelius, of Burlington City, account of the estate of, £324.6.1., by Rem Gerritsen (Garretson), survivor of his wife Catherine, late widow and executrix of said Cornelius, who reports on hand £141.5.11. [See for will, etc., N. J. Archives, Vol. XXX, p. 286]. Burl. Wills, 6131 C.

1750, Aug. 14. Laasheet, (Looshett), Johannes Peter, of Amwell Township, Hunterdon Co., yeoman; will of. Wife, Christina, sole Executrix of real and personal estate. Son, John. Provision made for "children" to come, who are to be placed under the guardianship of brother, Christian Loshett, and brother-in-law, Peter Wirt. Witnesses—Albortus Poppelsdorff, Andrew Tremer, Garr'd Williamson. Proved April 30, 1751. Lib. 7, p. 55.

1751, Apr. 16. Inventory, £62.7.2, by Andrew Tremer (Trimmer) and Garrard Williamson.

1756, July 22. Lacey, John, of Hopewell, Cumberland Co., husbandman also labourer. Int. Inventory, £94.13.10, incl. bonds and notes, £70.1.10; made by Jonathan Sayre and Richard Tarry.

1756, July 24. Sarah Lacy, the widow, refuses to administer.

1756, July 24. Bond of Timothy Brooks, chief creditor, as Adm'r; Jonathan Bowen fellowbondsman, both of Hopewell.

Lib. 8, p. 315.

1760, Sept. 23. Lacock, Henry, of Hardwick, Sussex Co., yeoman. Int. Inventory, £15.2.9, incl. 3 books, 2s.; made by Ephraim Darby and Henry Crosley.

1760, Oct. 8. Bond of William Lacock as Adm'r; Joseph Lacock fellowbondsman, both of Hardwick. Lib. 10, p. 464.

CALENDAR OF WILLS—1751-1760   189

1760, Aug. 27. Lacock, Joseph, of Hardwick Township, Sussex Co.; will of. Wife [not named]. Children—John, Nathan, Joseph, Sarah, Elizabeth, Henry and William. Real and personal estate. Executors—sons Joseph and William. Witnesses—Edward Pigot, Jeames Stark, Henry Crosley. Proved Oct. 8, 1760. Lib. 10, p. 465.
1760, Sept. 23. Inventory, £124.9.3, by Henry Crosley and Ephraim Darby.

1751, Dec. 29. Lacony, William, of Chester, Burlington Co., yeoman; will of. Children—Lecony, James, John, Mary and Katherine, the last two under age. Homefarm. Personal estate. Executors—the father and son James. Witnesses—David Walker, Patrick Jones, Samuel Atkinson. Proved May 24, 1759. Lib. 9, p. 291.
1759, May 7. Inventory, £166.17.7, incl. a negrowoman and child, £55; bonds, book debts and notes, £35.0.1; made by James and Elias Toy.

1760, Mar. 6. Lafollet, John, of Newtown, Sussex Co. Int. Bond of William Boyd and William Throckmorton, largest creditors, as Adm'rs, residents of "Mendum" and Roxbury, Morris Co., merchants.
Lib. G, p. 278.

1753, Jan. 16. Laing, John, of Elizabeth, Essex Co., yeoman. Int. Adm'rs—Benjamin Laing and Samuel Drake. Bondsman—James Manning, yeoman. Wtiness—Thomas Bartow. Lib. F, p. 84.
1753, Jan. 12. Inventory, £311.7.10, by James Manning and John Hepburn.
1753, Jan. 15. Account filed.

1751, Sept. 24. Lake, John, of Amwell, "Hondordon" Co., yeoman; will of. Wife, Sarah. Children—Hannah, John and Josep. Real and personal estate. Executors—the wife and brother-in-law, Daniel Baley (Bailis). Witnesses—Jacob Hortain (Horton), Mary Hortain, Jonathan Stout. Proved Nov. 2, 1751. Lib. 7, p. 221.
1751, Oct. 25. Inventory, £153.15.3½, of which £96.11.6 consist of value of 60 acres of land, a stack of wheat and two of rye; the balance personal; made by Jonathan Stout and William Allen, the one executor signing as Daniel Baylis, Jr.

1752, Feb. 20. Lake, John, of New Brunswick, Middlesex Co., yeoman; will of. Wife, Martinah. Children—Richard, Nailee, Hannah and Sarah. Granddaughter, Hanna, dau. of dec'd son John. Real and personal estate. Executors—son Richard and Daniel Bayleys (Baylis), Jr. Witnesses—Mathias Poland, Johannis Groenendyck, John Reynolds, Awrey Longstreet. Proved May 6, 1754. Lib. F, p. 172.
1753, Nov. 30. Inventory: Real estate, 157 acres in New Brunswick, £300; 266 ac. in Hunterdon Co., £350; personal, £122.9, incl. rents due, £21.19; made by John Reynolds and Awrey Longstreet.

1760, Mar. 7. Lake, John; will of. Wife (second), Elsia. Children—Elisabeth, Rachel and Gisburt, all under age; an expected child. Personal estate. Executors—Richard van Cleave, of Freehold, Daniel Lack, of Gravesend, L. I., and brother-in-law, Garrit Longstreat, of Squan. Witnesses—Hendrick Voorhees, Jr., and William Clark. Proved May 24, 1760. Lib. G, p. 224.

1758, Oct. 19. Lamb, Ann, widow of Jacob, of Northampton, Burlington Co., yeoman; will of. Children—Jacob (who has wife Elizabeth and sons Jacob and Joseph), Mary (wife of Zachariah Rossel). Personal estate. Executor—James Wills. Witnesses—Robert Hill, Thomas Folwell, John Ewan. Proved Dec. 19, 1758. Lib. 9, p. 142.
 1758, Dec. 18. Inventory, £166.6.8½, incl. bonds, £63.14.1; made by Thomas Budd and George Briggs.
 1758, Dec. 19. Bond of John Lamb as Adm'r with the will annexed; Abraham Hewlings, Esq., fellowbondsman, both of said Co.
Burl. Wills, 6135 C.

1760, Apr. 17. Lamb, John, of Northampton, Burlington Co.; will of. Wife [not named]. Children—Anne, Joseph and Jacob, all under age. Real and personal estate. Executors—brother, Jacob Lamb, and Abraham Leeds. Witnesses—Godfrey Hancock, Nathaniel Haines, John Fenimore. Proved May 22, 1760. Lib. 10, p. 210.
 1760, May 21. Inventory, £213.17, incl. a bond from William Budd, £29.6; the rest "sundries" of cattle, wheat, etc.; made by Henry Cooper and Jeremiah Hains (Haines).

1743, Sept. 16. Lamberson, John, of Freehold, Monmouth Co., yeoman; will of. Wife, Maycy. Children—(all called "Johnson"), John, Joseph, Rulef, James, Abraham, Anne, Else and Mary. Real and personal estate. Executors—the wife, Maycy Lamberson, son John Johnson, Tunis van der Veer and Garret Whycoff. Witnesses—John Sutfin, Hendryck Voorhes and Richard Pittenger. Proved May 27, 1760. Lib. G, p. 225.
 1760, July 9. Inventory, £237.9, incl. books, 6s.; made by John Longstreet and Timothy Lloyd (?).

1753, Nov. 27. Lambert, John, of Trenton, Hunterdon Co., tanner. Int. Inventory, £50.16.11, incl. a Bible 4s.; an English Dictionary, 8s.; 6 small books 4s.; made by Joseph Yard, Charles Axford and Edward Paxton.
 1753, Dec. 5. Bond of Nathan Beakes as Adm'r; Edmund Beakes fellowbondsman, both of Trenton. Hunt. Wills, 335 J.

1758, Aug. 17. Lambert, Joseph, of Essex Co., yeoman. Int. Adm'x —Elizabeth, his widow. Bondsman—Thomas Woodruff, yeoman.
Lib. F, p. 547.

1756, Aug. 17. Lambert, Samuel, of the Borough of Elizabeth, Essex Co., mariner, bound on a voyage to the Island of St. Kitts, W. I.; will of. Wife, Phebe. Children—names not given. Mother, Joanna Lambert. Real and personal estate. Executors—the wife and Jonathan Williams. Witnesses—John Spining, Phebe Spining, John Jones. Proved August 4, 1760. Lib. G, p. 272.

1760, Oct. 18. Lambson, Daniel, of Pen's Neck, Salem Co., yeoman; will of. Wife, Sarah, sole Executrix. Son, Thomas. Personal estate. Witnesses—Mathias Lambson, John Marshall and Christian Cornelouson. Proved Nov. 13, 1760. Lib. 10, p. 484.
 1760, Nov. 12. Inventory, £130.13.6, by Joseph Wright and Alexander Hill.

CALENDAR OF WILLS—1751-1760   191

1756, Nov. 4. Lampson, Daniel, of Newark, Essex Co. Int. Adm'x Unice, his widow. Bondsman—Nathaniel Ogden. Witness—Uzal Ogden.
Lib. F, p. 405.

1757, Apr. 29. Lane, John, of the "Burrough" of Elizabeth, Essex Co., "giner" (joiner); will of. Sister, Bobrow Lane, sole heiress. Stephen Burrowes sole Executor of real and personal estate. Witnesses—Samuel Olliver, William Springer, Jorge (George) Horess. Proved Dec. 3, 1757.
Lib. F, p. 496.

1751, Feb. 5. Langerfeldt, John, of Lebanon Twsp., Hunterdon Co. Int. Inventory: Real, 128 acres held by perpetual lease, £150; personal, £141.6, incl. 100 bush. of wheat, £17.10; made by Ralph Smith and Baltes Bickel (Pickel).
1751, Feb. 20. Bond of widow, Christina Langerfeldt, (who signs in German), as Adm'x; Baltes Bickel, of "Readingtown," said Co., tanner, fellowbondsman.
1756, May 31. Account of the estate by Christian Lambert, late Christian Langerfeldt, who has paid out £365.2.6, but does not state value of the inventory.
Hunt. Wills, 298 J.

1758, Sept. 6. Langlee, Thomas, of Morris Co. Int. Inventory: Real, forge and sawmill £180; a garden, 14s.; house on the hill, £2.4. Personal, £160, incl. bonds and book debts, £60.5.4; made by William Throckmorton and William Boyd.
1758, Sept. 25. Margret Langlee, widow, resigns her right of administration to Joseph Coe, Jr. Dated at "Musknecung, Roxbery Township, Morris Co."
1758, Oct. 9. Bond of Joseph Coe, yeoman, and one of the largest creditors, as Adm'r; Ezekiel Cheever, schoolmaster, fellowbondsman, both of Morris Co.
Lib. F, p. 554.

1759, May 24. Lanning, John, of Chester, Burlington Co. Int. Inventory, £157.2.11, by Samuel Atkinson and Jacob Hollinshead.
1759, May 29. Bond of Anne, widow, as Adm'x; Jacob Hollinshead, of Chester Township, said Co., fellowbondsman.
Lib. 9, p. 212.
1760, June 7. Account of the estate by his widow and administratrix, Anne Lanning, who has paid out in settling it £29.11.1.

1755, Mar. 11. Laqueer, Garrardus, of Amwell, Hunterdon Co.; will of. Wife, Ann. Children—John, Hannah, Mary and Joseph, all under age. Real and personal estate. Executors—the wife and John Williamson. Witnesses—Justus Reutzel, Johann Beorg Wagner, Anthony Blackford. Proved April 21, 1755.
1755, Mar. 31. Inventory, £271.13.3, incl. bills, bonds, book debts, cash and clothing, £80.10.6; a servant boy's time; made by Ichabod Leigh and Garret Schenck.
Hunt. Wills, 368 J.

1759, Oct. 3. Large, Ebenezer, of Burlington City, 76 years old; will of, signed with a facsimile stamp. Daughter, Jane Burling. Grandchildren—Mary, Jane and Hannah Burling; Thomas, Joseph and Samuel Pryor. Legacies to Monthly Meeting of Friends at Burlington and to the orphaned daughters of Benjamin Walker, "formerly my servant." House and lot in Burlington, bought of Dinah Bard; land in City limits; water gristmill, with house and land, in Salisbury Township, Bucks Co., Penna., bought of Ambrose Barcroft and now occupied by Thomas Pryor, Sr.; farm of 230 acres in Plumstead Township, Bucks Co., Penna. Personal property. Executors—the daughter, Jane Burling, and the three Pryor grandsons. Witnesses—Hannah Woolston, Hannah Kirkbride, Richard Smith. Proved Dec. 13, 1760. Lib. 10, p. 135.

1760, Dec. 9. Inventory, £2375.11.1, incl. bonds and mortgages, £1902.5.1; cash, £150.3.3; a silver watch, £6.10; a clock £10; a looking glass, £1.5; another do., 2s.6d.; another do., £2.10; a fourth do., £1.5; a fifth do., 15s.; a sixth, £3; silver plate, £67.19.3; 17 bush. of Indian corn, £1.18.3; books, £5.2; made by Edward Cathrall and John Hoskins.

1768, Feb. 6. Account by Thomas Pryor, Acting Executor.

1744, Dec. 24. Laughton, Benjamin, of Cape May Co., tailor; will of. Wife, Elisabeth. Son-in-laws (stepsons?). John Bancroft, and Nathan Newton. Legacy to William Laughton, of Salem Co. Home farm; land bought of Henry Young as trustee of Messrs Latouch & Hanes, of New York City, agents of the West New Jersey Society in England. Personal property incl. silver buttons. Executors—the wife and her son, John Bancroft. Witnesses—Thomas Bancroft, John Foster, John Chester, Jacob Spicer. Proved August 23, 1760. Lib. 11, p. 66.

1760, Aug. 27. Inventory, £186.18.5, by John Eldredge and Ebenezer Johnson.

1752, May 19. Laux, Johan, of Amwell Township, Hunterdon Co., yeoman; will of. Wife, Mary, sole heiress of personal estate. Legacy to brother Derrick's oldest son, "if he calls for it." Executors—the wife, Andrew Mandle and Peter Rocoveller, (Rockefeller), Jr. Witnesses—William Taylur, Herman Stittger (Stitter), Garr'd Williamson. Proved September 22, 1752. Lib. 7, p. 395.

1752, Sept. 26. Inventory, £1189.11.1, incl. bonds, £617.7.7; a mortgage on Jacob Arwin's land, £500; a clock, £7; books, 30s.; 2 looking glasses 6s.; made by John Opdyck and William Taylor.

1748, July 13. Lawrence, Benjamin, of Upper Freehold Township, Monmouth Co.; will of. Children—Mary, Elisabeth and Joseph. Real and personal estate. Executors—daughter Mary, son Joseph and cousin Robert Lawrence. Witnesses—Joseph Everingham, Samuel Davenport, Ruth Emley and Elizabeth Lawrence, Jr. Proved May 19, 1755. Lib. 8, p. 161.

1755, May 16. Inventory, £117.15, incl. a desk and clock, £8; 2 Bibles and other books, £3; a negro boy, £42; a negro girl, £35; made by Thomas Cox and John Chamberlin.

1753, Sept. 18. Lawrence, Thomas, of Philadelphia, merchant; will of. Wife, Rachel, £1,500 and my house, lot, wharf and stores where I dwell. Son, Thomas, my house and lot in New Brunswick, East Jersey, which I bought from William Coxe and contains 116 acres; also my Island farm bought of Henry Longfield, and lands on south side of Lawrence brook, bought of John Garret Keyser. Son, John, my Longbridge farm, consisting of the following purchases, besides the 800 acres already conveyed to him, viz., the 500 acre lot I bought from the heirs of Peter Sonmans; about 210 acre lot I bought from Peter Sonmans' surgeon; a lot of 127 acres bought from Benjamin Corle; a lot of 109 acres bought of Adraan Hegaman and a lot of 109 acres bought of Thomas Van Dyke, all lying together and making the said farm. My daughter, Mary, my lands in Jersey called Swego, bought of William Coxe; 130 acres, and land adjoining, bought of Peter Sonmans, Surgeon, 235 acres, and one of 220 acres of said Sonmans; also my land on banks of the Susquehanah, near Paxtan, formerly belonging to Peter Chartier and containing 600 acres; and, after my wife's death, the lot, house, stores and wharf on Water Street, where I dwell. Executors—sons, Thomas and John, and my daughter Mary. Witnesses—Henry Elvas, Richard Swan, Stephen Carmick. Proved May 4, 1754. Lib. 8, p. 125.

1757, June 25. Lawrence, William, of Shrewsbury, Monmouth Co. Int. Mary, widow, declines to administer.
1757, June 25. Bond of Thomas Tilton, Jr., Adm'r; Joseph Potter fellowbondsman, both of Shrewsbury, yeoman. Lib. F, p. 438.
1757, June 30. Inventory, £16.6.10, by William Osbourn, Daniel Havens and Gersham Bills. (Gives testator's residence as Squan).
Filed July 25, 1759. Account by the Administrator, who has sold the property for £19.11.7.

1759, Apr. 18. Leach, John, of Stow Creek, Cumberland Co. Int. Inventory, £7.7.6, by William Moss and Charles Davis.
1759, May 10. Bond of Francis Brewster, of Greenwich Township, said Co., merchant, as Adm'r; William Moss, of Cumberland Co., yeoman, fellowbondsman. Lib. 9, p. 256.

1751, Febr. 7. Leaming, Christopher, of Cape May. Int. Bond of Deborah Leaming as Adm'x; Recompence Hand fellowbondsman, both of Cape May Co. Cape May Wills, 153 E.
1751, Mar. 19-22. Inventory, £464.19, incl. a silver spoon, 17s.; a gold ring, £1; pair of silver buttons, £1.2; silver buckles and clasps, £2.3; three negro slaves, £93; 40 bush. of Indian corn, £4; 40 do. of wheat, £6.13.4; 5 bush. of salt, 6s.3d.; made by Joseph Ludlam and Jacob Spicer.

1753, Oct. 15. Leamyng, Christopher, Jr., only son and heir of Christopher Leaming of Cape May. Petitions that Jacob Spicer may be appointed his Guardian.
1754, Feb. 2. Bond of Jacob Spicer, of Cape May Co., as such Guardians; Isaac De Cow, Jr., of Burlington Co., gent., fellowbondsman. Cape May Wills, 167 E.

1754, Jan. 31. Leberger, Adam, of Piles Grove Township, Salem Co., yeoman; will of. Wife, Barbara, sole heiress and, with William Hall, Executors of real and personal estate. Legacies, however, to the poor and testator's brother in "High Germanie," and to two sisters. Witnesses—Jeremiah Wood, Daniel Bassett and Patrick Gray. Proved Nov. 30, 1758. Lib. 9, p. 374.
1758, Nov. 14. Inventory, £748.2.7, incl. a clock, £10; books; looking glass; bills, bonds, book accounts and indentures, £371.7.3; made by John Richman and Bateman Lloyd.

1759, Oct. 4. Lee, Abraham, Sr., of the "Borrough" of Elizabeth, Essex Co.; will of. Wife, Rachel. Children—William, Abraham, Mary and James, all under age. Home farm; part of Rahway meadows. Personal estate. Executors—brother Deacon (?) John

13

Lee and William Edgar, of Woodbridge. Witnesses—Richard Skiner (Skinner), Henry Baker, Jr., David Edgar. Proved Oct. 29, 1759.
Lib. G, p. 106.

1758, July 1. Lee, David, of Perth Amboy, Middlesex Co.; ward, being son of Joshua Lee, deceased, and an orphan of about 18 yrs of age. Guardian—Andrew Smyth. Bondsman—John Smyth. Witness—Thomas Bartow. Lib. F, p. 530.

1753, Dec. 29. Lee, Elihu, of Great Egg Harbour, Gloucester Co. Int. Inventory, £99.15, by Gideon Scull and Abel Scull.
1754, Apr. 25. Bond of Elezabeth Lee, of Great Egg Harbour, as Adm'x. Lib. 7, p. 463.
1756, June 7. Account by said Administratrix, who reports estate her debtor for £29.8.5.

1760, Jan. 26. Lee, Hezekiah, of Egg Harbour, Glouc. Co. Int. Inventory, £223.14.10½, incl. a piece of cedar swamp, shingles and swamp tools, £103.2.6; book debts, £36.2.4½; made by Nicholas Stillwill and John Bassett.
1760, Feb. 2. Bond of Margaret Lee and Nicholas Stillwell as Adm'rs. Lib. 9, p. 408.

1759, Mar. 6. Lee, John, of Woodbridge, Middlesex Co.; will of. Wife [not named]. Sons—John and Daniel. Daughters—Mary, Sary, Agness and Hannah. All children under age. Bequest to brother, Abraham Lee. Real and personal estate. Executors—David and William Edgar. Witnesses—Benjamin Pack, Samuel Freeman, Jonathan Freeman, Jr. Proved Nov. 12, 1759. Lib. G, p. 110.

1753, Feb. 1. Leeds, James, of Great Egg Harbour, Gloucester Co., yeoman; will of. Brother, Daniel Leeds, sole heir and Executor of real and personal estate. Witnesses—Sarah Leeds, Rebecca Leeds, Japhet Leeds. Proved May 8, 1754. Glouc. Wills, 549 H.
1755, Jan. 6. Inventory, £102.1, incl. a Testament and Young Man's Companion, 5s.; made by John Willing and Richard Harcurt.

1755, Feb. 15. Leeds, Titan, son of Felix, of Northampton, Burlington Co., gent., petitions, that his kinsman, Vincent Leeds, Esq. of Northampton, be appointed his Guardian.
1755, Feb. 15. Bond of Vincent Leeds as such Guardian; William Inskeep fellowbondsman. Burl. Wills, 5633 C.

1753, March 14. Leek, Stephen, of Little Eggharber, in Burlington Co., yeoman; will of. Wife, Sarah, to have use of house and land. Son, John (made Executor), the land after my wife's death. Daughter, Hannah Garrison, 10 shillings. Daughter, Rachel Ford, 10 shillings. Daughter, Sarah Leek, 10 shillings. Witnesses—Mathias Johnson, Lydia Gail, Samuel Lewis. Proved May 14, 1753.
1753, April 25. Inventory, £32.9.0, by Stephen Cramer and Samuel Lewis. Lib. 7, p. 334.

1754, May 28. Lefferson, Lefferd, of Upper Freehold, Monmouth Co., yeoman; will of. Wife, Margret. Children—sons and daughters, of whom only the eldest son, Aurt, is named. Real and personal estate. Executors—brother, Benjamin Lefferson, brothers-in-law, Garret

CALENDAR OF WILLS—1751-1760   195

Weackoff and William Williamson. Witnesses—John Polhemus, Lucas D. Wedt and William Dunterfield. Proved Sept. 16, 1755.
Lib. 8, p. 205.
1755, Sept. 16. Inventory, £364.18.6, incl. books, 15s.; a looking-glass 5s.; negro man, £50; made by John Lawrence and John Polhemus.

1751, Oct. 3. Leforge, Frances, of Piscataway, Middlesex Co., widow; will of. Sons—Abraham, Nicholas, David and Isaac. Grandchildren—John, Nathaniel, David, Frances (wife of Nathaniel Blackford), and Sarah, children of dec'd son John. Personal estate. Executors—son David and Jeremiah Field, both of Piscataway. Witnesses—Elisha Whitehead, Samuel Whitehead, Reune Runyon. Proved Oct. 31, 1755.
Lib. F, p. 287.
1755, Oct. 17. Inventory, £344.19.6, incl. bonds, cash and notes, £276.18.1; 3 French Bibles and other French books, 15s.; made by Reune Runyon and John Webster.

1759, June 12. Leforge, Nicholas, of Piscataway, Middlesex Co.; will of. Children—Nicholas, Jane, Fremis (?), Mary and Temperance. Homeplace; 52 acres between Reuney (Reune) Runyon and Benjamin Dotty, (Doty); 12 ac. adjoining Henry Mallison; other real and personal property. Executors—son Nicholas and Peter Runyon. Witnesses—John Hepburn, Cornelius Bice (Boice) and Joseph Mitchell. Proved August 14, 1759.
Lib. G, p. 93.
1759, Aug. 16. Inventory, £256.19.5, incl. cash and credits, £12.12.2; Bibles, Psalm book, etc., 10s.; looking glass, 14s.; made by Reune Runyon and John Hepburn, who, March 10, 1760, add an inventory of the goods left to dec'd. by Rynear Fontine, appraised at £17.4.6.

1757, Sept. 16. Lenard, Enoch, of "Mendum," Morris Co.; will of. Wife, Elizabeth, to inherit "all my estate" in New England. Legacy to grandson, John Arnold. Executor—Robert Arnold. Witnesses—Joseph Geren, Ebenezer Byram, Michel Corsman. Proved Oct. 19, 1757.
Lib. F, 460.

1759, Oct. 24. Lennox, Richard, of Essex Co. Int. Adm'x—Marcy Lennox, widow, of Elizabeth. Bondsman—Samuel Dunn, of Somerset Co., yeoman. Witness—Thomas Bartow.
1759, Oct. 18. Inventory, £162.12.11, by Samuel Drake and Daniel Fitz Randolph.
Lib. G, p. 105.

1759, April 11. Leonard, Henry, Jr., of New Hanover Co. in North Carolina; will of. To my father, Henry Leonard, all my lands and moveable estate, both at Cape May and in North Carolina. Executor—said father. Witnesses—John Leonard, Jr., William Goff, Dinah Robinson. Proved Oct. 4, 1760.
Lib. 10, p. 161.

1754, Mar. —. Leonard, Mary, of Shrewsbury, (Monmouth Co.), spinster. Int. Inventory, £127.1.2, incl. money at interest, £102.19.11; silver, 52s.; made by John Wardell and Thomas Eatton.
1754, Apr. 17. Joanna Parker and Joseph Leonard, sister and brother of, Mary Leonard, desire that administration may be granted to Thomas Brinley, husband of their elder sister Sarah, father and mother being dead.

1754, May 6. Bond of Thomas Brinley as Adm'r; William Brinley fellowbondsman, both of Shrewsbury, yeomen. Lib. F, p. 171.
1758, Aug. 7. Account by the Adm'r, reporting on hand £80.18.10.

1754, Apr. 2. Leonard, Samuel, of Perth Amboy, Middlesex Co.; will of. Wife ("now wife"), Ann. Daughters—Mary Berrien, Sarah Billop, Rachel Sarjant, Elizabeth (wife of Francis Goelet) and Ann Lawrence. Real and personal estate. Share of daughter, Elizabeth, given in trust to Executors, who are—sons-in-law, John Berrien, Samuel Sarjant and John Lawrence. Witnesses—Thomas Bartow, William Burnet and Andrew Smyth. Codicil of February 7, 1757, gives share of daughter, Mary, to her husband John Berrien in case of her death. Witnesses—James van Horne, John McIlhenney and Philipp van Horne. Second Codicil, of April 13, 1757, makes special bequest to son-in-law, John Lawrence, and provides for all grand children, of whom Elizabeth Lawrence only is mentioned by name. Witnesses— Jo. Christie, Obediah Higbe and William Bloodgood. Proved Feb. 13, 1758. Lib. F, p. 489.

1759, Aug. 6. Leonard, Samuel, of Essex Co. Int. Adm'r—Nathaniel Rusco, of Essex Co., at the request of Sarah Leonard, the mother of Samuel. Bondsman—Abraham Cadmus, of said Co. Witness— Thomas Bartow. Lib. G, p. 92.

1755, Dec. 6. Leonard Thomas, Esq., of Prince Town, Somerset Co.; will of. Nephew, Samuel Leonard, son of my brother Henry Leonard, deceased (whom I deem to be my heir-at-law) 20 shillings. Nephew, Thomas Leonard, brother to said Samuel, plantation in Amwell in Hunterdon Co., near the Delaware, of 300 acres; also the plantation at Fly Brook in Middlesex Co., of 100 acres, on condition that he pay to his brother Capt. Henry Leonard, £40. To nephew, Capt. Henry Leonard, all my claim to the Indian Purchase of land lying between Squam River and Metetieunk, of about 10,000 acres, which I had by deed from the above-named Samuel Leonard, brother of Capt. Henry Leonard; also to him, said Capt. Henry, house and lot in Kingstown, where Benjamin Maple did keep a tavern. To my nephew, John Leonard, son of my late brother John Leonard, dec'd, land on the northwest Branch of Cape Fear River, of 640 acres, near a place called Brumfiton. To nephew, Whitehead Leonard, house and lot I bought of Stephen Gudgeon, in Kingston, now in possession of widow Brunson. To said Whitehead Leonard and John Leonard, his brother (an infant under 21), my grist mill on North side of Opposite Brook in Middlesex Co. To my nephew, Daniel Leonard, son of my deceased brother James Leonard, house and lot in Princetown where Samuel Horner now lives, after the death or marriage of Abigail my now wife, he to pay £10 to his sister, Sarah Leonard, and £10 to my niece, Sarah Tindall, daughter of my said brother. John Leonard. To my said niece, Sarah Leonard, daughter of my late brother James, a lot at Amboy adjacent to a lot devised to her by her late father; also a small plantation in Middlesex Co. where Samuel Groves now lives, of 30 acres. To nephews, Whitehead Leonard, James Leonard and Thomas Leonard, sons of my said brother James, deceased, that land and saw mill in Middlesex Co. on Deep Run, of 1500 acres. To my niece, Nancey Eldridge, £5. All land I hold in partnership with my brother, Samuel Leonard, to go to said Thomas Leonard, son of my dec'd brother James. To my niece, Sarah Leonard, sister of last named Thomas Leonard, £10. To my sister's, Walker's two daughters, £15. To my nephew's, Captain Henry Leonard's, son (his eldest) £10. To niece, Sarah, daughter of my late brother Henry, decd, £10. To Hannah, wife of Richard Salter, Esq., £10. To Pamelia Leonard, daughter of my nephew Thomas, £10. To Lucy Leonard daughter of said Whitehead, £10. To Samuel Homer the plantation in Middlesex Co. I bought of Stephen Gudgeon, Samuel to pay to his daughter, Amey, £10. To the said Sarah Tindall, daughter of my said brother John, dec'd, that land in Middlesex Co. at a place called the Landing, on the Rariton River, above New Brunswick. To my friend, John Berrien, my house and about one acre of land in Kingstown, which I bought of Abraham Bonnell; and to his brother, Peter Berrien, house and lot in Somerset Co., adjoining the plantation where he lives. My wife, Abigail, while my widow, to have house and lot in Princetown where Samuel Homer lives, and, after her marriage or death, it to go to my nephew, Daniel Leonard. Also to my wife the house and lot in Princetown, where Richard Patterson dwells, which she bought of John Dare, Esq., Sheriff of Middlesex Co., and by her conveyed to me before our marriage, and after her death to go to her 3 daughters Hannah Doughty, Susanna Doughty and Deborah Doughty; also to my wife 5 acres of pasture land lying next to land I sold to Joseph Green. To the said Hannah Doughty the house and lot in Pensneck in Middlesex Co. To Charity, a daughter of my said nephew, Thomas Leonard, and to Mary, daughter of Whitehead Leonard, brother of said Thomas, that house and lot in Kingstown which I bought of Richard Huff. To Charity, another daughter of my nephew Whitehead Leonard, and to the said Deborah Doughty, my house and lot in Kingstown, where Richard Stippey lives. To Thomas Leonard, son of my said nephew Thomas Leonard (one of my Executors) my house and lot in Trenton. To my nephew, Whitehead Leonard, and to his brother, my said nephew Thomas Leonard, sons of my late brother James, the plantation in Middlesex Co. on Grist-Mill Brook, near Kingstown, joining land of Thomas Vandike and west by the Millston River, of 270 acres. To Thomas Leonard, son of my brother James, a tract in Princetown; also plantation where Nathaniel Runnion lives, of 20 acres; also my plantation called Man's Grove; also the plantation I had of the Stocktons; also my plantation called Cole Brook. To my nephew, James Leonard, son of my brother James, plantation in tenure of Nevill Furman; also plantation where Jeremiah Denton lives. To Thomas Leonard, of Crosswicks, son of John Leonard, my nephew, the house and lot in Kingstown where Martha Hide lives. My nephew, Thomas Leonard, son of my brother James, land in Prince Town of 130 acres. Executors— nephew, Thomas Leonard, son of my brother James, and my friend, John Berrien, of Rockyhill. Witnesses—Thomas Watson, Richard Patterson, Joseph Murrow.

1759, June 1. Codicil. Witnesses—Thomas Watson, Joseph Yard, Jr., Joseph Murrow. Proved Nov. 23, 1759. Lib. 10, p. 1.

1759, Aug. 6. **Leonard, William**, of Essex Co. Int. Adm'r—Nathaniel Rusco, of Essex Co., at the request of Sarah Leonard, mother of William. Bondsman—Abraham Cadmus, of said Co. Witness—Thomas Bartow. Lib. G, p. 92.

1728, May 20. **Leslie, George, Sr.**, of the City of Perth Amboy, Middlesex Co., gentleman; will of. Wife, Elizabeth. Children—

George Willocks, John, Edmund, James, Margret, all under age. Real property, 600 to 700 acres, inherited from uncle, George Willocks, in Amwell or Redingstown, on Westside of Alamitunck River, adjoining Lord Neal Campbell's 1,000 ac. tract; farm of Rudyard; land in East Jersey; houses and lots in Amboy; land above the Falls of Delaware in Pennsylvania, held in company with Clement Plumsted, Andrew Hamilton, Jeremiah Longhorn, dec'd, etc.; all mines and minerals with rights, derived from father-in-law, Col. Edmund Kingsland. Personal estate, incl. 11 negroes; pictures of George Willocks, his wife, Col. Kingsland; cartoons; ferry to Staten Island. Legacies to cousins on sister Richie's side and to sister, Anna Kingsland. Executors—the wife and son, George Willocks Leslie. Witnesses—Richard Frances, John Johnston, Rachel Johnston. Codicil of September 18, 1751, provides for son William, born since date of will. Witnesses—Edmund Roger Kingsland, Jonathan Nisbett, William Thorn. Proved Jan. 6, 1753. Lib. F, p. 85.

1753, Mar. 29. Lester, Mary, of Shrewsbury, Monmouth Co., spinster; will of. Divides personal estate between Mary (wife of Robert Citheart, of Shrewsbury, cloather), Hannah, (wife of William Lippincott), her daughter, Hannah and Samuel Parker, of Shrewsbury, cordwainer, making the last two Executors. Witnesses—Phebe Allen and Nancy White. Proved Nov. 6, 1753. Lib. F, p. 191.

1753, Nov. 7. Inventory, £58.6, incl. bonds £26.15; made by Jeremiah Tallman and Elihu Williams.

1760, Dec. 18. Lewis, Isaac, of Chester Township, Burlington Co. Int. Inventory, £26.1.9, by Joseph Morgan and Samuel Burrough.

1760, Dec. 20. Bond of George Pennistone (Pennistown) as Adm'r; Samuel Burrough, Jr., fellowbondsman, both of said County.

Burl. Wills, 6707 C.

1758, Nov. 16. Lewis, John, of Amwell, Hunterdon Co.; will of. Wife, Mary. Children—John, Jacob, Elizabeth, Rebecca, Paul, and Martha. Home farm; land in Trenton and in Kingwood. Personal property. Executors—Jacob Rumbah and Andrew Heath. Witnesses—Abraham Larew, Joseph Hull and John Rouse, Jr. Proved Dec. 5, 1758. Lib. 10, p. 117.

1758, Nov. 30. Inventory, £515.17.8, incl. bills, bonds and other "Duese," £463.9.6; made by Abraham Larew and Jacob Swallow.

1752, Mar. 5. Lewis, Paul, of Chesterfield, Burlington Co. Int. Inventory, £135.7.4; incl. bonds and book debts, £96.13.8; made by William Taylor and Henry Clarke.

1752, Mar. 9. Bond of widow, Hannah Lewis, and Robert Pearson, Esq., of Nottingham, as Adm'rs; William Taylor, of Chesterfield, and Philipp Welsh (Walsh), of Nottingham fellowbondsmen.

Lib. 7, p. 300.

1767, July 3. Account by the Administratrix.

1759, Dec. 7. Lewis, Samuel, of Great Eggharbour, Gloucester Co., blacksmith. Int. Inventory, £115.5, incl. 16 books, etc., 8s.; book debts and notes, £71.14.3; made by Edward Doughty and Samuel Risley.

1759, Dec. 15. Bond of Edward Doughty, Jr., as Adm'r; Edward Doughty, Esq., fellowbondsman, both of Egg Harbour, said Co.

Lib. 9, p. 394.

CALENDAR OF WILLS—1751-1760 199

1757, Apr. 16. Liddon, Benjamin, of "Greanwitch," Gloucester Co.; will of. Wife, Susannah, sole Executrix. Children—Samuel, Abraham and Alce Sidonia. Real and personal estate. Witnesses—Samuel Liddon, James Haines, Jacob Spicer. Proved May 12, 1757.
Lib. 8, p. 392.
1757, May 10. Inventory, £275.13.5, by Francis Batten and Jacob Spicer.

1754, Apr. 23. Liddon, Henry, of Greenwich Township, Gloucester Co., yeoman. Int. Inventory, £85.19.2, incl. books; made by Jacob Spicer and Enoch Haines.
1754, Apr. 26. Bond of widow, Elizabeth, as Adm'x; Enoch Haines, yeoman, fellowbondsman, both of Greenwich Township.
Lib. 7, p. 468.

1760, Dec. 10. Liddon, Samuel, of Greenwich Township, Gloucester Co., yeoman. Int. Bond of Joseph Stennard (Stinyard), of Greenwich Township, sawyer, as Adm'r; Joseph Tatem, of Deptford Township, said Co., cordwainer, fellowbondsman. Lib. 10, p. 289.
1761, ——— —. Inventory, £39.12.1, incl. bonds and book debts, £18.18; made by Joh. Franklin and Robart Maffit.

1759, Aug. 6. Liking, Ezekiel, of Essex Co. Int. Adm'r—Nathaniel Rusco, of Essex Co., by request of Michael Liking, brother of Ezekiel. Bondsman—Abraham Cadmus, of said Co. Witness—Thomas Bartow.
Lib. G, p. 92.

1760, Feb. 16. Liming (Lemmon), Dewilde, of Burlington City; will of. Mother, Dinah Lemmon. Brothers—Henry and Thomas Lemmon. Sisters—Dinah Everingham, Mary and Sarah Lemmon. Real and personal estate. Executors—brother, Thomas, and brother-in-law, Jeremiah Everingham. Witnesses—Isaac Heulings, Elizabeth Miller, George Eyre. Proved April 4, 1760. Lib. 9, p. 439.
1760, Mar. 4. Inventory, £32.6,9, incl. 2 books, viz., "Cambray's Dissertations" and "A Might into ye Treasury," 1s.6d.; made by William Smith and John Carty.

1757, June 14. Liming, John, Sr., of Upper Freehold Township, Monmouth Co., yeoman; will of. Wife, Dinah. Children—John, Henry, William, Thomas, De Wilda, Dinah Everingham, Mary and Sarah. Children of daughter, Kesiah Combs, viz., Lydia and Dinah. Home farm; land bought of Abraham Limon; meadow bought of Thomas Saltar; land bought of Richard Compton. Personal property. Executors—the wife, son William and Robert Hutcheson. Witnesses—John Johnston, John Combs and William Lawrence. Proved Dec. 22, 1757. Lib. 9, p. 54.

1757, Feb. 28. Linmire, Christopher, of Pens Neck, (Salem Co.). Int. Inventory, £193.1.2, incl. book debts, £40.14.10; made by Samuel Linch and John Helms.
1757, Mar. 2. Bond of Ann Linmire as Adm'x; John Helms fellowbondsman, both of said Co. Lib. 8, p. 445.

1758, May 26. Lippincott, Caleb, of Evesham, Burlington Co. Int. Inventory, £214.15.3, incl. two servantmen's time, £9; made by James Cattell and Micajah Wills.

1758, May 30. Bond of Joshua Lippincott as Adm'r; James Cattell fellowbondsman, both of said Co. Lib. 8, p. 533.
1769, Apr. 4. Account by the Administrator.

1748, May 21. Lippincott, Jacob, of Shrewsbury Town, Monmouth Co., yeoman; will of. Children—John, Jacob, Obadiah, Thomas, David and Margaret. Land, house and smith shop; blacksmith's tools, bought of Samuel Lippincott; homefarm, adjoining mother's; meadow, bought of Daniel Lippincott. Personal property. Executors—sons John, Jacob and Obadiah. Witnesses—Thomas Crafts, Anthony Dennis and Jacob Dennis. Proved Sept. 27, 1757. Lib. F, p. 451.
1757, Sept. 10. Inventory, £139.1.4, incl. bonds and notes, £48.11.7; a looking glass 11s.; another do., 2s.; made by Timothy Akin and Josiah Parker.

1757, June 30. Lippincott, Jacob, of Chester Township, Burlington Co., yeoman; will of. Wife, Grace, sole Executrix. Children—Jacob and Mary. Brothers—Thomas and Ezeakel, remaindermen. Real and personal estate. Witnesses—Robert French, Bartholomew Waricote, William Rudderow. Proved August 1, 1757. Lib. 8, p. 433.
1757, July 12. Inventory, £73.9.6, incl. 2 Bibles, 7s.6d.; made by John Cox and William Rudderow.

1754, Feb. 20. Lippincott, Jacob, of "Green weach" Township, Gloucester Co., yeoman; will of. Wife, Mary. Children—Joseph, Benjamin, Restore, Caleb, Jacob, Joshua, Samuel, William (under age), Mary Spicer, Hannah Lord and Sary Hains. Home farm, bought of Jacobus van Culin. Personal property. Executors—the wife, with sons Restore and Joshua. Witnesses—Archabell Silver, Abel Silver, Samuel Silver. Proved April 29, 1757. Lib. 8, p. 388.
1757, Apr. 25. Inventory, £708.18.1, incl. a clock, looking glass, silver tea spoons; bonds and book debts, £513.10.10; made by Samuel Lippincott and David Davis.

1759, Jan. 31. Lippincott, Jacob, of Shrewsbury, Monmouth Co. Int. Inventory, £193.19, incl. a large looking-glass, £5; a Bible and sundries, 13s.; made by Timothy Akin and Josiah Parker.
1760, Jan. 19. Bond of Lydia, widow, as Adm'x; George Woolley, of same place, yeoman, fellowbondsman. Lib. G, p. 176.

1752, July 9. Lippincott, James, Jr., of Northampton, Burlington Co., yeoman; will of. Children-in-law, Aaron and Judith, children of Aaron and Elizabeth Lippincott, (testator calling said Elizabeth, "my last wife, dec'd"). Cousin, William, son of brother Moses Lippincott. Brothers—Aaron, John, Daniel and Jonathan Lippincott. Sister, Increase (wife of Joshua Humphris). Cousin, Rachel Vinicomb. Personal estate. Executors—brothers-in-law, Joshua Humphris and Isaac Burroughs. Witnesses—Silvester Sharp, Samuel Lippincott, John Burr, Jr. Proved August 7, 1752.
1752, July 22-27. Inventory, £459.3.3, incl. a servant man's time, £9; a do. boy's time, £9; bonds of William Budd, Samuel Kemble, John Allen, Joshua Humphris, John Ewan, William Claypoole, James Lippincott, Michael Arnest, Thomas Shinn, Jr., Thomas Allinson and Joseph Burr, Jr., £48.11.6; the estate of his dec'd wife Elizabeth, £164.16, which includes 8 silver spoons, a thimble and a pocketbook £2.1.6, and debts due by Jacob Hugg, Thomas Cheesman, Joab Hill-

CALENDAR OF WILLS—1751-1760   201

man, Thomas Hackny, Abram Heas and John Hancock, £58.9; made by John Burr, Jr., and Thomas Allinson. Burl. Wills, 5047 C.

1760, Sept. 26. Lippincott, James, of Northampton, Burlington Co., yeoman; will of. Wife, Anna. Children—Daniel, Aaron, Increase, Anna and Jerusha. Grandson, Joseph, son of dec'd son John. Farm in Evesham; home farm in Bridgetown, between Ancokus Creek and the Milerace. Personal estate. Executor—son Daniel. Witnesses—William Jones, Alexander Ross, John Burr, Jr. Proved Dec. 20, 1760.
Lib. 10, p. 148.
1760, Nov. 20. Inventory, £243.18.8, incl. bonds and notes, £106; a girl's time; a clock; made by Joshua Ballinger and James Cattell.

1759, Feb. 12. Lippincott, Job, of Springfield, Burlington Co.; will of. Wife [not named]. Children—Job, Anne, (wife of Revel Elton) and Sary. Real and personal estate. Executor—brother, Samuel Lippincott. Witnesses—Edward Gaskill, Samuel Lippincott, John Fenimore. Proved June 11, 1759, when Samuel Lippincott refused to act as Executor. Lib. 9, p. 223.
1759, June 11. Anna Lippincott, widow, writes to Charles Read, that Samuel Lippincott, made Executor of her husband's will, refusing to act, she also declines in favour of her son, Job Lippincott.
1759, June 11. Bond of Job Lippincott as Adm'r; Henry Paxson and Samuel Lippincott fellowbondsmen, all of said Co.
1759, June 13. Inventory, £903.19.2, incl. his purse, £370.16.10; a silver watch; bills, bonds, etc., £316.7.3; household goods and furniture, £113.1.7; made by Henry Paxson and Samuel Lippincott.

1758, Feb. 28. Lippincott, Jonathan, of Northampton, Burlington Co., yeoman; will of. Wife, Ann. Sons—James, Levi William, Samuel (all under age). Home farm in Northampton, bought of father, James Lippincott, farm in Evesham, also bought of father; meadow adjoining, bought of brother, John Lippincott. In case sons James and Levi should die under age and without issue their shares to be given to Moses, son of brother Aaron Lippincott, and James, son of brother, Daniel Lippincott. Legacies to Rachael, daughter of Francis Vinecombe, and Joseph, son of brother John Lippincott. Executors—the wife and brother Daniel. Witnesses—James Lippincott, John Atkinson, John Burr, Jr. Proved June 16, 1759. Lib. 9, p. 229.
1759, June 11. Inventory, £262.4.1½, incl. books; made by Joseph Lippincott and Micajah Wills.

1751, Aug. 17. Lippincott, Joseph, of Monmouth Co.; will of. Wife, Susannah. Sons—Samuel, Robbart, Joseph, Benjamin and Thomas. Real and personal estate. Executors—sons Samuel and Joseph. Witnesses—Adam Brewer, John Morford, Remembrance Lippincott, John Fish. Proved Sept. 27, 1751. Lib. E, p. 549.

1760, Mar. 3. Lippincott, Margaret, of Shrewsbury, Monmouth Co., single woman; will of. Divides estate between cousins Dinah and Elisabeth, (daughters of dec'd brother Jacob Lippencott), Mary, wife, Lydia, daughter, and Jacob, son of brother John Lippencott; sister-in-law, Lydia Lippencott; Elisabeth, wife, and Jacob, son, of brother David Lippencott; brother, Thomas Lippencott, and Jacob, son of brother Obediah Lippencott. Brother, John, sole Executor. Wit-

nesses—Ann White, Elisabeth Borden and Sarah Lippencott. Proved May 15, 1760. Lib. G, p. 382.
1761, Mar. 6. Inventory, £76.1.6, by Joseph Hulit and John Allen.

1752, May 27. Lippincott, Moses, of Northampton, Burlington Co., yeoman; will of. Wife, Merriby. Children—William and Rachel, both under age. Legacies to mother, Anna Lippincott, brothers John, James, Daniel, Jonathan and Aaron Lippincott, sisters Increase, (wife of Joshua Humphris), Anna (widow of Thomas Taylor) and Jerusha (wife of Amos Rockhill), and cousin Rachel, daughter of Francis Vinicomb. Real and personal estate. Executors—brother-in-law, Joshua Humphris, and Francis Vinicomb. Witnesses—Thomas Allinson, John Burr, Jr., Mary Kemble. Codicil of same date gives legacy to cousin Merriby, daughter of Thos. Taylor, dec'd. Same witnesses. Proved August 7, 1752.
1752, July 21. Inventory, £200.14.6, incl. a Bible and other books, 6s.; a servant man's time, £10; debts due by Walker Atkinson, Thomas Foster, Adam Forker, Abraham Brian, John Clark, John West, Josiah White, Joseph Burr, Jr., Thomas Allinson, John Ewan, Jacob Parker, John Forken, Henry Paxson, Oddy Broek, £30.12.6; made by John Burr, Jr. and Thomas Allinson. Burl. Wills, 5055 C.

1759, Mar. 20. Lippincott, Samuel, of Evesham, Burlington Co., 75 years old; will of. Daughter, Mary (wife of Samuel Coles). Grandchildren—Abel and Samuel Lippincott; Samuel and Judith, children of dec'd son Aaron; Samuel, Sarah and Martha White, children of dec'd daughter Martha. Sister, Mary Peake. Housekeeper, Mary Hoel placed in charge of grandson Samuel Lippincott, and the farm, left to him, until he is of age. Real and personal estate. Executors—son-in-law, Samuel Coles, Abraham Allin and cousin, Joshua Lippincott. Witnesses—William Sharp, Isaac Buzby, Silvester Sharp. Proved March 6, 1760. Lib. 9, p. 410.
1760, Feb. 27, 28. Inventory, £1670.6.6, incl. purse or cash, £246.15.9; bills, bonds and book debts, £844.6.3; 4 silver tea and 6 do. large spoons, £6.10; a looking glass; Bible and 29 other books, £10.5.3; a servant man's time, £16; a clock, £9; made by Joshua Stokes, Joshua Ballinger and Enoch Roberts.
1763, June 2. Account by the Executors.

1755, May 23. Lippincott, Thomas, of Chester, Burlington Co., yeoman; will of. Children—Isaac, Nathaniel, Abigail, Esther and Mercy. Grandchildren—Thomas and Isaac, sons of Isaac, John, son of Nathaniel, Mary Wills, Meribah Rudderow, Daniel Wills, Pheby, daughter of dec'd son Thomas, Hannah and Pheby Andrews, daughters of dec'd. daughter Patience. Legacy to daughter-in-law, Rebecah Middleton, for "services done." Real and personal estate. Executors—sons Nathaniel and Isaac. Witnesses—Arthur Borradaill, John Matlack, Samuel Atkinson. Proved Oct. 7, 1757. Lib. 8, p. 462.
1755, Sept. 24. Inventory, £568.0.6, incl. bills and bonds, £436.4.8; a Bible and other books, 35s.; made by Joshua Humphris and John Cox.
1767, Sept. 19. Account by the Executors.

1760, Jan. 4. Lippincott, Thomas, of Shrewsbury, Monmouth Co., yeoman; will of. Wife, Hannah. Children, Sarah, Elizabeth, Mary, Rachel, Uriah, Thomas and Abula (under age). Children of daughter

Survyah. Granddaughter Elisabeth White. Real and personal estate. Executors—the wife, son Uriah and Thomas Borden, Jr. Witnesses—James Corliss, Samuel Curlies and Benjamin Boucher. Proved Feb. 5, 1760. Lib. G, p. 170.

1759, June 21. Littell, Abraham, of the Borough of Elisabeth, Essex Co.; will of. Wife, Mary. Sons—Abraham, Amasa and Amos, all under age. Real and personal estate. Executors—the wife and David Ross, Sr. Witnesses—John Woodruff, Henry Clarke, Jr., Ebenezer Price. Proved July 30, 1759. Lib. G, p. 90.
1759, June 28. Inventory, £103.4.2, by Cornelius Ludlam and John Williams, both of Elizabeth.

1760, Feb. 5. Littell, Benjamin, of the Borough of Elizabeth, Essex Co., yeoman; will of. Wife, Suzanah. Children—Isaac, Moses, John, Mary, Sarah and Suzanah. Real and personal estate. Executors—sons Isaac and Moses. Witnesses—John Stites, John Stites, Jr., Margaret Stites, Jr. Proved June 20, 1760. Lib. G, p. 235.

1751, Mar. 18. Little, John, Esq., of Shrewsbury. Inventory of the personal estate, £960.13, incl. a looking glass, £1; 3 silver teaspoons; books and pamphlets, £10; 3 negro men, 3 negro women and 2 children, £200; bonds and book debts, £367.17.8; made by Joseph Allen and Joseph Potter. [For will, see Vol. XXX, N. J. Archives, p. 302, where the dates of 1750 should read 1751].

1756, Feb. 21. Livingston, Robert, of Deerfield, Cumberland Co. Int. Inventory, £54.1.2, incl. a silver watch, £7; made by Charles Clark and Robert Dare.
1756, Feb. 26. Bond of Patiance Livingston as Adm'x; James Davis, fellowbondsman, both of Deerfield. Cumb. Wills, 140 F.

1753, Nov. 23. Lock, Israel, of Gloucester Township and County, yeoman. Int. Inventory, £63.15.11, incl. bills and bonds, £55.15; 2 old books; made by Isaiah Davenport and Walter Fawcet.
1754, Jan. 25. Bond of Thomas Duell, of Penns Neck Township, Salem Co., as Adm'r; Jacob Cozens, of Greenwich Township, Gloucester Co., fellowbondsman, both yeomen. Glouc. Wills, 552 H.

1759, May 8. Lock, Jesper, of "Grenage" Township, Gloucester Co.; will of. Makes brother's, Peter Lock's, youngest son, Jasper, sole heir of real estate and, in case of his death without issue, Peter's eldest son, Peter, to inherit the farm and meadow. Brothers, Charles, Jonas and Peter Lock receive the personal property, the latter two being named Executors. Witnesses—Isaiah Davenport, John Wilkinson, Mary Cox. Proved May 29, 1759. Lib. 9, p. 271.
1759, May 21. Inventory, £33.0.1, by Isaiah Davenport and Henry Hendrickson.

1749, June 5. Lockoney, James, of Chester, Burlington Co., yeoman; will of. Wife, Katherine and son, William, heirs and Executors of real and personal estate including two negro slaves. Legacy to the use of the poor in Chester Township. Witnesses—David Walker, Bartho Horner, Joshua Wright. Proved July 3, 1752, when William Lockoney qualifies as "surviving" Executor.
1752, June 20. Inventory, £147.18, incl. bills, bonds and book debts,

£85.2; a negro girl, £27; a gold ring, £1.5; two looking glasses, £1.1; made by David Walker and Samuel Davis. Burl. Wills, 5039 C.

1759, Sept. 29. Loftus, Ralph, of Philadelphia. Int. Jane, widow, refuses to administer on his estate but favoured Samuel Tucker, Jr. 1759, Oct. 12. Bond of Samuel Tucker, Jr., merchant, as Adm'r; Joseph Higbee fellowbondsman, both of Trenton, Hunterdon Co.
Lib. 9, p. 420.

1749, Oct. 7. Long, Ellenor, of Greenwich, Gloucester Co., widow; will of. Children—Peter, Abraham, Andrew, Dorothy, Deborah, Sarah. Grandchildren—Deborah, Paul, Susannah Lawrence, Catharine Bartleson, Sarah Long, Ellenor Thakery. Daughter Sarah and son-in-law, Alexander Randall residuary legatees and Executors of personal estate. Witnesses—Jonathan Fowler, John Wilkinson, Abel Randal. Proved Oct. 6, 1752. Lib. 7, p. 296.
1752, Oct. 6. Inventory, £178.13.1½, incl. a Bible £1, bills, bonds and notes, £157.6.10½, made by Jonathan Fowler and Jeffree Clark.

1759, Apr. 14. Long, Joseph, of Hopewell Township, Cumberland Co., yeoman; will of. Children—David, John (sole Executor), Malachi, Ellioner and Elizabeth. Real and personal estate incl. silver shoe buckle and a large Bible. Witnesses Azel Peirson Junior, George Peirson, Robert Nichols. Proved Oct. 17, 1760. Lib. 10, p. 203.
1760, Oct. 16. Inventory, £97.18.9, by Joseph Snethen and Daniel Stretch.

1754, Aug. 25. Long, Peter, of Stoe Creek, Cumberland Co., weaver; will of. Wife, Grace. Children—Ansell, David, Nathan, Eleonor Shipard, and Pleasant. Real and personal estate. Executors—the wife and son, Ansell. Witnesses—Dan Simkins, James MacFersen, Josep Simkins. Proved March 26, 1755. Lib. 8, p. 143.
1755, Apr. 11. Inventory, £408.2.3, incl. bills, bonds, book debts and library, £130.7.3; a negro man, wheat and corn, £35.8; made by John Rementon and John Finlaw.

1758, July 7. Longstreet, Cristofil, of Freehold, Monmouth Co.; will of. Wife [not named]. Children—Court and Cristina, both under age. Real and personal estate. Executors—brother, John Longstreet, brother-in-law, Aurt Zutphen, of Middletown, and Garret Schanck. Witnesses—Koert Schenck, Isaac Sutphen and Cornelius Couwenhoven. Proved Oct. 18, 1758. Lib. F, p. 557.
1758, Nov. 20. Inventory, £703.15.4, incl. bills, cash, bonds and book debts, £477.9.1; books, £1.5; two 'prentices, £20; made by Peter Cowenhoven, Dirik Zutphen, Jr., and Isaac Sutphen.

1755, Apr. 20. Longstreet, Gisbert, of Shrewsbury, Monmouth Co.; will of. Wife, Rachel. Children—Garret, Gisbert (both under age), Moyca, Nelley, Jane and Rachel. Real and personal estate. Executors—James Irons, Sr., Garret Scanck and John Longstreet, Sr. Witnesses—Koert Schenck, Garret Schanck and Nelley Schanck. Codicil of August 31, 1757, provides that a part of the bequest, given to dec'd daughter Jane, alias Onicha, be given to grandson, Guisberd Lake, mentions children of dec'd daughter Moica and a daughter Elizabeth. Witnesses—Moses Richards, Thomas Ellison and John Lake. Proved Nov. 8, 1758. Lib. G, p. 4.

CALENDAR OF WILLS—1751-1760   205

1758, Nov. 13. Inventory, £1265.15.10, incl. bills, bonds, book debts and cash, £704.18.4; 320 bush. of Indian corn, £32; 3 Dutch books, 10s.; others 12s.; half a book called "the Confesions," £1; two looking glasses, 16s.; 2 negroes, £100; made by Thomas Ellison, Ebenezer Cook and David Johnston, with James Irons, Jr., as clerk.

1752, Apr. 8. Longstreet, Moicae, of Shrewsbury Township, Monmouth Co., widow; will of. Children—Stoffel, Gisbert, Jeane, Cattren, Marcy, Sary, Masy and Anne. Personal estate. Executors—son Gisbert, John Little and William Hendrickson. Witnesses—Jeames Jorns (Trons), Gershom Bills, John Lake. Proved March 13, 1753. Lib. F, p. 105.
1753, Mar. 20. Inventory, £147.13, incl. half of a Bible, 15s.; a sermon book, 5s.; bonds and debts, £110.15.2; made by Thomas Ellison and William Osbourn.

1750, Aug. 14. Loosheet, Johannes Peter, of Amwell Township, Hunterdon Co., yeoman; will of. Wife, Christina to have household goods. Land to be sold and money to go to my wife and my son John. Brother, Christian, and brother-in-law, Peter Wirt, Guardian of my child. Executrix—my wife. Witnesses—Helbortus Poppels Dorff, Andrew Tremer, Garrard Williamson. Proved April 30, 1751.
1751, April 16. Inventory, £62.7.2, by Andrew Trimmer and Gerrard Williamson. Lib. 7, p. 55.

1753, Aug. 4. Lord, Abraham, of Piles Grove, Salem Co. Int. Inventory, £135.11.10, incl. books; made by Matthew Gill and Archabell Silver.
1753, Aug. 18. Bond of Ann Lord as Adm'x; Archabell Silver fellowbondsman, both of Piles Grove. Lib. 8, p. 92.

1756, Feb. 5. Lord, Abraham, Jr., of Salem Co., son of Abraham, petitions, that Archabald Silvers of said Co. be appointed his guardian.
1756, Feb. 5. Bond of Archabell (Archibald) Silvers as such guardian, Thomas Richards of Burlington Co. fellowbondsman.
Lib. 8, p. 254.

1752, Dec. 2. Lord, James, of "Debford" Township, Gloucester Co., yeoman; will of. Mother, Elizabeth Lord. Sister, Sarah (wife of Ebenezer Hopkins). Uncles—John Clark and Joshua Lord. Cousins—Sarah, wife of Joseph Gibson, Jr., Elizabeth Lord, James Cooper, David Cooper, Joshua Lord, Jr., Hannah Cooper, Eunice Lord, John Cooper, Ann, (wife of James Whitte), and Sarah, wife of John Brown. Legacy "for the Commendation of a Choole for the Bulders of the House"; also to Friends of Woodberry Creek Meeting "for the use of enclosing the grave yard." Land on Rackoone Creek in Greenwich Township; home farm; lot adjoining John Snowden and Henry Wood; other real and personal estate. Executors—the mother and cousin, John Cooper. Witnesses—Phineas Bond, William Hugg, Restore Lippincott, Jonathan Roberts. Proved Dec. 23, 1752.
Lib. 7, p. 396.

1759, Jan. 7. Lore, Ephraim, of Cumberland Co.; will of. Wife, Anna. Sons—John and Jonathan, both under 20 years old. David,

son of Hezekiah Lore, and Will'm, son of Seth Lore to be remaindermen. Real and personal estate. Executors—the wife and Seth Lore. Witnesses—Edmen Shaw, John Coleman, Amos Townsend. Proved March 1, 1759. Lib. 9, p. 227.
 1759, ——— ——. Inventory, £101.17.3, incl. books, £1.12.6; made by Amos Townsend and William Dalles.

1755, Feb. 27. Lott, Peter, of Trenton, Hunterdon Co., yeoman; will of. Wife, Hannah. Sisters—Antie and Maria. Brothers—Hendrick and Mourice Lott. Nephews—Peter (son of Hendrick Lott) and Peter (son of Jacob and Catrina Rappleye). Real and personal estate. Executors—the above named two brothers, Hendrick and Mourice, and Timothy Smith. Witnesses—Daniel Scudder, Samuel Hand, Amos Scudder. Proved May 6, 1755. Lib. 8, p. 164.
 1755, May 5. Inventory, £237.17.5, incl. his Libra, horse saddle and bridle, £17.8; a negro woman and negro girl, £60; a servant man's time £3; made by Garret Johnson and Benjamin Moore.
 1759, May 26. Account by the Executors.

1760, Nov. 15. Loutherback, Conrod, of Piles-grove, Salem Co. Int. Bond of widow, Eliza Loutherback, of Piles-grove as Adm'x; Lawrance Holsten, of the same place, and John Helm, of Penn's Neck, fellowbondsmen. Lib. 10, p. 446.
 1760, ——— ——. Inventory, £120.5.5, by Israel Lock and John Helm.

1742, July 7. Lovett, Jonathan, of Burlington City, saddler; will of. Wife, Sarah, sole Executrix. Children—Samuel, Jonathan, Mary and Sarah. Homestead on "Pirl" Str., adjoining Robert Smith; a water lot and wharf. Personal property. Witnesses—Robert Smith, John Bacon, George Eyres. Proved Jan. 15, 1754. Burl. Wills, 5479 C.

1750, Jan. 8. Low, Peter, of New York City, merchant; will of. Wife, Rachel, to have my real and personal estate, while my widow, and, after her death or marriage, to go to my sons Peter, Cornelius, Nicholas and John, and my daughters Helena, Margret, Jane, Rachel and Elizabeth. Executors—my wife, Rachel, and my two sons, Peter and Cornelius Low. Witnesses—John V. Cortlandt, Cornelius Wynkoop, Benjamin Wynkoop. Proved June 14, 1750. [Foregoing will omitted from preceding volume. County of probate unknown].
Lib. E, p. 425.

1759, Oct. 20. Loyd, Solomon, of Salem Town and Co., inn keeper; will of. Wife, Parcilla. Mother, Elizabeth Loyd. Brother, David. Executors—the wife and Joseph Sharp. Witnesses—John Hart, Branson Vanleer, and Edward Test. Proved Nov. 21, 1759. Lib. 10, p. 529.
 1759, Nov. 10. Inventory, £449.14.8, incl. cash and plate, £4.16.6; corn and a "melata geral," £3.10; book debts, £250.9.2; made by Thomas Rice and Thomas Goodwin.
 1759, Nov. 15. Joseph Sharp, one of the Executors named, "revokes" to act.

1760, Feb. 26. Lucas, Woolledge, of Piscataway, Middlesex Co., cordwainer. Int. Adm'r—Thomas Fitz Randolph, of said Co., who married a sister. Bondsmen—William Riddell and Benjamin Harris, both of Somerset Co., yeomen. Lib. G, p. 129.

CALENDAR OF WILLS—1751-1760

1760, Oct. 16. Luce (Luse), Matthias, of Morris Co. Int. Bond of Joseph Luce as Adm'r; Benjamin Luce fellowbondsman, both of said Co. Lib. G, p. 300.
1760, Feb. 11. Inventory, £47.18.2, by Nathaniel Reeve and Walter Brown. (Filed Mar. 26, 1761).

1760, Apr. 30. Luce (Luse) Zephaniah, of Morris Co. Int. Susannah, widow, declines to administer on his estate, in favour of Samuel Kimble, of New Brunswick, merchant, principal creditor.
1760, May 5. Bond of Samuel Kemble as Adm'r, Philipp French, Jr., fellowbondsman, both of New Brunswick. Lib. G, p. 188.
1760, May 12. Inventory, £141.19.8¼, by Nathaniel Drake and Benjamin Luse.

1753, Feb. 6. Ludlam, Joseph, Jr., of Cape May Co., yeoman; will of. Wife, Abigail. Children—Joseph, Henry, Thomas and daughters (names not given), all under age. Farm, now occupied by the father, on the seaside; marsh, called the Great Flat; right to the beach, called Ludlam's; land bought of the Society in England, adjoining Moses Crosley; land on East side of Jarret's Gut in Upper Precinct, said Co., between Barnabas Crowell, Lewis Cresey, Thomas Smith on the Westside of Dudecan's Branch, Thomas or Daniel Eldredge and William Goff; home farm in said Upper Precinct. Personal property. Executors—Daniel Norton, John Mackey and Providence Ludlam. Witnesses—John Goff, William Bond, Joseph Savage. Proved March 2, 1753.
1753, May 2-5; July 27. Inventory, £558.0.2, by Jeremiah Hand and Jacob Spicer, with a long explanation by said appraisers, giving reasons why they have not included in the inventory goods given by the will to the widow, Joseph (Tertius, the eldest son), Phebe, (the eldest daughter), Thomas, (second son), Alathear (second daughter) Esther (third daughter). Cape May Wills, 165 E.

1757, Jan. 22. Ludlam, Joseph, son of Anthony, of Cape May Co. Int. Bond of Providence Ludlam as Adm'r; John Mackey fellowbondsman, both of said Co. Lib. 8, p. 496.
1757, Jan. 23. Inventory, £73.10.10, by Henry Young and John Mackey.

1750, Sept. 4. Ludlam, Mary, of Barlebrough in the County of Derby, Eng., widow; will of. My lands in Pexeroft, in Town or Township of Sheffield, in county of York, and my land in Attercliffe in the Parish of Sheffield, County of York, to go to my nephew, Francis Bullus, one of the younger sons of my late brother, Samuel Bullus, dec'd, and at his death to his heirs; but if he have none, then to my nephew, John Bullus, eldest son of my said brother. To my said nephew, John Bullus, £100. To the three daughters of my late nephew, John Axspring, dec'd, £5 each. To my niece, Hannah, wife of John Dickeson, £10; to my niece Elizabeth, wife of Richard Woodcock, £10; to my niece Mary Bullus, daughter of my brother, William Bullus, dec'd £50; to my niece, Bullus Chambers daughter of my sister, Aspring dec'd, £50; to my niece, Elizabeth, wife of Thomas Dale, £10; to my niece, Alice Ann Lee, £10; to the two children of my late niece, Mary, late wife of George Marshall, dec'd, £5 each, when 21. To the Rev. Mr. Bower, minister of Barlebrough, £5 for the poor of the Parish; to my sister, Huldah Brierly, £4 yearly; to my servant, George Marshall, £5; to my nephew, John Bullus, my silver watch. My clothing to go to my sister, Huldah Brierly, the wife of my nephew, John Bullus, my said nieces, Mary Bullus, Bullus Chambers, Hannah Dickason, Elizabeth Woodcock, Elizabeth Dall, Ann Lee and the surviving daughter of my late niece, Mary Marshall. My plantation in Pennsylvania, America, of five hundred acres, to my nephew, John Bullus. My other plantation of two thousand acres in West New Jersey to my nephew, Francis Bullus. Executor—nephew, Francis Bullus. Witnesses—Elizabeth Smith, William Ward, Marm Carver. Proved April 30, 1757. Lib. 10, p. 313.

1760, Dec. 17. Ludlam, Samuel, Sr., of "Mendum," Morris Co. Int. Hanah, widow, declines the administration in favour of her eldest son, Samuel Ludlum, Jr.
1760, Dec. 22. Bond of Samuel Ludlum as Adm'r Samuel Arnold fellowbondsman, both of Morris Town. Lib. G, p. 370.

1759, Jan. 9. Luker, John, of Hanover Township, Morris Co. Int. Bond of Jacob Miller and Joseph Lasey (Lacey) as Adm'rs; Herrick Benjamin, fellowbondsman, all of Morris Town. Endorsed: "Jacob Miller is brother to the widow and relict of the deceased and Joseph Lacey one of the largest creditors and takes out letters of Administration at the Desire of the Widow." Lib. G, p. 71.

1755, Oct. 6. Lum, Daniel, of Hannover, Morris Co.; will of. Wife, Mary. Children—Sarah, Shuah, Anna, Squire, Matthew and Eunice, all under age; an expected child. Real and personal estate. Executors—the wife and brother, Matthew Lum. Witnesses—Gershom Mott, Sr., Benjamin Howell, Obadiah Cook. Proved October 21, 1755.
Lib. F, p. 285.
1755, Oct. 14. Inventory, £509.19.2, by Daniel Tuttle and Benjamin Howell.

1756, Oct. 7. Lum, Samuel, Esq., of Hanover, Morris Co.; will of. Wife, Martha. Children—Samuel, Israel, Nancy and Martha, all under age. Brother, John Lum, Town right to lands West of "Rakaway" River; other real and personal estate. Executors—the wife, David Lum and Thomas Day. Witnesses—Daniel Day, Benjamin Day, Samuel Rolfe. Proved Nov. 17, 1756. Lib. F, p. 405.

1759, May 28. Lundy, Joseph, of Hardwick Township, Sussex Co., weaver. Int. Inventory, £136.10.5, incl. 6 bush. of Indian corn, 15s.; books, 23s.8d.; made by Samuel Willson, Jacob Lundy and Samuel Lundy.
1759, May 28. Sara, the widow, declines to administer.
1759, May 29. Bond of Thomas Lundy as Adm'r; Samuel Lundy fellowbondsman, both of Hardwick. Lib. 9, p. 392.

1756, Nov. 1. Lundy, Richard, Jr., of Hardwick Township, Sussex Co.; will of. Wife, Anne, sole Executrix of real and personal estate. Ten children, names not given. Witnesses—Richard Lundy, Samuel Large, Joseph Lundy. Proved Dec. 7, 1756.
Lib. 8, p. 475.
1756, Nov. 20. Inventory, incl. a plantation, £150; personalty, £72.8; made by Samuel Willson, Peter Smoak and Jacob Lundy.

CALENDAR OF WILLS—1751-1760   209

1751, July 8. Lunn, Martha, of New Brunswick, Middlesex Co., spinster. Int. Bond of Peter Cochran, principal creditor, Adm'r; Andrew Norwood and John van Norden fellowbondsmen, all of New Brunswick.   Lib. E, p. 537.
  1751, July 13. Inventory, £95.18.11, incl. 73 oz. of "clipt" silver at 8s.4d., £30.8.4; 10¼ Spanish milled dollars, £4.8.10; 13 Engl. shillings and 2½ Engl. crowns, £1.19.6; 13s.3d. milled foreign coins and 3s.3d. in copper pence; 1½ pistol, good weight and 2 light do, £4.7.1; two 4 pistol pieces gold weight, £12.2.8; silver buckles, 15s.; a Common Prayer book and one of "Devotion," 2s.6d.; 2 vols. of the "Tatler," 1s.; made by William Ouke and Petrus Slegt.
  1751, Nov. 22. Account by the Adm'r who has bill against it for funeral charges, etc., £13.7.8; Dr. van Buren's bill of 17s.10d. [Enclosed in the account is a bill against dec'd for 6 years 9 months' board, washing and lodging, £81, and 2 months' attendance during her last illness, £5].

1758, Apr. 10. Lyon, Benjamin, of the "Borrough" of Elizabeth, Essex Co., yeoman; will of. Wife, Mary. Children—Benjamin, Mary and Martha, all under age. Homefarm, adjoining Stephen Hinds; lot in the Great Swamp, given by father Benjamin Lyon to testator and brothers Moses, Matthias and Daniel Lyon; 7 acres of Elizabeth Town Great Meadow on the Bound Creek; 2 acres at the lower end of the Neck; 17 acres bought of Josiah Congar between Israel Crane and Ezekiel Crane. Personal estate. Executors—the wife, brother, Samuel Lyon, and brother-in-law, Amos Day. Witnesses—Timothy Harrason, Joseph Jagger, Josiah Crane. Proved August 16, 1758.   Lib. F, p. 554.
  1758, Aug. 18. Inventory, £363.18.9, by Christopher Wood and John Ogden.

1754, Sept. 27. Lyon, Ezekiel, of "Mendum," Morris Co. Int. Inventory, £165.11.1, incl. books, 2s.; credits, £25.11.6., all at 8s. per oz.; made by Ebenezer Byram and John Royse.
  1754, Oct. 4. Bond of Rebeckah, widow, and John Cary as Adm'rs; John Royse fellowbondsman, all of "Mendum," said Co.
                                                                                        Lib. F, p. 231.
  1755, Oct. 3. Account by the Adm'rs, who have increased it to £555.2., by the sale of the forge for £127, and of the land, £185.

1760, Feb. 5. Lyon, James, of Baskenridge, Somerset Co., "having died intestate not worth £20." His widow, Fanny Lyon, declining the administration, Governor Francis Bernard writes to Thomas Bartow, it should be granted to James Miller, of Morristown, principal creditor.
  1760, Feb. 5. Bond of said James Miller as Adm'r; John Miller fellowbondsman, both of Morris Town, Morris Co., yeomen.
                                                                                        Lib. G, p. 125.
  1760, Feb. 7. Inventory, £12.10.5., by John Roy and Robert Moore.

1760, June 12. Lyon, Jedidiah, of Morris Town, Morris Co. Int. Bond of Betty, widow, as Adm'x; Benjamin Hatheway of said town fellowbondsman.   Lib. G, p. 289.

1760, Apr. 5. Lyon, Josiah, of Newark, Essex Co.; will of. Wife, Mary. Children—Abraham, Ann, David, Josiah, Phebe, Mary and

Elizabeth. Real and personal estate. Executors—the wife and Jonathan Lyon. Witnesses—Uzal Johnson, David Johnson, Jr., Alexander Vance. Proved June 3, 1760. Lib. G, p. 283.

1758, Dec. 13. Lyon, Thomas, of Newark Township, Essex Co., yeoman; will of. Children, of whom only the "youngest son," Daniel is named and appointed Executor with son-in-law, Samuel Bond. Witnesses—Nicholas Parcel, William Brant, Joshua Horton. Proved January 1, 1758. Lib. G, p. 11.
1758, Dec. 29. Inventory, £23.6.6, by Nicholas Basel and Thomas Denman, who report land sold for £116.18.10.

1759, Oct. 12. McAvalley, Edward, of Freehold, Monmouth Co., labourer. Int. Bond of William McKnight, principal creditor, as Adm'r; John Williams fellowbondsman, both of Freehold, yeomen.
Lib. G, p. 100.

1754, Feb. 25. McCain, James, of Baskinridge, Somerset Co., yeoman; will of. Wife, Mary. Children—Cathrine, Nelly, (both under age), James, Charles, John, Bryan, Richard, Hugh, Daniel, William, Susanna, (wife of Thomas McConnel). Real and personal. Executor —the wife, son John and James Macalhineys. Witnesses—Aaron Boylan, Cathrin Boylan, James McVicker. Proved April 10, 1754.
Lib. F, p. 167.

1759, Feb. 8. McCaine, James, of Sussex Co. Int. Inventory, £31.12.4, by Thomas Hutchison and John Anderson.
1759, May 31. Bond of Catherine McCaine as Adm'x; Thomas Hutchison (Hutchinson) fellowbondsman, both of Sussex Co.
Lib. 9, p. 393.

1756, Sept. 9. McCawley, Robert, of Burlington Co. Int. Bond of Eleazar Fenton as Adm'r; John Fenimore fellowbondsman, both of said Co. Lib. 8, p. 339.
1756, Nov. 24. Inventory, £28.9.2¼, by John Fenimore and James Childs.
1759, May 31. Account by the Adm'r, who reports balance of £1.8.9.

1755, Apr. 3. McCaye, Richard, of Windsor, Middlesex Co. Int. Bond of Jean McCaye and James Braden, both of said Co., Adm'rs; Moore Furman, of Trenton, Hunterdon Co., fellowbondsman.
Lib. 9, p. 95.
1755, Apr. 6. Inventory of the personal estate, £118.13.3., incl. a five year's lease of the farm £25.; made by Joseph Skelton and John Schenck.

1756, Oct. 28. McClassen, William, of Penn's Neck, Salem Co. Int. Inventory, £33.8.1, incl. cash, credits and notes, £27.11.1; made by Andrew Sinnickson and Robert Conaway (Conway).
1757, Feb. 10. Bond of Nicholas Smith as Adm'r; Edward Daugherty fellowbondsman, both of Penn's Neck. Lib. 8, p. 446.

1751, April 24. McComb, Joseph [of Somerset Co.], a seaman. Inventory, £33.0.6, by Thomas Fox and James Newell.
Somerset Wills, 142 R.

CALENDAR OF WILLS—1751-1760

1760, May 5. McCusker, Michael, of Piles Grove, Salem Co., "soger;" will of. Divides personal estate between Elesabeth Weltch, Margat Dunlap, David Purvine and Samuel Purvine, making the last two Executors (name signed in jurat as Purviance). Witnesses—John Stafford, Henrich Reul (signs in German script; called in jurat Henry Ryall) and Archibald McAlster. Proved Dec. 12, 1760. Lib. 10, p. 487.

1760, Dec. 5. Inventory, £62.12.4, incl. bills, bonds and bookdebts, £56.6.10; made by James Dunlap and John Creag.

1754, May 3. Mackdowell (McDowell), Baptist, of Cranberry in Middlesex Co., miller. Int. Adm'r—James Dye, principal creditor, of Cranberry. Bondsman—Francis Holman, of Cranberry, yeoman. Witness—Thomas Bartow.

1754, May 4. Inventory, £34.12.3¾, by James Farrill and Francis Holman. Lib. F, p. 171.

1754, May 4. Vendue List: Estate sold for £34.12.3, by Adm'r; incl. 3 books, 10d., and bonds £9.8.2. Francis Holman, crier; James Farrill, Clerk. Lib. F, p. 171.

1759, Aug. 22. McEowen, Robert, of Somerset Co., yeoman. Int. Bond of Mary McEown, widow of, and Robert Helm as administrators of the estate of, Brice Riky fellowbondsman. Lib. G, p. 94.

1758, Aug. 28. Inventory, £154.2.6, by John Kinnan and Hugh Campbell.

1761, Oct. 16. Account by the Administrators, Mary Cooper, late widow of Robert "McKown," and Robert Helm, who have sold it for £179.4.6, and paid out £68.12.1.

1751, April 28. McEvers, John, of New York City, merchant; will of. I desire to be laid in my vault in the Trinity churchyard by the side of my late wife, Catherine. Children—William, Charles, Mary, John, James, and Catherine Bayard; each to have £500. Rest of real and personal estate to go to my children. The 300 acres given to my son William at Rocky Hill by his uncles, Andrew and Abraham Van Horne, my wife and myself, he must put in my general estate to be divided among his brothers and sisters, or I cut him of any of my estate, for I desire what was left their mother by her father, John Van Horne, and my estate, shall go amongst all my children equally. The house where Judah Hays lives in must not come in a division, it being given to my son, John, by his grandfather. To my present wife, Catherine, late widow of Peter Cock, £50 yearly. To daughter Catherine Bayard the house James Clayton lives in, and, after her death, to her eldest child. Whereas my brother, Cornelius Van Horne, son and heir of his father, John Van Horne, dec'd, did assign to me Oct. 5, 1750, a deed of land purchased by his father from Mary Stout, wife and attorney of Harman Stout, of 607 acres in Middlesex Co., New Jersey, near Milstone River, to be sold by me in trust for the use of our niese and "couzen," Catherine Van Horne, daughter of Andrew Van Horne, my Ex'rs are to alien same. Executors—my sons, John and James, daughters Catherine Bayard and Mary McEvers, and my son Charles. Witnesses—Archibald Fisher, Isaac Goelet, Henry Bogert. Proved April 6, 1752.

1751, Dec. 14. John McEvers one of the Executors, was sworn.
Lib. F, p. 55.

1759, Feb. 7. McKenny, William, of "Mendum," Morris Co., yeoman. Int. Bond of Jacob Ford, Esq., of Morris Co., principal creditor, as Adm'r; Jonathan Freeman, of Woodbridge, yeoman, fellow-bondsman. Lib. G, p. 31.

1751, Dec. 18. McKetrek, (McKittre), Thomas, of Monmouth Co.; will of. Divides personal estate between Barns Smock, his son John, and nephews John, Robin and Moses Mollegin and Gisebert Lane. Disposes of a Bible and other books. Executors—Barns Smock and Hugh McCollum. Witnesses—Cornelius Couwenhoven, Johannis Smock, John Smock. Proved Feb. 18, 1752. Lib. F, p. 100.
1752, Jan. 22. Inventory, £115.2.3, incl. a silver watch, £2; bonds, book debts and notes, £90.12.7; made by Johannis Smock and John Bennet.

1753, Nov. 22. McKim, John, of Salem Co. Int. Inventory, £54.15, by Elisha Basset and Mounce Keen, Sr.
1753, Nov. 24. Bond of Mary McKim as Adm'x; John Walker fellowbondsman, both of Salem Co. Lib. 8. p. 91.

1759, Nov. 17. McKinney, Mordecai, Sr., of "Labenon" Township, Hunterdon Co.; will of. Wife, Mary. Children—John, Jacob, Daniel, David, Mordecai and Ann. Names Mordecai, son of son Daniel; children of son William, viz., Abraham, Ann, Mordecai and Mary. Real and personal estate. Executors—sons David and Mordecai, with Derick Molate. Witnesses—Adam Runcle, Luke van Boskerk and John Forrester. Proved July 5, 1760. Lib. 10, p. 385.
1760, May 28. Inventory, £1108.3.6, incl. books, £1, bills, bonds and cash, £563.3.10; 4 negromen, £195; one negro woman, £50; made by Joseph Hankinson and Thomas Bowman.

1759, Feb. 11. McKoan, John, of Mannington, Salem Co.; will of. Wife, Jane. Children of sister, i. e., James Reyne, Mary, William and Richard Parret. Real and personal estate. Executors—the wife and her brother, Robert Clark, of Piles Grove, said Co. Witnesses —William Harvey, George Clark and Bowes May. Proved March 12, 1759. Lib. 9, p. 383.
1759, Feb. 26. Inventory, £132.7.8, incl. the time of two servant boys and credits, £18.7.2; made by George Clark and William Harvey.

1757, Jan. 22. Macleese, Guysbert, of Middletown, Monmouth Co. Int. Bond of Rachael Macleese and Cornelius McCleese as Adm'rs; Harman Johnson fellowbondsman, all of Middletown.
Lib. F, p. 416.
1759, Sept. 5. Inventory, £36.18, by David Burdge and Uriah Burdge:

1752, Sept. 20. Macleese, John, of Middletown Township, Monmouth Co.; will of. Children—Peter, John, Gisbert, Margaret, Cornelius and Johnston, ("probably wife of Hermon Johnston"), who is to have a share of the real estate. Personal property, incl. a large Bible. Executors—sons Gisbert and Cornelius, and daughter, Margarett Mackleese. Witnesses—William Golding, William Bowne, Hugh Hartshorne. Proved Oct. 23, 1752. Lib. F, p. 72.

1760, Sept. 26. McLheny (McIlheney), James, of Bound Brook, (tavern keeper), in Somerset Co.; will of. Wife, Mary, and children, Mary,

CALENDAR OF WILLS—1751-1760   213

William, Ann and James to have my estate equally. Daughter—Susanna McWilliams. Executors—wife, Mary, David McWilliams and Thomas Carhart. Witnesses—Tobias Van Norden, Redman Conyngham, Charles Stewart. Proved Oct. 20, 1760.   Lib. G, p. 318.
  1760, Oct. 11. Inventory, £282.11.3, by Daniel Howell and Elias v. Court.

1753, Oct. 17. McMoland (McMuelin), Harvey, of Amwell Township, Hunterdon Co., yeoman; will of. Children—John, Ellenor and Elche, all under age. Daughter-in-law (stepdaughter?) Sarah, also under age. Real and personal estate. Executors—Samuell Fleming, Joseph Gordon and Robert Shields. Witnesses—William Peirson, John Edmonds, John Smith. Proved Nov. 8, 1753.   Lib. 7, p. 427.
  1753, Nov. 7. Inventory: Real—a farm of 56 acres, £100. Personal £67.2.10. Made by Jacob Gray and William Peirson.

1758, June 20. McNeese, Jacob, of Bridgetown, Burlington Co. Int. Adm'r—Daniel Jones, Jr., of Bridgetown. Bondsman—William Smith, Esq., of Burlington. Witnesses—Gabriel Blond and Samuel Blackwood.   Lib. 8, p. 181.

1758, June 20. McNeese, Jacob, of Bridgetown, Burlington Co. Int. Bond of Daniel Jones, Jr., of Bridgeton as Adm'r; William Smith, Esq., of Burlington City, fellowbondsman.   Lib. 8, p. 534.

1760, May 29. MacOwen (McQuown, McEowen), Sarah, of Somerset Co., widow of William. Int. Bond of Robert Helm, only brother, as Adm'r; Hugh Campbell fellowbondsman, both of said Co., yeomen.
  Lib. G, p. 222.
  1760, May 20. Inventory, £28.14.2, by John MackCollum and Joseph Gaston.
  1763, Jan. 26. Account by Robert Helm of "Barnerds," Somerset Co., the Adm'r.

1755, May 12. Maffet, Robert, of Greenwich Township, Gloucester Co., yeoman. Int. Inventory, £160.18, by Benjamin Lodge and George Flaningan.
  1755, June 18. Bond of James Maffet, of Greenwich Township, yeoman, as Adm'r; Samuel Maffet of Deptford Township, said Co., yeoman, fellowbondsman.   Lib. 8, p. 308.

1754, Nov. 25. Maharr, Thomas, of Penn's Neck, Salem Co. Int. Inventory, £32.17.10½, incl. cash in Daniel Myster's hands, £12.7.9; a penal bill in hands of John Streach, £15; made by William Pritchet and Cornelius Casperson.
  1754, Dec. 10. Bond of Joseph Hawkes as Adm'r; Cornelius Casperson fellowbondsman, both of Pen's Neck.   Lib. 8, p. 140.

1755, Nov. 17. Mahurin, Ebenezer, of "Paqunack," Morris Co., collyer. Int. Bathshua, widow, resigns her right of administration to Jacob Ford, one of the largest creditors.
  1755, Nov. 18. Bond of Jacob Ford, Esq., of Morris Co., as Adm'r; John Deare, Esq., of Perth Amboy, fellowbondsman. Lib. F, p. 294.
  1755, Dec. 8. Inventory, £86.5.8, as sold at vendue on 6 months' credit by order of the Adm'r.

1759, June 23. Mall, Robert, of Hopewell Township, Cumberland Co., yeoman; will of. Mikan Mall to receive 5s., "when he shall call

for the same." One third of the movable estate given to grandchildren, Elizabeth, Abijah and Seely Blew, and the child, "that Elannar Blew is grate with;" the other two-thirds and the "improvement I live on," to son-in-law, George Blew, who is also named Executor. Witnesses—Thomas Reeves and Sarah Jacson. Proved July 10, 1759.
Lib. 9, p. 338.

1759, July 4. Inventory, £147.17.11, incl. a servant boy, £15.1; made by Josiah Parvin and Jacob More.

1759, Sept. 11. Maloney, Richard, of Oxford Township, Sussex Co., labourer. Int. Bond of Richard Howell as Adm'r; John Pettit fellowbondsman, both of said Co. Lib. 9, p. 392.

1759, Nov. 6. Inventory, £14.10, by Leward Kuikendal and Edward Hunt.

1754, Aug. 10. Man, Joseph, Esq., of the Borough of Elizabeth, Essex Co.; will of. Wife, Elizabeth. Son, David. Grandson, Thomas Man. Real and personal estate. Executors—the wife and Matthias Hetfield. Witnesses—Benjamin Spinning, Timothy Higgins, Aaron Hetfield. Proved Feb. 3, 1759. Lib. G, p. 49.

1758, May 15. Inventory, £67.12.5, by Benjamin Crane and John Chandler

1750, Nov. 28. Man, Samuel, of Elizabeth Town. Int. Adm'x—Mary, his widow. Bondsman—Jacob Dehart. Witness—Robert Ogden. Lib. F, p. 149.

1757, Feb. 11. Manley, John, of Somerset Co., innkeeper; will of. "My now wife," Charity. Children—John Adrian, Thomas, Richard, Elizabeth and Mary, the last three under age; an expected child. Real and personal estate. Executors—the wife, son John and Simon Hegeman; the wife to be excluded, if she "should happen to "live unreaguler or unbecoming with any person." Witnesses—Wilhelmus Stoothof, Benjamin Hegeman and Andrew Brown. Proved Feb. 20, 1758. Lib. F, p. 500.

1758, Feb. 17. Inventory. Real—a house and lot of 10 acres, £200; a half-acre lot, £5; 315 acres of land, £945; a house and ¾ acre, £20. Personal, £307.0.2, incl. 2 looking glasses, £2; 7 silver teaspoons, 22s.; 3 pictures, 20s.; 2 negro men, £120; made by Andrew Brown, Wilhelmus Stoothof and Benjamin Hegeman.

1755, Nov. 2. Manning, Isaac, of North Precinct, Somerset Co.; will of. Wife, Cathron. Sons—John, Isaac and Clarkson. Real and personal estate. Executors—brothers, James Manning and James Clarkson, Jr. Witnesses—Isaac Jennings, Robert Clarkson, Jeremiah Manning. Proved Nov. 14, 1755. Lib. F, p. 293.

1755, Nov. 18. Inventory, £158.17.9, incl. a "Byble" and Psalm book, etc., 12s.; half a book called "The Law of the Province," 9s.; made by Samuel Drake and Peter Woodden.

1755, May 24. Marner, James, of Burlington City; will of. Sister, Christian Marner. Brothers—William and Alexander Marner. Names also Joseph Ferguson, Elizabeth Isdell and Sara, dau. of Thomas Isdell. The following names of legatees are crossed out in the original without explanation:—Campbell, Colin Campbell, Jr., John Campbell, Harkness (Tuckness?), Phebe Tuckness, James Tuckness,

CALENDAR OF WILLS—1751-1760 215

John Ferguson, Capt. Wrag and John Smith. Personal estate. Executor—Mr., also called Rev., Colin Campbell, and, in case of his death, Joshua Raper and Samuel Smith. Witnesses—Joseph Ellis, Jonathan Ferguson, Jo Smith. Codicil, without date, gives £15 in goods to intended wife, Ann Fisher, and divides what is over that sum between her and the above said brothers. Witness—John Hamilton. Proved Jan. 26, 1757. Lib. 8, p. 360.

1756, Sept. 24. Marsh, Daniel, Sr., of the Borough of Elisabeth, Essex Co.; will of. Wife, Mary. Children—John, Daniel, Henry, Christopher, Rolfe, Ephraim Markes, Phebe and Rhoda. Grandchild, Sary Dunnin. Homefarm; 3 acres of salt meadow, next to brother Mephiboshith Marsh; land bought of John Wood; land above the mountains. Personal estate incl. a silver watch. Executors—the wife, son Daniel and son-in-law, John Bishop. Witnesses—Isaac Noe, David Marsh, Mary Campbell. Codicil of same date states that the four youngest sons are under 15 years. Same witnesses. Proved Nov. 27, 1756. Lib. F, p. 394.
1756, Nov. 2. Inventory, £311.18.12, by Abraham Shotwell and Amos Morse.

1753, Oct. 5. Marsh, Henry, Sr., of the "Borrough" of Elizabeth, Essex Co., yeoman; will of. Wife, Johannah. Son, Henry. An expected child. Real and personal estate. Executors—the wife, brother-in-law, Abraham Crocheron, of Richmond Co., N. Y., yeoman, and Capt. Daniel Potter, of Elizabeth. Witnesses—Isaac Willis, Gershom Bonnal, Benjamin Bonnel. Proved Oct. 24, 1753. Lib. F, p. 149.
1753, Oct. 27. Inventory, £101.0.11, by Joseph Potter and Daniel Ogden.

1760, Feb. 21. Marsh, Joshua, of Elizabeth, Essex Co. Int. Adm'rs—Sarah Marsh, widow, and Abraham Marsh, of said place. Bondsman—Daniel Perrine, of said place. Witnesses—Thomas Tobin and Robert Ogden.
1760, Feb. 19. Inventory, £158.4.9, by Abraham Clark and Daniel Perine. Lib. G, p. 129.

1755, May 2. Marsh, William, Sr., of the Borough of Elizabeth, Essex Co., carpenter; will of. Wife, Mary. Children—Noah, William, John, Jesse, Sarah and Phebe, all under age; an expected child. Home lot; land, bought of Matthias Hetfield, Jr., between Samuel Miller and the parsonage land. Personal estate. Executors—father-in-law, Henry Clarke, brother, John Marsh, and brother-in-law, Samuel Miller. Witnesses—William Clark, Joanna Ross, Ebenezer Price. Proved June 30, 1755. Lib. F, p. 277.
1755, June 23. Inventory, £81.5.4, by Cornelius Ludlam and John Ross.
1757, June. Account by Executors.

1754, May 4. Marshall, John, of New Hanover Township, Burlington Co., yeoman; will of. Distributes real and personal estate between Solomon Whatkins, Elizabeth Whatkins, Benjamin Branson and Jonathan Branson, the last named being made Executor. Witnesses—Mary Jones, John Atkinson, Samuel Wright, Jr. Proved July 24, 1756. Lib. 8, p. 309.

1751, Oct. 30. Marshall, Joseph, of Deptford Township, Gloucester Co., tailor. Int. Inventory, £106.19.4, incl. books 5s.; made by James Hamilton and Henry Sparks.
 1751, Nov. 1. Bond of widow, Catherine Marshall, as Adm'x; Richard Sparks and Henry Weatherby, both husbandmen, fellowbondsmen, all of Deptford Township. Lib. 7, p. 154.
 1755, Mar. 12. Account by the Administratrix.

1755, July 1. Martin, Benjamin, of Piscataway, Middlesex Co.; will of, Wife, Philerato. Sons—Benjamin, Nathanael, Peter. Daughter, Zerviah, wife of Jeremiah Blackford. Grandchildren—Athanasius, James, and Luther; Jeremiah, Zephaniah, Ruben, sons of Benjamin; Mary, Isaiah and Benjamin, children of John and Hannah Blackford; Benjamin and Nehemiah, children of Nehemiah and Elizabeth Bonham; Zerviah, daughter of Zedekiah and Anna Bonham. Land bought of father, Benjamin Martin; homefarm on the Mill Brook, Woodbridge, bought in part of John Martin and in part of John Bloomfield; land bought of brother, Jonathan Martin; 16 acres in Essex Co., bought of Samuel Drake and Isaac Chandler; a lot at the Vinyard, bo't of Wm. Edinfield (?); a Proprietor's right in West Jersey; same at Florida, Woodbridge, bought of Richard Soper; same at South River, bought of Hezekiah Dunn; same bought of Kittrell Mundin. Personal estate. Executors—son, Benjamin, son-in-law, John Blackford, and cousin, James Martin. Witnesses—Samuel Martin, Jacob Martin and Azariah Dunham. Proved May 3, 1757.
                Lib. F, p. 422.
 1757, May 10. Inventory, £190.16.3, incl. his purse, £37.8.8; a large Bible, 10s.; "Acts of the Province," 14s.; a Bible in another tongue 3s.6d.; other books, £4.19; debts for rent £6.10; other debts £8.1.8; made by Reune Runyon and John Hepburn.
 1763, Apr. 8. Account by the Executors, who have sold it for £219.13.5, and charge £229.12.10 against it.

1752, Mar. 12. Martin, David, of Hunterdon Co. Int. Bond of Theophilus Severns and Joseph C. Cleayton, both of Trenton, Hunterdon Co., as Adm'rs; John Allen, of Trenton, fellowbondsman.
               Hunt. Wills, 318 J.
 1752, Aug. 28. Inventory, £2.7., appraised at Trenton, by John Allen and Joseph Higbee; £76.14, appraised at Sharon, by William Schooley and John Anderson on Sept. 26, 1752.
 1758, July 14. Account by Theophilus Severns, surviving Administrator, who has increased it to £1495.4.8, by the sale of the real property, and makes it his debtor for £53.16.2.

1760, Apr. 8. Martin, Hester, of Gloucester Co. Int. Bond of John Martin, of Gloucester Co., as Adm'r; Isaac Heulings, of Burlington City, fellowbondsman. Lib. 9, p. 415.

1757, June 6. Martin, John, of Piscataway, Middlesex Co. Int. Adm'r—James Martin, brother. Bondsman—Jonathan Martin, yeoman. Lib. F, p. 428.
 1757, June 9. Inventory, £175.9.6, incl. bonds and notes, £19.12.8; a looking glass, 2s.; made by Phineas Dunn and Samuel Drake.

1750, July 7. Martin, Joseph, of Woodbridge, Middlesex Co., yeoman; will of. Wife, Elisabeth. Children—William, Merrit, Valen-

CALENDAR OF WILLS—1751-1760   217

tine, Benjamin, John, Joseph, Katherine Codington, Sarah Connet, Rebecca Morgan, Susannah Kelly, Mary Coats. Names also Elisabeth and Anne, heirs of dec'd. daughter Hannah Trembly. Personal property. Executors—the wife, with sons William and Merrit. Witnesses—Benjamin Codington, Thomas Reed and Nugient Kelly. Proved June 7, 1757.   Lib. F, p. 429.

1755, Apr. 2. Martin, Peter, of Piscataway, Middlesex Co., will of. Wife, Sarah. Children—Robert, Peter, Zirviah Runyon, Priscilla, Mary Faurat and Sarah. Grandsons—Thomas (eldest son of dec'd. eldest son Mulford Martain), Mulford Martain and Samuel Martain. A lot of 39 acres in Woodbridge, adjoining Gershom Martain; salt meadow, bought of Richard Carmon; homefarm, adjoining John Wilson; a freehold lot; salt meadow in Martain's Neck; same at the mouth of the Great Pond. Personal property. Executors—son-in-law, Isaac Faurat, and brother-in-law, Samuel Martain. Witnesses—Nehemiah Dunham, Peter Martin, Jr., and Benjamin Martin. Proved March 17, 1756.   Lib. F, p. 328.
    1756, Mar. 11. Inventory, £135.12.9, incl. books, 10s.; appraised by Gershom Martin and Thomas Mundy.

1760, Sept. 1. Mason, Andrew, of Greenwich, Gloucester Co., labourer. Int. Bond of William Linsey (Lindsey), innholder, as Adm'r; Thomas Coles, yeoman, fellowbondsman, both of Greenwich Township.   Lib. 10, p. 293.
    1760, Sept. 3. Inventory, £38.6, incl. book debts, £22.15.2; made by George Cook and Benjamin Burroughs.

1755, Mar. 25. Mason, James, of Manington, Salem Co., yeoman; will of. Wife, Mary. Cousins—Joseph Wood, Gabriel Wood, William Smith, Sarah Young and Ann Nicholson. Sister, Sarah (under age). Children of sisters Mary and Martha. House and lot in Salem, now occupied by Ralph Walker; farm, occupied by John Thompson. Personal estate incl. a negro man. Executors—the wife and Benjamin Cripps. Witnesses—Preston Carpenter, Elizabeth Powell, Josiah Kay. Proved Sept. 1, 1755.   Lib. 8, p. 240.
    1755, Sept. 9. Inventory, £739.1.4, incl. plate, £24; 3 lookingglasses, £2.5; bonds, etc., £258.17.5½; one fifth of the brigantine, "Industry," £70; 350 gall. of rum, last brought in said brigantine, @ 2/8, £46.13.4; a negrowoman, £30; made by Jost Meller, and Preston Carpenter.
    1760, Jan. 5. Account by Mary Mason, surviving Executrix.

1759, Aug. 1. Mason, Samuel, of Manington, Salem Co., yeoman. Int. Inventory, £493.12.6, incl. a looking glass; plate; bond and notes, £39.2.6; John Beard's and Negro Jack's time, £75; made by Daniel Huddy and Jost Meller.
    1759, Sept. 8. Bond of widow, Hannah, as Adm'x; Daniel Huddy and Jonathan Woodnutt fellowbondsmen, all of Manington.
                                                        Lib. 10, p. 448.

1752, Feb. 21. Mathis (Matthews), John, of Hopewell, Hunterdon Co. Int. Inventory, £96.10.6, by Garrat Johnson and Joseph Severns.
    1752, Apr. 21. Bond of John Burroughs, of Trenton Township, as Adm'r; Garratt Johnson, of Hopewell, fellowbondsman.
                                                Hunt. Wills, 319 J.

1751, Apr. 8. Mathis, Thomas, and wife Rebecca, of Middlesex Co. Int. Robeart Mathis, by reason of his age, refuses to administer.
1751, Apr. 16. Bond of James Manning, of Essex Co., and Joseph Fitz Randolph, of Piscataway, as Adm'rs; Ephraim F. Randolph, of Piscataway, fellowbondsman, all yeoman. Lib. E, p. 514.
1751, Apr. 21. Inventory, £29.0.4., also £60.3.9, by Ephraim F. Randolph and Moses Randolph.

1757, Sept. 23. Matlack, Thomas, of Evesham, Burlington Co. Int. Inventory, £39.11.10, by John Cox and Silas Crispin.
1757, Nov. 14. Bond of Elizabeth Matlack, of Evesham Township, as Adm'x; John Cox, of Chester, said Co., fellowbondsman.
Lib. 8, p. 518.
1760, May 31. Account by the Adm'x, who makes it her debtor for £20.15.1.

1757, Dec. 29. Matson, Peter, of Deptford Township, Gloucester Co., yeoman. Int. Bond of John and Thomas Rambo as Adm'rs; John Hopper fellowbondsman, all of said Township, yeoman. Lib. 9, p. 72.
1758, Jan. 3 & 4. Inventory, £244.19.4¾, incl. bonds and cash, £211.10.3; made by Abram Chattin, Jr., and Richard Sparks.

1758, Jan. 10. Matson, Peter, son of Andrew, of Gloucester Co., yeoman, petitions, that Charles Hoffman and James Cooper, both of said Co., be appointed his Guardians. Same date bond of Charles Hoffman and James Cooper as such Guardians, John Brown fellowbondsman, all of Gloucester Co., yeomen. Lib. 8, p. 543.

1759, Aug. 6. Maxfield, Nathanial, of Essex Co., son of John Maxfield. Int. Adm'r—Nathaniel Rusco, of said Co. Bondsman—Abraham Cadmus, of said Co. Witness—Thomas Bartow. Lib. G, p. 92.

1753, Nov. 13. Maxfield, Samuel, of Elizabeth, Essex Co. Int. Ann Maxfield, the widow, renounced, in favor of his uncle, John Maxfield, and Moses Tompson, in presence of John Radley. The above John Maxfield renounced in favor of said Moses Thompson.
1753, Nov. 13. Adm'r—Moses Thompson, of Elizabeth. Bondsmen—John Maxfield and David Maxfield. Witness—Thomas Bartow.
1753, Nov. 16. Inventory, £89.0.5½, by Timothy Whitehead and Joseph Potter. Lib. F, p. 144.

1750, June 20. Maxwell, William, of Middlebush, Somerset Co., schoolmaster; will of. Wife, Gartrude. Children—William, Ann and Samuel, all under age. Remainderman, William Allibone. Provision made, if wife should go to live with her friends in Pennsylvania, the sons to be apprenticed to learn trades in the houses of Presbyterians. Real and personal estate, incl. books. Executors—John Maxwell, of Flatbush, Kings Co., on now "Saw Island," N. Y., tailor, Christian van Dorne and Abraham van Dorne, both of Middlebush, yeomen. Witnesses—Peter Wyckoff, Jacob Wyckoff, James Williamson. Proved April 20, 1752. Lib. F, p. 42.
1752, Apr. 17. Inventory, £129.18.7, by Aaron Van Dorne and Frederick Van Lawe.

1760, Jan. 21. Maydwell, John, of Philadelphia, merchant. Int. Inventory, taken at the house of Sarah Chubbs, in Trenton, N. J.,

£709.10.3, incl. 2 watches and a hat; silver shoes and knee buckles; gold sleeve buttons; bonds and book debts, £450.

1760, Jan. 21. Bond of Richard Footman, of Philadelphia, merchant, principal creditor, as Adm'r; John Allen, of Trenton, fellowbondsman. [In this bond dec'd is called as "of Trenton"].
Lib. 10, p. 416.

1753, Oct. 6. Meadlis, John, of Newark, Essex Co.; will of. Children—Samuel and Hannah. Granddaughters—Sarah (wife of Ephraim Canfield) and Elizabeth Buch. Legacy to First Presbyterian Church at Newark. Real and personal estate. Executors—son Samuel and Samuel Alling, of Newark. Witnesses—John Jenkens, Manasseh Hildreth, Stephen Foordham. Proved Dec. 28, 1756.
Lib. F, p. 410.

1757, Jan. 5. Inventory, £300.3.9, by John Crane and Samuel Huntington.

1757, Sept. 25. Meeker, Daniel, of the Borough of Elisabeth, Essex Co., yeoman; will of. Wife, Rachel. Son, Nathaniel. Bequests to Abraham Clark's daughters by his present wife; to John Thompson's daughters by his first wife; to Gabriel, son of Nathaniel Meeker; to Michael and Elihu, sons of Abner Woodruff. Real and personal estate. Executors—John Thompson and Abner Woodruff. Witnesses—Stephen Crane, John Pairson (Peirson), Ezekiel Cheever. Proved Oct. 29, 1757.
Lib. F, p. 532.

1761, —— ——. Account by John Thompson, Ex'r.

1759, Feb. 24. Meeker, Daniel, Sr., of the Borough of Elizabeth, Essex Co., yeoman; will of. Wife, Mary. Children—Mary (wife of Joseph Cory), Abigail (wife of David Conklin), Abraham and Daniel (an invalid). Grandchildren—John and Moses, sons of dec'd. son Moses; Susannah Meeker. Lot in said borough bought of Stephen and Joseph Hermon, John Thompson and James Hinds, Jr., between Samuel Williams and Ephraim Sayre; lot on Westside of Raway River, bought of Caleb Jefferies, other real and personal property. Executors—the wife, son in law, Joseph Cory, and Stephen Crane. Witnesses—Thomas Williams, John Johnson, Abraham Clark, Jr. Proved Oct. 8, 1760.
Lib. G, p. 312.

1757, Oct. 6. Meeker, Mary, widow of Michael (of Borough of Elizabeth); will of. Children—Phebe and Charity, both under age, with remainder to sister Abirgirl. Person's daughter Mary and sister Phebe Megie's daughter. Personal estate. Executors—brother, John Ogden and brother-in-law, John Megie. Witnesses—John Ogden, William Barnet, John Pairson (Peirson). Proved Oct. 19, 1757.
Lib. F, p. 506.

1755, May 26. Meeker, Michael, of the Borough of Elizabeth, Essex Co.; will of. Wife, Mary. Children—Phebe and Charity. Brother, Nathaniel Meeker. Real and personal estate. Executors—said brother and kinsman, Moses Ogden. Witnesses—John Ogden, Daniel Meeker, John Pairson (Peirson). Proved August 13, 1755.
Lib. F, p. 344.

1753, Oct. 12. Meeker, Moses, of Elizabeth Town, Essex Co. Int. Adm'x—Hannah Meeker, widow. Bondsmen—Joseph Cory and Stephen Crane. Witnesses—Moses Miller, Lewis Mulford, Thomas Bartow.

1753, May 7. Inventory, £196.9.9, by Elijah Davis and Joseph Haines. Lib. F, p. 143.

1759, Jan. 22. Petition of Daniel Williams and wife, Hannah, Daniel Meeker and others, showing that Moses Meeker, of Elizabeth, died intestate, leaving three children, Susannah, John and Moses; that his widow, Hannah Meeker, now wife of Daniel Williams, did administer and afterwards married and desires Guardian appointed for said children. The petitioner, Daniel Meeker, grandfather of said children, asks that Joseph Cory, of Elizabeth, being uncle to said children, may be appointed their Guardian. Request granted.

Essex Wills, 2699 G.

1759, July 23. Meeker, Rachel, of the Borough of Elizabeth, Essex Co.; will of. Children—Nathaniel, Sarah Clark and Rachel Woodruff. Granddaughter, Mary Ann Meeker. Bequest to daughters of John Thomson. Personal property. Executors—sons-in-law, Abraham Clark, and Abner Woodruff. Witnesses—Daniel Dayton, David Meeker, Joseph Ogden. Proved June 30, 1760. Lib. H, p. 29.

1758, Jan. 25. Meeker, Samuel, of Elizabeth Town in Essex Co. Int. Adm'x—Rachel Meeker. Bondsman—John Herriman, taylor, of said town. Witnesses—Josiah Ogden (3d) and Robert Ogden.

Lib. F, p. 511.

1760, Sept. 29. Merring, Thomas, of Salem, Salem Co. Int. Bond of Robert Johnson as Adm'r; Erasmus Kent and John Owen, fellowbondsman, all of Salem. Lib. 10, p. 440.

1760, Sept. 30. Inventory, £25.0.3, by Erasmus Kent and John Owen.

1760, July 19. Merry, Samuel, of Hanover, Morris Co. Int. Mary, widow, resigns her right of administration to Samuel Tuttle.

1760, July 21. Bond of Samuel Tuttle, of Morris Co., principal creditor, as Adm'r; John Ogden, Esq., of Newark, Essex Co., fellowbondsman. Lib. G, p. 290.

1753, June 22. Merseelis, Henry, of Trenton, Hunterdon Co., brewer; will of. Wife Hany (Hannah), sole Executrix of real and personal estate. Sister, Catherine Merseelis. Brothers—Peter and John Merseelis. Witnesses—Elijah Bond, Thomas Hooton, Thomas Cahill. Proved Sept. 3, 1754. Lib. 7, p. 519.

1754, Aug. 27. Inventory, £88.19.6, incl. a looking glass, £2.15; 11 small pictures; a servant lad's time, £18 ; made by Charles Oxford and Nathan Beakes.

1751, Nov. 17. Meserly, Daniel, of Deptford Township, Gloucester Co.; labourer. Int. Inventory, £24.1.1, by John Davis and Andrew Sloan.

1751, Nov. 19. Bond of Henry Wood as Adm'r; Andrew Sloan fellowbondsman, both of Deptford Township, yeoman.

Glouc. Wills, 503 H.

1759, Sept. 11. Messhow, John, of Deptford Township, Gloucester Co., husbandman. Int. Bond of widow, Elizabeth, as Adm'x; Benjamin Ward, tailor, fellowbondsman, both of said Township.

Lib. 9, p. 341.

CALENDAR OF WILLS—1751-1760   221

1756, Oct. 13. Mestayer, Daniel. Int. Bond of Mary Mestayer as Adm'x; George Trenchard fellowbondsman, both of Salem Co.
Lib. 9, p. 85.

1758, Sept. 9. Mickle, Archibald, of Newton, Gloucester Co., husbandman; will of. Children—Joseph, Sarah and Isaac, all under age. Executor—brother Isaac Mickle. Witnesses—Peter Breach, Samuel Spicer. Proved Nov. 11, 1758.
Lib. 9, p. 130.
    1758, Oct. 4. Inventory, £527.10, incl. a silver watch; book debts, cash and notes, £43.10.5; a looking glass; a negro man, £70; made by James Sloan and Robert Frd. Price.

1756, Jan. 30. Mickle, Mary, of Evesham Township, Burlington Co., widow; will of. Children—Ruth, Hannah, Rachel and Prudence. Grandchildren—Joshua and Rachel Wood; Jarvis, Jacob and Hannah Hews; Mary, John and Jonah Small; Jarvis Thomas. Daughter, Hanna, has son Jarvis. Son-in-law, John Small mentioned. Real and personal estate. Executor—son-in-law, John Stokes. Witnesses —John Dearnale, Matthew Allen, Noah Haines. Proved March 9, 1756.
Burl. Wills, 5723 C.
    1756, Feb. 27. Inventory, £ 172.8.8, incl. bonds £135, a looking glass 4s.; made by John Dearnale and James Cattell.

1760, June 6. Middleton, Nathan, of Chester, Burlington Co., yeoman; will of. Wife, Mary. Children—Bulia and Nathan, both under age. Real and personal estate. Executors—the wife and Samuel Stokes. Witnesses—Robert French, William Thomas, John Cox. Proved June 30, 1760.
Lib. 10, p. 31.
    1760, June 24. Inventory, £321.3.8, incl. a silver watch, £7; silver buckles, £2.3; "chania silver" tea spoons and sundries in cupboard. £3.13.6; a looking glass; the time of Martin Hesler, a Dutch lad, 4 years, £14; ditto, of Philipp Acreman, 6 years, £18; made by Joshua Humphris and Robert French.

1756, Nov. 20. Middleton, Samuel, of Greenwich Township, Gloucester Co., labourer. Int. Bond of Samuel Skill, of Philadelphia, boatman, as Adm'r; Gerret Vaneman, of Greenwich Township, fellowbondsman.
Lib. 8, p. 395.
    1756, Nov. 26. Inventory, £18.13, by Thomas Thomson (Thompson) and John Halmes (Helms).

1760, Mar. 5. Middleton, Thomas, of Burlington Co. Int. Inventory, £188.5., incl. bills, bonds, book debts and cash, £85.18.8; books 10s.; made by William Foster and James Allen.
    1760, Mar. 7. Bond of his widow, Hester, as Adm'x; William Foster fellowbondsman.
Lib. 9, p. 422.

1753, Dec. 5. Middleton, William, of Deptford Township, Gloucester Co., husbandman; will of. Son, William, under age, sole heir, and brother-in-law, John Ingle (Engle), Guardian of son and sole Executor of estate. Testator's mother still living. Witnesses— Elizabeth Price, Hugh Margin, William Wood. Proved Dec. 19, 1753 (the Executor signing as John Engle).
Lib. 7, p. 429.
    1753, Dec. 17. Inventory, £241.9.3, by George Kemble and William Wood.

1756, Dec. 29. Miller, Enoch, of Westfield, Essex Co. Int. Adm'x—Hannah Miller, widow. Bondsman—Daniel Pierson, yeoman, of same place. Witness—Thomas Bartow. Lib. F, p. 394.
1757, Jan. 17. Inventory, £112.18.1, by William Miller and Daniel Perrine.

1760, Aug. 13. Miller, Richard, Jr., of Elizabeth, Essex Co. Int. Adm'r—Stephen Crane, Esq., of Elizabeth Town. Bondsman—Benjamin Miller, of said Town, yeoman. Witnesses—Abraham Clark, Jr., and Robert Ogden. Lib. G, p. 298.

1735, Apr. 9. Miller, Samuel, of Elizabeth Town, Essex Co., carpenter; will of. Wife, Elizabeth. Children—William, John, Enoch, Aaron, Andrew, Moses, Hannah (wife of Mathias Hetfield), Elizabeth, (wife of Joseph Price), Joanna (wife of Nathanael Bonnel, Jr.), and Susanna. Homestead; 12 acres in Elizabeth Town Great Meadows, bought of Daniel Sayre; 100 acres in Southold, Suffolk Co., Long Island, bought of Benjamin Luce; 20 ac. adjoining brother, Richard Miller; other real and personal property. Executors—the wife, with sons William, Enoch and Aaron. Witnesses—Thomas Chapman, Nathaniel Mitchell, Elijah Davis. Proved Oct. 7, 1760. Lib. G, p. 308.

1753, Aug. 21. Millikan, Thomas, of Northampton Township, Burlington Co.; will of. To my brother, John Millikan, all my real and personal estate. Executors—James Dobbins and James Smith. Witnesses—John Cain and Alexander Ferguson. Proved Sept. 1, 1753.
1753, Aug. 29. Inventory, £38.3.1, by Thomas Budd and Vincent Leeds. Burlington Wills, 5211 C.

1759, July 31. Mills, John, Sr., of Elizabeth Town, Essex Co. Int. Adm'rs—Elizabeth Mills and John Mills, widow and son. Witness—Thomas Bartow.
1759, Aug. 10. Inventory, £98.14.4, by Jonathan Crane, Esq., and Samuel Brooks. Lib. G, p. 91.

1756, Nov. 19, Mills, Richard, of the Borough of Elizabeth, Essex Co., yeoman; will of. Wife, Sarah. Children—Samuel, Isaac, (both under age), Mary, (who receives cattle, given her by her dec'd grandmother, Mary Ogden), Sarah and Susannah. Real and personal estate, incl. land adjoining brother, James Mills. Executors—the wife and Stephen Burrowes. Witnesses—Phebe Clark, John Lee, Abraham Clark, Jr. Proved Feb. 14, 1757. Lib. F, p. 442.

1753, Oct. 17. Mills, Samuel, of the Borough of Elizabeth, Essex Co.; will of. Wife, Mary. Children—William, Samuel, Isaac, Joanna, Mary and Phebe. The sons to maintain "Sarah" (whoever she may be). Real and personal estate. Executors—the daughter, Mary, son William, and Thomas Woodruff. Witnesses—Thomas Willis, Stephen Woodruff, Ebenezer Price, Benjamin Woodruff. Proved Nov. 26, 1753.
Lib. F, p. 145.
1753, Nov. 20. Inventory, £62.6.7, by John Badgley and Daniel Perrine.
1758, Aug. 17. Account filed.

1751, July 17. Milton, Walter, of Cape May. Int. Inventory, £153.11.6, by Aaron Leaming and John Leonard.

1751, Aug. 7. Bond of Ann Milton as Adm'x; Annanias Osborne and Timothy Milton fellowbondsmen, all of Cape May.
Cape May Wills, 154 E.

1760, Aug. 1. Mink, Martin, of Mannington Precinct, Salem Co., yeoman; will of. Wife, Susannah. Children—John, Andrew (under age), and Sarah. Stepson, Samuel Tussey (under age). Real and personal estate. Executors—the wife and William Roberts. Witnesses—John Cornelius, Joseph Tussey and Samuel Whitehorne. Proved Sept. 1, 1760, when William Roberts qualifies as "surviving" Executor. Lib. 10, p. 485.
1760, Aug. 14. Inventory, £149.0.8, by Elisha Bassett, Jr., and William Harvey.
1763, Sept. 10. Account of the estate by Jonathan Roberts. Executor of William Roberts, above named, who reports as due to the estate a balance of £9.0.2.

1760, Sept. 15. Mire, Michael, of Alloways Creek, Salem Co., labourer, also called yeoman. Int. Inventory, £21.17.6, incl. 5 bush. of wheat £1.5; made by Michael Miller and Charles Clark. His widow, Anna Mire, refuses to administer on the estate in favor of Jacob Freese.
1760, Sept. 26. Bond of Jacob Freese of Alloways Creek as Adm'r; Charles Clark and Robert Dare, of Dearfield, Cumberland Co., yeoman, fellowbondsmen. Lib. 10, p. 440.
1761, Sept. 7. Account by said Adm'r who has sold estate for £29.1, and has paid Christopher Coolman per reading prayers, 5s.

1757, July 4. Mitchell, John, of "Menarsquon," Monmouth Co., yeoman; will of. Wife, Margrit, sole Executrix. Children—Daniel, Isaac, James and daughters (unnamed). Real and personal estate. Witnesses—Samuel Weston and Isaac Herbert. Proved Oct. 17, 1757.
Lib. F, p. 505.
1757, Oct. 14. Inventory, £57,12, by Timothy Willies and Isaac Herbert.

1756, May 17. Mitchell, William, of the Borough of Elizabeth, Essex Co.; will of. Wife, Elizabeth. Children—Elizabeth Maxfeald, Suzanah Pedit, Hannah Willis, Catron Ousborn, John (absent in the King's service). Mentions John's children and son-in-law George Pedit. Real and personal estate. Executors—Thomas Willis and John Milles. Witnesses—Thomas Thompson, John David Lamb, John Stits. Proved Nov. 24, 1757. Lib. F, p. 471.

1755, May 15. Monee, Abraham, Jr., of Woodbridge, Middlesex Co. Int. Elizabeth Monee, widow, declined to administer; witness, Andrew Hampton.
1755, May 15. Adm'r—Abraham Monee, of Richmond Co., on Staten Island, yeoman, father of said Abraham Monee Jr. Bondsman—Andrew Hampton, of Woodbridge, yeoman. Witness—Thomas Bartow.
Lib. F, p. 201.

1754, Oct. 5. Montgomerie, Thomas, of Middlesex Co. Int. Mary Montgomery, widow, renounced in favor of William Deare, in presence of John Dennisson and William Fielding.

1754, Oct. 8. Adm'r—William Deare, of Perth Amboy, Gent. Bondsman—Andrew Johnston, Esq., of same place. Witness—Thomas Bartow. Lib. F, p. 215.

1756, Apr. 12. Montgomery, James, of Upper Freehold, Monmouth Co., yeoman; will of. Wife, Mary. Children—Robart, Alexander, James, William, Burnet and Mary. Real and personal estate. Executors—sons Robart and Alexander. Witnesses—Stoffil Longstreet, John Robins and Ezekiel Smith. Proved April 26, 1759. Lib. 9, p. 317.

1759, Apr. 24. Inventory, £354.16.9, incl. purse and apparel, £68.17.7; book debts, £62.19.1; a negro boy, £60; a negro woman, £40; made by John and Moses Robins.

1760, Aug. 15. Account by Executors.

1754, Oct. 21. Moodey, James, of "Alaways" Creek, Salem Co., cooper; will of. Mother, Ruth Mudy. Friend and master, Robert Walker, of Alaways Creek, sole Executor. William, son of said Robert Walker to inherit personal estate. Witnesses—John Johnson, William Dickinson, Job Shepherd. Proved Dec. 20, 1754. Lib. 8, p. 246.

1755, Apr. 16. Moon, James, of Burlington City. Int. Else (Alice), widow, declines to administer, recommending William Smith, Esq., of said City.

1755, May 1. Bond of William Smith as Adm'r; Daniel Ellis fellowbondsman, both of said City. Lib. 8, p. 193.

1753, June 10. Moore, Benjamin, of Evesham, Burlington Co., yeoman; will of. Children—Benjamin, Thomas (both named Executors), Joseph, Samuel, Sarah (wife of Thomas Eayre) and Elizabeth, (wife of John Collins). Grandchildren—Joseph and Hannah, son and daughter of dec'd son-in-law, Jacob Heulings. Witnesses—James Lippincott, Benjamin Bispham, John Burr, Jr. Proved Dec. 5, 1754. Lib. 7, p. 521.

1754, Dec. 4. Inventory, £431.4.1, incl. bills, bonds, book debts & cash, £400.8.1; made by John Hiller and Henry Burr.

1758, Nov. 20. Moore, Benjamin, of Woodbridge, Middlesex Co., shopkeeper. Int. William Moore and John Moore renounced. Adm'rs —William Edgar and Joseph Moore, creditors. Bondsmen—Jonathan Bishop and Isaac Lane. Witness—Thomas Bartow. Lib. G, p. 6.

1757, Nov. 21. Moore, Daniel, of Rahway, Elizabeth Borough, Essex Co.; will of. Wife, Elizabeth. Children—Hope, Elizabeth, Rachel, Sarah, Hannah, Anne, Susannah, John and Daniel. Homestead; lot in Middlesex Co., adjoining John Lowe; lot, called the Pond "Paster" on the highway from Sarah Tucker's to the mill pond; farm in said borough, bought of dec'd brother Enoch, near the Riding-over Place, the 32d part of a "mind," in Essex Co., bought of John Davis. Personal estate. Executors—the wife, John Bishop and Joseph Moore, of Woodbridge. Witnesses—John Lee, Zachariah Codington, Edward Wilkinson, Jr. Proved Jan. 1, 1759. Lib. G, p. 13.

1760, Feb. 6. Moore, David, of Morris Town, Morris Co. Int. Bond of Elizabeth, widow, as Adm'x; Henry Primrose, of the same place, fellowbondsman. Lib. G, p. 160.

CALENDAR OF WILLS—1751-1760   225

1755, Jan. 10. Moore, Enoch, of the "Borrough" of Elizabeth, Essex Co., will of. Wife, Grace. Children—John (under age), Enoch, James, Samuel, Frances, Grace and Hope. Real and personal estate. Executors—the wife, nephew, Joseph Moore, and kinsman, Joseph Shotwell. Witnesses—John Vail, Samuel Marsh, Ann Wren. Codicil of October 6, 1755, provides for an expected child. Same witnesses. Proved Nov. 22, 1755. Lib. F, p. 294.

1759, June 19. Moore, Enoch, of Essex Co. Int. Adm'r—Henry Davis, of Elizabeth, yeoman ("empowered by the widow of Enoch Moor, late of Eliz: Town, to receive due to her son, Enoch, deceased"). Bondsman—William Line of Elizabeth, yeoman. Witness—Thomas Bartow. Lib. G, p. 83.

1760, Apr. 18. Moore, Francis, of Hackinsack, Bergen Co., yeoman; will of. Wife, Ganne, sole heiress and Executrix of real and personal estate. Witnesses—Abraham Van Buskirk, Mary Moore and Thomas Moore. Proved June 12, 1760. Lib. G, p. 284.
1760, May 30. Inventory, £213.13.3, incl. outstanding debts, £48.6.4, and a negro slave, £50; made by Abram Day and Garret Benson.

—, — —. Moore, Gershom, of Woodbridge, Middlesex Co.; will of. Wife, Rachel. Children—Thomas, Ruth, Rachel, Gershom, Enoch, Benjamin, Mary and Samuel, all but Thomas under age. Real and personal estate. Executors—the wife, son Thomas and brother Benjamin Islslee. Witnesses—Abraham Thorn, Jacob Shotwell, Abraham Thorn, Jr. Proved March 9, 1752. Lib. F, p. 21.
1752, Feb. 10. Inventory, £458.5.4, incl. bonds from Richard Nickels, £334; made by Abraham Thorn and Abijah Hubbell.

1759, March 22. Moore, Isaac, of Woodbridge, Middlesex Co., yeoman. Int. Elizabeth Moore, widow, renounced in presence of Kezia Bloomfield. Adm'r appointed—Joseph Moore, of Woodbridge. Bondsman—William Edgar, of same place. Witness—Thomas Bartow.
Lib. G, p. 48.

1755, Dec. 7. Moore, John, of Alloways Creek, Salem Co. Int. Bond of William Moore, of Manington, said Co., as Adm'r; no fellowbondsman. Lib. 8, p. 236.
1755, — —. Inventory, £27.5.6, incl. a Testament, 1s.; made by John Fitzpatrick and Francis Test.

1759, June 19. Moore, John and Samuel, sons of Samuel, deceased, of Woodbridge. Guardian appointed, John Blanchard. Lib. G, p. 85.
1759, June 26. John Blanchard released; Jonathan Alston appointed Guardian.

1757, Nov. 5. Moore, Joseph, of Hopewell, Hunterdon Co., yeoman; will of. Wife, Helena. Children—Stephen, Joseph, Daniel, John, Job, James, Phebe and Elizabeth. Land on the Scotch Road, bought of John and Abigail Alsop; land at John Carpenter's Corner; homefarm, bought of Timothy Temple. Personal property. Executors—son, Joseph, and brother, Benjamin Moore. Witnesses—John Moore, John Hutchinson and Josiah Ellis. Proved Nov. 26, 1757. Lib. 8, p. 487.
1757, Dec. 3. Inventory, £398.13.7, incl. a negro wench, £25; a negro man, £70; book debts, £46.19.7, a looking glass, 5s.; made by John Welling and John Moore.

15

1760, Feb. 14. Account by the Executors, who deduct from the inventory £80.10, for articles, disposed of in the will, and £14.7.5., for insolvent debts.

1758, March 21. Moore, Michael, of Woodbridge, Middlesex Co. yeoman. Int. Martha Moore renounced in favor of Jonathan Frazee, of Woodbridge.
1758, March 25. Adm'r—Jonathan Frazee. Bondsman—Timothy Frazee, of same place. Witness—Thomas Bartow.
1758, March 28. Inventory, £271.7.4, by Samuel Barrow and David Dunham (latter died before signing). Lib. F, p. 517.
1760, July 1. Account by Jonathan Frazee, the Administrator.

1753, Dec. 3. Moore, Moses, of Deerfield, Cumberland Co. Int. Inventory, £194.5.5, by John Jarman (Jerman), Jr., and William Stratton.
1754, Jan. 30. Bond of his widow, Elizabeth Moore, as Adm'x; Aaron Moore, of Hopewell Township, said Co., farmer, fellowbondsman. Cumb. Wills, 104 F.

1758, July 1. Moore, Nathaniel, of Hopewell, Hunterdon Co., yeoman; will of. Wife, Joanna. Children—John (oldest son), Benjamin (youngest son), Abigail, Samuel, Phebe and Joseph. Grandchildren— Joanna and Sarah (daughters of Benjamin Temple and wife Sarah) and Nathaniel (son of John Moore and wife Keziah). Home farm; lot of 10 acres in Newark; 50 ac. in Hopewell, bought of Ralph Hunt; lot in Queenstown, alias Pennington, adjoining Benjamin Ketcham, bo't of Philip Phillips; two lots bought of Samuel Tucker and William Cornell's heirs. Shares in the Pennington Schoolhouse lot and in the Trenton Library. Three negro slaves. Executors—the wife, with sons John and Samuel. Witnesses—William Kirkpatrick, Elnathan Baldwin, Josiah Ellis. Proved Sept. 15, 1759.
Lib. 10, p. 12.
1759, Sept. 19. Inventory, £600.18.1, incl. 3 negroes, £25, £80 and £65; share in Library, £6; in Schoolhouse lot, £6; a negro woman, £40; a large 4° Bible and other books, £1.11; made by John Welling and Reuben Armitage (Hermitage).
1760, June 24. Account by John and Samuel Moore, Executors.

1752, Apr. 11. Moore, Patrick, of Alloways Creek, Salem Co. Int. Bond of Mary Moore as Adm'x; Joseph Stretch fellowbondsman, both of Alloways Creek. Salem Wills, 866 Q.
1752, Apr. 11. Inventory, £28.13.8, by Jonah Platts and David Stretch.
1753, Mar. 26. Account of the estate, by the Administratrix, Mary Patrick, late Mary Moore, and her husband, John Patrick.

1753, Sept. 8. Moore, Sacket, of Hopewell, Hunterdon Co. Int. Inventory, £343.5.9, incl. 202¼ bush. of wheat, £50.15; made by John Welling and Joseph Hart.
1753, Sept. 30. Abigill Moore, widow, renounces in favour of her brother, John Moore, and brother-in-law, Benjamin Moore.
1753, Oct. 4. Bond of Benjamin and John Moore, both of Hopewell, as Adm'rs; John Allen, of Trenton, fellowbondsman.
Hunt. Wills, 337 J.
1760, Feb. 14. Account by the Administrators.

CALENDAR OF WILLS—1751-1760   227

1750, May 3. Moore, Samuel, of Woodbridge, Middlesex Co., merchant; will of. Wife, Mary. Sons—Joseph, Edward, Isaac, John and Samuel. Real and personal estate, incl. a negro wench. Executors—the wife and brother, Enoch Moore, of Essex Co., mariner. Witnesses—Robart Moores, Michael Moore, Isaac Prall, Nugient Kelly. Proved June 1, 1751.   Lib. E, p. 529.

1754, Oct. 29. Moore, Samuel, of Piles Grove, Salem Co.; will of. Wife, Rosannah, sole Executrix. Children spoken of as under age, but names not given. Real and personal estate. Witnesses—Erick Unander, Aaron Silver and Mary Barber. Proved May 27, 1758.
Lib. 9, p. 99.
1758, May 24. Inventory, £149.16.5, by Samuel Lippincott and Bateman Lloyd.

1758, Dec. 25. Moore, Samuel, of Evesham Township, Burlington Co.; will of. Wife, Abigail. Children—Vallariah, Mary, Anna, Sarah, Samuel, Thomas and Eber, all under age. Real and personal estate. Executors—Joshua Ballinger and Isaac Evens. Witnesses—Benjamin Moar, Habakkuk Eayre, Noah Haines. Proved April 8, 1759.
Lib. 9, p. 205.
1759, Apr. 7. Inventory, £351.14.4, incl. accounts and bonds, £49.2.6; made by James Allen and James Cattell.

1759, Oct. 5. Moore, Samuel, of Hopewell, Hunterdon Co.; will of. Wife (not named). Sons—Benjamin and Jonathan, both under age. Sister, Mary Moore, to have 100 acres in Bergen Co., if brother, Henry Moore, recovers the land by law. Land, 250 ac., in Woodbridge, E. J., inherited from uncle, Jonathan Moore. Other real estate and personal property. Executors—brethren, Henry Moore and Hezekiah Stout. Witnesses—Bn. Stout, John Hart and John Ballard. Proved Oct. 16, 1759.   Lib. 10, p. 118.

1755, Apr. 17. Moore, Stephen, of Greenwich, Cumberland Co. Int. Bond of Francis Brewster as Adm'r; Andrew Miller, fellowbondsman, both of said place.   Lib. 8, p. 158.
1755, Apr. 17. Inventory, £9.6.10, by Andrew Miller and John Asking.

1751, Apr. 13. Moore, William, of Hopewell, Hunterdon Co., weaver; will of. Wife, Easter. Children—Cornelius, Nancy, Marry, Nathan and Easter. Real and personal estate. Executors—the wife and John Phillips. Witnesses—Eliakim Anderson, Richard Phillips, Return Temple. Proved June 5, 1751.   Lib. 7, p. 73.
1751, Apr. 25. Inventory, "the place the widdo lives on & all Conveniencies," £20; personal, £92.0.7½; made by Eliakim Anderson and Return Temple.

1757, Feb. 23. Moores, George, of Woodbridge, Middlesex Co. Int. Adm'x—Mary Moores, widow. Bondsman—Robert Combes, of said place, yeoman. Witness—Thomas Bartow.   Lib. F, p. 404.

1756, May 31. Moores, Samuel, of Woodbridge, yeoman. Int. Adm'x —Experience Moores, widow.   Lib. F, p. 358.
1759, Feb. 8. The widow, Experience, having deceased, William Kent made Administrator.   Lib. G, p. 31.

1751, Oct. 6. Moores, Thomas, of Woodbridge, Middlesex Co.; will of. Wife, Rachel. Children—Marion, Anable, Mary and Sarah; sons spoken of, but names not given. Real and personal estate. Executors—the wife and brother, Daniel Moor. Witnesses—Daniel Moores, Charles Toms, Richard Frances, David Donham. Proved Oct. 21, 1751.
Lib. F, p. 1.

1751, Oct. 26. Inventory, £376, incl. books, 4s.6d.; 7 bush. of flax seed, £2.9; a looking glass, 8s.; 40 bush. of Indian corn in the chamber, £4.13.9; 100 do. in the field, £8.15; 6 do. of wheat in the barn, at 4s.6d., £1.7.; 60 do. of oats at 1s.6d., £4.10; a negro man, £60; a negro wench, £40; made by Jonathan Frazee and David Donham.

1751, Aug. 29. Mootrey, John, of Woodbridge, Middlesex Co., yeoman; will of. Wife, Elizabeth. Daughter, Annaple Kinsey, wife of Jonathan Kinsey, who have ch., Elizabeth, John, Mootrey and James Real and personal estate, incl. 4 negroes. Executors—Thomas Moore and George Brown, of Woodbridge. Witnesses—Edward Crowell, James Brown, Thomas Fox. Proved Sept. 14, 1752. Lib. F, p. 66.

1752, Aug. 7. Inventory; £368.7.1, incl. 3 silver spoons, £1.10; 2 negro men, £40 each; a negro girl, £30; a negro boy, £30; bonds. £68.10.7; given to the widow by the will, £41.16; made by Henry Martin and Abraham Tappen.

1752, July 10. Morehouse, James, of Elizabeth Town, Essex Co., blacksmith; will of. Wife, Mary; an expected child. Sister, Susanna Morehouse. Real and personal estate. Executors—the wife, father-in-law, Joseph Hinds, and Cornelius Hetfield. Witnesses—David Man, Alus Townby, John Ross. Proved July 23, 1752. Lib. F, p. 60.

1752, Nov. 30. Morehouse, John, of Morris Co., account of the estate, £206.16.2, by Matthias Hetfield and John. Ogden, Executors of David Morehouse of Elizabeth, who had been Executor of John Morehouse. Filed June 22, 1756. [See N. J. Archives, Vol. XXX, for will, etc.] Morris Wills, 99 N.

1759, ——— ——. Moreland, Lydia, 17 years old, and John, over 14, legatees of John Smith of Hopewell, Hunterdon Co., their uncle, petition that Samuel Tucker, Jr., of Trenton, merchant, be appointed their Guardian.

1759, Nov. 8. Bond of Samuel Tucker, Jr., as Guardian; Joseph Higbee of Trenton, saddler, fellowbondsman. Lib. 9, p. 455.

1751, Nov. 4. Morgan, Alexander, of Waterford, Gloucester Co., yeoman; will of. Wife, Hannah. Children—Joseph, Benjamin, Mary (wife of Edmund Hollinshead), Elizabeth (wife of William Miller), Lydia, Hannah, Sarah and Rachel, the last three under age. Farm in Newton Township, bought of brother-in-law, Joseph Cooper and already given to son, Joseph; home farm; land adjoining, bought of Samuel Burge; 23 acres in Burlington Co., adjoining Samuel Davis, Thomas Lippincot and ——— Clifton; 34 a. of meadow on Delaware River and N. E. side of Pensawking Creek, bought of Samuel Burroughs. Personal property. Executors—the wife and son Joseph. Witnesses—George Weed, Thomas Lippincott, Jr., Samuel Spicer. Proved Dec. 11, 1751. Lib. 7, p. 165.

1751, Nov. 28-29. Inventory, £1912.1.11½, incl. a watch, books, £5.17; plate £80.2; bonds and book debts, £724.4.2; clock, £17.10; looking glass, £2.10; pork and bacon of 9 hogs, £22.10; 24 cheeses, £3; a mulatto woman and mulatoo boy, £53; made by Thomas Spicer and Joshua Raper.

1754, Jan. 24. Morgan, Benjamin, of Somerset Co., blacksmith. Int. Inventory, £155.16.1, incl. a looking glass, 7s.; book debts, £51.6.9; made by Capt. John DeGroot and William Stewart, Esq., both of said Co., freeholders.

1754, Jan. 29. Bond of Jane, widow, as Adm'x; Benjamin Morgan, John Degroot and William Stewart fellowbondsmen, all of said county. Lib. F, p. 156.

1752, Aug. 23. Morgan, Cadwalader, of Newton, Gloucester Co., ferryman. Int. Inventory, £349.14.10¼, incl. his purse and apparel, £210.17.9¼; books 15s.; a silver tankard and 9 silver spoons, £15; made by Samuel Spicer and Archibald Mickell.

1752, Sept. 1. Bond of widow, Lydia, as Adm'x; Isaac Andrews and Joseph Morgan, both yeomen, fellowbondsmen, all of said county.
Lib. 7, p. 305.

1758, Sept. 2. Morgan, Daniel, of Chester, Burlington Co., yeoman; will of. Wife, Mary, to receive one-third of real (land in Gloucester Co.), and personal estate; the balance to be divided between Jonathan Haines, Joab Hains and his sister, Hester Davis, Jonathan Davis, Thomas Ridly, Joseph Morgan and Francis Collins, the last two being named Executors. Witnesses—Nathan Middleton, Thomas Stokes, James Cornish. Proved Sept. 25, 1758. Lib. 9, p. 57.

1758, Sept. 20. Inventory, £252.12.7½, incl. a clock and case, £8; old books, 6s.; an old looking glass, 2s.; made by Joseph Stokes and Samuel Stokes.

1759, Apr. 17. Morgan, George, of Deptford, Gloucester Co., yeoman; will of. Children—George, Randall, Jonathan, David, Ann Stiles, Martha and Abraham, the last two under age. Martha to be bound out to Rebekah Harrison, and Abraham to learn a trade. Farm bought of Aaron Jones; two farms bought of John Chew. Personal property. Executors—sons George, Randall and Jonathan. Witnesses—Johannes Huntzinger, Michaell Fisher, Charles Fisher, John Fisher. Proved May 16, 1759. Lib. 9, p. 236.

1759, May 12. Inventory, £294.12.10, by John Blackwood and Michaell Fisher.

1748, Jan. 12. Morris, David, of Salem, in Salem Co., will of. Mother, Jane Hart, to have all personal estate, and the benefits of two plantations, the same being in Mannington, during her life. Brother, John Hart, plantation in Elsenborough, when 21. Brother, William Hart (after my mother's decease), the plantation in Mannington (where John Hunt lives) when he is 21. Sister, Lilya Hart, (after mothers decease), my other plantation in Mannington (where Robert Dicky lives), when she is 18. Executors—Mother, Jane Hart, and my brother, John Hart. Witnesses—Daniel Mestayer, John Oakford, James Rodgers. Proved Nov. 26, 1751. Lib. 10, p. 445.

1752, Nov. 18. Morris David, of Greenwich, Morris Co., yeoman. Int. Bond of Samuel Morris, of White marsh Township, Philadelphia Co., Pa., miller, as Adm'r; Thomas Rodman, of Burlington City, gent., fellowbondsman. Lib. 7, p. 306.

1752, Dec. 9. Morris, Lewis, of Woodbridge, Middlesex Co. Int. Inventory, £90.2, incl. a wood boat, £47; made by Richard Wilkson and Jonathan Bishop.
1752, Dec. 13. Sarah, widow, declines the administration.
1752, Dec. 27. Bond of John Morris, Sr., Thomas Morris and Spencer Elstone, all of Woodbridge, yeomen, as Administrators.
Lib. F, p. 82.

1757, ——— —. Account by two Administrators, John Morris and Spencer Elstone, who charged £92.15.6 against the estate.

1752, May 13. Morris, Mary, widow of Robert Morris, of Northampton, Burlington Co.; will of. Divides real and personal estate between Alexander Bennet, John Bennet, sister Sarah Wilson and daughter Susannah, sister Mary Bennet, Elizabeth Clarke, Sarah Bennet, Sarah Fennemore, Rebekah Gamble, cousin Sarah Reeves, Sevill Wilson (son of sister, Sarah Wilson). Executors—sister Mary Bennet and her son, Alexander Bennet. Witnesses—Thomas Atkinson, Joseph Burr, Jr., Thomas Lawrance. Proved June 10, 1752.
1752, May 30. Inventory, £34.12.11, by Patrick Reynolds and Thomas Atkinson.
Burl. Wills, 5063 C.

1759, Feb. 12. Morris, Samuel, of Newark, Essex Co.; will of. Wife, Ellenor. Children—John, Mary, Sarah and Bettey, all under age. Real and personal estate. Executors—the wife, David Rogers and John Nisbut (Nesbit). Witnesses—John Ogden, Gabriel Ogden, Moses Ogden. Proved Mar. 10, 1759.
Lib. G, p. 42.

1758, Apr. 17. Morris, Stephen, of Great Egg Harbour, Gloucester Co. Int. Inventory, £84.15.6, by Joseph Ingersull and Gideon Scull.
1758, May 28. Bond of Ruth Morris as Adm'x; William Mapes fellowbondsman, both of Great Egg Harbour.
Lib. 9, p. 16.

1759, Nov. 1. Morrison, David (17 years old), son of John Morrison of Baskingridge, Somerset Co., yeoman. Bond of Joseph Kinnan, of same place, yeoman, as Guardian.
Lib. G, p. 109.

1751, June 17. Morrison, John, of Somerset Co., yeoman; will of. Wife, Margrete. Children—James, Sarah, Marey, Martha, Margrete, Agnes (the last three under age), David, Isaac and John. Real and personal estate, (incl. a Bible). Executors—the wife and Robeart Moore. Witnesses—William Flin, Levi Ayers, John Roy. Proved Oct. 25, 1753.
Lib. F, p. 141.
1753, Oct. 22. Inventory, £173.17.6, by James Miller and John Noy.

1757, Oct. 3. Moshell, George Frederick, of Burlington Co. Int. Inventory. £219.13.8, incl. gold and silver, £10.4.2; a looking glass and 2 pictures, 6s.; 8 glass pictures, 24s.; 6 paper pictures, 1s.; a large looking glass, £3; a French and English Dictionary, 10s.; 6 **English** books, 1s.; 10 Dutch books, 2s.; 2 lbs., 15 oz. of silver avoirdupois, £15.15; Anne Thomas' time £3; William Williams' time, £2.14; Jacob Frederick Wease's time, £6; a negro woman, £40; made by Thomas Barnes and Charles Axford.
1757, Oct. 28. Adm'x—Ester Moshell.
Lib. 8, p. 499.

1755, Feb. 26. Moslander, William, of Cumberland Co. Int. Inventory, £48.10.7, incl. 20 bush. of Indian corn, £2; made by Joseph Lord and Joseph Savage.

CALENDAR OF WILLS—1751-1760   231

1755, Mar. 1. Bond of Abraham Moslander as Adm'r; Joseph Low, fellowbondsman, both of Morris River, said Co.   Lib. 8, p. 158.

1752, Nov. 22. Mott, Thomas, of Burlington Co. Int. John, brother, writes to Joseph Catergood (Scattergood?): "Goot Sir—Those fiue Linys is To desier you To Laet Jeremiah Baker have Lutors of admanstrostion one my Brouther Thomes Mott a state. . . ."
1753, Jan. 15. Bond of Jeremiah Baker as Adm'r; James Pharo fellowbondsman, both of Burlington Co., yeomen.   Lib. 7, p. 307.
1753, Apr. 28. Inventory, £45.8.9, by Stephen Cramer and Samuel Lewis.
1757, July 25. Account, by the Administrator, who deducts from the inventory a bond for £25, due from Joseph Reeves and not recovered, and makes the estate a debtor for £15.15.2.

1757, Mar. 13. Mott, William, of Trenton, Hunterdon Co.; will of. Wife, Margret. Children—Sarah, John, Gershom and Asher. Lands with mill and water, bought of Samuel Leonard. Personal property. Executors—the three sons. Witnesses—John Howell, Daniel Laning and Mergret Annond. Proved Feb. 2, 1760.   Lib. 10, p. 67.
1760, Feb. 11. Inventory, £1794.17.3, incl. purse and apparel, £418.19.2; bonds, £374.13.5; 3 slaves, £120; 617 bush. of wheat, £173.13; 50 do. of Indian corn, £7.10; 2 looking glasses, £2.10; 40 yds. of ozenbriggs, £3; books, £12; book debts, £78.12.10; made by Thomas Barnes and Richard Green.

1758, Jan. 31. Mounson, John, of Penn's Neck, Salem Co., yeoman; will of. Wife, Elinor, sole heiress and Executrix of real and personal estate, with legacies to sister, Mary Keeves (Reeves?), Anne, Martha, John, James and Elizabeth Keeves (?), John Steedam, Jr. Anne Mounson, and, for the "palling" of the Churchyard in Penn's Neck. Remainder to daughter-in-law (stepdaughter?), Catherine Boon, after wife's death. Witnesses—Peter Boon, Israel Dalbow and Robert Howard. Proved March 8, 1758.   Lib. 9, p. 1.
1758, Feb. 15. Inventory, £267.9.6, incl. a servant lad's time and some "hoges," £8; made by Samuel Linch and John Helm.

1757, Aug. 14. Mount George, of Monmouth Co.; will of. Wife, Ordey, to have her living. To my 2 sons and daughter, my real estate, and, if my wife should be with child, it to have its share. To children that Peter Whit had by my sister, £5 each. Names also brother, Joseph Mount. Real estate to be sold. Executor—uncle, Thomas Mount, John Mount, Jr., and my brother, Joseph Mount. Witnesses—John Mount, David Eldrith, Joseph Tillton. Proved April 17, 1760.   Lib. K, p. 454.

1757, June 25. Mount, Nisbit, of Cranberry, Middlesex Co.; will of. Wife, Mary, and John Tomson. Executors of real and personal estate. Children, "males and females," spoken of, but names not given. Witnesses—John Tomson, Jr., Stephen Warne and Cornelius Tomson. Proved April 4, 1760.   Lib. G, p. 156.

1752, Dec. 27. Mount, Timothy, of Middletown, Monmouth Co.; will of. Wife, Elizabeth. Wife's mother, Elizabeth White. Daughters—Hannah, Jenyme and Elizabeth. Brothers—Joseph and George, remainder men. Real and personal estate. Executors—Thomas

Mount and James Grover. Witnesses—James Rice, Samuel Mount. Matthias Mount. Proved Jan. 31, 1753. Lib. F, p. 99.
 1753, Mar. 19. Inventory, £327.19.11½, incl. a looking glass, one-half of a boat, £60; bonds and book debts, £190.5.2½; made by Edward Taylor and Garret Morford.
 1763, June 22. Citation to James Grover and Thomas Mount, Executors. Whereas David Stout and wife, Hannah, Samuel White and Jemima his wife, which said Hannah and Jemima are daughters and legatees of said Timothy Mount, complains that you have failed to file an account; this is to cite you that you are to appear at Perth Amboy on the 6th day of July next at 10 o'clock and exhibit your account. Lib. H, p. 248.
 1763, July 5. Account filed by Executors.

1752, Oct. 7. Mulford, Christian, of Hopewell, Cumberland Co., widow; will of. Children—Mary, Moses, Aaron, Benjamin William and Daniel. John Miller sole Executor. Witnesses—Maskell Ewing, Stephen Mulford, Dorothy Padgett. Proved Oct. 19, 1752.
Cumb. Wills, 79 F.

 1752, Oct. 17. Inventory, £217,16.3, incl. bonds, bills and book debts, £52.3.6; made by Isaac Mills and Benjamin Mulford.

1752, Nov. 8. Mulford, Mary, of Hopewell Township, Cumberland Co., spinster. Int. Inventory, £53.1.6, by Isaac Mills and Stephen Mulford.
 1752, Nov. 10. Bond of Benjamin Mulford as Adm'r; Stephen Mulford fellowbondsman, both of Hopewell Township, yeomen.
Cumb. Wills, 80 F.

1754, ———— ——. Mulford, Moses, son of Aaron, of Hopewell Township, Cumberland Co., petitions that John Miller be appointed his guardian.
 1754, May 1. Bond of John Miller as such Guardian; Benjamin Mulford fellowbondsman, both of said township, yeomen.
Cumb. Wills, 105 F.

1760, July 8. Mulford, Moses, of "Greenwitch," Cumberland Co.; will of. Wife, Rachel, sole heiress and Executrix of real and personal property. Son, Joseph. Brother, Daniel Mulford, remainderman. Other brothers spoken of, but not named. Witnesses—Enoch Moore, Elnathan Ware, Thomas Maskell. Proved Sept. 5, 1760. Lib. 10, p. 186.
 1760, July 30. Inventory, £123.6.9, by Jonathan Stathem and Thomas Ewing.

1751, Nov. 28. Mulford, William, of Cape May Co.; will of. Wife, Charity. Children—Ezekiel, Thomas, Lewis, Daniel (sole Executor), and Mary. Real and personal estate. Witnesses—James Whilldin, Jane Whilldin, John Leek. Proved March 22, 1755. Lib. 8, p. 141.
 1755, Mar. 24. Inventory, £123.1, incl. bonds, bridle, saddle, divinity books and apparel, £85.14; made by Samuel Clark and Jeremiah Fithian.

1753, July 25. Mulica, Andrew, of Greenwich Township, Gloucester Co., yeoman. Int. Inventory, £83.1.1, by Hance Urion and John Jones.
 1754, June 26. Bond of widow, Mary, as Adm'x; Fredrick Urion, yeoman, fellowbondsman, both of Greenwich Township. Lib. 8, p. 117.

CALENDAR OF WILLS—1751-1760 233

1752, Oct. 8. Mullen, Edward, of Burlington Co., carpenter; will of. Son, Joseph, to have house where he lives. Wife, Mary, £4 yearly. Daughter, Eliza Mullen, £10 when 18. Son, John, the house joining Joseph's, and John to pay money to my wife and daughters Elizabeth and Martha Mullen. Son, Edward, house I live in, when 21. Daughters, named—Mary Burr, Meribeth Lippincot, Elizabeth and Martha Mullen. Executors—son John and son-in-law, Joseph Burr. Witnesses—James Lippincott, William Woolston, John Woolman. Proved May 1, 1753. Burl. Wills, 5276 C.
1753, May 29. Inventory, £523.14.0, by James Lippincott and John Woolman.

1757, —— ——. Mullen, Elizabeth, William and Mary, infant children of John Mullen, of Amwell, Hunterdon Co., shopkeeper, petition that Samuel Tucker, of Trenton, merchant, be appointed their Guardian.
1757, Sept. 29. Order of John Reading, President of the Council, to Secretary Charles Read, to make out letters of guardianship agreeable to preceding petition.
1757, Sept. 29. Bond of Samuel Tucker, Jr., of Trenton, Hunterdon Co., merchant, as Guardian; George Tucker, of same place, blacksmith, fellowbondsman. Hunt. Wills, 412 J.

1755, Nov. 1. Mullicar, Jacob, of Gloucester Co., shinglemaker. Int. Bond of Ezekiel Goodwin as Adm'r; Benjamin Lodge fellowbondsman, both of said Co. yeomen. Lib. 8, p. 383.
1755, Nov. 15. Inventory, £35.13.1, incl. book debts, £13.16.6; made by Benjamin Lodge and John Jones.
1758, Dec. 16. Account by Administrator.

1759, June 19. Mun, John, of Newark, Essex Co. Int. Adm'r. Joseph Mun, brother, of same place, yeoman. Bondsman—Samuel Plum, of same place, yeoman. Witness—Thomas Bartow.
Lib. G, p. 83.
1759, Sept. 7. Inventory, £38.1.0, by Thomas Baldwin and David Cory.

1753, Apr. 28. Murfin, Robert, of Nottingham, Burlington Co. Int. Bond of William Murfin, of Nottingham, as Adm'r; William Bunting, of Chesterfield, said Co., fellowbondsman, both yeomen. Lib. 7, p. 420.
1753, Sept. 13. Inventory, £18.17.4, by Preserve Brown and William Bunting.
1754, Feb. 5. Account by Administrator.

1759, April 25. Murphey, Cornelius, will of. Wife and children, names not given, living in Mile (Mill) Str., County Cork, to whom father Hardin of Philadelphia is to send their inheritance. Executor —Daniel Grady. Witnesses—Peter Bruere and John Bruce. Proved in Hunterdon Co., May 25, 1759, when Daniel Gready, the Executor named, had died, making John Bruce his sole Executor, to whom were granted letters of administration on the estate of Murphey.
Lib. 9, p. 320.

1757, April 26. Murray, Joseph, of New York City; will of. To Jane Pitt, of Dublin, widow of Thomas Pitt, and her children, £500. To the Honorable James Delancey, Esq., £200. To Col. Lewis Morris,

£200. Real estate to be sold. To the Trinity Church in New York, £100. To the Reformed Protestant Church of New York City, £50. To the French Congregation of New York, £20. To Presbyterian Congregation in New York, £20. To the Lutheran Congregation in New York, £10. All above to churches to be distributed among the poor of their congregations. To my Godson, Stephen DeLancey, and to my Goddaughter, the daughter of Lieutenant-Governor Delancey (whose Christian name I have forgot), to each £50. To my Godson, Richard Morris, £50. To Ann Williams and Grace Williams, the two daughters of Charles Williams, my Executor, £50 each. The rest of the money from the sales of real estate to the College of New York in the City of New York. Executors—Charles Williams and Thomas Jones, both of New York City. Witnesses—Isaac DePeyster, Richard Shuckburgh, Augustus Van Courtlandt. Proved May 2, 1757. Lib. F, p. 435.

1742, Mar. 25. Myer, Johannes, of Saddle River, Bergen Co., blacksmith; will of. Wife, Jannetie. Children—Marten, Cornelius, Johannes, Isaac, Abram, Jacob, Marytie Brevoort, Ragul Labagh. Real and personal estate. Executors—sons Marten, Cornelius and Johannes. Witness—Gerret van Horn, Joost Degroot and Paulus van der Beek. Proved April 10, 1755. Lib. F, p. 271.

1755, Apr. 9. Inventory, (partly destroyed), by Johannis Myer, appraised by Albert Terhun and Samuel Demarest.

1759, July 11. Myers, George, of Northampton, Burlington Co. Int. Bond of Mary, widow, as Adm'x; James Allen fellowbondsman.
Lib. 9, p. 287.

1759, July 19. Inventory, £28.18.9, by James Allen and Joseph Stokes.

1759, Apr. 12. Nealson, Matthias, of Penns Neck, Salem Co., husbandman; will of. Wife, Margaret, sole Executrix. "Children-in-law"—Jacob, Isaac, Rebecca and Catharine Derrickson; daughter Christianna Nealson. Real and personal estate. Witnesses—Cornelius Casperson, Samuel Whitehorne and Michael Miller. Proved June 9, 1759. Lib. 9, p. 379.

1759, June 9. Inventory, £122.17.11, incl. credits and desperate debts, £39.0.3; made by Alen Congelton and Samuel Whitehorne.

1754, March 13. Nefles, Garret, of Bergen Co. Int. Adm'x—Catherine, his widow. Bondsman—Cornelius Westervelt, of said Co. Witness—Uzal Ogden. Bergen Wills, 336 B.

1754, Apr. 12. Negus, Thomas, of Shrewsbury, Monmouth Co., blacksmith. Int. Bond of Levinah, widow, as Adm'x; Daniel Wainwrite, of the same place, yeoman, fellowbondsman. Lib. F, p. 240.

1758, May 10. Newbey, John, only son of Gabriel Newby, of Newton, Gloucester Co., petitions, that his father-in-law (stepfather?), James Baird, be appointed his Guardian.

1758, Apr. 28. Bond of James Baird, of Bristol, Pennsylvania, as such Guardian; John Eastlack, of Gloucester Co., fellowbondsman.
Lib. 8, p. 544.

1757, Jan. 10. Newbold, Barzillai, of Mansfield Township, Burlington Co., blacksmith; will of. Wife, Sarah, sole Executrix. Children

—Thomas, Joshua, Sarah, Hannah and Rachel, all but Thomas under age. Thomas to be trustee for Joshua. Home farm; Alling land and plantation in New Hanover Township, said Co., "whereon John Clevinger now dwells;" land in Morris Co. Personal estate, incl a clock. Witnesses—Thomas Folkes, Caleb Shreve, Philipp Bowne. Proved August 29, 1757. Lib. 8, p.434.

1757, Aug. 16. Inventory, £1437.2.5, incl. a watch; bonds and book debts, £848.18.6; meat and cheese, £16.7; wine and liquors, £10.12.6; made by Anthony Sykes and Thomas Folkes.

1743, Aug. 23. Newell, James, of Perth Amboy, Middlesex Co.; will of. Wife, Mary, sole heiress and Executrix of real and personal estate. Legacy to Ann McCoy, Jr., when of age. Witnesses—John Deare, William Jordan and Samuel Borrowe. Proved June 15, 1759.
Lib. G, p. 68.

1751, Oct. 11. Newhall, Eleazer, of Burlington City, peruke (wig) maker. Int. Bond of Charles Tonkin as Adm'r; Samuel How, victualler, fellowbondsman, both of Burlington. Lib. 7, p. 299.

1751, Dec. 5. Inventory, £7.10.2, by James Hancock and John Thomas.

1754, Jan. 21. Newton, Ebenezar, of Cape May. Int. Inventory, £87.10.8, by Isaac Newton and Daniel Stillwell.

1754, Jan. 26. Bond of Rachel Newton as Adm'x; Christopher Foster fellowbondsman, both of Cape May Co. Cape May Wills, 194 E.

1758, June 20. Nickinson, Nehemiah, of Cape May Co. Int. Inventory, £90.6, by John Willets and Daniel Gerretson.

1758, June 24. Bond of Deborah Nickison (Nickinson) of Tuckaho, Gloucester Co., as Adm'x; Joseph Goldin, of Cape May Co., fellowbondsman. Lib. 9, p. 16.

1755, Mar. 27. Nichols, Sarah, of Monmouth Co., widow of Dr. Nicols; will of. Brother, Josepeth (?) Throckmorton. Children of dec'd sister, Patiance Grandin, viz., Sarah, John, Rachel, Amos and Daniel. Children of brother, Samuel Throckmorton, viz., Hartness and Martille. Children of dec'd sister, Mary Grandin, viz., Daniel, John, Samuel and Philipp. Mentions also sister, Rebackah Helms; John, son of dec'd brother, John Throckmorton; another John Throckmorton; William Throckmorton; Thomas Throckmorton, Mary, wife of Reuben Foaster; Daniel Throckmorton; Job Throckmorton; Lewis Throckmorton; Elizabeth, daughter of said Job; and Ann Appelgate, all to receive legacies. Brother, Samuel Throckmorton, and Daniel Grandin to be residuary legatees and Executors. Witnesses—Thomas Leonard, John van Clafe and Mary Leonard. Proved July 1, 1755.
Lib. F, p. 279.

1751, Mar. 4. Nicholson, Abel, of Elsonburgh, Salem Co., yeoman; will of. Wife, Isabel. Children—William, Samuel, John, Ann Brick, Ruth Clemens. Grandchildren—Ann and Mary Mason. Real and personal estate. Executors—sons William and Samuel. Henry Stubbins to be Trustee to help the wife. Witnesses—Richard Vickery, Thomas Test, Samuel Abbott. Proved June 3, 1751. Lib. 7, p. 249.

1751, April 9. Inventory, £339.3, incl. a large Bible and other books, £4.19; a clock; looking glass; a servant man's time, £15; stock in the hands of Daniel Dorril, £126.8.6; made by Samuel Abbot and Joshua Thompson.

1753, Dec. 5. Nicholson, Isabel; will of. Children—William Daniel, Aaron Daniel and Elizabeth Winder. Legacies to sister, Martha Vickery, and Henry Stubbings, of "Elssinburg." Real and personal estate. Executors—son William Daniel and Henry Stubbings. Witnesses—Anthony Benezet and Joseph Howell. Proved June 29, 1754 (in Salem Co.). Lib. 7, p. 475.

1756, Mar. 1. Nicholson, Sarah, daughter of Samuel, of Gloucester Co., petitions that Daniel Hillman be appointed her Guardian.
1756, Mar. 6. Bond of Daniel Hillman as such Guardian; Joseph Nicholson fellowbondsman, both of Gloucester Co., yeomen.
Lib. 8, p. 544.

1753, Mar. 14. Nicholson, Williams, of Mennington, Salem Co. Int. Inventory, £1072.4.4, incl. bonds, £450.3.3; white servants and negroes, £120; a looking glass, £4.10; made by William Chandler and James Mason.
1753, May 15. Bond of Rachael Nicholson as Adm'r; Seth Smith fellowbondsman, both of Salem Co. Lib. 8, p. 90.

1760, July 31. Noe, Asher, of Bridgewater, Somerset Co., saddler; will of. Wife and children, names not given. Real and personal estate. Executor—Tobias van Norden, Esq., of Bridgewater. Witnesses—Mary Hutton, Benjamin Harris and Elias v. Court. Proved August 11, 1760. Lib. G, p. 268.
1760, Aug. 15. Inventory, £38.13.4, incl. a looking glass, 20s.; house & lot near Middlebrook, Bridgewater, £90; made by Elias v. Court and Thomas Carhartt.

1751, Apr. 23. Noe, Jean, of Woodbridge, Middlesex Co., gent; will of. Children—Peter, Isaac, Daniel, John, Margaret Always, Damaris Marsh and Magdalene Tooker. Real and personal estate. Executors—sons Isaac and Daniel, with son-in-law, John Marsh. Witnesses—George Brown, Daniel Moores, Thomas Brown. Proved Dec. 30, 1751. Lib. F, p. 12.

1751, Apr. 2. Norbury, Richard, of Woodbury Creek, Gloucester Co., tailor; will of. Mother and own sisters, names not given, inherit the estate. William Wood to be Executor and to sell the lot in Woodbury and pay Hannah Hannah for services done. Witnesses—Andrew Sloan, Abishai Chattin, Sarah Whiteal. Proved May 24, 1751. Lib. 7, p. 143.
1751, Apr. 27. Inventory, £45.9, incl. a silver watch, £4; made by Abraham Chattin and Joseph Gibson, Jr.

1751, Sept. 25. Norris, Henry, of Essex Co., yeoman. Int. Adm'r —Samuel Williams, of Essex Co., yeoman. Bondsman—Andrew Craig, of said Co., yeoman. Witness—Thomas Bartow.
Lib. F, p. 548.

1754, Aug. 6. Norris, John, of Waterford Township, Gloucester Co.; will of. Wife, Sarah. Sons—Thomas, John and Joseph (under age). Homefarm; land in Kensington between Thomas Norris and William

CALENDAR OF WILLS—1751-1760 237

Vaun. Personal property, incl. a negro man. Executors—the wife and son, Thomas. Witnesses—Benjamin Morgan and Thomas Willard. Proved July 15, 1755. Lib. 8, p. 193.

1759, Aug. 5. Norris, John, of New Hanover, Burlington Co., yeoman; will of. Wife, Sarah. Children—John (under age), Sarah and Hannah. Homefarm. Personal property. Executors—the wife and brother-in-law, Amos Wright. Witnesses—Thomas Wood, Sarah Dennis, Thomas Platt. Proved Jan. 30, 1760. Lib. 9, p. 388.
1760, Jan. 28. Inventory, £178.3, by Jacob Andrews and Samuel Emley.

1754, April 4. Norris, Martha, of the Borough of Elizabeth, Essex Co., widow. Int. Adm'r—John Cory, of Elizabeth. Bondsman—John Cory, Jr., of said Borough. Witness—Thomas Bartow. Lib. F, p. 166.
1754, June 3. Inventory, £114.10.4, by John Miller and John Cory.

1751, Aug. 6. Norris, Samuel, of the Borough of Elizabeth, Essex Co., yeoman; will of. Wife, Martha. Daughter, Frances. Brothers—Henry and Nathaniel Norris. Sisters—Mary (wife of Samuel Williams) and Margaret (wife of Nicholas Mooney). Real and personal estate, incl. land in said Borough and on Staten Island. Executors—father-in-law John Cory and Lewis Mulford. If either refuses, to be replaced by uncle, Joseph Cory. Witnesses—Jonathan Sayre, John Norris, Edward Griffing. Proved Aug. 29, 1751. Lib. E, p. 545.

1751, Sept. 25. Norris, Samuel, of Richmond Co.; Staten Island, yeoman. Int. Adm'rs—Andrew Craig and Samuel Williams, both of Essex Co., yeomen. Witness—Thomas Bartow. Lib. F, p. 548.

1753, June 26. Norris, Sarah, of Newton Township, Gloucester Co., widow; will of. Gives dwelling house, with lot and some personal estate, to Jonathan Axford, and the rest of the real and personal estate to daughter, Elizabeth Hinchman, and to granddaughters, Sarah and Mary Smith. Executor—Simeon Ellis. Witnesses—Thomas Bate, William Harrison, Jr., Joseph Harrison. Proved July 27, 1753. Lib. 7, p. 390.
1753, July 25. Inventory, £383, incl. silver spoons and buckles, £2; a Carolina horse, £3; 5 negro slaves, £142; made by Thomas Bate and Robert Friend Price.

1754, Mar. 26. Norton, Daniel, of Cape May Co.; will of. Wife, Phebe. Mentions Abigail, (wife of Jonathan Laurance) David, Nathaniel and Hannah, children of David Ogden, of Cumberland Co.; Hannah (wife of David Smith), Mary, daughter of brother Nathaniel Norton; sister, Mary Norton; nephew, George Norton, son of brother Nathaniel. Real and personal estate. Executors—the wife and George Norton. Witnesses—Richard Swain, Joseph Ludlam, Nathaniel Jenkins, Jr. Proved May 21, 1755. Lib. 8, p. 175.
1755, May 28. Inventory, £703.17.6, incl. merchandize, £102.10.5; two negroes, £86; a shallop and two canoes; bills, bonds and book debts, £209.15; made by John Shaw and Jeremiah Hand, who have excepted property valued at £28.4.10, and debts amounting to £21.14.3, as not recoverable.

1751, Oct. 30. Nuttman, Ephraim, of Morris Co. Int. Bond of Hannah, widow, as Adm'x; Zechariah Fairchild, of said Co., fellow-bondsman. Lib. F, p. 12.

1752, July 15. Inventory, £104.6.6, incl. a Bible and Psalm book, 4s., a "righting" book and pocketbook, 5s.; made by Daniel Gard and John Johnson.

1751, Aug. 28. Nuttman, John, of Newark, Essex Co., "clark;" will of. Wife, Phebe. Children of sister Mary Williams, viz., Nathaniel, James, Benjamin and Sarah. Children of dec'd sister Abigail Tuttle, viz., James and Phebe. Children of dec'd. sister Hannah Sergeant, viz., Hannah and Sarah Sergeant. Mentions also Jonathan Dod; Rachael, daughter of dec'd sister, Rachael Eagles; John, Phebe and Sarah, children of dec'd. brother, Isaac Nuttman. Brothers, Samuel, James and Ephream Nuttman, residuary legatees. Legacy to Deacon Joseph Tuttle for the benefit of the Congregation at Hanover, whereof Rev. Jacob Green is pastor. Real and personal estate. Executors—the three brothers abovenamed and Jonathan Sergeant. Witnesses—John Cleverly, Nathaniel Sherman, Nathaniel Potter. Proved Sept. 23, 1751. Lib. F, p. 18.
1752, June 10. Inventory, £810.1.2½ by Eliphalet Johnson, Esq., and Joseph Johnson.

1760, May 19. Nuttman, Phebe and Sarah, daughters of Isaac, deceased, of Essex Co. Dr. Moses Bloomfield, of Middlesex Co., appointed Guardian. Lib. G, p. 198.

1757, Sept. 19. O'Brian, Edmond, of Trenton, Hunterdon Co. Int.. Bond of widow, Mary, as Adm'x; Joshua Pitman, of Burlington Co., labourer, fellowbondsman. Lib. 8, p. 516.

1760, Nov. 4. Ogborn, John, of Middletown, Monmouth Co. Int. Bond of Mary Ogborne, widow, as Adm'x; John Stillwell, Jr., of the same place, yeoman, fellowbondsman. Lib. G, p. 319.
1760, Nov. 15. Inventory, £196.10.2, by Joseph Golden and William Crawford.

1751, Sept. 4. Ogden, David, of Essex Co. Int. Adm'x—Catherine, of Newark, widow. Bondsman—Josiah Ogden, of same place. Witness—Uzal Ogden. Lib. E, p. 552.

1759, Nov. 19. Ogden, David, of Fairfield, Cumberland Co.; will of. Wife, Mary, lately the widow of Thomas Bateman. Children—David, Nathaniel, Jason, Abigail (wife of Jonathan Lawrence), Hannah Jones, Elmer, Rachel Jamison, Abdon, Benjamin, and John, the last seven under age. Real and personal estate. Executors—sons David and Nathaniel, and brother, Joseph Ogden. Witnesses—Abigail Elmer, Daniel Elmer, Joanne Newcomb, Mary Doubleday. Codicil of November 27, 1760, changes bequest to wife. Witnesses—John Fithian, Zephaniah Ogden, Sarah Sayre. Proved Dec. 18, 1760.
Lib. 10, p. 190.
1760, Dec. 17. Inventory, £462.13.10, incl. a watch, £6.10; a looking glass; books, £5.1; bills, bonds and book debts, £89.2.3; made by David Wescote (Westcote) and David Sayers.

1754, Dec. 12. Ogden, Hannah, widow of Jonathan, of Deerfield, Cumberland Co.; will of. Sons—Richard, Jonathan and Joel, all under age. Land (6 acres) on the road in Deerfield, adjoining Sarah, widow of Benjamin Worton, bought of Stephen Jessup; marsh on

CALENDAR OF WILLS—1751-1760   239

Joneses Island; 29 ac. in Deerfield, between Joseph Peck and Stephen Jessup. Personal property inc. books. Executors—William Dare and Stephen Jessup. Witnesses—John Filler, Prudence Terrill, Charles Clark. Proved Jan. 6, 1755. Lib. 8, p. 99.
1755, Jan. 2. Inventory, £73.11.10, by Henery Seely and William Tullis.

1760, Feb. 29. Ogden, Joel, son of Jonathan and Hannah O. Ogden, of Deerfield, Cumberland Co., petitions that his uncle, Daniel Ogden, be appointed his Guardian.
1760, Feb. 29. Bond of Daniel Ogden, of Deerfield, weaver, as such Guardian; Thomas Ogden, of Fairfield, fellowbondsman.
Cumb. Wills, 222 F.

1759, April 16. Ogden, John, of Essex Co. Int. Adm'r—Daniel Pierson, Esq., of Newark, principal creditor. Bondsman—James Nuttman, of Newark. Witness—Uzal Ogden. Lib. G, p. 174.

1759, May 6. Ogden, John, Esq., of Fairfield, Cumberland Co.; will of. Wife (not named). Children—Zepheniah, Josiah, Samuel, Jedadiah, James, Elizabeth Shaw, Rhoda and Edward (first-born son). Real and personal estate. Brother, David Ogden, sole Executor. Witnesses—Beniaman Chard, Alice Coney, Jeremiah Buck. Proved June 21, 1759. Lib. 9, p. 303.
1759, June 14. Inventory, £166.9.5, incl. a Bible and other books;—, bills and bonds, £30.9.2; made by Benjaman Chard and William Newcomb.

1760, Nov. 8. Ogden, Josiah, of Burlington Co. Int. Bond of David Ogden, Esq., as Adm'r; Abraham Cottnam, Esq., fellowbondsman. Lib. 10, p. 169.

1760, Aug. 26. Ogden, Sarah, of Burlington Co. Int. Bond of David Ogden as Adm'r; James Mcletche (?) fellowbondsman, both of Northampton, said Co. Lib. 10, p. 70.

1758, Aug. 5. Ogden, Thomas, Jr., of the Borough of Elizabeth, Essex Co. Int. Elizabeth Ogden, widow, renounced, and desired Samuel Woodruff to act in her place. Signed in "Raway in Elizabeth Town," by Elizabeth Ogden's mark, in presence of Stephen Burrows. Adm'r—Samuel Woodruff, Esq., principal creditor. Bondsman—Stephen Burrows, of Elizabeth Town. Witnesses—Uzal Ogden and Lewis Ogden. Lib. F, p. 544.

1760, Sept. 13. O'Harrah, John, of Monmouth Co., yeoman; will of. Wife, Sarah. Children—George, Mary, James and Sarah, all under age. Real and personal estate. Executors—Samuel Forman and Lewis Forman. Witnesses—John Wiycoff, Andrew Shotwell and David Forman. Proved Sept. 22, 1760. Lib. G, p. 302.
1760, Sept. 23. Inventory, £358.15.8, incl. a sloop with sails, etc., £150; a negro man, £35; a silver watch, £7; a looking glass, 16s.; all York currency; made by Duncan Robertson and James Crawford.

1757, Jan. 13. Olden, John, of Windsor Township, Middlesex Co., yeoman; will of. Wife, Mary. Children—William (eldest), John, James, Thomas, Joseph, David, Mary, Benjamin (youngest). [Order

of foregoing uncertain]. Real and personal estate. Executors—John Clark and David Braillay. Witnesses—Samuel Worth, Thomas Middleton and Lewis Charles Faneuill. Proved May 3, 1757.
Lib. F, p. 420.

1752, May 7. Opdyck, Albert of "Maidehed," Hunterdon Co., yeoman; will of. Wife, Elisabeth. Children—John, Sarah, Catren, Joshua, Benjamin, William, Franch and Hannah. Real and personal estate. Executors—the wife and son Benjamin. Witnesses—Benjamin Stevens, Noah Gates, John Price. Proved August 6, 1752. Lib. 7, p. 275.
1752, July 25. Inventory, £165.1.5, incl. a servant man, £12; made by John Price and John Johnson.

1757, Dec. 6. Oppie, William, of Somerset Co. Int. Bond of William Oppie, Jr., as Adm'r; Henry Harrison fellowbondsman, both of said Co. Lib. 9, p. 175.

1758, Oct. 26. Osborn, Henry, mason, of Elizabeth Town, in Essex Co. Int. Adm'x—Margaret Osborn, widow. Bondsman—John Jewel, miller, of said town. Witness—Robert Ogden. Lib. G, p. 12.
1758, Oct. 28. Inventory, £109.11.0, by John Ogden and Daniel Ogden.

1754, Mar. 21. Osborn, Samuel, of Shrewsbury, Monmouth Co.; will of. Children—William, James, Samuel (all three made Executors), Alice Longstreet, Mary and Andria. Children of dec'd daughter, Catharine, wife of Aury Longstreet. Homefarm on Manasquam River; other farms. Personal property, incl. a folio Bible; two negro men manumitted. Witnesses—Zelpha Chamberlin, Mary Sherman, Anthony Woodward, Jr., Jacob Dennis. Proved May 1, 1754.
Lib. F, p. 175.
1754, May 3. Inventory, £297.7.3, incl. 6 silver spoons; a silver tankard, £13; made by Gisbert Longstreet, Jeames Irons and Henry Herbert.

1760, Feb. 12. Osborn, Samuel, of the Borough of Elizabeth, Essex Co.; will of. Sons—Samuel and Michael. Grandsons—Cooper Osborn and Adonijah Osborn, (under age). Lot at the Paper mill dam; a meadow called Osborn's Land; land on Eastside of the West branch of "Rahway" River, between Thomas Baylie, the highway, the river and the Jury Line. Other real and personal property. Executors—son Michael and James Carpenter. Witnesses—Daniel Ogden, Jr., Caleb Osborn, Thomas Taylor. Proved Feb. 19, 1760.
Lib. G, p. 143.
1761, Aug. 13. Inventory, £76.14.5 by Caleb Osborn and John Osborn.

1760, Sept. 1. Osborn, Samuel, of Piles Grove, Salem Co. Int. Inventory, £10.10.6, incl. a Bible; made by John Richman and Philipp Titus.
1760, Nov. 15. Bond of Robert Patterson, of Penns Neck, said Co., merchant, as Adm'r; John Richman, of Piles Grove, merchant, fellowbondsman. Lib. 10, p. 447.

1759, Nov. 27. Osborn, William, of Shrewsbury, Monmouth Co. Int. Inventory £594.5.4, incl. 2 negro boys, £100; 2 negro wenches

CALENDAR OF WILLS—1751-1760   241

and a child, £75; money due, £156.3.7; made by Zorobabel North, William Brand (?), Richard van Mater and Samuel Osburn.
1759, Dec. 3. Bond of Samuel Osborn and Richard van Mater as Adm'rs; Joseph Potter fellowbondsman, all of said Co., yeomen.
Lib. G, p. 142.

1759, Aug. 6. Osburn, Nathaniel, of Essex Co. Int. Adm'r—Nathaniel Rusco, by request of Joanna Osburn, widow. Lib. G. p. 92.

1757, Oct. 9. O'Sherky, Patrick, of Hopewell Township, Hunterdon Co.; will of. Gives estate to Patrick Keely, of Hopewell, with legacy to Leah Brown, of said Township. Executors—Wilson Hunt and Samuel Tucker. Witnesses—Samuel Keirstead and Edward Cornell. Proved Dec. 22, 1757.
Lib. 9, p. 165.

1760, June 16. Ouke, Jacob, of New Brunswick, Middlesex Co. Int. Bond of John Anderson, of Maidenhead, Hunterdon Co., farmer, as Adm'r; Theophilus Severns, of Trenton, merchant, fellowbondsman.
Lib. 10, p. 462.

1758, Aug. 14. Ourtman, Harman, of Reading Township, Hunterdon Co.; will of. Divides real and personal estate between Catharin and Hellana, eldest daughters of Tunis Hendrix, of said Township, making them Executrices. Land, 150 acres, in said Township, bought with said Tunis of the Coxes, late of Trentown. Witnesses—Powlus Hartounge, Tunis Hendrix, George Reading. Proved Sept. 25, 1758.
Lib. 10, p. 123.
1758, Sept. 20. Inventory, £48.15, by George Biggs and George Reading.

1752, Dec. 16. Overton, Joseph, of Nottingham, Burlington Co.; will of. To sister, Sarah Willits, or Richard Willits, 5 shillings; brother, Constantin Overton, and cousins, Samuel, Robart, James, John and Gabriel Wilson, my real and personal estate. Executor—cousin, James Wilson. Witnesses—Samuel Darwell, Mary Murfin, William Murfin. Proved Nov. 16, 1753.
1753, Nov. 14. Inventory, £107.3.2, by William Murfin and David Rockhill.
Burl. Wills, 5285 C.
1754, Nov. 6. Account, £107.3.2, by his Executor, who adds, as lately received, £53.18.8, but makes the estate a debtor of 13s.3d.

1752, Aug. 24. Owens, James, of Pen's Neck, Salem Co.; will of. Wife, Hannah, sole Executrix. Children—Thomas, Mary, Ann and Hannah. Farm of 64 acres in Duck Creek Hundred, Kent Co., on Delaware. Personal estate. Witnesses—Jeremiah Baker, David Price, Andrew Sinnickson. Proved Sept. 15, 1752. Lib. 7, p. 534.
1752, Sept. 2. Inventory, £103.10.4½, incl. books; made by John Mecum and Andrew Sinnickson.

1750, April 17. Pack, Job, of Elizabeth, Essex Co. Int. Adm'rs—Job Pack and Thomas Scudder, of Elizabeth. Bondsman—Daniel Clark, of same place. Witness—Thomas Bartow. Lib. E, p. 383.
1750, May 12. Inventory, £100.13.9, by Samuel Marsh and Eliphelet Frazee.
1755, March 1. Account by the Administrator.

16

1751, May 11. Padgett, Aaron, of Stow Creek Township, Cumberland Co., tailor. Int. Inventory, £175.9.4, incl. bills, bonds and book debts, £85.17.4; made by Ashbury Smith and Ephraim Milles (Mills).

1751, July 20. Bond of widow, Sarah Padgett, of same Township as Adm'x; Ephraim Milles, of Greenwich Township, Cumberland Co., farmer, fellowbondsman.   Cumb. Wills, 68 F.

1754, June 26. Page, John, of Chesterfield, Burlington Co.; will of. Wife, Sophia, sole Executrix. Sons—Asa and Henry, both under age. Real and personal estate. Witnesses—Roweth Beck, John Chapman, Jr., Joseph Reckless. Proved Sept. 6, 1754. Burl. Wills, 5487 C.

1754, Aug. 29. Inventory, £199.12.9, incl. "Pus, a Parril and book accounts," £104.10; a negro girl, £15; made by Roweth Beck and Solomon Ivins.

1748-9, Jan. 20. Pagett, Thomas, of Stow Creek, Cumberland Co., yeoman; will of. Wife, Dorothy. Children—John, David, Thomas, Mary Ewing and Abigail Harris. Real and personal estate. Son, David. Executor. Witnesses—Rich'd Butcher, William Daniel, John Barracliff. Proved Dec. 19, 1751.

1751, Dec. 17. Inventory, £170.7, by Ananius Sayre and Richard Butcher.   Cumb. Wills, 69 F.

1756, Mar. 4. Pain, Peter, of Woodbridge, Middlesex Co., husbandman; will of. Wife, Mary. Children—John (youngest son and under age), Peter (eldest son), Mary, (wife of John McCarter), Zeruiah (wife of John Sharp), Hannah (wife of John Bush), Alpheus, Abraham, Rachel and Elizabeth. Real and personal estate. Executors—the wife, sons Peter and Abraham, and Jonathan Frazee. Witnesses—Samuel Freeman, David Stuard, Jr., and Timothee Frazee. Proved July 26, 1756.   Lib. F, p. 370.

1759, Aug. 7. Pain, Peter, of Hopewell, Hunterdon Co.; will of. Wife, Hannah. Daughter, Davenport, who has children. Eliza and John Davenport. Only son, Peter Preston. Wife's daughter, Anna Johnson. Legacy to Dilly. Real and personal estate. Executors—said son and Benjamin Stevens, of Maidenhead. Witnesses—Nathaniel Moore, Amos Hart and John Guild. Proved Oct. 15, 1759.
      Lib. 10, p. 18.

1759, Oct. 11. Inventory, £223.16.6, incl. a large Bible, 6s.; 25 bush. of salt, £2.16.3; a book, 3s.; a negro wench, £55; a negro man, £5; made by Reuben Armitage and Benjamin Temple.

1760, May 21. Paine, Jonathan, of Lebanon Township, Hunterdon Co., wheelwright; will of. Children—Jonathan, Samuel and Elizabeth Cojear. The children of Patrick Hammell to receive one-fourth of the personal estate and he, with William Ball, both of said Township, are named Executors. Witnesses—John Burn and John Seal. Proved June 2, 1760.   Lib. 10, p. 113.

1760, May 22. Inventory, £64.4, incl. a Bible 10s.; made by Andrew Bray and John Burn.

1759, Nov. 7. Palmer, Samuel, of "Mendum" Township, Morris Co., gent.; will of. Children—Mary Boid, Thomas, Jacob, Lewis, James (under age), Jamimah, Anne, Charritie and Precilah. Personal estate.

Executor—Jacob Ford, of Morris Township. Witnesses—Thomas Hall, Abygail Hall, Ann McMurtry. Proved Nov. 29, 1759.
Lib. G, p. 137.

1756, Nov. 6. Pancoast, John, son of John, of Burlington Co., petitions that John Butler be appointed his Guardian. Same date, bond of John Butler, Jr., as such Guardian; Joseph Borden, Jr., fellowbondsman, both of Burlington Co. Lib. 8. p. 360.

1757, Sept. 29. Pancoast, John, of Burlington Co., account of the estate, £434.8.4, by the Executors, Mary Pancoast and Job Ridgway, who report on hand for distribution £314.16.4½. [For will, see Vol. XXX, N. J. Archives, p. 367]. Burl. Wills, 5731 C.

1753, Aug. 7. Pancoast, Thomas, of Mansfield Township, Burlington Co.; will of. Wife, Ann, and four daughters, viz., Grace, Phaney, Ann and Thomasin, to have personal estate. Wife to have profits of the farm where I dwell, until son Thomas is 21. Son, Thomas, to have farm when 21. Daughters said to be under 18. Executrix—Wife, Ann. Witnesses—Nathan Folwell, Jane Coles, Elizabeth Folwell. Proved Sept. 22, 1753.
1753, Sept. 21. Inventory, £389.15.11, by Thomas Folkes and Edward Tonkin. Burl. Wills, 5297 C.

1759, Aug. 3. Pangborn, William, of Newark, Essex Co. Int. Adm'r —Abraham Cadmus, of Newark. Bondsman—Benjamin Johnson, of same place. Witness—Lewis Ogden. Lib. G, p. 92.

1752, Aug. 4. Parke, Joseph, of "Grinig" Township, Morris Co.; will of. Wife, Marget. Children—David, Joseph. Refers to 6 sons and 4 daughters, (but only preceding two mentioned by name). Real and personal estate. Executors—brother, Jonah Parke, Robert Laning and Isaac Laning. Witnesses—Will Marritt, Thomas Silverthorn, William Hendrickson. Proved June 12, 1754. Lib. 7, p. 518.

1757, July 28. Parker, Adam, of Somerset Co. Int. Letter concerning administration on the estate, from Thomas Bartow, Perth Amboy, to Garret Lane at Lamitunk, stating that Andrew Reed has entered a caveat against granting administration to Lane, he, Reed, claiming as first cousin to dec'd. Endorsed, July 29, by Lane, agreeing to Reed's having letters.
1757, ———. Bond of Andrew Reed, "nearest kinsman" in the Province, as Adm'r; John Henderson and David English fellowbondsmen, all of Freehold. Lib. F, p. 441.
1757, Aug. 9. Inventory, £83.4.3, incl. books and pamphlets, 7s.; bonds and notes, £69.12.9; appraised by William Colwell and John Berry.
1758, Mar. 24. Account by the Administrator, who deducts the note for £1.17, of William McQuown, he "being dead insolvent at Oswego."

1751, Apr. 20. Parker, Elisha, of Middlesex Co. Int. Bond of Catherine, widow, as Adm'x; her father, James Alexander, and John Stevens, of Perth Amboy, merchant, fellowbondsmen. Lib. E, p. 514.

1753, Mar. 25. Parker, James, of Shrewsbury, Monmouth Co., saddler; will of. Wife, Johanna. Children—Samuel and Elizabeth; an expected child. Real and personal estate. Executors—the wife and brother, Joseph Parker. Witnesses—William Parker, John Flower, John Holdsworth. Proved June 14, 1753. Lib. F, p. 192.

1754, June 5. Joseph Parker, one of the Executors named in the will, refuses to act.

1754, Nov. 13. Parker, James, of Somerset Co.; will of. Leaves entire estate to father, Andrew Parker, and mother, Jannet, living in the Lordship of Nusie (?); Ireland, and, in case they are dead, to brother, Thomas Parker. Legacy to widow, Jeane Willson. Executor —Isack Powell. Witnesses—John McIlhenney, John Stel. Proved Jan. 28, 1755. Lib. F, p. 248.

1752, Jan. 15. Parker, John, of Shrewsbury, Monmouth Co. Int. Bond of Josiah Parker as Adm'r; Peter Parker fellowbondsman, both of Shrewsbury, yeomen. Lib. F, p. 16.

1756, Jan. 8. Parker, John, of Piscataway, Middlesex Co., tavern keeper. Int. Surviah Parker, widow, renounced in favor of Jacob Dunn.

1756, Jan. 15. Adm'r—Jacob Dunn, bondsman to a principal creditor of said deceased. Bondsman—Jeremiah Dunn. Witness—Thomas Bartow. Lib. F, p. 312.

1756, Jan. 19. Inventory, £59.14.5, incl. a Bible and Testament, 4s.; made by Reune Runyon and David Fitzrandolph.

1757, ——— ———. Account by the Administrator, who has sold estate for £74.14.11, and charges £81.12.5. against it.

1754, Feb. 14. Parker, Joseph, of Burlington Co. Int. Bond of Amariah Foster and wife, Mary, as Adm'rs; Jacob Woolston, yeoman, fellowbondsman, all of said Co. Lib. 8, p. 160.

1752, Sept. 28. Parker, Joshua, of BridgeTown, Burlington Co.; will of. Wife, Agnis. Son, Abraham, placed in charge of testator's parents, William and Jane Parker. Executor—brother, Jacob Parker. Witnesses—John Woolman, John Ewan, Thomas Conarro. [Jurat of proof dated October 30, 1752, but not executed, and instrument endorsed: "Mem.; nothing to be done with this Will as yet"]. Burl. Wills, 5069 C.

1752, Oct. 30. Inventory, £57.5.8, incl. silver spoons 18s.; looking-glasses; made by John Woolman and Thomas Conarro.

1752, Dec. 28. Jacob Parker, the Executor, named, refuses to act.

1760, Feb. 1. Parker, Lewis, Johnston, of Perth Amboy; will of. Sister, Mary Parker, and brothers, James and John Parker, heirs and Executors of real and personal estate. Legacy to John Smyth, of Perth Amboy. Witnesses—Samuel Sarjant, Jonathan Deare and John Smyth. Proved May 8, 1760. Lib. G, p. 320.

1754, Aug. 26. Parker, Nathaniel, farmer, of Morris Co. Int. Inventory, £88.2.10, by William Compton and Ezekiel Mulford.

1754, Sept. 25. Bond of Elizabeth, widow, as Adm'x; John Kinnan, of same Co., shopkeeper, fellowbondsman. Lib. F, p. 212.

———, ——— ———. Account of what Elizabeth Parker, widow of Nathaniel, has paid "or answd," amounting to £112.0.10., signed: "These are Chiefly known to me. **John Kinnan.**"

CALENDAR OF WILLS—1751-1760 245

1758, Mar. 28. Parker, Ursula, of Perth Amboy; will of. To nephews, James, John and Lewis Johnston Parker, and to niece, Mary Parker, are given debts due from the estate of dec'd brother, John Parker, and a share in the estates of dec'd father, Elisha Parker, and of sister, Mary Parker. Nephew, James Johnston, remainderman of real and personal estate, with annuity to Mrs. Mary Foster. Executor—nephew, James Parker. Witnesses—Margaret Smyth, Gertrude Skinner and John Smyth. Proved May 19, 1758. Lib. F, p. 525.

1756, Nov. 16. Parr, Hannah, of Chester, Burlington Co. Int. Inventory, £71.6.4, incl. a Bible and several "historeys," £1.6; made by Matthew Allen and William Allen.
1756, Nov. 17. Bond of Samuel Parr as Adm'r; Matthew Allen fellowbondsman, both of Chester Township, yeomen. Lib. 8, p. 345.

1752, Dec. 29. Parr, Samuel, of Waterford Township, Gloucester Co., gentleman; will of. Wife, Hannah. Children—John, Mary, James (all three under age), Samuel. House and lot in Turner's Alley, Philadelphia; one half of the 3,000 acres, bought of George Ohill (Okhill), of Philadelphia, merchant, (left in trust to Ohill for son John), which 3,000 ac. were patented by William Penn to the children of William Ashton, of Salford, Lancaster Co., Great Britain, and sold to said Ohill by Frances Legh and Mary, Wharburton, surviving children of said Ashton; farm in Springfield, Burlington Co., bought of heirs of Roger Merrick in Great Britain; home farm in Waterford. Personal estate. Executors—the wife, son Samuel and Thomas Say. Witnesses—Hannah Irvine, Robert L. Hooper, Jr., William Parr, Codicil of January 5, 1753, gives further directions to Trustee Okhill; appointed brother-in-law, John Burrows additional Executor, and provides that part of the orchard, where son Arthur lies buried, be laid out as a burialground for the family and for corpses taken up within the Cove. Witnesses—Richard Blackham, Robert Owen, Robert L. Hooper, Jr. Proved Feb. 12, 1753.
Lib. 7, p. 312.
1753, Feb. 5. Inventory, £277.5.9, incl. a servant girl's time, £10; a negroman, £50; made by John Shivers and Josiah Shivers.

1759, Feb. 4. Parrot, Richard, of Allaways Creek, Salem Co., farmer; will of. Wife, Elisabeth. Children—Mary, William and Richard, all of school age. Stepson, James Ryan. Legacy to Patrick Fegan, of Elsin borough, schoolmaster. Executors—the wife and Edward Kesley, and, in case Edward should refuse to act, brother-in-law, John McCoune. Witnesses—John McKoun, Margaret Fegan and Patrick Fegan. Proved March 12, 1759. Lib. 9, p. 290.
1759, Mar. 1. Inventory, £359.16.10, incl. 2 looking glasses; bonds and outstanding debts, £92.10.2; made by William Goodwin and Aaron Bradway.

1759, July 2. Passons, John, of Penns Neck Township, Salem Co. Int. Inventory, £17.2.5, by Andrew Vanneman and Henry Jeanes.
1759, July 13. Bond of Hugh Davis as Adm'r; Andrew Vanneman and Henry Jeanes fellowbondsmen, all of Penn's Neck.
Lib. 11, p. 3.

1750, Sept. 2. Paterson, James, of Salem Co., yeoman; will of. Wife, Elizabeth. Children—Michael, John, Thomas, Joseph and Jane.

Lot of 20 acres in the liberty of Salem, between Grace Smith, John Anderson, Robert Johnson and John Pearson. Personal property. Executors—the wife and son Michael. Witnesses—Amos Penton, Phebe Andrews, Francis Hinckley. Proved Sept. 18, 1751.
Lib. 7, p. 245.

1751, Sept. 11. Inventory, £92.16, by Amos Penton and John Whittall.

1756, Feb. 7. Paterson, John, of Bergen Co. Int. Else, widow, refuses to act as Administratrix, and recommends Josiah Paterson, the principal creditor, as Administrator.

1756, Feb. 17. Bond of Josiah Paterson of New York City, principal creditor, as Adm'r; Abraham Leydecker, of Bergen Co., fellowbondsman.
Bergen Wills, 361 B.

————, ———— ——, Patison, John, of Pen's Neck, Salem Co., farmer; will of. Wife, Elizabeth. Children—Mary (under age), James and John. Real and personal estate. Executors—the wife and Edward Caisbey (Keasbey). Witnesses—Hance Lambson, Daniel Tracey, John Marshall. Proved Dec. 13, 1754. Lib. 8, p. 145.

1754, Dec. 11. Inventory, £202.8.9., incl. a servant man's time, £5; made by Mathias Lambson and Andrew Sinnickson.

1754, Dec. 3. Edward Keasbey, one of the Executors named, refuses to act.

1759, Apr. 27. Patterson, John, of Chesterfield Township, Burlington Co. Int. Inventory, £72.18, by Joseph Reckless and John Edwards.

1759, Apr. 28. Jane, widow, refuses to administer on his estate.

1759, Apr. 28. Bond of William OBren (Obrian) of Rekless Town, Burlington Co., as Adm'r; John Shank, of Brunswick, Somerset Co., fellowbondsman.
Lib. 9, p. 210.

1759, Dec. 24. Patterson, Robert, of Middletown, Monmouth Co. Int. Inventory, £137.8.2, by Richard Crawford, Jr., William Crawford, Joseph Stilwell.

1760, Jan. 3. Bond of Elizabeth, widow, and John Patterson, yeoman, as Adm'rs; Joseph Patterson, yeoman, fellowbondsman, all of Middletown.
Lib. G, p. 192.

1753, Dec. 27. Paul, Nathan, of "Grenwich," Gloucester Co.; will of. Children—Samuel, Sarah, Nathan, David, Jeremiah, Joshua and Uriah, the last four under age. David to be apprenticed to "Alicksander" Randel, shoemaker, and Jeremiah to Ansel Long, weaver. The youngest two to be taken care of by Samuel and Sarah. Real and personal estate. Executors—son Samuel, and John Paul. Witnesses—William Cozens, Samuel Paul, George Cozens. Proved Jan. 25, 1754. Lib. 8, p. 27.

1754, Jan. 14. Inventory, £244.13.9, incl. books, £2; made by Jacob Cozens and Gerret Vanaman.

1754, Jan. 25. John Paul, one of the Executors, named, refuses to act.

1758, Apr. 21. Paullin, David, of Piles Grove Township, Salem Co., yeoman; will of. Gives plantation of 125 acres to brothers, Joseph and Jacob Paullin; Joseph named sole Executor, and to pay £60

CALDENDAR OF WILLS—1751-1760   247

to brother and sister, Whitlock and Easter. Witnesses—William Paullin and Peter Johnson. Proved June 22, 1758.   Lib. 9, p. 99.
 1758, May 30. Inventory, £55.9.1, by William Brick and George Dickinson.

1759, Dec. 14. Paulin, Whitlock, of Fairfield, Cumberland Co., joiner; will of. Wife, Rebecca, sole Executrix, with William Nucome as assistant. Children—Whitlock, Marget, John, Hannah, Elias and Jacob, all under age. Home farm; 2 acres of cedar swamp in Bucshutem. Personal property. Witnesses—Abel Siffin, Benjamin Bliszard, David Shepherd. Proved Jan. 19, 1760.   Lib. 10, p. 22.
 1760, Jan. 9. Inventory, £161.17.2, by, Benjamin Chard and David Shepherd.

1758, June 13. Paullin, Henry, Sr., of Pilesgrove Township, Salem Co.; will of. Divides personal estate between William, son of John Reay, dec'd (who is to be taken care of, until of age, by William Brick and wife Rachel), John Elwell, a sister's son, and Henry, son of brother William Paullin, giving to said Henry all real estate and making him sole Executor. Witnesses—Joseph Paullin, John Dickinson and Jacob Paullin. Proved Feb. 4, 1760.   Lib. 10, p. 578.
 1760, Jan. 15. Inventory, £59.9.6, incl. books, 7/6s.; made by Jacob Richman and Joseph Paullin.

1754, Sept. 23. Paullin, William, of Piles Grove Township, Salem Co.; will of. Children—David, Jacob (both named executors), Grace, Henry, Sarah and Hester Darvin. Real and personal estate. Witnesses—John Dickinson, Richard Stonebanks and Jacob Richman. Proved Nov. 12, 1757.   Lib. 9, p. 7.
 1757, Nov. 4. Inventory, £131.12.4, by Joseph Champneys and Jacob Richman.

1759, Apr. 12. Payne, William, of Stow Creek, Cumberland Co. Int. Inventory, £9.5.6, by Jacob Moore and John Carll.
 1759, Apr. 17. Bond of John Bereman (Berryman) of Stow Creek Township as Adm'r; Jacob More and John Carll, both of Hopewell, said Co., fellowbondsmen.   Lib. 9, p. 212.

1755, Oct. 4. Peachy, Joseph, of New Hanover Township, Burlington Co. Int. Bond of William Budd as Adm'r; Samuel How fellowbondsman, both of said Co.   Lib. 8, p. 224.

1759, June 14. Peacock, John, of Evesham, Burlington Co. Int. Inventory, £152.16, incl. a servant man, £12; made by James Allen and Jacob Prickit.
 1759, June 15. Bond of Elizabeth Peacock and Adonijah Peacock as Adm'rs; James Allen and Jacob Prickit fellowbondsmen, all of said Co.   Lib. 9, p. 230.
 1760, Jan. 8. Account by the Administrators, who have paid a dividend of cloath, @ £3.5.4¾. each, to Adonijah Peacock, Abner Peacock, John Peacock, Alexander Peacock and Melchizedeck Peacock, reporting a balance on hand for distribution of £111.16.11½.

1756, May 25. Pearsall, Samuel, of Cedar Brook, "Piscatqua," Middlesex Co., miller; will of. Wife, Martha. Children—John, Mary, Jacob and Phebe. Real and personal estate incl. negroes. Executors

—the wife, Jonathan Rowland and Capt. Samuel Drago. Witnesses—
David Leforge, Jr., Benjamin Monday and Laughten Fallon. Proved
June 10, 1756, when the Executor is called "Samuel Drake."
Lib. F, p. 259.
    1756, June 15. Inventory, £240.11.3, incl. a bond, £22; a looking
glass; books, 3s.; 5 negroes, £121; made by Richard Carman and
James Campbell.

    1754, June 24. Pearson, John, of Deptford Township, Gloucester
Co., husbandman. Int. Bond of widow, Sarah, as Adm'x; Elias
Hammitt, husbandman, fellowbondsman, both of said Township.
Lib. 8, p. 116.

    1751, Sept. 13. Pearson, Robert, of Nottingham, Burlington Co.;
will of. Wife, Mary, to have 1-3 of my movable estate. Son, Isaac,
the plantation purchased of John Rogers, and a tract joining the
lower side of said Roger's plantation on the Delaware River, which
contains 400 acres, and is part of plantation that formerly belonged
to Thomas Tindall. Son, Robert, the plantation where I dwell, of
540 acres, except 50 acres at the northeast end; also the rest of plantation that was Thomas Tindall's, that I have not given to Isaac;
also the tract I purchased of Nathan Allen, of 27 acres. To grandchildren, John, Robert, Richard, Nathaniel, Elizabeth, and Catherine
Parker, £100. My daughter, Elizabeth Hutchinson to have land which
my father, Robert Pearson, bought of John Hutchinson, of 500 acres,
and a part of the plantation I live on, of 50 acres, and, after her
death, said lands to go to her four sons, John, Robert, Jonathan and
Thomas Hutchinson; also to her five daughters, Sarah, Elizabeth,
Rachel, Ann and Mary, £5 each; and to her youngest son £5 also.
My daughter, Mary Nipe, to have 20 shillings, and her children,
Isaac, Robert, Daniel, Thomas, John, Moses, Aaron, and Mary Quigley £8 each. To my daughter, Rachel, £130, and to her children,
Alexander, Robert, and William, £5 each. Daughter, Ann Yard, to
have a house and lot in Trenton, where she lives, which I bought of
the Executors of Isaac Harrow; and to her two sons, James and
John Yard, £5 each. My grandson, George, to have a house and lot in
Trenton, but, if he die before 21, then to be sold and the money
given to my children, Isaac, Robert, Rachel, Ann, Achsah and Theodosia. Granddaughters, Elizabeth and Sarah Reed to have £5 each,
over and above the £50 each already promised Andrew Reed to be
given to them. My grandson, John Pearson, to have that tract I
bought of John Stevenson, of 160 acres, and 50 acres adjoining it.
My grandson, Robert Pearson, the tract I bought of James and Edward Draper, of 160 acres, and 60 acres adjoining. My granddaughters, Elizabeth and Catherine Pearson, £40 each when 21. My daughters, Achsah and Theodosia Pearson, the tract I bought of John
Morland, of 200 acres, and the rest of the land my father bought
of John Snowden, which is 250 acres. Executrix—wife, Mary. Witnesses—Joseph Yard, Phillip Welsh, Edmond Douglass, Anne Abbott. Proved June 22, 1753.
    1753, June 6. Inventory, £1876.7.8, by Joseph Yard and William
Murfin.
Burl. Wills, 5301 C.

    1758, Dec. 21. Pease, David, of Freehold, Monmouth Co., cooper.
Int. Elisabeth, widow, declines the administration in favour of Joseph Forman, Jr.

1758, Dec. 22. Bond of Joseph Forman, Jr., of Middletown Point, merchant, a creditor of the estate, as Adm'r; Obediah Buclew (Buckalew), of South Amboy, yeoman, fellowbondsman. Lib. G, p. 12.

1758, Mar. 8. Pedrick, Jacob, of Penn's Neck, Salem Co., husbandman; will of. Wife, Mary. Children—John, Jacob, Elizabeth and Mary, apparently all under age. John to live with Doctor Francis Halter "to learn his occupation." Land, incl. marsh over Salem Creek, bought of Francis Dunlap; land bought of Thomas Carter, for which his wife (widow?) is to give a deed; land bought of Matthias Neelson. Personal estate. Executors—the wife, Samuel Linch and John Pedrick. Witnesses—Peter Peterson, Samuel Whitehorne and Francis Halter. Proved Feb. 10, 1759. Lib. 10, p. 522.
1759, Feb. 9. Inventory, £191.16.3, incl. books; credits, £36.4.9; made by Joseph Wright and John Vanneman.
1759, Feb. 10. Samuel Linch, one of the Executors named, refuses to serve.

1754, Aug. 26. Peirson, Henry, of the Borough of Elizabeth Town, Essex Co.; will of. Wife, Unis. Children—David, William, Samuel, Abraham, Suruiah, Frances and Sarah, all under age. Real and personal estate. Executors—Caleb Brown and Amos Day. Witnesses—John Ogden, John Ogden, Jr., David Osborn. Proved Sept. 29, 1757.
Lib. F, p. 494.
1757, Oct. 4. Inventory, £127.5.5, by Timothy Whitehead and Josiah Crane.

1753, May 18. Peirson, Mahitabel, widow of Nathaniel Pierson, of Newark, Essex Co.; will of. Daughter, Joannah Pierson, under age. Sisters—Cleopatra Herrick, Deborah Herrick, Aanne Herrick and Abigail Herrick. Names also Rebeca Pierson and Joannah, wife of Peter Prudden. Personal estate. Executors—Peter Prudden and Rebeca Pierson. Witnesses—Jonathan Sergeant, Jonathan Pierson. Proved April 17, 1754. Lib. F, p. 233.
1754, Apr. 23. Rebeca Pierson, now Rebekah Lyon, one of the executors named, refuses to act.
1754, Apr. 13. Inventory, £91.19.4½, by Isaac Lyon and Thomas Longworth.

1751, Dec. 12. Penton, Abner, of Salem Co. Int. Bond of Rebecca Penton as Adm'x; John Ewen (Ewings) fellowbondsman, both of Alloways Creek, said Co. Lib. 8, p. 90.
1751, Dec. 16. Inventory, £381.10.10, incl. a clock; a looking glass & 2 pictures, £1.10; books and other things, 14s.; a negro boy, £30; a servant man, £8; book debts, £166.1.3; made by Amos Penton and John Andrew.

1760, Feb. 25. Penton, John, son of William, of Allaways Creek, Salem Co., yeoman, dec'd, and grandson of William Penton, petitions that Daniel Fogg, of Allaways Creek, yeoman, be appointed his Guardian.
1760, Feb. 25. Bond of said Daniel Fogg as such Guardian; Matthew Morrison and Charles Fogg fellowbondsmen, all of Allaways Creek, yeomen. Lib. 11, p. 23.

1757, Dec. 27. Penton, William, of Alloways Creek Township, Salem Co., yeoman; will of. Wife, Elner. Children—Philipp, Isaac, Joseph,

Ruth, Martha, Mary and Job. Executors—the wife and son, Job. Witnesses—Patrick Moore, Lawrance Delany and David James. Proved Jan. 13, 1758. Lib. 9, p. 10.
    1758, Jan. 3. Inventory, £107.4.6, by John Holme and Stephen Willis.

    1759, Mar. 28. Penyott, (Penquoit), John, of Gloucester Township and County, blacksmith. Int. Bond of Benjamin Collins as Adm'r; William Norcross fellowbondsman, both of said Township.
Lib. 9, p. 197.

    1759, May 17. Inventory, £7.10.4, by Henry Thorne and John Hider.
    1760, Apr. 14. Account of the estate by the Administrator, who adds £28 for house and lot sold.

    1754, June 26. Perriman, Robert, of "Greenwitch" Township, Gloucester Co., yeoman; will of. Wife, Joane. Daughters, Elizabeth Leddon, widow, who has son Perriman Leddon. Daughter-in-law, Mary, wife of Samuel Leddon, who has daughter Margarey. Granddaughters—Susannah, Elizabeth and Joannah Leddon. Legacy to Hannah Harris. Real and personal estate. Executors—the wife and daughter, Elizabeth. Witnesses—Joseph Stinyard, Catharene Osgood, Jacob Richman. Proved May 23, 1758. Lib. 9, p. 422.
    1754, July 16. Inventory, £193.9.3, by Jacob Spicer and Samuel Liddon.

    1752, Sept. 22. Perrine, Henry, of Cranberry, Middlesex Co., yeoman; will of. Wife, Martha. Children—Henry, Anthony, Nancey, John, William, Joseph, Martha, and James. Real and personal estate. Executors—the wife, John Perrine and Peter Perrine. Witnesses—John Davison, George Eggers, James Farrill. Proved March 6, 1753.
Lib. F, p. 92.

    1753, Mar. 3. Inventory: Real—a farm of 80 acres in Upper Freehold, Monmouth Co., £60; a farm of 80 ac. in the City of Amboy, Middlesex Co., £180; another there of 96 acres, £280. Personal, £265.5, incl. 2 looking glasses; a parcel of books; a negro girl, £42.10; bonds and notes, £129.10; made by Luycas Schanck, Patrick Vance and John Devison.

    1759, June 25. Perry, Frederick, of Essex Co. Int. Adm'x—Sarah Perry, widow. Bondsman—Thomas Gould, of said Co. Witness—Uzal Ogden. Essex Wills, 2725 G.

    1757, May 25. Perry, John, of Evesham, Burlington Co., tailor. Int. Inventory, £19.16.6, by John Cox and Thomas Gill.
    1757, June 7. Bond of Alexander Ferguson as Adm'r; Thomas Gill, yeoman, fellowbondsman, both of said Co. Alexander Ferguson engages, to obtain from said Perry's widow a renunciation of her right to administer on the estate. Lib. 8, p. 385.
    1758, Jan. 14. Account by the Administrator.

    1753, Mar. 31. Peters, Godfree, of Windsor Township, Middlesex Co.; will of. Wife, Margaret. Children—Henry, David, John, Abraham (under age), Philipp, Margrid Ranfeller, Elisebeth and Mary, the last two under age. Real and personal estate. Executors—the wife and son, Henry. Witnesses—Benjamin Sutton, Joseph South, Charles Sutton. Proved August 27, 1753. Lib. F, p. 130.

CALENDAR OF WILLS—1751-1760

1753, Aug. 22. Inventory, £182.7.2½, proclamation money, incl. Dutch books, 5s.; bonds and book debts, £72.16.2½; made by Benjamin Sutton and Henry Moore.

1759, July 14. Peterson, Aaron, of Morrises River, Cumberland Co., gent.; will of. Wife, Christianna. Children—Aaron, the youngest son, Frederick, William, and Permealy, all under age. Legacies to Abraham and Isaac, sons of Hance Peterson, of Carlinia, dec'd, payable, if Mary Hunter does not claim the amount as due by said Hance's estate in testator's hands. Real and personal estate. Executors—the wife, Christianna, and father-in-law, Peter Moslander. Witnesses—Joseph Savage, Marget Erexson (Erickson), Ealse Shaw. Proved August 25, 1759.
Lib. 9, p. 334.

1759, July (Aug. ?) 4. Inventory, £316.15.10, incl. 260 bushels of coal, £4.10.7; the improvements on Mr. Byerly's land, £40; made by Joseph Savage and William Cobb.

1759, June 8. Peterson, Ann, of Morrises River, Cumberland Co. Int. Inventory, £59.14, incl. beds, bedding and a looking glass, £5.10; made by Abraham Jones and John Bragg.

1759, June 9. Bond of John Peterson as Adm'r; Abraham Jones and John Bragg fellowbondsmen, all of Morrises River.
Lib. 9, p. 340.

1752, Feb. 1. Peterson, John, of Morris River, Cumberland Co.; will of. Wife (not named). Children—John, Dan and Ann. Daughters-in-law (stepdaughters?)—Sarah Cobb and Abia Garron. Real and personal estate. Executors—the wife and son, John. [In the body of the executors' oath they are called Sarah and John Peterson, while the signatures, by marks, are Mary and John]. Witnesses—John Carnickel, Mary David, Gibson Worrell. Proved Feb. 24, 1752.
Cumb. Wills, 81 F.

1752, Feb. 18. Inventory, £370.19.6, incl. a sloop, her rigging and freight, £165; cash and book debts, £87.4.4; made by William Cobb and Gibson Worrell.

1759, Aug. 22. Peterson, John, of "Morrises" River, Cumberland Co., yeoman. Int. Inventory, £96.18.10, by Joseph Lord and Joseph Savage.

1759, Aug. 25. Bond of his widow, Christiena Peterson, as Adm'x; William Cobb and Peter Moslander, both of Morrises River, fellowbondsmen.
Lib. 9, p. 340.

1759, Apr. 2. Peterson, Luke, of Fairfield Township, Cumberland Co. Int. Inventory, £49.12.3, by William Cobb and Gabrill Isurd (Iszard).

1759, May 14. Bond of Daniel Peterson, of Fairfield Township, yeoman, as Adm'r; William Cobb, of the same place, blacksmith, and Abraham Jones of Morrises River, fellowbondsmen.
Lib. 9, p. 256.

1755, Jan. 20. Peterson, Moses, of Middlesex Co., sawyer. Int. Inventory, £5.0.8, by George Williams and Thomas Loyd; also signed by John Throckmorton.

1755, Jan. 22. Rachel Peterson renounced her right, and John Throckmorton, of said Co., yeoman, appointed Adm'r. Witness—Thomas Bartow.
Lib. F, p. 241.

1751, May 28. Peterson, William, of Mourice River Township, Cumberland Co. Int. Christian, widow, refuses to administer on the estate.
1751, May 30. Bond of William Edgenton of Philadelphia, mariner, chief creditor of the dec'd, as Adm'r; William Jones, of Mourice Township, yeoman, fellowbondsman. Cumb. Wills, 70 F.

1759, June 11. Peterson, Zacheriah, of Greenwich, Gloucester Co., yeoman; will of. Children—Zacheriah (under age), Ruth, Britta, Magdalean Steelman and Sarah Shute. Real and personal estate. Executors—daughter, Ruth, and son-in-law, Joseph Shute. Witnesses—Thomas Denny, William Shute, Jr., James Hoffman. Proved Dec. 18, 1759. Lib. 9, p. 447.
1759, Dec. 13. Inventory, £229.12.2, by Thomas Denny and Samuel Hewes.

1758, Jan. 3. Pettit, Benjamin, Jr., of Essex Co. Int. Adm'r—Benjamin Pettit, of said Co. father of Benjamin, Jr. Bondsman—Joseph Potter, of Morris Co., yeoman. Witness—Thomas Bartow.
1757, Oct. 18. Inventory, £102.2.8, by William Jones and Richard Valentine Lib. F, p. 482.

1758, Dec. 1. Pettit, Thomas, of Newtown, Sussex Co. Int. Bond of Thomas Wolverton, of Sussex Co., as Adm'r; Moore Furman, of Trenton, Hunterdon Co., merchant, fellowbondsman. Lib. 9, p. 136.
1759, Jan. 17. Inventory, £26.5.6, by Elisha Robbins and Ephraim Darby.
1760, Feb. 12. Bond of Mary Shermon as administratrix de bonis non of said Pettit; Ephraim Darby fellowbondsman, both of Newtown.
1760. Feb. 20. Inventory, of the estate, left unadministered on by Thomas Woolverton, £12.1.8; made by Ephraim Darby and Aaron Doud. Same date, account filed by Adm'x.

1760, Jan. 29. Petty, Ebenezar, of Cumberland Co. Int. Bond of David Sayers (Sayre) of Fairfield, said Co., as Adm'r; John Whitecur (Whitaker) and Enoch Seeley, both of the said place, fellowbondsmen. Lib. 10, p. 110.
1760, Jan. 30. Inventory, £97.1.4, incl. book debts, £39.13.6; a suit of new cloaths sent down from Philadelphia, £5; made by Silas Newcomb and John Whitecur (Whitaker).
1761, Nov. 14. Account by the Adm'r, who, among other items, charges £15. "due to me by agreement with the deceased for bringing up his childe from 18 months ould," and reports due to the estate and his hand, £47.5.3.

1753, Jan. 19. Pew, John, of Middletown Township, Monmouth Co., "cordwainer." will of. Wife, Susana. Children—Marey Wall, Ann Dorset, Katern Daueson and James. Executors—the son, son-in-law, Gerrat Wall, and James Dorset. Witnesses—John Willit, George Gilbert and Joseph Dennis. Proved May 3, 1757. Lib. F, p. 474.
1757, Apr. 6. Inventory, £254.9.2, incl. 17 books, 12s.; 4 other books; two negro girls, £85; one negro boy, £40; made by Nichols Johnson and James Mott.

1757, Nov. 17. Pharo, James, of Chesterfield Township, Burlington Co., yeoman; will of. Cousin, James, son of Jarvis Pharo dec'd.

CALENDAR OF WILLS—1751-1760   253

Names said cousins children, Jarvos, Amos, Timothy, James, Elizabeth and Ann; Avis, wife of Samuel Scholey; cousin, George Holloway and his sons, Isaac and George; John and George, sons of John Holloway, dec'd. Cousin, James Holloway, residuary legatee and Executor. Land, 120 acres, at Barnagat; home farm. Personal property. Witnesses—Joseph Reckless, Isaac De Cow, Sam Harris. Proved March 28, 1760. Lib. 9, p. 427.
1760, Mar. 25. Inventory, £120.14.8, incl. bonds, £50.8; made by Isaac De Cow and Joseph Reckless.
1765, Feb. 4. Account by Rebekah Holloway, sole Executrix of James Holloway, the Executor named above, who reports the estate her debtor for £73.2.5.

1751, July 26. Philips, Adolph, Esq., of New York City. Int. Adm'r—Joseph Reade, of New York, merchant [who deceased in New Jersey]. Bondsmen—Cornelius Van Horn and Philip French, of New Jersey, gent. Witness—Thomas Bartow. Lib. E, p. 538.

1751, July 26. Inventory, £1059.14.7, all bonds and credits.
Morris Wills, 55 N.

1760, Jan. 30. Phillips, Cornelius, of Hunterdon Co. Int. Bond of Robert Muir, of Princetown, Middlesex Co., as Adm'r; Samuel Tucker, Jr., Trenton, Hunterdon Co., fellowbondsman. Lib. 10, p. 416.

1760, Aug. 8. Phillips, Peter, of Evesham Township, Burlington Co.; will of. Wife, Sarah. Children—Mary Brooks, Hannah Allin, Elizabeth Prickit, John and Samuel, the last two under age. Real and personal estate. Executors—son, John, and Micajah Wills. Witnesses—John Inskeep, John Eves, Rebecca Wills. Proved Dec. 20, 1760. Lib. 10, p. 139.
1760, Dec. 18. Inventory, £625.2.7½, incl. bonds and other debts, £267.2.1; purse and apparel, £100.13.5; books; made by Joshua Ballinger and Daniel Lippencott.

1760, Dec. 10. Phillips, Sarah, widow of Peter, of Burlington Co.; will of. Children—John, Samuel, Mary Brooks, Hannah Allen and Elizabeth Prickit. Executors—son, John, with sons-in-law, Thomas Brooks, James Allen and Jacob Prickit. Witnesses—William Evens, Daniel Lippencott, Micajah Wills. Proved Dec. 27, 1760.
Lib. 10, p. 360.

1750, May 26. Phillpot, John, of Salem Co., yeoman; will of. Wife, Catteren. Sons—Nickles and John, both Executors of real and personal estate. Witnesses—Jeremiah Baker, Timothy Coner (Conner), Allice Conaway. Proved Jan. 21, 1752. Lib. 7, p. 247.
1752, Jan. 20. Inventory, £249.10.10, incl. a prayer book; a looking glass; a servant woman's time, £9; bills, bonds, book debts and cash, £117.8.10; made by Jeremiah Baker and Andrew Sinnickson.

1755, Feb. 11. Phillpott, Nicholas, of Penns Neck, Salem Co.; will of. Divides real and personal estate between mother, Catherine Phillpott, Rebecca Richmond and her daughter, Ann Richmond, Penn's Neck Church, aunt Jane Harrison and Sarah, daughter of brother, John Phillpott. Executors—the mother and said brother,

John. Witnesses—Marten Mink, Elisabeth Coper (Copner), Oliver Webb. Proved Feb. 27, 1755. Lib. 8, p. 136.
1755, Feb. 26. Inventory, £109.8.3½, incl. bills, bonds and book debts, £66.17.9½; a watch; made by Andrew Sinnickson and John Marshall.

1749, June 3. Pierson, Abraham, of Newark, Essex Co.; will of. Wife, Hannah. Children—Benjamin, Abraham, Isaac (sole Executor), and Mary Plum. Land in Morris Co.; land in Essex Co. Personal estate. Witnesses—Epenetus Beach, Timothy Pierson, David Ogden. Proved March 8, 1756. Lib. F, p. 365.

1744, Oct. 6. Pietersen, Hessel, of Essex Co., yeoman; will of. Children—Pitter, Vroutje, Mettje, Antje, Elizabath, Reachell, Ghertje, Klaesje. Real and personal estate, incl. 3 negro girls. Executors—son, Pitter, and Philipp Schuyler. Witnesses—Hartman Vrelant and Hendrick Post. Proved April 7, 1753. Lib. F, p. 137.
1753, Apr. 5. Inventory, £226.9.6½ by Hartmand Vreelant and Johannes Vrelant.

1756, Jan. 1. Pimm, John, of Evesham Twsp., Burlington Co. Int. Mary, widow, declines to administer in favour of her son-in-law, Daniel Lippincot.
1756, Jan. 3. Bond of Daniel Lippincott as Adm'r; James Cattell, fellowbondsman, both of said Co., yeomen. Lib. 8, p. 304.
1756, Jan. 3. Inventory, £256.10.1, incl. a silver watch, £4, a negro woman, £25; bills, bonds and book debts, £154.14.1; made by Abram Haines and James Cattell.

1743, Aug. 5. Pintard, Anthony, of Shrewsbury, Monmouth Co., yeoman; will of. Wife, Abigail. Children—Anthony, Abigail, Katherine, Samuel, Florinda, John and Poncet Stelle Pintard, all under age. Real and personal estate. Executors—the wife, brothers John and Samuel Pintard, and brother-in-law, John Halstead. Witnesses—Samuel Dennis, Samuel Pintard, Isaac Palmmar (Palmer) and Joseph Gifford. Proved June 3, 1755. Lib. F, p. 335.
1755, Jan. 11. Inventory, £111.9.6, incl. a looking glass, a coffee mill and coffee pot, a "grate" Bible, the "Whole Duty of Man," and other books; made by David Hilldreth, David Killey and Samuel Throckmorton.

1756, Aug. 21. Pintard, Samuel, of Shrewsbury, Monmouth Co. Int. Inventory, £12.1.6, by Daniel Wainwright and John Okeson; signed also by Abigail Lewis, "late Abigail Pintard," Administratrix.
1756, Aug. 27. Bond of Abigail, widow of Anthony Pintard and mother of Samuel, as Adm'x; Josiah Halstead, of Shrewsbury, yeoman, fellowbondsman. Lib. F, p. 442.

1756, Feb. 6. Pinyard, William, of Greenwich Township, Gloucester Co., husbandman. Int. Bond of Thomas Davis, cordwainer, as Adm'r; Isaac Low, yeoman, fellowbondsman, both of said Township.
Glouc. Wills, 593. H.

1757, Aug. 19. Pitt, Samuel, of Perth Amboy, Middlesex Co., schoolmaster. Int. Adm'r—John Deare, Esq., of Perth Amboy, principal creditor. Bondsman—Obadiah Ayers, of same place, carpenter. Witness—Thomas Bartow. Lib. F, p. 442.

CALENDAR OF WILLS—1751-1760 255

1757, Aug. 20. Inventory, £50.13.6, incl. silver ware, 54 oz., 3 gr., at 7s. per oz., £19.1.3; broken gold buttons, gold ring and gold girdle, in all 3 pw. 18 grs., at £6 per oz., £3.16.1; a looking glass, 4s.4d.; books, £2; made by Andrew Robinson and Thomas Skinner, Jr. [Note says the goods were sold for £70.6.11].

1759, May 21. Plats, Thomas, of Greenwich, Cumberland Co.; will of. Divides personal estate between Mary and Lidia, daughters of brother Jones Plats, cousin Jean, daughter of Jacob Evens, and William, son of William Daniel. Executor—Benjamin Tiler. Witnesses—John Shepherd, Benjamin Johnson, Mark Reeve. Proved June 21, 1759.
Lib. 9, p. 300.
1759, June 13. Inventory, £93.0.1, incl. bonds and book debts, £37.14.1; made by Philipp Dennis and Mark Reeve.

1760, Dec. 12. Platts, Jonah, of Alloways Creek Precinct, Salem Co. Int. Inventory, £585.6.4, incl. a young negro girl, £25; bills, bonds and debts, £64.12.10, made by John Stewart and Thomas Sayre.
1760, Dec. 17. Bond of Joseph Stretch as Adm'r; John Stewart and Thomas Sayre fellowbondsmen, all of Allaways Creek, yeomen.
Lib. 10, p. 440.

1759, June 19. Plum, Samuel, Jr., of Essex Co. Int. Adm'r—Samuel Plum, his father, of Newark, yeoman. Bondsman—Joseph Man, of Newark, yeoman. Witness—Thomas Bartow.
Essex Wills, 2727 G.

1759, July 17. Poling, William, of Hunterdon Co., yeoman; will of. Wife, Sarah. Eldest son, Cornelis. Other sons and daughters but names not given. Real and personal estate. Executors—the wife and son, Cornelis. Witnesses—Samuel Wyckof, Tunis Johnson and Nicolas Wyckof. Proved Sept. 10, 1759.
Lib. 10, p. 452.
1759, Sept. 1. Inventory, £105.6.3, by Nicolas Wyckof, Aaron Lane and Nicolas Wyckoff, Jr.

1756, Jan. 12. Pomyea, Peter, of Somerset Co., cooper; will of. Executors—wife, Mary, and only son, Peter. Wife to have real estate, while my widow, and to support all my unmarried children. Mentions children of my eldest daughter, Ann Boudwine (wife of Jeremiah Boudwine). Daughters—Susanna, Sarah, Mary, Margaret, Dorcus and Elizabeth, eight children in all. Will signed "Piter Pownrey." Witnesses—Joseph Gifford, Simon Hegeman, William Walling. Proved Oct. 27, 1756.
Lib. F, p. 384.
1756, Oct. 23. Inventory, £900.3, incl. bonds, £685.4.9; 5 negroes, £118.10; clock, £5; French Bible and other French books, 8s.; 2 looking glasses, £1.15; made by William Walling, Simon Hegeman, Joseph Gifford and Johannes van der Veer.

1752, Feb. 24. Pool, Robert, of Morris Town, Morris Co., labourer. Int. Susana, widow, declines to administer in favour of Jacob Ford, the principal creditor.
1752, Mar. 20. Bond of Jacob Ford, Esq., of Morris Town, as Adm'r; Barnardus Lagrange, Esq., of Middlesex Co., fellowbondsman.
Lib. F, p. 32.
1752, Apr. 6. Inventory, £72.2.10, incl. books, £9; made by Jacob Ford, the Administrator.
1756, Sept. 7. Account by Administrator.

1752, Feb. 4. Popeno, Peter, of Manington Township, Salem Co., weaver; will of. Wife, Mary. Children—James, Peter (both under 24), and Abigail (under 21). Home farm and 70 acres of marsh, bought of Thomas Haynes. Personal estate. Executors—the wife and the two sons. Witnesses—David Seley, Richard Hackett, George Trenchard. Proved March 12, 1755. Lib. 8, p. 139.
1755, Mar. 8. Inventory, £224, by Isaac Johnson and William Harvey.

1754, Mar. 20. Poppelstorff, Johan William, of Amwell, Hunterdon Co.; will of. Children—Alburtus, sole Executor, and Marya Coevert. Real and personal estate. Witnesses—Johannis Houschilt (Housell), Henry Landis and Philip Ringo. Proved April 27, 1757.
Lib. 8, p. 424.

1757, Aug. 31. Porter, William, of the Borough of Elizabeth, Essex Co., miller; will of. Children—John, Philipp, Abigail Norris, Sarah Oliver and Susannah Stanberry. Lot between Daniel Traubles, Mephibosheth Marsh and David Watkins; lot between William Oliver, Solomon Brick, said Traubles and Marsh; meadow; all foregoing subject to a payment of £30 to Isaac Noe. Also home farm; meadow between the road, the creek and David Marsh, subject to a payment of £50 to Daniel Traubles. Personal estate. Executors—son, John, and Joseph Morss. Witnesses—Joseph Morss, Jr., John Layer, Jacob Stanbery. Proved September 2, 1760. Lib. G, p. 290.
1760, June 12. Inventory, £19.18.0, by Amos Morss and Abraham Shotwell.
1760, Sept. 2. John Porter, one of the Executors named, refuses to act.

1759, Feb. 5. Potter, Isaac, of Hanover, Morris Co.; will of. Wife, Sarah. Children—Sarah, David, Jemimah and Loes. Real and personal estate. Executors—Jacob Ford and Joseph Potter. Witnesses—Benoai Thomas, Abraham Cory, David Cory. Proved Feb. 23, 1759.
Lib. G, p. 52.

1759, Sept. 10. Potter, Noadiah, Esq., of the Borough of Elizabeth, Essex Co.; will of. Wife, Phebe. Children—Joseph, Phebe, Sarah (foregoing under age), Noadiah, Nathaniel, and David. Home farm, between Thomas Bailey, Jr., the road to Elizabeth Town and Joshua Horton; salt meadows; mills and farm on West branch of "Raway" River. Personal estate. Executors—the wife, with sons Nathaniel and Noadiah. Witnesses—William Burnet, Phebe Baker, Sarah van Winckle. Proved Oct. 10, 1759. Lib. G, p. 114.
1759, Oct. 10. Phebe Potter, named Executrix in the foregoing will, "protests" against serving as such.

1746, Dec. 27. Potter, Samuel, of the Borough of Elizabeth, Essex Co., yeoman; will of. Wife, Mary. Children—Daniel, Joseph, Noadiah, Sarah, Hanna, Elizabeth and Mary. Grandsons—Isaac, Samuel and Joseph, sons of dec'd son, Samuel. Land, adjoining John van Winkle on Westside of "Rahaway" River; Proprietary rights in Indian purchase, Morris Co.; homefarm; salt meadows; right to the Blue Mines, so called; land at the Hurtleberry Swamp. Personal estate, incl. a great Bible. Executors—sons Joseph and Noadiah. Witnesses—Charles Hole, John Clark (3d), Elizabeth Hole. Proved Jan. 6, 1756, at which time Charles Hole is deceased. Lib. F, p. 312.

CALENDAR OF WILLS—1751-1760   257

1754, Jan. 30. Potts, Thomas, of Mansfield Township, Burlington Co.; will of. Wife, Rebecca. Children—Nathaniel, Joshua, William, Ann, (wife of William Folwell), Mary (wife of John Cox). Grandchildren, children of daughter, Rebecca Cox and of Thomas Potts. Real and personal estate incl. two negroes. Executors—sons Joshua and William Potts, and son-in-law, Thomas Cox. Witnesses—Jonathan Bates, Jeremiah Bates, Thomas Folkes. Proved Feb. 21, 1754.
Burl. Wills, 5491 C.

1754, Feb. 22. Inventory, £836.6, incl. books, £1.15; bonds, £550; a pocket compass; made by George Folwell and Thomas Biddle.

1752, May 2. Pound, John, of Piscataway, Middlesex Co., yeoman; will of. Sons—Thomas, John, Elijah and Joseph. Legacy to Rachel, wife of John Leforge. Personal estate. Executors—Reune Runyon and David Fitz Randolph. Witnesses—George Marlett, John Long, Abraham Marlett. Proved August 26, 1752. Lib. F, p. 64.

1752, Aug. 28. Inventory, £419.16.2, incl. a looking glass, 3s.; a Bible and other books, 9s.; bonds, £329.11.8; made by George Marlett and Peter Runyon, Jr.

1757, July 15. Pound, Matthew, of Somerset Co., mariner; will of. Makes John Thompson, of Somerset Co., sole heir and Executor of all his estate and prize money. Witnesses—H. Gaine, John Cregier and Evan Jones. Proved August 23, 1758, by the Executor only, the witnesses living in New York. [Power of attorney appears, from said Pound to said Thompson, to collect prize money due from the Privateer Brig "True Briton," Capt. Christopher Miller, or any other vessel].

1758, Aug. 22. Inventory, in the possession of John Thomson, £3.12.9; made by Tobias van Norden and William Riddel. A second inventory, made by William Riddel and James Willson, adds £3.3.6, to which John Thomson add 15s. as received at York.
Somerset Wills, 225 R.

1758, May 1. Pound, Thomas, of Piscataway, Middlesex Co.; will of. Wife, Audrey. Children—John, Mary, Esther, Johannah and Isaac, all under age. Real and personal estate. Executors—brother, Elijah Pound, and David Corriel. Witnesses—Isaac Stelle, John Hepburn and Reune Runyon. Proved August 11, 1758.
Lib. F, p. 544.

1758, June 14. Inventory, £302.17.7, incl. bonds and book debts, £73.19.6; a lookingglass, 6/6; a Bible and other books, 7s.; insolvent book debts, £6.2.1; made by Reune Runyon and John Hepburn.

1749, Nov. 2. Powell, Arthur, of Newton Township, Gloucester Co., yeoman; will of. Wife, Mary. Children—James (under age) and Rachel. Names Lewis, a grandson Samuel Kent. Real and personal estate. Executors—the wife and Joseph Ellis. Witnesses—Robert Stephens, Edward Hampton, Joseph Harrison. Proved March 30, 1751.
Lib. 7, p. 148.

1759, Feb. 28. Powell, John, of Northampton, Burlington Co., yeoman; will of. Children—Jacob, Grace (wife of Joseph Gaskill), Elizabeth (wife of William Jones), Sarah, John, Joseph and Christopher, who is sole Executor. Real and personal estate. Witnesses—Amariah Foster, Johan (?) Insling (?) [called in jurat, Henricus Enslising], John Burr, Jr. Proved June 7, 1759. Lib. 9, p. 216.

17

1759, June 4. Inventory, £297.12.4, incl. 3 negroes, £64; made by Thomas Budd and George Briggs.

1739, Aug. 6. Praa, Peter, of Bushwick, Kings Co., Nassau Island, New York; will of. Wife, **Mary,** use of all real and personalty while my widow. Grandsons, Peter Praa Vanzandt and Johannes Vanzandt to have my two houses in the North ward in New York City; my daughter, Elizabeth Miseroll, that tract of land I purchased of Derick Volkertse adjoining land I now live on upon west side thereof, and bounded by land of John Miseroll and, after her death, to go to her children. My daughter, Annietie Boddee, wife of Daniel Boddee, to have land on east side of Mespets Kill, or creek, in Newtown, in Queens Co., commonly called Dominees Hook, except the little Island in the said land which my old negro, Jack, is to have while he lives, if he maintains himself; and I give the said Island also to my daughter Annietie, and, at the death of Annietie, to her children. To my daughter Christiana Provoost to have house and ground where she lives; also 2 houses I have by lease from Jan Harperdink, and, at her death, to her children. Executors—grandsons, Jacobus Collier and Isaac Bergon, and Johannes Alberts. Witnesses—John Van Derspiegal, Abraham Lodge, Bartholemew Crannell. Proved Mar. 20, 1752.

1752, July 16. "Received the original will of Peter Praa in order to return the same into the Secretary's Office at New York."
"Jonathan Provost." Lib. F, p. 22.

1757, Sept. 8. Prance, Job, of Woodbridge, Middlesex Co., yeoman. Int. Sarah Prance declines to administer an estate of her husband, but desires it should be performed by Rezia Runyon.

1757, Sept. 14. Adm'r—Reziah Runyon, of Woodbridge, yeoman. Bondsman—Joseph Ayers, of same place, yeoman. Witness—Thomas Bartow. Lib. F, p. 447.

1757, Oct. 9. Praten, Elizabeth, of Cape May; will of. Son-in-law (stepson?) James Praten. Son, Thomas Praten. Daughter, Hulda Hand. Sister, Lydia Osborne. Brother, Annios Osborne. Personal estate. Executors—Annias Osborne and James Pratten. Witnesses—John Leonard and William Smith. Proved Jan. 7, 1758.

1758, —— ——. Inventory, £13.0.8, by William Smith and John Leonard. Cape May Wills, 191 E.

1760, Nov. 20. Pratten, James, of Cape May Co.; will of. Brother, Thomas Pratton, sole heir of real and personal estate, but, if he dies under age, to go to cousin, Judith, daughter of Abner Corsen. Executor—Daniel Hand, of the Middle Precinct. Witnesses—Jeremiah Hand, Jonathan Cresse, Jesse Hand. Proved Dec. 23, 1760.
Lib. 11, p. 71.

1760, —— ——. Inventory, £50.9.2, not itemized; made by Jonathan Cresse and Jesse Hand.

1752, Feb. 11. Preston, Isaac and Levi, sons of Isaac, of "Fairefield" Township, Cumberland Co., Bond of Josiah Wheeler, of said Township, as Guardian; John Dare, of Deerfield Township, same Co., fellowbondsman, both farmers. Cumb. Wills, 82 F; 84 F.

1752, Dec. 1. Preston, John, of Hopewell Township, Cumberland Co. Int. Inventory, £93.14.1, incl. a legacy, from grandfather Pres-

CALENDAR OF WILLS—1751-1760   259

ton, to be paid by Levi Preston, £20; made by Samuel Miller and John Woodruffe, of said Co., yeoman.

1753, May 26. Bond of widow, Sarah Preston, as Adm'x; Samuel Miller, of the same place, yeoman, fellowbondsman.
Cumb. Wills, 86 F.

1750, Feb. 19. Preston, Levi, of Cumberland Co., yeoman; will of. Daughters—Mary Bishop, Abigail Stratton and Freelove Dare. Daughter-in-law, Elizabeth, widow of son Isaac. Grandchildren—Levi, Isaac, William, John and Joseph, sons of son Isaac Preston; John, son of John Preston; Freelove, Thomazine and Elizabeth Stratton, Elizabeth Preston and Mary Bennet. Son-in-law, Samuel Bennet. Real and personal estate. David Wescote sole Executor. Witnesses—Jonathan Stratton, Jonathan Lorance. Proved Feb. 4, 1752.   Lib. 7, p. 215.

1752, Jan. 29. Inventory, £113.8.3, by Joseph Daten and Joseph Ogden.

1753, June 30. Preston, William, of Freehold, Monmouth Co., yeoman; will of. Wife Sarah. Sons—Joseph, Samuel and William. Grandson, William Mount. Real and personal estate. Executors—Garven Watson and John Anderson. Witnesses—Anna Anderson, Elizabeth Anderson and William Whitlock. Proved March 23, 1756.
Lib. F, p. 332.

1756, Mar. 12. Inventory, £106.10.2, incl. 17 bush. of wheat, £4.5; made by Thomas Tonison and Michael Johnston.

1759, Nov. 24. Price, Benjamin, of the Borough of Elizabeth, Essex Co.; will of. Wife, Mary. Children—George, Benjamin, Anthony, John (under age), Prudy (wife of Wm. Gartwite), Mary, Elizabeth, Margaret and Anna, the last four under age. Homestead of 10 acres, given by father, Benjamin Price; other real and personal property. Executors and Guardians of children—the wife, son George and kinsman Abraham Clark, Jr. Witnesses—John Donington, Merget Vaunse, Robert Ogden. Proved October 27, 1760.   Lib. G, p. 345.

1753, Sept. 6. Price, Edward Radolphus, of Burlington Ctiy, attorney-at-law. Int. Robert Friend Price and Hannah Price, son and daughter, renounce their right of administration. Bond of Thomas Rodman as Administrator; Elias Hughes and Joseph Scattergood fellowbondsmen, all of Burlington City.   Lib. 7, p. 422.

1753, Sept. 6. Inventory, £105.15.0., by John Bacon and Elias Hughes.

1755, Jan. 27. Price, Joseph, of the "Borough" of Elizabeth, Essex Co., planter; will of. Wife, Eliza. Children—Hannah, Daniel (under age), Moses, Jonathan and Eliza. Home farm; 100 acres in Westfield, adjoining William Darby, bought of William Miller; land between Robart Bond, Steven Meeker's stone house, and the Great Swamp brook; meadow near Daniel Dehart, given to testator by his father and his uncle, Capt. Daniel Price. Personal estate. Executors—the wife, sons Jonathan and Moses, and Capt. Joseph Lyon. Witnesses—Joseph Lyon, John Cahune, Moses Lyon. Proved April 4, 1757.
Lib. F, p. 432.

1757, Aug. 26. Price, Solomon, of Maidenhead, Hunterdon Co.; will of. Wife, Eleanor. Daughter, Sarah (under age). Sisters—Sarah

Updike, Letticia and Mary Price. Azariah Hunt sole Executor. Witnesses—John Potts, David Price. Proved March 28, 1758.
Lib. 9, p. 167.
1758, Mar. 21. Inventory, £111.8.6, by John van Cleave and Josiah Furman.

1749-'50, Feb. 10. Price, Thomas, of Elizabethtown, Essex Co., cordwainer; will of. Children—Thomas, John, Elijah, Rebacka (wife of John Reessel), Mary, Phebe (wife of John Ramsden), and Jane. Real and personal estate. Executors—son Thomas and daughter Mary. Witnesses—Jonathan Thompson, Abraham Woodruff, Josiah Woodruff. Proved August 26, 1752. Lib. F, p. 241.
1752, Aug. 24. Mary Price, now Mary Howell, named Executrix, refuses to serve.

1756, Nov. 6. Price, Thomas, of Nottingham, Burlington Co. Int. Inventory, £577.1.6, incl. a looking glass in the bar; a servant maid's time, £3; bills, bonds and bookdebts, £441.5.6; made by William Bunting and Jacob Lawrance.
1756, Nov. 10. Bond of widow, Ruth Price, as Adm'x; George Tucker, of Trenton, Hunterdon Co., blacksmith, fellowbondsman.
Lib. 8, p. 397.

1760, May 14. Price, Thomas, of Northamton, Burlington Co. Int. Bond of Edith Price as Adm'x; James Budd fellowbondsman, both of said Co. Lib. 9, p. 417.
1760, May 17. Inventory, £61.13.6, by Thomas Budd and James Budd.

1753, Jan. 22. Prickett, Zachariah, of Northampton, Burlington Co.; will of. Son, Richard, to have house and lot in Mount Holly, known by the name of Robert Stevens' place; also the house and 7 acres where I live. Daughters, Patience Smith, Sarah Simons, Mary Paullis Miers, each 5 shillings. Daughter, Hannah Prickett, £60 when 18. Daughter, Hope, £100 when 18. Son, Zachariah, plantation where he lives, except what I give to my son Richard as above. Executor—brother, Jacob Prickett. Witnesses—William Foster, John Goldy, James Allen. Proved Jan. 30, 1753.
1753, Jan. 28. Inventory, £443.10.5, by George Briggs and Thomas Budd.
1755, Oct. 17. Account of Executor. Burl. Wills, 5221 C; 5637 C.

1757, Mar. 15. Probasco, Frederick, of Amwell Township, Hunterdon Co., husbandman; will of. Wife, Margaret. Children—sons and daughters, all under age, spoken of but not named. Real and personal estate. Executors—the wife, Abraham Deremer and Abraham Praall. Witnesses—William Poast, Richard Hudnut and Garrard Williamson. Proved April 27, 1757. Lib. 8, p. 422.
1757, Apr. 25. Inventory, £317.8.6, incl. bills, bonds and book debts, £132.17.5; made by Garrard Williamson and Richard Green.

1752, Dec. 22. Probasco, Jacob, of Somerset Co., farmer; will of. Children—Christopher (living at Middlebush), Jacob, Frederick, John, Hendrick, Deyna (wife of John Hogelandt), Ida (wife of William Post), Mary (wife of George Berrege). Home farm; farm at Middlebush; land on the Westside of Millstone River, formerly belonging to Steven Courten; 260 acres in Amwell, Hunterdon Co. Personal es-

CALENDAR OF WILLS—1751-1760   261

tate. Executors—sons Christopher and John, and son-in-law, John Hogelandt. Witnesses—John Smock, Tise Smock, John Brokaw. Proved Nov. 25, 1755. Lib. F, p. 297.

1755, Nov. 7. Inventory, £435.13.11, incl. 19½ Dutch ells of home-made linen @ 2s., £1.19; a silver cup & 2 silver spoons, £3.10; 3 books, 6s.; 3 negroes, £150; 100 bush. of wheat, £25; 40 do. of Indian corn, £5; 30 do. of buckwheat, £2.5; bonds and cash, £99.13; made by Benjamin Thomson, Peter Perrine and Abraham Couwenhoven.

1749, Oct. 21. Probasco, Jan, of Middlebush, Somerset Co., yeoman; will of. Wife, Helletie. Children—John and others, names not given, all under age. Real and personal estate. Executors—the wife, brother-in-law, Tunniss Rappleyea, cousin, Christopher (son of Jacob Probasco), and Gerrit Voorheese, blacksmith, all of said Co. Witnesses—Yacob Wyckof, Peter Wyckof, William Maxwell. Proved Jan. 27, 1752. Lib. F, p. 16.

1752, Feb. 18. Inventory, £306.8.5, by Christian Vandorn and Henry Van Lawe and Frederick Van Lawe.

1755, Sept. 3. Prosser, John, of Gloucester Township and County, sawyer. Int. Inventory, £19.4.7, incl. 4 books, 12s.; made by John Blackwood and Joseph Hedger.

1755, Oct. 16. Bond of John Irven (Irwin), husbandman, as Adm'r; John Blackwood, fuller, fellowbondsman, both of Deptford Township, said Co. Lib. 8, p. 384.

1754, Feb. 25. Prout, Ebenezer, of Trenton, Hunterdon Co.; will of. Wife, Elizabeth. Daughter, Love Prout. Grandchildren—Ebenezar, Eliza, Phebe, Deborah and Patience Rose, all children of son-in-law, Stephen Rose. Son-in-law, George Ely. Real and personal estates. Executrix—daughter, Love, with William Mott and Daniel Laning as advisers. Witnesses—Daniel Howell, John Reed, Hannah Haines. Proved Nov. 12, 1754. Lib. 8, p. 80.

1754, Nov. 4. Inventory, £172.10.3, incl. a looking glass and a house Bible, £1.10; made by Arthur Howell and David Howell.

1752, Oct. 18. Prudden, John, of Morris Co. Int. Bond of Solomon Munson as Adm'r; Peter Dickinson fellowbondsman, both of said Co. Lib. F, p. 70.

1753, Nov. 22. Pryer, Casparus, of the Town of Bergen, miller; will of. Wife, Sarah. Children—Anderies, Nicolas, and others, names not given. Real and personal estate. Executors—Joris Vrelandt, of "Pimmer Pogh," David Abeel, of New York, and sons Anderies and Johannis. Witnesses—Johannes van Wagenen, Johannes van der Hof and Jacobus Abeel. Proved March 13, 1759.
Lib. G, p. 43.

1757, July 21. Purkins, John, of New Stafford, Monmouth Co.; will of. Wife, Jane. Children—John, Amy Cosaboom, Sarah and William (under age). Executors—the wife and Stephen Birdsell. Witnesses—Lem Cramer, David Andreson and John Conklin. Proved Oct. 26, 1757. Lib. F, p. 462.

1760, Mar. 5. Putland, Penthesilea, of Perth Amboy, Middlesex Co.; will of. Divides personal estate between the wife of Dr. William

Mercer, of New Brunswick, Mrs. Elizabeth Skinner, (widow of Rev. William Skinner), her daughter Gertrude, and granddaughter Elizabeth Skinner, and Gertrude, (wife of John Barberie of Perth Amboy). Executors—Miss Gertrude Skinner and Capt. William Bryant. Witnesses—John Waterhouse, Sophia Waterhouse and Elizabeth Pringal. Proved April 9, 1760. Lib. G, p. 171.

1760, Mar. 15. Pyatt, Thomas, of Piscataway, Middlesex Co.; will of. Wife, Martha. Son, Asa, under age. Sister, Mary Veiland. Names also Jane Pyatt; brother-in-law, Joseph Drake, and his children; mother, Ruth Pyatt; First Day Baptist Church of Christ at Piscataway; brother, James Pyatt, who is residuary legatee of real and personal estate. Executors—the wife, said brother James, and Henry Sutton. Witnesses—Bouley Arnold, Michael Moore and Samuel Pelston. Proved April 17, 1760. Lib. G, p. 173.

1760, Apr. 31 (?). Inventory, £163.3.2, by Isaac Steele and Nehemiah Dunham.

1760, Apr. 14. Quest, James, of Burlington City, innholder. Int. Bond of Rebecca Quest, spinster, as Adm'x; Abraham Hewlings fellowbondsman, both of said City. Lib. 9, p. 416.

1760, Apr. 16. Inventory, £107.5.6, incl. a looking glass; another do., £3; a Bible, and 6 other books, 5s.; a large and 6 small silverspoons, £1; 2 coffee mills; made by Abraham Hewlings and Thomas Scattergood.

1754, Dec. 7. Quicksall, Joshua, of Mansfield, Burlington Co., yeoman; will of. Wife, Mary. Children—Joshua, Samuel, Sary and Rebeckah, all under age. Home farm of 125 acres of upland, and 7 ac. of marsh, on Cross Weeks Creek; land in Bristow Township, Bucks Co., Penna.; 6 ac. of marsh near Bordentown, on the Point of Crossweek. Personal property. Executors—the wife and her brother, Joseph Church. Witnesses—Mary Church, Jacob Swain, James Rockett. Proved Dec. 26, 1754. Lib. 7, p. 61.

1754, Dec. 16. Inventory, £236.7.11, incl. a looking glass, 43s.; books, 3s.; made by Joseph English and Thomas Biddel.

1760, Jan. 13. Quicksall, William, of Chesterfield, Burlington Co., yeoman; will of. Wife, Sarah. Children—Sarah Taylor, Daniel, William and Thomas. Real and personal estate. Executors—the wife, and sons Daniel and William. Witnesses—Jonathan Quicksall, Ann Quicksall, John Grimes. Proved April 7, 1760. Lib. 9, p. 445.

1760, Mar. 7. Inventory, £190.10.9, incl. bills, and bookdebts, £35.4.2; made by Jonathan Quicksall and Samuel Taylor, Jr.

1759, Apr. 11. Quigly, Daniel, of Nottingham Township, Burlington Co., yeoman; will of. Wife, Susanna. Children—Terrance, Mary Burns, Sarah, Susanna, Bridget, James, Phillop, Daniel, John, Neall and William. Real and personal property. Executors—the wife and John Tealer. Witnesses—John Abbott, Jonathan Knipe and David Silver. Proved June 1, 1759. Lib. 9, p. 322.

1759, May 25. Inventory, £124, by David Silver and Jonathan Knipe.

1756, Apr. 15. Quinton, Edward, of Alaways Creek (Salem Co.). Int. Inventory, £164.3.8, incl. books; made by Job Shepherd and Samuel Sims.

CALENDAR OF WILLS—1751-1760   263

1756, Apr. 16. Bond of Temperance Quinton as Adm'x; Edward Keasbey and Edmund Wetherby fellowbondsmen, all of Salem Co.
Lib. 8, p. 303.

1760, Feb. 16. **Radley, John,** of Elizabeth Town, Essex Co.; will of. Wife, Elizabeth, sole Executrix. Children—John, and others spoken of, but names not given. Home lot, bought of Rev. Mr. Vaughan, adjoining John May's; other real and personal estate. Witnesses—Abraham Keteltas, William Crissy, Thomas Tobin. Proved March 20, 1760.
Lib. G, p. 269.

1759, Mar. 16. **Ragan, Timothy,** of Greenwich, Gloucester Co., yeoman; will of. Wife, Margrett, principal heiress of real and personal estate, with legacies to the Poor of the Townships of Greenwich and Newtown, said Co. Cousin, Timothy, son of John Yong, of Pennsylvania. Brother-in-law, William and John Yong. Mentions the Meeting of Gilbert Tennant in Philadelphia. Witnesses—Robert Pond, Able Pond, Benjamin Lodge. Proved April 4, 1759.
Lib. 9, p. 201.
1759, Apr. 2. Inventory, £293.14.1., incl. bonds, books debts and cash in silver and paper, £46.2.9; silver teaspoons; a servant boy and a negro girl, £60; two lots of land in Greenwich, £80; made by Benjamin Lodge and Archibald Maffett.

1755, May 9. **Rain, John,** of Gloucester Co. Int. Bond of Samuel Hewes as Adm'r; Thomas Denny and John Rambo fellowbondsmen, all of said Co.
Lib. 8, p. 161.
1755, June 7. Inventory, £411.2.11, incl. debts on specialties, desperate bonds and book debts, £391.7.8; a silver watch; made by Thomas Denny and Mathew Gill.

1753, Apr. 18. **Rambo, Peter,** of Gloucester Co.; will of. Children—John, Mounce, (under age), Benjamin, Gabriel, Elizabeth Denny, Madlena and Marta; Gabriel, Madlena and Marta also under age. House in Vicacou, Philadelphia Co., Penn., subject to groundrent and now occupied by son John; 150 acres of "Poyn" land on Poplar's Branch, Gloucester Co.; 335 ac. at Mantu Creek, said Co., sold to Isak Stephens, already living on the premises, but no deed given for it. Personal property, incl. silver shoe buckles and gold sleeve buttons. Executors—son John and son-in-law, Thomas Denny. Witnesses—Erick Unander, Samuel Cabb (Cobb), Mathew Gill. Proved May 5, 1753.
Lib. 7, p. 361.
———, ——— ———. Inventory, £915.16, incl. "Sweeds" books, £2.10; pair of silver buckles, 15s.; three silver teaspoons, 7/6; debts due, £822; made by Joseph Applin, William Gerrard and Alexander Randall.

1752, Feb. 3. **Rand, Simon,** of Piles Grove Precinct, Salem Co.; will of. Makes Henry van Meter, of said Co., sole heir and Executor of personal estate. Witnesses—James Johnson, John Bishop, William Garrison, David van Meter. Proved May 1, 1752. [He died February 3].
1752, Feb. 14. Inventory, £58.16.4, by Joshua Garrison and John Frankling.
Salem Wills, 824 Q.

1759, June 20. **Randell, Christopher,** of Manington, Salem Co.; will of. Wife, Mary, sole heiress and Executrix of real and personal

estate. Witnesses—John Sims, George Warners and Reese Williams. Proved July 25, 1759. Lib. 9, p. 286.
1759, July 2. Inventory, £147.18, by Thomas Sayre and John Sims.

1760, Aug. 9. Raper, Joshua, of Burlington City and County, shopkeeper; will of. Children—Mary (wife of John Hoskins), Abigail and Sarah (wife of Daniel Smith, Jr.). Sister, Martha Barker, widow. Grandchildren—Sarah, Raper, Ruth, and Joseph Hoskins and Joshua Raper Smith. Niece, Mary Barker. Real and personal estate. Executors—daughter, Abigail, and sons-in-law, John Hoskins and Daniel Smith, Jr. Witnesses—Thomas Pryor, Jr., Robert Smith, Jr., Richard Smith. Proved August 30, 1760. Lib. 10, p. 70.

1756, April 26. Rattoone, Thomas, of Perth Amboy, Middlesex Co., ferryman. Int. Adm'x—Elizabeth Rattoone, widow. Bondsmen —James Newell and Daniel O'Brien, of Perth Amboy. Witness— Thomas Bartow. Lib. F, p. 341.

1760, April 28. Raymond, Edward, of Essex Co., Ward, son of Peter Raymond, late of Essex Co., deceased. Guardian—Christopher Seely, of Morris Co., until Edward is 21. Lib. G, p. 169.

1760, Mar. 21. Raymond, Peter, of Newark, Essex Co., carpenter; will of. Wife. Christiana. Children—Edward, James, Seth, Mercy Bedford, Hannah, Susannah, Rebeckah and Rachel. Real and personal estate. Executors—son-in-law, Jonah Bedford, and Ebenezer Byram, of Mendham, Morris Co. Witnesses—Israel Ward, Joseph Budd, Gershom Mott. Codicil, of same day, provides for an expected child. Same witnesses. Proved April 16, 1760. Lib. G, p. 279.
1760, Apr. 17. Ebenezer Byram, one of the Executors named, declines the trust.

1749, Jan. 4. Reagain, Thomas, of Cumberland Co.; will of. Sons —Lazerus, Gaberall, Benjamin and Nebucadnezer. Real and personal estate. Executors—sons Lazerus and Gaberall. Witnesses— William McGlaughlin, Mary Bell, Elizabeth McGlaughlin. Proved July 27, 1751.
1751, July 17. Inventory, £101.16.8, by George Hollinshead and James White. Cumb. Wills, 71 F.

1753, Aug. 29. Reaney, George, of Springfield Township, Burlington Co., labourer; will of. Divides real and personal estate between John Sevenar and Jonathan Hough, both of Springfield, making the last named sole Executor. Witnesses—Steven Addams, Sarah Addams, Jonathan Taylor. Proved March 11, 1760. Lib. 9, p. 436.

1756, May 4. Reckless, Joseph, of Burlington Co. Int. Bond of Joseph Reckless as Adm'r; Michael Newbold fellowbondsman, both of said Co. Lib. 8, p. 306.

1753, May 31. Redmonds, Francis, of Newark, Essex Co. Int. Adm'r—Thomas Eagees, principal creditor, of Newark. Bondsman— Jonathan Sergeant, of said place. Witness—Uzal Ogden.
Lib. F, p. 136.
1753, May 29. Inventory, £157.13.10¼, by Samuel Huntington and Jonathan Sergeant.

1752, Apr. 26. Ree, John, of Salem Co., yeoman; will of. Wife, Sarah. Children—John, Samuel, William, Jeams, Elisabeth, Agnes and Susannah, all but John and Elizabeth under age. Homefarm; farm adjoining Samuel Smith, bought of Jeams Dunlap; land bought of Peter Pappino; other real and personal property. Executors—the four sons. Witnesses—William Sharp, John Sharp, Jacob Richman. Proved July 28, 1752. Lib. 8, p. 49.
 1753, July 15. Inventory, £303.18.5, incl. bills, bonds and bookdebts, £178.8.9; 5,000 white oak hogshead staves, £15; made by Jacob Richman and John Mayhew, Jr.

1754, Mar. 8. Reed, Thomas, of Hunterdon Co. Int. Bond of Jonathan Reed, of Amwell, Hunterdon Co., as Adm'r; Henry Ringo, of Hopewell, said Co., fellowbondsman.
 1754, Mar. 11. Inventory, £5.9.9, by Francis Labaw and Gershom Menns. Lib. 7, p. 464.

1759, Mar. 30. Reeve, David, of Cumberland Co. Account of the estate, £188.16.8., by David Padgett, Executor of Thomas Paget, who had been Executor of Reeve's will. [No other papers, or record].
Cumb. Wills, 196 F.

1760, Aug. 28. Reeve, Elizabeth, of Burlington Co. Int. Inventory, £11.16.6, incl. a prayerbook, made by John Cliffton and Peter Allinson.
 1760, Aug. 28. Bond of Samuel Reeve (Reeves) as Adm'r; Peter Allinson fellowbondsman, both of Northampton Township, Burlington Co., yeomen. Lib. 10, p. 102.

1759, July 21. Reeve, Hezekiah, of Roxbury, Morris Co.; will of. Wife, Easter, to have lands and movable effects during her life; also the goods she had before we married. My brother, Manassah Reeve, lands and movables after my wife's death, he to pay to my brothers, Jonathan, William, Jesse, Silas and Puryer, each £10. Executors—wife, Easter, and brother, Manassah. Witnesses— William Hopkins, Rebekah Robinson, William Griffing. Proved Nov. 29, 1759.
Lib. G, p. 136.
 1759, Aug. 10. Inventory, £171.19.9, by David Luse, Esq., and William Hopkins.

1757, May 27. Reeve, Jonathan, of Morris Town, Morris Co., carpenter; will of. Wife, Elizabeth. Children—Nathan, John, Samuel, Martha, Mary and Rachel. Real and personal estate. Executors—the wife, Thomas Cleverly and Capt. Samuel Day, both of Morris Town, yeomen. Witnesses—Stephen Hedges, Silas Day, Timothy Johnes. Proved Oct. 21, 1759. Lib. G, p. 103.

1753, Dec. 29. Reeve, Nehemiah, of Northampton Twp., Burlington Co. Int. Inventory, £34.14.8, by Thomas Atkinson and Patrick Byrne.
 1754, Jan. 25. Bond of Samuel Reeve as Adm'r; Thomas Atkinson fellowbondsman, both of said Township. Lib. 8, p. 38.

1753, May 28. Reeve, Walter, of Northampton Township, Burlington Co., yeoman; will of. Children—Samuel, Micage, Jonathan, Berzila, Ruth, Rebeckah, Ann and Sarah. Mention of three sons of son, Walter. Some property given to Samuel "and Elisabeth," but without explanation of Elisabeth's relationship. Home farm in the Fork of Ancokes; land on the North Branch of Ancokes Creek; 200 acres in Mannington Township, Salem Co.; land bought of John Blumount and of Samuel Goldy; farm, formerly father's, on the Northside of the North branch of Ancokes; Proprietary rights to 200 ac., bought of John Allen. Personal estate. Executors—Thomas Pancost, sons Micage and Samuel Reeve. Witnesses—Thomas Mecue (McCue), Richard Buckston, Samuel Clark. Proved April 11, 1754.

1754, Apr. 11. Inventory, £310.4.4, incl. bills and bonds, £207.17.6; made by Henry Paxson and Patrick Reynolds.

1758, May 22. Account, £311.5.7, by Micajah Reeve and Samuel Reeve, as Executors, who report on hand for distribution £255.17.9.

Burl. Wills, 5505 C.

1759, April 30. Reeves, John, of Deptford Twp., Gloucester Co., carpenter. Int. Inventory, £82.7.10½, by John Sparks and Joshua Lord, Jr.

1759, May 21. Adm'r—Thomas Reeves, of said Co. Bondsman—John Sparks, yeoman, of same place. Witnesses—Samuel Mickle and John Ladd. Lib. 9, p. 234.

1760, June 3. Account by the Administrators.

1760, Feb. 1. Reeves, Rebecca, of Northampton Township, Burlington Co., single woman; will of. Sister, Sarah Patisson. Jonathan, son of Marmeduke Fort. Cousins—John, son of Water Reeves, and Ann, daughter of Micajah Reeves. Personal estate. Marmeduke Fort, sole Executor. Witnesses—Mathew Allen, George Shinn, William Shinn. Proved March 24, 1760. Lib. 9, p. 413.

1760, Mar. 22. Inventory, £6.10.10, incl. a Bible 6s.; a prayerbook, 6d.; made by William Shinn and Thomas Budd.

1760, July 1. Account by the Executor, who has increased the estate by adding a bond in suit against James McCleiche (?) for £27, and reports as on hand balance of £9.5.8.

1753, Aug. 6. Remmington, John, of Newton, Gloucester Co., labourer. Int. Inventory, £24,13.5, by Jacob Clement and Richard Weeks.

1753, Aug. 6. Bond of John Hinchman, Jr., innholder, as Adm'r; Richard Weeks, schoolmaster, fellowbondsman, both of Newton.

1758, Sept. 29. Account, £24.13.5, by the Administrator, who reports £11.9.5 on hand for distribution. Glouc. Wills, 521 H.

1757, Sept. 23. Reynolds, Patrick, of Northampton, Burlington Co., carpenter; will of. Children—Thomas, Margrett Bispham, Mary, Ann, Ruth and Lydia, the last four under age. Grist and saw mill; cedar swamp; pine and other land, owned in partnership with Daniel Smith, Robert Smith and David Budd; meadow between Joseph Burr and John Munrow, bought of Edward Gaskill and Thomas Shinn; one half of the Board Landing lot, bought of Nathaniel Cripps; other real and personal property. Executors—son Thomas, son-in-law John Bispham, and Henry Paxson. Witnesses—Daniel Quigg, George Windsor, Daniel Jones, Jr. Proved Sept. 30, 1757.

Lib. 8, p. 457.

1757, Sept. 28. Inventory, £1187.18.5½, incl. a watch; bills, bonds and book debts, £555.18.8½; two servants, £22; a flat and scow, £35; boards, plank, scantling and slabs, £254.10; made by Thomas Shinn and Daniel Hopewell.

CALDENDAR OF WILLS—1751-1760

1757, Sept. 22. Reynolds, William, of Freehold, Monmouth Co., carpenter; will of. Wife, Anna. Children—William, John and daughters, names not given. Real and personal estate. Executors—the wife and Robert Cumming. Witnesses—Gavin Watson, William McKnight and John Perkeson. Proved Oct. 20, 1757. Lib. F, p. 461.
1757, Sept. 29. Inventory, £101.11, by Gavin Wattson and William McKnight.

1760, July 31. RhineHart, Nicholas, of Cumberland Co. Int. Bond of Silas Newcomb as Adm'r; Benjamin Thompson fellowbondsman, both of Fairfield, Cumberland Co. Lib. 10. p. 178.

1759, June 13. Rhinehart, Philipp. Int. Inventory (filed in Salem County), £108.19.3, incl. book debts, cash and notes, £98.15.3; made by John Holme and Joseph Thompson.
1759, June 14. Bond of Benjamin Thompson and William Wentzel as Adm'rs; John Holme and Joseph Thompson fellowbondsmen, all of Allaways Creek, Salem Co. Lib. 9, p. 351.

1749, Jan. 19. Richards, Thomas, of Newark, Essex Co.; will of. Wife, Mehetibel. Children—Thomas, Nathaniel and Mary; all under age; an expected child. Aaron Richards and the surviving children of David Ward, Jonathan Ward and John Mun remaindermen of real property. Uncle, John Mun, to have the use of certain land. Real and personal estate. Executors—the wife and brother-in-law, William Crane. Witnesses—John Ogden, Jr., Thomas Williams, David Ogden, Jr. Proved Jan. 30, 1758. Lib. F, p. 512.

1751, Feb. 16. Richardson, Edward, of Deepford Township, Gloucester Co., yeoman; will of. Wife, Mary, sole Executrix. Children—Jesse, Amey, Tabitha, Anna, all under age and put into the charge of James Whiteall and James Lord, in case the wife remarries. Real and personal estate. Witnesses—Johannes Volschlaeger (German), Ruth Snowden, Joshua Lord. Codicil, without date, disposes of shares given to daughters Ann and Amey, who have died. Witnesses—Ruth Ross, Ann Houghstedtre, William Wood. Proved Oct. 16, 1752.
Lib. 7, p. 282.
1752, Oct. 17. Bond of James Whital (Whiteall) and James Lord, both of Deptford Township, yeomen, Adm'rs, with the will annexed, David Cooper, of the same place, fellowbondsman; Mary, the Executrix named in the will, being dead.
1752, Oct. 17-19. Inventory, £1187.19.7, incl. cash and plate, £32.18.10; a looking glass; bonds, £810.19.11; a servant man's time, £9; a servant woman's time, £1.10; made Joshua Lord and David Cooper. [James Whiteall is called "surviving" administrator April 20, 1753].
1758, Sept. 28. Account by surviving Adm'r, James Whitall.

1758, Sept. 28. Richardson, Jesse, son of Edward, of Gloucester Co. Bond of James Whital (Whiteall) as Guardian; James Cooper fellowbondsman, both of Deptford Township, said County, yeoman.
Lib. 8, p. 544.

1760, Feb. 11. Richardson, John, of "Morris" River Twsp., Cumberland Co. Int. Inventory, £5.8.0, by Peter Vaneman and Thomas Flinter.
1760, Feb. 12. Adm'r—Gabriel Vanman, of said place. Bondsman—

Peter Vaneman of same place. Witnesses—Henry Shaw and Jonathan Elmer. Lib. 10, p. 178.

1757, Feb. 4. Richman, Oeldrick, of Salem Co. Int. Inventory, £301.1.7, incl. a negro lad, 2 beds and furniture, £39; books, bonds and book debts, £124.13.7; made by Elisha Bassett and Joseph Chanymeys.

1757, Feb. 21. Bond of Sarah Richman as Adm'x; David Seley (Seely) and Mounce Keen fellowbondsman all of Salem Co.
Lib. 8, p. 445.

1759, Nov. 7. Richmond, James, of New Brunswick, in Middlesex Co., mason. Int.. Adm'x—Jane Richmond, of said place, widow. Bondsman—Benjamin Dasigny, of same place, cordwainer. Witness —Thomas Bartow. Lib. G, p. 109.

1759, Nov. 13. Inventory, £196.12, incl. book debts and notes, £161.4.2; taken before John Lyle and William Hall; followed by an affidavit of Ann McKarty and Hanah Jorden, taken February 6, 1760, that dec'd. had said on his "deth Beed," that he left all to the management of his wife for her and the family's use and support.

1756, (?) Nov. 10. Rickey, John, of Baskingridge, Somerset Co. Int. Inventory, £117.17.7, incl. 45 bush. of Indian corn, £4.10; 60 do. of buckwheat, £4.10; a Dutch book 2s.; 2 spelling books 3s.; made by John Roy and Joseph Kinnan. [Filed June 7, 1757].

1757, June 7. Bond of Ariantie, widow, as Adm'x; Brice Riky, of said Co., yeoman, fellowbondsman. Lib. F, p. 428.

1760, Mar. 13. Riddle, Andrew, of Monmouth Co. Ind. Bond of John Lawrence, surveyor, as Adm'r; Hugh Hartshorne fellowbondsman, both of Burlington Co. Lib. 9, p. 410.

1754, Jan. 1. Riggs, Miles, of Newark, Essex Co. Int. Elizabeth Riggs, the widow, renounced in favor of Joseph Riggs, Jr., brother of said Miles, in presence of Sarah Riggs.

1754, Jan. 1. Adm'r—Joseph Riggs, Jr., of Newark, Essex Co. Bondsman—Daniel Riggs, of same place. Witness—Uzal Ogden.
Lib. F, p. 229.

1754, Jan. 14. Inventory, £68.2.3, by Joseph Day and Thomas Canfield.

1757, Apr. 21. Ringo, Philipp, of Amwell, Hunterdon Co.; will of. Wife, Catrina. Sons—Albartus, Henry, John, Cornelius (under age), all by a former wife. Legacy to Philipp, son of Henry Ringo. Real and personal estate. Executors—sons Albartus and Henry, with brother, Cornelius Ringo. Witnesses—Ichabod Leigh, Henry Landis and George Trout. Proved May 23, 1757. Lib. 8, p. 490.

1757, May 21. Inventory, £582.16, incl. bills and bonds, £313.8.2; his libra, £5.8; three looking glasses, £2.2; a negro woman and boy, £50; made by Jonathan and Timothy Smith.

1755, July 10. Ritchie, Anne. Int. Petition of John Burnet and William Burnet, of Perth Amboy, Middlesex Co., to be appointed Administrators. Claiming on a legacy of £200 left by George Willocks to Ann Ritchie, which was not administered by her husband, John Ritchie, now also deceased. Same appointed. Witness—Thomas Bartow. Lib. F, p. 266.

CALENDAR OF WILLS—1751-1760   269

1754, Sept. 17. Rite, Isaac, of Piscataway Township, Middlesex Co., yeoman; will of. Son Isaac, under age, "if he be living," principal heir. Legacies, payable in case Isaac is dead, to Mary Weavers, Edmond Crede and Jeremiah Drake. Personal property. Jeremiah Drake sole Executor. Witnesses—Thomas Holtom, Jonathan Randolph. Proved Oct. 3, 1754. Lib. F, p. 212.
1754, Oct. 10. Inventory, £82.15, incl. bonds, £66; made by Joseph Fitz Randolph and Thomas Holtom.

1759, Aug. 6. Risley, George, a soldier. Int. Bond of Abner Phillips, of Hunterdon Co., as Adm'r; Moses Hart, of the same Co., fellowbondsman. Hunt. Wills, 476 J.

1756, Jan. 14. Robarts, John, of Morris Town, Morris Co., cooper; will of. Wife, Abigail, Children—Abigail, Sarah, Elizabeth, Hannah, Joseph, Samuel, Stephen and John. Real and personal estate. Executors—brother, Samuel Robarts, of Morris Town, Jonathan Sergeant and Thomas Canfield, of Newark. Witnesses—David Dille, Isaac Winans, Ebenezer Sturgis, Jr. Proved June 2, 1757.
Lib. F, p. 531.
1757, June 8. Inventory, £463.13.7, by Henry Primrose and Zechariah Fairchild.

1751, Mar. 20. Robbins, Richard, Sr., of "Morrises" River, Cumberland Co., farmer; will of. Wife, Marey. Children—Sarah, Richard, John, Priscilah, Marey Hand, Masey Sulevan and Ruth Glen. Real and personal estate. Executors—the wife and daughter, Sarah. Witnesses—John Maers, John Pearson, James Mares. Proved April 8, 1755. Lib. 8, p. 156.
1751, Apr. 1. Inventory, £48.9.6, by John Bragg and [name illegible].

1760, Mar. 18. Robbins, Richard, of Dividing Creeks, Cumberland Co., farmer; will of. Wife, Sibbel. Daughters, Theodosia and Judith. Legacy to Tamson, daughter of Rebecca Blizard. Real and personal property. Executors—the wife and Joseph Savege. Witnesses—John Bragg, William Blizard, Anne Hand. Codicil of March 22, 1760, gives direction for sale of land. Witnesses—John Bragg, William Blizard, Henry Walker. Proved June 19, 1760. Lib. 10, p. 194.
1760, June 17. Inventory, £150.16.4, by John Bragg and Richard Lore.
1762, Jan. 21. Account by the Executors.

1757, Sept. 29. Robenson, Thomas, of Greenwich Township, Sussex Co. Int. Bond of Alexander White, of Greenwich, as Adm'r; Samuel Henry, of Trenton, Hunterdon Co., merchant, fellowbondsman.
Lib. 8, p. 500.
1757, Oct. 18. Inventory, £61.9.5, by William Scholey and John Stuart.
1759, May 24. Account, £61.9.5, by the Administrator, who reports £31.2.11, on hand after settling the estate.

1753, July 28. Roberson, William. of the Borough of Elizabeth, Essex Co., yeoman; will of. Wife, Elizabeth. Children—William, Phebe, Elizabeth and "my youngest daughter," name not given, all under age. Real and personal estate. Executors—the wife and Henry

Clarke. Witnesses—Abigail Person, Mary Denman, Ebenezer Price.
Proved Sept. 10, 1753. Lib. F, p. 133.
    1753, Sept. 13. Inventory, £57.5.2, by Daniel Perrine and John Scudder.

1758, Aug. 7. Roberts, Hannah, of Newton Township, Gloucester Co., widow; will of. Children—Jacob and Daniel Roberts, Ruth Powel, Keziah Albertson and three other daughters, names not given, all under age. Personal property. Executor—Robert Fred. Price. Witnesses—Thomas Edgerton, Jr., Samuel Boggs, Richard Weekes. Proved August 28, 1758. Lib. 9, p. 124.
    1758, Aug. 21. Inventory, £130.3.11, incl. bills, bonds, book debts and cash, £84.0.7; a looking glass; made by Thomas Redman and Richard Weekes.

1749, Dec. 2. Roberts, Jacob, of Waterford, Gloucester Co., husbandman; will of. Wife, Hannah, sole Executrix. Children—Ephraim, Keziah, Joseph, Jacob, Elizabeth and Hannah, all under age; an expected child. Personal estate. The sons to be bound out to learn a trade. Witnesses—Mary Champion, Elizabeth Champion, Samuel Spicer. Proved March 26, 1752. Lib. 7, p. 185.
    1752, Feb. 7. Inventory, £283.10.10¾, incl. bills, bonds and book debts, £103.11.7¾, made by Thomas Spicer and Josiah Shivers.

1759, Aug. 16. Roberts, Richard, of New Hanover, Burlington Co. Administration on the estate of Richard, who died at the house of Samuel Wright, on the 14th inst., recommended by said Samuel to be granted to Joseph Wright, who is, with Samuel, the largest creditor.
    1759, Aug. 17. Bond of Joseph Wright as Adm'r; Joseph Arney fellowbondsman, both of Burlington Co. Lib. 9, p. 243.
    1759, Aug. 25. Inventory, £191.6.7½, incl. bills, bonds and notes, £116,10.5½; bills & bonds "we think worth little or nothing," £52.17.8; made by Thomas Woodward and Joseph Arney.

1751, July 1. Roberts, Thomas, of Hopewell, Hunterdon Co.; will of. Wife, Sarah. Children—Richard (sole Executor), John, Thomas, Ezra, Ruth Corwine, and Deliverance Phelp. Real and personal estate. Witnesses—Jonathan Smith, Margret Burrowes, John Akers. Proved Dec. 10, 1751. Lib. 7, p. 206.
    1751, July 8. Inventory, £108.3, incl. what testator gave to his widow, £16.16.6; made by Jonathan Smith and John Akers.

1751, Oct. 21. Robertson, David, of Middletown, Monmouth Co., yeoman. Int. Margret, widow, declines the administration, favour of Duncan Robertson and Robert Savage, of Middletown, traders.
    1751, Oct. 22. Bond of Duncan Robertson and Robert Savage as Adm'rs; Thomas Kearney, also of Monmouth Co., fellowbondsman.
    1751, Oct. 21. Inventory, £130.15.1, by Richard Frances and Peregrine Van Emburgh. Lib. E, p. 551.
    1768, Jan. 9. Account by Administrators.

1754, Jan. 8. Robertson, Elizabeth, of New York City, spinster. Int. Bond of Arthur Brown as Adm'r; Duncan Robertson, Robert Savage and Charles Rhodes, all of Middletown, Monmouth Co., fellowbondsmen. Lib. F, p. 155.

CALENDAR OF WILLS—1751-1760   271

1755, Apr. 18. Robertson, John, of Middletown Township, Monmouth Co., bricklayer; will of. Divides estate between brothers, Patrick and Dunkan Robertson (who is sole Executor), and sisters, Christen Sickels, Isabel Leppard and Jane Brown. Witnesses—Chris. ven Pelt, Sarah van Brackle and James van Brakle. Proved Sept. 17, 1757.   Lib. F, p. 448.

1753, Sept. 15. Robertson, William, of Middletown Point, Monmouth Co. (who dec'd September 8). "Pa." Robertson, of Perth Amboy, one of the children, declines the administration, stating, that the mother is unable to undertake it and that the brother, Duncan, being heavily indebted to the estate, "cannot be esteemed a proper person; administration is therefore asked to be granted to the mother and some proper, honest person."
1753, Sept. 25. John Robertson, Christian Sickles, Isabella Lepper, Jane Brown and Duncan Robertson, all children of William, declare that their mother, Mary Robertson, ought to be the Administratrix with the assistance of Capt. John Anderson.
1753, Sept. 27. Bond of widow, Mary Robison (Robertson) and John Anderson as Adm'rs; Samuel Forman, merchant, and Charles Rhodes, schoolmaster, fellowbondsmen, all of Monmouth Co. Lib. F, p. 136.
1753, Oct. 24. Inventory, £1683.19.3½ by Charles Rhodes, Thomas Roberts and Lewis Forman.

1757, Oct. 18. Robeson, Thomas, of Granage, Hunterdon Co. Inventory, £61.9.5, by William Schooley and John Stuart.
Hunterdon Wills, 418 J.

1759, April 6. Robins, Aron, of New Hanover, Burlington Co.; will of. Wife, Elizabeth. Children—Samuel, Aron, Daniel, Elizabeth Quicksal, Abigail Buck. Grandchildren—Margrate Quicksal, Margrate Holloway, Mary and Margret Stuard, James Robens. Names also the two eldest daughters of Josiah Smith and children of son Ephraim, viz., James, Lucia, Ephraim and Mergrate. Personal estate. Executors—sons Daniel Robins and Moses Robins (not mentioned before), of Allens Town. Witnesses—Benjamin Kirby, Joseph Arney, William Lawrie. Proved April 19, 1759.   Lib. 9, p. 326.
1759, Apr. 12. Inventory, £213.9.6, incl. bonds and mortgages, £169.6; made by Isaac Forman and William Lawrie.

1759, Jan. 15. Robins, Benjamin, Sr., of Nottingham Township, Burlington Co., yeoman; will of. Wife, Judith. Children—John, William, Deliverance (widow of John Taylor), Benjamin, Obadiah, Ann (wife of Samuel Cheshire) Nathaniel and Richard. Grandchildren—Benjamin, Joseph, Jessee, Moses and Aaron, sons of Benjamin. House and lot in Allentown; other real and personal estate. Executors—sons, Nathaniel and John. Witnesses—Moses Robins, Nathan Robins, John Lawrie, Benjamin Clarke. Proved Dec. 3, 1760.
Lib. 10, p. 146.
1766, Dec. 1. Inventory, £151.7.10, by Moses Robins and Thomas Tyren.

1759, Mar. 30. Robins, Ephraim, of Monmouth Co. Int. Inventory, £52.9.6, incl. John McDaniel, a servant lad, £18; made by John and Moses Robins.
1759, Apr. 19. Bond of Marcey Robins as Adm'x; Moses Robins fellowbondsman, both of Monmouth Co.   Lib. 9, p. 316.

1756, Jan. 19. Robins, Job, of Amwell Township, Hunterdon Co., yeoman; will of. Wife, Abigail. Children—Daniel, Rachel, Amie, Andrew, Mary, Elizabeth and Lydia, all under age. Mother, Mary Robins. Real and personal estate. Executors—the wife and son Daniel. Witnesses—Thomas Carroll, Vincent Robins, Chris. Search. Proved May 17, 1756. Lib. 8, p. 327.

1756, Apr. 2. Inventory, £467.15.2, incl. bills, bonds and book debts, £215.14.8; a servant's time, £15; made by John Emley, Thomas Kitchin and Vincent Robins.

1759, May 14. Robins, Samuel, of Upper Freehold, Monmouth Co., yeoman; will of. Wife, Margrate. Children—Nathan, Randolph, Aaron, Samuel, Mary, Margaret, Martha and Lydia. Granddaughter, Permela Stillwell. Homefarm, between York "Rode" on the South and "Inden" Run on the North; 50 acres on Northside of "Inden" Run; part of the lot bought of Nathan Allen; land bought of John Evilman; land on Southside of York Road; two on Southside of Mill Pond and South of the road to the pines, bought of Gershom Silver and William Lawrance. Personal estate. Executors—sons Nathan and Randolph. Witnesses—Moses Robin, William Page, Thomas Lawrie. Proved May 25, 1759. Lib. 9, p. 331.

1760, Feb. 11. Robins, Vincent, of Amwell, Hunterdon Co. Int. Inventory £85.3.4, by Daniel Robins and William Barns.

1760, Feb. 18. Bond of Ann Robins as Adm'x; Daniel Robins fellowbondsman, both of Amwell. Lib. 10, p. 416.

1752, Feb. 24. Robinson, Deborah and Thomas, children of John Robinson and Dearie Robinson (daughter of Ichabod Smith), placed under the guardianship of Thomas Robinson of Perth Amboy; Andrew Robinson and James Newell, of the same place, fellowbondsmen. Lib. F, p. 32.

1756, Dec. 1. Robinson, James, of New Brunswick, Middlesex Co., cordwainer. Int. Margaret Robinson, the widow, renounced in presence of David Gano.

1757, Sept. 16. Adm'r—William Crawford, of Perth Amboy, principal creditor. Bondsman—John Smyth, of same place.
Lib. F, p. 447.

1757, Dec. 26. Inventory, £12.1.8, incl. a looking glass 14s.; a Bible and sermon book, £1.5; 6 silver teaspoons, 18s.; made by David Gano and Henry Guest.

1755, Jan. 10. Robinson, John, of Cumberland Co. Int. Inventory, £51.5.4, by Dan Bowen and Josiah Parvin.

1755, Jan. 13. Bond of Abigail Robinson as Adm'x; Dan Bowen and John Garrison fellowbondsmen, all of Cumberland Co. Lib. 8, p. 98.

1759, Jan. 8. Robinson, William, of Perth Amboy, Middlesex Co., ship carpenter. Int. Mary Robinson, his widow, renounced. Same date Adm'r—Thomas Johnson, of Perth Amboy. Bondsman—Robert Iselstine, of same place. Witness—Thomas Bartow. Lib. G, p. 15.

1755, Jan. 9. Rock, William, of Essex Co. Int. Adm'rs—John Vanderpool and Apphia Vanderpool, his wife, of Newark. Bondsman—Nathaniel Anderson, of same place. Witness—Uzal Ogden.
Lib. F, p. 257.

CALENDAR OF WILLS—1751-1760 273

1752, May 4. Rodgers, James, of Salem Co. Int. Bond of William McIlvaine as Adm'r; James Barkly (Bartley) fellowbondsman, both of said Co.
1752, May 4. Inventory, £136.0.3½, incl. merchandise, £61.10.6½; debts due, £74.9.9; made by James Barkley and William Siddons.
Salem Wills, 867 Q.

1753, Aug. 13. Rodgers, Robert, of Salem Co. Int. Bond of John Nicholson as Adm'r; Josiah Kay fellowbondsman, both of said Co.
Lib. 9, p. 94.

1756, June 3. Rodman, John, of Burlington City and County; will of. Wife, Mary. Children—John, Thomas, William, Samuel, Scamon, Anna and Elizabeth. Grandsons—John and Joseph Johnson, sons of daughter Mary. Homefarm in City bounds; 300 acres in Warwick Township, Bucks Co., Pa., now occupied by grandsons' father, John Johnson; 300 ac. adjoining, now occupied by William and John Boogs; 500 ac. adjoining the last, now occupied by Charles Wulker and David Linsey; 400 ac. adjoining the first, now occupied by Alexander Harvey and Charles McMekin; 400 ac. more in said Township; house and lot on High Street, Burlington, bought of Caleb Raper; orchard of 5 ac. on said street, adjoining, bought of Nathaniel Cripps; 500 ac. in City bounds, bought of Samuel Bayard; land in Bensalam Township, Bucks Co., Pa.; other lands and personal property incl. cattle on Block Island or New Shorum, Rhode Island, (and also negroes). Executors—Sons Scamon and Samuel. Witnesses—Daniel Smith, Hugh Hartshorne, Thomas Wetherill, Jr., Daniel Smith, Jr. Proved Sept. 14, 1756.
Lib. 8, p. 306.

1758, Jan. 25. Roe, Grace, of Evesham, Burlington Co., widow. Int. Bond of David Roe as Adm'r; Richard Chew fellowbondsman, both of Gloucester Township and County.
Lib. 9, p. 73.

1754, Apr. 17. Roelefson, Catherine, of Monmouth Co. Int. Bond of Roelof Roelofson, husband, Adm'r; Leonard Stright, (Streit) and Harman Roelofson fellowbondsmen, all of New Jersey. Lib. F, p. 171.

1756, Aug. 6. Rogers, Samuel, of Upper Freehold, Monmouth Co., shopkeeper; will of. Children—Samuel, Isaac, Elisabeth Borden, Mary Kirkbride. Farm below the Dead Creek, now occupied by John Collens and William Bower, between Mr. Jacoon, Mr. English, John Horsfield and John Lawrence down to Crosswicks Creek; another farm, now occupied by Elisabeth Boultonhouse, bought of Marmaduke Horsman; a third now occupied by Robert Newil, bought of John Lawrence. Executors—the two sons. Witnesses—James Jolley, Peter Lott, Jr., and Safety Meghee. Proved Sept. 22, 1756. Lib. 11, p. 333.

1758, June 5. Rogers, Samuel, of Burlington City; will of. Wife, Elizabeth. Children—Elizabeth, Martha, Ann, John and Samuel, all under age. Personal estate. Executors—the wife and Abraham Hewlings. Witnesses—William Blake, Thomas Rogers, Daniel Ellis. Proved August 28, 1758.
Lib. 9, p. 38.
1758, Aug. 24. Inventory, £446.17.2½, incl. bonds and notes, £24.17; 3 negroes, £92.10; a "prentis" boy's time, £10; made by John Deacon and John Antram.

18

1757, Nov. 23. Rogers, William, of Burlington Co. Int. Bond of Thomas Patterson as Adm'r; Micajah Reeves fellowbondsman, both of said Co., yeomen. Burl. Wills, 5937 C.

1757, Mar. 31. Rolf, Josiah, of Salem, Salem Co. Int. Inventory, £660.6.6, incl. a clock, two looking glasses, books, a silver bowl, tankard, spoons and sundrys, £40.6.1; stock and rent in hands of Daniel Dorril (?), £108.8.1; rent in hands of Parrot & Ambler, £13.10; bonds, book debts and notes, £129.14.5; made by H. Stubbines and Joshua Thompson.
1757, Apr. 6. Bond of Sarah Rolfe as Adm'x; Joseph Zane (Zeans) and H. Stubbines fellowbondsmen, all of Salem Co. Lib. 8, p. 444.

1758, Sept. 6. Rolfe, Nathaniel, of New Brunswick, in Middlesex Co. Int. Elizabeth Rolfe renounced in favor of Samuel Neilson of South River, in Middlesex Co., in presence of Jonathan Rolfe and William Collins.
1758, Sept. 6. Inventory, £12.17.8, incl. 2 books, 2s.; made by Jonathan Rolfe and William Collins.
1758, Sept. 15. Adm'r—Samuel Neilson, of South Amboy, principal creditor. Bondsman—John Deare, Esq. Witness—Thomas Bartow.
 Midd. Wills, 3163 L.

1748, Feb. 13. Rolph, John, Sr., of Borough of Elizabeth in Essex Co.; will of. All real and personal estate to be sold. Wife, Sarah £40, and the overplus to be divided between wife and four children, Henry, Hannah, Elizabeth and John Rolph, and "the child my wife is big with," provided my son Henry returns to this place by the time my youngest child is 21, but, if he does not, then his share to go to the others. Executrix—my wife, Sarah. Witnesses—Samuel Smith, William Hall, Joseph Shotwell. Proved March 26, 1750. Lib. E, p. 374.
1750, March 20. Inventory, £1410.8.1, by Samuel Marsh and Eliphalet Frazee.

1756, Aug. 10. Roosa, Jan Aldert, of "Manissink," Sussex Co., yeoman; will of. Wife, Catherin. Children—Isaac, Jacob, Marya and Rebecca. Real and personal estate. Executors—brothers Dirk and Isaac Rosa, both of Ulster Co., N. Y., and brother-in-law, Anthony Westbroek, of Sussex Co. Witnesses—James McCarthy, Elizabeth McCarthy, William Ennes. Proved Nov. 2, 1756, and April 1, 1758.
 Lib. F, p. 521.

1757, Mar. 27. Rose, Christifar, of Bucks Co., farmer; will of. Wife, Martha. Children (names not given). Executors—the wife and John Beats. Witnesses—Robert Gardner, Samuel Dunbar, Moses Toner. Proved July 11, 1757 [in Hunterdon County]. Lib. 8, p. 481.

1755, Mar. 20. Rose, John, of Manington, Salem Co. Int. Elizabeth, widow, resigns her right of administering to his eldest son, Abraham Rose.
1755, Mar. 21. Inventory, £196.4.10, of which a cow, household goods and plantation tools, valued at £21, he had by his wife, to whom they were returned again; made by John Mayhew, Jr., and Jacob Elwell.
1755, Mar. 26. Bond of Abraham Rose as Adm'r; Thomas Mayhew fellowbondsman, both of Piles Grove, Salem Co. Lib. 8, p. 234.

CALENDAR OF WILLS—1751-1760 275

1760, Dec. 17. Ross, Benjamin, of Elizabeth, Essex Co. Int. Nathaniel Ross, brother, renounced in favor of Recompence Stanbery.
1760, Dec. 19. Adm'r—Recompence Stanbery, of said place. Bondsman—James Miller, of same place. Witnesses—Phebe Ross and Robert Ogden. Lib. G, p. 345.

1755, April 7. Ross, James, of Woodbridge, Middlesex Co., merchant. Int. Catharine Ross, widow, renounced and gives it over to her brother, John Ross.
1755, April 11. Adm'r—John Ross, of Woodbridge, shopkeeper. Bondsman—Robert Ross, of Piscataway, yeoman. Witness—Thomas Bartow. Lib. F, p. 257.
1755, April 15. Inventory, £748.3.3, by John Ross, Adm'r.

1754, Aug. 20. Ross, John, Esq., of Elizabeth Town, Essex Co.; will of. Wife, Sarah. Children—John, David, Andrew, Jacob, Sarah Crane, Mary Baldwin, Elizabeth, Phebe and Joanna. Homefarm, with an oil mill; meadow near Piles's Creek; land, adjoining Cooper Woodruff and Joseph Magee, bought of John Broadwell; meadow on the Northside of Woodruff's Creek; land bought of John Ramsden; land in New Brittain; land adjoining John Spinning, Joseph Littel, John Clawson and Matthias Baldwin. Personal property. Executors —the wife, son John and son-in-law, Matthias Baldwin. Witnesses— Matthias Hetfield, Benjamin Spining, George Emott. Proved Sept. 9, 1754. Lib. F, p. 307.
1754, Sept. 19. Inventory, £366.1.5, by Matthias Hetfield and William Winans.

1751, Aug. 8. Ross, Thomas, "an unworthy member of the Church of Scotland"; will of. Wife, Masey [signs later as Marcy]. Children —William, Christopher, Hannah, Lydia, Thomas. Real and personal estate. Executors—the wife and son, Thomas. Witnesses—William Bowness, James Hedges, Peter Toullard. Proved Oct. 1, 1751.
Cape May Wills, 155 E.
1751, Oct. 4. Inventory, £225.17.2, incl. books; made by Elisha Hand and Elijah Hughes.

1755, Mar. 5. Ross, Thomas, of Cape May Co. Int. Inventory, £134.2.1, incl. a bond and cash, £122.16.6; made by John Eldredge and Samuel Crowell.
1755, Mar. 6. Bond of William Ross as Adm'r; Samuel Crowell fellowbondsman, both of said Co. Lib. 8, p. 158.

1757, Nov. 9. Rossell, Barzillai, of Northampton, Burlington Co. Int. Inventory, £184.17, by Samuel Cripps and Samuel Kemble.
1757, Dec. 7. Bond of Rebecca Rossell as Adm'x; Samuel Cripps fellowbondsman, both of Northampton. Lib. 8, p. 499.

1760, Jan. 23. Rowand, John, of Waterford, Gloucester Co.; will of. Wife, Sarah. Children—Jacob, John, Joseph, Alexander, Abigail and Mary, all under age; an expected child. Real and personal estate. Executors—brother, James Rowand, and uncle, John Hillman. Witnesses—John Maxell, Mary Matlack, George Weed. Proved Feb. 21, 1760. Lib. 9, p. 400.
1760, ——— ——. Inventory, £191.15, incl. a watch; made by Thomas Bate and John Maxell.

1758, Dec. 12. Rowe, Henry, of Newark, Essex Co. Int. Adm'x—Mary Rowe, of same place. Bondsman—Robert Ward, of same place. Witnesses—Uzal Ogden and Lewis Ogden. Lib. G, p. 22.

1755, Feb. 1. Rue, Matthew, of Manalapon, Middlesex Co., yeoman; will of. Wife, Margaret to have 1-3 of my movables and her maintenance on my plantation by my six sons, while she remains my widow. Son, Joseph, to have 100 acres of the lower end of my plantation where I live. Son, Samuel, 100 acres, purchased of Patrick Brown in Cranbury; son, William, 100 acres, the remainder of my plantation at the upper end; son, Matthew, 100 acres, purchased of Arthur Brown in Cranbury; son, James, 100 acres of plantation, at upper end, purchased of John Rue, Jr., in Manalapon; son, Mathias, 100 acres, the remainder of said plantation at lower end; son, John, £180. Daughters, Ellnor, Jean and Margarit Rue 2-3 of my movable estate. Executors—brothers, William Rue and Joseph Rue. Witnesses—James Peairs, Henry Perine, Matthias Johnson. Proved Nov. 13, 1755. Lib. F, p. 290.

1755, Nov. 6. Inventory, £467.1.9, incl. 2 looking glasses, £1.4; a negro man £65; a negro woman, £55; made by John Barclay and John Perine.

1754, Dec. 12, Rueberry, James, of Gloucester Township and County, flatman. Int. Bond of Richard Cheesman as Adm'r; Edward Williams fellowbondsman, both of said Township, yeoman. Lib. 8, p. 120.

1755, Feb. 1. Inventory, £101.2.1, by John McColloch and John Brian.
1755, Nov. 27. Account by the Administrator.

1760, July 4. Rumford, John, of Greenwich Township, Gloucester Co.; will of. My mother to have all real and personal estate, and, at her death, same to go to my brothers and sisters. Executors—brothers Elias, Thomas and Jonathan Rumford, and my mother. Witnesses—Nathan Boys, Nathan Roberts, James Urian. Proved Aug. 5, 1760. Lib. 10, p. 53.

1760, July 17. Inventory, £598.9.1¼, by Nathan Boys and Mathew Gill.
1764, June 8. Account made by Ann Weatherby and Elias Thomas, Executors.
1770, Aug. 17. Account again by Executors. Lib. 15, p. 47.

1760, May 16. Runyon, Joseph, of Piscataway, Middlesex Co., yeoman; will of. Wife (not named, but otherwise known to be Elizabeth). Children—Peter, Joseph (oldest son), Philipp, and daughters, names not given, all under age except Joseph. Real and personal estate. Executors—the wife and brothers Peter and Benjamin Runyon. Witnesses—Elijah Pound, Jeames Gieles and Elias v. Court. Proved July 14, 1760. Lib. G, p. 261.

1760, July 2. Inventory, £883.17.4, incl. cash, £263.0.4; bonds and notes, £234; a Bible and other books, 20s.; a looking glass 12s.; 3 deerskins, £2.15; taken by the executors and appraised by George Marlett and Elijah Pound.

1750, Sept. 20. Runyon, Peter, of Piscataway, Middlesex Co.; will of. Wife, Providence. Children—Joseph, Peter (both made Execu-

tors), Richard, Benjamin, Ann Layton, Grace Cooper, Rosannah Davison and Providence, (wife of John Bowman). Real and personal estate. Witnesses—James Campbell, Jeames Giles, Reune Runyon. Proved Nov. 3, 1755. Lib. F, p. 288.
    1755, Nov. 17. Inventory, £1563.8.11, incl. bonds and cash, £1359.17.3; a Bible and other books, £1.5; made by David Fitzrandolph and David Coriell.

    1759, Jan. 18. Runyon, Providence, widow of Peter, of Piscataway, Middlesex Co.; will of. Children—Joseph, Peter, Richard, Benjamin, Ann Begle, Rosannah Davis, Providence Bowman. Grandchildren of dec'd. daughter, Grace Cooper, viz., Daniel, John, Benjamin, George, Rosannah, Providence and Ann. Personal estate. Executors—sons Joseph and Peter. Witnesses—John Moore, David Pound and Reune Runyon. Proved July 14, 1760. Lib. G, p. 264.
    1760, July 4. Inventory, £362.9, incl. cash, £140.15; bonds, £204.4.6; taken by the Executor, Peter Runyon; appraised by George Marlett and Elijah Pound.

    1738, Oct. 30. Runyon, Thomas, of Hopewell Hunterdon Co.; will of. Wife, Martha. Children—only Vinson and Thomas spoken of by name and they with the wife, Martha, to be Executors. Witnesses—Josiah Furman, Elizabeth Furman, Roger Woolverton. Proved April 16, 1753. Lib. 7, p. 408.
    1753, Mar. 20. Inventory, £402.2.8, incl. bills and bonds, £305.13.6; made by Willson Hunt and Timothy Smith.
    1753, Nov. 12. Account by the Executors.

    1754, Mar. 16. Rutan, Peter, of Morris Co. Int. Inventory, £121.13.6, incl. books, 5s.; a pair of silver clasps and band, 6s.; made by James Calwall and William Johnston.
    1754, Mar. 28. Bond of Sarah, his widow, as Adm'x, with David Day, Esq., of Elizabeth, fellowbondsman. Lib. F, p. 164.

    1759, Mar. 6. Ryker, Jacob, of Horseneck, Essex Co. Int Adm'x—Catherine, the widow. Bondsman—Isaac Varmes, of Horseneck. Witness—Lewis Ogden. Essex Wills, 2741 G.

    1755, Apr. 7. Ryley, James, of Cohansey, Cumberland Co., husbandman; will of. Wife, Martha. Children—James, Jonathan, David, Nathan, Levi, Sarah Ogden, Elizabeth and Lornamy. Real and personal estate. Executors—the wife and David Sayers. Witnesses—John Sheppard, Jr., Thomas Test, Elizabeth Dixon. Proved May 19, 1755.
Lib. 8, p. 185.
    1755, May 16. Inventory, £92.4.9., incl. books; made by Abraham Smith and Phillipp Shephard.

    1759, May 19. Saint, Thomas, of New Hanover, Burlington Co. Int. Elisabeth, widow, transfers her right of administration to her "suning-law," John Ansley.
    1759, May 19. Inventory, £87.2.9, incl. book accounts and notes, £8.17.3; books; made by Jonathan Branson and Samuel Wright.
    1759, May 21. Bond of John Ansley as Adm'r; Joseph Lamb fellowbondsman, both of Burlington Co., yeomen. Lib. 9, p. 229.

    1760, Jan. 21. Salmon, Stephen, will of. Children—Abener and Hannah. Personal estate, part of it on Long Island. Executors—

father, Abner Frost, and brother, Nathaniel Salmon. Witnesses—Jonathan Barkley, Jonathan Dayton the 3d, Jonathan Dayton, Jr. Proved March 1, 1760 (in Essex County). Lib. G, p. 146.

1757, Dec. 12. Salnave, Peter, of Elizabeth Town, tanner. Int. Widow, Abigail, renounced in favor of her brother, William Barnet. Witness—Josiah Winans. Same date William Barnet, of same place, Adm'r. Bondsman—James Marshall, of same place. Lib. F, p. 477.

1752, Jan. 9. Sanders, Elizabeth, of Deptford Township, Gloucester Co., widow. Int. Inventory, £216.16.6, incl. plate, bills, bonds and book debts, £136.8.3; a clock; made by Abraham Chattin and John Wilkins.
1752, Mar. 4. Bond of Thomas Wilkins, of Greenwich Township, innholder, as Adm'r; Abraham Chattin, of Deptford Township, yeoman, fellowbondsman. Lib. 7, p. 546.

1760, Mar. 13. Satterthwaite, Richard, of Chester Township, Burlington Co; will of. Children, William, Joshua and Elizabeth, all under age. Real and personal estate. Executors—brothers-in-law, Joshua and Joseph Wright, and friend, John Cox. Witnesses—Darby Durell, William Holcraft, Rebecah Lippincott. Proved April 2, 1760.
Lib. 10, p. 93.

1760, Apr. 11. Satterwaite, David, of Burlington Co. Int. Inventory, £185.15.2., incl. Europian shop goods, £8.19.6; a negro boy, £60; made by Stacey Potts and Joseph Hall.
1760, Apr. 14. Bond of widow, Mary Satterwate (Satterwaite), of Notingham Township, said Co., as Adm'x; Stacy Potts, of Trenton, Hunterdon Co., fellowbondsman. Lib. 10, p. 417.
1760, Apr. 1. Inventory, £557.6.8, incl. a looking glass; an 8-day clock and case, £11; bills and bonds, £181.9.11; 100 bush. of rye, @ 3s., £15; a servant girls' time, about a year, £3; made by Joshua Humphris and Enoch Roberts.

1757, July 8. Savery, Peter, of Perth Amboy, Middlesex Co., barber. Int. Esther Savery, widow, renounced and desires that William Burnet be Administrator, he being a creditor.
1757, July 11. Adm'r—William Burnet, of Perth Amboy, merchant. Bondsman—John Stylls, of same place. Witness—Thomas Bartow.
Lib. F, p. 438.

1751, Aug. 23. Savoy, Isaac, of Pen's Neck, Salem Co. Int. Bond of Robert Clark (Clarke), as Adm'r; George Clarke, fellowbondsman, both of Pile's Grove, said Co., yeomen.
1751, Aug. 23. Inventory, £67.2, incl. bonds due by Lawrence Dalboe and Charles Dolbo, £38; made by Joseph Woods and Patrick Morgan. Salem Wills, 841 Q.

1759, May 1. Sayre, Abraham, of Fairfield, Cumberland Co. Int. Inventory, £49.13.8, incl. books; made by Thomas Ogden and Theophilus Elmer.
1759, June 6. Bond of his widow, Mehetabel Sayre, as Adm'x; Thomas Ogden and Theophilus Elmer, both of Fairfield, fellowbondsmen. Lib. 9, p. 336.

CALENDAR OF WILLS—1751-1760 279

1752, July 12. Sayre, Caleb, of Newark, Essex Co.; will of. Wife, Martha, sole Executrix. Children—Icabod and others, names not given, all under age; an expected child. Real and personal estate. Witnesses—Stephen Baldwin, Caleb Wheler, David Ogden. Proved August 19, 1752. Lib. F, p. 70.

1760, Jan. 7. Sayre, Daniel, of Morris Co. Int. Bond of John Sayre, son, and Samuel van Court, of Middlesex Co., son-in-law, as Adm'rs; John Smalley, of Somerset Co., fellowbondsman.
Lib. G, p. 121.
1760, Jan. 9. Inventory, £177.18.6, incl. a looking glass, £1; 20 bush. of corn, £3; 2 do. of flax seed, 12s.; books, 15s.; made by Jacob Carl and Thomas Baker.

1760, Feb. 22. Sayre, Daniel, of the Borough of Elizabeth, Essex Co., blacksmith; will of. Wife, Rebeka. Children—Sarah (wife of John Owen, who has children, Mary, Rebekah and Hanna), David, Benjamin, Jedadiah and John. Real and personal estate. Executors —the wife and son, David. Witnesses—Benjamin Connet, Daniel Owen, Ebenezer Price. Proved April 16, 1760. Lib. G, p. 248.
1760, Mar. 11. Inventory, £124.16.3, by Benjamin Connet and John Clark.

1760, Dec. 5. Sayre, Samuel, of Hopewell Township, Cumberland Co. Int. Bond of John Bishop as Adm'r; Timothy Brooks and Nicholas Johnson, fellowbondsmen, all of said Township. Lib. 10, p. 178.
1761, Jan. 19. Inventory, £40.8, by Seth and Timothy Brooks.

1758, Feb. 10. Sayre, Stephen, of Hopewell Township, Cumberland Co.; will of. Wife, Patience. Three sons, under age, names not given. Executors—the wife and brother, Ananias Sayre. Witnesses— Thomas Sayre, Jonathan Bowen, David Fithian. Proved July 25, 1758.
Lib. 9, p. 15.
1758, Mar. 6. Inventory, £108.13, by Samuel Fithian and Samuel Miller.

1760, June 14. Sayres, Samuel, of Somerset Co. Int. Adm'r—Samuel Sayres, of said Co. Bondsman—Josiah Broadwell, of Essex Co. Witness—John Smyth. Lib. G, p. 228.
1760, June 4. Inventory, £111.8.6, incl. bond of £50 by Samuel Dunn and Amos Sutton.

1742, Aug. 13. Scattergood, Joseph, of Burlington City and County, mariner; will of. Wife, Rebecca, sole Executrix. Son John, under age. Father still living. Cedar Swamp in the "Sak of Wading River," bought of Jonathan Wright; water lot on the Northside of Pearl Street, Burlington, bought of Elizabeth Bass, Catherine Peirce and Ann Pidgeon; land in Wrightston, bought of Joseph Govett. Personal estate, incl. books and mathematical instruments. Brother Thomas Scattergood asked to assist wife in the sale of land. Witnesses—Joseph Govett, Nathan Lovett, Bennit Bard. Proved Nov. 4, 1754. Lib. 7, p. 531.

1752, June 6. Scattergood, Joshua, of Mansfield Township, Burlington Co. Int. Inventory, £43.7.9, incl. a bill due from John Stogdel, £7; made by Joseph Pope and James Davies.

1752, June 10. Elizabeth, widow, resigns her right of administration to Caleb Scattergood.
1752, June 11. Bond of Caleb Scattergood as Adm'r; Joseph Pope, yeoman, fellowbondsman, both of Mansfield. Lib. 7, p. 303.

1760, May 28. Schamp, George, of Reading Township, Hunterdon Co., yeoman; will of. Wife, Margaret. Children—George, Hendrick, Stonchy (a married daughter) and Hannah. Grandchildren—George, Aerian and Antia, children of son Nicholas (probably deceased); George, Peter, Margret, Phebe, Sarah, Knorcha and Hannah, children of son George; and children of dec'd daughter Yanika, wife of Derick Merlot. Land over South Branch of Raritan River, adjoining John Monfort and New Shanick; homefarm; land adjoining homefarm and Abraham Church, late Michel Church. Personal property. Executors —son Hendrick, George Reading and son-in-law, Jacobus Cocks. Witnesses—Edward Wilmot, Dirck van Vliedt and John Emans. Proved June 14, 1760. Lib. 10, p. 592.
1760, June 10. Inventory, £439., incl. a Dutch Bible and other books, £1.4; a silver cup; a looking glass; five negroes, £195; made by David Cock and Dirck van Vliedt.

1752, Nov. 30. Schamp, Nicholas, of Somerset Co. Int. Bond of Anne Schamp, widow, as Adm'x; Adriaen Aten, of Hunterdon Co., and Teunis Middagh, of Somerset Co., fellowbondsmen. Lib. F, p. 78.
1752, Oct. 23. Inventory, £182.6, by John Monfoort and Peter Monfoort, Jr.
1754, Jan. 3. Account by Administratrix.

1760, Mar. 28. Schamp, Peter, of Reading Township, Hunterdon Co.; will of. Brother, Hendrick Schamp, sole Executor and, with sisters Stonchy (wife of Jacobus Cox), Hannah (wife of Jerome van Fleet), and nephews, George (son of Hendrick Schamp) and George (son of George Schamp), heirs of real and personal estate. Witnesses— Benjamin Alleger, Anderis Anderisen and Edward Wilmot. Proved June 14, 1760. Lib. 10, p. 596.
1760, May 26. Inventory, £299.15.5, incl. 4 books, 4s.; bonds, £138.4.11; made by Edward Wilmot and David Cock.

1750, Oct. 16. Scharffenstein (Sharpenstine), Mathias, of Reading Township, Hunterdon Co., yeoman; will of. Wife, Anna Geertride. Children by present wife, of whom only the second son, Johonas Ievry, is mentioned by name, all under age. Real and personal estate. Executors—Baltis Pikle [Pickel] and Harmon Cline. Witnesses —Michael Bochler (Bailor, who signs in German script), Marius Glanvill, William Richason. Proved Oct. 7, 1756. (Testator signs in German script). Lib. 8, p. 419.
1756, Sept. 8. Inventory, £250.0.7, incl. a Bible and other books, £2.10; bonds and notes, £58.15; made by Abraham van Horn and Marius Glanvill, who state, that said Sharpenstine "died August 29, last past."

1759, Oct. 8. Schellinks, Abraham, of Cape May Co. Int. Inventory, £52.10.11, incl. books, 2s.; made by William Readey and George Taylor.
1760, Feb. 9. Bond of Jane Schellinks as Adm'r; George Taylor fellowbondsman, both of Cape May Co. Lib. 9, p. 409.

CALENDAR OF WILLS—1751-1760   281

1746, Sept. 11. Schenck, Jan, Sr., of Middletown, Monmouth Co., yeoman; will of. Wife, Sarah. Children—John, Roelof, Peter, Sarah (who had children by Johannis Vorious (Voorhees) and by Hendrick Vorious) and 6 other daughters, names not given. Real and personal estate. Executors—the wife and son, Roelof. Witnesses—Roelyf Couenhoven, Garrit Schanck and Thomas Craven. Proved June 3, 1755.   Lib. F, p. 262.

1757, Sept. 28. Schenck, Garret, of Monmouth Co. Int. Inventory, £1713.0.7, incl. a looking glass, £5.10; 3 pictures and a wooden clock, with stand, 13s.; another looking glass, 10s.; a large Dutch Bible and 2 Testaments, £4.14; books and pamphlets, £1.7; 100 bush. of Indian corn in the crib, £11.5; 90 do. of wheat in the mill, £20; 3 negro slaves, £150; bonds and book debts, £868.15.4; made by William Hendrickson and John Bowne.
1757, Sept. 27. Adm'rs—Jannetie Schenck widow of Garret, late of Middletown, yeoman, Albert Schenck and Hendrick Van Brunt.
   Lib. F, p. 450.

1760, May 26. Schnuck, (Snook), William, of Amwell, Hunterdon Co., yeoman; will of. Wife, Cateron. Children—John, Caterin Steenman, Elizabeth Volbart, Christian Roteham, Ann Wombock, Mary Abbut, William, George and Philipp. Real and personal estate. Executors—the wife, with sons John and William. Witnesses—Timothy Smith, Timothy Brush and Hieronymus (Jerome) Mengus (Mingus). Proved June 18, 1760.   Lib. 10, p. 575.
1760, June 13. Inventory, £301.10.11, incl. apparel, bills, bonds, book debts and purse, £75.4.9; made by Timothy Smith and Timothy Brush.

1756, Dec. 15. Scholey, John, of Hanover Township, Burlington Co., yeoman; will of. Wife, Rachel, sole Executrix of real and personal estate. Daughter, Frances, under age; if she should die without issue, her share to go to testator's brother, Jonathan Scholey and sisters, Mary Black, Isabel Ridgway, Rebecka Wright and Sarah Horner. (Susannah Newbold apparently the wife of Jonathan Scholey). Witnesses—Daniel Doughty, Anthony Sykes, Rebekah Wright. Proved Feb. 7, 1757.   Lib. 8, p. 354.
1757, Feb. 4. Inventory, £525.4.4, incl. bonds and book debts, £131.15.7; a servant lad, £15; made by Michael Newbold and Anthony Sykes.

1751, Oct. 15. Scholey, Samuel, of Springfield, Burlington Co., yeoman. Int. Bond of John Scholey as Adm'r; John Warren fellowbondsman, both of said Co., yeoman.   Lib. 7, p. 299.
1751, Dec. 4. Inventory, £202.17.2½, incl. bills, bonds and book debts, £144.13.2½; made by Anthony Sykes and John Warren.

1758, Dec. 14. Schooley, Jonathan, of Springfield Township, Burlington Co. Inventory, £734.7.5, incl. purse and apparel, £267.19.9; a silver watch £7.10; a clock; books; bills and bonds, £28.8.5; two negro children, "worth to them that incline to buy or keep slaves," £20; made by Daniel Doughty, William Stockton and Jonathan Hough.
1758, Dec. 19. Bond of his widow, Mary, as Adm'x; William Stockton and Jonathan Hough, both of Burlington Co., fellowbondsmen.
   Lib. 9, p. 142.

1754, Sept. 25. Schorp, Fredrick, of Burlington Co. Int. Bond of Mary Schorp, as Adm'x; no fellowbondsman. Lib. 7, p. 498.

1752, Sept. 19. Schwart (Swart) George, of Lebanon Township, Hunterdon Co.; will of. Wife, Sara. Children—Samuel, Peter, Catherean, Barbara and Anna. Real and personal estate. Executors—Samuel Bernhard and Balthes Pikel (Pickel). Witnesses—Johannis Singer, Adam Dafford, John Albert Weygand. Proved Oct. 31, 1752.
Lib. 8, p. 170.
1752, Oct. 25. Inventory, £262.8.1, incl. 4 bonds of "Hones Sager," and cash due by Meheal Helebrant, £107.12.9; made by Francis Lucas and Pilifs (Philip) Veiss.
1754, May 28. Account by the Executors.

1758, Jan. 21. Scoby, William, of the South Ward of Perth Amboy, Middlesex Co. Int. Adm'r—Andrew Smyth. Bondsman—John Smyth. Witness—William Crawford. Lib. F, p. 497.

1758, Jan. 23. Scoggins, Jonah, of Allaways Creek Township, Salem Co., bricklayer. Inventory, £693.17.2, incl. his purse, £100.10.8; books and looking glass; 100 sheep, £25; a negro woman, £45; made by John Nicholson and Samuel Sims.
1758, Mar. 15. Bond of Ann Scoggin as Adm'x; Robert Johnson and John Nicholson fellowbondsmen, all of Salem Co. Lib. 8, p. 529.

1752, Apr. 20. Scompt (Schomp), George, Jr., of "Riddingtown," Hunterdon Co., will of. Wife Keneartea (Knearte). Children—Jost, Margaret, Seaby, Sarah, Knertea, Anatie and Peater. Farm bought of Kort Johnson. Personal estate. Executors—the wife, Peater Monfort, and Dirca Marlatt. Witnesses—Cornelius Lane, George Scompt, Sr., Adam Arey. Proved August 4, 1752. Lib. 7, p. 278.
1752, July 28. Inventory, £219.5, by Cornelius Lane and Abraham Croom.

1751, Oct. 16. Scott, Alexander, of Hopewell, Hunterdon Co., yeoman; will of. Wife, Abigail. Children—Henry, Jonathan, More, Timothy, John, Thomas, Hester, Hannah and Alexander, all under age. Personal estate. Executors—the wife and Willson Hunt. Witnesses—John Phillips and Edward Burrows. Proved Jan. 14, 1752.
1751, Nov. —. Inventory, £255.13.7, by John Phillips and Edward Burrows. Hunt. Wills, 321 J.

1760, Aug. 15. Scott, Ebenezer, of New Windsor, Middlesex Co. Int. Patience Scott, his widow, renounced.
1760, Nov. 14. Adm'r—John Clark, of Windsor, Middlesex Co. Witness—John Smyth. Lib. G, p. 320.

1750, May 13. Scott, Elizabeth, of Gloucester Township and County, spinster; will of. Children—Elizabeth (sole Executrix), Amy (left to care of sister, Joana Williams), Temperance (left to care of sister, Jean Hutchinson). Personal estate. Witnesses—Michaell Fisher, Elizabeth Roe, Bathsheba Williams. Proved April 30, 1751.
Lib. 7, p. 141.
1750, May 21. Inventory, £34.16.5, by John Marten and Benjamin Liddon.

CALENDAR OF WILLS—1751-1760

1751, Dec. 4. Scott, Jonathan, of Burlington City, wheelwright; will of. Wife, Mary, sole Executrix. Sons—John and Samuel, both under age. Real and personal estate. Witnesses—John Raworth, William Heulings, Rowland Ellis. Proved Feb. 20, 1756.
Lib. 8, p. 250.

1760, Mar. 18. Widow, Mary, having administered on part of the estate and died, David Carslake appointed Adm'r with will annexed. Bondsmen—John Buffin and Henry Delatush, both of Burlington Co. Witness—S. Blackwood.
Lib. 9, p. 450.

1760, Jan. 8. Scott, Mary, of Burlington City, widow of John Scott. Int. Bond of David Carslake as Adm'r; Henry Delatush and John Buffin fellowbondsmen, all of Burlington Co.
Lib. 9, p. 450.

1759, May 13. Scott, William, of Penn's Neck, Salem Co., husbandman; will of. Wife, Susanna. Children—William, John, Ann, Mary, Elizabeth, Susanna, Robert and Joseph, the last two under age. Real and personal estate. Executors—the wife and Henry Jeanes. Witnesses—Samuel Whitehorne, John Brown and Joseph Jaquat. Proved May 26, 1759.
Lib. 9, p. 356.

1759, May 25. Inventory, £232.6.8, incl. credits and desperate debts, £60.13.2; made by Alen Congelton and Samuel Whitehorne.

1753, June 21. Scriner, Peter, of Salem Co. Int. Adm'r—Richard Wistar.
Lib. 8, p. 89.

1758, April 22. Scudder, John Jr., of Elizabeth Town, Essex Co. yeoman. Int. Adm'r—Thomas Scudder, of same place. Bondsman—Andrew Bloomfield, of Woodbridge. Witness—Thomas Bartow.
Lib. F, p. 524.

1754, Mar. 2. Scudder, Capt. Richard, of Trenton, Hunterdon Co., yeoman; will of. Children—Rebeckah, Joannah Pierson and Joseph. Grandchildren—Deborah Hart, Daniel, Amos, Jedadiah and Ephraim Scudder. Daughter-in-law (widow of son John). Names also Phebe Scudder, who has ch., Jedidiah, Ephraim, Katurah, Prudence and Jemima. Real and personal estate. Executors—son, Joseph, and Arthur Howell. Witnesses—Daniel Clark and Peter Lott. Proved March 19, 1754.
Lib. 7, p. 443.

1754, Mar. 20. Inventory, £166.9, incl. 100 bush. of clean wheat, £22.10; made by Daniel Clark and Peter Lott.

1751, Nov. 25. Scull, Daniel, of Eggharbor, "Glossester" Co. Int. Inventory, £95.4.8, incl. a lookingglass; a Bible and three other books, 10s.; made by James Somers and Recompense Scul, sworn to by Hannah Scull as administratrix.
Glou. Wills, 507 H.

1751, Jan. 12. Scull, Peter, of "Turkey Hoe," Cape May Co. Int. Inventory, £218.7.9, incl. books, £1.15; made by James Hathorn and James Godfrey.

1751, Feb. 23. Bond of John Scull as Adm'r; James Hathorn fellowbondsman, both of Cape May Co., gentlemen.
Cape May Wills, 156 E.

1751, Oct. 10. Seagrave, William, of Piles Grove Township, Salem Co., farmer; will of. Wife, Esther. Son, Onesimus, sole Executor, and real property entailed to him and his male descendants. Grandchildren—William, Samuel and Rebecca, children of dec'd son William. Witnesses—Peter Burr, Rebecca Burr, Elizabeth Garrison. Proved Nov. —, 1753.   Lib. 8, p. 47.

1753, Oct. 23. Inventory, £264.6.3, incl. book debts, £18.18.10; a negro man, £35; books, £2.9.8; made by Henry van Metere.

1757, Sept. 5. Search, Christopher, of Amwell, Hunterdon Co.; will of. Wife, Lydia, sole Executrix. Son, William, and small children, names not given. Witnesses—Charles Woolverton, Joseph Howell, Jr., William Carroll. Proved Oct. 18, 1757.   Lib. 8, p. 478.

1757, Oct. 14. Inventory, £113.5.4, incl. book debts, £34.19.4; books, £8; surveying instruments, £2.15; a prospect glass, 10s.; two looking glasses, 7/6; not included "debts supposed to be insolvent," £43.3.8; made by John Harrison and Joseph Howell, Jr.

1758, Oct. 5. Account by the Executrix, Lydia McMasters, late Lydia Search.

1760, May 6. Searing, Jacob, of Essex Co. Int. "We, Apphia Searing, Daniel Searing and Nancy Searing, resign our right to administer to John Stite, Esq., and Isaac Woodruff.

1760, May 9. Adm'rs—John Stites and Isaac Woodruff, both of Essex Co. Witness—John Smyth.   Lib. G, p. 192.

1760, Apr. 6. Searing, Phebe, of Essex Co.; nuncupative will of. Gives her estate to sister, Amey Pryer, and cousins, Cattyroun and Mascey, daughters of sister, Sary Wade. Josiah Broadwell to be Executor. Witnesses—Mary Townsley, Apphia Ball, Hannah Colie. Proved August 26, 1760.   Lib. G, p. 293.

1760, Aug. 26. Bond of Josiah Broadwell as Executor. Bondsman—Andrew Pryor, of Essex Co. Witness—John Smyth.

1760, Mar. 29. Searing, Simon, of the Borough of Elizabeth, Essex Co., yeoman; will of. Wife, Affa. Children—Jacob, Daniel, Jonathan, Nancy, and Marey Parsons. Real and personal estate. John Stits and Isaac Woodruff to divide the real property. Son, Jacob, and John Stits Executors. Witnesses—David Ball, David Russell, James Colie, Jr. Proved May 9, 1760.   Lib. G, p. 194.

1752, July 24. Sebring, Roelof, of Somerset Co.; will of. Wife, Angenitje. Children—John, Cornelius, Volkert, Dirck, and Annatje, wife of Harpert Peterson. Wife's son, Paul Leboiteux. Real and personal estate. Executors—sons Volkert and Cornelius, and said Paul Leboiteux. Witnesses—William Ouke, Abraham Heyer and Minne van Voorhies. Proved March 26, 1756.   Lib. F, p. 337.

1756, Jan. 20. Inventory, £235.2.5., incl. a silver porringer, £3; 6 silver spoons, £6; an old French Bible and other books, 10s.; a young negro wench, £40; a negro man, £60; a large Dutch Bible, £2.10; a Dutch Testament and other books, 15s.; 2 looking glasses, 8s., bonds and cash, £39.16.10; 33½ bush. of wheat @ 5s.9d., £9.12.7; 10 do. of Indian corn, £1.10; 10 do. of oats, 17s6d.; made by Folkert Sebring, Cornelius Sebring and Paul le Boyteux.

1758, May 28. Sedden, John, of "Always" Creek, Salem Co.; will of. Wife, Mary, sole heiress and Executrix of real and personal estate. Witnesses—James Young, James Wiggins and Hannah Wiggins. Proved August 15, 1758.   Lib. 9, p. 107.

CALENDAR OF WILLS—1751-1760

1758, June 30. Inventory, £89.1, incl. a Bible; a looking glass; 15 bush. of wheat, £2.12.6; made by Edmund Wetherby and Jonathan Bradway.
1760, Nov. 5. Account by the Administratrix.

1760, June 17. Seeley, Joseph, of Fairfield Township, Cumberland Co. Int. Inventory, £27.11, by David Husted and Benjamin Chard.
1760, June 17. Bond of Job Seely as Adm'r; David Husted fellowbondsman, both of Fairfield. Lib. 10, p. 177.
1760, June 23. Account by the Administrator.

1754, Feb. 24. Segler, Daniel, of Somerset Co.; will of. Son, John to have 10 shillings; son, Thomas, 10 shillings; son, Henry, 30 acres of woodland on the mountain. Youngest son, James, to have house and lot at Second River. Daughter, Catherine Sickelere, to have 10 shillings. Household goods to daughter's, Catherine Sickelere's, children. To Catherine Huffman all my high Dutch books. My smith tools in John Ditcher's shop in Newark to my five children. Executors—my friends Peter Berrien and John Clunn. Witnesses—Joseph Badcock, John Powers, Benjamin Yates. Proved March 29, 1754.
1754, March 29. Peter Berrien and John Clunn renounced.
1754, March 30. Admr's, with will annexed—Thomas Segler and William Wheaten, both of Newark. Bondsman—Nathaniel Wheeler, Jr., of same place. Witnesses—Thomas Bartow and Uzal Ogden.
Lib. F, p. 165.

1757, Feb. 12. Segler, Henry, of Elizabeth Town, Essex Co., weaver. Int. Adm'r—James Marshall, of Elizabeth Town, yeoman, principal creditor. Bondsman—Josiah Winans, of same place, yeoman. Witness—Thomas Bartow. Lib. F, p. 403.

1755, Dec. 19. Serjent, Daniel, of Morris Co. Int. Bond of John Tichenar and wife, Mary, of Morris Co., as Adm'rs; Jonathan Sergeant, of Newark, Essex Co., fellowbondsman. Lib. F, p. 325.

1751, June 3. Seward, Obadiah, Jr. Int. Bond of Izabel Seward, of Morris Co., widow, as Adm'x; William Solmon, of said Co., fellowbondsman. Lib. F. p. 94.
1754, May 14. Inventory, £116.8, incl. a Bible, 4/6; by David Luse and William Solmon.

1750-1, Jan. 24. Sexton, Charles, of Hopewell Township, Hunterdon Co., yeoman, "stricken in years;" will of. Wife Sarah. Children—Charles, George, Joseph, Nathaniel, Jared, Nehemiah, Japhath, Esther Rogers, Elisabeth Adams, Kezia Brush, Bathsheba Hill and Mabel Stout. Names Sarah, wife of William Hallock. Grandchildren—Charles and Nathaniel, sons of Charles; children of daughter Hannah and Zephaniah Platt. Homefarm of 160 acres; land in Huntington Township, Suffolk Co., N. Y.; other real and personal estate. Executors—the wife, Timothy Brush and Henry Wollsey. Witnesses—Isaac Eaton, Stephen Barton, John Gano. Proved April 13, 1752.
Lib. 7, p. 224.
1752, Apr. 16. Inventory, £228.1.4, incl. 22 bush. of wheat, £4; a lookingglass, 5s.; a silver cup and 2 spoons, £5; gold buttons and silver buckles, £1; made by William Waters and John Hart.

1756, July 27. Shaftner, Jacob, of Alaways Creek, (Salem Co.), tailor. Bond of Mary Shaftner as Adm'x; Adam Leberger fellowbondsman, both of said Co. Lib. 8, p. 446.
  1756, July 28. Inventory, £49, by Richard Willets and John Dickeson.

1759, July 2. Sharp, Elizabeth, of Township and Co. of Gloucester, spinster; will of. Cousin, John Sharp, son of John Sharp, of Burlington Co., yeoman, £50. Cousin, Elenor Thomlinson, £100. Cousin, Elizabeth Lippincott, wife of Aaron, of Burlington Co, £25. Cousin, Margaret Boucher, daughter of Thomas Boucher, of Burlington, Co., £15. Cousin, Lydia Thomlinson, £10. Uncle, William Sharp (my father's brother), 10 shillings. Hugh Sharp, eldest son of uncle William, 10 shillings. Cousin, Isaac Thomlinson, residue, he paying £20 to his mother, Mary Thomlinson. Executor—said Isaac Thomlinson. Witnesses—Daniel Tomlinson, Michael Fisher and Benjamin Davis. Proved June 17, 1760. Lib. 10, p. 84.
  1760, June 16. Inventory, £425.18.8, by John Hillman and Michael Fisher.

1754, Sept. 25. Sharp, Fradrick, Inventory of personal estate, £63.2.6, made by Thomas Fennimore and Daniel Haines, sworn to by Mary Schorp as administratrix. Burl. Wills, 5515 C.

1757, Oct. 29. Sharp, Samuel, of Gloucester Co. Int. Bond of John Eastlack as Adm'r of estate left unadministered by Robert Down and Henry Siddons, both dec'd, late Administrators; Aaron Aronson fellowbondsman, both of said Co. Lib. 9, p. 62.

1759, Aug. 4. Sharp, William, Sr., of Evesham Township, Burlington Co., yeoman; will of. Wife, Hannah. Children—Jane, Susannah, Isaac, Josiah, Elizabeth (all under age), Mary Strattan, Hannah Heanes, Sarah Pricket, Easter Heanes, Hugh, William, Samuel. Real and personal estate. Executors—sons Hugh and William. Witnesses—Thomas Parkinson, Thomas Shinn, Isaac Haines. Proved September 7, 1759. Lib. 9, p. 276.
  1759, Sept. 6. Inventory, £285.0.6½., incl. book accounts, £59.6.4½; made by Robert Braddock and Joshua Ballinger.
  1766, Aug. 23. Account by Edmund Haines, surviving Executor of William Shorp, Jr., during Edmund Haines' life, and of Edmund's Executors, Joseph Warrington and Elizabeth Haines.

1760, Apr. 7. Sharp, William, Jr., of Evesham Township, Burlington Co.; will of. Wife, Mary. Children—William and Mary, both under age. Real and personal estate, incl. a negro and money left by the father to brother Isaac, when of age. Executors—the wife and brother-in-law, Edmond Haines. Witnesses—William Foster, David Strattan, Thomas Shinn. Proved Oct. 1, 1760. Lib. 10, p. 130.
  1760, June 4. Inventory, £453.9.4, incl. a servant boy, £16; a negro wench, £25; bills, bonds and book debts, £150.12.11; made by William Foster and Joshua Ballinger.

1760, June 2. Sharpenstine, John Peter, of Roxbury, Morris Co. Int. Executrix—Anne, widow, of said place. Bondsmen—John Hendershott, yeoman, of same place and John Hagar, of Roxbury Township. Lib. 10, p. 111.

CALENDAR OF WILLS—1751-1760

1760, June 2. Inventory, £467.12.5, by John Hendershott and William Larson.

1762, Feb. 27. Account by Anne Pisher, late Anne Sharpenstine.

1756, Oct. 22. Sharpenstine, Paul, of Lebanon, Hunterdon Co.; will of. Wife, Elsa. Godchildren—Paul Clover, Paul Sharp, Paul Engel and Paul Eick. Executors—Joh: Dilse, of Amwell, and Jacob Gerhart, Jr., of Lebanon. Witnesses—Jacob Eick, Jacob Anders (signs in German script), David Fetter. Proved Nov. 20, 1756. Lib. 8, p. 412.

1756, Nov. 17. Inventory, £301.6.1, incl. bonds and book debts, £108.0.7; 3 books; 6 years of a servant boy's time, £6; made by Edward Wilmot and David Fetter.

1753, Jan. 23. Shaw, John, of Hopewell Precinct, in "County of Cumberland Cohansie," yeoman; will of. Wife, Sarah. Daughters—Lucy, Temperance and Elishabe. Grandson, Jonathan Fithian, Jr. Real and personal estate. Executors—the wife, daughter Lucy and Ananias Sayres. Witnesses—Samuel Harris, Moses Platts, Benjamin Worton. Proved March 2, 1753.

1753, Feb. 26. Inventory, £122.15.3, by Samuel Harris and Moses Plats. Cumb. Wills, 87 F.

1758, Aug. 22. Shaw, Richard, of "Morrss" River, Cumberland Co.; will of. Wife [not named]. Children—Richard ("if ever he returns"), Jeremiah, John, Ichabod, Aaron and Nathan. Real and personal estate. Executor—son Jeremy. Witnesses—Thomas Peterson, Dean Grover, Thomas Flinter. Proved Sept. 7, 1758. Lib. 9, p. 134.

1758, ——— ———. Inventory, £141.7.6, incl. a shalop, £65; a Bible, 4s.; made by Abraham Jones and Thomas Peterson.

1760, Apr. 17. Shaw, Richard, of Cumberland Co. Int. Inventory, £21.14, by Silas Newcomb and Jonathan Lore.

1760, May 10. Bond of Edmond Shaw as Adm'r; Silas Newcomb fellowbondsman, both of Fairfield Township, Cumberland Co. Lib. 10, p. 177.

1759, Jan. 2. Shaw, Thomas, (Lieut.-Colonel), of Burlington City. Int. Bond of Daniel Ellis as Adm'r; Joseph Hollinshead, Esq., fellowbondsman, both of said City. Lib. 9, p. 176.

1759, May 16. Inventory, £80.4.1, incl. bonds and notes, £43.3.7; a silver spoon and lace for a hat, £1; a book; a pair of gold buttons, 19s.; a silver-hilted sword, £6; a silver watch, £5; made by Jonathan Smith and Samuel Peart.

1753, May 21. Shaw, William, of Monmouth Co., miller and single man. Int. Certificate by John Henderson, that Eleanor Shaw is the only sister of the whole blood, and that Thomas Craig is a freeholder in said Co., owning 100 acres.

1753, May 24. Bond of Eleanor Shaw as Adm'x; Thomas Craig fellowbondsman. Lib. F, p. 123.

1753, May 22. Inventory, £53.17, incl. silver buckles, £1.16; a pair of gold buttons and a gold ring, £3; a silver watch and seal, £7; made by Michel Sweetman and William McKnight.

1754, June 3. Account by the Administratrix, who claims to have received from the sale only £50.8.11, and has paid out £18.10.11.

1754, Apr. 23. Sheldon, Lemuel, of Northampton, Burlington Co., labourer. Int. Inventory, £44.18, by Thomas Atkinson and John Woolman.

1754, Apr. 24. Bond of Joseph Sheldon as Adm'r; John Woolman fellowbondsman, both of said place, yeoman. Lib. 7, p. 467.

1751, May 17. Shephard, Thomas, of Middleton, Monmouth Co.; will of. Wife, Deborah. Children—Joseph, Sarah Stilwill, Rebeckah Coscoe, John, Deborah Burros, Hannah Still, Mary, Thomas and Ebenezer, the last two to be Executors of real and personal estate. Witnesses—Henderick Bennet, William Bennet, Joseph Wardell. Proved May 20, 1751. Lib. E, p. 526.

1751, July 30. Inventory, £655.1.4, incl. two looking glasses; silver spoons; a Bible; an old negro man, £25; an old negro wench, £10; a young negro, £50; a negro girl, £25; bonds, £209.17.10; made by Henderick Bennet, John Patterson and Edward Taylor.

1754, June 18. Shepherd, David, of the Southside of Cohansey, Cumberland Co.; will of. Wife, Sarah. Children—Ephraim, David, Joseph, Philipp and Phebe. Farm of 150 acres, on which father, David, lived and died, now occupied by Jonathan Shepherd; land South of Abraham Smith; 50 ac. bought by the father of Capt. William Dare, called Kuldry (?). Personal estate. Executors—sons Ephraim and David. Witnesses—Stephen Mulford, James Broocks, Abigail Wescott. Proved May 19, 1755. Lib. 8, p. 188.

1755, May 10. Inventory, £71.4., incl. books, made by Abraham Smith and David Sayers.

1759, Nov. 19. Shepherd, Ebenezer, of Middletown, Monmouth Co. Int. Bond of Catherine, widow, as Adm'x; Thomas Shepherd, of same place, yeoman, fellowbondsman. Lib. G, p. 112.

1759, Nov. 14. Inventory, £299, incl. negro, £75, by Cyrenius van Mater, John Smock and James Grover, Jr.

1757, Feb. 9. Shepherd, Job, of Salem, Salem Co.; will of. Wife, Kathrine. Children—Elnathan, Job, Beelbe, Daniel, Cumberland, Rebeca, Cathrine, Martha, Keziah and Ruth, the last six under age. Old farm in Cumberland Co.; land there adjoining Seth Brooks, inherited from brother, Joseph Shepherd; another lot in the same Co., on the North side of the main road to Cohansey Bridge, adjoining Ephraim Shepherd. Personal property. Executors—the wife and brother, Captain Benoni Dare. Witnesses—John Holme, William Crow and Agnes Gray. Proved May 14, 1757. Lib. 8, p. 450.

1757, Apr. 23. Inventory £103.3.2, by John Holme and John Whittall.

1753, Sept. 1. Shepherd, Joseph, of Middletown, Monmouth Co.; will of. Wife, Rebecca. Children—Thomas, Moses, Catherine, Deborah, Sarah, Mary and Hannah. Real and personal estate. Executors—the wife, son-in-law, Richard Crawford, and Cornelius van de Vear. Witnesses—Andrew Winter, John Louden, John Taylor. Proved Sept. 10, 1753. Lib. F, p. 134.

1753, Sept. 14. Inventory, £251.19.8, incl. a looking glass, a servant man, 6 silver spoons, 3 old books, 3s.; made by Andrew Winter and Nathaniel Leonard.

CALENDAR OF WILLS—1751-1760

1756, Dec. 7. Shepherd, Joseph, of Cumberland Co. Int. Inventory, £236.0.3, incl. books; bonds and debts, £186.11.3; made by Benjamin Mulford and Jonathan Bowen.

1756, Dec. 7. Bond of Job Shepherd, of Salem Co., clerk, as Adm'r; Benjamin Mulford and Jonathan Bowen, both of Cumberland Co., yeoman, fellowbondsmen.   Lib. 8, p. 347.

1752, Nov. 17. Shepherd, Moses, of Fairfield Township, Cumberland Co., yeoman; will of. Children—Nathan, John, Moses, Rachel Reminton (who has son Moses Reminton), Sarah and Mary. Real and personal estate. Executors—sons Nathan and John. Witnesses—Joseph Reeve, Thomas Conner, Mark Reeve. Proved January 19, 1753.

1753, Jan. 13. Inventory, £404.8.7, incl. books; a servant man; made by David Shepherd and Mark Reeve.   Cumb. Wills, 88 F.

1755, ——— ——. **Shepherd, Moses** (son of Moses, dec'd), of Farefield, Cumberland Co., petitions that Mark Remington, of said Co., yeoman, be appointed his Guardian.

1755, Apr. 22. Bond of Mark Remington as such Guardian; John Remington, Esq., of Cumberland Co., and Hugh Blackwood, of Salem Co., fuller, fellowbondsmen.   Lib. 8, p. 159.

1759, Dec. 6. Shepherd, Silvanus, of Cohansey, Cumberland Co., yeoman; will of. Divides personal estate between brothers, Samuel Shephard and Abraham Shephard (under age), Mary and Sary Prestons, Grace Pawling, Phebe (daughter of Silas Ireland), and Joseph Ireland. Executor—Henry Westcoat. Witnesses—David Sayers, Silas Ireland, Mary Ireland. Proved Feb. 5, 1760.   Lib. 10, p. 29.

1760, Jan. 15. Inventory, £77.11.9, by Nathan Lorance (Lawrence) and Lewis Whitacar (Whitaker).

1761, Nov. 14. Account by David Westcoat, Executor of Henry Westcoat, deceased, who was Executor of Silvanus Shepherd.

1757, Oct. 20. Shepherd, Stephen, of Fairfield Township, Cumberland Co., yeoman; will of. Wife, Ruth. Children—Joseph (under age), Stephen, Peter, Gibbons, Martha and Lovice. Homefarm, on the Main and the little Creek, adjoining brother John Shepherd; a lot, called the Hickory Land, between Laufet Saruel and William Pauling; marsh on Delaware Bay, below Padget's Point, encompassed by the creek called Sow and Pigs; marsh at Flax farm, bought of Dickerson Shepherd; 200 acres of marsh below Smith's Islands, bought of Joseph Reevs; farm now occupied by Whitlock Pauling. Personal estate. Executors—the wife, with brethren David Shepherd and William Pauling. Witnesses—William Newcomb, Silvanus Shepherd, Samuel Shepherd. Proved Dec. 24, 1757.
   Lib. 8, p. 508.

1757, Dec. 7. Inventory, £199.11.9, by David Sayers and Ephraim Shepard (Shepherd).

1755, Dec. 31. Sherd, Cathrine, of Trenton, Hunterdon Co., widow woman; will of. Children—Anna, Mary, Frances, Lucy and William, the last named under age. Personal property. Executors—daughters Mary and Anna, with brother Hezekiah Anderson. Witnesses—Enoch Anderson, Alexander Anderson. Proved March 26, 1756.   Lib. 8, p. 274.

19

1756, Mar. 26. Inventory, £25; incl. 3 silver teaspoons, 12s.; a looking glass and picture, 2s.; made by Enoch Anderson and William Yard.

1758, Aug. 18. Sherwin, James, of Gloucester Co.; will of. Wife, Edith. Children—names not given, all under age. Real and personal estate. Executors—the wife, Jacob Spicer and Alexander Randall, who are directed to execute a conveyance for land in Greenwich, said Co., sold to Isaac Inskip. Witnesses—John Ab. Lidenies, William Guest. Proved Sept. 19, 1758. Lib. 9, p. 44.
1758, Sept. 16. Inventory, £1651.10.8, incl. bills, bonds and book debts, £934.14.9; leases and specialties, £78; shop goods, £293.17; furniture, £161.5.7; made by William Guest and Thomas Denny.
1762, Dec. 14. Account of Edith Abit, late Edith Sherwin, Executrix, by her second husband, Burroughs Abit, who charges £136.6.10. for keeping the children of dec'd, viz., Rebecca, George and James Sherwin for 3 years and 8 months.

1754, Sept. 9. Sherwin, William, of Chester, Burlington Co., yeoman; will of. Wife, Sarah. Daughter, Grace, under age; an expected child. Real and personal estate. Executors—the wife and Darling Connaroe (Conroe). Witnesses—Matthew, Allen, William Allin, John Cox. Proved Oct. 28, 1754. Lib. 7, p. 508.
1754, Oct. 8. Inventory, £325.4.2, incl. bills, bonds and book debts, £175.1.6; made by Thomas Hackney and Joseph Stokes.
1769, June 7. Account by Darling Conroe.
1770, May 4. Second account by same.

1752, Apr. 30. Shinn, Caleb, of Burlington Co. Int. Mehetabel, widow, refuses the administration, recommending Thomas Atkinson, of said Co., innholder, the principal creditor.
1752, Apr. 30. Bond of Thomas Atkinson as administrator, Bennet Bard, of said Co., yeoman, fellowbondsman. Lib. 7, p. 303.

1751, Nov. 19. Shinn, George, of Bridgetown, Burlington Co., chairmaker; will of. Wife, Sarah, sole heiress and Executrix of real and personal estate. Witnesses—James Lippincott, Joshua Humphris, John Burr, Jr. Proved Feb. 11, 1752. Burl. Wills, 5077 C.

1751, June 8. Shinn, James, of Burlington Co. Int. Inventory, £36.19.6, by William Budd and Abraham Kille (Killey).
1751, June 14. Bond of Joseph Shinn, of Hanover, as Adm'r; Samuel How, of Burlington City, butcher, fellowbondsman.
1751, Aug. 1. Account by the Administrator, who charges "for nursing and watching the deceased when he had the numb palsie, 4 years & 3 months, at £9. the year, £36.5;" has paid for the coffin to Edward Mullin, £1.15; for "sundrys" at funeral to John Ewans, 8s.; and charges for administration expenses, £3.1. Burl. Wills, 4855 C.

1753, July 16. Shinn, James, of Burlington Co. Int. Bond of Thomas Budd as Adm'r; Henry Paxton fellowbondsman, both of Northampton, said Co., yeomen. Lib. 7, p. 421.
1753, July 17. Inventory, £98.8.7, by George Briggs and Patrick Reynolds.
1754, Feb. 7. Account by Administrator.

CALENDAR OF WILLS—1751-1760   291

1759, Feb. 15. Shinn, Joseph, of New Hanover, Burlington Co. Int. Bond of William Shinn as Adm'r; George Briggs fellowbondsman, both of Northampton, said Co., yeomen.   Lib. 9, p. 177.
   1759, Feb. 15. Inventory, £28.12.2, by George Briggs and David Budd.
   1759, Mar. 29. Account of the estate by the Administrator, who makes it his debtor for £3.8.5.

1751, Oct. 10. Shinn, Thomas, of Burlington Co.; will of. Daughter, Susannah Atkinson to have my chair in which I ride. Son, Earll, my lot on Elbo Alley when 21. Son, Gamaliel, two houses on Elbo Alley when 21. Daughter, Elizabeth Shinn, a lot when 21, and the house in which I live to son, Aquilla, when 21. Daughter, Postrema Shinn, £60. I have given to my daughter, Martha Paxson, a negro called Pleasant, and to my daughter, Mary Allinson, one called Jude. Son, Thomas, 20 shillings, as he has already been advanced. My plantations and lands not given away to be sold. The rest to be given to my nine children, Susannah Atkinson, Martha Paxson, Thomas Shinn, Jr, Mary Allinson, Elizabeth Shinn, Earl Shinn, Gamaliel Shinn, Aquilla Shinn and Postrema Shinn. Executors—son-in-law, Henry Paxson and friend, John Woolman. Witnesses—Benjamin Bispham, Joseph Humphris, John Clark. Proved March 10, 1753.
   1753, May 17. Inventory, £1893.9.11, by Peter Andrews, Thomas Lawrence, Henry Paxson and John Woolman. Burl. Wills, 5325 C.

1759, Feb. 24. Shmidt, Wilhelm, of Stow Creek, Cumberland Co., yeoman; will of. Divides estate between John Luts, Marget Ramsted, cousin William Smick and friend, Philipp Smick. Executor—Azel Peirson. Witnesses—Beniman (Benjamin) Calooper, Azel Peirson, Jr., George Peirson. Proved March 6, 1759. [Testator signs in German script].   Lib. 9, p. 225.
   1759, Mar. 5. Inventory, £24.11.11, by Jacob More and Adam Schaffer.

1757, June 20. Shotwell, Abraham, Sr., of "Piscatua," Middlesex Co.; will of. Children—John, Abraham, Deborah, Sarah Vail, Elizabeth Webster. Grandchildren—Hannah (daughter of son-in-law Daniel Shotwell and Debory), Abraham, (son of John and Sarah Vail) and Hannah (daughter of Joseph and Elizabeth Webster). Personal estate. Executors—son, Abraham, son-in-law, Daniel Shotwell, and Nathaniel Fitzrandolph. Witnesses—Agnes Boomfield (Bloomfield), Jacob Thorn and Joseph Shotwell, Jr. Proved Nov. 2, 1757, when Nathaniel Fitz Randolph refuses to act as Executor.   Lib. F, p. 465.

1757, Nov. 17. Shotwell, John, Sr., of Woodbridge, Middlesex Co., yeoman; will of. Wife, Anna. Children—John, Mary and Jesper. Real and personal estate. Executors—the wife, Recompence Stanbery and James Clarkson. Witnesses—Jeremiah Wright, Benjamin Shotwell and Robert Clarkson. Proved Jan. 3, 1758.   Lib. F, p. 481.
   1758, Jan. 3. Inventory, £846.14.2, incl. bonds, £609.14.6; other debts, £9.4.1; sworn to October 5, 1763, by David Edgar as appraiser, the other appraiser being dead.

1758, July 3. Shotwell, Joseph, Jr., of Woodbridge, Middlesex Co., carpenter; will of. Wife, Rachel. Children—Benjaman, Rachel and Lyda, all under age. Real and personal estate. Executors—brother,

Benjaman Shotwell, and brother, Peter Martain. Witnesses—James Fitz Randolph, Rebekah Fitz Randolph and David Edgar. Proved July 29, 1758. Lib. F, p. 541.

1757, Feb. 12. Shotwell, Peter, of Elizabeth Town, Essex Co., laborer. Int. Adm'r—James Marshall, principal creditor, yeoman, of same town. Bondsman—Josiah Winans, yeoman, of same place. Witness—Thomas Bartow. Lib. F, p. 403.

1758, June —. Shoulter, Jacob, of Gloucester Co. Int. Inventory, £58.9.4, incl. an apprentice boy's time, £7.; made by Robert Zane and John Lock.

1758, June 14. Bond of Alexander Randall, Esq., as Adm'r; Simon Sparks, innholder, fellowbondsman, both of Gloucester Co. Witnesses—Jacob Hugg and John Ladd. Lib. 9, p. 197.

1759, Mar. 2. Account by Administrator.

1750-1, Mar. 14. Shreve, Benjamin, of Mansfield, Burlington Co., yeoman; will of. Wife, Rebecca. Children—Keziah, Sarah, Caleb, William, Israel, Benjamin and Samuel, all but Caleb under age. Homefarm; a farm bought of Preserve Brown, part in Mansfield, part in Chesterfield; a farm bought of Jacob Ong, of Hanover; 100 acres inherited from father. Personal estate, incl. a negroman, to be liberated. Executors—Daniel Doughty and Michael Newbold. Witnesses—Barzillai Newbold, Levi Nutt, Robert Bland. Proved March 29, 1751.

1751, Apr. 18. Inventory, £1980.4.1, incl. an old negroman, £5; bills, bonds and book debts, £1300.17.3½; made by William Cooke, Thomas Black and Anthony Sykes. Burl. Wills, 4861 C.

1756, May 3. Shreve, Jonathan, of Burlington Co. Int. Inventory, £28.15.2, by Thomas Hall and Abram Shreve.

1756, May 4. Bond of John Shreve as Adm'r, Thomas Hall fellowbondsman. Lib. 8, p. 305.

1757, Oct. 1. Shreve, Joseph, of Mansfield Township, Burlington Co. Int. Inventory, real estate, £15; personal, £17.13.6; made by Isaac De Cow and Thomas Hall.

1757, Oct. 15. Bond of Thomas Shreve as Adm'r; Abraham Shreve, fellowbondsman, both of said Co. Lib. 8, p. 517.

1757, Oct. 24. Account by the Administrator, of the sale of the goods for £29.1.7.

1751, March 30. Shreve, Joshua, of Springfield Township, Burlington Co.; will of. Daughters, Mary Curtis, Sarah Shreve, Marcy Mattheries and Faith Butteer, to each 5 shillings. Sons-in-law, John Beck and William Shinn, each one shilling. Wife, Jean, use of my new house, and benefit of my boy, Eastwood Allen, and my girl, Mary Smith. Son, James, 5 shillings. Son, Caleb, my plantation where I live. Grandson, John, son of my son, Caleb, and grandson Joshua, son of James, a gun each. Executor—son, Caleb. Witnesses—Joseph Shreve, Samuel Wright, Jr., Isaac De Cow. Proved April 2, 1753.

1753, April 4. Inventory, £186.9, by Thomas Earl and Jonathan Branson. Burl. Wills, 5223 C.

CALENDAR OF WILLS—1751-1760

1759, May 21. Shreve, Sarah, dau. and legatee of Benjamin, of Mansfield, Burlington Co., asks that her brother Caleb Shreeve, be made her Guardian.

1759, May 29. Bond of Caleb Shreve as such Guardian, Wm. Skeeles fellowbondsman, both of Burlington Co. Burl. Wills, 6451 C.

1753, June 21. Shriner, Peter, of Salem Co. Int. Jane, widow, resigns her right of administration to Richard Wistar.

1753, June 21. Bond of Richard Wistar, of Philadelphia, as Administrator. Lib. 8, p. 88.

1758, Mar. 11. Shurts, George, of Reading Township, Hunterdon Co., yeoman; will of. Wife, Jane, sole heiress of real and personal estate for the education of the children (whose names are not given). Executors—the wife and brother, John Shurts. Witnesses—Nicholas Egbert, Hendrick Devooer (Devore) and Susanah French. Proved April 19, 1758. Lib. 9, p. 163.

1758, Apr. 19. Inventory, £162.0.4, by David Cock and Nicholas Egbert.

1759, Sept. 3. Shurts, Michael, of Reading Township, Hunterdon Co., yeoman; will of. Wife, Elizabeth. Children—John, Abraham, Anne, Eve and Margaret. Children of son George Shurts, viz., Michael, Elizabeth, Mathew, Rachael and John. Wife's son Hanes Fetter. Real and personal estate. Executors—sons John and Abraham. Witnesses—Daniel DeVhore (Devore), David Cock, Jr., George Reading. Proved November 26, 1759. Lib. 10, p. 96.

1759, Oct. 8. Inventory, £235.5.7, incl. bonds, £82.15.1; made by John Anderson and David Cock.

1754, Feb. 24. Sickeler (Segler), Daniel, of Somerset Co., late of Essex Co., miner; will of. Children—John, Thomas, Henry, James and Catherine Huffman. Home lot on Second River; land on the Mountain next to one Cockefor. Personal estate, incl. 4 pair of silver buckles; 2 gold rings; High Dutch books; money due from Thomas Combs, of Newark, saddler. Executors—Petter Berrien and John Clunn. Witnesses—Joseph Badcock, John Powers, Benjamin Yates. Proved March 29, 1754, in Essex Co. Lib. F, p. 165.

1754, Mar. 29. Peter Berrien and John Clunn, the Executors named, depute William Wheaten and Thomas Siglar, the son of testator, to act in their stead. Dated at Ten-Mile Run, Somerset Co.

1759, Aug. 7. Sickle (van Sickle), Abraham, of Morris Co., yeoman; will of. Wife, Sarah. Only child, Elisabeth. Real and personal estate. Executors—the wife and "Ensyn" Thomas Baker, of the Congregation of New Providence in the "Borrough" of Elizabeth. Witnesses—Jonathan Elmer, Piter Rutan, Abraham Rutan. Proved Dec. 10, 1759. Lib. G, p. 139.

1751, July 25. Siddons, Henry, of Newtown Township, Gloucester Co., yeoman. Int. Inventory, £168.6.7, incl. a watch; bonds and cash notes, £56.16.10; made by Robert Stephens and Joseph Ellis.

1752, Apr. 4. Bond of widow, Elizabeth, as Adm'x; Joseph Ellis, yeoman, fellowbondsman, both of Newton Township.

Glouc. Wills, 508 H.

1755, Oct. 3. Siddons, William, of the Town and County of Salem; will of. Wife, Mary. Children—William, Ezekiel, Edward, Isaac (all under age), Deborah, Elizabeth and Hannah. Real and personal estate, incl. a clock and case. Executors—the wife and son William. Witnesses—John Budd, Daniel Mestayer, Mary Mestayer. Proved Oct. 24, 1755. Lib. 8, p. 248.

1755, Oct. 21. Inventory, £1534.14.6¾, incl. bills, bonds, etc., £1209.1.11¼; 2 looking glasses; shop goods, £49; 2 servants, one 1 year 8 mo., the other 5 yrs, £24; a shallop, boat and "batto," £83; made by Henry Stubbines and Aaron Bradway.

1754, Oct. 28. Siliman, John, of Freehold, Monmouth Co., yeoman; will of. Stepmother, Susna (?) Silliman, who has three daughters. Sisters—Jean Blayer, Isbel Clarke and Elizabeth Gibson. Legacies to John Gaston and his son James; Hugh McFarrin, his son Robert and Archebal Laird; the heirs of sister, Margret McFerrar, and sister, Susnah Laird, to be residuary legatees. Executors—William Laird and John Gaston. Witnesses—David Barclay, Elisabeth English and John Tomson, Jr. Proved June 2, 1755. Lib. F, p. 261.

1755, May 28. Inventory, £224.10.2, incl. silver clasps, 4/6; bills, bonds and book debts, £209.4.2; made by Thomas Davies, David Barclay and Alexander Laird.

1757, June 4. Silver, James, Jr., of Upper Freehold, Monmouth Co.; will of. Wife, Hesther. Children—Mary, John, Rebecca and Amos, all under age. Real and personal estate. Executors—brothers, John Silver and John Foord. Witnesses—Isaac Price, James Newell and Thomas Lawrie. Proved Nov. 9, 1757.
Lib. 8, p. 465.

1757, Nov. 3. Inventory, £132.14; incl. bills, bonds, bookdebts and cash, £70.12; books; 225 lbs. of new iron, £3.7; a looking glass; made by Moses Robins and Bartholo West.

1758, Sept. 30. Silver, James, of New Winsor Township, Middlesex Co., yeoman; will of. Wife, Mary. Children—John, David, Job (under 14), Archibald, Gershom, Mary (wife of Francis King). Children of dec'd son James, viz., Mary, John, Rebecca and Amos. Real and personal estate. Executors—son John, Isaac Coverly and Nathaniel Robins. Witnesses—John Foord, Thomas Foord and Stephen Foord. Proved Jan. 24, 1759. Lib. G, p. 149.

1758, Dec. 28. Inventory: Real, being a plantation £800; personal, £144.0.7, incl. a book, "General Acts of N. J. Assembly," 15s.; made by John Hammell, Jr., and John Foord.

1755, Sept. 5. Simkins, Francis, of Stow Creek Township, Cumberland Co., yeoman; will of. Wife [not named]. Children—John, David, Abraham, Francis, Benjamin (all under age), Mercy, Rachel, Johanna; an expected child. Homefarm; 5 acres of salt marsh on the other side of Stow Creek in Salem Co.; 55 ac. bought of Joseph Brick. Personal estate. Executors—son John and Stephen Mulford. Witnesses—Harbert Peck, Ann Broen, Robert Nicholls. Proved Sept. 19, 1755. Lib. 8, p. 212.

1755, Sept. 15. Inventory, £201.0.3, incl. 10 books; made by John Finlaw and Richard Butcher, Jr.

1752, Mar. 20. Simons, Barant, of Reading Township, Hunterdon Co., cordwainer; will of. Wife, Appolonia. Children—Aaron, Simon,

CALENDAR OF WILLS—1751-1760

Catharen Frew, Nelly Johnson, Vankey Wimmer. Granddaughter, Deborah Froom (under age). Personal estate. Executors—Thomas Bowman, Sr., and Jacob Vanderbilt. Witnesses—Vinard Vandivendure, Teunis Lou (Low), Patrick Fitz Gerald. Proved Oct. 14, 1752. Endorsed: "No probate issued for want of the proof of the Executors."
Lib. 7, p. 405."

1752, Feb. 14. Simonson, (Symonse), Isaac, of Somerset Co.; will of. Wife, Neeltje. Children—Isaac, Peter, Symon, William, Antje, Jaques, Arius and Deborah, all under age. Real and personal estate. Executors—Cornelius Stoothoff and Hendrick Cortelyou, both of said Co. Witnesses—David Nevius, Peter van Pelt, John Bennet. Proved April 15, 1752.
Lib. F, p. 33.

1760, May 21. Simpson, John, of the City of London, merchant. Int. Bond of John Hackett as Adm'r; Samuel Johnson fellowbondsman, both of Bethleham, Hunterdon Co.
Lib. 9, p. 420.

1751, June 26. Slaney, Anne, of Bordentown, Burlington Co., widow of Edward Slayney; will of. Daughter, Ann Gamble. Granddaughter, Henrieta Gamble. Executors—Aron, son of Marmaduke Watson, dec'd, and Thomas Watson, cooper. Witnesses—Edward Wheat Craft, William Weatherel, John Collings. Proved August 24, 1751.
Lib. 7, p. 125.

1751, Aug. 21. Slaney, Edward, of Bordentown, Burlington Co., joiner. Int. Inventory, £111.10.8½, by William Pancoast and Thomas Folkes.
1751, Aug. 24. Bond of Thomas Watson, cooper, as Adm'r; Aaron Watson, joiner, fellowbondsman, both of Bordentown, said Co.
Lib. 7, p. 298.

1751, ——, ——. Sleeper, John, son of Jonathan and Hannah Sleeper, of Burlington Co., over 14 years old, petitions that Peter Andrews be appointed his Guardian.
1751, Apr. 8. Bond of Peter Andrews, of Burlington Co., yeoman, as Guardian; Joseph Clowes, of Burlington City, merchant, fellowbondsman.
Burl. Wills, 4881 C.

1752, Oct. 13. Sleeper, Mary, of Bridgetown, Northampton, Burlington Co., "taylores;" will of. Sister, Leah, widow of Jonathan Atkinson, who has son Jonathan Atkinson. Brothers—John and Jonathan Sleeper. House and lot in Bridgetown. Personal estate, incl. a Bible, a book, "Journal of Thomas Chalkley." Executors—sister Leah and Peter Andrews. Witnesses—Josiah White, Mary Owen, Henry Paxson. Proved Nov. 6, 1752.
1752, Oct. 30. Inventory, £76.16.2, incl. 6 silver spoons and a pair of silver studs, £1.1.6; a looking glass 9s.; a Bible and "Chalkley's Journal," 7/6; small books 1s.; made by Henry Paxson and Josiah White.
Burl. Wills, 5081 C.

1756, Oct. 1. Slingerlant, Theunis, of "Peremus" Precinct, Bergen Co., yeoman; will of. Eldest son, John. Other children, under age, mentioned, but not by names. Executors—Abraham van Gelder and Andries de Bow. Witnesses—Peter Vouck, Cunrat van Allman, Autie van Allman. Proved May 18, 1757.
Lib. F, p. 454.

1759, Oct. 12. Slocum, Nathaniel, of Shrewsbury, Monmouth Co., yeoman; will of. Wife, Susanah. Daughters—Margrate, Athaliah and Ruth. Real and personal estate. Executors—the wife and brother, Pelick Slocom. Witnesses—Job Cook, Joseph Allen and Meribah Taber. Proved Nov. 16, 1759. Lib. G, p. 256.
1759, Dec. 15. Inventory, £101.10.6, incl. a looking glass, 14s.; made by Job Cook and Joseph Allen.

1759, July 20. Slocum, Peter, of Shrewsbury, Monmouth Co., yeoman; will of. Wife, Katharine. Children—Susanah, Elizabeth, John, Jonathan and Hannah, all under age. Real and personal estate. Executors—the wife and Job Cook. Witnesses—Susanna Holmes, Jabez Treadwell and George Boniface. Proved Nov. 3, 1760.
Lib. G, p. 447.
1760, Sept. 13. Inventory, £183.3.5, incl. bonds and book debts, £58.12.4; a looking glass, 10s.; an old sloop, £30; made by Joseph Allen and Daniel Williams.

1754, May 6. Smalley, John, Jr., of Piscataway, son of Benjamin. Guardians appointed—Benjamin Stelle and Azariah Dunham. Bondsman—Richard Fitz Randolph. Midd. Wills, 2723 L.

1760, Feb. 18. Smalley, John, of Piscataway, Middlesex Co.; will of. Mother, Anna Dottey. Brothers—Benjamin Smalley, Joshua Smalley. Brother-in-law, Garrit van Camp. Real and personal estate. Executors—friend and brother, Samuel Jones, and Truston Manning. Witnesses—John Breadbilck (?), Henry Kinter and Joseph Davis. Proved May 3, 1760. Lib. G, p. 188.

1760, Mar. 19. Smalley, Joshua, Jr., of Piscataway, Middlesex Co.; will of. Wife, Sarah. Children—Mary and James. Real and personal estate. Executors—the wife, father, Joshua Smalley, and father-in-law, James Larrence. Witnesses—Isaac Stelle, Hannah Swaim and Adam Heiller (signs in German script and remark says, "In English is Adam Hyler"). Proved April 18, 1760. Lib. G, p. 175.
1760, Apr. 17. Inventory, £151.15.5, incl. a looking glass and a small Bible; made by Henry Welch and Isaac Stelle.

1756, Febr. 19. Smallwood, John, of Gloucester Township and Co., yeoman. Int. Bond of William Smallwood, of Gloucester Township, as Adm'r; John Down, of Deptford Township, said Co., fellowbondsman, both yeomen. Lib. 8, p. 307.
1756, Mar. 1. Inventory, £124.3.9, incl. a large Bible and 2 small books, £1.15; debts due, £76.11; made by Abrahem Flewellen and Daniel Hillman.

1756, Feb. 2. Smart, Nathan, of "Elsonburrow," Salem Co., yeoman; will of. Wife, Deborah. Children—Isaac, Mary Siddons and Hannah Humphries. Granddaughter, Catherine Smart. Real and personal estate, incl. six silver spoons and looking glass. Executors—the wife and son. Witnesses—Joshua Thompson, Aaron Bradway and John Firth. Proved May 13, 1757. Lib. 8, p. 452.
1757, Oct. 4. Inventory, £385.10.8, incl. 2 Bibles, 2 journals, "Sewil's History" some old books and some lawbooks, etc., 11.8, a map of the Province;—, a silver tankard and case; knives and forks; the time of 2 servants, £8; bills, bonds and book debts, £28.10.2; made by Aaron Bradway and H. Stubbines.

CALENDAR OF WILLS—1751-1760   297

1760, May 24. Smith, Abijah, of Shrewsbury, Monmouth Co., yeoman; will of. Wife, Mary. Four children, of whom only John and Jesse are named all under age. Real and personal estate. Executors—the wife, Amos White and Benjamin Woolley, Jr. Witnesses—Joel White, Joshua Boude and Esebel Maccoy. Proved July 1, 1760, and again March 3, 1761. Lib. H, p. 497.
1760, July 2. Inventory, £428.5., incl. apparel, bills, bonds, book debts and cash, £269.3.6; made by James Woolley and Jacob Brewer.

1755, Aug. 13. Smith, Able, of Bergen Township, Bergen Co., farmer; will of. Wife [not named]. Sons—Daniel, Job, James, Able. Daughters—Elezebeth Flewerding (?), Sarah Hockings, Dabrow (Deborah) Hitfield, and Mary, dec'd, who left son Able. Real and personal estate. Executors—sons James, Able and Job. Witnesses—Nathaniel Whitaker, Job Prance and Dennes Donham. Proved Sept. 19, 1755. Lib. F, p. 282.

1751, Dec. 17. Smith, Alexander, of Cumberland Co., yeoman; will of. Wife, Ruth, "who was called Ruth Foster and whose maiden name was Ruth Dark." Sons—Nathan, Alexander and John, the last two under age. Executors—the wife and Samuel Harris. Witnesses—Jeremiah Bacon, Elinor Smith, John Bee. Proved May 19, 1758.
Lib. 9, p. 33.
1758, June 23. Inventory, £83.4.1, by David Padgett and Andrew Miller.

1760, June 24. Smith, Ashbury, of Greenwich Township, Cumberland Co. Int. Inventory, £211.17.6, incl. the library, £4.9.9; a negro woman, £12; made by Jonathan Stathem and Thomas Ewing.
1760, June 30. Bond of his widow, Lydia Smith, as Adm'x; Jonathan Stathem, of said Township, fellowbondsman. Lib. 10, p. 176.
1763, July 23. Account by Lydia Smith, Adm'x.

1747, Mar. 31. Smith, Benjamin, of Trenton, Hunterdon Co.; will of. Wife, Sarah. Brothers—Daniel and Robert Smith. Brother-in-law, James Burling. Sister, Katherine Kallender. Mills and 50 acres of land in Amwell; 7 acres next to Emanuel Corrials (Corriel); 10 ac. bought of John Winder; farm in Trenton, bought of James Gould; lots with stonehouse in Trenton, fronting on King and Queen Street, bought of James Trent; lot on King Street, bought of William Plasket; 500 acres in Hanover Township, bought of Thomas Saint; 170 ac. in "Aimwell," bought of Thomas Stevenson; lot on King Street, Trenton, near the Stone Bridge. Personal property, incl. a negro girl. Executors—brother Robert Smith of Burlington and James Burling, of New York. Witnesses—Samuel Tucker, Jr., John Jenkins, Gideon Bickerdike, Wm. Morris, jun. Proved December 31, 1755. Lib. 8, p. 232.

1754, Apr. 19. Smith, Catharine, of Greenwich Township, Gloucester Co., widow. Int. Bond of Alexander Randall as Adm'r; Jonathan Fowller (Fowler) fellowbondsman, both of said Township.
1754, ———. Inventory, £62.17.4, incl. book debts, £41.1.5; made by George Flaningam and Benjamin Lodge. Glou. Wills, 557 H.
1755, Oct. 11. Account by the Administrator.

1760, Feb. 15. Smith, Daniel, of Newtown Township, Gloucester Co. Int. Inventory, £192.15.7, incl. book debts, £29.19.7; a looking glass; rents paid by Thomas Gill and Benjamin Thackry, £57.10; made by James Sloan and Isaac Mickle.

1760, Feb. 16. Bond of Aaron Smith as Adm'r; Thomas Wetherill fellowbondsman, both of Burlington Co. Lib. 9, p. 394.

1756, July 1. Smith, Ebenezer, of Newark, Essex Co. Int. Adm'x—Jane Smith, the widow, of Newark. Bondsmen—Joseph Smith and William Crane, of said town. Witness—Uzal Ogden.

1756, July 5. Inventory, £89.16.7, by Samuel Freman, Jr., and Jedidiah Freeman. Lib. F, p. 404.

1754, Dec. 26. Smith, Elisha, of Great Egg Harbour, Gloucester Co.; will of. Wife, Zeruiah. Children—Jonathan, David (both under age), Elisha, Elijah, Elias, Sarah, Rachel, Joshua and Priscilla. Real and personal estate. Executors—the wife and sons Elisha and Elijah. Witnesses—David Scull, Francis Holder, John Town, Jr. Proved May 25, 1755. Lib. 8, p. 177.

1755, May 8. Inventory: Real—sawmill on the river; meadow on Chandler Run; 10 acres of land, £25; 50 ac. of swamp, £25; 25 ac. of cedarswamp, £12.10; 100 ac. of land at landing, £15; a tract of 50 ac, £2; homefarm of 216 ac., £200. Personal, £216., incl. bills, bonds and cash, £81.13.11; made by James Somers and George May.

1757, Sept. 17. Smith, Hannah, of "Manninton," Salem Co., widow; will of. Children—Pile, Hannah Carpenter (who has sons Samuel and William Carpenter), and Elisabeth Sharp, who has daughter Hannah. Farm in Piles Grove, now occupied by Sparks; 128 acres in "Manninton" Township, formerly William Johnson's, adjoining Racheal Huddy; house and lot, now occupied by Jane Jones, adjoining Edward Test; 50 ac. inherited from daughter, Mary Anne; lot in Salem Town, formerly belonging to William Griffin and wife Sarah. Personal property, incl. 3 negroes; a silver mug, marked "H. H.;" a silver spoon, marked "W. H." Executors—sons-in-law, Isaac Sharp and Preston Carpenter. Witnesses—John Walker, Bartholomew Wyate, Jr., and William Walker. Proved July 29, 1758.
Lib. 9, p. 109.

1758, July 24. Inventory, £943.14, incl. bills, bonds and accounts, £714.11; two negroes and a white girl's time, £65; books; made by Josiah Kay and Robert Johnson.

1759, Mar. 26. Smith, Henry, Sr., of the Borough of Elizabeth Town, Essex Co.; will of. Wife, Sarah. Children—Henry (cut off with £1 from sharing in real and personal estate), Mary, Sarah Hoel and Hannah Meeker. Grandson, William, son of son Henry. Executors—son (-in-law?) Isaac Meeker and James Carpenter. Witnesses—John Ogden, John Jewel, Nicholas Baker. Proved June 16, 1759.
Lib. G, p. 78.

1759, Apr. 20. Inventory, £136.10.0 by Daniel Thompson and John Ogden.

1752, Aug. 17. Smith, Hugh, of Philadelphia, boat builder. Int. Bond of widow, Johanna, of Philadelphia as Adm'x; Joseph Bun, Sr., and John Woolman, both of Northampton, Burlington Co., yeomen, fellowbondsmen. Lib. 7, p. 304.

1751, Oct. 5. Smith, Ichabod, carpenter, of Woodbridge, Middlesex Co.; will of. Mother [not named]. Brothers—Leggit Smith and

Benjamin Smith and sister, Mary Comton, heirs of personal estate, with legacy to John Pierson, minister at Woodbridge. Executors—Jonathan Dennis and David Dunham. Witnesses—Norris Thorp, Thomas Kinnan, Edward Griffin. Proved Nov. 4, 1751. Lib. F, p. 4.

    1751, Nov. 4. The Executors, named in the will, refuse to act.

    1751, Nov. 4. Bond of Legget Smith, brother of Ichabod, as Adm'r, with the will annexed; William Compton fellowbondsman, both of Freehold, Monmouth Co.

    1752, Jan. 9. Inventory, £57.8.9, incl. a black "wigg," 10s.; a Bible and Psalm book, £1.5; a negro boy, about 6 years old, £20; made by Peter Savery and Thomas Kinnan. The executor, Legget Smith, adds two bonds of David Perkins for £48, and a few other things, not appraised.

1755, Aug. 30. Smith, Isaac, of Cohansey Bridge, Deerfield Township, Cumberland Co. Int. Bond of Phebe, widow, as Adm'x; Seth Brooks, of said Co., fellowbondsman. Lib. 8, p. 231.

    1755, Oct. 11. Inventory, £86.4, incl. books and a looking glass; made by Daniel Ogden and Robert Livingston.

1754, Sept. 11. Smith, Jasper, Jr., of Hunterdon Co. Int. Bond of Kezia Smith and Waters Smith as Adm'rs; Thomas Stevens fellowbondsman, all three of Maidenhead. Lib. 7, p. 64.

    1754, Oct. 8. Inventory, £407.18.6, incl. a looking glass, silver spoons, a negro girl and other small things, £44.4; bills and bonds, £158.12.6; made by Henry Mershon and John Vancleave.

1751, Jan. 10. Smith, John, of Hunterdon Co.; will of (made on board the schooner "Charming Polly," at sea, lat. 28°40′ N.). Second sister's children—Jacob, John and Lydia Moreland, to inherit estate both by sea and land, paying a legacy of £10. to oldest brother, Joseph Smith, who is to be placed in the care of Peter Pain and Nathaniel Moore, both of Hopewell, the Executors. Personal estate in Newport, R. I.; half of said schooner; half of the sloop "Mulbery"; bonds and bills at Joseph Hammond's in Newport; a negro boy and girl at Peter Pain's. Witnesses—William Gibbs, Anthony James. Proved at Newport, June 1, 1752. [Note by Theo. Severns: "Both the Ex'rs are dead"]. Hunt. Wills, 324 J.

1752, Sept. 15. Smith, John, of Cape May Co., yeoman; will of. Children—Carman, Uriah, Elihu, John and Judith Chesnut. Home farm on Gravely Run Creek; land back of it; a cedar swamp. Personal estate, incl. a great Bible. Executors—sons Carman and Uriah. Witnesses—Shamgar Hand, Joseph Hewit, Nathaniel Jenkins, Jr. Proved Nov. 15, 1752. Cape May Wills, 161 E.

    1752, Nov. 14. Inventory, £185.12.1, by Nathaniel Jenkins, Jr., and Jeremiah Hand.

1757, Nov. 16. Smith, John, formerly of Woodbridge, but late of Hunterdon Co. Int. Ellanor, widow, refuses the administration in favor of their son, Jabez Smith.

    1757, Nov. 18. Bond of Jabez Smith, of Somerset Co., as Adm'r; Timothy Bloomfield, Jr., of Middlesex Co., yeoman, fellowbondsman. Hunt. Wills, 422 J.

1758, Feb. 20. Smith, John, son of Ebenezer Smith of Greenwich, Cumberland Co. Bond of Samuel Fithian of Hopewell as Guardian; Ebenezer Miller, of Greenwich, fellowbondsman. Cumb. Wills, 161 F.

1760, Feb. 13. Smith, John, of Eggharbour, Gloucester Co. Int. Inventory, £134.10; incl. Barclay's "Appolligy," and other books 5s.; bonds and book debts, £47.18.9; a negro woman, £20; made by Henry Woodward and Japhet Leeds.
1760, Apr. 12. Bond of Noah Smith, son, as Adm'r; Henry Woodward fellowbondsman, both of said place.
1765, Mar. 25. Account by Administrator.
Lib. 9, p. 415.

1760, Feb. 21. Smith, John, of the Town of Bridgetown or Northampton, Burlington Co., blacksmith. Int. Bond of Nathaniel Smith as Adm'r; John Forker (Forqueher), fellowbondsman, both of Bridgetown, Burlington Co.
Lib. 9, p. 397.

1760, Nov. 29. Smith, John, of Bethleham, Hunterdon Co. Int. Bond of Rachel Smith as Adm'x; Barefoot Brunson fellowbondsman, both of said Co.
Lib. 10, p. 461.

1752, Aug. 10. Smith, Jonathan, Bond of Joseph Smith of Monmouth Co., as Guardian, Peter Wilson of the same Co. fellowbondsman.
Mon. Wills, 911 M.

1744, May 27. Smith, Joseph, of Manington Precinct, Salem Co.; will of. Wife, Sarah, sole Executrix. Children—Thomas, Elisabeth, Phebe and Susnah. Personal estate. Witnesses—Robert Raines, William Nicholson and William Barratt. Proved June 8, 1758.
Lib. 9, p. 102.
1758, May 30. Inventory, £109.3.10, by Daniel Huddy and Samuel Mason.
1760, June 19. Bond of Job Smith, of Allaways Creek, Salem Co., as Adm'r with the will annexed, the Executrix, Sarah Smith, having died intestate; Joseph Fogg, of Allaways Creek, and Peter Brynbery, of Pen's Neck, blacksmith, fellowbondsmen.
Lib. 11, p. 3.

1753, Feb. 27. Smith, Joseph, of Somerset Co. Int. Bond of widow, Elizabeth, of Somerset Co., and Jeremiah Smith, of Hopewell, Hunterdon Co., farmer, as Adm'rs; Smith Cornell, of Hopewell, fellowbondsman.
Lib. 7, p. 419.

1758, Feb. 11. Smith, Joshua, of Burlington Co., cooper. Int. Bond of Thomas Smith, of Mansfield Township, Burlington Co., yeoman, as Adm'r; John Buffin, of the same place, fellowbondsman.
Lib. 8, p. 519.
1759, Feb. 26. Account of the estate, £19.16.11, by the Administrator, who charges for bringing the corpse from Jonathan Thomas', and makes the estate his debtor for £1.9.10.

1753, Sept. 7. Smith, Lazarus, of Piles Grove, Salem Co. Int. Inventory, £165.1.6, by Thomas Mayhew and John Mayhew, Jr.
1753, Oct. 12. Bond of Mary Smith as Adm'x; John Mayhew, Jr., and Thomas Mayhew fellowbondsman, all of Piles Grove. Lib. 8, p. 91.
1753, Oct. 12. Inventory, £165.1.6.

1753, Sept. 8. Smith, Matthis, of Amwell Township, Hunterdon Co., yeoman; will of. Wife, Christeen. Children—John, Lowdawick, Mathis, Abraham, Jacob and Christeen, some of them under age. Real and personal estate. Executors—sons John, Lowdawick and

Mathis. Witnesses—Samuel Hill, Jacob Baum (signs in German script), Samuel Flaming (Fleming). Proved June 26, 1755.
Lib. 8, p. 225.
1755, June 4. Inventory: Real, being 214¼ acres of land, £588.13.9. Personal, £153.9.4. Made by William Peirson and John Wood.

1760, Aug. 28. Smith, Richard, of Long Island, N. Y. Int. Bond of Gilbert Smith as Adm'r; J. Smith fellowbondsman, both of Burlington Co. Lib. 10, p. 70.

1750, Mar. 31. Smith, Richard, Sr., of Burlington; will of. Sons—Richard, James, William and Jonathan. Daughter, Rachel Pole, who has children, viz., Anna, John, Edward and Richard Pole. Other grandchildren named are Anna, Elizabeth and Samuel Lovett Smith. Lot on High Street, Burlington, given by brother-in-law, James Marshall, dec'd, with dwelling and bolting house and other buildings (alley named between the bolting house and the barber shop); lots No. 1, 2, 3, 4, 5, 6 and 7, of meadows in Burlington; house and lot on High Street, bought of cousin, Joseph Smith, dec'd; smith shop on High Street, with lot, 26 feet front and rear, from the corner of the Meeting House stable South to the next street; homestead, i. e., house and lot bought of Joseph Scattergood, dec'd; two orchards, bought of Abraham Brown, Jr., and Benjamin Furnis; lot opposite; tract at the Mountain bought of James Beck, dec'd; lot over the Tan House Run, bought of cousin Joseph Smith, dec'd; orchard bought of Jacob Gamble; 6 acre lot of upland and meadow in Burlington, bought of John van Horn, late of New York, dec'd. Personal property, incl. a gold watch; gold buttons; books relating to physics and "chy surgery"; a case of instruments, mostly silver; mortgage, given by William Wright, of "Bethlem" Township; a large new Bible. Kinsmen, Richard Smith, Daniel Smith and Robert Smith appointed referees in case of dissensions among the heirs. Executors—son-in-law, John Pole, and the four sons. Witnesses—John Allen, William Lovett Smith, R. Hartshorne. Proved Jan. 5, 1751. Lib. 7, p. 117.

1754, Aug. 16. Smith, Richard, of Stoe Creek, Cumberland Co., blacksmith; will of. Wife, Mary. Children—William, Clark, Mary, Eleoner, Charity, Sarah, Elizabeth and Hannah. Real and personal estate. Executors—the wife and son, William. Witnesses—Joseph Feadall (?), James Jackson, Peter Long. Proved Sept. 16, 1754.
1754, ———— ——. Inventory, £446.7.3, incl. a clock, watch and other goods, £124.2.7; made by Richard Butcher and Peter Long.
Cumb. Wills, 106 F.

1760, June 12. Smith, Richard, of Newton, Gloucester Co., yeoman; will of. Wife, Hannah. Children—Richard, Daniel, James, John, Experience, Rachel, Judith and Hannah, all but the first two under age. Speaks of "five daughters," but names only four as above. Real and personal estate. Executors—the wife, son Richard and brother, Daniel Smith. Witnesses—Isaac Mickle, Joseph Coffey, J. Harrison. Proved June 24, 1760. Lib. 10, p. 82.
1760, June 26. Inventory, real and personal as sold at Cape May, £1523.16.9; made by Jacob Stokes and Isaac Mickle.

1750, Dec. 25. Smith, Richard, Jr., of Burlington, merchant; will of. Children—Samuel, John, William Lovett, Richard (under age),

Elizabeth. Grandchildren—Abigail, Joseph, James, Sarah, and Sarah Logan Smith. Annuity to Sarah Morris, to be paid as long as she remains unmarried. Homestead; meadows on the creek, bought of Thomas Hunloke, Henry Clothier, John Allen and Cornelus Clawson, where there is now a nursery; farm, called Red Hill; another house and lot; a store; lot and wharf; two pieces of "townbound" land; 50 acres bought from Isaac Williams and wife Mary, and from Ann Carlile; an orchard; 25 ac. on the Salem road, bought of Henry Clothier; 257 ac. on the South branch of Ancokas Creek, bounded E. by John Hiler, North by Henry Cooper, West by Abram Farington, who wants to buy it. Personal property, incl. two negro slaves; a large silver tankard, a silver teapot and chinaware. Executors—sons Samuel, John and William Lovet Smith. Witnesses—Joseph Noble, Joseph Clowes, Robert Smith. Proved Nov. 18, 1751. Burl. Wills 4875 C.

1759, May 18. Smith, Sarah, of Maninton Precinct, Salem Co. Int. Inventory, £79.7.4, by Joseph Fogg and John Thompson.

1759, May 21. Bond of Job Smith as Adm'r; Joseph Fogg, of Alloways Creek, and John Thompson, of Maninton, fellowbondsmen, all yeomen. Lib. 9, p. 352.

1754, Dec. 12. Smith, Sylvanus, of Great Egg Harbour, Gloucester Co. Int. Inventory, £132.17.1, incl. a servant boy, £11; 2 books, 3s.; 20 bushels of "Endgen" corn @ ¼, £1.6.8; book accounts and notes, £18.16.5; made by Henry Woodward and Nehemiah Leeds.

1754, Dec. 17. Bond of Evi Smith as Adm'x; Nehemiah Leeds fellowbondsman. Lib. 8, p. 66.

1755, Dec. 20. Account by the Administrator who makes the estate his debtor for £6.14.10.

1754, Nov. 12. Smith, Thomas, of Greenwich, Gloucester Co. Int. Adm'r—Alexander Randall. Bondsman—Michael Fisher.

1755, Mar. 22. Inventory, £20.19.3, all being due on bonds, book accounts and notes; made by Benjamin Lodge and George Flaningan.

1755, Oct. 11. Account by the Administrator. Glouc. Wills, 559 H.

1756, Feb. 23. Smith, Tunis, of Perth Amboy Corporation and of Monmouth Co. Int. Inventory, £21.16.3, incl. 11 books, 5s.6d.; made by Hendrick Hendrickson and Ephraim Donham.

1756, May 3. Bond of Margaret Smith and Daniel Morgan as Adm'rs; Samuel Ellison fellowbondsman, all of Perth Amboy.
Lib. F, p. 344.

1757, June. List of debts paid for the estate, £39.5.10., by the administrators, who report having sold it for £40.9.8.

1759, Apr. 12. Smith, William, of Stow Creek Township, Cumberland Co. Int. Inventory, £144.15.8, by Ananias Sayre and Samuel Fithian.

1759, Apr. 14. Bond of his widow, Sarah, as Adm'x; Samuel Fithian, of Hopewell, said Co., fellowbondsman. Lib. 9, p. 211.

1756, Jan. 12. Smith, William, Jr., of Cape May Co. Int. Inventory, £22.8.5, by John Leonard and Jeremiah Hand.

1756, May 20. Bond of widow, Phebe, of Cape May Co., as Administratrix. Lib. 8, p. 307.

CALENDAR OF WILLS—1751-1760   303

1746, Nov. 29. Smock, Hendrick, of Piscataway, Middlesex Co., farmer; will of. Wife, Antie, sole Executrix. Children—Hendrick, Elizabeth Denys, Ann; all, except Elizabeth, under age. Homefarm; farm of 131 acres at Bound Brook; 40 ac. of woodland; 2¾ ac. of meadow; all in said Co. Personal property, incl. a negro girl. Witnesses—George Anderson, William Williamson, Peter Leboyteuix. Proved August 29, 1754.   Lib. F, p. 210.

1754, Sept. 24. Smock, Johannis, of Middletown, Monmouth Co., yeoman; will of. Wife, Catherine. Children—Barnes, Ann (wife of John Teunison), Morritey (wife of Cornelius van de Vear). Grandchildren—Johannis, Garrat, Barnes, Nelly and Catherine, children of dec'd son Hendrick. Real and personal estate. Executors—son, Barnes, sons-in-law, John Teunisson and Cornelius van de Vear, and grandson, Johannis Smock. Witnesses—Benjaman van Mater, Joseph van Mater and Edward Taylor. Proved Jan. 24, 1755.   Lib. F, p. 245.

1754, Dec. 18. Inventory, £1079.13.5, incl. bills, bonds and book debts, £374.18.8; books, 20s.; a silver tankard, £12; table cloths, etc., £32.3; 10 negroes (one a child), £285; made by Benjaman and Joseph van Mater.

1760, Mar. 1. Smock, John, of the Eastern Precinct of Somerset Co.; will of. Wife, Leah. Children—Tice, Charles, John, Ryneir, Jacob, Abraham, Lena (wife of Powel Powelson), Elizabeth, Maria, Leah, Ghartie, Catharine and Jane. Real and personal estate. Executors—the wife, son Tice and Jacob van Tine. Witnesses—Abraham van Buren, W. Thomson and Samuel Brewer. Proved April 29, 1760.   Lib. G, p. 179.

1755, April 30. Smock, Sarah, of Somerset Co. Int. "Sarah Smock, of Somerset, died leaving considerable personal estate, and left one son, John Smock, and one daughter, Sietie Boyce. The said John has sold part and is in possession of the remainder of said estate, claiming the whole, and refuses to administer, and I have advised Sietie Boyce and her husband to apply for letters." Signed, David Ogden.

1755, May 2. Adm'rs—George Boyce and Sytie, his wife, late Sytie Smock, daughter of said Sarah Smock, of Piscataway. Bondsman—Jacob Boyce, of same.   Lib. F, p. 260.

1751, Dec. 30. Smyth, Lawrence, Esq., of Perth Amboy, Middlesex Co. Int. Bond of Andrew Johnston, the principal creditor, as Adm'r; John Smyth fellowbondsman, both of Perth Amboy. (The widow, Margaret, renounced Dec. 2, 1748).   Lib. F, p. 13.

1754, Oct. 29. Sneyder (Snyder) Jacobus Peter, of Amwell, Hunterdon Co., Inventory, £150.14, incl. 2 Bibles and other books, £3.11; made by Francis Beson and Job Robins.

1755, Apr. 17. Bond of Elizabeth Snyder as Adm'x; William Snyder fellowbondsman, both of Amwell.   Lib. 8, p. 170.

1759, May 3. Sockquil (Sockwell), Lancit, of Fairfield Precinct, Cumberland Co.; will of. Wife, Eve. Children—Jonadab, (sole Executor), Lancit, Leah, Rachel, Eve, Elizabeth, Phebe, Experience and Patience. Homefarm; land of Enoch Shepherd; land and marsh on the Southside of the homestead and on Annekeys Creek, and the

road to John Bedent's marsh below John Bedent's on the Southside of Sow and Pigs Creek. Personal estate. Witnesses—Jonadab Shepherd, Enoch Shepherd, William Paullin, John Ogden. Proved June 8, 1759.
Lib. 9, p. 263.

1759, May 30. Inventory, £174.0.11, incl. books; made by William Paullin and David Shepherd.

1770, Apr. 23. Account by the Executor, Jonadab Sockwell.

1754, Nov. 19. Somers, Samuel, Jr., of Great Egg Harbour, Gloucester Co., yeoman; will of. Wife, Hannah, sole Executrix. Daughter, Martha (under age). Personal estate. Witnesses—John Badcock Mathew Garreson, Marget Brandref (Brandrath). Proved at Cape May February 1, 1755.
Lib. 8, 154.

1755, Feb. 1. Inventory, £252.3.2, incl. books, £1.5; a looking glass; bonds, book debts and notes, £134.17.4; made by Nicholas Stillwell and John Willets.

1752, Jan. 13. Sorter, Jacob, of Somerset Co. Int. Bond of Johannes Peter Sorter, of Somerset Co., yeoman, as Adm'r; William Skinner, Jr., of Perth Amboy, merchant, fellowbondsman.
Lib. F, p. 14.

1752, Jan. 6. A citation was issued to Johannes Sortor, son of Jacob Sorter, to show cause why he does not administer, and why letters should not be given to Jacob Vastbinder, who married a daughter of deceased.

1752, Jan. 28. Inventory £73.9.0 made by Geisbert Sutfin, Peter Berrien and Peter Nevius.

1748, May 6. South, Thomas, of New Brunswick Corporation, Middlesex Co., miller; will of. Wife, Dorothy. Sons—Joseph and Daniel. House and lot in Kingston; other real and personal property. Executors—the wife and son, Daniel. Witnesses—John Steel, William van Tibagh (Tilburgh) and John Dalley. Proved Sept. 16, 1757.
Lib. F, p. 447.

1755, Mar. 27. Southwick, Elizabeth, of Gloucester Co. Int. Bond of Maham (Mayham) Southwick as Adm'r; Johannes Huntzinger (signs in German script), fellowbondsman, both of Gloucester Township and County, yeomen.
Lib. 8, p. 150.

1759, July 2. Sparks, Elizabeth, of Gloucester Township and Co., spinster; will of. Cousins—John (son of John Sharp of Burlington Co.), Elenoar Thomlinson, Elizabeth (wife of Aaron Lippincott of Burlington Co.), Margaret (daughter of Thomas Boucher of the same Co.), and Lydia and Isaac Thomlinson, children of Mary, uncle (father's brother), William Sharp and his son, Hugh. Executor—cousin, Isaac Thomlinson. Witnesses—Daniel Tomlinson, Benjamin Davis, Michaell Fisher. Proved June 17, 1760.
Lib. 10, p. 84.

1760, June 16. Inventory, £425.18.8, incl. bonds, £373.7.8; made by Michael Fisher and John Hillman.

1755, Sept. 23. Sparks, Elizabeth, of Wiccacoe, Philadelphia Co., widow of Henry; will of. Children—Isaac Barringer, Sarah Davis, Margaret Snowdon and Elizabeth Barringer. Real and personal estate. Executors—kinsman, Josiah Albertson, and William Wood, both of Gloucester Co. Witnesses—Joseph Bond, Francis Holton, Edward Teaw. Proved June 20, 1760.
Lib. 10, p. 104.

CALENDAR OF WILLS—1751-1760   305

1760, Apr. 24. The two Executors named in the will refuse to act, recommending Isaac Ballenger, the son of dec'd, as Administrator.

1760, June 9. Inventory, £100.8., incl. book debts, £59.5; made by Samuel Ladd and Jonas Cattell.

1760, June 20. Bond of Isaac Ballinger as Adm'r with the will annexed, William Snowden fellowbondsman, both of Deptford Township, Gloucester Co.

1748, July 27. Sparks, Henry, of the Town and County of Gloucester, innholder; will of. Sons—Robert, Henry and George (all under age), John and Simon. Legacies to "relation," Joanna Pearson, to children of daughter, Mary Sparks, and to son-in-law, John Sparks. Real and personal estate. Executors—sons, John and Simon, with John Parrock as overseer and quasi-guardian of sons Henry and George. Witnesses—William Edgerton, Thomas Sparks, Joseph Harrison. Proved March 19, 1756.   Lib. 8, p. 261.

1751, May 25. Spear, Hendrick, of "Horsneck," Essex Co., yeoman. Int. Adm'r—Tunis Spear, the eldest son, of Horsneck. Bondsman—Sanders Egbertson, of same place. Witness—Uzal Ogden.
Lib. E, p. 529.

1752, Apr. 24. Spence, Samuel, of Perth Amboy Corporation, yeoman; will of. Wife, Rachel. Nephew, Alexander Spence (apparently living abroad), principal heir of real and personal estate, which, if he does not claim it within four years, is to go, one-half to the Presbyterian Congregations of Monmouth Co. for the Presbyterian poor in Freehold, the other half to Rev. William Tennant. Executors—Joseph Ker, Matthew Rue, John Davison, blacksmith, and John Anderson. Witnesses—William Whitlock, John Wall and Elizabeth Anderson. Proved June 21, 1757.   Lib. F, p. 434.

1757, June 18. Inventory, £63.9.6, by Charles Hibbits, John Egbert and John Lloyd.

1759, Jan. 4. Spicer, Thomas, Sr., of Waterford, Gloucester Co.; will of. Wife, Abigail. Sons Jacob—Thomas and Samuel. Grandchildren—Abigail Rudderow, Jacob Spicer, Abigail (daughter of Samuel) and Thomas Spicer. Farm in Greenwich, said Co.; land and meadow in Waterford on Cooper's Creek, adjoining Abel Nicholson; land bought of Samuel Nicholson; two farms between Samuel Burrough, John or Joseph Osler, cousin Jacob Spicer and Richard Wood; land in Waterford Township; homefarm. Personal property. Executors—sons Jacob and Samuel, with kinsman, Jacob Spicer, of Cape May Co. Witnesses—William Hepard, Susanna Bradshaw, Charles Day. Proved Nov. 7, 1759.   Lib. 9, p. 308.

1759, Sept. 17, 18. Inventory, £1421.0.8, incl. his purse, £170.12.8; bills, bonds and book debts, £739.19.11; books, £6; a looking glass, £3; a clock, £8; 8 maps, 12s.; a negro man, £35; 2 negro boys, £20; 2 do. girls, £20; made by Henry Wood and Joseph Morgan.

1760, May 14. Spicer, Thomas, of Waterford Township, Gloucester Co., farmer; will of. Wife, Rebecca. Daughter, Abigail. Real and personal estate. Executors—the wife and Henry Wood. Witnesses—James Johnson, Samuel Osler, John Daniel. Proved Dec. 6, 1760.
Lib. 10, p. 386.

1760, Oct. 27. Inventory, £371.1.6, incl. purse and apparel, £277.18.6; plate, £1; a looking glass; made by William Stone and Samuel Osler.

1751, Nov. 14. Spoonemer, Johan Jerry, of Somerset Co. Int. Jacob Coll (Cobb?) and Robert Bolmer, sons-in-law desire that letters of administration be granted to Barnardus Lagrange.

1752, Jan. 22. Bond of Barnardus Lagrange, of Raritan Landing, as Adm'r; Courtland Skinner, of Perth Amboy, fellowbondsman.
Lib. F, p. 16.

1759, Feb. 3. Squire, Nathan, of Essex Co. Int. Adm'r—Joseph Riggs, Jr., of said Co. Bondsman—Thomas Dean, of same place. Witness—Uzal Ogden.

1759, Feb. 6. Inventory, £77.0.2, by Ebenezer Hedden and Ezekiel Johnson.
Lib. G, p. 40.

1756, Mar. 7. Stalkop, Catherine, of Pen's Neck, Salem Co., widow; will of. Daughters—Catherine (wife of Henry Gilljohnson) and Christian. Grandson, John Stalkop. Real and personal estate. Executors—the son-in-law and his wife. Witnesses—John Marshall, Jeremiah Baker, Oliver Webb, John Parke and William Edwards. No jurat, or proof. [Entered in 1756].

1756, June 18. Inventory, £14.13.5, incl. books; made by John Marshall and John Parke.
Salem Wills, 968 Q.

1752, June 22. Stallcop, Jonas, of Penn's Neck, Salem Co. Int. Inventory, £59.14, by Martin Skeer and Samuel Copner.
Lib. 8, p. 92.

1752, Aug. 3. Bond of Jane Stallcop as Adm'x; Timothy O'Conner fellowbondsman, both of Pen's Neck.

1754, Mar. 4. Stanly, Ownesiphorus, of Pen's Neck, Salem Co., yeoman; will of. Wife, Catherine. Son, Andrew Stanley, sole Executor, charged to pay a bond of £15 to John Thompson, when of age, given to said John's uncle Claud Johnson. Real and personal estate. Witnesses—John Marshall, Hance Lambson, Mathias Lambson. Proved March 20, 1754.
Lib. 8, p. 53.

1754, Mar. 16. Inventory, £121.19.6½, incl. 17 bush. of wheat @ 4s.5d., £3.15.1; made by John Marshall and Andrew Sinnickson.

1758, Oct. 25. Staples, Thomas, of Burlington City, yeoman; will of. Children—Mary (wife of Josiah Gaskill), Dorothy (wife of Joseph Pearson), Ann (wife of Thomas Rogers). Son-in-law (stepson?), John Tompson, who has children Thomas and Uriah. Grandchildren—Rachel Tompson, Rebecca Tompson, Elisabeth Tompson, Staples Tompson, Rebecca Hancock, Martha and Mehetable Staples, Mehetable and Mary Rogers. Personal estate, incl. a negro girl. Executors—John Antram and George Deacon. Witnesses—Joseph Antram, Elnathan Stevenson, Joseph King. Proved April 18, 1759.

1759, Apr. 18. Inventory, £353.0.11, incl. bonds, £288.16; a negro girl, £40; made by John Deacon and Joseph Antram.
Burl. Wills, 6455 C.

1755, May 7. Steelman, Haunce, of Greenwich, Gloucester Co., yeoman; will of. Wife, Alce. Sons—James, Haunce, Charles, John and Daniel. Real and personal estate. Executors—son, John, and Alex-

ander Randall. Witnesses—Charles Lock, Andrew Lock, Bridgett Dalbo. Proved Dec. 29, 1760. Lib. 10, p. 409.
1760, Dec. —. Inventory, £337.16.1, incl. ready cash, £55.0.10; a clock, £5; bonds, book debts and notes, £101.4.9; made by Thomas Thomson and Charles Lock.

1758, Apr. 20. Stelle, Benjamin, Sr., of Piscataway, Middlesex Co.; will of. "Present wife," Lydiah. Children—Benjamin, Isaac, Susanah Hull and Rachel Fitzrandolph. Children of dec'd. son John. Grandsons—Thomson Stelle and Lewis Stelle. Real and personal estate. Executors—sons Benjamin and Isaac, with Runey Runyon. Witnesses—James Pyatt, Boley Arnold and Thomas Pyatt. Proved Feb. 22, 1759. Lib. G, p. 31.

1754, Dec. 22. Stelle, John, of New Brunswick, Middlesex Co.; will of. Wife, Rachel. Children—Experience, Thomson, Lewis, Charity and Phebe. Homestead; salt meadows, bought of John Bodine and of heirs of John Parker; land in Piscataway. Personal property, (incl. part of the scow Betty and Rachel). Executors—the wife, father-in-law James Thomson, and brother Benjamin Stelle. Witnesses—William Ouke, George Coryell, Azariah Dunham. Proved Feb. 17, 1755. Lib. F, p. 254.

1758, Dec. 30. Stelle, Samuel, of Nottingham Township, Burlington Co.; will of. Wife, Rachel. Children—John, Elizabeth and Rachel, all under age. Real and personal estate. Executors—the wife and Joseph Chambers. Witnesses—Isaac Cubberley, Robert Chambers, Samuel Langstaff. Proved March 2, 1759. Lib. 9, p. 319.
1759, Feb. 29. Inventory, £38.6, by John Hammell, Jr., and Isaac Cubberley.

1759, May 5. Stellsts, Anthony, of Roxbury, Morris Co. Int. Inventory, £341.1.2, incl. a Bible, £2; other books, 8s.; a pair of show boots, 12s.; a looking glass, 1s.; a servant boy, £20; the improvement £50; made by William Larason and Jabesh Dell.
1759, May 29. Bond of Mary Stellsts as Adm'x; Antony Waldorff, farmer, fellowbondsman, both of "Rocksberry," Morris Co.
Lib. 9, p. 316.

1757, July 25. Stephens, Isaac, of Deptford Township, Gloucester Co., yeoman; will of. Wife, Rachel. Children—John, Isaac, James, Sarah and Rachel, all under age. Brothers—Robert and James Stephen. Cousin, Thomas Edgerton. House and lot in Willmington, owned in partnership with brother James; other real and personal property. Executors—the two brothers above named. Witnesses—William Wilkins, William Wilkins, Jr., Joseph Harrison. Proved August 10, 1757. Lib. 8, p. 439.
1757, Aug. 9 & 10. Inventory, £2021.9.1, incl. bills, bonds, book debts and cash, £1783.1.7; two silver spoons; a clock; a desk, £10; made by William Wilkins and Joseph Lord.

——, ——. Stephens, Robert, of Newtown, Gloucester Co., yeoman; will of. Wife, Mary. Daughters—Mary Redmond, Susanna and Elizabeth Lotton. Names also wife's son, James Kaighn; cousin, Thomas Edgerton, Jr.; Joseph Saul, of Philadelphia; brothers, Henry and James Stephens. Real and personal estate. Executor—brother,

James. Witnesses—Isaac Mickle, Jonathan Norton, James Sloan. Proved May 28, 1759. Lib. 9, p. 234.
 1759, June 8. Inventory, £496.19.7, by Isaac Mickle and James Sloan.
 1761, Mar. 4. Account of the estate by the Executor, who, by collection of debts and sale of real and personal property, had increased it to £1658.9.7.

 1759, July 23. Stetson, Joshua, of Great Egg Harbour, Gloucester Co. Int. Bond of James Somers, Jr., as Adm'r; George May fellowbondsman, both of said Co. Lib. 9, p. 347.
 1759, July 26. Inventory, £201.14.10, by Andrew Blackman and John Badcock.
 1759, Nov. 7. Account by the Administrator.

 1753, July 13. Stevens, Henry, of Dearfield, Cumberland Co., mariner; will of. Wife, Mary. Sons—Jonathan, Ezekiel (sole Executor), and Henry. Real and personal estate. Witnesses—Jeremiah Parvin, Jacob Shull, Zeruiah Fithan. Proved May 28, 1755.
Lib. 8, p. 187.
 1755, May 23. Inventory, £101.3, by Jeremiah Parvin and Archbald McColster.

 1748, Apr. 23. Steward, Josiah, of Upper Freehold, Monmouth Co.; yeoman; will of. Wife, Sarah. Children—Joseph, Martha, Sarah, Josiah and Abraham, the first three called under age; an expected child. Real and personal estate. Executors—brothers John and Joseph Steward. Witnesses—John Brown, Samuel Emley, Abraham Brown, Jr., Thomas Earl. Proved Jan. 2, 1752. Burl Wills, 5089 C.
 1751, Dec. 12. Inventory, £353.6.1, incl. bonds and book debts, £64.15.5; made by Samuel Emley and William Folwell.

 1760, Dec. 10. Stewart, John, of Bridgwater, Somerset Co. Inventory, £41.10.3, incl. 2 looking glasses, £2.10; made by Elias v. Court and Thomas Carhartt.

 1751, May 27. Stewart, Neill, of Salem, Salem Co., surgeon; will of. Divides estate between Curtis, son of George Trenchard, and Merriam Merrien, George Trenchard to be sole Executor. Witnesses—David Russell, Daniel Mestayer, Henry D. Mestayer. Proved June 3, 1751. Lib. 7, p. 541.

 1758, Apr. 28-29. Stewart, Doctor Patrick, of Cape May. Int. Inventory, £47.1.10, incl. apparel, cash, medicines, surgical instruments, etc., £19.2.1; debts £27.19.9; made by Jeremiah Hand and Jacob Spicer.
 1758, Oct. 2. Bond of William Smith as Adm'r; Jacob Spicer fellowbondsman, both of Cape May Co. Lib. 9, p. 313.
 1760, Nov. 13. Account by Adm'r, William Smith.

 1758, Oct. 30. Stewart, William, of Elizabeth, Essex Co., schoolmaster. Int. Adm'r—John Moores of Woodbridge, innkeeper, principal creditor. Bondsman—Samuel Beasly, of same place, cooper.
Lib. F, p. 560.

 1760, May 21. Stewart, William, of Bridgwater, Somerset Co.; will of. Wife, Priscilla. Children—all under age, names not given. Real

and personal estate. Executors—the wife, brother-in-law, John Lefferty, and John Degroot. Witnesses—Asa Kelly, William Kelly and Elias v. Court. Proved Dec. 29, 1760. Lib. G, p. 340.
1760, Dec. 10. Inventory, £41.10.3, by Elias v. Court and Thomas Carhart.

1758, Oct. 2. Stiles, Jonathan, of Pequanack, Morris Co., yeoman; will of. Children—Joseph, John, Jonathan, Ephraim, Thomas, Ebenezer, Hanah Smith, Rebecker Primrose and Stephen. Grandchildren—Rebecker Parret and Daniel Smith. Real and personal estate. Executors—son Jonathan and son-in-law, Henery Primrose. Witnesses—Joseph Wood and John Plume. Proved Nov. 30, 1758. Lib. G, p. 21.

1750, Nov. 16. Stilley, Morton, of Greenwich, Gloucester Co., yeoman; will of. Wife, Elinor. Children—John, Daniel, Jacob and Johanna, all under age. Real and personal estate, incl. two gold rings, silver buckles, silver spoon, a gold piece. Executors—Jacob Spicer and Zachariah Petterson, both of Greenwich Township. Witnesses—Jestah Homan, Lawrance Cemp, William Guest. Proved Oct. 9, 1752.
1752, Sept. 29. Inventory, £105.18.6, incl. books; made by Mathew Gill and Thomas Denny. Glou. Wills, 509 H.

1752, June 1. Stillwell, John, of Cape May Co.; will of. Son, Daniel, use of plantation, and, after his death, to his youngest son. Daughter, Patience Shaw, warming pan. Grandson, Nicholas Stillwell, £5. Grandchildren, John Evans, David Evans and Elizabeth Evans (now Skull), 20 shillings each. My children, Richard Stillwell, Daniel Stilwell and Patience Shaw rest of personal estate. Executors—sons Richard and Daniel. Witnesses—Susannah Hand, Isaiah Hand, John Leek. Proved May 9, 1753. Lib. 8, p. 180.

1760, Dec. 11. Stillwell, Joseph, Esq., of Middletown, Monmouth Co. Int. Bond of Sarah, widow, and John, son, as Adm'rs; Edward Taylor, of the same place, gent., fellowbondsman. Lib. G, p. 360.

1759, Dec. 20. Stillwell, Nicholas, of Shrewsbury Township, Monmouth Co., weaver; will of. Wife, Mary. Children—Obadiah, Martha, William, Mary, Rebecca, Lydia, Priscilla, Elias and Joseph, the last three under age. Real and personal estate. Executors—the wife and kinsman, Job Throckmorton, of Freehold. Witnesses—William Hankinson, Joseph Burdge and George Rhea. Proved March 19, 1760. Lib. G, p. 193.

1759, May 2. Stillwell, Richard, of Cape May Co., yeoman; will of. Wife, Mary. Children—Elijah, Elizabeth, Zerviah, Stites, Phebe. Grandson—John Foster. Real and personal estate, incl. a negro man. Executors—son Elijah and son-in-law, Richard Stites. Witnesses—Benjamin Laughton, David Bancraft, William Sinkins. Proved June 7, 1759. Lib. 9, p. 245.
1759, June 6. Inventory, £177.13.1, incl. a negro, £28; books, £2.9.2; made by Christopher Foster and John Leek.

1753, Nov. 2. Stillwell, Samuel, of Upper Freehold Township, Monmouth Co., yeoman; will of. Wife, Margaret. Son (not named), under age. Brothers, (of whom only Daniel is spoken of by name) and sisters remaindermen of real and personal estate. Executors—

Anthony Woodward and William Tapscott. Witnesses—John Brittin, Richard Loyd, John Lawrence. Proved Nov. 10, 1753.
Lib. 7, p. 370.
 1753, Nov. 12. Inventory, £373.15.11½, incl. a "Palitine" boy, £18; a negro wench and child, £40; a young negro wench, £40; made by Thomas Duglass and Joseph Groven.

 1753, Oct. 26. Stilwell, Thomas, of Kings Co., N. Y., yeoman. Int. Bond of Thomas Shreve (Shreeve) of New York City, carpenter, and Jeremiah Brower, of Kings Co., miller, as Adm'rs. Lib. G, p. 105.

 1754, Sept. 23. Stites, George, of Cape May Co., yeoman; will of. Wife, Esther. Sons—William, George, Thomas, Nathan, Adonijah and Daniel, all but the first two under age. Real and personal estate. Executors—the wife and son George. Witnesses—Mary Taylor, Jane Doubledee, Francis Taylor. Proved Sept. 27, 1754. Lib. 8, p. 67.
 1754, Oct. 15. Inventory, £168.7.5, by Christopher Foster and Joshua Shaw.

 1757, Jan. 17. Stockbridge, Moses, of Morris Town, Morris Co. Int. Reabeckah, widow, resigns her right of administering to Peter Condict, one of the largest creditors.
 1757, Jan. 18. Bond of Peter Condict, of Morris Co., as Adm'r; Edward Sale, of Essex Co., fellowbondsman. Lib. F, p. 433.
 1757, Jan. 28. Inventory, £9.17.7, by Peter Cundict, Adm'r.

 1759, June 2. Stockman, Abigail, of Newark, Essex Co. Int. Adm'r—Benjamin Freeman (father), of Newark. Bondsman—John Ogden, of same place. Witness—Lewis Ogden. Lib. G, p. 76.

 1756, Dec. 9. Stockman, John, of Essex Co. Int. Adm'x—Abigail Stockman, the widow. Bondsman—Benjamin Freeman, of said Co. Witnesses—Nathaniel Ogden and Uzal Ogden. Lib. F, p. 407.

 1758, May 9. Stockton, John, Esq., of Princeton, Somerset Co.; will of. Children—Richard, sole Executor and Guardian of John, Philipp, Samuel, Hannah, Abigail, Susannah and Rebecca; all but Richard under age. Land on the Northside of the road from Princeton to Maidenhead to be divided between son Richard and Robert Stockton. Homefarm on the Southside of said road; meadow on Stoney Brook; a farm now leased to Ruluff Bushart. Personal estate. Witnesses—Ame Stockton, Elias, Boudinot, Jr., and Joseph Reed, Jr. Proved June 9, 1758. Lib. 8, p. 539.

 1760, Feb. 15. Stockton, Joseph, Jr., of Princeton, Somerset Co.; will of. Brothers—Daniel, Doughty, Samuel and John, all under age; their respective shares of the real and personal estate to be kept by parents, Joseph and Elizabeth Stockton, who are also named Executors. Witnesses—Mary Stockton, Sarah Pitcock and Onrey Gaffin (Gaphin). Proved April 12, 1760. Lib. 10, p. 455.

 1756, June 28. Stockton, Richard, son of Joseph, of Burlington Co., petitions that Vincent Leeds be appointed his Guardian.
 1756, June 29. Bond of Vincent Leeds as such Guardian; William Stockton fellowbondsman, both of said Co. Burl. Wills, 5775 C.

CALENDAR OF WILLS—1751-1760   311

1760, Mar. 19. Stockton, Richard, of Windsor Township, Middlesex Co. Will of. Only son, John. Grandson, Samuel Scott. Nephew, Jacob, son of Samuel Stockton. Daughter, Ruth Scott. Son (in-law?), John Scott. Land in Hopewell and Amwell; farm, now tenanted by William Porter. Personal property. Executors—nephew, Samuel Stockton, and Lewis Charles Faneuil. Witnesses—Arthur Keeffe, Samuel Tatum and Jemime Knox. Proved April 4, 1760.
Liber. 10, p. 458.

1750, Sept. 23. Stokes, Elizabeth, widow of John Stokes, of Willingbrough Township, Burlington Co.; will of. Children—John Stokes (sole Executor), Mary Mullin, Sarah Biddle. Grandchildren—Elizabeth Blackham, William Blackham, Elisabeth Mullins, Isaac, Rebecca and John Rogers, children of Sarah Biddle; Edward Mullin, Sally and and Patty Mullin, Mary and John Stokes. Sister, Jane Green. Personal estate. Witnesses—Joseph Green, James Gaskill, Gabriel Blond. Proved July 20, 1751.
1751, July 20. Inventory £146.10.6, incl. bonds of Joseph Biddle and Edward Mullin, £112.14.6; made by Thomas and John Buzby.
Burl. Wills, 4085 C.

1753, Oct. 24. Stokes, John, of Waterford, Gloucester Co. Int. Bond of widow, Ann Stokes, of Waterford, as Adm'x; John Cox, of Chester township, Burlington Co., innholder, fellowbondsman.
Lib. 7, p. 423.
1753, Oct. 17. Inventory, £296.3, by Josiah Shivers and Aaron Aronson.

1757, Dec. 28. Stokes, Joseph, Sr., of Chester, Burlington Co., "advanced in age"; will of. Wife, Anne. Children—Mary, Elisabeth (under age), Samuel, Joseph, John (under age), Hannah Gosling, Martha Allin, Rebecca Roberts, Judith (wife of William Allin), and Bersheba Evins. Grandchildren—John Coles and Joseph Coles. Homefarm and other land in Chester Township; farm at Cocxing, Evesham Township. Personal estate. Executors—the wife and son-in-law, Joshua Roberts; they also made Guardians of the two minor children. Witnesses—Joshua Raper, Samuel Allinson, Gabriel Blond. Proved June 28, 1759.
1759, June 18. Inventory of the personal estate, £1241.6.11, incl. bills, bonds and notes, £807.1.8; 2 looking glasses at £2; a small do. 7s.6d.; a black walnut desk, £8; 6 silver spoons, £6. Additional inventory, made June 27, £71.2, incl. the "History of Josephus, 45s.; a large Bible, 35s.; both made by Samuel Coles, Joshua Ballinger and Enoch Roberts.
1768, Jan. 15. Account of the estate by Anna Stokes, acting Executrix, who reports on hand £147.18.1.
Burl. Wills, 6467 C.

1756, Nov. 15. Stone, Joshua, of Woodbridge; will of. Wife, Rhoda. Son, Jeremiah. Real and personal estate. Executors—the wife and Benjamin Thorp. Witnesses—Samuel Jaquess, John Moore and Mary Alston. Proved Sept. 1, 1757.
Lib. F, p. 445.
1757, Sept. 5. Inventory, £69.15.6, by John Carlile and John Blancher.

1760, Jan. 24. Stone, Robert, of Woodbridge, Middlesex Co. Int. Adm'r—William Stone (father), of Woodbridge. Bondsman—Samuel Sarjant, of Perth Amboy. Witness—Thomas Bartow. Lib. G, p. 123.

1760, Jan. 30. Inventory, £472.1.4, incl. a Bible and other books, 10s.; a large looking glass, 110s.; gold buttons, 38s.; silverspoons, £4; silver buckles and thimble, 28s.; a negro wench, £60; made by Jonathan Frazee and Daniel Moores.

1758, Mar. 21. Stoothoff, Albert, (Elbert), Jr., of Somerset Co. Int. Bond of Abraham Low, husband of Ida, late widow of Albert, as Adm'r; Cornelius Low fellowbondsman, both of said Co., yeomen.
Lib. F, p. 517.

1753, —— ——. Inventory, £223.3.8, incl. a coffee mill, 5s.; a negro man, £60; a negro wench, £53, and 2 negro children, £10; made by Peter Bekman (Beekman), Martin Beekman. (Filed Mar. 21, 1758).

1756, Sept. 7. Stoothoff, Elbert, of Somerset Co., yeoman; will of. Children—William, John, Johanna (wife of Abraham, Hoogland), Cornelia (wife of John Hoogland), Adrjana (wife of Peter Dimon) and Abraham. Grandchildren—Margaret, Johanna and Sarah (daughters of eldest son Garret, dec'd.), Albert Stotehoff and his sister, Anatje. Homefarm of 330 acres; 61 acres in Middlesex Co., on the road from New Brunswick to Rocky hill, bought of John Parker. Executor of John Harrison; 150 ac. on the South branch of Raritan River in Somerset Co., conveyed to testator by Harmanus Hoogland, May 12, 1739. Personal estate. Executors—sons William and John, and son-in-law, Abraham Hoogland. Witnesses—Cornelius Stoothoff, Henry Cortelyou and Petrus Nevius. Proved Nov. 18, 1756. Lib. F, p. 388.

1756, Nov. 20. Inventory, £778.13.11, incl. bonds and cash, £265.1.6; a silver cup and 3 spoons, £10; 4 negroes, £220; made by Cornelius Stoothoff and Henry Cortelyou.

1750, Sept. 3. Story, William, of New Brunswick, Middlesex Co., yeoman; will of. Children—Thomas, John, Joseph, Elisabeth (wife of Stephen Ketcham), Mary (wife of Samuel Bayles) and Hannah (wife of Joseph Wilson). Real and personal estate. Executors—sons Thomas and John, with son-in-law, Joseph Wilson. Witnesses—Richeard Sparks, Walter Wall and Stephen Warne. Proved Oct. 13, 1760.
Lib. G, p. 306.

1754, Aug. 8. Stout, James, of Hunterdon Co. Int. Bond of Jemima Stout as Adm'x; Timothy Titus fellowbondsman, both of Hopewell, Hunterdon Co. Lib. 7, p. 63.

1755, Dec. 18. Account by the Administratrix.

1760, Jan. 31. Stout, Jeams, of "Srosbery" Township, Monmouth Co.; will of. Children—John (sole Executor), Mary Potter and Enelephe. Grandchildren—John Stout, Daniel Stout and Jeams Wells. Real and personal estate. Witnesses—John Potter, Jeams Wels and Jacob Baker. Proved March 28, 1760. Lib. G, p. 215.

1760, Mar. 6. Inventory, £100.15.9, by Jacob Applegate and John Tillton.

1758, Jan. 14. Stout, John, of Middletown, Monmouth Co., boatman. Int. Bond of Samuel Tilton principal creditor, as Adm'r; William Compton fellowbondsman, both of Middletown, yeomen.
Lib. F, p. 485.

CALENDAR OF WILLS—1751-1760   313

1758, Jan. 17. Inventory, £17.8.6, incl. 2 Bibles and 2 books, 6s.9d.; a silver buckle, 2s.; made by Samuel Carman, Cornelius Compton, Samuel Legg and Samuel Tilton.

1760, May 14. Stout, Joseph, of Amwell, Hunterdon Co.; will of. Wife, Marey. Sons—Eliiah, Beniaiah and apparently others, all under age. Real and personal estate. Executors—the wife and brother, John Stout. Witnesses—Joseph Higgins, James Young and John Ringo. Proved July 4, 1760. Lib. 10, p. 552.
1760, June 17. Inventory, £618.15.7, incl. bonds, £476.7.9; made by Joseph Higgins, Sr., and Joseph Higgins, Jr.

1753, June 3. Stout, Samuel, of Somerset Co., blacksmith. Int. Bond of widow, Sarah, as Adm'x; Arte Sutven (Arthur Sutphen), fellowbondsman, both of said Co. Lib. 8, p. 14.
1753, June 27. Inventory, £81.16.4, incl. 35 lbs. of German steel, 15s.; 64 lbs. of Bristol do., £1; made by Arte Sutven, Joseph Newton and Zebulon Stout.

1759, Nov. 15. Stouten, Edward, of Amboy; nuncupative will of. Leaves all to his wife, giving his brother, Joseph Stouten, a legacy. Proved by the testimony of James Brooks, who wrote the will, Jean Brea and Thomas Inglis, Dec. 24, 1759, when Elizabeth Stouten, widow of dec'd, is granted administration. Lib. G, p. 113.

1755, Aug. 1. Stow, John, of Salem Town and Co. Int. Bond of William Hall as Adm'r; Edward Test fellowbondsman, both of said Co. Lib. 8, p. 302.
1755, Aug. 2. Inventory, "excepting such part as was before distrained for rent by William Siddons," £11.19, incl. books, 7s.6d.; made by John Firth and Josiah Kay.

1751, July 13. Stratton, Benjamin, of Cohansey, Cumberland Co., yeoman; will of. Wife, Abigail. Children—Abigail Harris, Jonathan, Benjamin, Preston, Freelove, Thomazine, Elizabeth, Levi and John, the last six under age. Real and personal estate. Executors—sons Jonathan and Benjamin. Witnesses—Richard Powell, Silvanus Shepherd, Jonathan Lorance. Proved Sept. 18, 1751. Lib. 7, p. 137.
1751, Sept. 17. Inventory, £405.16.1, by Thomas Harris and David Wescote.

1759, Feb. 9. Stratton, Benjamin, of "Poilsgrove" Township, Salem Co.; will of. Wife, Sarah, sole Executrix. Sons—Benjamin and James. Real and personal estate. Witnesses—Henry Brooks, Jonathan Smith and Peter Austen. Proved June 6, 1759. Lib. 9, p. 367.
1759, Apr. 25. Inventory, £359.13.5, incl. bills, book debts and cash, £102.6.17; books and "sundreys," £6.11; a "Servent made," £8; made by Joseph van Meter and Samuel Sherry.

1753, —— ——. Stratton, Hezekiah, son of Isaac, of Deerfield Township, Cumberland Co., petitions that Charles Clarke, of said township, tailor, be appointed his Guardian.
1753, Sept. 4. Bond of Charles Clark as such Guardian; Jeremiah Buck, of Fairfield Township, yeoman, fellowbondsman.
Cumb. Wills, 90 F.

1752, Dec. 15. Stratton, Isaac, of Deerfield, Cumberland Co. Int. Inventory, £109.18.3, by Charles Clark and Robert Dare.
1753, Jan. 5. Bond of widow, Mary, as Adm'x; Charles Clark, tailor, fellowbondsman, both of Deerfield Township. Cumb. Wills, 91 F.

1759, Mar. 16. Stratton, Jonathan, of Fairfield, Cumberland Co. Int. Inventory, £236.3.10, incl. a servant boy, £15; books; bills, bonds and book debts, £65.13.3; made by Jonathan Lorance (Lawrence) and Joseph Ogden.
1759, Mar. 26. Bond of his widow, Cathrine Stratton, as Adm'x; Jonathan Lorance and Henry Sparks, both of Fairfield, fellowbondsmen. Lib. 9, p. 211.
1762, Jan. 6. Account by the Administratrix.

1760, Jan. 5. Stratton, Levi, son of Benjamin, of Fairfield, Cumberland Co., petitions that Joseph Daiton be appointed his Guardian.
1760, Jan. 5. Bond of Joseph Daten (Dayton) as such Guardian; Henry Pearson and Zadok Thompson fellowbondsmen, all of Fairfield. Cumb. Wills, 233 F.

1755, June 19. Stratton, Mark, of Evesham, Burlington Co., yeoman; will of. Wife, Ann. Children—David (sole Executor), Daniel, John, Isaac, Enoch, Ruth (wife of Thomas Shinn), Ann (wife of Hugh Sharp), Elizabeth (wife of William Berry) and Jane (wife of Joshua Norcross). Real and personal estate. Witnesses—William Garwood, John Prickitt, John Burr, Jr. Codicil of October 14, 1756, directs, how the bequests to daughters should go in case of daughters' death. Same witnesses. Proved April 8, 1759. Lib. 9, p. 202.
1759, Apr. 6. Inventory, £37.3, by James Allen and Francis Austin.

1759, July 30. Stratton, William, of Deerfield, Cumberland Co., yeoman; will of. Wife, Phebe. Children—William, Jonathan, Sarah Parvin, Phebe Woodruff, Fithian Ephraim and Aaron. Wife's daughter, Hannah Royal. Real and personal estate. Executors—sons, Jonathan and Fithian. Witnesses—Noah Harris, Samuel Ogden, Charles Clark. Proved Sept. 22, 1759. Lib. 10, p. 49.
1759, Aug. 24. Inventory, £332.2.6, by Charles Clark and Noah Davis.
1761, Feb. 4. Account by the Executors.

1759, Feb. 10. Street, Nathaniel, of Alloways Creek, Salem Co.; will of. Wife, Lydia. Children—William, Edward, Aaron (all three under age), Elizabeth and Mary. Real and personal estate. Executors—the wife and son William. Witnesses—William Wadington, Jess Carll and William Stretch. Proved Feb. 21, 1759. Lib. 9, p. 362.
1759, Feb. 17. Inventory, £224.10.8, incl. bonds, book debts and notes, £24.10.10; made by Thomas Sayre and Benjamin Allen.

1760, Dec. 17. Stretch, Peter, of Alloways Creek, Salem Co., yeoman, son of Peter, petitions that Joseph Stretch, of the same place, yeoman, be appointed his Guardian.
1760, Dec. 17. Bond of said Joseph Stretch as such Guardian; John Stewart and Thomas Sayre fellowbondsmen, all of Alloways Creek Township, yeomen. Lib. 11, p. 24.

1750, Nov. 30. Stretch, Sarah, of Salem Co. Int. Inventory, £365.5, incl. outstanding debts, £140.18.9; made by Joseph Warl and Jonathan Bradway.

CALENDAR OF WILLS—1751-1760 315

1751, Apr. 22. Bond of John Stretch as Adm'x; Jonathan Bradway fellowbondsman, both of Alloways Creek, said Co.
Salem Wills, 839 Q.

1754, Feb. 21. Style, John, Sr., of Newark, Essex Co. Int. Rebekah Style, widow, renounced. Witness—Theophilus Pierson.
1754, March 1. Adm'r—John Style, oldest son, of Newark. Bondsman—Joseph Johnson, of same place. Witness—Uzal Ogden.
Lib. F, p. 230.

1759, Jan. 17. Sullivan, Owen, of Windsor, Middlesex Co., yeoman. Int. Adm'r—Neil McConnely (husband of Eleanor, lately widow of Owen Sullivan). Bondsmen—Francis Bodine and Joseph Wilson, Jr., both of said county.
Lib. G, p. 17.
1759, Jan. 8. Inventory, £82.5.6, incl. 20 bush. of "Engen" corn, £2.10; bonds and notes, £22.14.6; made by Richard Hutchinson and Samuel Bonnel. Endorsed: "Windsor, Jan'y 9th, 1759. Please to admit the Bearer hereof, my Husband Neil McConnelley, to a Letter of Administration on the Estate of my Husband, Owen Sullyvan, Deceased."
——— ——— —. Additional inventory by Neil McConnelly, of debts due, £49.17.4.

1759, Apr. 7. Sutten, Mary, of Mansfield, Burlington Co., widow; will of. Children—John Jackson, Daniel Jackson (under age), Jean, Mary and Elizabeth. Farm in Gloucester Co. Personal property. Executors—daughter Mary and son Daniel. Witnesses—William Folwell, Thomas Boulton, Jonathan Fenimore. Proved Dec. 31, 1759.
Lib. 9, p. 305.
1759, Dec. 17. Inventory, £796.8.11., incl. bonds and book debts, £367.13.11; made by Jonathan Fenimore and William Folwell.
1761, Mar. 11. Account by Joseph Cox and wife, Mary, late Mary Sutton, the Executrix named above, who report for distribution a balance of £680.16.3.

1758, Aug. 22. Swaim, Anthony, of Elizabeth, Essex Co., joiner. Int. Adm'x—Abigail Swaim, of same place, his widow. Bondsman—Samuel Brooks, of said town. Witness—Thomas Bartow.
1758, Aug. 16. Inventory, £84.17.5, by Jacob Brookfield and Philip Denman, both of Elizabeth.
Lib. F, p. 547.

1754, May 1. Swaime, John, of New Winsor Township, Middlesex Co., yeoman; will of. Daughters—Jane, Saitye, Elisabeth. Sarg, Katerine and Anne. Grandchild—Mary Bustedo. Benjamin Maple, sole Executor. Witnesses—Benjamin Maple, Jr., Thomas Shinkfield and John Parker. Proved Oct. 25, 1757.
Lib. 8, p. 472.
1757, June 17. Inventory, £128.10.9., incl. a note of hand on Joshua Bostedo, £1; a bond of Benj. Maple, Sr., £115, and a debt due by Jane Swaim, 12s.; made by Joseph Skelton and Thomas van Dick.

1755, Dec. 12. Swain, Ebenezer, of Cape May Co., mariner; will of. Wife, Mary. Children—Daniel, James, Silas, Mary Townsend, Ruth Mulford. Homefarm; land adjoining Timothy Hand; interest upon Five-Mile Beach; part of a mill; land between Reuben and Daniel Swaine; personal estate. Executors—sons Daniel and Silas. Witnesses—Ruth Swain, Mary Forkland, Francis Taylor. Proved May 18, 1756.
Cape May Wills, 179 E.

1758, Feb. 21. Swain, Reubin, of Cape May Co. Int. Inventory, £362.1.1, incl. bonds, book debts, cash and notes £131.6.1; a negro man, £50; made by Amos Johnson and Richard Stites.
1758, Feb. 22. Bond of George and Judith Taylor as Adm'rs; Amos Johnson fellowbondsman, all of Cape May Co.
1758, Oct. 27. Additional inventory, £15.8.8, incl. a pilot boat and tackle, £10.13.4; made by the same appraisers. Cape May Wills, 193 E.

1760, July 14. Swain, Reuben, Jr., son of Reuben, of Cape May Co., asks, that his brother-in-law, George Taylor be made his Guardian.
1760, July 23. Bond of George Taylor as such Guardian; John Taylor, fellowbondsman, both of Cape May Co. Lib. 10, p. 602.

1759, May 10. Swayze, Samuel, of Mendum, Morris Co., gent.; will of. Wife, Susannah. Sons—Samuel, Barnebus, Richard, Iseral, Caleb. Daughters and other children of the dec'd, but no names given. Grandson-in-law, John Carns. Homefarm; land on the road to the Iron works, bought of Jacob and Caleb Shins; farm, bought of Daniel Zeale; 150 acres bought of Jonathan Kite; land on the Morris Town road; personal estate. Executors—David Luse, of Roxbury Township, and Daniel Lindsly, of the Township of Morris, both in Morris Co. Witness—Benjamin Doutey, Hanah Burwill, Jonathan Pitney. Proved June 13, 1759. Lib. G, p. 669.
1759, May 23. Inventory, £226.16.10, incl. a Bible and other books, £1.15; made by Alexander Aikman and Jonathan Pitney.

1749, Jan. 4. Sweet, Elisabeth, of "Always" Creek, Salem Co.; will of. Gives homestead bought of William and Clement Hall, to "son by law," Jeremiah Sneathen (Snetten) and wife Elisabeth, with a lien for his life to Edward Maker (Meeker?). Personal estate to go without exception to said Jeremiah and wife. Executors—Jeremiah Snethen and William Oakford. Witnesses—Isaac Oakford, John Galoucher (Gallaher), Samuel Purviance. Proved Oct. 21, 1751.
Lib. 9, p. 11.
1751, Oct. 12. Inventory, £14.5.6, by Isaac Oakford and Samuel Purviance.

1758, Apr. 27. Swinney, Deborah, of Hopewell Township, Cumberland Co.; will of. Children—Joseph (sole Executor), Deborah Bower, Ann Ayres. Grandchildren—Sarah, Jess, Joseph, Elisha, Ruth, Valintine and Mary. Personal estate. Witnesses—Caleb Ayers, Rebekah Ayers, Hugh Dunn. Proved May 8, 1760. Lib. 9, p. 451.
1760, Apr. 10. Inventory of the personal estate, £100.6.4, made by Stephen Ayars (Ayers) and Josiah Parvin.

1756, Feb. 9. Swinney, John, of Hopewell Township, Cumberland Co., husbandman; will of. Wife, Martha, sole Executrix. Children—Elisha, Valentine, Rachel, Ruth and Mary, all under age. Salt marsh near Greenwich, bought of Ebenezer Miller; do. adjoining Jonathan Holms, Esq., bought of Timothy Brooks; personal property. Witnesses—Seth Brooks, Noah Bowen, Robert Kelsey. Proved April 16, 1756.
1756, Apr. 16. Inventory, £111.16, by Enoch Shepherd and Jonathan Bowen. Cumb. Wills, 142 F.
1770, May 9. Account by **Martha Shepperd,** late **Martha Swinney,** Executrix.

CALENDAR OF WILLS—1751-1760 317

1754, Oct. 30. Sydenham, John, of Newark, Essex Co.; will of. Wife, Martha. Children—Sucke, David, John, William, Thomas. Personal estate. Executors—Joseph Farrand, Caleb Harrison and Jonathan Sergeant. Witnesses—Solomon Crane, John McGinnis, Mary Longworth. Proved Nov. 6, 1754. Lib. F, p. 267.
    1754, Nov. 11. Inventory, £159.5, incl. a negro girl, £40; made by Isaac Lyon and John Crane. [Note at the bottom: "Joseph Farrand is dead; Isaac Lyon is dead."]
    1772, Oct. 24. Account by Caleb Harrison, one of the Executors, who has increased it to £244.9.5, and has spent £286.18.

1755, Nov. 14. Taggert, Jonathan, of Salem Co. Int. Bond of Mary Tagart, widow as Adm'x; Charles Ellet, of said Co., and Joshua Tagart, of Pennsylvania, fellowbondsman. Lib. 8, p. 236.
    1755, Nov. 14. Inventory, £339.8.7½, incl. book debts, £179.9.1½; shop goods, £103.14.6; made by Joshua Tagart and Charles Ellet.

1756, Mar. 23. Talman, James, late of Gloucester, N. J., now of Philadelphia, gentleman; will of. Wife, Keziah. Sons—Hinchman and James, both under age. Farm of 400 acres on Oldman's Creek. Greenwich, Gloucester Co.; other real and personal estate. Executors —the wife and uncle, Joseph Talman, of Burlington Co. Witnesses— Susannah Badger, Asher Mott, John Reily. Codicil of August 23, 1758, makes slight changes. Witnesses—Stephen Ayars, Halbidge Ayars, Joseph Harrison. Proved Sept. 16, 1758. Lib. 9, p. 126.
    1758, Sept. 4. Inventory, £1928.19., incl. a large Bible and 2 other books, £2.3; plate, china ware and glass, £56.15; a white servant's time, £13; 4 negroes, £160; bills, bonds, book debts and notes, £1394.6.6; made by Joseph Harrison and Richard Sparks.

1758, Jan. 6. Talman, Job, of Burlington Co., yeoman; will of. Daughters—Sarah and Martha Talman, principal heiresses and Executrixes, with kinsman, Gilbart Smith, one of the legatees, as assistant. Legacy to kinswoman, Catharina Watters. Real and personal estate. Witnesses—Joseph Talman, John Antram, Thomas Folkos. Proved Feb. 11, 1758. Lib. 9, p. 62.

1754, Mar. 23. Tatem, Mary, of Deptford Township, Gloucester Co., widow. Int. Bond of Joseph Tatem, cordwainer, as Adm'r; John Hopper, yeoman, fellowbondsman, both of said Township.
Lib. 7, p. 468.

1757, Apr. 25. Taylor, Aaron, son of John Taylor, of Burlington Co., asks, that George Taylor be appointed his Guardian.
Burl. Wills, 5961 C.

1754, Nov. 27. Taylor, Charles, of Bordentown, Burlington Co. Int. Inventory, £38.8.5, by Jonathan Quicksall and Samuel Farnsworth.
Lib. 8, p. 66.
    1754, Nov. 30. Bond of John Thorn, innholder, as Adm'r; Jonathan Quicksall, turner, fellowbondsman, both of said Co.

1758, July 30. Taylor, Davie, of Newark, Essex Co. Int. Adm'r— Samuel Thompson, of Elizabeth Town, principal creditor. Bondsman—Isaac Crane, of same place. Witness—Uzal Ogden.
Lib. F, p. 542.

1749, Feb. 27. Taylor, Edward, of Upper Freehold, Monmouth Co.; will of. Wife, Hannah. Children—Edward, Catherine, James, Hannah, Lawrence, Mehatebel, Deborah, all under age. Real and personal estate. Executors—the wife, her brother Jacob Lawrence, and James Holms. Witnesses—Joseph Taylor, John L. Illey, John Brittain. Proved May 17, 1751. Lib. 7, p. 82.

1751, Mar. 27. Inventory, £268.10.10, incl. a silver cup, 5 silver spoons and tea ware, £6.13; 4 Bibles and other books, £3; made by Elisha Lawrence, William Tapscott and Joseph Taylor.

1751, July 4. Taylor, Elias, of Cape May Co., gentleman; will of. Children—Thomas, Elias and Mary Flowers. Real and personal estate. Executor—Ebenezer Johnson, with Elisha Hand as assistant. Witnesses—John Eldredge, John Bock (Buck), John Crandel. Proved March 7, 1752. Lib. 9, p. 53.

1757, Dec. 31. Inventory, £47.9, by William Simkins and John Eldredge.

1758, Jan. 4. Bond of Mary Taylor as Adm'x (estate being intestate), William Simkins fellowbondsman, both of Cape May Co.

1750, Sept. 10. Taylor, Hugh, of Middlesex Co. Int. Adm'x—Frances Taylor, widow. Bondsman—Lewis Johnston, Esq. Inventory, £485.8.6, by John Barclay, John Combs and John Throckmorton.
Lib. E, p. 452

1759, Mar. 30. Taylor, Martha, of Cape May Co. Int. Inventory, £39.9.6, by Jonathan Smith and Carman Smith.

1759, Apr. 2. Bond of Joshua Hildreth as Adm'r; Amos Johnson, fellowbondsman, both of Cape May Co., gentlemen. Lib. 9, p. 314.

1760, Feb. 12. Taylor, Mary, of Greenwich Twsp., Gloucester Co. Int. Adm'r—Nathan Boys, of same place, yeoman. Bondsman—Samuel Chester of said place, yeoman. Witnesses—Sarah Howell and John Ladd.

1760, Jan. 28. Inventory, £10.0.5, by Thomas Roberts and Alexander Ware. Lib. 9, p. 421.

1755, Dec. 30. Taylor, Robert, of Chesterfield, Burlington Co.; will of. Children—Anthony (sole executor), Isaac, Robert, Mary; all but Anthony under age. Granddaughter, Idaleasa Taylor. Real and personal estate. Witnesses—Preserve Brown, John Taylor, Sarah Taylor. Proved February 27, 1758. Lib. 8, p. 510.

1758, Feb. 3. Inventory, £188.1.5, incl. bills, bonds and notes, £93.3.11; made by Joseph Reckless and William Wood.

1752, Feb. 17. Taylor, Thomas, of Chesterfield, Burlington Co.; will of wife, Anna. Children—James, Lucretia, Meribah, all under age. Land on north side of Millpond between Chapman's place, Joseph Reckless, Raworth Beck and the road; meadow bought of Robert Chapman and Richard Satterthwaite; farm, now occupied by William Letts; personal property. Executors—the wife, brother Samuel Taylor and David Rockhill. Witnesses—Joshua Humphris, William Steward, Joseph Reckless. Proved April 9, 1752. Lib. 7, p. 194.

1752, Apr. 1. Inventory, £722.3.3, incl. horses, cattle, sheep and swine, £143.7; bills, bonds and book debts, £298.5.7; "sarvants" and provisions, £74.8.8; made by John Rockhill and Joshua Humphris.

CALENDAR OF WILLS—1751-1760   319

1759, June 2. Account by Ann and Samuel Taylor, two of the Executors above named, who have increased it to £822.3.3, by the sale of land, and paid out £859.0.3. in discharging debts due to James Lippincott, Samuel Hardgrove, Thomas Douglass, George Taylor, Sarah Thorne, William Black, George Bliss, Nathan Richardson (schoolmaster), Thomas Ryan (blacksmith), William Baker, Abram Sherin, Thomas Lawrie, William Leets, Joseph Borden, George Briggs, Isaiah Foulke, Abraham Brown, Caleb Carman, Jonathan Thomas, Moses Ivins, John Collins, Joseph Richards, Thomas Quicksall, Barzillai Newbold, Deliverance Taylor, William Taylor, Francis Hall, Philipp Marott, Thomas Haines, Benjamin Taylor, John Page, Robert Taylor, Joiada Schooley, John Imlay, Samuel Harris, Phineas Bunting, Thomas Foster, William Pancoast, Rawarth Beck, Richard Allison, Alexander Moore, Hezekiah Jones, and Godfrey Beek.

1760, June 3. Taylor, Thomas, of Amwell Township, Hunterdon Co. Int. Hannah, the widow, relinquishes her right of administration, to her brother-in-law, Edward Taylor.
1760, June 3. Inventory, £224.18.4, incl. bills, bonds, book debts and other dues, £80.4.6; made by Abraham Larew and Richard Rounsavell, Jr.
1760, June 9. Bond of Edward Taylor as Adm'r; Richard Rounsavell, Jr., fellowbondsman, both of Amwell, yeoman.   Lib. 10, p. 463.

1743, Apr. 25. Taylor, William, Sr., of Chesterfield, Burlington Co.; will of. Wife, Rebecah. Children—William (eldest son) and others, names not given, all under age. Land on West side of the Mill road, adjoining brother John Taylor; personal property. Executors—the wife and Robert Rockhill. Witnesses—Godfrey Beck and Benjamin Busson. Proved Nov. 12, 1756.
1756, Oct. 28. Inventory, £136.12.7, by Abraham Brown, Jr., and Samuel Cheshire.   Burl. Wills, 3645 C.

1736, Sept. 2. Temple, Abraham, of Hopewell, Hunterdon Co.; will of. Wife, Rebecca. Children—Abraham, Benjamin, Johanna, Elizabeth, Return and Timothy, the last two under age. Real and personal estate. Executors—sons Abraham and Benjamin. Witnesses—Edward Hart, John Hart, Bartholomew Corwine. Proved Jan. 24, 1754.   Lib. 7, p. 435.

1750, Feb. 15. Temple, Timothy, of Hopewell, Hunterdon Co., yeoman; will of. Wife, Sarah. Children—John, Nathaniel, Sarah and Joanna, all under age. Real and personal estate. Executors—the wife, with brothers Benjamin Temple and John Hart. Witnesses—David Cowell, John Guild, Return Temple. Proved May 27, 1751.
Lib. 7, p. 71.
1751, Mar. 26. Inventory, £184.5.8, incl. bonds and notes, £60.10; made by Joseph Moore and Stephen Burrowes.

1758, Mar. 24. Ten Brook, Elizabeth and Jacob, of Somerset Co., minor children of Wessel, petition that Samuel Stout, Jr., son of Samuel Stout, Esq., present husband of their mother, Eleanor ten Brook, be appointed their Guardian.
1758, Mar. 25. Bonds of Samuel Stout, Jr., of Hopewell, Hunterdon Co., farmer, as their Guardian; Samuel Tucker, Jr., of Trenton, merchant, fellowbondsman.

1753, Apr. 3. ten Brook, John, son of John, an infant above 14 and under 21 years. Ward. Bond of Conrad ten Eyck and Mathew ten Eyck as Guardians; Fisbert Crom and Francis Cossaart fellow-bondsmen, all of Somerset Co. Lib. F, p. 108.

1752, June 25. ten Eyck, Jacob, of Somerset Co., farmer; will of. Wife [not named]. Children—Mathew, Coenraet, Jacob, Peterus (under age), Katrien, Janetje, and Anaetje. Real and personal estate. Executors—the four sons. Witnesses—Teunis Post, William McKinney, Hendrick Bries. Proved March 28, 1754. Lib. F, p. 162.

———, ——— ———. Inventory, £1224.12., incl. silver spoons and silver cup, £6.6; books, £3.9.6; negroes, £361; bonds and notes, £335.9; made by Jan van Neste, Anderies Teneyck, Teunis Post. [Filed Mar. 23, 1754].

1759, Mar. 5. Terryl (Terril), Daniel, of Deerfield Township, Cumberland Co. Int. Bond of Mark Ryley, cooper, as Adm'r; John Dare and Thomas Joslin (Joslane), yeomen, fellowbondsmen, all of said Township. Lib. 9, p. 211.

1759, Apr. 14. Inventory, £24.10.3, by John Dare and Thomas Joslin.
1762, Feb. 13. Account by the Administrator.

1759, Sept. 25. Test, Edward, of Salem, Salem Co., gent.; will of. Son, Edward, under age. Son-in-law, Joseph Burroughs. Sons of sister, Elizabeth Bacon, viz., John, David, Job and Thomas Bacon. Sister, Ann Dennis. Real and personal estate, incl. 3 negro slaves, set free and a clock. Executors—son Edward and Philip Dennis, Sr., of Cohansie. Witnesses—John Paschall, William Clancy and Ann van Hist. Proved Oct. 19, 1759. Lib. 10, p. 336.

1759, Oct. 11. Inventory, £1691.18.5, incl. apparel, cash and plate, £209.0.4; meat book debts, £63.2.7; tavern book debts, £476.12.10; a servant man's time (7 years), £28; a negro man, £70; a negro girl, £25; made by Joshua Thompson and Thomas Goodwin.

1753, Jan. 22. Test, Elizabeth, daughter of, Joseph and wife Sarah, of Salem Co. Ward. Bond of Joseph Test of Salem, yeoman, as Guardian, until she is 14 years old; Jonathan Thomas, of Burlington City, innholder, fellowbondsman. Salem Wills, 850 Q.

1759, Mar. 3. Test, Hanah, of Salem Township, West Jersey, widow; will of. Son, Joseph Sidden, "if he be living." Cousin, Elizabeth Boss. Grandchildren—William and Henry Siden, James Chamless, Mary Siden and Jacob Chamless. Widow, Mary Thomson. Daughters of brothers Elisha and Daniel. Personal estate. Executors—Charles Fogg and Elisha Bassett, Jr. Witnesses—John Hart, Hannah Hart and William Hart. Proved Dec. 13, 1760. Lib. 10, p. 491.

1760, May 30. Inventory, £109.4.11, by Grant Gibbon and Thomas Rice.

1755, Dec. 27. Test, Joseph, of Salem Town and Co., hatter; will of. Wife, Hannah. Son, John. Granddaughter, Elizabeth. Daughter of son Joseph. Real and personal estate. Executors—son John and Philipp Dennis. Witnesses—Edward Draper, Mary Thompson and Josiah Kay. Proved Jan. 22, 1756. Lib. 8, p. 299.

1756, Jan. 22. Inventory, £158.14.8½; incl. book debts, £27.4.3½; rents and interest due, £9.11.9; a negro woman, £5; John Darcy's time, £5; made by Thomas Hancock and Joshua Thompson.

CALENDAR OF WILLS—1751-1760   321

1752, Nov. 3. Test, Joseph, Jr., of Salem Co. Int. Bond of Joseph Test as Adm'r; Edward Test fellowbondsman, both of Salem Town and County. Lib. 7, p. 292.
1752, Nov. 24. Inventory, £92.5.5. incl. a silver watch, £5; silver spoons, 25s.; gold and silver buttons, £1; book debts and cash, £37.1.5; a looking glass; made by Edward Test and Fortunatus Woods.

1753, Jan. 20. Test, Sarah, widow of Joseph, Jr., late Sarah Mason, daughter of Samuel Mason, of Salem Co., dec'd. Int. Bond of Joseph Test as Adm'r; Edward Test fellowbondsman, both of said Co.
Salem Wills, 889 Q.

1749, Dec. 31. Test, William, of Salem Town and Co., hatter; will of. Wife, Priscilla. Children—Rebecca, Grace, Sarah, Walker, Richard, Edward and William. Real and personal estate. Executors—the wife, with sons Walker and Richard. Witnesses—John Andrews, Edward Test, George Trenchard. Proved Sept. 20, 1752. [Endorsed: "The Exec. died before she proved the will."] Lib. 7, p. 539.
1752, Sept. 20. Bond of Francis Test and Edward Test as Adm'rs with the will annexed; Joseph Test fellowbondsman, all of Salem Co.
1752, Sept. 22. Inventory, £118.3.8, by Joseph Ware, Sr., and John Fitzpatrick.

1756, July 21. Test, William, Jr., of Salem Co., son of William, petitions that Francis Test be appointed his Guardian.
1756, Aug. 9. Bond of Francis Test as such Guardian; John Sheppard fellowsbondman, both of Salem Co., yeomen. Lib. 8, p. 315.

1751, June 10. Tetsward, Stephen, of Morris Co. Int. Adm'x—Sarah Tetsward, of Morris Co. Bondsmen—George McKenney and Cornelius Devore, both of said Co. Witnesses—James Rutherford and Hezekiah Howell. Inventory, £21.18.9, by George McKenny and Henry ———? Lib. 7, p. 70.

1745, Jan. 3. Thomas, Edward, of the Borough of Elizabeth, Essex Co., innholder; will of. Wife, Sarah. Children—Rachel, Edward, Sarah, John and Anne, all under age. Real and personal estate. Executors—the wife and John Blanchard. Witnesses—John deWitt, Matthias Williamson, Robert Drummond. Proved August 5, 1756.
Lib. F, p. 402.

1759, Mar. 26. Thomas, John, of Hunterdon Co. Int. Bond of Eva, widow, as Adm'x; Abraham van Horne fellowbondsman, both of Hunterdon Co. Hunt. Wills, 480 J.

1752, Aug. 21. Thomas, Nathaniel, of Burlington City, Esq.; will of. Wife, Lydia. Daughter, Rebecca, under age. Real and personal estate, incl. 3 large silver spoons, six silver tea spoons and a gold ring. Legacy to William Sheeles, who, with Henry Paxson, is made Executor and Guardian of the daughter. Witnesses—Isaac De Cow, Jr., James Scattergood, John Lamb. Proved Nov. 23, 1754.
Lib. 7, p. 502.

1727, Feb. 28. Thomasee, Johannes, of Newark, Essex Co., yeoman; will of. Wife, Mary, to have use of real and personal estate during her life and to bring up my children, except what is hereafter disposed of. Eldest son, Thomas, the plantation where I dwell. My children, now living, Abraham, Aria, Aneltie, Mary, Johanus, Rachel and Cornelius, £80 equally. Executors—wife Mary. Overseers—friends, John Stoutenburgh and John Cooper, of Newark. Witnesses—John Cooper, John Stoutenburgh and Barnt Fransee.

1748, Nov. 25. Codicil gives to son, Johannes Codmus, 1-3 of plantation "where I dwell." Witnesses—Jonathan Sergeant and Lawrance Ward. Proved March 22, 1759. Lib. G, p. 72.

1759, Dec. 18. Inventory, £31.10, by Lawrance Ward and John King, Jr. Executors—May Cadmus, Thomas Cademus, Cornelis Yoraleman.

1757, Apr. 25. Thompson, Aaron, of the Borough of Elizabeth, Essex Co., yeoman; will of. Wife, Charetree. Children—Thomas, Celib and Patiance, all under age. Real and personal estate. Executors—Thomas Baker and John Lamb. Witnesses—Jonathan Crane, Abner Frost, John Stits. Proved Sept. 17, 1757. Lib. F, p. 446.

1754, Sept. 13. Inventory, £76.7.5, by John Littell and Job Mulford.

1760, April 17. Thompson, Benjamin, of Essex Co. Int. Adm'rs—Phebe Thompson, widow, and George Frazee, both of Elizabeth, said Co. Bondsman—Samuel Chandler, of same place. Witnesses—Robert Ogden and Thomas Tobin. Lib. G, p. 244.

1760, Sept. 20. Thompson, Henry, of Mansfield, Burlington Co. Int. Inventory, £121.2.10, incl. old books, 5s.; book debts, £5.5.5; made by Joseph Talman and Henry Delatush; affirmed by Mary Thompson as Administratrix.

1760, Sept. 23. Bond of Mary Thompson as Adm'x; Henry Delatush and Samuel Rockhill fellowbondsmen, all of said Co.

Lib. 10, pp. 102, 171.

1762, ———— —. Account by Thomas Shinn, blacksmith, of goods unadministered on by Mary Thompson, Adm'x, deceased. Plantation sold for £241.4.

1758, Sept. 1. Thompson, Isaac, Esq., of Allaways Creek, Salem Co. Int. Inventory, £185.17.6, by William Oakford and Daniel Fogg.

1758, Sept. 2. Bond of widow, Hannah Thompson, and John Thompson as Adm'rs; William Oakford and Daniel Fogg fellowbondsmen, all of Allaways Creek. Lib. 9, p. 95.

1759, Mar. 30. Thompson, John, of Mansfield Township, Burlington Co., yeoman; will of. Disposes of real and personal estate to three daughters (names not given), and younger sons Uriah and Staples, (all under age) subject to disposition to be made by father-in-law, Thomas Staples, of his estate. Executors—sons Daniel and Henry Thompson. Witnesses—Richard Gibbs, William Brown, Isaac De Cow. Proved July 7, 1759. Lib. 9, p. 280.

1759, July 5. Inventory, £114.18.10, by Benjamin and Joseph Talman.

1760, Aug. 4. Account by the Executors, who add to the value the amount received for the land sold, £341.14.

1759, July 23. Thompson, Mulford, of Fairfield, Cumberland Co. Int. Bond of Zadok Thompson as Adm'r; Henry Pearson (Pierson) and Abial Shaw, fellowbondsmen, all of Fairfield. Lib. 9, p. 450.

CALENDAR OF WILLS—1751-1760   323

1753, Dec. 1. Thompson, Nathanael, of Alloways Creek, Salem Co., yeoman; will of. Brother, Isaac Thompson, sole heir and Executor of real and personal estate, but with legacy to brother John Thompson. Witnesses—Samuel Test, Mary Thompson, Benjamin Thompson. Proved May 12, 1755. Lib. 8, p. 239.
   1755, May 10. Inventory, £228.1, incl. a servant and staves, £32, made by William Oakford and Benjamin Holme, Jr.

1760, April 24. Thompson, Rachael; ward. Daughter of Nathaniel Thompson of Essex Co., dec'd. Guardian—James Chandler, of said Co. Lib. G, p. 166.

1749, May 8. Thompson, William, of Alaways Creek, Salem Co.; will of. Wife, Elisabeth. Children—Nathaniel, Isaac, Andrew, John, Hannah, Rebeccah and Elisabeth. Homefarm; 100 acres, bought of Henry Cornelius; 25 ac., bought of Joseph Thompson; personal property. Executors—the wife, with sons Andrew and Nathaniel. Witnesses—Benjamin Holme, Samuel Thompson, Benjamin Thompson. Proved Nov. 21, 1751. Lib. 7, p. 244.
   1751, Nov. 21. Elisabeth Thompson, the widow, declines acting as Executrix.
   1751, Nov. 21. Inventory, £372.11.6, incl. bills, bonds and book debts, £65.17.6; silver spoons and books; made by Joseph Ware and William Oakford.

1760, Jan. 30. Thomson, Agness, of Middletown Point, (Monmouth Co.); will of. Daughters—Sarah and Phebe. Granddaughters—Anne Bates and Agness Brown. Personal estate. Executors—sons-in-law, Richard Bates and Hendrick Hendrickson, Jr. Witnesses—Peter Clark, Owen Evans and John Voorhees. Proved March 31, 1760. Lib. G, p. 155.
   1760, Feb. 6. Inventory, £36.3, incl. a pair of gold buttons, £1.10; a silver snuff box, 16s.; a large Dutch Bible and other books, £2.2; a looking glass, 25s.; made by Richard Franses and Owen Evans. (House and lot not appraised).

1759, Aug. 6. Thomson, Azariah, of Essex Co. Int. Adm'r—Nathaniel Rusco, of said Co. Bondsman—Abraham Cadmus. John Thomson, the father of above Azariah, renounced. Witness—Thomas Bartow. Lib. G, p. 92.

1759, March 8. Thomson, John, of Perth Amboy, Middlesex Co., yeoman. Int. Adm'x—Anne Thomson, widow. Bondsmen—James Newell and Francis Letts, of same place. Witness—Thomas Bartow. Lib. G, p. 38.
   1759, Mar. 9. Inventory, £3.13.6, by Richard Hews and Thomas Inglis.

1760, April 7. Thorn, Jacob, of Middlesex Co. Int. Adm'r—Andrew Bloomfield, of Woodbridge, principal creditor. Bondsman—Joseph Thorn, of said place. Witness—John Smyth. Lib. G, p. 153.

1758, Apr. 8. Thorn, John, of Bordentown, Burlington Co., yeoman; will of. Divides real and personal estate between cousin, Jonathan Quicksall, of Bordentown, chairmaker, who is also named sole Execu-

tor, and John, son of John Taylor, of said place, dec'd. Witnesses—Richard Allison, Israel Butler, John Grimes. Proved May 29, 1759.
Lib. 9, p. 213.

1759, May 28. Inventory of the estate: real, three houses and lots in Bordentown and a lot some distance off. £450; personal, £59.17.11., incl. 6 silver teaspoons, and silver pair of buckles; 29 silver buttons, £1.8.9; made by Richard Allison and Israel Butler.

1759, Aug. 4. Thorn, Joseph, of the "Sitte" of Amboy, Middlesex Co. Int. Inventory, £19.15.2, by Thomas Cox and Joseph Lawrence.

1759, Aug. 13. Mary, widow, empowers Richard Duglass, of Upper Freehold, Monmouth Co., to administer on her late husband's estate.

1759, Aug. 14. Bond of Richard Duglass as Adm'r; John Shaw, of Burlington, fellowbondsman.
Lib. 9, p. 243.

1757, Oct. 1. Thorn, Thomas, of Waterford, Gloucester Co. Int. Inventory, £297.14.4, incl. a clock £12; books, 10s.; a negro man, £40; made by William Ellis and Charles Farguison.

———, ——— —. Bond of his widow, Letitia Thorn, as Adm'r; James Hinchman, of Greenwich, said Co., yeoman, fellowbondsman.
Lib. 9, p. 38.

1751, Sept. 26. Thorne, Henry, of Township and County of Gloucester, yeoman. Int. Adm'r—Joseph Hedges, yeoman, of said place. Bondsman—Michael Fisher, Esq., of Deptford Township in said Co. Witnesses—John Mickle and John Ladd.

1751, Sept. 28. Inventory, £69.16.0, by Richard Cheesman and Richard Chew.
Glou. Wills, 490 H.

1751, July 29. Thorne, John, of Gloucester Township and County, sawyer; will of. Wife, Elizabeth. Children—Zacheus, Richard, John and a daughter, name not given. Farm, where father Henry Thorne and wife now live; sawmill; personal estate. Executors—the wife and her brother, William Cheesman. Witnesses—Henry Thorne, Henry Thorne, Jr., Michaell Fisher. Proved Sept. 21, 1751.
Lib. 7, p. 146.

1751, Aug. 24. Inventory, £144.13.1½, by Richard Cheesman and Michaell Fisher.

1755, Sept. 3. Account by the Executors, Elizabeth, (wife of Richard Tice, late Elizabeth Thorne) and William Cheesman.

1753, Apr. 14. Thorne, John, of Middletown, (Monmouth Co.). Int. Inventory, £384.4, incl. bonds and book debts, £64.12.7; a boat, £45; books 15s.; looking glasses; a negro man, negro wench, child, boy and girl, £100; made by Nicholas Johnson, William Hendrickson and Edward Taylor.

1753, Dec. 24. Bond of Sarah, widow, as Adm'x; William Hendrickson, of said Co., fellowbondsman.
Lib. F, p. 156.

1759, May 10. Thorne, Thomas, of the Town and County of Gloucester, yeoman; will of. Daughters—Abigail, wife of William Harrison, Jr., and Elizabeth. Real and personal estate. Executors—daughter Elizabeth, son-in-law William Harrison, Jr., with brothers Samuel Harrison, Jr., and Joseph Harrison. Witnesses—Nathan Albertson, John Glover, Thomas Ellis, Jr. Proved Dec. 17, 1760.
Lib. 10, p. 411.

CALENDAR OF WILLS—1751-1760   325

1760, Dec. 1. Inventory, £609.13.2, incl. book debts and notes, £156.4.4; live stock, £228.7.6; made by Jacob Albertson and Samuel Clement, Jr.

1755, July 3. Thorp, Samuel, of Middlesex Co. Int. Bond of Robert Montgomery, of Monmouth Co., as Adm'r; William Clayton, of Trenton, Hunterdon Co., fellowbondsman.   Lib. 8, p. 309.

1750, Oct. 16. Thorp, Solomon, of Woodbridge, Middlesex Co., yeoman. Int. Adm'rs—Hannah Thorp, the widow, and William Moore, both of Woodbridge. Bondsman—Thomas Thorp, of said place. Witness—Thomas Bartow.   Lib. E, p. 458.
1750, Oct. 18. Inventory, £178.18.6, by James Brown and Edward Crowell.

1759, Aug. 1. Throckmorton, Joseph, of Middletown, Monmouth Co.; will of. Wife [not named]. Children—John (under age), Rebecca, Alice, Catherine and Mary. Children of daughters Sarah, Ann and Patience. Executors—son, Job Throckmorton, and John Campbell, Jr., both of Freehold Township. Witnesses—John Stout, Jonathan Stout and John Mount, Jr. Proved August 13, 1759.
    Lib. G, p. 100.
1759, Aug. 24. Inventory, £435.17.11, incl. bonds, £127.2.5; books; a negro man, woman and child, £115; made by Jared Morford and ———— Thomamont.

1758, Dec. 15. Throckmorton, Samuel, of Freehold, Monmouth Co. Int. Bond of Daniel Grandin as Adm'r; Edmond Lafetra fellowbondsman, both of said Co., yeoman.   Lib. G, p. 38.

1751, Nov. 5. Tichener, Joseph, of town and Co. of Morris. In his will he did not appoint Guardians for his children, Joseph, James and Jane, and they, being above 14 years of age, pray that Thomas Woodruff, Jr., of Elizabeth be appointed their Guardian, which was so ordered.   Lib. F, p. 48.

1754, Dec. 12. Tietsort, Abraham, of Bridgewater Township, Somerset Co., carpenter; will of. Wife, Geertruy. Children—Abraham, Peter, Isaac, John, Margaret, Catheline, all under age; an expected child. Legacy to Dutch Reformed Church of the North Branch congregation. Real and personal estate. Executors—brother, William Tietsoort, brother-in-law, Isaac Hoff, and Dirck Lou. Witnesses—John Hoff, Antie Schamp, Teunis Middagh. Proved July 2, 1755.
    Lib. F, p. 281.

1753, Aug. 16. Tilsilver (Tielshofir), Michael of Stow Creek Township, Cumberland., farmer; will of. Wife, Elizabeth. Children—Martin, Simon, John, George, Margaret, Christian and Jacob, all under age. One hundred acres in Deerfield Twsp, bought of Jonathan Fithian; improvement bought of Eliakim Carle, Jr.; 5 ac. in Greenwich Town marsh, bought of Samuel Harrice; personal estate. Executors—the wife and son Martin. Witnesses—Hugh Dunn and John Carll. [Will signed in German script]. Proved Sept. 19, 1753.
    Cumb. Wills, 89 F.
1753, Sept. 17. Inventory, £530.2.1, incl. bills, bonds and book debts, £132.4.5; servants, £34; made by Hugh Dunn and Samuel Moore.

1751, Apr. 10. Tindall, Benjamin, of Alaways Creek, Salem Co., yeoman; will of. Wife, Esther. Son, Joseph, under age. Real and personal estate. Executors—the wife and John Steward. Witnesses—Jonathan Bradway, Joshua Thompson, Samuel Abbott. Proved April 15, 1751. Lib. 7, p. 258.

1751, May 3. Inventory, £607.14.4, incl. bills, bonds, book debts, cash and notes, £200.0.2; books; 2 looking glasses; a servant man's time, £15; made by Samuel Abbott and Joshua Thompson.

1756, —— ——. Titsilver, Martin, son of Michael, dec'd, of Cumberland Co., petitions, that Jacob Freese, of Salem Co., yeoman, be appointed his Guardian.

1756, Dec. 7. Bond of Jacob Freese as such Guardian; Charles Clark, of Deerfield, Cumberland Co., tailor, and Fill (Philipp) Sauter, of Hopewell, said Co., yeoman (who signs in German script) fellowbondsmen.

1756, Dec. 21. Bond of Jacob Freese, of Alaways Creek Township, Salem Co., yeoman, and Charles Clark of Deerfield, tailor, as administrators of the estate of Michael Titsilver with his will annexed, the executrix named therein, his wife Elizabeth, being dead and the son Martin a minor. Joseph Peck, of Deerfield, Esq., and Filb Sauter of Hopewell, said Co., fellowbondsmen.

1757, Feb. 8. Inventory of the estate, £306.5.10, left unadministered by Elizabeth Titsilver, made by Joseph Peck and Jonathan Davis.

1764, June 11. Account by Jacob Freese, Adm'r, and Daniel Clark, representing Charles Clark, deceased Adm'r.

1757, Nov. 16. Titsoort, Isaac, of Newtown, Sussex Co. Int. Letter from Henry Simson, Joseph Byram, John Anderson, Thomas Woolverton and Joseph Parry to "Your Honour," stating, that Isaac Titsoort had gone with Col. Jacob Ford and Col. Abraham van Campen, to make a treaty with the Indians on the "front Tears," where he is said to have been killed. The widow, being "considerabley Bereaved of hur naturall Reason," the writers recommend the eldest son, Lenard Titsoort, as Adm'r of the estate.

1757, Nov. 17. Bond of Lenard Titsoort as Adm'r; Constant Hart fellowbondsman, both of Newtown. Lib. F, p. 466.

1758, Jan. 21. Inventory, £176.8.4, incl. a new beaver hat, £1.18; 21 bush. of wheat @ 4s., £4.4; made by Constant Hart and George Havens.

1757, Apr. 25. Titus, Timothy, of Hopewell, Hunterdon Co.; will of. Wife, Mary. Children—Timothy, Philipp (now abroad), Dennis, Susanna, Jemima, Phebe and Mary. Children of dec'd daughter, Hannah. Personal estate. Executors—Edward Hunt and Henry Woolsey. Witnesses—William Waters, Richard Hoff, John Guild. Proved June 14, 1757. Lib. 8, p. 483.

1757, June 20. Inventory, £178.10, incl. books, £1.10; cash and notes, £18.4; made by William Waters and Timothy Smith.

1759, Feb. 6. Tobin, James, of Hunterdon Co. Int. Bond of William Allen, of Amwell, Hunterdon Co., as Adm'r; Richard Reading, of the same place, fellowbondsman. Lib. 9, p. 454.

1757, Sept. 22. Toele, George, of City of New York, mariner; will of. "To my friend, Garret Van Wert, of said City, innkeeper, all my

real and personal estate, and I appoint him Executor." Witnesses—Jacobus Stoutenburgh, Christopher Steymets, Richard Baucker. Proved Oct. 28, 1757.
Lib. F, p. 463.

1759, Apr. 7. Tomlins, James, of Greenwich, Gloucester Co., yeoman. Int. Inventory, £90.9.4, by William Sharp and Thomas Joyce. 1759, Apr. 14. Bond of widow, Mary Tomlins, as Adm'x; Mathew Tomlins, yeoman, fellowbondsman, both of Greenwich Township.
Lib. 9, p. 233.

1755, Jan. 2. Tomlinson, John, of Gloucester Township and County, yeoman; will of. Wife, Mary. Children—Isaac, Hannah and Eleanor (under age). Real and personal estate. Executors—the wife, son Isaac, and brother Joseph Tomlinson. Witnesses—Benjamin Davis, Josiah Hillman, Alexander Crawford. Codicil of same date gives a legacy to mother and empowers wife and son to deed property to brother Joseph. Same witnesses. Proved March 25, 1755.
Lib. 8, p. 146.
1755, Feb. 18. Inventory, £264.18.6, made by Michael Fisher and John Hillman.

1758, Aug. 23. Tomlinson, Joseph, of Gloucester Township and Co., yeoman; will of. Wife, Catherine. Children—Joseph, Samuel, and three daughters, names not given. Real and personal estate. Executors—the wife, son Joseph and cousin Isaac Tomlinson. Witnesses—Joseph Davis, Benjamin Davis, Patience Mallock. Proved October 9, 1758.
Lib. 9, p. 122.
1758, Sept. 29. Inventory, £218.9.10, by Michael Fisher and John Hillman.

1759, Feb. 9. Tomlinson, Samuel, of Waterford Township, Gloucester Co., carpenter; will of. Wife, Ann, sole heiress and Executrix of real and personal estate, with legacy to brother, Daniel Tomlinson. Witnesses—Enoch Roberts, Samuel Collins, Alexander Crawford. Proved Feb. 20, 1759.
Lib. 9, p. 183.
1759, Feb. 15. Inventory, £250.13.1, by George Matlack and Enoch Roberts.

1751, July 15. Tompkins, Samuel, of Newark, Essex Co., planter; will of. Divides real and personal estate between cousins, James Smith (made sole Executor), Joseph Smith, John Smith, David Smith, Samuel Robards, Mary Smith, Sarah Smith, Hanah Farin, Joana Plumb, Mary Harison, Unice Baldwin, Unice Tomkins, Easter Tomkins, David Tompkins and Ebnezer Orsborn. Witnesses—Moses Baldwin, Ezekiel Johnson, Phebe Johnson. Proved July 20, 1751.
Lib. F, p. 540.
1751, July 23. Inventory, £69.11.5, by Moses Baldwin and John Gildersleeve.

1751, Nov. 12. Toms, John, of Greenwich Township, Gloucester Co., yeoman. Int. Inventory, £22.5.6, by James Currie and Anthony Hooper.
1751, Nov. 19. Bond of widow, Hannah Toms, as Adm'x; Anthony Hooper, yeoman, fellowbondsman, both of Greenwich Township.
Glou. Wills, 491 H.

1756, Jan. 1. Toms, Joseph, of Woodbridge, Middlesex Co., yeoman; will of. Wife, Susannah. Children—Richard, John, Jonathan, Elisabeth, Rachel, Catherine, Susannah and Ann, all under age. Real and personal estate. Executors—the wife, Jonathan Fraze and David Edgar. Witnesses—Joseph Oliver, James Elston and Thomas Alston. Proved Jan. 20, 1756. Lib. F, p. 316.

1753, Dec. 31. Tooker, Joseph, Sr., of Elizabeth Town, Essex Co., gentleman; will of. Wife, Mary. Children—Susannah (wife of Benj. Little), Joseph, Sarah. Grandchildren—Joshua Tooker and children of dec'd daughter, Elizabeth. Property left to son Joseph in trust for Mary, wife of Thomas Jeffers. Real and personal estate. Executors—son Joseph, and son-in-law, Joseph Hinds. Witnesses—John Bird, Philipp Blacklidg, John Ross. Proved Feb. 25, 1754.
Lib. F, p. 170.

1756, Aug. 22. Townley, Charles, of the Borough of Elizabeth, Essex Co.; will of. Wife, Abigail. Children—Effingham, Sarah Herriman, Mary, Ann Tucker and Elizabeth. Grandson, Richard Townley, son of Effingham and wife Rebekah. Real and personal estate. Executors—son (in-law?) John Herriman and Joseph Morse. Witnesses—John Cleverly, Jonathan Allen, Thomas Tobin. Proved Sept. 13, 1756. Lib. F, p. 413.

1760, June 12. Townsend, Amos, of Dividing Creek, Fairfield Township, Cumberland Co. Int. Inventory, £151.7, by John Bragg and Jonathan Lore.
1760, June 19. Bond of his widow, Martha, as Adm'x; Jonathan Lore, of Turkey Point, said Co., fellowbondsman. Lib. 10, p. 179.

1759, June 20. Townsend, Richard, of Penn's Neck, Salem Co., yeoman. Int. Inventory, £354.4.7, incl. bonds, cash and credits, £226.17.11; made by Andrew Sinnickson and Joseph Wright.
1759, June 26. Bond of widow, Sarah Townsend, as Adm'x; Daniel Brandreth and Andrew Sinnickson, fellowbondsmen, all of Penn's Neck. Lib. 9, p. 352.
1760, June 25. Account by the Administratrix.

1753, May 25. Toy, Nicholas, of Gloucester Co., yeoman, will of. Children—Abigail and Savory, both under age. Brother, Daniel Tay. Sisters—Mary Wullis, Marget, Rebecca and Gerterew Tay. Land bought of brother Elias and sold, but not yet conveyed, to John Ogg; personal property. Executors—brothers Elias and Daniel Tay. Witnesses—Amos Haines, Nathan Haines, Samuel Atkinson. Proved Sept. 3, 1753. Lib. 7, p. 353.
1753, July 30. Inventory, £364.18, incl. bonds £260; a "flaet" and sail, £48; made by Thomas Middleton and Robert Hunt.

1758, Sept. 13. Toy, Nicholas, of Northampton, Burlington Co., cordwainer; will of. Wife, Susannah, sole heiress and, with Henry Paxson, Executrix of real and personal estate. Witnesses—John Goldy, Samuel Budd, Daniel Jones, Jr. Proved Oct. 14, 1758.
Lib. 9, p. 75.
1758, Oct. 11. Inventory, £80.15.4, by Daniel Jones, Jr., and Zachariah Rossell.

CALENDAR OF WILLS—1751-1760   329

1714, Dec. 23. Tranbles, Jean (John), of Raways Neck, Elizabeth Town bounds, Essex Co.; will of. Wife, Mary, sole Executrix. Children—Peter, John, Mary, Margrate, Anne, Elizabeth, the daughters all under age; an expected child. Homefarm of 156 acres and 44 ac. of meadow, called Raways Neck, as described in patent of Governour Carthwrite (Carteret) to testator; a parcel of upland, 50 ac., and meadow, 10 ac., bought of William Oliver, of Elizabeth Town dec'd; 34 ac. of upland between Ellin Scott, Rosses' Brook, Mrs. Thomas and the Commons; 4 ac. of meadow on Raways Neck, between Millers meadow and James Hains; 230 ac. of upland on the West branch of Raway River, as patented by said Governour; personal property. Witnesses—Johannis Sleght, Abraham Lee, H. Lindley. Proved October 22, 1754, by the testimony of Jacob Dehart as to the signature of Lindley, "who had taught him to write." Peter Tranbles and John Tranbles are made Administrators with the will annexed.

Lib. F, p. 216.

1755, Feb. 24. Inventory, £265.3.8, by William Oliver and William Porter.

1756, April 30. Account by the Administrators.

1754, Feb. 26. Treadway, John, of Deptford Township, Gloucester Co., yeoman. Int. Bond of widow, Sarah, as Adm'x; Henry Treadway, yeoman, fellowbondsman, both of said Township. Lib. 7, p. 468.

1754, ——— ——. Inventory, £102.1.8, by John Sparks and John Wilkins.

1754, Nov. 7. Trimmer, Tunis, of Roxberry, Morris Co., weaver; will of. Wife, Eleasabath. Children—Paul, Mary and Anthony, all under age. Real and personal estate. Executors—Mathias Trimmer and Johannes Hager. Witnesses—Roelof Roelofson, Johann Wilhelm Welsh, Johannes Petter Scharfenstein (the last two signing in German). Proved Dec. 24, 1754. Lib. 8, p. 77.

1754, Dec. 3. Inventory, £211.17.7, incl. outstanding debts, £60.11.10, 5 old books, 3s.; made by John Hendershart and Roelof Roelofson.

1753, Sept. 3. Trotter, Benjamin, of Elizabeth Town, Essex Co., gentleman; will of. Children—William, John Cavalier, Katharine, Elizabeth; mother-in-law, Mary Jewet. Houses and land in Elizabeth Town, inherited from father Benjamin Trotter, late dec'd; do. bought of Stephen Crane; do. on the Island of Jamaica, inherited from Col. John Cavalier. Personal property, incl. a silverheaded cane, silver shoebuckles, gold sleeve buttons, a pearl necklace with a solitaire, a silver girdle buckle, set with pearls, and an old "Diman" ring. Executors—John Troop (Troup), of New York City, merchant, and Joseph Ogden, of Elizabeth Town. Witnesses—Jonathan Crane, Jr., Humphrey Spining, Jacob Mitchell. Proved August 6, 1754.

Lib. F, p. 220.

1754, Nov. 1. Trout, John, of Mansfield, Burlington Co. Int. Inventory, £39.9.6, by Edward Rockhill and Joseph English.

1754, Nov. 2. Bond of John Rockhill as Adm'r; Joseph English and Edward Rockhill, fellowbondsmen, all of said Co. Lib. 8, p. 65.

1751, Sept. 21. Trusdill, William, of Great Egg harbour, Gloucester Co., tanner; will of. Children, but only daughter, Mary, spoken of by name. John English sole Executor. Witnesses—Edward Doughty,

Jr., Mary Gandy, William English. Proved June 1, 1752, when John English refused to act as Executor and John Price was sworn in as administrator on June 2. Lib. 8, p. 108.
 1751, Dec. 13. Inventory, £24.15.3, by Andrew Blackman and Stephen Morris.

 1759, April 23. Tucker, William, of Essex Co. Int. Mary Tucker, widow, renounced and desired Justus Morris to administer.
 1759, April 26. Adm'r—Justus Morris, of Raway in Essex Co., yeoman. Bondsman—Samuel Shotwell, of same place, yeoman.
Lib. G, p. 57.

 1759, July 26. Tuckniss, Henry, of Burlington City, cordwainer; will of. Wife, Ann, sole Executrix. Children—Robert, John, James and Mary. House and lot, bought of George Reading and wife, Rebeckkah. Personal estate. Witnesses—William Smith, Isaac Heulings, Aquila Rees. Proved Nov. 20, 1759. Lib. 9, p. 287.

 1757, Oct. 23. Tunison, Tunis, of Somerset Co., yeoman; will of. Wife, Ariantje. Children—Tunis, Abigall, Sarah, Cornelius, Altje, Geartje and Johannis. Homefarm, bought of Charles Coxe; another farm, bought of the same. Personal estate, incl. negro slaves. Executors—the wife and son Tunis. Witnesses—Barnardus Lagrange, Philip Tunison and Cornelius Tunison, Jr. Proved Dec. 22, 1757.
Lib. F, p. 478.

 1759, Dec. 25. Turner, George, of Evesham Township, Burlington Co.; will of. Wife, Hannah, sole Executrix; an expected child. Mother, Jane Middleton. Brothers-in-law—William Matlock and John Risdrell. Homefarm and cedar swamps, bought of Daniel Lippincott. Personal estate. Witnesses—James Cattell, Noah Haines, Margery Kirkbride. Proved May 3, 1760. Lib. 10, p. 15.
 1760, Apr. 18. Inventory, £135.10.7, by James Cattell and Benjamin Haines.

 1756, Oct. 12. Turner, John of Gloucester Township and County; will of. Wife, Mary. Children—John, Milsin (Milicent?), Mary, Rachel and Anne, all under age; an expected child. Personal estate. Executors—the wife and John Hider, of Newtown Township, said Co. Witnesses—Alexander Patterson, John Davis, Samuel Clark. Proved Nov. 16, 1756. Lib. 8, p. 337.
 1756, Dec. 15. Inventory, £269.14, incl. a servant lad, £10; made by Gabriel Davies and William Davis.

 1754, Feb. 15. Turner, William, Sr., of Newark, Essex Co; will of. Children—Lillis and Mary, by former wife, apparently daughter of Benjamin Thompson. Present wife, Mehitabel, who had Lydia, William, Daniel and Peter; all the children under age. Real and personal estate, latter incl. a silver-hilted sword, a silver watch, a silver-headed cane. Executors—the wife, stepson, Jabez Canfield, and friend James Nutman. Witnesses—Joseph Riggs, Daniel Farrand, Court Low, Jr. Proved March 14, 1754. Lib. F, p. 232.

 1754, Dec. 14. Tuttle, Timothy, of Hanover, Morris Co.; will of. Wife, Cissel. Children—Daniel, Isaac, Thomas, Stephen, Mary, Joanna, Abraham (under age). Homefarm; a grist mill; land, where the old pond was, between the race and the river; other real and personal estate. Executors—the wife, son Daniel, and son-in-law Jonathan Stilles. Witnesses—Lodawick Wortman, Matthew Lum, Ezekiel Cheever. Proved March 24, 1755. Lib. F, p. 269.

1753, June 12. Tyle, Margret, of Depford Township, Gloucester Co., widow; will of. Children—Naomi Tyle and Samuel Graves (both under age and children by former husband, Samuel Graves); an unborn child. Other children, names not given. Naomi to be given to Debora Dun or to Massey Jefferis; son Samuel not to go to his uncle's. Sister, Mary Kimsey, and husband's brother, John Tyle, remaindermen. Executor—James Cooper. Witnesses—Abram Chattin, William Fletcher, John Wood. Proved Nov. 20, 1754. Lib. 8, p. 113.
1754, Nov. 19. Inventory, £56.4, incl. bonds and book debts, £38.17.6; a looking glass, Bible and other books, 15s. 6d.; made by John Brown and Gabriel Rambo.
1761, Apr. 20. Account by the Executor, who adds to it £9.3.9, and makes it his debtor for £6.18.2.

1758, Dec. 16. Tyler, David, of Deerfield Township, Cumberland Co. Int. Adm'r—John Tyler. Lib. 9, p. 178.

1760, Dec. 26. Urion, Andrew, of Greenwich, Gloucester Co., waterman. Int. Bond of Hans Urion as Adm'r; John Jurin (Urion) fellowbondsman, both of said Co., yeoman. Lib. 10, p. 291.
1761, Jan. 2. Inventory, £24.1.10, by Mathew Gill and Thomas Roberts.

1748, July 15. Vahan (Vaughn), John, of Upper Freehold, Monmouth Co., yeoman; will of. Wife, Rachel. Children—James, Richard, Azariah (all three under age), Esther, Tabitha, Rebecca and Rachel. Real and personal estate. Executors—the wife, brother William Vaughn and Thomas Cox. Witnesses—Thomas Clayton, Robert Hankinson, Robert Lawrence. Proved April 29, 1752. Lib. F, p. 51.
1752, Apr. 8. Inventory, £189.18.2, by John Cox and Thomas Cleayton.

1754, May 1. Vail, John, of the "Burrough" of Elisabeth, E. J.; will of. Wife, Mary. Children—John, Daniel, Isaac, David, Jacob, Abraham, Benjamin, Joseph and Christien. Real and personal estate. Executors—brother, Steven Vail, and Abner Hamton. Witnesses—David Coryell, Micaiah Dunn, Mary Mullen. Proved June 4, 1754.
Lib. F, p. 181.
1754, June 6. Inventory, £703.14.7, incl. what is given to the widow by will, £54.12.6; bonds, book debts and cash, £39.5.1; 3 looking glasses, 20s.; 2 Bibles and other books, £1.17; made by Reune Runyon and John Hepburn. [Heading of inventory states he is of "Somerset Co."]

1751, Oct. 27. Valentine, James, of the Township and County of Gloucester, yeoman; will of. Devises to cousin, Richard Arrell, of Philadelphia, all real estate, and makes him Executor, charged with paying legacies to Israel Williams; to nephew, Richard Burch, when of age; to the mother and half-brothers, Edward Bennett and David Bennett, and sister Ruth Burch. Witnesses—Thomas Cuthbert, Ann Cuthbert, Paul Isaac Voto. Proved Nov. 26, 1751. Lib. 7, p. 155.

1751, Nov. 12. (Prior to proof of will), widow, Ann Bennett, appointed Adm'x. Bondsman—Edward Williams, of said place, yeoman. States that the above James Valentine was sometimes called James Bennett. Witnesses—Hannah Cooper and John Ladd.

1749, July 6. Valleau, Magdalen, of Bergen Co.; will of. Children—Theodorus, Peter and Fauconnier Valleau, John Bard, Ann and Susannah, the last two in New York. Real and personal estate. Executors—the four sons. Witnesses—Abraham Lerou, Stephen Bour Dett, Necklaes Ackerman. Proved June 24, 1755. Lib. F, p. 324.

1755, June 6. Peter Valleau resigns as Executor in favor of his brothers, Theodore and John Bard, because he lives at a great distance from Hackensack.

1755, June 26. Fauconnier Valleau resigns likewise, because he lives in another county.

1753, Apr. 4. van Aersdalen, Abraham, of Somerset Co., yeoman; will of. Wife, Mary. Children—Isaac, Willim, Catrin, Cornelius and Abraham, all under age; an expected child. Personal estate, incl. a large Bible. Executors—brothers Simon and Jacobus van Arsdalen and John Stryker. Witnesses—Gerrit van Aersdalen, Johnnis van Aersdalen, John van Dike. Proved May 7, 1753. Lib. F, p. 119.

1753, Apr. 13. Inventory, £174.9, incl. a negro woman and negro boy, £60; books, £2; a silver cup, £1.10; made by Sachyyos van Vooryes, Petris Quick, Simon van Aersdalen, Johannes Stryker and Jacobus van Aersdalen.

1757, March 30. Van Allen, Peter, of Saddle River Precinct, Bergen Co., yeoman; will of. Son, Hendrick, 20 shillings, for birthright. Wife, Tryntie, to have real and personal estate while my widow. Son, Anderis, the farm where I live, reserving a portion for my son Jacob. Executors—sons Anderis and Jacob. Witnesses—George Ryerse, Pieter Post, Hassel Garritse. Proved Oct. 6, 1759.

Lib. H, p. 58.

1748, Sept. 24. van Brakle, James, of Middletown Township, Monmouth Co., mariner; will of. Wife, Sarah. Four children, names not given, all under age. Real and personal estate. Executors—the wife and brother John (van Brackle). Witnesses—Johannes Heyer, David Allen and Thomas Bullman. Proved May 9, 1760. Lib. G, p. 197.

1760, May 10. Inventory, £174.11.3, incl. silver buckles, buttons and pieces of spoons, £1.4; 6 books; bonds and notes, £120.4.9; 2 navigation books, 7s.; made by John Smith and Thomas Bullman.

1750, Nov. 7. van Buskirck, Lawrence, Esq., of Minachquay, Bergen Co., will of. Fytie. Children—Cornelius, Janitie (wife of Jacob van Hoorne), Metie (wife of Johannes Legrange, they having children), John, Geytie (Feytie) and Jannetie), Geytie (or Feytie) (wife of John Roll of Staten Island), Anna (wife of Thomas Brown, mariner). Real and personal estate, incl. negro slaves. Executors—the wife during widowhood, son Cornelius, and the three sons-in-law. Witnesses—John Coo, Jr., William Lewis, Abram Lodge. Codicil of May 27, 1752, revokes appointment of son Cornelius as Executor. Witnesses—Jorys Vrelandt, Samuel Ten Eyck, Abram Lodge. Proved April 12, 1753.

Lib. F, p. 109.

CALENDAR OF WILLS—1751-1760   333

———, ——— —. **van Camp, John,** of Sussex Co.; will of. Sons—Isaac and Gilberd. Grandchildren—John Van Wye and Magdalen van Wye. Personal estate, incl. a negro man and negro girl. Executors—the two sons. Witnesses—John Rosenkrans, Thomas Sartworth (Swartworth) and John Riky. Proved March 17, 1759.
Lib. 9, p. 327.
1758, Dec. 15. Inventory, £164.9, incl. a negro man, £50; a negro woman, £50; made by Jacobus Cole and Andreas Faubert (in German script and very indistinct).

1757, Aug. 11. van Campen, (van Kamp), Jacob, of Sussex Co., killed by the Indians. Inventory, £47.8.4.
1757, Dec. 7. Bond of Geisbert van Kampe, of Redingtown, as Adm'r; Joseph Yard, of Trenton, fellowbondsman.
Hunterdon Wills and Lib. 9, p. 145.

1751, May 18. Vance, Bridget, of Alloways Creek, Salem Co., widow; will of. Leaves homefarm to James Morgan for five years free of rent; then to Samuel, son of John Vance, his heirs, etc.; both are named Executors. Witnesses—John Rolfe, Joseph Zane, Josiah Kay. Proved May 31, 1751.
1751, May 30. Inventory, £59.12, made by Thomas Thompson and Josiah Kay.
Salem Wills, 847 Q.

1747, July 26. Vance, John, of Newark, Essex Co., turner; will of. Wife, Alice. Children—Anne Norwood, Elizabeth Henry, Edward, William, Thomas, Esther, Alexander, the last two under age. Grandson, John Vance, son of son James. Real and personal estate. Executors—the wife, John Johnson, tanner, and Ichabod Grammon, weaver, both of Newark. Witnesses—Stephen Meeker, Henry Lyon, Charles Hole. Proved Dec. 21, 1751.
Lib. F, p. 29.
1752, Jan. 30. Inventory, £190.11.7, by Christopher Wood and Joseph Lyon.

1754, Sept. 23. van Court, Thomas, of Middlesex Co.; will of. Brothers—Samuel (sole Executor), Moses, John and Michael, the last under age. Estate inherited from father. Witnesses—Daniel Sayre, Brice Rikey, William Leddel. Proved Dec. 10, 1755.
Lib. F, p. 303.
1756, Jan. 7. Inventory, £133.2.7, incl. bonds, book debts and notes, £103.8.7; a watch, £10; made by John Hepburn and William Olden.

1756, Sept. 5. van de Mark, Jeremiah, of New Urley (Hurley), also of Wallpack, Sussex Co., weaver; will of. Wife, Lea. Children—Benjamin, Peter, Jeams, Elias, John, Samuel, Jeremiah and Elizabeth. Real and personal estate. Executors—sons Benjamin and Peter, with Hendry, son of Nichloss Schoonover. Witnesses—Lambert Barns, Dirck van Vliet, Dirck Karmer. Proved Nov. 21, 1760. Lib. 10, p. 473.
1757, May 26. Inventory, £89.5.6., by Dirck Karmer and Henry Schoonover.
1762, June 3. Account by the Executors, who add for the farm sold, £403.12, and for grain not appraised, £38.

1753, July 12. van der Cook, Henry, of Perquaneck Precinct, Morris Co., yeoman, will of. Wife Cathrine. Children—Michael, Peter, Henry, John, Cathrine, Sarah and Anne. Real and personal estate.

Executors—brother Francis Vandercook and brother-in-law, Peter Post. Witnesses—Peeter Post, Joseph Barham, Livina Francisco. Proved Nov. 24, 1755. Lib. F, p. 322.

1755, Dec. 22. van der Hoofe, Gilbert, of Morris Co. Int. Bond of John, eldest son, as Adm'r; Lemuel Bowers and Nicholas Stagg fellowbondsmen, all of said Co. Lib. G, p. 23.

1756, Mar. 24. van Deventer, Jacob, of Somerset Co., yeoman; will of. Wife, Elizabeth. Sons—Jacob and Jeremiah. Real and personal estate. Executors—Michael Field and Jeremiah Field. Witnesses—Isaac van Deventer, John Harris and John Hodghon. Proved April 12, 1756. Lib. F, p. 334.
1756, Apr. 5. Michael Field of Bound Brook, one of the Executors named above, refuses to qualify, and, on April 12, Jeremiah Field does the same.
1756, Apr. 26. Bond of Elizabeth Van Deventer, widow, as Adm'x with will annexed, Stephen Crane, Esq., of the Borough of Elizabeth, fellowbondsman.
1756, Apr. 28. Inventory, £248.5.4, incl. a silver box, etc., £1.5.6; a "grate" Bible; a bond, £71.19.6; made by Ebenezer Tingley and Samuel Dunn.

1757, Jan. —. van Dien, Cornelius, of Bergen Co.; will of. Divides property between Hendrickje, daughter of Reynier van Giesen; brother, Derck van Dien; Gerret and Janniette, children of brother Albert van Dien; brother, Hendrick van Dien; sister, Geertruy Kip, and children of sister Hendrickje. Executors—Hendrick Kip and Rynier van Giesen. Witnesses—Jacop Kip, Pieter Kip and Isack Kip. Proved April 9, 1757. Lib. F, p. 452.
1757, Apr. 8. Inventory, £175 incl. 2 negroes, £75; made by Egbert and Lawrence Accerman.

1750, Nov. 12. van Duehren, Johannes Bernhardus, minister of the Lutheran Congregation of Schamenie (Neshaminy?), living at Rachewe, (Rockaway), Jersey; will of. Wife, Maria. Children—Godfried, Johannes, Barbara, Maria, Dorithea, Anna, David, Elizabeth, Sarah and Joanna. Real and personal estate, incl. slaves, books, a Bible in three volumes. Executors—Domine Albert Weygandt and Mr. Barrend van Horren. Witnesses—Albert Weygand, Abraham van Deventer, Francis Lucas, Harman Roelofsun. Proved May 10, 1751. Lib. 7, p. 63.
1751, May 6. Inventory of the estate: Real—land at Lebanon, £150; 500 acres above Albany, not valued. Personal—£521.3, incl. bonds, £290; silver spoons, £2; gold sleeve buttons, 19s.; a silver watch, £7; 187 books, [56; made by John Nicklas Bickel (Pickel) and Francis Lucas.

1751, Dec. 2. van Dyck (van Dyke), Hendryecus, of Middelbush, Somerset Co., yeoman; will of. Wife, Maregrieta. Children—Johanis, the oldest son; other children, names not given, all under age. Real and personal estate. Executors—brother, Peter van Dick and cousin, Gerrit Terhune. Witnesses—Gerrit Gerritsen, Jr., Simon Wikoff, Jr., and Gerrit Gerritsen. Proved Feb. 9, 1756.
Lib. F, p. 326.
1756, Mar. 16. Inventory, £165.8.9., incl. a looking glass and pic-

CALENDAR OF WILLS—1751-1760   335

tures, 10s.; a Testament with silver clasps, 12s.; other books, 12s.; a negro wench, £41; made by Petrus Wyckof, Frederick van Lawe (Liew), and Jacob Wyckoff.

1750, Aug. 18. Van Dyke, Francis, of Essex Co., gunsmith; will of. Children—Nicholas, Francis, Elizabeth Broadberry, Marritie van Winckle and Hanah. Land in Newark Township, bought of Jonathan Seers, bounded N. by Second River, E. by Paysayack. Personal estate. Son-in-law, Richard Broadberry sole Executor. Witnesses—Adrian P. Post, Abraham Gerretse, James Billington. Proved August 24, 1752. Lib. F, p. 63.

1753, Apr. 3. Vaneman, Samuel, of Salem Town and Co. Int. Bond of Josiah Kay as Adm'r; John Andrews fellowbondsman, both of said Co. Lib. 8, p. 88.

1751, July 22. Van Geeson, Bosteon, of Essex Co. Int. Adm'r—Hendrick Van Geesen, of Newark, said Co., eldest son. Bondsman—Isaac Lyon, of same place. Witness—Uzal Ogden. Lib. E, p. 541.
  1751, Aug. 1. Inventory, £535.12.8, by Isaac Lyon and Joseph Johnson.

1753, June 23. Van Giesen, Abraham, Sr., of Essex Co., gentleman; will of. Wife [not named]. Children—Reinier, Andris, Isaac, Abram, Dirkje, Anna Maria, Catharine and heirs of daughter Printie van Giesen. Home farm, adjoining "Huntentun's" patent; share of land, formerly belonging to Johannis van Giesen, dec'd; 500 acres in Morris Co., called Achquach, or Tewahhaw. Personal estate, incl. a silver mug. Executors—sons Reinier, Andris and Isaac. Witnesses—Alexander Cockafair, Jr., Margrit Degarmo, Peter DeGarmo. Proved May 1, 1758. Lib. F, p. 538.
  1759, May 4. Inventory, £284.9.1, by Daniel Pierson and Peter Degarmo.

1753, Sept. 24. Vangiesen, Andreas, of Essex Co. Int. Adm'r—Abraham Vangiesen, only son, of Essex Co. Bondsman—Peter Degarmo, of same place. Lib. F, p. 136.
  1754, Feb. 11. Inventory, £72.6.9, by John King, Jr., Elias Vreeland, Johannes Woutersse and Peter Degarmo.

1758, Dec. 29. van Horn, Abraham, of Hunterdon Co.; will of. Wife, Antia. Children—Abraham (youngest son and under age), Margaret, wife of Herman Rulefson, Phicha, Antia, Neeltie, Matthew (oldest son, married), Cornelius. Children of son Matthew, viz., Abraham, William, Matthew and Cornelius. Homefarm of 250 acres with a gristmill; another farm of 200 ac.; other real estate and personal property, incl. 7 negro slaves. Executors—sons Cornelius and Abraham, with son-in-law Tobias ten Eyck. Witnesses—Cornelius van der Bilt, Edward Wilmot, David Cock. Proved Dec. 5, 1759. Lib. 10, p. 73.
  1760, Feb. 9. Inventory, £576.11.6, incl. bonds and book debts, £201.9.5; books, £2.14; 5 looking glasses, £4; 200 bush. of wheat, a skreen and a skoop, £64; made by Michal Demott and Edward Wilmot.

1757, Dec. ——. van Horn, John, of Bergen Co.; will of. Wife [not named]. Children—John (under age), Linah (under 18). Neettie (wife of Helmagh Vreelandt), Annatie (wife of Cornelius van Vorst), Jannatie (wife of Cornelius Garrabrants). A farm and plantation. Personal property, incl. 5 slaves, a silver tankard, a silver teapot, six silver teaspoons. Executors—the three sons-in-law. Witnesses— Peter Stuyvesant (signs by mark), Tunas Gerbrants and David Mathews. Proved Dec. 29, 1757. Lib. F, p. 479.

1757, Dec. 30. Inventory, £2280.11.10, incl. 13 small pictures; one silver tankard, £10; a silver teapot, £8; a silver bowl, £5; two silver cups, £4.5; 51 large and small silver spoons, £13.10.0; 6 slaves, £185; a Psalm book with silver clasps; mortgages from Myndent Garrabrants, £213; Cornelis Bogart, £106; cash in York currency, £245; bonds for York currency, £1272.10; made by Joris Belant and Hendrick Blinkerhoff. Bergen Wills, 389 B.

1760, May 28. van Horn, Luykes, of Hackensack; will of. Wife [not named]. Children—Marytye, Jannitje, Gritye, Elsye, Sietsye, Annatye, Angenitye and Rachel. House and land on both sides of the highway. Personal estate. Executors—David van Buskerk and Peter Demarest, Jr. Witnesses—William Campbell, Dr. Abraham van Horn and William van Horn. Proved June 19, 1760. Lib. G, p. 234.

1760, June 18. Inventory, £113.13.0, by Johannes Demarest and William Campbell.

1755, April 12. Vanhuys, Ouke, of Perth Amboy, Middlesex Co., yeoman; Int. The widow renounced. Adm'r—James Vanhuys, son of said Ouke, of same place. Bondsman—John Vanhuys, of said Co., yeoman. Witness—Thomas Bartow. Lib. F, p. 257.

1760, May 23. van Iman, (Vannaman), Garrat, son of David, of Greenwich, Gloucester Co., yeoman; will of. Wife, Ruth. Children—Isaac, Joseph, and Elenor, wife of Thomas Bright. Homefarm; meadow on Clanmell and Lowland Creeks; 100 acres of cedar swamp; other real and personal property. Executors—the wife, son-in-law, Thomas Bright, and Thomas Clark. Witnesses—Alexander Randall, Andrew Long, John Rumford. Proved June 28, 1760.
Lib. 10, p. 90.

1760, June 24. Inventory, £622.4.10, incl. an old negro man and negro girl, £70; a looking glass, £1; book debts, £169.11.6; made by Alexander Randall and William Nickle.

1760, Aug. 31. van Kirk, Arthur, of the South Ward of Perth Amboy, Middlesex Co., yeoman; will of. Wife, Mary. Children—Elce, William, Jennison, Annah, Sarah and Elizabeth, all under age; an expected child. Real and personal estate. Executors—brother, William van Kirk, and brother-in-law, Robert Davison. Witnesses— Stephen Warne, Barent Hegeman and Henry Disbrow. Proved Sept. 22, 1760. Lib. G, p. 304.

1760, Sept. 4. Inventory, £166.14, by Luycas Schanck and Barent Hegeman.

1763, Jan. 7. Account by the Executors, who have sold the personal estate for £228.17.7, and the plantation for £556; and have paid out £774.5.4, among the items being tavern tax, or license, for 6 months, £1.3.4. and £30 to the widow for release of dowry.

1752, May 2. van Meter, Henry, of Piles Grove Township, Salem Co.; will of. Children—Joseph, David, John, Ephraim, Fetters, Benjamin, Jacob, Elesabeth, and Rebecca. Homefarm of 350 acres; farm of 300 ac., now occupied by Philipp Sutter; farm of 350 ac., now occupied by Joshua Garrison; farm of 350 ac. adjoining the homefarm; 900 ac., bought of Langhorn Biles and Jeremiah Bates. Personal property, incl. a negro girl. Executors—sons Joseph and David. Witnesses—Joshua Garrison, Benjamin Worton and Onesimus Seagrave. Proved Dec. 8, 1759. Lib. 10, p. 507.

1758, Nov. 28. van Meter, Isaac. Inventory of part of his estate found in Salem Co., in the custody of Jost Millar, viz., a negro man, "if he arrives at the age of 21 years," £50, proclamation money; a negro girl, £15, "if she arrives to full age." Signed by Bateman Lloyd and Joseph van Meter. Salem Wills, 1049 Q.

1760, Feb. 14. van Meter, John, of Piles Grove Township, Salem Co., yeoman; will of. Wife, Sarah. Daughters—Catthreain and Sarah, both under age. Executors—brothers Joseph and Ephraim van Meter. Witnesses—William Conkelyn, David Gagers and Azubah Concklyn. Proved Dec. 24, 1760. Lib. 10, p. 336.
1760, Mar. 3. Inventory, £103.0.2, by James Dunlap and Samuel Sherry.

1754, Feb. 15. Vanmetre, Isaac, of South Branch of the Potowmack, in Frederick Co., Va.; will of. Wife, Hannah, to have £20 yearly and negro named Hannah. Lands in New Jersey, with the stock thereon, to remain under the leases now granted till they expire, then to be sold, and money to go to my children, viz., Henry, Jacob, Garret, Sarah Richman, Catherine Vanmetre, Rebecca Hite, Helita Vanmetre. Lands in Virginia I bought of James Cebrun, located by Abraham Hite and Jonathan Heath, of 600 acres, to be divided, and the upper 200 I give to my son Garrett, the middle 200 to my son Jacob and the lower 200 to my son Henry, whereon he now lives. The land I purchased of Michael Hyder I give to my daughter Catherine, if she incline to dwell thereon, and, if she does not, then to be sold. The 200 acres which is in dispute, if it goes to me, then I give it to Abraham Hite, husband of my daughter Rebecca, joining his lot, and the other 200 acres I give to my daughter Hellita. If my daughters Catherine and Hellita die without marriage or issue, then my daughter Sarah, the wife of John Richman, to have said land. If sons Jacob or Garret die without marriage or issue, then their part to go to the surviving children. Executors—sons Henry, Jacob and Garret. Witnesses—Ebenezer Holme, Abel Randell, Joseph Carrell. Will proved Dec. 14, 1757, in Hampshire County, Va. Lib. 12, p. 119.

1755, Dec. 10. Vanneman, Petter, of Pens Neck, Salem Co., weaver; will of. Wife, Cathrine. Children—Israel, Lawrence, Petter, Elizabeth and Sarah. Real and personal estate. Executors—the wife and brother, Garrett Vanneman. Witnesses—Christopher Lenmier, Ann Lenmire and William Guest. Proved March 2, 1757.
Lib. 8, p. 148.

1757, Feb. 22. Inventory, £80.9.1, incl. two Bibles and other books, 7/6; made by Samuel Linch and John Vannemen.

1751, Oct. 30. van Nest, Jacob, of Somerset Co., yeoman. Int. Bond of Gisbert Boogart, Jr., and wife, Elizabeth, late Elizabeth van Nest, of Pennsylvania, as Adm'rs; Frederick Bodin, living in Somerset Co., fellowbondsman. Lib. F, p. 61.

1751, —— ——. Inventory, £71.5, by Martin Beekman, Henry V. Middleswaert and Andres Stott. [Made Apr. 24, 1747].

1751, June 10. van Neste, Barnardus, of Somerset Co., yeoman; will of. Wife, Catherine. Children—Barnardus, Mary, Catherine, Elizabeth. Real and personal estate, incl. negro slaves. Executors —the son and brother, John van Nest. Witnesses—Tunis Tunison, Abraham Tunison, Edward Willmott. Proved August 28, 1751.
Lib. E, p. 543.
1751, Aug. 7. Inventory, £752.4.10, by Dirck Van Veghten and Kennes Kennessen.

1752, Apr. 2. van Neste, Jacob, of Bridgewater Township, Somerset Co., yeoman; will of. Wife, Caterine. Children—Peter, Jacob and Jemima (under age). Real and personal estate. Executors—the wife and Thomas van Horne. Witnesses—Jacob Tenyke, Francis Cossaart, Jacomintie ten Eyck. Proved April 3, 1753. Lib. F, p. 107.
1753, Jan. 9. Inventory, £569.2.10, by Gisbert Crom and Francis Cossaart.

1760, Oct. 1. Vanniman, Ruth, of Greenwich, Gloucester Co., widow; will of. Sons Isaac and Joseph, both under age. Real and personal estate. Executor—Thomas Clark. Witnesses—Mary Reaves, John Spencer. Proved October 11, 1760. Lib. 10, p. 372.
1760, Oct. 16. Inventory, £340.10.9, incl. a negro girl, £55; book debts and cash, £76; made by Alexander Randall and William Mickle.

1753, July 5. van Noordstrand, Johannes Folkertse, of Somerset Co.; will of. Wife, Ann. Son, Folkert. Grandchildren—John and Angenitje van Noordstrand. Real and personal estate. Executors— son Folkert, Cornelius Bennet of Middlesex Co., and Christopher Probasco of Somerset Co. Witnesses—William Ouke, Minne van Voorhies and Jacob Weiser. Proved April 5, 1756. Lib. F, p. 339.

1760, Dec. 29. Van Norder, of New Brunswick, Middlesex Co. Int. Adm'r—John Van Norder, eldest brother, of said place. Witness— John Smyth. Lib. G, p. 340.

1757, May 2. Vanomon, Ephraim, of Hunterdon Co. Int. Bond of Henry Woolsey as Adm'r; Josiah Howell fellowbondsman, both of Hopewell, said Co. Lib. 8, p. 398.
1757, May 13. Inventory, £5.16.6, by Joseph Brown and Cornelius Polhemus.

1757, Nov. 15. Van Riper, Dirk Thomassa, of Essex Co. Int. Adm'r —Dirch Van Riper, of said Co. Bondsman—George Vreeland, of same place. Witness—Uzal Ogden. Lib. F, p. 409.

1757, Nov. 12. Van Riper, John, of Essex Co. Int. Adm'r—Jury Peterson, of Essex Co., principal creditor. Bondsman—Adrian Post, Jr., of Acquacknong, in Essex Co. Witness—Uzal Ogden.
Lib. F, p. 509.

1755, Jan. 27. Van Riper, Tomas, of Essex Co. Int. Margaret, the widow, renounced, to Adrian Post, principal creditor, of said Co., who became Adm'r. Bondsman—Gerret Gerretsen, of same place. Witness—Uzal Ogden. Lib. F, p. 265.

1756, Mar. ———. van Schuiver, Jacob, son of John, of Burlington City, petitions, that John Tylee, of said City, be appointed his Guardian.
1756, Mar. 2. Bond of John Tylee, cordwainer, as such Guardian; Joseph Hollinshead fellowbondsman, both of said City.
Burl. Wills 5779 C.

1754, May 24. van Sicklan, Abraham, of Readington, Hunterdon Co. Int. Bond of Anne van Sickland as Adm'x; John van Sickle fellowbondsman, both of Redingtown. Lib. 8, p. 63.
1754, ——— ———. Inventory, £166.13, by John Marlatt, Jr., and Harmen Lane.

1754, Oct. 22. van Sicklan, Peter, of Lebanon, Hunterdon Co. Int. Bond of Sarah van Sicklan as Adm'x; Nathaniel Foster fellowbondsman, both of Lebanon Township. Lib. 8, p. 86.
1754, ——— ———. Inventory, £102.13.3, by Nathaniel Foster and Andrew Bray.
1755, June 25. Account by the Administratrix.

1759, Aug. 25. van Sickle, Abraham, of Morris Co. Int. Inventory, £333.2.10., incl. 62 bush. of corn in the ear; 17 do. of buckwheat; bonds, cash and notes, £150.4.7; made by William Broadwell, Abraham Rutan, Thomas Baker and Sarah van Sickel.

1757, Oct. 20. van Sickle, Fardinandus and Richard, sons of Renier, of Hunterdon Co., petition as follows: Fardinandus that John Bennit, of Pensylvania, be appointed his Guardian; Richard asks for appointment of Evan Jones of Pensylvania as his Guardian.
Burl. Wills, 426 J.

1754, Feb. 4. Van Voorhees, Koert, of Perth Amboy, Middlesex Co., yeoman; will of. To only son, Stephen, silver tankard and spoons; to wife, Sarah, spoons. Remainder to said wife Sarah and son. Executors—friends James Peairs and Luycas Schenck. Witnesses—Stephen Warne, John Collins, Matthias Johnson. Proved Jan. 20, 1756. Lib. F, p. 318.
1755, Aug. 27. Inventory, £102.19.3, incl. 4 silver spoons, £1.5; a Bible, 14s.; made by Daniel Disbrow and Richard Jewell.

1733, June 13. van Vorst, Cornelis, of Horessimese, Bergen Co., yeoman; will of. Wife, Fytye. Children—Gerrit, Johannes, Cornelius, Janneke and Maritie. Real and personal estate, incl. a negro slave. Executors—son Cornelius and Walter Hier (Spier?). Witnesses—Hendrick Bogert, Paroclus Parmyter, H. Demeyer. Proved August 15, 1753. Lib. F, p. 128.

1757, May 14. van Wagenen, Garret, of Readings Town, Hunterdon Co. Int. Cathrone, widow, relinquishes her right of administration to her brother, Coenrat ten Eyck, and John Stoll.
1757, May 16. Bond of Coenrat ten Eyck, of Somerset Co., and John Stoll, of Hunterdon Co., as Adm'rs; David McWilliam, of Somerset Co., fellowbondsman, all yeomen. Lib. 8, p. 432.

1757, May 18. Inventory, £128.19.1, incl. a looking glass, 3s.; 3 books, 1/6; a small Dutch Bible, £1; book debts, £40.13.5; made by Abraham Bodine and John van Sickle, who also report as bad debts, £84.2.1.

———, ——— ———. van Wagenen, Johannis, of Bergen Co.; will of. Wife, Cathallyne. Children—Cornelius, Jacob, John, Jane, (wife of Hendrick de Moat). Grandson—Johannis, son of dec'd's eldest son Helmigh. Real and personal estate. Executors—sons Cornelius, Jacob and John. Witnesses—Hendrick Siggles (Sickles), Zacharias Sickles and David Abeel. Proved Nov. 8, 1759. Lib. G, p. 118.

1753, Aug. 14. van Wickle, Symen, of Somerset Co., yeoman; will of. Wife, Dinah. Children—Evert, Nicholas, Anne, Mary, Dinah, Elsee, Mattje and Seytje. Homefarm on Rartian River; a lot of 31 acres over the river and on the Northside of the Raritan road, bought of son-in-law, Joseph Mount; 10 acres of meadow. Personal estate, incl. negroes and plate. Executors—the two sons. Witnesses—Dirrik Rappaljee, Cornelus Sebring, Barnardus Lagrange. Proved Jan. 3, 1755. Lib. F, p. 237.

1757, Mar. 2. van Wicklen, Evert, of Somerset Co., yeoman; will of. Wife, Cornelia. Daughter, Antje. Brother, Nicholas van Wicklen. Brother-in-law, Ram Lupardus. Sisters—Mattja (wife of George Anderson, Jr.), Seytje (wife of John Boyce), Dinah (wife of John Probasco), Antje (wife of Jacob Suydam). Children of dec'd sister Elsee, late wife of Joseph Mount. Real and personal estate. Executors—brother, Nicholas, and brother-in-law, Ram Lupardus. Witnesses—John van Bueren, Barnardus Lagrange and Brunt Neume— (in German script, very indistinct). Codicil of March 3, 1757, provides that outset, given to wife Cornelia, by father, Christianus Lupardus, and devised to daughter Antje, shall go, in case of Antje's death without issue, to wife's sister Anatje, wife of Cornelius Duryea, of Long Island. Witnesses—John van Bueren and Barnardus Lagrange. Proved March 17, 1757. Lib. F, p. 411.

1757, Mar. 24. Inventory, £720.11.8, incl. bonds and notes, £197.6.1; an old negro wench, £5; a negro man, £60; a negro boy, £45; 52 bush. of wheat and £88.9 of goods, given by the codicil to the child with remainder to Antje, wife of Cornelius Duryea; this additional list includes 2 silver snuffboxes; a Dutch Psalm book, 20s.; a gold ring and gold locket, £2. The whole appraised by Cornelus Sebring and Denys van Duyn.

1759, June 13. van Winkle, John Sr., of the Borough of Elizabeth, Essex Co., yeoman; will of. Wife, Magdalen. Children—Simeon, Alexander, Jacob, Abraham, Merrinus, Hannah, Mary, Leah, Rachel, Magdalen (?), Sarah Duley (?). Grandchildren—John and Tunis, children of dec'd son John; children of dec'd daughter Catharine Marsh. Personal estate. Executors—Simeon Briant (Bryant) and Joshua Horton. Witnesses—Henry Earle, Isaac Woodruff, Joseph Bruen. Proved August 4, 1759. Lib. G, p. 256.

1760, June 16. van Winkle, John, Jr., of Elizabeth. Int. Adm'r—James Black, weaver, principal creditor, of Elizabeth. Bondsman—David Ball of same place. Lib. G, p. 290.

CALENDAR OF WILLS—1751-1760   341

1757, June 8.   van Yderstyn, (Eydersteyn), Casparus, of Bergen Co. Inventory, £93.18.4, by Tadeus van Eydersteyn, administrator, and appraised by Isaac Kingsland and John Vreland.   Lib. H, p. 14.

1750, July 5.   Verplanck, Gulian, of New York City, merchant; will of. To mother, Aryaentie Warmstal, widow, £60 yearly. Sister, Anne Verplanck, £30 yearly. Wife, Mary, furniture, slaves, etc., and an annuity of £200, and the rent of my house in Wall Street, where I live, till my son is 23, and, if he die, then till my eldest daughter is 21. Son, Samuel, farm in Dutches County called Mount Gulian, but if he die before 21, then to my daughter Aryentie Verplanck. I am entitled to part of a large tract of land in the Counties of Albany and Ulster, which was granted by Patent to Johannes Hardenbergh and Company, and by a division there was released to me my portion; part of which I give to my son Samuel, part to my daughter Anne Verplank, part to daughter Mary Verplanck, and part to daughter Aryaentie Verplanck. Should there be another child born, it is provided for. Executors—Wife, Mary, Gabriel Ludlow, Robert Crommeline and Charles Crommeline. Witnesses—Thomas Duncan, David Vanhorne, Samuel Van Horne. Proved April 9, 1752.   Lib. F, p. 35.

1748, Dec. 6.   Verree, James, of Burlington; will of. Wife, Rachel. Children—William, Mary (wife of George Harris), James, Samuel, Robert, Joseph and Isaac. Grandson, James Thomas. Real and personal estate, incl., a mulatto girl. Executors—the wife, son James and Richard Wright. Witnesses—Sarah Hooper, John Watkinson, George Eyre. Codicil of December 2, 1749, confirms the will. Witnesses—Anne Butterworth, Paul Watkinson, Rowland Ellis. Proved April 30, 1751.

1749, Dec. 29. Inventory, £112.6, almost all carpenter's and joiner's tools; made by Abraham Hewlings and Jonathan Lovett.
Burl. Wills, 4891 C.

1758, Feb. 17.   Vickers, Philipp, of Cohansey, Cumberland Co., yeoman; will of. Wife, Sarah, sole Executrix. Daughter, Mary, (under age). Farm in the "Wodes," left to wife, but to go at her death to Joseph Fithing, Hannah, Thomas and Sarah Ewings. Legacies to son-in-law, Edmond Dare, and daughter-in-law, Ann Dare. Land in Greenwich Precinct. Personal property. Witnesses—Abel Shepperd, William Carll, Isabel Carll. Proved March 22, 1758. Lib. 9, p. 146.

1758, Mar. 7. Inventory, £349.15.7., incl. watches, books, a looking-glass, etc.; made by Obadiah Robins and Mark Reeve.

1759, June 4.   Vickery, Richard, of Allaways Creek, Salem Co. Int. Inventory, £53.18.6.

1759, June 6. Bond of Bradway Keasbey, of Allaways Creek as Adm'r; Edward Keasbey, of the Town of Salem, and Samuel Nicholson, of Elsinburrough, fellowbondsmen, all yeomen.
Lib. 9, p. 351.

1759, June 30.   Vickery, Thomas, of Pen's Neck, Salem Co.; will of. Wife, Sarah. Children—Thomas, Ann and Rebecca, all under age. Real and personal estate. Executors—John Dun and Edmond Wetherby, Jr. Witnesses—Jacob Vanemen, Cathrie Dunn and Mary Kilchrist. Proved July 25, 1759.   Lib. 10, p. 525.

1759, July 23. Inventory, £359.19.11, incl. bonds and book accounts, £64.8.8; made by Daniel Garrison and Francis Miles.

1752, Oct. 13. Viele, Elizabeth, of New York City, widow; will of. Daughter, Sarah Viele to have the use of my real and personal estate during her life, same to be held in trust by my cousins, Andries Abrahams and Ariantie Seymour, and, after the death of said daughter, I give my above cousins my plate and jewels. To the children of my cousin, Sarah Leaycraft, dec'd, the apparel at death of my daughter. My slaves to be freed. Parts of residue to my cousins, Elizabeth Beekman, Cornelia Bowey, Margaret Showet, Cornelia Bogart, and to children of my cousin Elizabeth Deforest, dec'd. Executors—cousins Andries Abrahams and Ariantie Seymour. Witnesses—Jasper Farmer, Luke Romine, Cornelius Sebring. Proved April 17, 1753. Lib. F, p. 117.

1752, June 18. Vleet, John, of Six-Mile Run, Somerset Co., yeoman; will of. Wife, Grietje. Children—John, Geertje, Simon and Grietje. Real and personal estate. Executors—the wife and Folkert van Noort Strant. Witnesses—Daniel Vleet, Jabish Ashmore, John Michael Sperling. Proved Oct. 2, 1752. Lib. F, p. 67.

1752, Sept. 24. Inventory of real and personal estate, £820.0.9, made by Adrian Hegeman and Jocobus Williamson. Includes "200 acres of land, £600."

1722, Dec. 1. Vliet, John, of Six-Mile Run, Somerset Co., yeoman; will of. Wife Geertie. Children—John, of Ten-Mile Run, brewer; Geertye (wife of Simon Wickoff), Sarah, Rebecca, Maria (wife of Adrian Hegeman), Derrick, dec'd, who left a daughter, Dirrickje. Lot No. 6, 500 acres, bought of Theodore Polhemis, Sr., of Jamaica, L. I., on the road from Inions Ferry to Delaware Falls. Personal property, incl. negro slaves. Executors—son John and son-in-law, Simon Wickoff. Witnesses—Francis Harrison, Dirck van Aersdalen, Fredrick van Leewes (Liew). Proved May 30, 1754. Lib. F, p. 178.

1752, Nov. 4. Volckers (Folkerson), Dirck, of "Milston" River, Somerset Co., farmer; will of. Wife, Gerttie. Children—Volker Derrickson (oldest son, who has children Derrick, Frederick, Mary, Volkert, Dinah, Peter, Johannis, Deborah, Jacobus and Abraham); Deborah (wife of Hendrick Rosaboome, who has son Garret Rosaboome); Hannah Dally (who has children, Mary, Elezabeth, Annatje and Gertje); Mary (wife of Peter Schenk). Real and personal estate, incl. negro slaves. Executors—the wife, son-in-law, Peter Schenk, and John Brokaw, of Somerset Co. Witnesses—Hendrick Schenk, Yoseph Folkersen, Sarah Folkerson. Proved August 5, 1754. Lib. F, p. 199.

1751, Apr. 3. Voorhees, Peter, of the Corporation of New Brunswick, Middlesex Co., yeoman. Int. Bond of Mary, widow, as Adm'x; Lucas Voorhees and John Ryder (Rider), both of said Corporation, fellowbondsmen. Lib. E, p. 504.

1750, Aug. 16. Voorhees, Roeloff, Sr., of New Brunswick, Middlesex Co., yeoman; will of. Wife, Maregrieta. Children—Helena, Johanis, Marya, Catlyna, Luke, Gerrit, Roeloff, Johana and Janitie. Real and personal estate, incl. a Dutch Bible, other books, a negro man, money received on behalf of children's grandfather, Gerrit

CALENDAR OF WILLS—1751-1760 343

Stoothoff. Executors—the four sons. Witnesses—Gerrit Voorhees, Johannes, Martinus van Harlingen, Jr., Arnoldus van Harlingen. Proved April 25, 1751. Lib. E, p. 518.

1756, March 29. Vreeland, Isaac, of Newark, Essex Co. Int. Adm'r—Garrabrant Garrabrants, Jr., principal creditor.
1756, April 6. Inventory, £16.4.4, by Daniel Pierson and Humphry Nichols. Lib. F, p. 369.

1754, Apr. 27. Vreeland, Nicholas, of Acquechenong Precinct, Essex Co., yeoman; will of. Wife, Aelse. Sons—Hartman, Hassel, Dirrick, Elyas, and three other children, names not given. Real and personal estate. Executors—sons Elyas and Dirrick, and Micheal Vreeland. Witnesses—John Wanshaer, Christoffel van Rypen, Metye Vanrypen. Proved Oct. 24, 1757. Lib. F, p. 464.

1760, Apr. 11. Vrelandt, Hartman, of Pecquanack Township, Morris Co. Int. Bond of Claas Vreelandt, eldest son and heir, as Adm'r; Marten van Duin fellowbondsman, both of said place. Lib. G, p. 289.
1760, Apr. 25. Inventory, £56.14, by Peter Young and Hendrick Mandeviel.

1756, Oct. 9. Vroom, Christian, of Hunterdon Co., yeoman. Christian, son, gives up his right of administering on the father's estate to Edward Antill, or Hendrick Lane, creditors.
1756, Oct. 12. Bond of Hendrick Lane, of Middlesex Co., yeoman, as Adm'r; Barnardus Lagrange, of the same Co., gent., fellowbondsman. Hunt. Wills, 387 J.

1756, Dec. 2. Vroom, George, of Piscataqua, Middlesex Co., yeoman. Int. Sarah Vroom, his widow, renounced. Adm'rs—Hendrick Vroom and John Vroom, farmer of Middlesex Co. and later of Somerset Co. Bondsman—Peter Vroom, of Somerset Co. Witness—Thomas Bartow.
Lib. F, 392.
1757, Mar. 3. Inventory, £689.18.5, incl. 6 negroes (one a child), £133; a Dutch folio Bible and Dutch sermon book, £1.17; other books, £1.5; 40 Spanish dollars, £17.6.8; bonds and book debts, £126.8.6; made by Edward Antill and Cornelius Low.

1760, Apr. 24. Wade, Benjamin, of the "Borrough" of Elizabeth, Essex Co., yeoman; will of. Wife, Deborah. Children—Jothan, Sarah, Hannah and Rachel. Real and personal estate. Executors—Timothy Whitehead, Esq., and brother, Daniel Wade. Witnesses—James Colie, Samuel Thompson, Jotham Clark, Jr., John Wade, Jr. Proved August 4, 1760. Lib. G, p. 275.

1751, Sept. 9. Wadington, Jonathan, of Alloways Creek Precinct, Salem Co., farmer; will of. Wife [not named]. Children—Isaac, Robert, Sarah (who has children), Mary and Ann. Real and personal estate. Executors—the wife and the two sons. Witnesses—Nathaniel Chambless, Thomas Waithman, Richard Bradford. Proved July 8, 1752. Lib. 8, p. 57.
1752, June 8. Inventory, £489.12.7., incl. apparel, cash, a horse, bridle & saddle, £175.3.10; debts due, £75.2.9; made by Jonathan Bradway and Joseph Hancock.
1752, June 9. Joan Waddinton, the widow, declines serving as Executrix, "being aged."

1759, June 29. Wadington, Robert, of Alloways Creek, Salem Co.; will of. Sister, Sarah Fogg. Cousins—William, Jane and Elizabeth Wadington. Real and personal estate. Cousin, William Wadington, sole Executor. Witnesses—William Beavan, Thomas Thompson and William Stretch. Proved July 23, 1759. Lib. 9, p. 368.
   1759, July 18. Inventory, £885.10.2, incl. bills, bonds, notes and outstanding debts, £445.17.10; made by Samuel Wood and John Diviny.

1759, June 21. Wady, Humphrey, of Shrewsbery, Monmouth Co., yeoman; will of. Wife, Sarah. Children—John, Catherine Russell, Mary Wood, Ann Williams, Phebe Kirkbride and Humphrey (under age). Grandchildren—Sarah and Humphrey Williams (who is to have a silver tankard, formerly belonging to his grandfather George Williams), John Wood, Ann Wood, Mary Williams, Amos Williams, Elisabeth Wood, Daniel Wood and Lydia Corles. Real and personal estate. Executors—sons-in-law, John Kirkbride and Elihu Williams. Witnesses—John Williams, David Knott and Joseph Hulit. Codicil of September 18, 1759, gives directions for sale of homestead. Witnesses—John Lippincott, Jr., Richard Lawrence and Joseph Hulit. Proved Nov. 30, 1759. Lib. G, p. 181.

1753, May 16. Wainrite, (Wainwright), Mary, of Little "Egharbor," Burlington Co.; will of. Children—Susanna, Pornellopy (Penelope), Rebacah, John. Real property. Personal estate includes a legacy from Old England, collected by cousin Stephen Painter. "My maiden name was Mary Jacobson, daughter of Isaac and Ann Jacobson, living in Bormudus, whom I likewise Constetut, make and ordaine my Executors; my son-in-law, James Wainrite, and my son, John Stout." Witnesses—John Ridgway, Samuel Andrews, Mary Andrews. Proved Oct. 2, 1754. Lib. 8, p. 100.
   1754, May 8. Inventory, £19.6, by Joseph Lippincott and Jonathan Pettit.

1750, Aug. 26. Wainrite, (Wainwright), Nicholas, of Little Eggharbor, Burlington Co., yeoman; will of. Wife, Mary. Children—Jeames and Patience, who has child Anne. Speaks of children of Richard Vollintine. Real and personal estate. Executors—son Jeames and John Ridgway. Witnesses—Mordica Andrews, Nehemiah Andrews, Jonathan Pettit. Proved May 25, 1752. Burl. Wills, 5101 C.
   1752, July 29. Inventory, £315.9.9, by Robart Ridgway and Jonathan Pettit.

1753, Feb. 22. Walker, Benjamin, of Burlington Co. Int. Bond of George Nicholson as Adm'r. of estate left unadministered by Phebe Walker, late Administratrix; Isaac De Cow, Jr., fellowbondsman, both of Burlington Co. [First administration in 1745]. Burl. Wills, 3849 C.

1753, July 27. Walker, David, of Chester Township, Burlington Co., yeoman; will of. Wife, Mary. Children—Samuel, Sarah and John. Grandchildren—Edward, Rebekah, Mary, Sarah and Hannah [parents not stated]; children of son, John, viz., Elizabeth, Martha and one lately born. Son Abraham's widow, Rebekah. Real and personal estate. Executors—the two sons. Witnesses—Joseph Burr, Jr., Joshua Bispham, Samuel Atkinson. Proved Dec. 9, 1758.
                                                                    Lib. 9, p. 136.
   1758, Nov. 17. Inventory, £31.8, by Elias Toy and James Toy.

CALENDAR OF WILLS—1751-1760   345

1753, Sept. 17. Walker, Richard, of Springfield Township, Burlington Co.; will of. To Abner Foster my chest. To Thomas Foster rest of personal and real estate. Executor—said Thomas Foster. Witnesses—Amariah Foster, Joshua Foster, Thomas Nickolson. Proved Oct. 6, 1753.
1753, Sept. 28. Inventory, £27.18.4, by Joshua Foster and Amariah Foster.
Lib. 7, p. 359.

1754, Jan. 16. Walker, William, of Mourice River, Cumberland Co. Int. Inventory, £115.16.9, by William Dalles and Joseph Savage.
1754, Jan. 17. Bond of Daniel Walker, of same place, as Adm'r; Joseph Savage, of Cape May Co., fellowbondsman, both yeomen.
Cumb. Wills, 107 F.

1750-1, Mar. 13. Wall, James, of Middlesex Co.; will of. Wife, Hannah. Children—Martha, Rebeccah, Abigaill, Neomia, Walter and James (all under age). Real and personal estate. Executors—John and Joseph Story. Witnesses—Stephen Warne, Richards Sparks and John Bazley. Proved April 4, 1760.
Lib. G, p. 87.

1758, Nov. 20. Wallace, Thomas, Sr., of Chester, Burlington Co., yeoman; will of. Wife, Hope. Children—Thomas, Hope and Mary (all under age). Wife's daughter, Rebeckah. Farm in Evesham, now occupied by William Higbee; land on Eggharbour River; other real and personal estate. Executors—the wife, brother, John Wallace, and brother-in-law, Joshua Lippincott. Witnesses—Andrew Anderson, John Cox, Elizabeth Jones. Proved Dec. 18, 1758. Lib. 9, p. 139.
1758, Dec. 11. Inventory, £689.3.11, incl. bills, bonds and book debts, £306.9.7; a looking glass, 60s.; silver spoons, 30s.; a Bible and other books, 15s.; a negro man, £40; made by Joseph Stokes and Andrew Anderson.
1767, Mar. 9. Account by Henry Jones and wife Hope, late Hope Wallace, one of the executors named above, who have increased it to £996.16.5. by the sale of a house and lot in Burlington, land at Blew Anchor, and other real property and report on hand £776.2.4, charging, among other items, £25. paid to Doctor John Kaighin for doctoring Thomas Wallace, the son, in his last illness, and $40. for nursing him during twelve weeks.

1752, Mar. 31. Wallis, (Wallace), Philipp, Jr., of Evesham Township, Burlington Co. Int. Inventory, £372.11.10, incl. a servant lad's time, £15.9; made by Samuel Coles and Freedom Lippincott.
1752, Apr. 2. Bond of widow, Mary Wallace, of Evesham Township, as Adm'x; Samuel Coles, of Waterford, Gloucester Co., yeoman, fellowbondsman.
Burl. Wills, 5107 C.

1753, Aug. 25. Wallis, (Wallace), Philipp, of Chester Township, Burlington Co.; will of. Children—Jane Jones, Sarah Venable, Hester Cooper, Rachel Atchinson (?), Abigail Hullings, Thomas, John. Grandchildren—Philipp Elwood, and five children of dec'd son Philipp Wallis, names not given. Land in Gloucester Co., i. e., 100 acres bought of Samuel Cole; farm at mouth of Rancokus Creek; home-farm on Pensawing Creek. Personal estate. Executors—the two sons. Witnesses—Thomas Lippincott, Meribah Wills, Gabriel Blond. Proved March 24, 1755.
Lib. 8, p. 128.

1755, Mar. 21. Inventory, £918.11.7, incl. bills, bonds and book debts, £672.6.9; a looking glass; 11 bush. of rye, at 3s., £1.13; a clock and case, £3; a negro boy and a servant lad's time, £42; made by Samuel Stokes and Darling Connarve.

1753, Mar. 6. Walmsley, Jonathan, of Salem Town and County. Int. Inventory, £36.14.6, incl. books, made by William Tuft and John Firth.
1753, Mar. 17. Bond of widow, Rachel, as Adm'x; John Smith and William Tuft fellowbondsmen, all of said Co. Lib. 8, p. 91.

1760, Nov. 17. Wannicoate, Bartholomew, of Gloucester Co. Int. Bond of Thomas Helmes as Adm'r; Isaac Jones fellowbondsman, both of said Co. Lib. 10, p. 169.
1760, Nov. 17. Inventory, £22.12.8, by Thomas Willet and Isaac Jones.

1752, June 26. Ward, Bethuel, of Newark, Essex Co., cordwainer; will of. Wife, Sarah. Children—Zenas, Rebecca, Easter, Mary; an expected child. Real and personal estate. Executors—brothers Daniel and Isaac Ward, with Daniel Lamson. Witnesses—Eleazar Lamson, Isaac Williams, Daniel Lamson. Proved July 17, 1752.
Lib. F, p. 94.

1755, July 5. Ward, Daniel, of Newark, Essex Co., yeoman; will of. Wife, Mary. Children—Amos, Samuel, Jemima and Hannah, all under age, Jemima being the oldest. Real and personal estate. Executors—the wife and brother (in-law?), Amos Harrison. Witnesses—Caleb Smith, Joseph Dod, Daniel Lamson. Proved Nov. 4, 1755. Lib. F, p. 504.
1755, Nov. 6. Inventory, £93.11.11, by Eleazer Lamson and John Dodd.

1760, Feb. 25. Ward, Edward, of Achquechnonk Precinct, Essex Co., surgeon; will of. Makes Hester Devosne, John Ludlo, Richard D. Vreeland, Margret, daughter of Derrick Vreeland, Rev. David Marinus, all of Achquechkenonk and Duncan Kirkland, heirs of personal estate, incl. three shares of all prizes taken by the brig "Johnson," Nicolis Horton Commander; notes due by William Duffele, in hands of Stephen Schinner, Commander of the brig Delancey, and by Thomas Dannold, John Smith and Duncan Kirkland; one note in hands of Mr. Mills, of New York, sheriff; deed from Charles Hamilton; drugs, medicines, instruments, etc., in the shop, belonging to widow Devosne, to be sent to Doctor John Brown of New York. Executors—John J. Ludlo and Rev. David Marinus. Witnesses—John Wanshaer, Dirrick Vreeland, John Wanshaer, Jr. Proved July 15, 1760. Lib. G, p. 287.

1754, Feb. 7. Ward, Elemuel, of Morris Co. Int. Bond of Hannah, his widow, as Adm'x; Daniel Pierson, Esq., of Essex Co., fellowbondsman. Morris Wills, 68 N.

1752, Feb. 6. Ward, Hannah, of Deptford Township, Gloucester Co.; will of. Desires to be buried in Woodbury Meetinghouse yard; gives personal property, incl. a negro girl and Bible, to sisters, Sarah, Mary and Elizabeth Ward (last named under age), and brother, Josiah Ward, who is made sole Executor. Witnesses—James Maffett, Seavil Willson, George Chism. Proof, April 7, 1752. Lib. 7, p. 544.

CALENDAR OF WILLS—1751-1760   347

1752, Mar. 5. Inventory, £21.16, incl. a negro girl, £20; made by Thomas Kimsey and Abraham Chattin.

1752, Apr. 7. Josiah Ward, the Executor named in the will, refuses to act.

1752, Apr. 7. Bond of Sarah Willson, a widow, as Adm'x of the estate, with will annexed; Thomas Kimsey, yeoman, fellowbondsman, both of Deptford Twsp.

1760, Apr. 3. Ward, Hannah, of Newark, Essex Co.; will of. Children—Samuel, Sarah and Elizabeth. Personal estate. Brother, Thomas Canfield, sole Executor. Witnesses—Lewis Ogden, Abraham Canfield, Sarah Beach. Proved July 12, 1760.   Lib. G, p. 286.

1754, Dec. 20. Ward, Isaac of Essex Co. Int. Adm'x—Rebecca Ward, the widow, of Newark. Bondsman—Henry Bonnal of said County.   Lib. F, p. 265.

1751, Oct. 4. Ward, John, Jr., of Burlington Co. Account, £21.12.10., by the Administrators, William and Ruth Ward, who charge against it for the coffin to Geo. Matlock (£1.10), and for debts paid to John Ward, Reuben Jackaway, Benjamin Ward, John Green, Arthur Borradaill, Joshua Bispham, Benjamin Allen, Rebecca Sherwin, Joshua Wright, Ezekiel Harding, John Appleton, and Samuel Atkinson. [see N. J. Archives, Vol. XXX, p. 514].   Burl. Wills, 4900 C.

1753, Mar. 26. Ward, John, of Chester Township, Burlington Co., yeoman. Will of. Wife, Abigail. Children—Benjamin, Nicholas, Peter, Richard, Sarah Cox, Edith van die Grifth, Abigail and Mary. Grandson, George Standley. Homefarm of 110 acres. Personal estate. Executors—the wife and son, Nicholas. Witnesses—Thomas Hackney, Samuel Stokes, John Cox. Proved April 25, 1755.
Lib. 8, p. 150.

1755, —— ——. Inventory, £67.6.4, by Thomas Hackney and Hugh Hollinshead.

1759, Dec. 29. Ward, Mary, of Deptford Township, Gloucester Co., single woman, ill of small pox; will of. Sisters—Sarah and Elizabeth Ward. Brothers—George and Isaac Ward, Isaac being under age. Intended husband, James Wilkins. Names also Rachel Wilkins, Sarah (wife of John Wilkins), John Wilkins, Jr., Ann (daughter of James Wood), Mary (daughter of Henry Wood), as the heirs of her personal estate. Brother George Ward to be Executor. Witnesses—William Wood, Stephen Ayars and John Wilkins. Proved May 2, 1760.   Lib. 10, p. 77.

1760, May 1. Inventory, £92.15.10, incl. bonds, book debts and cash, £59.15.10; made by William Wilkins and John Wilkins.

1754, Nov. 29. Ward, Moses, of Deptford Township, Gloucester Co., yeoman; will of. Wife, Mary. Children—James (oldest son), Joseph, Moses, Jonathan, Benjamin, Jahu (youngest son), and Mary, the last four under age. Homefarm; another farm, bought of the Sheriff, formerly John Tatom's, on Woodbury Creek; a third farm on South-side of said creek, which descended to testator as heir-at-law of nephew, Samuel Ward. Personal estate. Executors—sons James and Joseph, with brother William Clark as overseer. Witnesses—John Hopper, Thomas Andrews, David Cooper. Proved Feb. 3, 1755.
Lib. 8, p. 93.

1754, Dec. 31. Inventory, £434.9.5, incl. a watch, £6.10; looking glass; books, 5s.; a Dutch girl's time, £5; bonds and book debts, £38.2.8; made by John Hopper and David Cooper.

1754, Oct. 12. Ward, Nathaniel, Jr., of Newark, Essex Co.; will of. Wife, Sarah. Children—Sarah, Mary, Jabez, Abraham and Nathaniel. Real and personal estate. Executors—the wife, brother Abner Ward and David Bruen. Witnesses—Jonas Winter, Thomas Winter, Jonathan Sergeant. Proved June 16, 1755. Lib. F, p. 275.

1752, July 23. Ward, Samuel, of Newark, Essex Co.; will of. Children—Ebener (Ebenezer), Tama Munson, Elisabeth Henman, Ann Davis, Jemima Higgins. Grandson, Uzal Ward. Children of son, John Ward. Homestead between David Ogden, dec'd, Nathaniel Farrand, John Cochrun and the street; 10 acres in the Great Neck, next to Elihu Crane, dec'd; lot in the Great Swamp, next to Josiah Ogden; salt meadow near Joseph Bruen's; do. at the mouth of Maple Island Creek, adjoining Caleb Wheeler. Personal property. Executors—son Ebenezer and grandson Uzal Ward. Witnesses—Joseph Johnson, Josiah Ogden, Jr., Gabriel Ogden. Proved April 16, 1759.
Lib. G, p. 71.

1752, May 26. Ward, Thomas, of Morris Co. Int. Bond of Susana, widow, as Adm'x; Gideon Hedges, of the same Co., fellowbondsman.
Lib. F, p. 70.
1752, June 1. Inventory, £80.7.7, incl. a silver teaspoon; a wooden horse to shave with 1s.; a looking glass; made by William Dixon and David Young.

1753, May 8. Ward, William, of Chester Township, Burlington Co. Int. Bond of widow, Ruth, as Adm'x; Thomas Wallis, yeoman, fellowbondsman, both of said Township. Lib. 7, p. 420.
1753, Sept. 26. Account by Administratrix.

1755, Oct. 27. Ward, William, of Cumberland Co. Int. Inventory, £75.9.5, by David Jenkins and Samuel Harris, Jr.
1755, Nov. 4. Bond of Benjamin Harris as Adm'r; Samuel Harris fellowbondsman, both of Cumberland Co., weavers. Lib. 8, p. 229.

1758, Nov. 6. Ware, Andrew, of Gloucester Township and County, shingle maker. Int. Bond of Gabriel Daveis (Davis) as Adm'r; William Davis, fellowbondsman, both of said Township, yeomen.
Lib. 9, p. 126.
1758, Nov. 13. Inventory, £12.13, incl. books, made by William Hampton and William Davis.
1759, Aug. 9. Account by the Administrator.

1753, Apr. 18. Ware, Joseph, of Allaways Creek Township, Salem Co. ,yeoman; will of. Son, Joseph; his wife Elizabeth and their four youngest children, Rebecca, Joseph, Elija and Jane. Daughter, Elizabeth Thompson. Residuary legatees and Executors—son, John Ware, and son-in-law, Benjamin Thompson. Witnesses—William Daniel, Ruth Sayers, James Daniel. Proved Oct. 20, 1753.
Lib. 8, p. 59.
1753, Sept. 20. Inventory, £179.19.7, incl. bonds £148.3.4; books 11/6; made by James Daniel and John Stewart.

1754, May 3. Ware, Joseph, Jr., of Alleways Creek, Salem Co. Int. Bond of Sarah, widow, as Adm'x; Benjamin Allen, of the same place, fellowbondsman.
Lib. 8, p. 89.

1754, —— ——. Inventory, £51.19. ,incl. a looking glass and a gun £2; made by John Fitzpatrick and Benjamin Allen.

1760, Sept. 10. Ware, Solomon, of Allaways Creek, Salem Co., yeoman. Int. Inventory, £452.9, incl. cash, bridle and saddle, a great Bible, a clock, made by Jonathan Bradway and John Stewart.

1760, Nov. 24. Bond of widow, Sara Ware, as Adm'x; John Stewart and John Ware fellowbondsmen, all of Allaways Creek.
Lib. 10, p. 443.

1757, Mar. 26. Warford, Job, of Amwell, Hunterdon Co. Int. Bond of widow, Sara, as Adm'x; John Phillips, Esq., of Hopewell, said Co., fellowbondsman.
Lib. 8, p. 516.

1757, Apr. 7. Inventory, £76.15, by John Phillips and George Ely.

1758, Aug. 4. Warne, Joshua, of South Amboy, Middlesex Co., yeoman; will of. Wife, Elizabeth. Children—Job (youngest son), Thomas, Joshua, John, William, James Ezekiah, Joseph, Mary, Elizabeth and Catherine, all under age. Real and personal estate. Executors—the wife, with sons Thomas and Joshua. Witnesses—Richard Franses, Samuel Warne and Robert Savage. Proved August 28, 1758.
Lib. F, p. 549.

1758, Apr. 6. Warrell, Joseph, of Belleville, near Trenton, Hunterdon Co.; will of. Children—Joseph, Elizabeth (wife of Abraham Cottnam) and Grace. Homestead and other lands. Personal property, incl. 4 large silver spoons, 8 tea do., a silver marrow spoon, silver cup and salver, wife's pedigree roll, own family pedigree, family pictures, silver buttons, law and other books, two negro women. Executors—son Joseph, Andrew Reed, of Trenton, merchant, and John Berrien, of Rocky Hill, with son-in-law, Abraham Cottnam, as Assistant. Witnesses—David Cowell, Peter Kemble, Jr., John Kolb. Proved June 12, 1758.
Lib. 9, p. 26.

1756, Feb. 27. Warren, John, of Hannover, Burlington Co.; will of. Wife, Susannah. Children—Fellwell, Rebekah, Mary, Samuel, Achsah, Gamaliel and John. Real and personal estate. Executors—the wife and her brother, Samuel Farnsworth. Witnesses—John Scholey, Rachel Scholey, George Cole. Proved April 15, 1756.
Lib. 8, p. 258.

1756, April 14. Inventory, £263.16.8, incl. bonds and book debts, £126.18.6; made by John Scholey and Anthony Sykes.

1758, Oct. 12. Watkins, Benjamin, of Woodbridge, Middlesex Co.; will of. Wife, Phebe. Children—David and Mary, both under age; an expected child. House and lot in Woodbridge, bought of David Wright; house and lot in "Perscatua" (Piscataway), bought of John Jaquess. Personal property. Executors—the wife and Daniel Moores. Witnesses—Peter Ellston, Martha Britten and Anne Perlee. Proved Oct. 21, 1758, when the widow, Phebe Watkins, refuses to act as Executrix.
Lib. F, p. 556.

1753, May 15. Watkinson, Mary, of Burlington City, widow; will of. Sisters—Judith Nield and Jane Ely. Brothers—Elias, Nathaniel and Jonathan Pettit. Personal estate. Executors—Joshua Raper and Rev. Colin Campbell, both of said City. Witnesses—Joseph Allinson, John Saunders, Sarah Raper. Proved Febr. 2, 1754.

1754, —— ——. Inventory, £168.10.11, incl. money due from the estate of her late husband, Paul Watkinson, £53.15; bills and bonds, £109.2.9. Burl. Wills, 5535 C.

1752, July 7. Watkinson, Paul, of Burlington, cordwainer; will of. Wife, Mary. Brothers—Godfry and John Watkinson. Sisters—Susannah Watkinson and Elizabeth Ashbury. Legacies to Isaac Heulings; Church of St. Anne's in Burlington to have house, lot and orchard, left to wife, after her death. Other real estate, incl. 500 acres in Morris Co. and personal property. Executors—the wife, Joshua Raper and Rev. Colin Campbell. Witnesses—Thomas Wetherwill, Mary White, Row'd Ellis. Proved August 8, 1752.

1752, Aug. 19. Inventory: Real (500 acres in Morris Co. £200); personal, £831.16.2, incl. bonds and book debts, £683.19.11; made by Isaac Heulings and Abraham Hewlings.

1761, Dec. 21. Account, by the surviving Executor, Colin Campbell, who deducts from the inventory £200, for the land, it being unsold; £201.11.3, as having been given by the will to the widow, and £12.6. insolvent debts, and has paid debts due to Richard Smith, Thomas Clifford, William Martin (bill of exchange for £100, for which £167.10. is paid, with 1s.8d. for postage). Burl. Wills, 5111 C.

1756, May 31. Watson, Abram, of Middletown, Monmouth Co.; will of. Wife, Elizabeth. Grandchildren—Abraham, Sarah and Elizabeth Watson. Real and personal estate, incl. a negro boy. Executors—John Burrowes and William Hendrickson, both of Middletown. Witnesses—Thomas Walling, Joel Beddle and Edward Taylor. Proved August 11, 1756. Lib. F, p. 372.

1753, Feb. 14. Watson, Mathew, of Gloucester Co., pedlar. Int. Bond of Mathew Usher, of Philadelphia, merchant, as Adm'r; Henry Sparks, of Deptford Township, Gloucester Co., yeoman, fellowbondsman. [Endorsed: "Before letters were made out letters were granted to Abram Usher, the within named Matthew being also dead."]

1754, Jan. 14. Bond of Abraham Usher, of Philadelphia, as Adm'r; Abraham Hewlings, of Burlington City, fellowbondsman.
Lib. 8, p. 87.

1756, Aug. 20. Watson, Richard, of Morris Co., cordwainer. Int. Bond of Nathaniel Foster, of Hunterdon Co., blacksmith, the principal creditor, as Adm'r; Nathaniel Foster, Jr., of Morris Co., blacksmith, fellowbondsman. Lib. F, p. 373.

1756, Nov. 13. Inventory: Real estate, £20; personal, £33.12.8., mostly debts due, made by Isaac Jones and David Ogden. Followed by an account of the Administrator, who deducts from the value of the inventory £12, for a bond of George Morris, "absconded without having any effects," and £3.10, due by William Jolly, not recoverable.

1751, Nov. 8. Watson, William, of Freehold, Monmouth Co., yeoman; will of. Daughters—Euphunea Johnston and Margaret. Peter and Gawen, sons of brother, Gawen Watson, remaindermen. Real and personal estate. Executors—Joseph Ker and William Tapscot.

CALENDAR OF WILLS—1751-1760   351

Witnesses—Michael Sweetman, Jane Sweetman, John Henderson.
Proved March 12, 1752.   Lib. F, p. 34.
   1752, Jan. 14. Inventory, £225.19.1., incl. bonds, £65; 40 bush. of Indian corn, £4.13.4; the time of two negroes, £38; made by Jacob Morris, Michael Sweetman, and John Henderson.

1758, Oct. 9. Watson, William, of Greenwich, Gloucester Co., yeoman; will of. Wife, Sarah. Children—John Tubman, James Ward, Mary, wife of William England, and William Watson, who is made sole Executor of real and personal estate. Witnesses—Elizabeth Helms, Catherine Helmes, John Rumford. Proved May 25, 1759.
                                                Lib. 9, p. 268.
   1759, May 22. Inventory, £84.15.1, incl. several old books 10/6; made by Isaiah Davenport and Jussta Lock.

1760, Jan. 29. Watson, William, of Greenwich, Cumberland Co. Int. Inventory, £205.16.4, incl. bills and bonds, £133.7.6; made by Samuel Clark and Thomas Ewing.
   1760, Feb. 2. Bond of his widow, Mary, as Adm'x; Samuel Watson, of Greenwich, fellowbondsman.   Lib. 10, p. 109.

1751, Apr. 22. Wattkins, Joseph, of Bergen Co. Bond of Herman Luckens of said Co., principal creditor of dec'd., as administrator of the estate, Jacob Toers fellow-bondsman.   Bergen Wills, 312 B.

1752, June 18. Wattson, Thomas, of New Barbadoes, Bergen Co.; will of. Wife, Marritye, sole heiress of real and personal estate during life, with remainder to Thomas, eldest son of brother William. Executors—Jacob Titsort and Johannes Demarest. Witnesses—Abraham Ackerman, Abraham Stagg, Guilliam Bertholf. Proved August 13, 1752.   Lib. F, p. 62.
   1752, Aug. 10. Inventory: Real—house and land in Bergen Co., £250; personal—£87.3.2, incl. a negro boy, £45; a looking glass, 15s.; and English Bible, 8s.; made by Abraham Ackerman and Pieter Zabriskie.

———, ——— ———. Weatherby, William, of Greenwich, Gloucester Co., yeoman; will of. Wife, Ann. Children—Benjamin, Daniel, David, Henry, Mary Sielden, Elizabeth Sparks, Cathrine Marshall and Rachael. A stepson, name not given. Personal estate. Executors—the wife and Edward Weatherby. Witnesses—Mathew Gill, James Aran, William Guest. Proved Sept. 24, 1753.   Lib. 7, p. 432.
   1753, Sept. 18. Inventory, £242.4.8, incl. debts due on specialties, £159.17.10; made by Matthew Gill and Thomas Denny.
   1754, May 29. Account by Ann Weatherby, one of the Executors.

1755, May 13. Weatherby, William, of Greenwich Township, Gloucester Co., cordwainer. Int. Bond of Henry Weatherby, of Greenwich Twsp., yeoman, as Adm'r; Thomas Sparks, of Deptford Township, said Co., yeoman, fellowbondsman.   Lib. 8, p. 307.
   1755, May 14. Inventory, £26.0.1, incl. books 5s.; made by Joseph Wilkinson and Richard Sparks.

———, Dec. 13. Webb. George, of Woodbridge, Middlesex Co.; will of. Wife, Jerusha, sole Executrix. Children—John, Elizabeth, Jane, Pheby and Deborah, all under age. Real and personal estate. Witnesses—Griffin Disbrow, Matthew Lofbrow, Margret Waller. Proved Jan. 15, 1753. Lib. F, p. 84.

1753, Oct. 13. Webley, Benjamin, of Somerset Co., schoolmaster; will of. Makes Hannah, wife of Philip van Arsdarl, sole heiress and Executrix of personal estate. Witnesses—Samuel Poland, Abraham v. Middleswart. Proved Sept. 20, 1755. Lib. F, p. 284.

1754, Jan. 21. Webster, Sarah (widow of Thomas), of Gloucester Co. Int. Bond of Thomas Andrews of Gloucester Co. as Adm'r; Peter Andrews, of Burlington Co., fellowbondsman, both yeomen.
Lib. 8, p. 38.
1754, July 15. Inventory, £129.9.10, by John Woolman and Josiah White.

1759, May 21. Welding, John, of "Burdenstown," Burlington Co., blacksmith. Int. Hannah, widow, resigns her right of administration to her uncle, John Beaumont.
1759, May 22. Bond of John Beaumont, of Pensylvania, as Adm'r; Edward Wheatcraft of "Burdentown" fellowbondsman. Lib. 9, p. 212.
1759, May 21. Inventory, £205.19.11, incl. bills and bonds, £130.13.11; a looking glass; a silver watch £6.10; made by Samuel Farnsworth and Edward Wheatcraft.
1760, Sept. 8. Account by the Adm'r, who makes it his debtor for £25.14.8.

1760, Oct. 20. Wells, Thomas, of Shrewsbury, Monmouth Co. Int. Bond of Penelope, widow, as Adm'x; William van Ort, of said Co., yeoman, fellowbondsman. Lib. G, p. 300.

1760, Feb. 14. Wescote, Henry, of Fairfield, Cumberland Co., farmer; will of. Wife, Sarah. Sons—Amos, Lewis, Ezra and Josh. Real and personal estate. Executor—David Wescote. Witnesses—Robt. Low, Daniel Powel, Freelove Whitackar. Proved March 8, 1760.
Lib. 10, p. 105.
1760, Feb. 29. Inventory, £557.7.6, incl. books, £1.6; 35 bush. of corn, £4.16.3; bills, bonds, etc., £160.12.3; 50 bush. of wheat, £11.5; made by Robert Low and Joseph Ogden.
1761, Nov. 14. Account by the Executor.

1760, June 1. Wescott, Ziba, of Eggharbour, Gloucester Co. Int. Inventory, £167.19.3, incl. book debts and notes, £105.12.11; made by Elijah Clark and Wallis Hurd.
1760, June 19. Bond of Richard Westcote as Adm'r; Wallis Hurd, fellowbondsman. Lib. 9, p. 449.
1763, Aug. 24. Account by the Administrator.

1753, Sept. 15. West, John, of Burlington Co. Int. Bond of widow, Mary West of Northampton Township, as Adm'x; William West and Henry Cooper, both of the same place, yeomen, fellowbondsmen.
Lib. 7, p. 422.
1753, Sept. 7. Inventory, £535.0.11, by Henry Paxton and Henry Cooper.
1757, Nov. 23. Account by the Adm'x, £2665.19.6, incl. personally, £1535.0.11, and a farm sold for £1130.18.7; deducting as wrongly inventoried and not recoverable debts amounting to £1143.10.4., makes the estate her debtor for £86.19.9.

CALENDAR OF WILLS—1751-1760   353

1759, Apr. 17. West, Mary, of Shrewsbury (Monmouth Co.). Int. Bond of her daughter, widow Mary Throckmorton, as Adm'x; John Williams fellowbondsman.   Lib. G, p. 56.

1759, Oct. 4. West, Richard, of "Greanwitch," Gloucester Co.; will of. Wife, Rachel. Children—Thomas (who has son Uriah), John, Israel, Richard and Elisabeth. Real and personal estate. Executors— the wife, with sons, Israel and Richard. Witnesses—Sarah Willson, Restore Lippincott, Jacob Spicer. Proved Jan. 22, 1760.
Lib. 9, p. 443.

1758, Feb. 8. West, Stephen, of Shrewsbury, Monmouth Co., yeoman; will of. Children—Thomas, Eunis, Uriah and Abigail. Real and personal estate. Executors—son Thomas, Samuel Scott and John West. Witnesses—Joseph West, Asher West and John West. Proved Feb. 10, 1759.   Mon. Wills, 2403 M.

1756, Aug. 20. West, Webley, of Shrewsbury Township, Monmouth Co., will of. Wife [not named]. Children—Webly (absent a long time), John, William, Daniel, Joseph, Mary Price, Elizabeth Halsted, Sarah Hewett, Deborah, Rebekah, Cathrina and Susannah. Children of dec'd daughters, Ann Bills and Zilpha Halsted; Webly West, son of daughter Mercy West. Real and personal estate. Executors— sons John and William. Witnesses—Thomas Lepper, Joseph West and Thomas West. Proved Sept. 1, 1756.   Lib. L, p. 205.

1755, June 26. Westbroek, Anthony, of "Manissink," Sussex Co., yeoman; will of. Wife, Aeltie. Children—Johannis, Jacob, Saloman, Gideon, Anthony, Jennetie (wife of Simon Westvael), Magdalin, (wife of Abraham Shimer), and Maria (wife of Daniel Westvael). Real and personal estate. Executors—sons Johannes and Jacob. Witnesses—Jane Keater, Cornelis Westbroek, William Ennes. Proved Feb. 24, 1759.   Lib. G, p. 34.
  1760, Nov. 6. Inventory of goods, left out of the appraisement, made by Capt. Johannis Westbroek, £20.12, incl. a book, "Ye Young Man's Companion," 2s.; made by Joseph Westbrook and William Ennes.

1760, Sept. 26. Westbroek, Anthony, of Montagu Township, Sussex Co., yeoman. Int. Inventory of the personal estate of, £96.10.10., incl 3 Dutch books, 3s.6d., a large Dutch bible, £2.5., a lookingglass, a negro man £15., made by Jacob Westbroek and William Ennes.
  1760, Nov. 6. Bond of widow, Susannah Westbroek, as Adm'x; Abraham van Aken fellowbondsman, both of Sussex Co.
Lib. 10, p. 464.

1755, Sept. 12. Westbroek, Dirk, of Namenock, Wallpeck Township, Sussex Co., yeoman; will of. Wife, Janneke. Children—Joseph, Abraham, Johannes, Terck van Keuren, Marya (wife of Johannes C. Westbroek), Sarah (wife of Jacob Gunsalis), Elizabeth and Lidea. Land in New Jersey and in New York. Personal property. Executors—the four sons. Witnesses—Cornelis Westbroek, Philipp Windematt (Wintermute), William Ennes. Proved Dec. 8, 1757.
Lib. F, p. 475.

23

1759, Nov. 12. Westbroek, Gideon, of Mountagu Township, Sussex Co., miller. Int. Inventory, £126.2.11., incl. 2 Dutch Testaments, 4s.; a "bay natural paising hipshot mair" 19s.; outstanding debts, £14.15.10; made by Abraham Shimer and William Ennes.
1759, Nov. 19. Bond of widow, Jane Wasbrook (Westbroek) as Adm'x; Jacob Westbroek fellowbondsman, both of Mountagu.
Lib. 10, p. 110.

1755, Jan. 4. Westbroek, Solomon, of Matshepeconck, Sussex Co., miller; will of. Wife, Esther, to be "master and ruler" of all real and personal estate. Children—Luwis and Altie (under age). Eight acres of woodland, bought of Cornelius Brinck. Executors—father, Anthony Westbroek, and brother, Gideon Westbroek, both of said Co. Witnesses—Cornelius Brinck, Jr., Jacob Westbroeck, William Ennes. Proved Feb. 24, 1759. Lib. G, p. 36.
1759, Feb. 24. Bond of Johannis Westbroek, brother of Salomon, as Adm'r with the will annexed, the Executors named and the widow being dead. Fellowbondsman, Jacob Westbroek, both of Sussex Co.
1759, Apr. 24. Inventory, two grist mills, with houses, barns, orchard and lot, and another lot of 8 acres on the stream, £400; personal, £109.3.7½, incl. 2 Dutch Testaments, 7s.; bonds and notes, £70.0.9½; made by Johnnis Westvael and William Ennes.

1760, Jan. 3. Westcote, Jonathan, of Deerfield Township, Cumberland. Int. Bond of Henry Sparks as Adm'r; Henry Pearson (Pierson) and Joseph Westcot (Westcote) fellowbondsman, all of Fairfield, said Co. Lib. 10, p. 108.

1759, Jan. 10. Weston, William, of Piles Grove, Salem Co.; will of. Wife, Hannah. Grandchildren—George Coleson and Mary More. Daughter-in-law (stepdaughter?), Hannah Oakfoot (Oakford). Personal estate. Executors—the wife and son-in-law (stepson?) John Oakfoot. Witnesses—Isaac Barber, John Moor and David Davis. Proved Feb. 21, 1759. Lib. 9, p. 370.
1759, Jan. 18. Inventory, £148.7.9, incl. bonds and book debts, £85.5; made by David Davis and Bateman Lloyd.

1760, May 7. Wetherby, John, of Salem Co. Int. Bond of widow, Mary, as Adm'x; Charles Ellot (Elliot), merchant, and Isaac Johnson, yeoman, fellowbondsmen, all of Manington, Salem Co.
Lib. 10, p. 449.

1748, Sept. 15. Wetherill, Thomas, of Burlington City, yeoman; will of. Wife, Ann. Children—Christopher, Thomas, Elizabeth Johnston, Samuel, Ann, (wife of James Moor). Grandchildren—Thomas Bishop, son of daughter Ann Moor; Joseph, son of Christopher; granddaughters, names not given. Speaks of six children, but names only the five as above. Houses and lots on York Str., Broad Str., High Str., and Mountholly Road; land in Amwell Township, Hunterdon Co.; land at "Attapunck Hana." Personal estate. Executors—the three sons. Witnesses—Peter Fearon, Dan Smith, Daniel Smith, Jr. Codicil of October 1, 1758, makes a bequest to granddaughter, Abigail Bishop, and granddaughters born since date of will, and gives names of daughters as Mary, Elizabeth and Ann. Personal estate disposed of, including silver spoons, silver tankard and books. Witnesses—Daniel Smith, Daniel Smith, Jr., Richard Smith. Proved Sept. 10, 1759. Lib. 9, p. 247.

CALENDAR OF WILLS—1751-1760   355

1759, Sept. 4. Wheaten, Peter, of Woodbridge, Middlesex Co. carpenter. Int. Adm'r—Samuel Wheaten, Jr., of Bound Brook, Somerset Co., yeoman, brother of said Peter. Bondsman—John Smith, of Woodbridge, yeoman. Witness—Thomas Bartow.   Lib. G, p. 95.
 1759, Sept. 5. Inventory, £86.1.9, incl. bonds and book debts, £25.3.9; made by John Campbell, Edward Wilkison and John Smith.

1751, May 25. Wheeler, David, of Hanover, Morris Co.; will of. Wife, Charity. Children—Mary, Phebe, Rhoda, Sarah, David, John, the last two under age. Real and personal estate. Executors—the wife, Gershom Mott, Jacob Ford, Timothy Tuttle, and John Ross. Witnesses—Timothy Tuttle, Daniel Tuttle, Thomas Dickson. Proved July 29, 1757.   Lib. F, p. 439.

1755, Apr. 19. Wheeler, Jehiel, of Fairfield Township, Cumberland Co. Int. Elizabeth, widow, refuses to administer.
 1755, Apr. 19. Bond of Mathew Parvin as Adm'r; Alexander Moore fellowbondsman, both of Deerfield, said Co.   Lib. 8, p. 159.
 1755, Apr. 24. Inventory, £89.14.6, by David Ogden and Jeremiah Buck.

1751, Aug. 6. Whilldin, Mathew, of Cape May Co. Int. Adm'r—James Whilldin, of same place, gentleman. Bondsman—Jeremiah Hand, of said Co., gentleman. Witnesses—Jacob Hughes and Jonathan Smith.
 1750, Oct. 11. Inventory, £86.4.10, by Thomas Hand and Jeremiah Hand.   Cape May Wills, 157 E.

1752, Dec. 13. Whitaker, Nathaniel, of Fairfield Precinct, Cumberland Co., husbandman; will of. Children—Ambrose, Lemuel, Lewis, Daniel, Sarah, Hannah and Ruth. Real and personal estate. Executors—son Ambrose and Joseph Daton. Witnesses—Jeremiah Buck, Abigail Wescot, Jehiel Wheeler. Proved Jan. 19, 1753.
Lib. 7, p. 329.
 1753, Jan. 18. Inventory, £127.0.6., incl. books, made by Jeremiah Buck and Jehiel Wheeler.

1760, May 3. Whitaker, Elizabeth. Int. Bond of David Husted as Adm'r; Henry Pearson (Pierson) fellowbondsman, both of Fairfield Township, Cumberland Co.   Lib. 10, p. 31.
 1760, May 10. Inventory, £38.13.7, by Thomas Ogden and Jonathan Lorance (Lawrence).

1759, June 25. Whitaker, Richard, of Fairfield, Cumberland Co.; will of. Wife, Elizabeth. Children—Richard, Lawrana, Elizabeth, Vashti, Susanna, Lydia, Elnathan and Reuben. Real and personal estate. Executors—the wife and David Sayre. Witnesses—Israel Petty, Enuch Bowen, John Whitecur (Whitaker). Proved July 18, 1759.   Lib. 9, p. 337.
 1759, July 18. Inventory, £125.15.7, by Henry Pearson and Thomas Ogden.
 1760, Oct. 31. Account by David Sayre, one of the Executors, who has increased it by the sale of land to £200.15.2, and reports on hand £142.6.11.

1751, Mar. 19. White, Daniel, of New Brunswick, Middlesex Co., farmer; will of. Wife, Rebecca. Daughter, Abigail; another child, name not given. Personal estate. Executors—Edmund Bainbridge, Sr., and George Wetherill. Witnesses—John Sperling, John Hoogland, John Michael Sperling. Proved April 11, 1751. Lib. E, p. 512.

1751, Oct. 30. Inventory, £44.11, by John Buckerlo and Piter Miserol; George Wetherill adds a bond, given by John White to Daniel, Jan. 30, 1733-'4, for £33.

——— ——— —. Vendue list of the estate, sold for £48.6.10, and signed by George Wetherill.

1755, Mar. 15. White, James, of Mourice River, Cumberland Co. Int. Inventory, £358.10.11, incl. rigging, etc., of a shalop, £75; book debts and notes £63; made by Gabrill Isard and Thomas Petersen.

1755, Apr. 28. Bond of James and Leaming White as Adm'rs; Gabrill Isard and Thomas Petersen fellowbondsmen, all of Maurice River. Lib. 8, p. 172.

1754, Oct. 27. White, Joseph, of Burlington City and County, yeoman; will of. Wife, Mary. Children—William, Anne (widow of Joseph Heulings), Mary Brian and Elizabeth. Grandsons—James and Joseph Claypole. Farm in City limits on Southside of Assisconk Creek, bought of Thomas Stevenson, William Stevenson, William Bassnet and Thomas Postgate; homestead with waterlots; lot of 6½ acres on Southside of Broad Str., adjoining said creek; farm also in City limits on both sides of the Brickyard Road, bought of Thomas Cuttlar, the Executors of Richard Allison and William Pettit; a corner lot and orchard, N. E. corner of York and Pearl Str. Personal property. Executors—the wife and son. Witnesses—Anthony Elton, Mary Campbel, William Heulings. Proved Dec. 2, 1754.

Lib. 7, p. 522.

1754, Dec. 7. Inventory, £373.3.8, incl. plate, £8.13; bonds, £116.15.2; servants, £30; made by Thomas Scattergood and William Heulings.

1754, Aug. 8. White, Joseph, Jr., of Burlington City and Co., yeoman; will of. Parents—Joseph and Mary White, sole Executors of personal estate. Sister, Mary Brian. Nephews—James and Joseph, both under age, sons of James and Rebecca Claypole. Witnesses—Isaac Heulings, Elisabeth Elton, William Heulings. Proved Dec. 2, 1754. Lib. 8, p. 134.

1758, Jan. 18. White, Mary, of Burlington City; will of. Son, William White; daughters, Elizabeth White, and Mary Bryan. Late husband's great-grandsons, William Snowden Heulings (under age, son of Isaac Heulings), Joseph Heulings, Thomas Polegreen Heulings and his brother, Abraham Heulings. Grandsons—James and Joseph Claypole, sons of James Claypole. Sister, Hannah Leeds. House and lot on corner York and Pearl Streets; other real and personal property. Executors—daughter, Mary Bryan, and Abraham Heulings. Witnesses—Esther Heulings, Fretwell Wright, William Heulings. Proved May 13, 1760. Lib. 10, p. 140.

1760, May 13. Inventory: Real—143 acres of land, £250. Personal—£269.13, incl. bonds, £228.18; a silver cup and old silver, £6; 3 gold rings, £2.10; 9 books and a looking glass, £1.15; made by William Heulings and Isaac Heulings.

CALENDAR OF WILLS—1751-1760   357

1750, Dec. 14. White, (Wheten) Peter, of Middletown, (Monmouth Co.). Int. Inventory, £11.15.6, by Matthias Johnson, John Layton, Jr., and Edward Taylor; Jacob Johnson administrator.
Lib. G, p. 95.

1759, Feb. 12. White, Samuel, of Upper Freehold, Monmouth Co.; will of. Wife, Anne, to have her marriage inheritance, also £100, etc. Children—Thomas and Meribah, both under age. Father, Thomas White, to be guardian of son Thomas. Legacies to brother, Thomas White, and brother-in-law, David Curtis, both being named Executors. Personal property, incl. surveyors instruments, books, a silver watch, carpenter's and turner's tools. Witnesses—Thomas Cox, Robert Hutchinson and William Liming. Proved Oct. 9, 1759.
Lib. 9, p. 282.
1759, Oct. 10. Inventory, £345.10.9, incl. a watch and snuffbox, £7.10; made by Thomas Cox, Robert Hutchinson and William Liming.

1758, May 16. White, Zephaniah, of Middletown, Monmouth Co.; will of. Brothers—Amos and Andrew White. Sisters—Avis Fisher and Hannah Layton. Cousins—Leah Stout, Richard Stout, Jonathan Stout, Jr., Mary Stout and Hester Stout. Friend, Elenah Huff, daughter of John Stout. Gravestone to be bought and placed on the grave of cousin Hanah Stout. Executors John Taylor and John Wall, both of Middletown. Witnesses—George Taylor, Samuel Tilton and Richard Norris. Proved June 29, 1758. Lib. G, p. 96.

1754, Oct. 19. Wilkerson, Mary, late of N. Y. City, now of Middletown, Monmouth Co., widow; will of. Daughters—Grace Applegate and Susannah Bedloe. Grandchildren—Daniel Lewis, Philipp Lewis and their sister Elizabeth Oblith. Homestead in Middletown, bought of Timothy Mount; personal estate. Executors—grandson-in-law, John Tompson, and Jonathan Stout. Witnesses—James Grover, John Mount and Matthias Mount. Proved Feb. 28, 1758. Lib. F, p. 535.
1758, ——— ——. Inventory, £231.11.4, incl. bonds and notes, £225.18.10; made by John Stout and Thomas Stillwell.

1751, Oct. 26. Wilkerson, Samuel, of Cape May Co. Int. Adm'r—Ephraim Kent, cordwainer. Witnesses—Henry Young and John Mackey.
Cape May Wills, 158 E.

1757, Sept. 24. Wilkins, Isaac, of Evesham Township, Burlington Co. Int. Bond of Elizabeth Willkins (Wilkins) as Adm'x; Joshua Ballinger fellowbondsman, both of Evesham. Lib. 8, p. 442.
1757, Sept. 21. Inventory, £203.13, incl. servant man, £7.10, by Joshua Ballinger and Micajah Wills.

1758, Mar. 4. Wilkins, William, of Evesham Township, Burlington Co.; will of. Wife, Elizabeth. Children—William and Lydia, both under age. Real and personal estate. Executors—brothers, Thomas and Amos Wilkins. Witnesses—Benjamin Nayler, Esther Naylor, Noah Haines. Proved July 2, 1758. Lib. 9, p. 74.
1758, Mar. 22. Inventory, £485.13, incl. bonds, £202.17.6; 22,600 feet of boards, £50.17; negroes, £95; made by Benjamin Moar (Moore) and James Cattell.

1758, Dec. 15. Willard, Rebacah, of Waterford Township, Gloucester Co. Int. Inventory, £97.8.9, incl. an apprentice girl, £1; a negro man, £30; a Bible and Prayer book, 7s.6d.; a "Numberiello," 2s.; a boat and sail, £4; made by Henry Wood and Joseph Morgan.

1758, Dec. 18. Bond of Benjamin Willard (Woolard), Jr., as Adm'r; John Wallis (Wallace) and Andrew Anderson fellowbondsmen, all of Burlington Co.   Lib. 9, p. 176.

1751, Sept. 12. Willbor, Peleg, of Perth Amboy, Middlesex Co. Int. Bond of Thomas Fox, gent., as Adm'r; Andrew Johnston, Esq., fellowbondsman, both of Perth Amboy.   Lib. E, p. 547.

1758, Feb. 3. Willcox, William, of Kingstown, Middlesex Co. Int. Bond of Elizabeth Wilcocks, of Kingstown, as Adm'x; Jacob Skillman, of Somerset Co., fellowbondsman.   Lib. 9, p. 175.

1757, Dec. 31. Willets, Richard, of Alloways Creek Township, Salem Co.; will of. Wife, Sarah. Children—Richard Machai, Elizabeth Stilwel, Deliverance Birdcill and Amos. Grandsons—Amos Bunten and Richard Stilwel. Brother, John Willis, of Cape May. Privileges granted to his negroes. Personal estate. Executors—the wife and son, Richard. Witnesses—John Test, Elizabeth Wethman and Robert Nicholls. Proved March 2, 1759.   Lib. 9, p. 378.
1759, Apr. 16. Inventory, £880.4.8, incl. bonds and notes £381.6.8; negro slaves, £200; made by Thomas Sayre and Samuel Wood.

1760, May 16. Willhellmess (Wilhelm), Michael, of Philipsburg, Sussex Co., yeoman. Int. Inventory, £263.15.6, incl. 12 books, £2; book debts, £53.16.11; made by Christoffel Bittenbender and Jacob Sachwitz (Savage), (both signing in German script).
1760, Sept. 23. Bond of widow Margaret Willhelm as Adm'x; Lodwick Titman and Christian Minneer fellowbondsmen, all of Sussex Co.   Lib. 10, p. 464.

1753, Mar. 12. Williams, Amos, Esq., of Newark, Essex Co.; will of. Wife, Mary. Children—Nathaniel, Benjamin, James, Sarah, all but the first under age. Home farm; land over the mountain; meadow on Fishing Creek; personal estate. Executors—son Nathaniel and Aamos Harrison. Witnesses—Samuel Harrison, Timothy Williams, Daniel Lamson. Proved August 3, 1754.   Lib. F, p. 502.
1754, Dec. 9. Inventory, £750.4.7, by John Dod and John Cundict.

1760, Feb. 29. Williams, Ebenezar, of the Borough of Elizabeth, Essex Co., blacksmith; will of. Wife, Sarah. Children—Benjamin, Enoch, Ebenezer (all three under age), Sarah and Mindwell; an expected child. Real and personal estate. Executors—the wife and brother-in-law John Doobs (Dobbs). Witnesses—Joseph Hindes, Thomas Williams, Robart Clark. Proved June 10, 1760.
  Lib. G, p. 250.

1759, Jan. 19. Williams, Edward, of Gloucester Township and Co., yeoman; will of. Wife, Joana. Children—Joana, Rachel (both under age), and Jonathan. Real and personal estate. Executors—the wife and son. Witnesses—Israel Williams, Thomas Chew, Aaron van Scyhawke. Proved March 5, 1759.   Lib. 9, p. 184.
1759, Feb. 22. Inventory, £263.5.2, incl. bonds and book debts, £62.16.2; made by Michaell Fisher and John Marten.

CALENDAR OF WILLS—1751-1760 359

1751, Aug. 6. Williams, Samuel, of the Borough of Elisabeth, Essex Co.; will of. Wife, Johnah. Sons—Abraham and David. Personal estate. Executors—son, David, and brother, David Williams., of Newark. Witnesses—Moses Smith, John Ogden, Jr., John Ogden. Proved Feb. 12, 1759. Lib. G, p.387.
1759, Feb. 17. Inventory, £137.1.2., by John Ogden and Timothy Harrison.

1758, Jan. 4. Williamson, Abraham, of Wellingborough Township, Burlington Co. Int. Inventory, £27.7, incl. 50 bush. of Indian corn, £5; made by Joseph Fenimore and Benjamin Butterworth.
1758, Jan. 7. Bond of widow, Rachel, as Adm'x; Abraham Hewlings, Esq., of Burlington City; fellowbondsman. Lib. 8, p. 519.
1758, Oct. 27. Account Administratrix, who makes estate her debtor for £1.2.4.

1760, May 20. Williamson, Garrard, of Amwell Township, Hunterdon Co., yeoman; will of. Wife, Margrett. Daughter, Sarah, under age, the only child mentioned by name, but "children" spoken of. Real and personal estate. The wife sole Executrix, with George Trout as Assistant, if she should wish to dispose of the farm. Witnesses—Joseph Johnson and Thomas Sutton. Proved August 13, 1760. Lib. 10, p. 577.
1760, Aug. 11. Inventory, £1269.17.9, incl. bills, bonds, book debts and cash, £1164.1.9; made by Joseph Johnson and George Thomson.

1752, Jan. 13. Williamson, Joseph, of the "Burrough" of Elisabeth, "Summerset"(?) Co., yeoman; will of. Wife, Jane. Children—William, Aron (both under age), Robert, Daniel and Elisabeth. Home farm by Green Brook; personal property. Executors—the wife and son, William. Witnesses—John Vail, John Vail, Jr., and John Shotwell, Jr. Proved July 3, 1759. Lib. G, p. 88.

1760, Aug. 19. Williamson, Nicholas, of Amwell Township, Hunterdon Co.; will of. Eldest son, Benjamin to have £50. Wife, Rachel, £50, over and above the shares of my two daughters, Mary and Catherine, and also the profits of my real and personal estate, till my youngest son, William, is 21; then my realty to be divided among my three sons, Benjamin, Jacob and William. Executors—the wife and son Benjamin. Witnesses—Jacob Mattison. Peter Prall, Jr., Abram Prall. Proved Dec. 18, 1760.
1760, Dec. 13. Inventory, £486.11.0, by Thomas Atkinson and Jacob Mattison. Lib. 10, p. 567.

1758, May 10. Willis, Henry, of Elizabeth, Essex Co., enlisted as a soldier in his Majesty's Provincial Forces against the common enemy; will of. Divides estate between Nancy and Mary, daughters of sister, Mary Nox, brother Samuel Willis, and sister Patience Willis. Capt. Daniel Potter, of Elizabeth, sole Executor, directed not to dispose of the estate in less than 7 years from date without full and legal proof of death. Witnesses—Abraham Wade, David Willis, Benjamin Bonnel, Reuben Cherry. Proved December 8, 1758.
Lib. G, p. 10.
1758, Dec. 6. Inventory, £113.14.2, by James Hindes and John Ogden.

1759, Aug. 4. Willis, Henry, of New Brunswick, Middlesex Co., servant of James Thomson. Int. Adm'r—James Thomson, of New

Brunswick, innkeeper, principal creditor. Bondsman—Courtland Skinner, Esq., of Perth Amboy. Lib. G, p. 91.

1756, June 1. Willis, Isaac, of Essex Co. Int. Adm'x—Hannah Willis, of Essex Co. Bondsman—Daniel Potter, of said Co. Witness —Thomas Bartow.
1756, June 2. Inventory, £123.3.4, by John Ogden and Daniel Potter.
Lib. F, p. 358.

1752, Sept. 1. Willis, Joseph, of Elizabeth Borough, Essex Co., blacksmith; will of. Children—Joseph, Benjamin, Mary (wife of Robert French). Grandchildren—Anne, Mary and Hannah, daughters of Benjamin Pearse. Real and personal estate. Executors—Timothy Whitehead and kinsman, Isaac Willis, both of said Borough. Witnesses—Benjamin Bonnel, Samuel Littel, Jacob Littell. Proved February 26, 1753. Lib. F, p. 103.
1753, Feb. 28. Inventory, £87.11.1, by James Hinds and Thomas Thompson, yeomen, of Elizabeth.

1759, May 9. Willis, Stephen, of Alloways Creek, Salem Co.; will of. Wife, Mary, sole Executrix. Children—David, Stephen, Hannah and Elizabeth, the last two under age. Real and personal estate. Witnesses—Robert Walker, Job Smith and James Smith. Proved June 25, 1759. Lib. 9, p. 259.
1759, June 21. Inventory, £660.8.10, incl. a negro boy, £50; bonds and book debts, £295.7.10; made by Daniel Smith and Jost Meller.

1751, Oct. 26. Willkerson, Samuel, of Cape May Co. Int. Bond of Ephraim Kent, of Cape May, cordwinder, as Adm'r.
Cape May Wills, 158 E.

1760, Nov. 29. Wills, Daniel, of Northampton, Burlington Co., yeoman; will of. Eldest son, Daniel, 5 shillings, as he has had his share. Lands to be sold. Daughter, Mary Buzby, widow of William Buzby, £80. Granddaughter, Elizabeth Buzby, daughter of my son-in-law, William Buzby, £20. My son, Aaron, £200. My son, Moses, £50. Daughters, Hope, wife of Benjamin Lippincott, and Hannah, wife of Caleb Lippincott, £10 each. Son, Moses, £50. Executors—sons Aaron and Moses. Witnesses—Isaac Hillier, Edward Hillier, John Burr, Jr.
1760, Nov. 29. Codicil. To my son, Aaron, my right of Propriety to land in West, not taken up. Witnesses—John Stokes, Elizabeth Delap by her mark, John Woolman, John Burr Jr. Edward Hillier. Proved Dec. 9, 1760. Lib. 10, p. 143.
1760, Dec. 3. Inventory, £160.2.11½, incl. silver spoons, an old watch and "Doc's Instriments," £3.5; made by Asher Woolman and George Elkinton.

1754, Oct. 26. Wills, George, son of Daniel, of Northampton, Burlington Co., merchant, petitions that Vincent Leeds, of the same place, be appointed his Guardian. Same day bond of Vincent Leeds as such Guardian; Philo Leeds, Jr., fellowbondsman.
Burl. Wills, 5475 C.

1754, July ——. Wills, Hannah, daughter of Daniel, of Northampton Township, Burlington Co., merchant, petitions that Vincent Leeds of said Co. be appointed her Guardian.

CALDENDAR OF WILLS—1751-1760   361

1754, July 24. Bond of Vincent Leeds, yeoman, as such Guardian; Jonathan Thomas, of Burlington City, innholder, fellowbondsman.
Burl. Wills, 5547 C.

1757, Dec. 12. Wills, James, of Northampton Township, Burlington Co.; will of. Wife, Elizabeth. Children—Lettice Dobbin and Micaja Wills, latter made sole Executor. Grandchildren—Margaret Wills, the daughter of Ruth Woolstone, "who was one of the daughters of Samuel Woolstone," Sarah and Elizabeth Dobbin, Joab Dobbins, Zabede Dabin, Sarah and James Dabin, children of daughter Lettice. Legacy to Ann, daughter of Joshua Woolstone, dec'd. Land, bought of John Bolsby and Raches Williamson. Real and personal estate. Witnesses—Jonathan Hough, Zachariah Roswell, Jr., Thomas Lawrence. Proved March 31, 1759.   Lib. 9, p. 192.
1759, Mar. 28. Inventory, £1568.2.3, incl. bills, bonds, book debts and notes, £1136.17.4; books; a negro boy, £34; made by Thomas Budd and George Briggs.

1754, May 23. Wills, John, of Morris Co. Int. Inventory, £56.14.2., incl. books and a Bible, £1.4.8; made by Joseph Carson and Ebenezer Byram.
1754, July 12. Abigail, widow, resigns her right of administration to her son, Thomas Wills.
1754, Aug. 2. Bond of Thomas Wills as Adm'r; Samuel Palmer fellowbondsman, both of Morris Co.   Lib. F, p. 197.

1754, Dec. 18. Wills, Margaret, of Burlington Co. Account of the estate, £930.6.11, by the Administrators, Noah Wills and Jacob Hugg, who add to it interest on a bond for £476, i. e., £32.6.4., and report on hand for distribution £556.0.10. [See N. J. Archives, Vol. XXX, p. 536].   Burl. Wills, 5551 C.

1758, Mar. 7. Wills, Noah, of Trenton, Hunterdon Co. Int. Inventory, £125.19, incl. a silver watch, £5; a servant boy, £5; a looking glass 15s.; book debts, £40; made by Daniel Clark and Richard Green.
1758, Apr. 4. Bond of widow, Mary Wills, of Trenton, as Adm'x; William Harrison, of Gloucester Co., fellowbondsman.
Lib. 9, p. 173.

1759, Dec. 29. Wills, Thomas, of Northampton, Burlington Co., yeoman; will of. Wife, Mary. Children—Keziah, Mary and William, all under age. Real and personal estate. Executors—Thomas Budd and George Briggs. Witnesses—Jacob Lutz, Grace Bowker, John Burr, Jr. Proved Feb. 1, 1760.   Lib. 9, p. 389.
1760, Jan. 30. Inventory, £485.17.4, incl. a silver watch, £6; bills and bonds, £213.18.6; a negro woman and child, £35; made by Francis Venicomb and James Dobbin.

1757, Dec. 29. Willson, Andrew, of Deptford Township, Gloucester Co., flattman. Int. Bond of widow, Martha Willson, of Mooreland Township, Philadelphia Co., Pa., as Adm'x; John Perce, of Deptford Township, fellowbondsman.   Lib. 9, p. 61.
1757, Dec. 31. Inventory, £18.16, by Levi Perce and Jonas Cattell.

1754, Feb. 21. Willson, Jane, of New Brunswick, Middlesex Co., single woman; will of. Sisters—Rachell and Euphamia. Brother,

James Wilson. They heirs of personal property, incl. legacy due and in the hands of David Rhee. Executors—uncles Duncan Campbell and John Tomson. Witnesses—Stephen Warne, John Predmore, Margery Willson. Proved March 14, 1754. Lib. F, p. 160.

1754, Mar. 16. Inventory, £119.15.5, incl. bonds and debts, £102.0.5; made by Duncan Campbell and John Tomson.

1760, Jan. 30. Willson, Joseph, of Wantage, Sussex Co., yeoman. Int. Bond of Andrew Willson, of Wantage, as Adm'r; John Willson, of Hardwick, said Co., felowbondsman. Lib. 10, p. 111.

1760, Feb. 4. Inventory, £17.4.7, by John Willson, Jr., and Benjamin Willson.

1761, June 15. Account by said Adm'r, who adds to the inventory, £23.1.6½ for an improvement and has expended £17.8.4½.

1757, Sept. 2. Willson, Peter, of Middletown, Monmouth Co.; will of. Gives real and personal estate to sisters, Margareet, Mary and Martha; 10s. to stepbrother, John Willson. Executors—John Taylor and John Wall. Witnesses—Edward Taylor, Helena Stout and George Taylor, Jr. Proved Oct. 5, 1758. Lib. G, p. 95.

1756, Mar. 31. Willson, Susannah, of Amwell, Hunterdon Co. Int. Bond of Peter Willson, of Amwell, farmer, as Adm'r; Moore Furman, of Trenton, merchant, fellowbondsman. Lib. 8, p. 309.

1757, Sept. 15. Willson, Thomas, yeoman; will of. To Jane Wilson, daughter of James Wilson of Bound brook, New Jersey, 1-8 of my estate; 1-4 of estate to Mary Sharp, daughter of Joseph Sharp of Bound brook; the rest to my father, Adam Wilson, of Pennsylvania. Executor—James Wilson, of Boundbrook. Witnesses—H. Gaine, Andrew Stewart, John Steel. Proved Oct. 12, 1758. Lib. F, p. 556.

1755, March 22. Wilson, Ebenezer, gent., who at the time of his death was of the City of New York. Int. Adm'r—William Smith, of Middlesex Co. Bondsmen—John Deare and Nathaniel Heard, both of Middlesex Co. Witness—Courtland Skinner. Lib. F, p. 253.

1751, May 25. Wilson, Hezekiah, of Burlington Co. Account of the estate, £39.17.6., by the Administratix, Christian Wilson, who has increased it to £60.3.1, by sale of the goods, and paid debts due to Preserve Brown, William Cooke and Charles McClane, charging £6.5. for the funeral and £9.15. for administration fees. [See N. J. Archives, Vol. XXX, p. 536]. Burl. Wills, 4906 C.

1759, May 5. Wilson, James, of Middlesex Co.; will of. Son, James, to have land on south side of Raritan River, purchased of Pontius Stelle, he paying to his sisters £200 when he is 21. Daughters, Anne, Hannah and Elizabeth, the residue, when 18. The house where Peter Lot lives to be let to him for 7 years, and the ferry to be let also. Executors—Thomas Bartow, John Smyth and Andrew Smyth. Witnesses—Peter Lott, Jr., John Burrow, John Roe. Proved May 28, 1759.

1759, May 13. Inventory, £254.4.5, by Robert Sproull and Peter Lott, Jr. Lib. G, p. 58.

1759, May 13. Inventory, £254.4.5, incl. an old negro, £3; negro boy, £60; half a boat, £80; made by Peter Lott and Robert Sproull.

1755, July 26. Wilson, Peter, of Freehold, Monmouth Co., yeoman. Int. Hannah, widow, resigns her right of administration to her uncles, William Waters and William Hankinson, and friend John Anderson.
1755, July 28. Bond of William Waters, William Hankinson and John Anderson as Adm'rs; Joseph Taylor and John van der Veer fellowbondsmen, all of Freehold. Lib. F, p. 282.
1755, Aug. 9. Inventory, £266.3.7, incl. a man servant; £25; a negro woman, £40; a pew in the Meetinghouse, £10.10; a large Bible; made by John van der Veer and Richard Hulst.

1758, Mar. 21. Windsor, George, of Northampton, Burlington Co., innholder. Int. Bond of Daniel Jones as Adm'r; Zachariah Rossell, Jr., fellowbondsman, both of Northampton, inn holders. Lib. 8, p. 534.
1758, March 24. Inventory, £162.9.5, by Zachariah Rossell and John Clark.

1757, Nov. 1. Wines, Isaiah, of Hanover Twsp., Morris Co., yeoman. Int. Bond of Zerviah, widow, as Adm'x; Benjamin Hallsey, of said Co., fellowbondsman. Lib. F, p. 465.
1757, Nov. 8. Inventory, £196.10.8, incl., 11 books, 10s.; a looking glass; a negro man, £55.15; made by Daniel Lindsley and Matthew Fairchild "for Zurviah Windes," the Administratrix.

1755, May 13. Winget, Reuben, of Morris Town, Morris Co., merchant; will of. Wife and children; names not given. Real and personal "and next" estate. Executors—Robert Goble, Gideon Riggs and Ezekiel Cheever. Witnesses—Samuel Ollouer, Stephen Wiggins, Stephen Munson. Proved Oct. 2, 1755. Lib. F, p. 284.
1755, Sept. 13. Inventory: Real—the homestead; £175; the meadow lot, £50. Personal—£265.5.1., incl. books and pamphlets, 16s.; a looking glass, 2s.; book debts and cash, £168.1.7; made by Benjamin Conger and Jonathan Stiles, Jr.
[The Executors sold the homestead of 50 acres to John Gano for £136; 21½ a. of meadow to Gideon Riggs for £51.15, and account for £503.4.8½].

1759, May 28. Wingfield, Abraham, of Wantage, Sussex Co., yeoman. Int. Inventory, £28.10.10, by Martines Decker and Andrew Willson.
1759, May 28. Bond of widow, Mary, as Adm'x; Peter Decker fellowbondsman, both of said Co. Lib. 10, p. 110.
1760, May 28. Account by the Administratrix, who has sold the goods for £45.4.9, York money, and expended the whole amount.

1755, May 8. Winne, Peter, of Newark, Essex Co.; will of. Wife, Leah. Children—Marte, John, Abraham (the last two under age), Catherine and Margaret. Real and personal estate. Executors—the wife, son John and son-in-law, Abraham Vanriper. Witnesses—William Dow, John Kipp, Jr., Jonathan Sergeant. Proved May 10, 1756.
Lib. F, p. 366.

1760, Feb. 28. Winter, Andrew, of Middletown, Monmouth Co., yeoman; will of. Children James (who has daughter Deborah), Moses, Catherine, Ann and Hannah. Daughter-in-law, Mary Winter. Real and personal estate. Executors—son James, John Taylor and Nathaniel Leonard. Witnesses—Matthew Lofborow, John Layton and John Young. Proved April 30, 1760. Lib. 38, p. 83.

1760, Dec. 17. Winton, John, of Piles-grove, Salem Co. Int. Inventory, £145.10.2, by Thomas Davis and David Davis.
1760, Dec. 19. Bond of Samuel Lippincott as Adm'r; Thomas Davis and David Davis fellowbondsmen, all of Piles-grove, yeomen.
Lib. 10, p. 443.

1760, Apr. 14. Wodington, William, of Aloways Creek, Salem Co.; will of. Wife, Elizabeth, sole Executrix. Sons—Jonathan and Robert, both under age. Homefarm, received from uncle Robert Wodington; lower farm, also received from said uncle and bought of Benjamin Tylor; farm in Stoe Neck, inherited from father; personal estate. Witnesses—Nathaniel Hancock, Edward Hancock and Thomas Sayre. Proved June 2, 1760. Lib. 10, p. 516.
1760, May 26. Inventory, £630.7.6, incl. bills, bonds and book debts, £136.7.4; made by Nathaniel Chamless and John Diviney.

1758, Nov. 20. Wood, Christopher, of Lyons Farms, Essex Co.; will of. Wife, Phebe. Sons—Elias and John. Children of dec'd daughter, Mary Lyon, viz., James, Henry and Hannah. Child of dec'd daughter, Abigail Horton, viz., Phebe. Real and personal estate. Executors—the wife, brother-in-law, Timothy Johnes and Capt. Joseph Lyon. Witnesses—Joseph Lyon, Jr., Obadiah Meeker, John Cahune, Timothy Johnes. Proved Feb. 22, 1759. Lib. G, p. 40.

1760, Mar. 16. Wood, Henry, of Depford Township, Gloucester Co., yeoman; will of. Wife, Ruth. Children—Mary, David, John and Jacob, all under age. Real and personal estate. Executors—the wife and cousin, William Wood. Witnesses—Thomas Cooper, Robert Cooper, Ann Cooper. Proved April 3, 1760. Lib. 9, p. 427.
1760, Mar 26. Inventory, £394.8.7, incl. book debts, £83.8.7; a clock, £5; books; 2 looking glasses; made by William Wilkins and John Wilkins.

1754, Oct. 30. Wood, Jehu, only son and heir (7 years old) of Jeremiah Wood, of Gloucester Co., yeoman, and wife Deborah (both deceased), petitions that William Hanby, of said Co., only uncle of Jehu and brother of said Deborah, be appointed his Guardian in preference to James and Henry Wood, because they, as brothers of said Jeremiah, would inherit the real estate, if the child should die.
Glou. Wills, 543 H.
1756, Jan. 1. Petition of Hannah Hanby, grandmother, and Jonathan Sell, father-in-law (stepfather?), that William Wood, nearly related to Jehu, be appointed his Guardian.
1756, Jan. 9. Bond of William Wood, of Deptford, Gloucester Co., as such Guardian, Samuel Shivers, of Greenwich Township, said Co., fellowbondsman, both yeomen. Lib. 11, p. 126.

1752, July 22. Wood, Jeremiah, of Gloucester Co. Account of the estate, £191.11.5, by Jonathan Sell and wife, Deborah, late Deborah Wood, Administrators. [See N. J. Archives, Vol. XXX, p. 541].
Lib. 6, p. 78.

1757, Aug. 16. Wood, Jeremiah, of Piles Grove, Salem Co. Int. Bond of Jechonias Wood as Adm'r; John Davis and John Loyd fellowbondsmen, all of Piles Grove. Lib. 9, p. 80.

CALENDAR OF WILLS—1751-1760   365

1757, Sept. 13. Inventory, £640.14.2, incl. 306 hides and 93 calf skins in the tanyard, £270.4.9; 22 cords of bark, £11; a negro man, £45; bills, book debts and notes, £143; made by Isaac Sharp and Bateman Lloyd.

1759, Apr. 22. Wood, John, of Newark, Essex Co.; will of. Wife, Tabitha. Daughter, Phebe. Remainder to brother, Elias Wood. Nephews—James and Henry Lyon and nieces, Hannah Lyon and Phebe Horton. Real property, inherited from father, Christopher Wood, lately dec'd. Personal estate. Executors—the wife, father-in-law, Abraham Clark and Abraham Clark, Jr. Witnesses—Richard Verguson, Samuel Clizbe, Benjamin Price. Proved June 6, 1759.
Lib. G, p. 86.

1754, Sept. 27. Wood, Joseph, of Morris Co. Int. Bond of Mary, widow, and Timothy Tuttle as Adm'rs; Daniel Tuttle fellowbondsman, all of said Co. Lib. F, p. 230.

1760, Feb. 7. Wood, Joseph, of Upper Penn's Neck, Salem Co., innkeeper. Int. Inventory, £124.12.8, incl. credits and desperate debts, £35.12.3; made by Thomas Sparks and Sam'l Whitehorne.
1760, Feb. 8. Bond of widow, Jean Wood, as Adm'x; John Thompson and Samuel Whitehorne fellowbondsmen, all of Penn's Neck.
Lib. 10, p. 447.

1757, Jan. 24. Wood, Matthew, of Kingwood Township, Hunterdon Co., yeoman; will of. Wife, Rebecca. Children—Aaron (sole Executor), James (eldest son) and Margret. Grandson, Matthew Wood. Bequest of real property to housekeeper, Rachel Gibson. Real and personal estate. Witnesses—William Hogeland, George Meldrum and Robert Sitlinton. Proved April 27, 1757. Lib. 8, p. 416.
1757, Apr. 23. Inventory, £101.12.4, by William Hogeland and Joshua Waterhouse.

1751, Apr. 14. Wood, Nathan, of Deerfield Township, Cumberland Co.; will of. Sister, Mary Brual. Brothers—Elnathan Wood and Job Wood (of East Jersey). Legacies to Alexander Foster, Hannah, wife of James Ayers, and widow, Abigail Brooks. Personal property, incl. a gold ring and silk handkerchief. Executors—Alexander Moore and James Ayers. Witnesses—Hance Woolson, Samuel Woodroff, Benjamin Sayre. Proved June 14, 1751. Cumb. Wills, 73 F.

1755, Jan. 31. Wood, Obediah, of Greenwich, Cumberland Co. Int. Bond of Samuel Wood, of Allaways Creek, Salem Co., as Adm'r; Silas Parvin and Samuel Clark, both of Cumberland Co., fellowbondsman.
Lib. 8, p. 101.
———, ——— —. Inventory, £46.11.7, by Samuel Clark and Thomas Ewing.

1756, Apr. 26. Wood, Samuel, of Chesterfield Township, Burlington Co., carpenter; will of. Wife, Hannah, sole heiress and, with Marmaduke Watson. Executors. Witnesses—Anne Tantum, Mary Bunting, Mary Duglass. Proved Feb. 7, 1757. Lib. 8, p. 356.

1759, May 26. Wood, William, of Somerset Co., innkeeper; nuncupative will of. Gives all his estate to his sister's son, William

Wood, of New York. Proved by the testimony of John Letts, Francis Flatt and his brother, William Flatt. Lib. G, p. 63.
 1759, May 28. Cataren, widow authorizes William Wood to administer on her late husband's estate. Same date bond of William Wood, of New York City, carman, Adm'r; John Kent, of Woodbridge, yeoman, fellowbondsman.
 1759, May 29. Inventory, £96.9.6, incl. a silver spoon, 17s.4d.; a bond and a note £17.17; made by Joseph Gifford and Andrew Brown.
 1760, Mar. 10. Account by the Adm'r, who charges £43.11.1. as given to the widow, Catherine Wood.

1753, Oct. 15. Woodbridge, Deodat, of Salem, Salem Co., surgeon. Int. Mary, widow, declines the administration in New Jersey, Pennsylvania or the three Lower Counties on the Delaware.
 1753, Oct. 15. Bond of George Trenchard as Adm'r; Daniel Mestayer fellowbondsman, both of Salem Co. Lib. 8, p. 88.

1759, May 20. Woodnutt, Joseph, of Manington Precinct, Salem Co., yeoman; will of. Brother, Richard Woodnutt, of said Precinct, sole Executor. Nephews—Joseph, son of Elisha Bassett and wife Mary, and Joseph, son of Samuel Hedge and wife Hannah. Nieces—Rebecca Hedge and Rachel Bassett. Real and personal estate. Witnesses—Job Butcher, Bartholomew Wyatt, Jr., and Malachi Kille. Proved June 29, 1759. Lib. 11, p. 192.
 1759, June 13. Richard Woodnutt, named as Executor above, refuses to serve.
 1759, June 18. Inventory, £176.1.4, incl. credits and desperate debts, £63.3.6; made by John Robertes and John Thompson.
 1759, June 29. Bond of Elisha Bassett, Jr., of Manington, as Adm'r; John Thompson, of the same place, and Charles Fogg, of Allaways Creek, fellowbondsmen.
 1765, Mar. 6. Account by the Administrator.

1759, June 17. Woodnutt, Richard, of Manington Precinct, Salem Co., yeoman; will of. Daughter, Elizabeth, under age. Sisters—Hannah Hedge (who has son Joseph), and Mary Bassett. Legacies to Mary Mason, Prudence Rugg, cousins Jonathan and Henry Woodnutt, and wife, Elizabeth, and children of William Hall, namely, Nathaniel, Mary and Edward. Real and personal estate. Executors—William Hall and Jonathan Woodnutt. Witnesses—Ann van Histe, Henry Woodnutt, Bartholomew Wyatt, Jr., and J. Budd. Proved August 21, 1759. Lib. 10, p. 514.
 1759, July 25. Inventory, £381.13.2, by Whitten Cripps and John Nicholson.

1755, Aug. 4. Woodruff, Ebenezer, of Deerfield, Cumberland Co., yeoman; will of. Wife, Meriam, sole Executrix. Children, Isaac, Ebenezer, Mary, Phebe, Rachel, Meriam and Hannah, all under age. Real and personal estate. Witnesses—Jeremiah Parvin, Onesimus Seagrave, William Stratton. Proved Sept. 13, 1755. Lib. 8, p. 207.
 1755, Aug. 23. Inventory, £129.10, by Jeremiah Parvin and Daniel Ogden.

1755, May 1. Woodruff, John, of Hopewell Township, Cumberland Co., weaver; will of. Wife, Lidia. Children—John (under age), Jesse, Benjamin, Ester, Lidia, James, David, Timothy and Catura, the

CALENDAR OF WILLS—1751-1760   367

last six under age. Real and personal estate. Executors—the wife and Jonathan Holmes. Witnesses—Andrew Hunter, Samuel Miller, Isaac Penton. Proved May 23, 1755. Lib. 8, p. 183.
1755, May 16. Inventory, £251.10.3, incl. bonds and book debts, £75.4.4; made by Benjamin Lapton and Thomas Brown.

1759, Aug. 6. Woodruff, Joshua, of Essex Co. Int. Adm'r—Nathaniel Rusco, of said Co., appointed at the request of the brother, Cooper Woodruff. Bondsman—Abraham Cadmus, of said Co. Witness—Thomas Bartow.   Essex Wills, 2737 G.

1753, Dec. 7. Woodruff, Samuel, of Westfield, Elizabeth Borough, Essex Co.; will of. Wife, Elizabeth. Children—Abigail, Rachel, Samuel, Mathias, Abner and John, all under age. Real and personal estate. Executors—the wife, John Corey and Joseph Corey. Witnesses—Jonathan Woodruff, John Woodruff, Ebenezer Price. Proved Oct. 9, 1754. Lib. F, p. 208.

1752, Mar. 11. Woodruff, Thomas, of Elizabeth Town, Essex Co., cordwainer; will of. Wife, Hannah. Daughter, Sarah, wife of Ellet Cresey. Grandsons—Thomas Woodruff Cresey and Mathias Ward. Real and personal estate. Executors—the wife and son-in-law, Ellet Cresey, (signs Crisey). Witnesses Matthias Baldwin, John May, Robert Ogden. Proved May 13, 1754. Lib. F, p. 222.

1756, Aug. 15. Woods, Richard, of Morris Town, Morris Co., blacksmith, will of. Wife, Rebecca. Children—Abijah, Richard, Hopestill, Hannah, Sarah and Phebe, all under age. Executors—Ezekiel Cheever, of Morris Town, schoolmaster, and brother, Christopher Woods. Witnesses—John Whitehead, Christopher Woods, Philip Price. Proved Sept. 3, 1756. Lib. G, p. 97.
1756, Sept. 22. Account of goods sold at vendue for £56.10.3. by the Executors. Some goods bought by widow, Rebecca Woods.
1756, Oct. 15. Inventory: Real—farm at Rockeway £95; homestead, £57.10; shop £2.1.1. Personal—£76.1.11, incl. a looking glass, 7s., signed by the Executors and by Caleb Fairchild, John Whitehead and Samuel Tuthill, Inspectors.
1760, May 29. Account by the Executors.

1756, Aug. 21. Woodward, Hannah, of Upper Freehold, Monmouth Co., widow of Anthony; will of. Sons—Thomas, Anthony and Joseph, who has wife Hannah, and children Anne Reckless, Joseph and Appollo. Legacy for use of Poor Women, and Friends of Chesterfield Monthly Meeting. Real and personal estate, incl. dec'd husband's estate in Great Britain and 5 negroes. Executors—son Joseph, his son Joseph, and Joseph Reckless. Witnesses—William Lawrie, Joseph Fowler and Rebekah Terry. Proved Sept. 30, 1760.
Lib. 10, p. 421.
1756, Sept. 20. Inventory, £235.17.6, incl. bonds, £110; 2 negro boys and 3 negro girls, £110; made by William Lawrie and Joseph Fowler.

1752, Sept. 25. Woolley, Rachel, of Shrewsbury, Monmouth Co., widow; will of. Divides real and personal property between the following: Mary Lawrence, daughter of John and Mary Cambell, dec'd; Leah, daughter of John and Leah Den dec'd; Hannah, daughter of John and Elisabeth Field; William Lawrence, son of Mercy Field;

the Indian School; Abigail Longstreet; Lydia Bordin; Mary, daughter of Parnell and Content Cleyton, dec'd; the Friends' Meeting at Shrewsbury (to make backs for the women's benches); Catherine, wife of Peter Knott; Mercy Field and her daughter Catherine Lawrence; Elisabeth Lewis and her son Lemuel; Rachel Hubbard, alias Yates; Hannah, daughter of John Williamson; Elisabeth, daughter of James and Mary Corliss; Mary, wife of Thomas Leonard; Hannah Vandeverton (the money for her to be left in the hands of Daniel Wainright to pay for her children's schooling); Richard Lawrence and daughter Catherine; Jedidah Wainright; Hannah Little; Jerushea and Lydia Wainwright; Catherine Knott, Jr., and her sister, Abigail Knott. Disposes of a lot in Perth Amboy, silver tankard, gold chain, and gold buttons. Executors—Jerushea Wainright and David Knott. Witnesses—Stephen West, Joseph West, Andria West, Sarah West. Proved Feb. 25, 1754. Lib. F, p. 203.

1754, Feb. 25. Inventory, £292.14.9½, incl. silver tankard, £8; lookingglass, 5s.; a silver bodkin, 1/3; an "arethmetaick" book and another, 18s.; 2 pistoles at £2.18. York money, £3.2.6. light; a gold chain, £2; pair of gold buttons at £1.9. York, £1.11.3, light; bonds and notes, £227.12.3; made by Webley West and Stephen West; Sarah West assisting in the appraisal of the clothing.

1753, Feb. 3. Woolston, Job, of Northampton, Burlington Co. Int. Bond of Michael, father, as Adm'r; Francis Briggs fellowbondsman, both of Northampton.

1753, Jan. 29. Inventory, £113.9.9, by Francis Briggs and Robert Hill.

1754, Sept. 6. Bond of James Wills as Adm'r of the estate left unadministered by Michael Woolston; Henry Paxson fellowbondsman, both of said Co. Lib. 7, p. 308.

1752, Nov. 14. Woolston, John, of Northampton, Burlington Co., yeoman; will of. Son, Jacob, house where I live, with the west part of the plantation of 170 acres. Son, Melentus, east part of said plantation. Son, Cornwell, one-half of the land at the mountains at Musquenica. Son, Newbold, the other half of land at Musquenaca. Land at Blue Anchor, of 146 acres, to be sold and the money to be paid to my wife, Hannah. Daughters—Prudence, Ruth, Epicarius, Hannah and Sarah; they to have my land at Mount Holly bought of Blackham. Rest of estate to my wife, Hannah, and my five daughters. Executors—son, Jacob, and my wife, Hannah. Witnesses—Lott Ridgway, Gabriel Blond. Proved Nov. 21, 1753.
Burl. Wills, 5335 C.

1753, Nov. 20. Inventory, £524.1.8¾, incl. bills and bonds, £124.10.10; a Bible and other books, £1.12; a servantman's time, £15; made by Thomas Budd and Francis Briggs.

1755, Jan. 10. Account of the estate by Joseph Belcher and wife Hannah, Executors, who have spent only £87.12.7.

1753, May 23. Woolston, Joshua, of Northampton, Burlington Co., yeoman; will of. Mother, Sarah Woolston, to have use of my plantation till my brother, Barzillai Woolston, is 21. To brother Barzillai all my lands. Sisters, Lettice and Ann Woolston, £50 each. Executor—my uncle James Wills. Witnesses—Thomas Millikam, John Carman, John Burr Jr. Proved June 9, 1753. Burl. Wills, 5349 C.

1753, June 16. Inventory, £72.13.8, by George Briggs and Thomas Budd.

1753, Feb. 23. Woolston, Michael, of Northampton, Burlington Co., yeoman; will of. The land I bought of Henry Cooper, lying in Mount Holly near the house in which William Murrill dwelt, I give to my daughter, Lettice Woolston. The plantation I bought of Stephen Murfy & Son, whereon Robert Hill lives, to my daughter, Ann Woolston. Son, Barzillai, other land. Son, Joshua, house and part of plantation where I live. Son, Joseph, rest of the plantation. Father-in-law, John Stockton. Wife, Sarah. Son, Joseph, is a minor. To John Carman, £5. Cousin, Michael Woolston, who lives with me, £5. Executor—son Joshua. Witnesses—James Wills, Thomas Millickan, John Woolman.

1753, March 5. Inventory, £517.17.2, by George Briggs, Jr., and James Wills.
Burl. Wills, 5257 C.

1754, Oct. 26. Woolston, Ruth, daughter of John, of Northampton Township, Burlington Co., petitions, that Vincent Leeds, of said Co., yeoman, be appointed her Guardian. Same date bond of Vincent Leeds as such Guardian, Philo Leeds, Jr., fellowbondsman, both of said Co.
Burl. Wills, 5559 C.

1759, July 2. Woolverton, Thomas, Esq., of Newtown, Sussex Co. Int. Bond of Mary Woolverton and Ephraim Darby, both of Newtown, and Nathaniel Pettit, Jr., of Bethlehem, Hunterdon Co., yeoman, as Adm'rs; Peter Schmuck, Esq., of Hardwick, Sussex Co., fellowbondsman.
Lib. 9, p. 392.

1760, Jan. 7. Inventory, £338.4.4., incl. a watch and chain, £7; 3 looking glasses, 8s.; 2 glass pictures, 2s.; 2 paper pictures, 1s.; 2 books; a Bible, spelling book and Psalter 6s.; made by Sam'l Willson, Japheth Byram and Peter Schmuck.

1759, Jan. 12. Worthington, Ephraim, of "Allawares" Creek, Salem Co. Int. Bond of Sarah Worthington as Adm'x; John Fitzpatrick and John Stretch fellowbondsmen, all of said Creek. Lib. 9, p. 350.

1759, —— —. Inventory, £140.0.4, by John Fitzpatrick and Samuel Wood.

1760, June 21. Worthley, John, of Shrewsbury, Monmouth Co., yeoman. Int. Bond of Lydia, widow, as Adm'r; John Williams, of Freehold, yeoman, and Richard Lawrence, of Shrewsbury, yeoman and trader, fellowbondsmen.
Lib. G, p. 241.

1739, Sept. 24. Worton, Benjamin, of Dearfield, Salem Co., cordwainer; will of. Wife, Sarah, sole heiress and Executrix. Witnesses—Simon Rands and Thomas Yapp. Proved Nov. 28, 1754.
Cumb. Wills 108 F.

1754, Nov. 26. Inventory, £266.0.8, incl. bonds and book debts, £32.0.2; an apprentice boy; made by William Stratton and Henry Stevens.

1756, May 21. Wright, Elizabeth, of Pen's Neck, Salem Co., widow; will of. Grandchildren—Catherine Doughaty, William Carty, Joseph Corbet, and Rebecca Doughaty. Son-in-law, Edward Doughaty and his wife, Elizabeth, residuary legatees and Executors of real and personal estate. Witnesses—John Scott, Jean Enlows, Jean Grooms and John Marshall. Proved May 29, 1756. Lib. 8, p. 456.

1756, May 29. Inventory, £30.8.6, by John Marshall and Andrew Sinnickson.

1759, Apr. 27. Wright, John, of Hardwick Township, Sussex Co.; will of. Wife, Alyday. Daughter, Eve. Real and personal estate. Executors—the wife and Nathan Armstrong. Witnesses—Thomas Robinson, Samuel Willson, Samuel Willson, Jr. Proved May 5, 1760.
Lib. 10, p. 112.

1760, Apr. 3. Inventory, £139.11.7, incl. an old negro wench, £15; a young negro, £30; an English Bible, £1; made by Thomas Robinson, Samuel Willson and Peter Schmuck.

1760, May 5. Nathan Armstrong, one of the Executors named, refuses to act.

1750-1, Mar. 22. Wright, Joshua, of Chester, Burlington Co., yeoman; will of. Wife, Thomasin. Children—Joshua, Joseph (both under age), Elizabeth, Mary, Thomasin, Anna and Susanna. Homefarm on Delaware River, near Plum Point, adjoining Robert Bishop; house and smith shop, now occupied by John Jackson; land (200 acres) above or back of Bristol, Penna.; 200 ac. near the head of Timber Creek, Gloucester Co.; land on S. E. side of the new great road; 1-3 of 27 acres a mile out of Trenton, held with Mahlon Wright and Isaac Knight; personal property. Executors—the wife, brother-in-law, Thomas Folkes, of Bordentown, and Samuel Stokes, of Chester. Witnesses—Thomas Potts, Rabekah Potts, Charles Farguison. Proved July 20, 1751. Lib. 7, p. 105.

1751, July 15. Inventory, £612.11.10, incl. bills, bonds and book debts, £169.11.8; "libria," £1; "chinia" and silver tea spoons, £2.5; a looking glass, 8s.; a "cofey" mill and sundries, 12s.; a servant man's time, £6.10; made by Darling Conarroe and Joseph Stokes.

1756, Sept. 28. Wright, Joshua, (son of Robert), of Burlington Co. Int. Bond of John Ware as Adm'r; John Buffin, Sr., fellowbondsman, both of said Co. Lib. 8, p. 340.

1754, June 24. Wright, Josiah, of Mansfield, Burlington Co., yeoman; will of. Wife, Ann. Children—David, Abednego, Susannah, Prudence, Elizabeth (wife of Antohny Allcut), Charity (widow of John Garwood), and Israel. Homefarm, bought of brother, Jonathan; personal property, Son, David, sole Executor. Witnesses—Enoch Fenton, William Fenimore, John Fenimore. Proved August 26, 1755.
Lib. 8, p. 201.

1755, Dec. 10. Inventory, £70.19, by John Fenimore and William Hancock.

1755, Jan. 14. Wright, Meriam, of Chesterfield Township, Burlington Co. Int. Bond of Harmanus King as Adm'r; Ralph Woodward and Obadiah Ireton Jr., fellowbondsmen, all of Burlington Co.
Lib. 8, p. 87.

1752, May 22. Wright, Nathan, of Trenton, Hunterdon Co., yeoman; will of. Wife [not named]. Son, Nathan. Bequests made to Lititia Wright, William Wright and "the youngest child," but it does not appear whether they are testator's children, he saying the young-

CALENDAR OF WILLS—1751-1760 371

est must not become a charge on the estate. If son, Nathan, die in his minority or without issue the estate, left to him, to go to testator's brothers, Mahlon and David Wright (the Executors), and sister Rebekah Terry. House and lot in Trenton; 52 acres in Stockins Hollow; 100 ac. at the Burnt Swamp; 50 ac. at the Mountains, had from Joseph Decow. Witnesses—Joseph Steward, Joseph Fowler, Joseph Smithier (?). No jurat of proof, but Executors named sworn in as such on June 4, 1752. Lib. 7, p. 240.

1752, June 8. Inventory, £551.15.11, incl. a small looking glass and 2 pictures, 1s.6d.; bills and bonds, £306.10; made by Joseph Yard and William Ely.

1755, Oct. 4. Wright, Richard, of Burlington City, gent.; will of. Children—Joseph, Esther Maxwell, Sarah Wright (sole Executrix), Elizabeth Imlay, Martha Furnis. Grandchildren—James Maxwell, who has sisters, names not given; two daughters of dec'd son George, names not given; George, Mary and Lydia, children of dec'd son Richard. Land (300 acres) in Monmouth Co., bought of Robert Montgomery and Martha De Cow; house and lot; homestead; land on the Southside of the creek around Burlington Island, bought of Thomas Scattergood; wood field on Salem road, bought of George Emmet; lot of land, called the Barnfield; personal property. Witnesses—Benjamin Fornis (Furniss), Samuel Jones, Gabriel Blond. Proved Sept. 24, 1756. Lib. 8, p. 324.

1756, Sept. 25. Inventory, £3108.7.4, incl. bonds, £2898.17.4; a negro man and negro woman, £90; made by Abram Hewlings and Joseph Imlay.

1763, July 20. Account, by Edmund Woolley and wife, Sarah, formerly Sarah Wright, the Executrix, who reports on hand for distribution, 29 sh.

———, ——— —, **Wright, William,** "of Allawares" Creek, Salem Co., carpenter; will of. Wife, Mary, sole Executrix, with assistance of David Wood to settle accounts. Children—John and Ann, both under age. John to have all books and "instrewments belonging to the art of Survaying and Navigation," and to learn "the Busniess of Survaying." Personal estate. Witnesses Joseph Hildereth, John Smith and James Sayer. Proved March 2, 1759. Lib. 9, p. 284.

1759, Feb. 27. Inventory, £175.4.8., incl. bonds and book debts, £64.6.2; surveying instruments, £14.1; made by Jonathan Wright and James Sayer.

1752, Mar. 7. Wright, William, of Morris Co. Int. Inventory, £76.8.10, by John Arrison and Lazarus Adams.

1752, Mar. 12. Bond of John Wright as Adm'r; Lazarus Adams fellowbondsman, both of Morris Co., yeomen. Morris Wills, 51 N.

1756, Sept. 11. Wyckoff, Cornelis, of the "Milston, Summersett Co.," yeoman; will of. Also signed by Maddelenti Wyckoff, probably the wife. Children—Pieter and Willentie, both under age. Real and personal estate. Executors—brother Marten Wyckof; brother-in-law, Cornelis Derye, and Joseph Cernell (Cornell). Witnesses—Peiter Stryker, Barnt Stryker and Jacobus Stryker. Proved May 16, 1757. Lib. F, p. 425.

1757, May 14. Inventory, £441.2, incl. 4 negroes, £165; a backplate, £1.10; a looking glass, with 7 pictures, 20s.; a Bible and other books, £3; a bond, £56; a note, £3; **made by William Baird, Maertynis Hogelandt, Peter Stryker and Cornelius Duryee.**

1759, July 1. Wyckoff, Cornelius, Jr., of Readington, Hunterdon Co.; will of. Wife, Mary. Children—Coruelius, Adriaentie and another daughter, name not given. Father, Cornelius Wyckoff. Real and personal estate. Executors—the wife, John van Buscark and Cornelius Lane. Witnesses—Abram Emans, Jeromas Emmans and Marge Henry. Proved Oct. 3, 1759. Lib. 10, p. 58.
1759, Aug. 6. Inventory, £283.17, incl. a negro man, £25; a Bible, a dictionary and other books £3; a looking glass; made by Thomas Atkinson and Pieter Middagh.

1756, July 1. Yager, Johannis, Jr., of Amwell Township, Hunterdon Co., carpenter; will of. Wife [not named]. Children, of whom only son John mentioned by name. Executors—father, John Peter Yager, Tunis Case, Francis Beson and Peter Case. Witnesses—William Wilgus and Garrard Williamson. Proved Sept. 27, 1756. Lib. 8, p. 410.
1756, Sept. 24. Inventory, £145.2.5, incl. bonds, book accounts and cash, £105.16.5; made by Christ. Kaull and Garrard Williamson.

1756, Sept. 21. Yager, Hans (John) Peter, of Amwell Township, Hunterdon Co., yeoman; will of. Wife [not named]. Son, Philipp. Grandsons—John, Peter, Philipp and William, sons of son John. Real and personal estate. Executors—John Houshel, Philipp Kemple and Christopher Coul, Jr., who are also named trustees for the grandsons. Witnesses—Garrard Williamson, Chr. Kaull (Coul). Proved Nov. 15, 1756, when John Houshel, above named, signs jurat as Johannis Hauschilt in German script. Lib. 8, p. 418.

1759, May 29. Yard, William, of Trenton, Hunterdon Co. Int. Bond of widow, Margaret Yard, and Benjamin Yard, of Trenton, as Adm'rs; Samuel Tucker, Jr., and Alexander Chambers, of the same place, merchants, fellowbondsmen. Lib. 9, p. 315.
1759, May 30. Inventory, £717.10.11., incl. a looking glass and 7 pictures, £2.10; another looking glass, £1; a negro man, £50; a negro boy, £35; bonds and notes, £195.14.7; made by Theodore Severns and Samuel Tucker, Jr.

1757, Feb. 4. Yates, Thomas, of Middlesex Co. Int. Adm'r—William Yates, of Middlesex Co., yeoman. Bondsman—William Cheesman, Jr., of said Co. Witness—Thomas Bartow. Midd. Wills, 2729 L.

1754, Jan. 6. Yates, Thomas. Inventory of the personal estate, £234.5.3, incl. a book, the work of Samuel Houron, £1 ; 12 other books, 20s.; a looking glass, £1.10; 3 negroes, £145; made by Peter Berrien and John Clunn, also signed by William Yates.
Feb. 4, 1754. Bond of William Yates as Adm'r. Bondsman—William Cheesman, Jr., both of same county. Witness—Thomas Bartow.
Lib. F, p. 156.

1756, Oct. 8. Young, Elizabeth, of "Deepford" Township, Gloucester Co., widow; will of. Daughters—Mary Davis, Susanna Griffith, Phebe Cosens and Amy, wife of Samuel Chester, Jr. Personal estate. Executors—sons-in-law, Thomas Davis and William Cosens. Witnesses—James Snoden (Snowden) and Nixon Chattin. Proved Oct. 29, 1756. Lib. 8, p. 374.

1756, Oct. 25. Inventory, £95.15.7, incl. bonds and book debts, £28.8.6; a 'prentice boys' time, £20; made by Gabriel Rambo and Ebenezer Brown.

1754, June 17. Yuriansen, (Juriansen) Harmen, of Achquechenonk, Essex Co., yeoman; will of. Wife, Judith. Children—Jurrie, Fredrick, Abraham, Johannes, Christoffel, Marytje, Jacob, Isaac, Sarah, Gerrit, Geurt, Thomas and Christyna, all called "van Rype." Homefarm of 200 acres on the N. M. side of Pessaick River, between Madlene van Giese and Claas Vreland No. 4; other land in Achquechenonk patent; land in Orange Co., N. Y.; personal estate. Executors—sons Abraham and Jacob. Witnesses—David Marinus, Johannis Wanshaer, Richard Bradberry. Proved May 14, 1756. Lib. F, p. 355.

1756, July 1. Zabriski, Jacob, Sr., of "Peremus," Bergen Co.; will of. Grandson, Andries Zabriski. Granddaughter, Antie Zabriski, heiress of testator's oldest son Albert. Children—John, Steven, Jacob, Henritie, Fitie. Grandchildren—Andris and Jacob, sons of daughter Jannetie and Abraham Hoppe. Other children's or heirs' names destroyed. Land east of the Steenbergh; land at Weeramus; land over the Slink, an island, formerly part of Class Janse Romyne's patent; personal property. Executors—sons John, Stephen and Jacob. Witnesses—Bn. van der Linde, John Ackerman, Johann Henrich (———?). Proved September 26, 1758. Lib. G, p. 1.

1758, May 5. Inventory, £157, incl. a negro man, £80; made by John Ackerman and Roelef Westervelt.

1759, May 19. Zane, Joseph, of Salem Town and Co., tanner; will of. Wife, Rebecah. Children—Thomas, Isaac and Rebeckah, all under age. Real and personal estate. Executors—the wife and Joshua Thompson. Witnesses—Samuel Tyler, Isaac Zane and Josiah Kay. Proved June 7, 1759. Lib. 9, p. 358.

1757, May 23. Zans, (Zanns, Zane), Joseph, of New Town, Gloucester Co.; will of. Wife, Mary. Daughters, Esther Collins, Rhoda Zanns, and Rachel Jones, the first two called "dutiful," the third "undutiful." Real and personal estate. Executors—brother, Isaac Zanns and son-in-law, Richard Collins. Witnesses—Henry Hill, Anne Hill, James Mulock. Proved June 12, 1759. Lib. 9, p. 238.

1759, July 16. Inventory, £476.5.8, incl. bills and bonds, £297.2.4; a looking glass, 7s.; made by James Graisbury and Jacob Stokes.

INDEXES

I. INDEX OF NAMES OF PERSONS
II. INDEX OF PLACE-NAMES

Index of Names of Persons

NOTE.—The names of testators, intestates, etc., printed in heavy type in the preceding text, are not repeated in this Index, except in the case of some alternate spellings, since they are already placed in strict alphabetical order.

Where surnames or Christian names, in common use to-day, or at least with well-known spellings, are unusually or curiously used in the text, the current modern spelling is substituted in this Index in order to facilitate reference. A few exceptions are of some Dutch or German names, or where names are uncertain.

A

Aaronson, Ann, 5
  Benjamin, 5
  Hannah, 5
  John, 5
  Joseph, 5
  Mary, 5
  Sarah, 5
  (see Aronson, Arison)
Abbett, (Abbot, Abit), Abdon, 6
  Aldon, 5
  Anne, 248
  Benjamin, 5, 6
  Burroughs, 290
  Edith, 290
  Hannah, 5
  James, 115
  John, 82, 184, 262
  Joseph, 5
  Kezia, 5
  Martha, 5
  Mary, 281
  Samuel, 10, 235, 236, 326
Abeel, David, 261, 340
Abel, Andreas, 5
  Jacobus, 261
  Maria, 5
  Mathias, 5
  Michael, 5
  Paul, 5
Abraham, Abraham, 6
  John, 92
Abrahams, Andries, 342
Acker (see Aker)
Ackerman, Abraham, 6, 351
  Abraham L., 6
  Altie, 6
  David, 6
  David A., 6
  Egbert, 334
  Garret, 6
  Jannetie, 6
  Johannes, 6
  John, 373
  Lawrence, 6, 334
  Margaret, 6
  Nicolas, 332
  Philip, 221
  Rachel, 6
Acret, Sarah, 133
Acton, John, 56
Adams, Charles, 136
  David, 6
  Elizabeth, 6, 285
  Hannah, 172
  Isaac, 6
  James, 6, 133
  Jeremiah, 6
  John, 130
  Joseph, 6, 7, 70, 74
  Lazarus, 371
  Mackdole, 6
  Margaret, 6
  Matthew, 6
  Samuel, 6
  Sarah, 15, 264
  Steven, 264
  William, 6
Addis, Ann, 7
Addleton, Elizabeth, 82
Afflack, Paul, 7
  Robert, 7
  William, 7
Agnew, Sarah, 7
Aherrin, John, 86
Aikman, Alexander, 7, 316
  Jean, 7
  William, 7
Aker (Akers), Anne, 7
  John, 270
  Peter, 7
  Robert, 185
Akin, Timothy, 29, 200
Alberts, Johannes, 258
Albertson, Anglechea, 8
  Ann, 7
  Enoch, 7
  Garret, 8, 61
  Hannah, 8
  Isaac, 7
  Jacob, 7, 8, 104, 325
  Jonathan, 7
  Josiah, 158, 176, 304
  Keziah, 270
  Lætitia, 7
  Mathias, 142
  Nathan, 8, 324
  Nehemiah, 7
  Rosanna, 142
  Sarah, 8
  Simeon, 8
  William, 8
Albright, John, 179
Alderman, Abigail, 8
  Elizabeth, 8

Joel, 8
Mary, 8
Rachel, 8
Sarah, 8
Susanna, 8
Tabitha, 8
William, 8
Alexander, Anne, 8
  David, 8
  Elizabeth, 8
  James, 8, 75, 76, 88, 116, 243
  John, 115
  John Provost, 8
  Katherine, 8
  Mary, 8
  Susannah, 8
  William, 8, 9, 102
Allcut, Anthony, 176, 370
  Elizabeth, 370
Allegar, Benjamin, 64, 280
Allen (Allin), Aaron, 10
  Abraham, 9, 11, 13, 136, 141, 156, 202
  Agnes, 11
  Benjamin, 9, 10, 11, 52, 109, 167, 314, 347, 349
  Champles, 10
  Charles, 10, 35
  Catharine, 9
  David, 10, 130, 150, 175, 332
  Eastwood, 292
  Elisha, 10
  Elizabeth, 9, 10
  George, 9, 10, 29, 41, 134, 160
  Hannah, 253
  James, 30, 31, 38, 157, 221, 227, 234, 247, 253, 260, 364
  James, Jr., 31
  Jedediah, 9, 10, 56
  Job, 130
  John, 10, 123, 163, 200, 202, 216, 219, 225, 226, 266, 301, 302
  Jonathan, 10, 92, 328
  Joseph, 9, 203, 296
  Judiah, 10, 311
  Margaret, 10
  Martha, 311
  Mary, 10, 11, 24, 41, 61
  Matthew, 10, 46, 148, 221, 245, 266, 290
  Mathias, 10, 11
  Miriam, 10
  Nathan, 10, 248, 272
  Nehemiah, 159
  Patience, 9
  Phebe, 10, 198
  Ralph, 10
  Rebecah, 10, 11
  Robert, 11
  Ryley, 10
  Samuel, 9
  Sarah, 10, 11, 156
  Thomas, 11
  Timothy, 59, 88
  West, 10
  William, 10, 11, 189, 245, 290, 311, 326
Aller, Elizabeth, 183
  John, 72
  Peter, 183
Allibone, William, 218
Alling, Job, 150
  Martha, 11
  Samuel, 20, 219
Allinson, Elizabeth, 11

Jacob, 11
John, 95
Joseph, 11, 62, 64, 350
Mary, 11, 291
Peter, 11, 64, 127, 265
Richard, 319, 324, 356
Samuel, 11, 49, 311
Sarah, 12
Thomas, 11, 200, 201, 202
Alsop, Abigail, 225
Alston, David, 12, 105
  Jonathan, 30, 225
  Mary, 12, 82, 311
  Thomas, 105, 328,
Alston (see Elston)
Alward, Benjamin, 100
  Daniel, 66
Always, Margaret, 236
Amack, Thunis, 40
Ambler, Jacob, 113
  John, Jr., 113
Anders, Jacob, 287
  Nathaniel, 164
Anderson, Abraham, 12
  Alexander, 289
  Andrew, 12, 280, 345, 358, 152
  Ann, 12
  Anna, 259
  Catherine, 12
  Cornelius, 111, 147
  David, 261
  Eleanor, 12
  Eliakim, 227
  Elizabeth, 12, 13, 259, 305
  Enoch, 289, 290
  Ephraim, 33
  Esther, 13
  George, 303
  George, Jr., 340
  Grace, 152
  Hannah, 12, 13
  Hezekiah, 289
  Isaac, 12, 13
  Jacob, 12
  James, 12
  John, 77, 94, 145, 146, 178, 200, 216, 241, 246, 259, 271, 293, 305, 326, 363
  Joseph, 13
  Judith, 142
  Lydia, 12
  Mary, 12, 13, 111
  Mattja, 340
  Nathaniel, 79, 272
  Rebecca, 85
  Sarah, 77
  Simon, 13
  Thomas, 13
  William, 12
Andrews, Azubah, 14
  Benajah, 13, 14
  Beulah, 13
  Catherine, 14
  Dorcas, 13
  Ebenezer, 13
  Edward, 13
  Elizabeth, 13
  Esther, 13
  Hannah, 13, 43, 202
  Isaac, 45, 158, 229
  Jacob, 13, 93, 237
  John, 14, 144, 154, 160, 187, 249, 321, 335
  Leah, 295
  Mary, 13, 344

INDEX OF NAMES OF PERSONS

Mordica, 344
Nehemiah, 344
Patience, 202
Peter, 13, 14, 291, 295, 352
Phebe, 13, 202, 246
Samuel, 123, 344
Temperance, 13
Thomas, 13, 14, 96, 347, 352
Annond, Margaret, 231
Ansley, John, 164, 277
Antill, Edward, 55, 343
Antonides, Hannah, 73
Antram, Ann, 14
  David, 14
  George, 89
  Hester, 14
  Isaac, 14
  Job, 14
  John, 13, 14, 89, 129, 273, 306, 317
  Joseph, 13, 306
  Margaret, 14
  Thomas, 14
Applegate, Alse, 14
  Ann, 235
  Benjamin, 14
  Daniel, 14
  Grace, 357
  Jacob, 312
  Jemima, 14
  Johannah, 14
  John, 14
  Joseph, 14
  Mary, 14
  Moses, 14
  Richard, 14
  Thomas, 14
  William, 14, 68
Appleton, John, 347
  Joseph, 14
Applin, Joseph, 99, 263
  Mary, 99
Arans, James, 8, 351
Archad, Israel, 14
  Jacob, 15
Archer, Ananias, 15
  Andrew, 15, 93
  Austen, 15
  Benjamin, 15, 117
  Elizabeth, 15
  Hannah, 15
  Jeremiah, 15
  John, 15
  Joseph, 31, 141
  Meleson, 15
  Sarah, 15
Archord, Jacob, 15
Arey, Adam, 282
Arison, Aaron, 15
  Benjamin, 15
  Hannah, 15
  John, 15, 186, 371
  Joseph, 15
  Mary, 15
  (see Aronson)
Armitage, Reuben, 32, 98, 155, 226, 242
Armor, John, 150
Armstrong, Nathan, 370
  Thomas, 81, 188
Arnest, Michael, 200
Arney, Joseph, 130, 181, 270, 271
  Joseph, Jr., 119
Arnold, Bouley, 262, 307
  John, 195

Rachel, 16
Robert, 195
Samuel, 16, 150, 208
Aronson, Aaron, 311, 286
  Anne, 16
  Joseph, 16
  (see Aaronson)
Arrell, Richard, 158, 331
Arrowsmith, Edmund, 42
  Joseph, 42
Arwin, Jacob, 192
Ashbrook, John, 158
  Susannah, 21
  Thomas, 21
Ashbury, Elizabeth, 350
Ashead, Amos, 110
  Elizabeth, 110
  John, 110
Ashfield, Mary, 76
  Richard, 174
Ashmore, Jabish, 342
Ashton, Hannah, 111
  Robert, 139
  William, 245
Asking, John, 227
Aspden, Mathias, 148
Atchinson, Rachel, 345
Aten, Adrian, 16, 280
  Ann, 16
  Cateline, 16
  Derick, 16
  Garret, 16
  Gerardus, 62
  Hendrick, 16
  Jacobje, 16
  John, 16
  Judah, 16
  Mary, 16
  Thomas, 177
Atkinson, Aaron, 16
  Abigail, 16
  Anne, 136
  Elizabeth, 16, 17
  Hannah, 17
  Hester, 17
  Hope, 17, 36
  James, 16, 130
  Jean, 118
  John, 16, 40, 108, 118, 201, 215
  Jonathan, 295
  Joseph, 118
  Leah, 295
  Levina, 16
  Lidia, 16
  Mary, 16, 17
  Rebecca, 17
  Samuel, 16, 136, 155, 175, 189, 191, 202, 328, 344, 347
  Samuel, Jr., 136
  Sarah, 15, 16, 118
  Susannah, 16, 291
  Thomas, 11, 16, 17, 27, 31, 39, 83, 125, 130, 139, 148, 230, 288, 265, 290, 359, 372
  Walker, 138, 202
  William, 15, 16, 30
  (see Hatkinson)
Atmore, Thomas, 108
Aubray, Letitia, 148
Austen (Austin), Amos, 137
  Cornelius, 17
  Esther, 137
  Francis, 139, 158, 314
  Jonathan, 139, 167
  Peter, 313

Robert, 117
Sarah, 133
Seth, 137
William, 139
Avery, Edward, 165
Axford, Charles, 96, 190, 230
  Charles, Jr., 14
  Jonathan, 237
Axspring, John, 207
Axtell, Bethanah, 17
  Calvin, 17
  Hannah, 17
  Henry, 17
  Jemima, 17
  Luther, 17
  Phebe, 17
Ayers (Ayres, Ayars), Aaron, 18
  Abijah, 18
  Anne, 18, 316
  Benjamin, 18
  Burgin, 181
  Caleb, 22, 316
  Daniel, 18
  Deborah, 18
  Elelus, 18
  Frasee, 34, 123
  Halbridge, 17, 18, 317
  Hamilton, 18
  Hannah, 17, 365
  Heziah, 18
  Hume, 18
  James, 365
  Joanna, 18
  John, 18
  Joseph, 101, 258
  Keziah, 101
  Levi, 7, 230
  Mary, 18
  Nathaniel, 96, 181
  Obadiah, 18, 33, 254
  Peter, 7
  Phebe, 18
  Philip, 18
  Phineas, 78
  Rachel, 18
  Rebecca, 17, 18, 316
  Reuben, 18
  Robert, 18, 174
  Sarah, 17, 18
  Seth, 18
  Stephen, 18, 316, 317, 347
  Susannah, 18
  Tabitha, 17, 18
  William, 18
Aynsley, Elizabeth, 18

B

Babbit, Isaac, 17
Bacon, Amos, 92
  Benjamin, 10
  Daniel, 92
  David, 18, 320
  Elizabeth, 18, 320
  Jeremiah, 297
  Job, 18, 320
  John, 18, 19, 65, 92, 116, 148, 206, 259, 320
  Joseph, 19, 22, 116
  Margaret, 19
  Mary, 92
  Thomas, 18, 19, 320
  William, 19
Badcock, Hannah, 19
  John, 304, 308

Joseph, 19, 285, 293
Mary, 19
Naomi, 19
Rachel, 19
Sarah, 19
Badger, Susannah, 317
  William, 54
Badgley, Anthony, 19, 66
  Anthony, Jr., 19
  Elizabeth, 19
  George, 19, 133
  Hannah, 19, 183
  Jean, 19
  John, 19, 222
  Katherine, 19
  Mary, 19
  Moses, 19
  Phebe, 19
  Rachel, 19
  Robert, 19
  Ruth, 66
  Sarah, 19
  Uphamey, 19
  William, 19
Badley, James, 183
Baggs, Sarah, 142
Bailer, Michael, 280
Bailey, James, 133
  Thomas, Jr., 256
Bainbridge, Edmund, 356
  John, 170
Baird, James, 234
  John, 40
  Williams, 372
Baker, Barbara, 20
  Cornelius, 19
  Daniel, 20, 88, 159
  Henry, 19
  Henry, Jr., 194
  Jacob, 19, 84, 159, 312
  Jeremiah, 23, 67, 70, 125, 145, 231, 241, 253, 306
  Jeremiah, Jr., 68
  John, 84
  Joseph, 125
  Mary, 19, 84, 159
  Martha, 20
  Mathias, 19
  Mercy, 20, 84
  Nicholas, 298
  Patience, 20
  Phebe, 20, 256
  Thomas, 20, 26, 59, 83, 149, 279, 293, 322, 339
  William, 19, 319
Baldwin, Abraham, 171
  Caleb, 17, 20
  Catherine, 20
  Dorcas, 20
  Eleazer, 20
  Elizabeth, 20
  Elnathan, 226
  Hannah, 20, 50
  Israel, 63
  Jabesh, 20
  James, 20
  Jemima, 20
  Johanna, 20
  Jonathan, 20
  Joseph, 20, 48
  Leah, 50
  Mary, 20, 275
  Mathias, 157, 275, 367
  Moses, 20, 21, 48, 327
  Nehemiah, 79

INDEX OF NAMES OF PERSONS

Noah, 20
Phebe, 20
Samuel, 20
Sarah, 79
Silvanus, 178
Stephen, 21, 279
Thomas, 33, 48
Unice, 327
Zenus, 50
Balen, James, 30
Ball, Aaron, 21
  Apphia, 284
  Catherine, 21
  Charity, 21
  Daniel, 21
  David, 182, 284, 340
  Deborah, 21
  Esther, 21
  Hannah, 21
  Jemima, 21
  John, 21, 69
  John, Jr., 69
  Jonas, 21
  Joseph, 21, 94, 112
  Kezia, 21
  Margaret, 21
  Nathaniel, 21, 182
  Rachel, 21, 116
  Rebecca, 21
  Richard, 69
  Sarah, 21
  Silas, 21
  Timothy, 21
  Uzal, 21
  William, 89, 242
Ballard, John, 86, 227
Ballinger, Amariah, 21
  Elizabeth, 21
  Isaac, 21, 23, 305,
  Joseph, 148
  Joshua, 11, 21, 49, 81, 104, 110, 125, 126, 132, 138, 156, 164, 201, 202, 227, 253, 286, 311, 357
  Mary, 21
  Samuel, 21
  Sarah, 21
  Thomas, 21, 104, 126
Baly, Abigail, 21
  Henry, 21
  Jonathan, 21
  Phebe, 21
  Thomas, 20, 21
  (see Bayley)
Bancker, Evert, 8
  Evert, Jr., 8, 9
Banckson, Peter, 113
Bancroft, David, 309
  John, 192
  Thomas, 142, 192
Bantow, Cornelia, 33
Barber, Alledee, 21
  Aquilla, 21
  Cornelius, 21
  Elizabeth, 21
  Hannah, 21
  Isaac, 154, 354
  James, 21
  Jemima, 22
  John, 21, 35, 52, 53
  Mary, 21, 227
  Rachel, 22
  Susannah, 21
Barberie, Gertrude, 262
  John, 262

Barclay, David, 294
  John, 276, 318
Barcroft, Ambrose, 191
Bard, Bennet, 148, 153, 279, 290
  Dinah, 153, 191
  John, 332
  Peter, 54
  Theodore, 332
Bardan, John, 146
Baremore, Phebe, 43
Barham, Joseph, 334
Barkalow, Daniel, 22, 152
  Margaret, 22
Barker, Abigail, 62
  Elizabeth, 62
  Joshua, 62
  Martha, 264
  Mary, 264
  Richard, 22
  William, 148, 182
Barkestead, Joshua, 115
Barkley, Jonathan, 278
Barnes, Abraham, 22
  Andrew, 9
  Benjamin, 87
  John, 22
  John, Jr., 163
  Jonathan, 22
  Lambert, 333
  Samuel, 34, 115
  Thomas, 22, 230, 231, 163
  William, 272
Barnet, William, 219, 278
Barracliff, John, 49, 92, 242
Barrett, Abigail, 22
  Caleb, 22
  Catherine, 23
  Elizabeth, 23
  Gwin, 23
  James, 22
  Joshua, 22
  Rachel, 23
  Rebecca, 22
  Sarah, 22
  Thomas, 80
  William, 300
  Zurviah, 101
Barringer, Elizabeth, 304
  Isaac, 304
Barron, Samuel, 95, 122, 226
Bartleson Andrew 162
  Catherine, 204
  John, 162
  William, 23
Bartley, James, 273
Barton, Ann, 23
  Edward, 23
  Elizabeth, 23
  Gilbert, 150, 164
  John, 23, 127
  Jonathan, 31
  Joseph, 119
  Sarah, 23
  Stephen, 52, 184, 285
  Thomas, 23
  William, 23
  (see Borton)
Bartow, Daniel, 61, 85
  Gilbert, 164
  Thomas, 51, 54, 58, 59, 61, 63, 78, 79, 89, 90, 95, 97, 101, 118, 121, 122, 123, 131, 133, 140, 151, 152, 155, 171, 174, 176, 189, 194, 195, 196, 197, 199, 209, 211, 218, 219, 222, 223,

224, 225, 226, 227, 233, 236, 237, 241, 243, 244, 251, 252, 253, 254, 255, 258, 264, 268, 272, 274, 275, 278, 283, 285, 292, 311, 315, 323, 325, 336, 343, 355, 360, 362, 367, 372
Bartram, Ann, 23
  John, 23
  Mary 23
Barwell, Samuel, 241
Basel, Nicholas, 210
Bass, Elisa, 148
  Elizabeth, 279
  George, 50
Bassett, Ann, 113
  Daniel, 21, 106, 193
  Elisha, 65, 106, 138, 167, 212, 268, 366
  Elisha, Jr., 152, 223, 320, 366
  John, 194
  Joseph, 366
  Mary, 366
  Rachel, 366
  Samuel, 113
Bassnet, William, 356
Bastedo, Joshua, 315
  Peter, 126
Bate, Thomas, 57, 69, 158, 183, 237, 275
  William, 24
  (see Bates)
Bateman, Aaron, 24
  Abigail, 24
  Elizabeth, 24
  Hannah, 24
  James, 24
  Jane, 24
  Job, 115
  John, 38
  Joseph, 24
  Louina, 24
  Manoah, 24
  Martha, 24
  Mary, 24, 45, 238
  Moses, 24
  Nathan, 24
  Nehemiah, 24
  Peter, 24
  Phebe, 24
  Rebecca, 24
  Timothy, 24, 115
  Thomas, 24, 115, 238
  William, 24
Bates, Abigail, 24
  Anne, 323
  Daniel, 111
  Elizabeth, 24
  Hannah, 24, 25
  Jeremiah, 257, 337
  Job, 25
  John, 24, 25
  Jonathan, 257
  Joseph, 77
  Lidda, 24
  Martin, 24
  Pamal, 24
  Richard, 323
  Sarah, 24, 25
  William, 125
  (see Bate)
Batten, Ann, 57
  Francis, 57, 199
Baucker, Richard, 327
  (see Boucher)
Bauer, Michael, 127

Baum, Jacob, 301
Baxter, Samuel, 45
Bayard, Catherine, 211
  James, 147, 148
  Samuel, 273
Bayles, Mary, 312
  Samuel, 312
Bayley, Thomas, 240
Baylis, Benjamin, 66
  Daniel, 189
  Daniel, Jr., 189
  Samuel, 66, 167
Bazley, John, 345
Beach, Abner, 24
  Epenetus, 254
  Ephraim, 23
  Hannah, 25
  Junia, 25
  Peter, 69
  Phebe, 25
  Sarah, 25, 347
  Susannah, 25
  William, 25
Beakes, Edmund, 190
  Nathan, 163, 190, 220
Beard, John, 217
Beats, John, 274
Beaumont, John, 352
Beavan, William, 344
Beavers, Joseph, 61
Bebout, Jacob, 121
  Sarah, 59
Bechinhead, Thomas, 139, 157
Beck, Godfrey, 319
  James, 301
  John, 139, 292
  Raworth, 318, 319
  Roweth, 25, 164, 242
Bedell, Ann, 25
  Catherine, 25
  Henry, 25
  Jacob, 25
  Jacob (3rd), 26
  Joel, 350
  John, 25, 179
  John, Jr., 177, 179
  Susannah, 26
Bedent, John, 304
Bedford, Jonah, 264
  Mercy, 264
  Sarah, 26
  Zophar, 26
Bedloe, Susannah, 357
Bee, John, 297
Beebe, Nehemiah, 60
Beech, David, 26
  Hannah, 26
  John, 26
  Capt. Joseph, 20
  Martha, 26
  Moses, 26
  Samuel, 26
  Sarah, 26
  Stephen, 26
  Waldron, 26
Beekman, Christopher, 75
  Elizabeth, 342
  Martin, 312, 338
  Peter, 312
  Sarah, 75
  William, 75
Beeks, Godfrey, 319
  Edmond, 89
  Nathan, 89
Beem, Cornelia, 108

INDEX OF NAMES OF PERSONS 383

Beesly (Beasly), John, 10, 93, 171
  Mary, 26
  Samuel, 50, 308
Begle, Ann, 277
Belant, Joris, 336
Belcher, Andrew, 26
  Elizabeth, 26
  Hannah, 368
  Jonathan, 26
  Joseph, 167, 368
  Louisa, 26
Bell, Jabesh, 307
  Joseph, 22
  Mary, 264
  Thomas, 117
Benezet, Anthony, 236
Beng, Frances, 27
  Elizabeth, 27
  Mary, 27
  William, 27
Benjamin, Herrick, 102, 208
Bennet (Bennett), Alexander, 83, 230
  Ann, 27, 332
  Cornelius, 338
  David, 331
  Edward, 331
  Ezekiel, 85, 27
  Hendrick, 27, 288
  James, 332
  Johannes, 27, 187
  John, 212, 230, 295, 339
  Mary, 230, 259
  Oryonche, 27
  Samuel, 259
  Sarah, 230
  Susannah, 27
  William, 27, 288
Benson, Garret, 225
Benz, John Eberhardt, 188
Bereman, John, 24
  Sarah, 24
Bergen, Isaac, 258
Bernard, Gov. Francis, 58, 209
Bernhard, Samuel, 282
Berrege, George, 260
  Mary, 260
Berrien, Benjamin, 27
  Cornelius, 27
  Elizabeth, 27
  Jacob, 27
  Janetie, 27
  John, 27, 33, 196, 197, 349
  Mary, 196
  Nicholas, 27
  Peter, 27, 136, 197, 285, 293, 304, 372
  Samuel, 27
Berry, David, 28
  Ebenezer, 28
  Elizabeth, 28, 314
  Isabel, 28
  John, 28, 155, 243
  Sidney, 28
  Thomas, 28
  William, 314
Berryman, John, 247
Bertholf, Guilliam, 33, 351
Bescherer, Abraham, 28
  Barbara, 28
  Catherine, 28
  Elizabeth, 28
  Jacob, 28
  John, 28
  Margaret, 28
  Mary, 28
Beson, Francis, 303, 372
Betts, John, 145, 148
Beverly, Joshua, 126
Bevis, Elizabeth, 28
  Isachar, 28
  Margaret, 28
Bickel (see Pickel)
Bickerdike, Gideon, 297
Bickham, Caleb, 28
  Elizabeth, 28
  Joshua, 28
  Margaret, 28
  Patience, 28
  Thomas, 28
Biddle, Joseph, 311
  Sarah, 311
  Thomas, 25, 37, 139, 256, 262
Bigger, James, 29
  Joseph, 29
  Martha, 29
  Robert, 29
Biggs, Daniel, 173
  Francis, 133
  George, 64, 241
Biglow, Thomas, 68
Bilderback, Catherine, 29
  Hans, 87, 94
  Matthias, 108
  Peter, 70, 71
Biles, Langhorn, 337
Billieu (Bilyeu), Barbara, 177
  Daniel, 26
  Isaac, 26
  Jacob, 26
  John, 77
  Lucas, 35
  Peter, 26
  Ruth, 26
Billington, James, 335
Billop, Sarah, 112, 196
Bills, Ann, 353
  Gershom, 29, 145, 193, 205
  Mary, 29, 35
  Richard, 29
  Silvanus, 29
  Thomas, 29
Bird, John, 328
  Joseph, 184
  Reuben, 184
  Sarah, 29
Birdsell, Deliverance, 358
  Abigail, 29
  Stephen, 261
Bishop, Aaron, 31, 85
  Abigail, 354
  Anne, 354
  Benjamin, 30
  Daniel, 29, 30
  David, 30
  Elizabeth, 354
  Hannah, 30
  James, 31
  John, 30, 137, 215, 224, 263, 279
  Jonathan, 12, 30, 105, 133, 224, 230
  Joseph, 29, 30
  Levi, 30
  Martha, 30
  Mary, 12, 30, 31, 259, 354
  Moses, 30, 131
  Noah, 12
  Preston, 179
  Rachel, 30

Robert, 30, 31, 370
Thomas, 30, 354
William, 153
Bispham, Benjamin, 11, 112, 130, 167, 224, 291
Elizabeth, 31
John, 31, 266
Joseph, 31
Joshua, 31, 87, 110, 139, 155, 168, 344, 347
Margaret, 266
Thomas, 31
Bittenbender, Christoffel, 358
Bivins, Joseph, 18
Thomas, 18
Blachley, Ebenezer, 125
Black, Achsah, 31, 32, 61
Amy, 31
Ann, 31
Edward, 31, 32, 61
Ezra, 31, 61
James, 340
John, 31, 32, 61
Mary, 31, 281
Nancy, 32
Samuel, 31, 32, 61
Sarah, 31, 32, 61
Thomas, 292
William, 31, 32, 61, 114, 174, 319
Blackall, Anne, 32
Elizabeth, 32
Francis, 32
Jacob, 32
Mary, 32
Robert, 32
Thomas, 32
Blackledge, Philip, 328
Willempe, 155
Blackford, Anthony, 191
Benjamin, 216
Frances, 195
Hannah, 216
Isaiah, 216
Jeremiah, 216
John, 97, 216
Mary, 216
Nathaniel, 195
Zerviah, 216
Blackham, Mr., 368
Elizabeth, 311
Richard, 245
William, 311
Blackly, Francis, 28
Blackman, Andrew, 308, 330
Anna, 130
Zachariah, 130
Blackwell, Ann, 32
Elizabeth, 32
Francis, 32
Jacob, 32
Mary, 32
Robert, 32
Thomas, 32
Blackwood, Hugh, 289
John, 172, 229, 261
Samuel, 50, 94, 113, 152, 172, 213, 283
Blake, Sarah, 32
William, 273
Blanchard, John, 31, 225, 321
Blancher, John, 311
Bland, Robert, 292
Blaw (Blew), Abijah, 214
Eleanor, 214
Elizabeth, 214

Frederick, 33, 55
George, 214
Jane, 55
John, 55
Seely, 214
Blayer, Jean, 294
Blim, Philip, 150
Bliss, George, 319
John, 165
Blizard, Benjamin, 121, 247
John, 121
Rebecca, 269
Tamson, 269
William, 269
Blond, Gabriel, 11, 36, 41, 75, 94, 103, 109, 110, 127, 137, 142, 213, 311, 345, 368, 371
Bloodgood, Aaron, 33
Geach, 18, 33
Joshua, 33
Martha, 33
Mary, 33
Mather, 147
Moses, 33
William, 18, 196
Bloomfield, Agnes, 291
Andrew, 133, 171, 283, 323
Benjamin, Sr., 34
Elizabeth, 33
Ezekiel, 18
Jeremiah, 33
John, 216
Kezia, 225
Mary, 34
Dr. Moses, 20, 238
Nathaniel, 34
Phebe, 34, 55
Reuben, 33
Richard, 34
Ruth, 34
Samuel, 34
Sarah, 34
Timothy, 100
Timothy, Jr., 299
Ursula, 34
Blumont, John, 266
Blundon, Elizabeth, 90
Board, David, 23
James, 23
Boatman, Matthias, 112
Bochler, Michael, 280
Bockee, Abraham, 20
Boddee, Annietie, 258
Daniel, 258
Bodine, Abraham, 34, 163, 340
Amiantie, 177
Annetie, 34
Cornelius, 34
Francis, 315
Frederick, 34, 163, 337
Isaac, 34
John, 307
Bogart (Bougaert), Abram, 37
Angenietie, 37
Antie, 37
Cornelia, 342
Cornelius, 336
Elizabeth, 337
Gisbert, Jr., 337
Hendrick, 211, 339
Isaac, 33
Jacobus, 37
Luykes, 37
Steven, 37
Willimptie, 37

INDEX OF NAMES OF PERSONS 385

Boggs, John, 273
  Samuel, 270
  William, 273
Boice, Cornelius, 118, 195
  Jacob, 118
  John, 34
  Lena, 34
  Leonard, 34
  Mary, 34
  Siche, 34
  (see Boyce)
Bolmer, Abraham, 35
  Albert, 55
  Allabortes, 35
  Elizabeth, 35
  Jenny, 35
  John, 35
  Magdalen, 35
  Marcy, 35
  Mary, 35
  Robert, 35, 306
  Rosena, 35
Bolsby, John, 361
  Rachel, 116
Bolton, Henry, 46
  (see Boulton)
Boltinghouse, Joseph, 35
Bond, Benjamin, 35
  Elihu, 35
  Elijah, 124, 220
  Jacob, 35
  John, 149
  Joseph, 304
  Mary, 35
  Phebe, 35
  Phineas, 121, 158, 205
  Robert, 35, 259
  Samuel, 210
  Sarah, 35
  Stephen, 35
  Susannah, 35
  William, 207
Bonham, Anna, 216
  Benjamin, 216
  Elizabeth, 216
  Malakiah, 120, 172, 178
  Nehemiah, 120, 216
  Patience, 22
  Samuel, 153
  Zedekiah, 216
  Zerviah, 216
Boniface, George, 296
Bonnel, Abraham, 11, 108, 111, 197
  Benjamin, 20, 21, 54, 106, 215, 359, 360
  Edward, 131
  Gershom, 215
  Henry, 347
  Joanna, 222
  Nathaniel, 80, 103
  Nathaniel, Jr., 222
  Samuel, 315
Booline, John, 50
Boon, Catherine, 231
  Peter, 71, 231
Boorom, John, 118
Booth, Elizabeth, 35
  Jane, 35
  Ruth, 35
  Sarah, 35
Borden, Amy, 13, 35
  Anne, 36
  Benjamin, 35, 36, 71, 160
  Charity, 58
  Ebenezer, 13

Elizabeth, 35, 202, 273
Esther, 36, 160
Francis, 35
James, 36, 148
Jean, 35
John, 35, 71
Jonathan, 9, 36, 165
Joseph, 35, 36, 139, 160, 319
Joseph, Jr., 114, 180, 243
Lydia, 368
Mary, 35, 36
Richard, 35
Safety, 58
Samuel, 36
Thomas, 35
Thomas, Jr., 203
Borous, Stephen, 184
Borradaill, Arthur, 167, 202, 347
  John, 36
  Margery, 36
  Ruth, 36
  Sarah, 36, 61
  William, 36, 186
Borrowe, Crawley, 117
  Samuel, 235
Borton, Abraham, 36, 90
  Elizabeth, 36
  Hannah, 41
  William, 36
  (see Barton)
Boss, Catherine, 36
  Elizabeth, 320
  John, 36, 37
  Joseph, 36
  Nicholas, 36
Boucher, Benjamin, 203
  Margaret, 286, 304
  Thomas, 286, 304
  (see Baucker)
Boude, Joshua, 297
Boudinot, Elias, 37
  Elias, Jr., 310
Boudwine, Ann, 255
  Jeremiah, 255
Boulton, Edward, 37, 44
  Elizabeth, 37
  Isaac, 37
  Mary, 37
  Sarah, 37
  Thomas, 315
  William, 44
  (see Bolton)
Boultonhouse, Elizabeth, 273
Bouman, Cornelius, 37
  Thomas, 37
  (see Bowman)
Bourten, Elizabeth, 67
Bowen, Daniel, 93, 116, 126, 272
  Elijah, 116
  Enoch, 22, 115, 177, 365
  Jeriel, 142
  Jonathan, 30, 123, 173, 188, 279, 289, 316
  Joseph, 18
  Mary, 84, 86
  Noah, 316
  Phebe, 22
Bower, David, 38
  Deborah, 316
  William, 273
  Rev., 207
Bowers, Lemuel, 145, 334
Bowey, Cornelia, 342
Bowker, Grace, 361
  Richard, 44

25

Bowlby, John, 147
  Richard, 148
Bowman, John, 37, 100, 277
  Providence, 277
  Thomas, 212, 295
  (see Bouman)
Bowne, Esther, 37, 68
  John, 27, 95, 112, 187, 281
  Peter, 43
  Philip, 235
  Safety, 175
  William, 212
Bowness, William, 275
Boyce, Elias, 120, 166
  George, 303
  Jacob, 303
  John, 166, 340
  Nathan, 62, 163, 276, 318
  Richard, 90
  Seytje, 303, 340
  (see Boice)
Boyd, Ann, 114
  Mary, 242
  Robert, 178
  William, 189, 191
Boylan, Aaron, 55, 131, 187, 210
  Catherine, 210
Boyles, Alexander, 39
Boynsette, Peter, 49
Bozorth, Andrew, 37, 38
  Barzillai, 30
  Experience, 37
  John, 37
  Mary, 30, 37, 38
  Samuel, 37
  Thomas, 37
Bradberry, Richard, 182, 373
Braddock, Robert, 126, 286
Bradford, Martha, 177
  Richard, 343
Braden, James, 210
Bradshaw, Susannah, 305
Bradway, Aaron, 95, 142, 171, 245, 294, 296
  Jonathan, 52, 92, 285, 314, 315, 326, 343, 349
  William, 35
Bragg, John, 120, 121, 122, 251, 269, 328
Brailey, David, 39, 240
  Benjamin, 38
  John, 12
  Elizabeth, 38
  Rachel, 38
  Sarah, 38
  (see Brearley)
Braman, Benjamin, 38
  Martha, 38
  Sarah, 38
Brand, William, 241
Brandreth, Catherine, 38, 39
  Daniel, 38, 328
  Elizabeth, 39
  Jacob, 38
  Judah, 38
  Marget, 304
  Millicent, 39
Branson, Benjamin, 215
  Jonathan, 49, 215, 277, 292
  Mary, 46
  William, 148
Brant, Barnabas, 39
  Joseph, 102
  Phebe, 39
  William, 210

Brass, Adolph, Jr., 183
  Henry, 39
  Lucas, 39
Bray, Andrew, 22, 39, 242, 339
  Anne, 39
  Daniel, 39, 55
  Elizabeth, 39
  Hannah, 39
  James, 39
  John, 39
  Susanna, 39
Brayman, John, 38
  Sarah, 39
  Thomas, 38
Brea, Jean, 39, 313
Breach, Peter, 221
Breadbilck, John, 296
Bready, John, 47, 141
Brearley, Benjamin, 39
  Elizabeth, 39
  John, 39, 40
  Rachel, 39
  Rebecca, 39
  Sarah, 39
Breckenridge, Esther, 40
Brevoort, Marytie, 234
Brewer, Adam, 9, 201
  Anne, 40
  Deborah, 9
  George, 9
  Jacob, 297
  Lazarus, 9
  Lydia, 145
  Margaret, 9
  Samuel, 303
  William, 9
Brewster, Francis, 116, 193, 227
Brian, Abraham, 40, 202
  Esther, 40
  Haran, 40
  Jacob, 57
  Joannah, 40
  John, 276
  Joseph, 40
  Mary, 40, 356
  Rebecca, 40
  Samuel, 40
  Susannah, 40
  Thomas, 40
  Uriah, 40
  (see Bryan)
Brick, Ann, 41, 235
  Elizabeth, 52
  Hannah, 40, 41
  Jane, 41
  John, 40, 41, 176
  Joseph, 40, 41, 85, 294
  Joshua, 40
  Rachel, 247
  Richard, 116
  Ruth, 41
  Solomon, 256
  William, 40, 87, 247
Bridge, Benjamin, 41
  David, 41
  Elizabeth, 41
  John, 41
  Mary, 41
  Pamela, 41
  Ralph, 41
  Sarah, 41
  Thomas, 41
Brierly, Huldah, 207, 208
Bries, Hendrick, 320
Briggs, Francis, 41, 46, 83, 368

INDEX OF NAMES OF PERSONS 387

George, 17, 30, 36, 41, 44, 46, 78, 107, 113, 130, 137, 190, 258, 260, 290, 291, 319, 361, 369
  George, Jr., 360
  Levi, 46
  Thomas, 17
Bright, Eleanor, 336
  John, 38
  Thomas, 41, 336
Brinck, Cornelius, 354
  Cornelius, Jr., 354
  Mathewes, 165
Brinckerhoff, Antie, 33
  George, 33
  Hendrick, 33, 336
  Jacob, 33
  Jacobus, 33
  Joris, 33
  Nickasie, 33
Brinley, Sarah, 195
  Thomas, 195, 196
  William, 196
Brittin (Brittain), Charity, 41
  Isaac, 41
  John, 148, 310, 318
  Joseph, 41
  Martha, 349
  Nicholas, 169
  Rachel, 41
  William, 56
Broadberry, Elizabeth, 335
  Richard, 335
Brock, Elizabeth, 103
  Massy, 157
  Oddey, 112, 202
  Ralph, 102
  Richard, 103
  Susanna, 103
  Tabitha, 103
Brockholls, Henry, 68
Broderick, David, 12, 136, 158
  Judith, 12
Brodwell, Ann, 159
  Henry, 10, 53
  Jean, 159
  John, 275
  Josiah, 35, 54, 59, 88, 279, 284
  William, 339
Broen, Ann, 294
Brokaw, Abraham, 42
  Catrine, 41
  Isaac, 42
  John, 42, 99, 261, 342
  Jude, 41, 42
  Margaret, 41
Brookfield, Catharine, 42
  Charles, 42, 139
  Jacob, 315
  William, 148
Brooks, Abigail, 365
  Elizabeth, 20
  Hannah, 33, 34
  Henry, 42, 313
  James, 62, 288, 313
  Jonathan, 33, 34, 171
  Judith, 143
  Mary, 253
  Mathias, 139
  Samuel, 222, 315
  Seth, 279, 288, 299, 316
  Thomas, 161, 253
  Timothy, 123, 173, 188, 279, 316
Brower, Jeremiah, 310
Brown, Abia, 44
  Abraham, 319

Abraham, Jr., 25, 102, 301, 308, 319
Agnes, 323
Alice, 44, 74
Andrew, 152, 214, 386
Anna, 332
Arthur, 270, 276
Benjamin, 64, 107
Caleb, 87, 249
Carlile, 43, 44
Chatfield, 14
David, 43
Ebenezer, 373
Elizabeth, 36
Esther, 44
Frederick, 90
George, 12, 42, 51, 84, 122, 228, 236
Greer, 42
Hendrick, 43
Hume, 43, 44
Isabel, 42
Jacobus, 42, 43
James, 43, 44, 82, 88, 154, 173, 228, 325
Jane, 42, 271
John, 14, 42, 43, 44, 45, 51, 77, 92, 138, 176, 205, 218, 283, 308, 331, 346
Jonathan, 44, 45
Joseph, 42, 338
Leah, 44, 241
Lyndon, 43
Margaret, 43
Martha, 42, 44, 45
Mary, 12, 42, 43, 44
Patrick, 276
Preserve, 114, 233, 292, 318, 362
Prudence, 138
Richard, 44
Robert, 110
Samuel, 44, 45
Sarah, 42, 44, 109, 205
Stephen, Jr., 44
Thomas, 12, 42, 43, 44, 51, 84, 115, 236, 332, 367
Walter, 207
William, 7, 42, 43, 44, 82, 105, 322
Zebulon, 44, 45
Brual, Mary, 365
Bruce, John, 109, 133, 233
Bruen, David, 348
  Eleazer, 178
  Joseph, 340, 348
  Obadiah, 151
Bruere, Peter, 133, 134, 233
Brundage, Mary, 45
Brunson, Barefoot, 45, 111, 156, 300
  John, 45, 165
  Samuel, 45
  Thomas, 45, 165
  Widow, 196
Brush, Timothy, 281, 285
  Kezia, 285
Bryan, Abraham, 45
  Ann, 45
  Benjamin, 45
  Cornelius, 112
  Jacob, 45
  John, 45, 148, 149
  Mary, 45, 356
  Peter, 138, 148, 167
  Robert, 45

Samuel, 45
Thomas, 46
  (see Brian)
Bryant, Daniel, 51
  Simeon, 340
  William, 109, 165, 262
Brynberry, Peter, 71, 140, 300
Bryte, B., 140
Buch, Elizabeth, 219
Buck, Abigail, 271
  Elizabeth, 219
  Jeremiah, 22, 38, 46, 85, 115, 142, 146, 239, 313, 355
  John, 46, 318
  Mary, 46
Buckelew, Abram, 46
  Ann, 46
  Frederick, 46, 151
  George, 46
  John, 46, 356
  Mary, 46
  Obediah, 249
  Peter, 46
  Priscilla, 46
  Rebecca, 46
  Susannah, 46
  Thomas, 46
  William, 46
Buckingham, Margaret, 177
Buckman, Elizabeth, 156
Buckston, Richard, 266
Budd, Catherine, 46
  Daniel, 46
  David, 28, 130, 266, 291
  Henry, 46
Budd, J., 366
  James, 50, 54, 55, 260
  John, 11, 83, 113, 125, 130, 163, 294
  Jonathan, 36
  Joseph, 46, 264
  Mary, 36
  Samuel, 36, 328
  Susanna, 36
  Thomas, 17, 20, 30, 36, 41, 46, 52, 78, 107, 137, 163, 190, 222, 258, 260, 266, 290, 361, 368, 369
  William, 36, 46, 130, 190, 200, 247, 290
Budden, Elizabeth, 46
  Haney, 46
  Mary, 46
Buffin, John, 28, 283, 300, 370
Bullman, Thomas, 125, 332
Bullock, John, 47, 101
  Joseph, 47, 92
  Mary, 47
  William, 47
Bullus, Francis, 207, 208
  John, 207, 208
  Mary, 207, 208
  Samuel, 207
  William, 207
Bunn, Edward, 47
  Garret, 47
  Joseph, Sr., 298
  Lawrence, 47
  Mary, 47
  Matthew, 47
Bunten, Amos, 358
Bunting, Anthony, 111
  Mary, 365
  Phineas, 319
  William, 66, 233, 260
Burch, Richard, 331

Ruth, 331
Burden, Rebecca, 157
Burdge, David, 212
  Jonathan, 120
  Joseph, 309
  Patience, 47
  Samuel, 228
  Uriah, 212
Burgess, Moses, Sr., 47
Burling, Hannah, 47, 191
  James, 297
  Jane, 191, 192
  Jane L., 47
  Mary, 47, 191
Burn, John, 242
Burnet, John, 268
  William, 196, 256, 268, 278
Burns, Mary, 262
Burr, Aaron, 16, 47, 48
  Elizabeth, 47
  Esther, 47
  Henry, 103, 224
  John, 139, 361
  John, Jr., 14, 31, 45, 50, 127, 129, 130, 138, 200, 201, 202, 224, 257, 290, 314, 360, 368
  Joseph, 137, 200, 233, 266
  Joseph, Jr., 52, 183, 202, 230, 344
  Mary, 233
  Peter, 47, 48, 284
  Rebecca, 284
  Sarah, 47, 48
  Solomon, 148
  Thaddeus, 16
Burroughs (Burrough), Benjamin, 98, 217
  Deborah, 48, 176
  Hannah, 137
  Isaac, 15, 98, 200
  Jacob, 26
  John, 22, 48, 217
  John, Jr., 15
  Joseph, 320
  Josiah, 48
  Phebe, 48
  Samuel, 198, 228, 305
  Samuel, Jr., 48, 198
  Thomas, 48
Burrowes, Charity, 48
  Deborah, 288
  Edward, 282
  Forster, 48
  Job, 48
  John, 43, 245, 350, 362
  Margaret, 270
  Mary, 48
  Rebecca, 48
  Stephen, 34, 48, 191, 222, 239, 319
Burt, Deborah, 48
  John, 133
  Jonathan, 38
  Mary, 48
  Richard, 48
  Sarah, 48
Burtis, Ann, 47
  Sarah, 47
Burton, John, 48
  Robert, 12
  William, 12
Burwill, Hannah, 316
Bush, Hannah, 242
  John, 242

INDEX OF NAMES OF PERSONS

Bushart, Ruluff, 310
Busson, Benjamin, 164, 319
Bustedo, Mary, 315
Butcher, Anne, 49
  Elizabeth, 49
  Esther, 49
  Hannah, 49
  James, 49
  Job, 366
  John, 10, 49, 112
  Joseph, 49
  Mary, 49
  Patience, 49
  Prudence, 49
  Richard, 49, 86, 92, 242, 301
  Richard, Jr., 294
  Samuel, 49
  Thomas, 49
Butler, Elizabeth, 49
  Israel, 22, 139, 324
  John, 148, 243
  John, Jr., 115, 117, 243
Butteer, Faith, 292
Butterworth, Anne, 341
  Benjamin, 359
  Moses, 103
Buxton, Margaret, 158
Buzby (Busby), Amos, 49
  Anne, 50
  Daniel, 49
  Elizabeth, 50, 360
  Grace, 50
  Hannah, 50
  Isaac, 49, 110, 137, 141, 202
  Jabez, 50
  John, 50, 148, 311
  Joseph, 49, 50
  Margaret, 138
  Mary, 50, 360
  Samuel, 50
  Thomas, 39, 50, 75, 134, 138, 165, 311
  William, 50, 360
Bycount, Elizabeth, 63
  Solomon, 63
Bye, Hezekiah, 172
  Mary, 172
Byram, Abigail, 50
  Ebenezer, 17, 50, 68, 186, 195, 209, 264, 361
  Eliab, 50
  Hannah, 50
  Japheth, 50, 55, 369
  Joseph, 326
  Martha, 50
  Mary, 50, 55
  Naphtily, 50
  Perkin, 50
  Sarah, 50
Byrne, Patrick, 125, 265

C

Cadmus (Codmus), Abraham, 54, 140, 196, 197, 199, 218, 243, 323, 367
  Charity, 63
  Elizabeth, 43, 63
  Johannes, 146, 322
  Malicut, 63
  May, 322
  Peter, 63
  Thomas, 63, 322, 182
  (see Codemus)
Cafarty, John, 160

Cahill, Thomas, 220
Cahune, John, 259, 364
Cain, Catherine, 50
  Charity, 50
  Josiah, 130
  John, 83, 222
  (see Kain)
Cairns, Cornelia, 6
  Don, 6
  John, 316
  William, 6
Caldwell, James, 177, 179, 277
  John, 179
  Joseph, 82
  Rebecca, 51, 64
Calopper, Benjamin, 291
Calz, Cathrina, 103
Cameron, Isaac, 128
  Richard, 139, 181
  (see Comron)
Camp, Caleb, 35, 159
  Joseph, 51
  Lawrance, 309
  Phebe, 147
  Samuel, 159
Campbell, Alexander, 51
  Archibald, 148
  Catherine, 61
  Charles, 51
  Rev. Colin, 36, 215, 350
  Colin, Jr., 214
  David, 21, 51
  Duncan, 88, 173, 362
  Elizabeth, 53
  Eneas, 51
  Esther, 51
  Hugh, 186, 211, 213
  James, 51, 114, 248, 277
  Jesse, 51
  John, 51, 61, 214, 355, 367
  John, Jr., 325
  Mary, 51, 52, 215, 356, 367
  Neil, 112, 198
  Obediah, 51
  Phebe, 51
  Robert, 51
  Sarah, 51
  William, 336
Campion, Francis, 84
  John, 167
  Mary, 110
Campton, James, 52
  John, 52
  Mary, 52
  Moses, 52
  William, 52
Canfield, Abraham, 347
  Ephraim, 219
  Jabez, 330
  Jemimah, 52
  Sarah, 51, 219
  Thomas, 52, 268, 269, 347
Cannon, Mary, 25
Cargel, Daniel, 183
Carhart, Cornelius, 177
  Thomas, 213, 236, 308, 309
Carlile, Ann, 302
Carline, Benjamin, 139
Carll, Eliakim, 52
  Eliakim, Jr., 325
  Elizabeth, 52
  Henry, 52
  Isabel, 341
  Jacob, 279
  Jesse, 52, 53, 314

Jeremiah, 52
John, 18, 100, 247, 311, 325
Phinehas, 52, 53
William, 52, 53, 341
Carman, Caleb, 319
  Hannah, 53
  Hezekiah, 53
  Jacob, 117
  Rev. James, 58
  John, 53, 368, 369
  Richard, 117, 217, 248
  Samuel, 313
Carmick, John, 53
  Stephen, 53, 193
Carmickel, John, 251
Carney, Thomas, 108
Carpenter, Elizabeth, 53
  Hannah, 298
  James, 240, 298
  John, 53, 57, 155, 225
  Michael, 240
  Phebe, 53
  Preston, 10, 81, 217, 298
  Samuel, 298
  Sarah, 53
  William, 298
Carroll, Ann, 54
  Daniel, 91
  Joseph, 337
  Thomas, 272
  William, 284
Carslake, David, 283
Carson, Daniel, 150
  John, 72
  Joseph, 361
  Richard, 156
Carter, Abigail, 54
  Ann, 129
  Barnabas, 54
  Bate, 54
  David, 54
  Daniel, 54, 58
  Eleaner, 54
  Eunice, 54
  George, 54
  Hannah, 54
  James, 54
  John, 54
  Joseph, 12
  Luke, 54
  Martha, 54
  Mary, 54, 55, 141
  Moses, 141
  Nancy, 54
  Phebe, 54
  Rhody, 54
  Sarah, 54
  Stephen, 54
  Thomas, 54, 249
Carteret, Governor, 329
Carty, John, 199
  William, 369
Carver, Marm, 208
Cary, Beriah, 20
  Daniel, 20
  Ezra, 50
  John, 17, 209
  Phebe, 50
Casaboom, Amy, 261
Case, Peter, 372
  Philip, 183
  Tunis, 372
  (see Kaes)
Caskie, Thomas, 148

Casperson, Cornelius, 213, 234
  Tobias, 71
Cassiday, James, 119
Castner, Daniel, 55
  David, 55
  Helena, 55
  Jacob, 55
  James, 55
  Juliana, 55
  Mary, 55
  Peter, 55
  Sarah, 55
Cathcart, Joseph, 55
Cathrall, Edward, 47, 192
Cattell, James, 9, 11, 13, 23, 36,
  90, 94, 123, 136, 137, 138, 156,
  164, 168, 200, 201, 221, 227,
  254, 330, 357
  Jonas, 305, 361
  William, 93
Cavelier, John, 141, 182, 329
Cebrun, James, 337
Chalkley, Thomas, 295
Chambers, Alexander, 100, 372
  Aspring, 207
  Bullus, 207, 208
  John, 73
  Joseph, 307
  Robert, 82, 307
Chamberlain, C. Mary, 55
Chamberlin, Caty, 55
  Jane, 55
  John, 14, 192
  Zelpha, 240
Chamless, Jacob, 320
  James, 320
  Joseph, 106, 268
  Nathaniel, 10, 343, 364
  Sarah, 113
Champion, Elizabeth, 270
  Mary, 149, 270
  Robert, 149
Champneys, Joseph, 65, 106, 247
Chandler, Abigail, 56
  Hannah, 56
  Isaac, 216
  James, 323
  Jane, 37
  John, 9, 10, 13, 56, 214
  Joseph, 56
  Mary, 56
  Moses, 56
  Nathaniel, 56
  Rebecca, 105, 106
  Samuel, 56, 322
  Thomas B., 37
  William, 236
Chapman, Edward, 56
  John, 56, 89
  John, Jr., 242
  Philip, 153
  Robert, 318
  Thomas, 63, 66, 222
  William, 164
Chard, Benjamin, 142, 239, 247, 285
Charlton, John, 56
Chartier, Peter, 193
Chattin, Abishai, 236
  Abraham, 28, 236, 278, 331, 347
  Abram, Jr., 218
  Nixon, 15, 28, 372
Cheesman, Azubeth, 57
  Benjamin, 57, 58

INDEX OF NAMES OF PERSONS 391

Bersheba, 57
Catherine, 58
Esther, 57
Hannah, 57
John, 58
Joseph, 58
Jotham, 57
Lydia, 58, 75
Martha, 57, 58
Mary, 58
Peter, 149, 180
Richard, 46, 58, 141, 152, 159, 276, 324
Samuel, 58
Thomas, 81, 158, 200
William, 57, 58, 75, 324
William, Jr., 372
Cheever, Ezekiel, 102, 191, 219, 331, 363, 367
Cherry, Reuben, 359
Cheshire, Ann, 271
 Samuel, 271, 319
Chester, Amy, 372
 John, 76, 77, 92
 Lydia, 120
 Samuel, 318
 Samuel, Jr., 372
 William, 76
Chestnut, Judith, 299
Chetwood, Margaret, 58
Chew, Abigail, 58
 Constantine, 58
 Eleanor, 58
 Elizabeth, 127
 John, 127, 142, 229
 Nathaniel, 58
 Richard, 58, 152, 273, 324
 Thomas, 58, 172
 William, 58
Childs, James, 49, 210
Chinoph, Thomas, 136
Chism, George, 346
Christie, John, 58
 Joseph, 196
Chubbs, Sarah, 218
Church, Abraham, 280
 Edward, 143
 Joseph, 262
 Mary, 262
 Michel, 280
 Silas, 81, 82
Cirdrite, Joseph, 73
Citheart, Mary, 198
 Robert, 198
Clancy, William, 320
Clark (Clarke), Abigail, 59, 60
 Abraham, 19, 29, 121, 183, 184, 215, 219, 220, 365
 Abraham, Jr., 53, 60, 78, 121, 122, 219, 222, 259, 365
 Abraham (3rd), 66
 Anne, 59
 Benjamin, 60, 134, 271
 Charles, 46, 86, 134, 203, 223, 239, 313, 314, 326
 Cornelius, 158
 Daniel, 55, 59, 241, 283, 326, 361
 David, 60
 Deborah, 59
 Elias, 59
 Elijah, 60, 352
 Elizabeth, 60, 230
 Esther, 60
 George, 73, 103, 212, 278
 Hannah, 60

 Henry, 198, 215, 269, 270
 Henry, Jr., 19, 203
 Isabel, 294
 Jabesh, 59
 Jacob, 83
 James, 59
 Jane, 60
 Jeffery, 204
 Jeremiah, 59
 Joanna, 60
 John, 59, 134, 156, 165, 202, 205, 240, 279, 282, 291, 363
 John (3rd), 256
 Joseph, 78
 Jotham, 59
 Jotham, Jr., 343
 Keturah, 59
 Keziah, 60
 Latham, 150
 Margaret, 179
 Mary, 59, 103, 124
 Mary Ann, 59
 Peter, 323
 Phebe, 60, 222
 Rachel, 59
 Rebecca, 59, 87, 113
 Richard, 53, 60, 130
 Robert, 59, 93, 212, 278, 358
 Samuel, 59, 116, 129, 130, 232, 266, 330, 351, 365
 Sarah, 59, 60, 220
 Stephan, 53, 59
 Thomas, 59, 60, 80, 152, 153, 336, 338
 William, 158, 189, 215, 347
Clarkson, James, 18, 60, 105, 116, 291
 James, Jr., 214
 Robert, 60, 214, 291
Clawson, Cornelius, 61, 302
 John, 275
 Mary, 61
 Sarah, 124
 William, 61
 Zachariah, 61
Claypoole, James, 356
 James, Jr., 356
 Jehu, 165
 Joseph, 356
 Rebecca, 356
 William, 200
Clayter, Alice, 61
Clayton, Asher, 135
 Content, 368
 Elizabeth, 85
 James, 211
 John, 85, 111
 Joseph C., 216
 Mary, 368
 Parnell, 368
 Thomas, 148, 331
 William, 68, 76, 89, 325
Clemens, Ruth, 235
Clement, Elizabeth, 168
 Jacob, 124, 266
 Jacob, Jr., 128
 Samuel, 57, 158, 164
 Samuel, Jr., 65, 70, 325
 Thomas, 148
Cleverly, John, 238, 328
 Thomas, 265
Clevinger, John, 90, 235
Clifford, Anne, 61
 James, 61
 John, 61

Margaret, 61
Mary, 61
Sarah, 61
Thomas, 350
Clifton, Amy, 61
  John, 265
  Mary, 61
  Rachel, 61
  Simon, 61
  Mr., 228
Cline, Herman, 158, 280
  William, 81
  (see Klein)
Clizbe, Samuel, 365
Clothier, Henry, 61, 302
  James, 11, 61
  Mary, 11
Clowes, Joseph, 295, 302
  Patience, 62
Clover, Paul, 287
Clunn, John, 285, 293, 372
Clyme, Martin, 83
Coate, Esther, 62
  Henry, 62
  William, 148
Coates, John, 55
  Mary, 217
Cobb, Jacob, 306
  Rachel, 62
  Samuel, 182, 263
  Sarah, 251
  William, 85, 93, 159, 173, 251
Cochran, John, 348
  Peter, 209
Cock, Cornelia, 62
  David, 280, 293, 325
  David, Jr., 293
  Eleanor, 62
  Henry, 62
  Jacob, 62
  Jacobus, 280
  John, 62
  John, Jr., 140
  Peter, 211
  Samuel, 62
  Thomas, 62
  William, 62
  (see Cox)
Cocker, Samual, 177
  William, 177
Coddington (Codington), Abigail, 62
  Ashur, 63
  Benjamin, 63, 217
  Daniel, 62, 66
  David, 62, 63
  Elizabeth, 63
  Isaac, 63
  James, 62
  John, 62, 63, 117
  Jotham, 63
  Katherine, 217
  Margaret, 62
  Mary, 63, 116
  Rebecca, 63
  Reuben, 63
  Robert, 62
  Sabrah, 63
  Sarah, 62, 66
  Thomas, 63
  Uzziah, 63
  Zachariah, 224
Codemus, Abraham, 63
  Anne, 63
  Cornelius, 63

Frances, 63
Jane, 63
Katherine, 63
Malechi, 63
Margaret, 63
Mary, 63
Rachel, 63
Sarah, 63
(see Cadmus)
Coe, Joseph, Jr., 191
Coffery, Joseph, 301
Cojear, Elizabeth, 242
Cole, Benjamin, 64, 72, 186
  David, 64
  Dennis, 64
  Elizabeth, 64
  Ezekiel, 64
  Gertrude, 72
  George, 349
  Isaiah, 64
  Jacobus, 333
  James, 64
  Johanna, 64
  John, 64
  Joseph, 64
  Kendal, 110
  Mary, 64, 128
  Phebe, 64
  Samuel, 104
  Sarah, 64
  Tunis, 64
  William, 64, 161
  (see Cool, Kaull)
Coleman, Anne, 64
  John, 206
Coles, Jane, 243
  John, 311
  Joseph, 311
  Kendal, 105
  Mary, 202
  Samuel, 105, 138, 202, 311, 345
  Thomas, 217
Colie, Hannah, 284
  James, 343
  James, Jr., 284
Colket, James, 64
Collard, Elijah, 64
Collier, Jacobus, 258
  John, 7
Collings, George, 130
  John, 65
  Jonathan, 111
  Mary, 65
Collins, Benjamin, 58, 65, 250
  Elizabeth, 224
  Esther, 373
  Francis, 229
  John, 183, 224, 273, 295, 319, 339
  Matthew, 88, 136, 150
  Priscilla, 65
  Richard, 373
  Samuel, 327
  William, 105, 274
  Mrs., 147
Collum, Elizabeth, 65
  James, 65
Colson, David, 65
  George, 65, 354
  Hannah, 65
  Jonathan, 65
  Sarah, 65
  William, 65
Colver, Timothy, 175
Colwell, William, 28, 243

INDEX OF NAMES OF PERSONS 393

Combes (Combs), Dennis, 34
  Dinah, 66, 199
  James, 66
  John, 66, 199, 318
  Jonathan, 58, 88, 173
  Kesiah, 66, 199
  Lydia, 66, 79, 199
  Robert, 227
  Thomas, 58, 174, 293
Commines, Abigail, 6
Compton, Cornelius, 313
  David, 66
  John, 66
  Mary, 299
  Richard, 199
  Samuel, 66
  William, 66, 244, 299, 312
Comron, Richard, 172, 181
  (see Cameron)
Conarro, Darling, 346, 370
  Grace, 67
  Isaac, 151
  Thomas, 244
Condit (Condict), John, 83, 358
  Peter, 166, 310
  Rebecca, 83
  Samuel, 83
Condon, Richard, 126
Coney, Alice, 239
Congelton, Allen, 70, 71, 93, 100, 106, 108, 172, 175
Conger, Bathia, 66
  Benjamin, 363
  Enoch, 66
  Esther, 66
  Job, 66
  Josiah, 209
  Kezia, 66
  Moses, 66
Conine (Conyn), Andrew, 66, 101, 146
  Catlinty, 66
  David, 66
  Derrick, 66
  Elizabeth, 67
  Jacob, 66
  John, 66
  Philip, 66
  Rachel, 67
  Richard, 67
Coningham, Redman, 213
Conkling, (Conklin), Abigail, 66, 219
  Azubah, 337
  David, 219
  John, 29, 66, 261
  Joseph, 60
  Josiah, 66
  Matthew, 66
  Stephen, 66
  William, 337
Connelly, Domine, 23
  John, 61
Conner, John, 148
  Morgan, 148
  Morris, 148
  Thomas, 289
  Timothy, 253
Connet, Anna, 67
  Benjamin, 67, 279
  Elizabeth, 66
  Gardner, 66, 67
  Hester, 67
  James, 67
  John, 66
  Mary, 67
  Matthew, 67
  Rebecca, 67
  Ruth, 66
  Samuel, 66
  Sarah, 66, 217
Connoway, Ann, 67
  Margaret, 67
  Mary, 67
Conover, Matthias, 187
  Roleph, 187
Conseljey, Uriah, 74
Conway, Alice, 253
  John, 34
Coo, John, Jr., 332
Cook (Cooke), Abel, Jr., 57
  Abiel, 57
  Abiel, Jr., 59
  Asa, 68
  Catherine, 162
  Ebenezer, 205
  Eleanor, 170
  Elizabeth, 111
  Ellis, 68
  Epaphras, 68
  Faith, 68
  George, 217
  Hannah, 68
  Henry, 170
  Jacob, 17
  Job, 175, 296
  John, 68, 115, 162
  Jonathan, 68
  Joseph, 68
  Mary, 68, 162
  Nathaniel, 57, 59
  Obadiah, 208
  Rebecca, 68
  Sarah, 68
  Thomas, 68
  William, 68, 292, 362
Cool, Abraham, 8
  Christopher, Jr., 372
  Coartrout, 73
  Paul, 183
Cooley, Mary, 68
Coolman, Christopher, 223
Coon, Thomas, Jr., 93
Cooper, Ann, 127, 277, 364
  Benjamin, 68, 69, 70, 277
  Benjamin, Jr., 69
  Caleb, 70
  Catherine, 69
  Constant, 69
  Daniel, 277
  Daniel, Jr., 100
  David, 13, 43, 66, 205, 267, 347, 348
  Deborah, 70
  Edward, 56, 98
  Eleanor, 68
  Elizabeth, 68, 69
  Esther, 69
  George, 69, 277
  Grace, 277
  Hannah, 58, 265, 332
  Henry, 69, 157, 190, 302, 352, 369
  Hester, 17, 68, 139, 345
  Ichabod, 69
  James, 114, 139, 176, 205, 218, 267, 331
  Jerusha, 69
  John, 69, 205, 277, 322
  Jonathan, 69

Joseph, 69, 70, 228
Josiah, 68
Margaret, 74
Martha, 70
Mary, 70, 74, 158, 211
Obadiah, 68
Phebe, 68
Providence, 277
Robert, 364
Rosannah, 277
Thomas, 69, 74, 364
William, 70, 139
William S., 158
Copland, Susannah, 117
Copner, Elizabeth, 254
  Isaac, 70
  Joseph, 70
  Samuel, 101, 306
  Sarah, 70
Corbet, Ann, 70
  Daniel, 148
  Joseph, 369
  Mary, 70
  William, 70
Cordeary, Edmund, 7, 70
Coreman, Michael, 195
Corle, Benjamin, 192
  Syche, 152
Corliss (Corlies), Elizabeth, 368
  James, 71, 203, 368
  John, 36, 71
  Joseph, 10, 71
  Lydia, 344
  Mary, 111, 368
  Samuel, 71
  William, 71
  Zilpha, 71
Cornel (Cornell), Adrian, 71
  Cornelius, 71
  Edward, 241
  Jacobus, 71
  Jannetje, 71
  Joseph, 371
  Sarah, 72
  William, 71, 226
Cornelison, Catharine, 71
  Charles, 71
  Christian, 190
  Cornelius, 116
  George, 71
  John, 95
  Judith, 71
  Michael, 71
Cornelius, Henry, 323
  John, 223
Cornish, James, 229
Corsen (Corson), Abner, 258
  Arianty, 72
  David, 174
  John, 72, 173
  Joseph, 131, 169
  Judith, 258
  Nathan, 174
  Yannetie, 72
  (see Coursen)
Cortelyou, Hendrick, 295, 312
Cortrecht, Gerritje, 72
  Hendrick, 72
  William, 72
Corwine, Bartholomew, 319
  Ruth, 270
Cory, Abraham, 256
  David, 233, 256
  Elnathan, 88
  John, 59, 237, 367

John, Jr., 19, 237
Joseph, 132, 219, 220, 237, 367
Mary, 219
Coryell (Corriell), Cornelius, 72
  David, 73, 257, 277
  Emanuel, 72, 297
  George, 307
  John, 72
  Samuel, 67
  Sarah, 72
Cosart (Cossart), Anthony, 73
  Benjamin, 73
  Derick, 73
  Elizabeth, 73
  Francis, 55, 320, 338
  Jacob, 73
  Jane, 73
  John, 73
  Stynche, 146
Coscoe, Rebecca, 288
Cosens (see Cozens)
Coshan, Joshua, 125
Coshow, Benoni, 93
  John, 102
  Joshua, 125
Cosman, John, 58
Costigan, Francis, 76
Cotten, Henry, 82
Cotting, Elias, 30, 42, 67, 116, 126
  Elizabeth, 84
Cottnam, Abraham, 239, 349
  Elizabeth, 349
Couger, Enoch, 63
  Job, Jr., 63
  Lydia, 63
  Zillah, 63
Coulon, John, 143
Coulton, Anne, 109
Coursen, Matte, 72
  Tunis, 72
  (see Corson)
Courten, Steven, 260
Courtney, Benjamin, 73
  Jane, 73
  John, 73
  Sarah, 73
  Thomas, 73
Couwenhoven (Covenhoven), Abraham, 170, 261
  Cornelius, 88, 204, 212
  Elias, 73
  Gertrude, 27
  John, 148
  Mary, 74
  Peter, 73, 148, 204
  Patience, 73
  Roelif, 281
  Sarah, 6
  William, 27, 67, 73
  William C., 27
  (see Kouwenhoven)
Covert, Francis, 74
  Maria, 256
Coverly, Isaac, 294
Cowan, John, 11
  Robert, 52, 184
Coward, Alice, 74
  Elizabeth, 74
  John, 57, 59, 74
  John, Jr., 75
  Jonathan, 74
  Joseph, 74
  Patience, 74
  Rebecca, 74
  Thomas, 74

INDEX OF NAMES OF PERSONS 395

Cowell, David, 76, 85, 319, 349
Cowgill, Elizabeth, 130
  George, 41
  Isaac, 41
  John, 41
  Rachel, 41
  Thomas, 136
Cox, Abram, 75
  Andrew, 74
  Ann, 74
  Catherine, 75
  Charles, 76, 135
  Cornelius, 75
  Daniel, 75, 76
  David, 112
  Dorothy, 74
  Elizabeth, 74, 75
  Else, 74
  Elisha, 74
  Grace, 76
  Hannah, 75
  Isaac, 74
  Jacobus, 280
  James, 74
  John, 16, 36, 46, 74, 75, 105, 109, 110, 123, 124, 139, 155, 168, 200, 202, 218, 221, 250, 257, 290, 311, 331, 345, 347
  Jonas, 75
  Jonathan, 75
  Joseph, 75, 315
  Longfield, 75
  Magdalen, 74
  Mary, 75, 203, 257, 315
  Moses, 75
  Nathaniel, 74
  Peter, 93
  Rachel, 74
  Rane, 75
  Rebecca, 74, 75, 257
  Richard, 75
  Samuel, 75
  Sarah, 75, 109, 347
  Stonchy, 280
  Thomas, 74, 75, 96, 192, 324, 331, 357
  Walter, 75
  William, 75, 81, 147
    (see Cock)
Coxe, Abigail, 75
  Charles, 330
  Daniel, 75, 170
  Grace, 75
  Hannah, 36
  Parthena, 75
  William, 76, 192, 193
Cozens (Cosens), Amy, 76
  Eleanor, 76
  Elizabeth, 76
  George, 76, 246
  Hannah, 57
  Jacob, 38, 128, 139, 203, 246
  John, 76
  Joshua, 76
  Phebe, 372
  Samuel, 76
  Sarah, 76
  William, 76, 246, 372
Craft, Ann, 77
  George, 77
  Gershom, 77
  Edward, 295
  Elizabeth, 77
  Hannah, 77
  James, 77, 141
  Margaret, 77
  Samuel, 77
  Sarah, 77
  Thomas, 77, 200
Craig, Alexander C., 77
  Andrew, 59, 77, 78, 184, 236, 237
  Andrew, Jr., 78
  Ann, 77
  David, 78
  Elizabeth, 47, 77
  James, 77
  John, 55, 77, 78, 101, 126, 211
  Margaret, 77
  Mary, 77
  Moses, 77, 132
  Robert, 77
  Samuel, 77
  Sarah, 59
  Thomas, 287
  Timothy, 77, 78
  Ursula, 77
  William, 77
  William Linn, 77
Cramer, David, 78
  Lemuel, 261
  Levi, 29
  Stephen, 42, 194, 231
Cramwell, Platt, 18
Crandel, Adorithy, 161
Crane, Benjamin, 80, 214
  Caleb, 56, 78, 79
  Christopher, 79
  Daniel, 78
  David, 78, 79
  Demaris, 78
  Elihu, 348
  Elizabeth, 78, 79, 178
  Ezekiel, 209
  Gamaliel, 78
  Isaac, 79, 87, 317
  Israel, 159, 209
  Jacob, 78
  Jane, 80
  Jeremiah, 78, 79
  Joanna, 79
  Job, 78
  John, 20, 21, 178, 219, 317
  John, Jr., 87, 132
  Jonathan, 56, 79, 132, 322
  Jonathan, Jr., 329
  Joseph, 80
  Josiah, 21, 25, 44, 79, 87, 164, 209, 249
  Lydia, 78, 79
  Mary, 79
  Mathias, 80, 164
  Nathaniel, 78, 79
  Nehemiah, 78
  Noah, 78, 79
  Patience, 79
  Phebe, 78, 79
  Phineas, 78, 79
  Rebecca, 78
  Samuel, 21, 79, 80
  Sarah, 78, 275
  Silas, 78
  Solomon, 317
  Stephen, 26, 56, 122, 219, 222, 329, 334
  Timothy, 79
  William, 78, 79, 267, 298
Crannell, Bartholomew, 258
Cranstone, John, 147
Craven, Thomas, 45, 133, 281

Crawford, Alexander, 110, **327**
  Benjamin, 80
  Eleazer, 144
  Gertrude, 80
  Hannah, 77
  Isachar, 80
  James, 239
  Lewis, 80
  Lydia, 80
  Margaret, 80
  Naomi, 80
  Rachel, 80
  Richard, 162, 169, 288
  Richard, Jr., 246
  William, 58, 77, 92, 160, 162, **238**, 246, 272, 282
  William, 58, 282
Crede, Edmond, 269
Cregier, John, 257
  (see Kreager)
Creighton, Hugh, 124
  Mary, 124
Cresse (Cressy), Aaron, 80
  Ellet, 367
  Eunice, 80
  Israel, 80
  James, 80
  Jeremiah, 258
  Jonathan, 177
  Lewis, 80, 144, 207
  Mary, 80, 179
  Robert, 177, 179
  Ruth, 80
  Salathiel, 80
  Sarah, 367
  Thomas W., 367
  William, 263
Cripps, Benjamin, 56, 129, 133, 217
  John, 80
  Mary, 80
  Nathaniel, 50, 266, 273
  Samuel, 30, 40, 50, 127, **275**
  Whitten, 23, 56, 80, 366
Crishan, Sarah, 81
Crispin, Benjamin, 167
  Patience, 137
  Silas, 13, 81, 104, 137, 218
Crocheron, Abraham, 215
Croker, Elizabeth, 81
Crom, Abraham, 282
  Gisbert, 107, 320, **338**
Crommeline, Charles, 341
  Robert, 341
Crosby, Elizabeth, 81
  John, 81, 113
Crosley, Aaron, 81
  Abraham, 81
  George, 81
  Hannah, 81
  Henry, 28, 169, 188, 189
  Mary, 64
  Moses, 81, 207
  Robert, 64
  Sarah, 81
Crosman, Phebe, 82
Cross, Thomas, 124
Crow, George, 82
  Samuel, 151
  William, 288
Crowell, Agnes, 82
  Annable, 82
  Barnabas, 207
  Edward, 82, 103, **228**, **325**
  Jacob, 144
  James, 44, 82
  John, 82, 116
  Loes, 80, 82
  Samuel, 21, 25, 82, 169, **275**
  Seth, 54, 103
  Thomas, 82
Cubberley, Anne, 82
  Isaac, 82, 307
  James, 82
  James S., 60
  John, 39, 82
  Mary, 82
  Thomas, 82
  William, 82
Cull, Catherine, 45
Culwell, Joseph, 82
Cumine, (Cumin), James, 41, 82, 89
  Margaret, 82
  Mary, 82
  Sarah, 82
  Thomas, 82
Cumming, Rev. Alexander, 48
  David, 141
  Robert, 73, 90, 267
Cummins, Abigail, 6
  James, 52
  Jane, 83
  Margaret, 83
  Martha, 83
  Robert, 83
  Rosey, 83
  William, 83
Cupper, Mary, 57
Curlies, Samuel, 203
Currie, (Curry), James, **327**
  Mary, 83
  Thomas, 56
Curtis, Barnabas, 125
  David, 130, 145, 357
  David, Jr., 83
  John, 83
  Joseph, 37, 61, 77, 103
  Lydia, 83
  Mary, 292
  Mercy, 61
  Meriby, 145
  Peter, 83
  Solomon, 45
  Thomas, 45, 83
  William, 83
Cushman, Thomas, 83
Cuthbert, Ann, 331
  Thomas, 331
Cutler, Jane, 83
  Thomas, 356
  William, 151
Cutter, Agnes, 84
  Christian, 84, **85**
  Ebenezer, 84
  Ephraim, 84, 133
  James, 84
  John, 84
  Joseph, 84
  Keziah, 84
  Kilsey, 84
  Mary, 84
  Mercy, 84, 183
  Rebecca, 84
  Richard, 84
  Samuel, 44, 84
  William, 84
Cuzens, Hannah, 57
  (see Cozens)

INDEX OF NAMES OF PERSONS 397

D

Dafford, Adam, 282
Dagworthy, Ely, 85
  John, 85
  Mary, 85
  Sarah, 85
Dahlman, Peter, 44
Dalbo (Dalbow), Bridget, 307
  Charles, 278
  Israel, 231
  Lawrence, 278
  Peter, 166
  William, 100, 181
Dale, Elizabeth, 207
  Thomas, 207
Dall, Elizabeth, 208
  John, 160
Dalles, William, 206, 345
Dalley (Dally), Annatje, 342
  Cornelius, 66
  Elizabeth, 342
  Gertje, 342
  Hannah, 342
  John, 304
  Mary, 342
Daniel, Aaron, 92, 236
  Henry, Jr., 161
  James, 348
  John, 61, 88, 305
  William, 236, 242, 255, 348
Daniels, Abigail, 85
  Benjamin, 85
  Edward, 85
  Jeremiah, 85
  John, 85
  Jonathan, 67
  Mary, 85, 131
  Randol, 160
  Sterlin, 85
  Uriah, 85
Danielson, Ann, 145
  Gabriel, 23, 145
Dannold, Thomas, 346
Danser, George, 14, 135, 136
Darby, Ephraim, 54, 169, 188, 189, 252, 369
  William, 259
Darcy, John, 320
Dare, Abigail, 86
  Amy, 86
  Ann, 341
  Benoni, 85, 86, 288
  Edmond, 341
  Eleanah, 67
  Elizabeth, 85
  Elkana, 85
  Freelove, 86, 259
  Hannah, 85
  John, 24, 258, 197, 320
  Jonathan, 85, 86
  Levi, 86
  Rachel, 86
  Robert, 203, 223, 314
  William, 86, 239, 288
Dark, Ruth, 297
Darkin, Ann, 86
  Hannah, 86
Darling, Benjamin, 16
  Thomas, 103
Darnal, John, 102
Darvin, Hester, 247
Dasigny, Benjamin, 268
Daton (see Dayton)
Daugherty, Edward, 210

Davenport, Abraham, 86
  Ebenezer, 86
  Eliza, 242
  Elizabeth, 86
  Henry, 23
  Isaac, 162
  Isaiah, 166, 203, 351
  John, 86, 242
  Parnel, 86
  Samuel, 192
David, Hugh, 245
  Sarah, 304
Davies, James, 279
  Gabriel, 330
  George, 76
  Thomas, 294
Davis, Ann, 87, 348
  Benjamin, 87, 286, 304, 327
  Caleb, 87
  Charles, 19, 41, 193
  David, 41, 87, 154, 200, 364
  Dorothy, 87
  Elijah, 79, 220, 222
  Elizabeth, 102
  Elnathan, 18
  Esther, 18
  Ezekiel, 87, 99
  Gabriel, 87, 141, 142, 348
  George, 42
  Hannah, 42, 87
  Henry, 108, 225
  Hester, 229
  Hugh, 159
  Isaac, 42, 87
  Jacob, 87
  James, 70, 87, 99, 175, 203
  John, 87, 99, 220, 224, 330, 364
  Jonathan, 18, 22, 101, 167, 229, 326
  Joseph, 87, 296, 327
  Josiah, 105, 163
  Jude, 42
  Lydia, 87
  Margaret, 42
  Mary, 42, 43, 86, 251, 372
  Massey, 58
  Noah, 314
  Peter, 42
  Phebe, 87
  Rosannah, 277
  Samuel, 61, 87, 204, 228
  Sarah, 87, 101
  Solomon, 151
  Timothy, 176
  Thomas, 65, 254, 364, 372
  William, 21, 23, 87, 99, 117, 168, 330, 348
Davison, Agnes, 88
  Amaziah, 88
  Ananias, 88
  Andrew, 88
  Ann, 45, 88
  Catherine, 257
  George, 88
  James, 88
  Jean, 88
  John, 88, 250, 305
  Josiah, 88
  Mary, 88
  Nathaniel, 88
  Robert, 336
  Rosannah, 277
  Sarah, 88
Dawes, John, 50
Day, Abigail, 54

Abram, 225
Amos, 35, 87, 209, 249
Artemas, 88
Benjamin, 88, 208
Charles, 88, 89, 154, 305
Daniel, 88, 208
David, 277
Derrick, 96
Desire, 88
Ezekiel, 88
Hannah, 69
Henry, 78
James, 67
Jane, 88
Jemima, 88
Jeremiah. 88
Joseph, 268
Marcy, 88
Mary, 88
Nehemiah, 88
Rebecca, 88, 89
Samuel, 16, 54, 88, 265
Sarah, 88
Silas, 265
Spicer, 89
Susanna, 88
Thomas, 208
Timothy, 88
Dayton (Daton), Daniel, 220
  Ephraim, 105
  Jonathan, 159
  Jonathan, Jr., 278
  Jonathan (3rd), 278
  Joseph, 22, 38, 86, 177, 259, 314, 355
  Lucy, 132
  Peter, 132
  Ruhamaleo, 105
Deacon, George, 89, 306
  John, 50, 137, 273, 306
Deal, Mary, 89
  Sarah, 89
Dealy, William, 140
Dean, Thomas, 306
Deare, John, 34, 43, 89, 213, 235, 254, 274, 362
  Jonathan, 89, 98, 147, 244
  Margaret, 89
  William, 89, 119, 223, 224
Dearnal, Edward, 89
  Hannah, 89
  Jemima, 89
  John, 42, 137, 156, 221
  Lewis, 89
Dearwin, Jehiel, 105
De Bonrepos, David, 116
Deborgh (Debow), Agnes, 183
  Andries, 295
  Francis, 90
  Hannah, 90
  Lawrence, 90
  Sarah, 90
  Solomon, 90
  Van Hook, 90
Debs, Ann, 91
  John, 91
  Mary, 91
  Peter, 91
  Sarah, 91
DeCamp, Elizabeth, 90
  Lawrence, 183
Decker, Martines, 363
De Cow, Anne, 90
  Frances, 90
  Hannah, 90

Isaac, 5, 62, 90, 142, 149, 253, 292, 321, 322
Isaac, Jr., 130, 193, 344
Joseph, 12, 41, 90, 124, 371
Martha, 62, 90, 371
Mary, 41, 110
Sarah, 90, 110
Deforest, Elizabeth, 342
Degamo (Degarmo), Lucretia, 90
  Margaret, 335
  Peter, 42, 335
DeGroot, John, 229, 309
  Joost, 234
DeGuele, Elizabeth, 139
Dehart, Abigail, 80
  Anne, 90
  Baltus, 90
  Catherine, 90
  Daniel, 90, 259
  Elizabeth, 90, 91
  Jacob, 80, 91, 214, 329
  John, 94
  Margaret, 90
  Mathias, 90
  Samuel, 90
  Sarah, 90
  Yocomyntie, 136
Delancey, James, 233
  Lieutenant-Gov., 234
  Stephen, 234
Delany, Lawrence, 250
Delap, Elizabeth, 360
Delaplain, Phebe, 112
Delatush, Henry, 283, 322
Delsz, Henrich, 91
Demarest, Anna, 91
  Cornelius, 6
  David, 91
  Elizabeth, 91
  Jacobus, 91
  Johannes, 91, 336, 351
  Martie, 6, 91
  Mary, 91
  Peter, 91
  Peter, Jr., 336
  Rachel, 91
  Samuel, 234
  Sarah, 91
  William, 91
Demeyer, H., 339
Demoney, Augustus, 91
  Henry, 91
  Henry, Jr., 105
  Susannah, 91
DeMott, Clasie, 91
  Hendrick, 91, 340
  Jacob, 91
  Jane, 340
  Joris, 91
  Lawrence, 140
  Maritie, 91
  Michael, 91, 335
  Ontie, 91
Dempsy, Mark, 182
Denham, Abigail, 92
  James, 92
  John, 92
  Margaret, 92
  Obadiah, 92
  William, 92
Denman, Elizabeth, 53
  Lydia, 92
  John, 92
  Mary, 270
  Philip, 315

INDEX OF NAMES OF PERSONS 399

Thomas, 210
Denn, David, 92
  Elizabeth, 92
  James, 92
  John, 10, 92, 109, 367
  Leah, 367
  Lydia, 92
  Paul, 92
  Rachel, 92
  Rebecca, 92
Dennis, Agnes, 93
  Anne, 92, 320
  Anthony, 200
  Dorcas, 122
  Elizabeth, 92, 303
  Ellinor, 47, 92
  George, 92
  Hannah, 84, 92, 93, 94
  Jacob, 9, 71, 92, 135, 169, 200, 240
  James, 92, 93
  John, 65, 83, 92
  Jonathan, 100, 299
  Joseph, 93, 252
  Mary, 98
  Philip, 19, 41, 49, 92, 115, 255, 320
  Rachel, 92, 93
  Robert, 93, 100
  Samuel, 184, 254
  Sarah, 237
  Thomas, 8
  William, 92
Dennison, John, 223
Denny, Elizabeth, 263
  John, 15, 120, 153, 182
  Thomas, 15, 87, 120, 152, 166, 252, 263, 290, 309, 351
de Normandie, John Abraham, 54, 180
  Doctor, 83
Dent, Robert, 69
Denton, Ann, 93
  Anthony, 33
  Ellena, 93
  Jeremiah, 197
  Mary, 93
Denys, Jaques, 107
DePeyster, Isaac, 234
Deremer, Abraham, 178, 179, 260
Derrickson, Abraham, 342
  Catherine, 234
  Christian, 93
  Deborah, 93, 342
  Derrick, 342
  Dinah, 342
  Eleanor, 93
  Erick, 93
  Frederick, 342
  Isaac, 234
  Jacob, 234
  Jacobus, 342
  Johannis, 342
  John, 15, 93
  Mary, 342
  Peter, 342
  Rebecca, 234
  Volkert, 342
  William, 93
Devansue, Easter, 93
Devenny, George, 93
  Leah, 93
  Mary, 93

Richard, 6
William, 93
Devereux, Thomas, 148
Devore, Cornelius 321
  Daniel, 293
  Hendrick, 293
Devosne, Hester, 346
DeWitt, Jacob, 9
  John, 321
Dickerson, Daniel, 125
  Margaret, 94
  (see Dickinson)
Dickey, Deborah, 94
  James, 68
  Robert, 94, 229
Dickinson, George, 247
  Hannah, 207, 208
  John, 9, 184, 207, 247, 286
  Peter, 261
  William, 180, 224
  Rev. Mr., 157
Dickson, Thomas, 355
Dilkes, Aaron, 157, 166
  Abraham, 94
  Ann, 94
  Isaac, 47, 94
  James, 94
  John, 94
  Joseph, 94
  Rachel, 94
  Thomas, 94
Dill, Henry, 90
Dille, David, 269
Dillon, Margaret, 55
Dilly, Mr., 242
Dilts, Ann, 183
  Hendrick, 183
  John, 287
  Philip, 183
Dimon, Adrjana, 312
  Peter, 312
Dingee, Judith, 94
  Mary, 94
Disbrow, Benjamin, 94
  Daniel, 177, 339
  Griffin, 352
  Hannah, 94
  Henry, 177, 336
  John, 58, 80, 94
  Mary, 94
Ditcher, John, 285
Ditmars, Rem, 170
Diviny, John, 344, 364
Dixon, Elizabeth, 277
  Sarah, 116
  William, 68, 69, 348
Dobb, John, 358
Dobbin, Elizabeth, 361
  Lettice, 361
  Sarah, 361
  Zabede, 361
Dobbins, Anne, 152
  James, 52, 139, 157, 222, 361
  Joab, 361
Dod (Dodd), John, 346, 358
  John, Jr., 94
  John (3rd), 79
  Jonathan, 238
  Joseph, 20, 346
  Nathaniel, 20
Dodsworth, John, 180
Dole, Richard, 84
Dollas, Ann, 122
  Elizabeth, 122

Done, Mary, 61
Donham (see Dunham)
Donington, John, 259
Doody, Elinor, 95
Doolhagen, Martha, 95
Dopson, Peter, 96
Doremus, Abraham, 96
  Aeltje, 96
  Cathreen, 96
  Cornelius, 96
  Elizabeth, 96
  John, 96
Dorlandt, Aeltje, 95
  Antje, 95
  Gertje, 95
Dorne, Anne, 95
  Catharine, 95
  Cornelius, 95
  Deatluf, 95
  Elinor, 95
  John, 8
  Joseph, 95
  Nicholas, 95
Dorrell, Daniel, 100, 236
Dorset, Ann, 252
  James, 125, 126, 252
  Joseph, 65
Doty, Anna, 296
  Benjamin, 195, 316
  Ebenezer, 130
  Rachel, 96
Doubleday, Jane, 310
  Mary, 122, 238
Doud, Aaron, 252
Dougherty, Catherine, 369
  Elizabeth, 369
  Rebecca, 369
  William, 124
Doughty, Daniel, 14, 31, 46, 281, 292
  Deborah, 197
  Edward, 172, 198, 369
  Edward, Jr., 70, 198, 329
  Hannah, 197
  Susannah, 197
Douglas, Alexander, 96
  Althalannah, 96
  Edmond, 248
  George, 96, 111
  John, 96
  Mary, 365
  Richard, 75, 324
  Thomas, 164, 310, 319
  William, 96
Dove, David James, 33
Dow, William, 63, 363
Down, Ann, 97
  Aquila, 96
  Jemima, 96
  John, 96, 97, 296
  Robert, 96, 286
  Sarah, 96
  William, 96
Downey, Burrows, 96
  George, 96
  Mary, 96
  Nathaniel, 96
  Nicholas, 96
  John, 96
  Tabitha, 96
  William, 96
Doxey, Janetje, 33
  John, 33
Drago, Samuel, 248

Drake, Andrew, 97
  Ann, 97
  Benjamin, 98
  Daniel, 97, 98, 109
  Edmond, 97, 98
  Ephraim, 98
  Esther, 97
  Fitz Randolph, 97
  Francis, 98
  Hannah, 97
  Hugh, 97
  Isaac, 97
  Imle, 98
  Jeremiah, 97, 98, 269
  Joseph, 98, 262
  Kezia, 97
  Martha, 97
  Nathaniel, 28, 97, 207
  Reuben, 98
  Samuel, 85, 97, 189, 195, 214, 216, 248
  Sarah, 97, 98
  Simeon, 98
  Susannah, 61, 98
  Thomas, 97, 98
  William, 98
  Zachariah, 32, 97
Draper, Edward, 21, 106, 154, 167, 248, 320
Drummond, Robert, 321
Dubois, Abraham, 98, 99
  Elizabeth, 126
  Garret, 98
  Jacob, 8, 98, 126, 135
  Louis, 98
  Margaret, 98
Dudley, Francis, 13, 168
Duell, Gain, 99
  John, 99
  John, Jr., 65
  Thomas, 99, 148, 203
Duffele, William, 346
Dukemaneer, Hannah, 87, 99
  Lydia, 99
Duley, Sarah, 340
Dumont, Abraham, 99, 100
  Annatje, 99
  Dirck, 99
  Femmetje, 99
  John, 99
  Peter, 99
Dunbar, James, 148
  Samuel, 274
  Sarah, 100
Duncan, Thomas, 341
Dunham (Donham), Amy, 101
  Azariah, 101, 116, 216, 296, 307
  David, 63, 84, 97, 101, 122, 151, 173, 226, 228, 299
  Dennis, 297
  Ephraim, 302
  Joseph, 184
  Keziah, 100
  Lewis, 100
  Mary, 95
  Nehemiah, 101, 217, 262
  Phebe, 100
  Rachel, 100
  Robert, 95
  Ruth, 97
  Sarah, 95
  Susannah, 60
Dunkin, Elizabeth, 100
Dunlap, Elizabeth, 40
  Francis, 23, 249

INDEX OF NAMES OF PERSONS 401

James, 54, 55, 71, 100, 157, 211, 265, 337
John, 100
Margaret, 211
Mary Ann, 55, 100
Thomas, 100
Dunn, Amy, 101
  Benjamin, 98
  Catharine, 341
  Deborah, 331
  Esther, 101
  Hezekiah, 216
  Hugh, 17, 60, 101, 160, 167, 316, 325
  Jacob, 244
  Jeremiah, 116, 244
  John, 67, 101, 116, 163, 180, 341
  Joseph, 163
  Micajah, 135, 331
  Nicholas, 133
  Phinehas, 101, 216
  Rachel, 100
  Samuel, 101, 181, 195, 279, 334
Dunnin, Sarah, 215
Dunphy, Thomas, 121
Dunterfield, William, 45, 195
Dupuy, Daniel, 53
Durell, Darby, 278
Duryea, Anatje, 340
  Cornelius, 340, 371
Dusenberry, John, 19
Duvall, Eunice, 178
  Joel, 178
Dye, Catharine, 101
  Hannah, 101
  Isaac, 33, 101
  James, 211
  Sarah, 101
  Ussallar, 101
  Vincent, 88

E

Eacrit, John, 130
Eagees, Thomas, 264
Eagles, Rachel, 238
Eakin, James, 101
  John, 101
  Margaret, 101
  Mary, 101
  Thomas, 101
Earle, Anglica, 170
  Antlebee, 102
  Ebenezer, 170
  Edward, 102
  Elizabeth, 102
  Henry, 340
  Hester, 102
  John, 102
  Judith, 102
  Mary, 137
  Morris, 102
  Philip, 102
  Robert, 102
  Tanton, 137
  Thomas, 102, 292, 308
  William, 102
Easley, Mary, 149
Eastlack, Francis, 109
  John, 32, 97, 234, 286
  William, 109
Easton, Dorcas, 102
  Sarah, 102
Eastwood, Mary, 102
Eaton, Benjamin, 148

Isaac, 285
John, 135
Joseph, 29
Thomas, 10, 195
Eddy, Garvin, 103
  Hannah, 103
Edgar, Alexander, 34, 151, 152
  David, 7, 43, 44, 84, 85, 105, 116, 132, 194, 291, 292, 328
  Experience, 60
  William, 30, 31, 63, 194, 224, 225, 305
Edgers, George, 250
Edgerton, Thomas, 307
  Thomas, Jr., 270, 307
  William, 252
Edinfield, William, 216
Edmonds, John, 213
Edwards, David, 116
  Elizabeth, 48
  Ephraim, 174
  Hannah, 35
  Jemima, 103
  John, 180, 246
  Joseph, 10, 125, 131
  Lucy, 48
  Mary, 39
  Owen, 111, 103
  Sarah, 48
  Timothy, 48
  William, 306
Egbert, John, 305
  Nicholas, 293
Egbertson, Sanders, 305
Eggers, George, 64
Eglington, John, 103
Eick, Jacob, 287
  Paul, 287
Eiler, George, 103
  Henry, 103
  Jacob, 103
  John, 103
  Leonards, 103
  Margreta, 103
  Mary, 103
  Susannah, 103
Einott, George, 21
Eldreth, David, 231
  Lydia, 179
Eldridge, (Eldredge), Abraham, 104
  Abigail, 104
  Daniel, 104, 207
  Enoch, 104
  Esther, 104
  Ezekiel, 130, 143
  Hannah, 122, 143
  Isaac, 104
  James, 104, 137
  Jeremiah, 143
  John, 104, 142, 143, 144, 169, 192, 275, 318
  Levi, 104, 169
  Lydia, 143
  Mary, 143
  Nancy, 196
  Nathan, 169
  Persilah, 104
  Reuben, 148
  Samuel, 143
  Thomas, 103, 207
  William, 104, 143, 174
Elkinton, George, 50, 75, 360
Ellet, Charles, 317
  Mary, 85

Elliot, Charles, 40, 354
Ellis, Abigail, 156
  Catherine, 105
  Daniel, 23, 45, 52, 65, 113, 121, 142, 224, 273, 287
  Joseph, 32, 57, 97, 104, 158, 215, 257, 293
  Josiah, 225, 226
  Mary, 104
  Rebecca, 104
  Rowland, 62, 283, 341, 350
  Sarah, 45
  Simeon, 237
  Thomas, Jr., 324
  William, 324
Ellison, Samuel, 302
  Thomas, 204, 205
Elmer, Abigail, 85, 238
  Daniel, 51, 238
  Daniel, Jr., 42
  Elizabeth, 105
  Jonathan, 268, 293
  Ramolia, 105
  Samuel, 105
  Silvanus, 105
  Susanna, 105
  Theodorus, 105
  Theophilus, 46, 60, 105, 115, 278
Elston (Elstone), Abraham, 105
  Agnes, 105
  Anna, 105
  Benjamin, 183
  Benjamin, Jr., 43
  Elsia, 105
  Enoch, 105
  Hannah, 105
  Isaac, 105
  James, 328
  John, 105
  Jonathan, 105
  Margaret, 105
  Mary, 105
  Peter, 349
  Rhoda, 105
  Ruth, 183
  Samuel, 105
  Spencer, 230
  (see Alston)
Elton, Anne, 201
  Anthony, 356
  Elizabeth, 356
  Hannah, 36
  Revell, 157, 201
Elvas, Henry, 193
Elwell, Esther, 105, 106
  Jacob, 8, 274
  John, 105, 247
  Joseph, 106
  Mary, 106, 175
  Rachel, 105, 106
  Rebecca, 98
  Samuel, 106
Elwood, Philip, 345
Ely, George, 106, 261, 349
  Jacob, 106
  Jane, 349
  John, 14
  Puah, 106
  William, 106, 371
Emans (Emmons), Abraham, 107, 108, 272
  Andries, 106, 107
  Ann, 107
  Benjamin, 106, 107, 136
  Catherine, 107
  Elinor, 107
  Hendrick, 107
  Jacobus, 107
  Johannes, 107
  John, 107, 280
  Jerome, 108, 372
  Nicholas, 107
  Rachel, 107
  Rebecca, 107
  Sarah, 107
  Sycha, 108
  Teuntje, 107
Emley, Elijah, 111
  Elisha, 108
  John, 107, 108, 111, 272
  Johnson, 188
  Mary, 107
  Robert, 108
  Ruth, 192
  Samuel, 92, 93, 237, 308
  Sarah, 107
  Thomas, 102, 119
  William, 120
Emott (Emmett), George, 91, 182, 275, 371
  John, 37
  Mary, 37
Empson, Ebenezer, 108
  James, 108
Endicott, John, 139, 157
England, Mary, 351
  William, 351
Engle, John, 23, 139, 167, 221
  Nicholas, 108
  Paul, 287
English, Ann, 172
  Elizabeth, 294
  David, 243
  David, Jr., 67
  Joseph, 32, 177, 262, 329
  Moses, 139
  Sarah, 61
  William, 7, 330
  Mr., 273
Enlising, Henricus, 257
Enloes, Jean, 370
  Joseph, 108
  Peter, 108
  Tenah, 108
Ennes, William, 72, 165, 274, 353, 354
Enoch, John, 139
Ensley, Thomas, 119
  (see Insley)
Eoff, Jacob, 35
  Jacob, Jr., 35
Erickson, Andrew, 93
  Marget, 251
  Michell, 67
Erwen, Ann, 127
  David, 148
  John, 148
  Martha, 11
  Mary, 138
  Sarah, 108
  (see Irwin)
Eselow, Christian, 107
Eserson, Richard, 94
Estell, Joseph, 108
Evangame, Mary, 109
Evans, Benjamin, 109
  Bethsheba, 30, 311
  David, 84, 109, 131, 309
  Elizabeth, 109
  Evan, 110

INDEX OF NAMES OF PERSONS 403

Hannah, 109, 110
Isaac, 30, 132, 110, 168, 172, 227
Jacob, 23, 255
James, 9
Jean, 255
Jerusha, 109
John, 309
Katherine, 82
Martha, 110
Mary, 56, 109, 110
Owen, 323
Richard, 97, 98
Sarah, 109, 110
Thomas, 172
William, 19, 109, 172, 253
Everingham, Dinah, 199
  Jeremiah, 199
  Joseph, 192
Everitt, Daniel, 39
  Elizabeth, 120
  Francis, 63
  Samuel, 61
  William, 19
Everse, Jan, 108
Everson, Nicholas, 46, 154, 174
Eves, John, 110, 253
  Joseph, 110
  Thomas, 110, 136
  Thomas, Jr., 110
Evilman, John, 109, 272
  Mary, 109
  William, 109
Ewan, Absalom, 127, 130
  Hannah, 127
  John, 83, 130, 190, 200, 202, 244, 290
  Julius, 148
Ewar, Sarah, 36
Ewing (Ewings), John, 249
  Mary, 242
  Maskell, 59, 114, 232
  Robert, 96
  Sarah, 341
  Thomas, 59, 114, 116, 132, 232, 297, 351, 365
Exceen, Job, 111
  John, 111
  Nuell, 111
Eyre (Eayre), George, 60, 148, 165, 183, 199, 206
  Habakkuk, 139, 227
  Richard, 102, 103
  Sarah, 103, 224
  Thomas, 103, 224

F

Fabre, Heinrich, 57
Fain, Elizabeth, 114
Fairchild, Caleb, 367
  Hannah, 111
  Matthew, 363
  Zechariah, 237, 269
Fallon, Laughton, 248
Fancher, Joseph, 144
Faneuill, Lewis C., 240, 311
Fanning, Dr., 83
Farand, Samuel, 94
Farguison, Charles, 48, 102, 324, 370
Farin, Hannah, 327
Farley, Caleb, 170
Farmer, Jasper, 342
  John S., 149

Richard, 32, 33
Sarah, 53
Farnsworth, Amariah, 111
  Daniel, 103, 111
  Hannah, 111
  Henry, 111
  John, 12, 111
  Mary, 165
  Nathaniel, 111
  Samuel, 25, 96, 111, 117, 174, 317, 349, 362
  Thomas, 111
Farquhar, Adam, 127
  John, 300
Farr, Thomas, 57, 59
Farrand, Catharine, 112
  Daniel, 112, 178, 330
  Enos, 112
  Hannah, 112
  James, 112
  John, 112
  Joseph, 317
  Lydia, 112
  Margaret, 112
  Nathaniel, 112, 348
  Sarah, 112
  Stephen, 112
Farrell, James, 123, 211, 250
  Robert, 50, 130
Farrington, Abram, 302
  Joseph, 112
  Mary, 112
  Samuel, 112
Farrot, Henry, 112
Fasey, Ann, 35
Faubert, Andreas, 333
Faurat, Isaac, 163, 217
  Mary, 217
Fawcet, Grace, 112
  Hannah, 112
  John, 112
  Jonathan, 112
  Margaret, 112
  Nathan, 112
  Walter, 203
Feadall, Joseph, 301
Fearon, Peter, 354
Fegan, Margaret, 245
  Patrick, 245
Fennimore, Anne, 90
  Elizabeth, 113
  James, 113
  John, 39, 40, 149, 174, 190, 201, 210, 370, 113
  Jonathan, 16, 49, 113, 118, 315
  Joseph, 113, 359, 112
  Joshua, 113
  Mary, 112
  Richard, 112, 113
  Sarah, 113, 125, 230, 112
  Thomas, 286
  William, 113, 370
Fennin, Katherine, 15
Fenton, Abigail, 174
  Eleazar, 145, 210
  Elizabeth, 31
  Enoch, 145, 370
  Robert, 113
  Stacy, 174
  Thomas, Jr., 74
Ferguson, Alexander, 13, 45, 222, 250
  Charles, 15
  Hannah, 119
  John, 59, 215

Jonathan, 215
Joseph, 214
Richard, 365
Fetter (Fetters), David, 81, 158, 188, 287
  Johannes, 293
  Mary 113
  Rebecca 113
Fidler, John, 113
  Mary, 113
  Nathan, 113
  Sarah, 113
  Thomas, 113
  Timothy, 113
Field, Ambrose, 139
  Benjamin, 32, 146
  David, 195
  Elizabeth, 367
  Hannah, 367
  Jeremiah, 67, 101, 146, 195, 334
  John, 165, 367
  Joseph, 139
  Mary, 165
  Mercy, 367, 368
  Michael, 66, 334
  Patrick, 130
  Robert, 114, 139
  Samuel, 114, 165
  Sarah, 114, 165
Fielding, William, 223
Fight, Catharine, 114
  Elizabeth, 114
  Susanna, 114
Filler, John, 239
Findall, Anna, 130
Fine, John, 136
Finlaw, David, 114
  Elizabeth, 114
  James, 114
  Jane, 114
  John, 114, 204, 294
  Nathan, 114
  Rebecca, 114
  Sarah, 114
  William, 114
Firth, John, 170, 296, 313, 346
Fish, Beersheba, 114
  Isaac, 114, 161
  John, 114, 201
  Michael, 114
  Samuel, 27
  Thomas, 27
Fisher, Ann, 215
  Archibald, 211
  Avis, 357
  Charles, 229
  Folkert, 42
  Hendrick, 118, 123
  Janetje, 42
  John, 229
  Jonathan, 43, 115
  Michael, 58, 87, 152, 155, 229, 282, 286, 302, 304, 324, 327, 358
Fitch, James, 169
  Samuel, 133
  Thomas, 20
Fithian, Aaron, 115
  Abigail, 115
  David, 46, 115, 279
  Ephraim, 115
  Isaac, 115
  Jeremiah, 116, 232
  John, 115, 238
  Jonathan, 115, 287, 325
  Joseph, 115, 341

Josiah, 115
Lot, 115
Mary, 115
Phebe, 184
Samuel, 96, 115, 116, 176, 178, 179, 279, 299, 302
Sarah, 115, 116
Temperance, 115
Zeruiah, 115, 308
Fitzgerald, Patrick, 295
Fitzpatrick, John, 13, 139, 140, 167, 225, 321, 349, 369
Fitz Randolph, Ann, 116
  Benjamin, 116, 117, 149, 151
  Catherine, 116
  Daniel, 195
  David, 97, 100, 146, 244, 257, 277
  Deliverance, 74
  Edward, 116, 117
  Elizabeth, 117
  Ephraim, 218
  George, 116, 117
  Hartshorne, 116
  Hull, 116
  Isaac, 63, 116
  Jacob, 116, 117, 163
  Jale, 86
  James, 292
  Jane, 86
  Jenett, 116
  Jeremiah, 117
  Jonathan, 100, 116
  Joseph, 97, 116, 218, 269
  Joseph, Jr., 98
  Katherine, 117
  Malachi, 100
  Mary, 116, 117
  Moses, 116
  Nathaniel, 95, 116, 117, 165, 178, 291
  Rachel, 116, 307
  Rebecca, 292
  Reuben, 116, 117
  Richard, 60, 94, 117, 131, 173, 174, 296
  Robert, 116
  Samuel, 63, 117
  Sarah, 86, 116
  Thomas, 116, 117, 206
Flamenfeld, Zachary, 158
Flaningan, George, 94, 115, 130, 213, 297, 302
  Sarah, 176
Flatt, Francis, 366
  William, 366
Fleming, Jean, 117
  John, 149
  Joseph, 117
  Nicholas, 117
  Rachel, 149
  Samuel, 213, 301
  William, 53
Fletcher, William, 331
Flewellen, Abraham, 296
Flewerding, Elizabeth, 297
Flick, Philip, 13
Flin, William, 230
Flinter, Thomas, 267, 287
Flintham, John, 167
  Sarah, 117
Flinton, John, 139
Flomerfelt (see Flamenfeld)
Flower (Flowers), John, 244
  Mary, 318

INDEX OF NAMES OF PERSONS 405

Fogg, Charles, 10, 40, 56, 249, 320, 366
  Daniel, 118, 249, 322
  Joseph, 118, 300, 302
  Sarah, 118, 344
Folkerson, Gerittie, 342
  Joseph, 342
  Philip, 177
  Sarah, 342
Folkes, Thomas, 31, 103, 111, 139, 235, 243, 257, 295, 317, 370
Folwell, Ann, 118, 257
  Elizabeth, 47, 118, 174, 243
  George, 25, 37, 118, 149, 257
  John, 5, 118
  Mary, 118, 174
  Nathan, 14, 118, 243
  Sarah, 118
  Thomas, 118, 190
  William, 44, 174, 257, 308, 315
Fondrill, William, 98
Fontine (Fontyn), Abraham, 118
  Anna, 118
  Charles, 118
  John, 118, 119
  Lida, 118
  Rynear, 195
  Yacus, 118
Footman, Richard, 219
Forbes, Hugh, 156
  Mary, 119
  Robert, 119
Force, Samuel, 44
Ford, Charity, 119
  Charles, 66
  Demas, 119
  Eunice, 119
  Hannah, 119
  Jacob, 10, 43, 64, 119, 211, 213, 243, 255, 256, 326, 355
  James, 119
  John, 184, 294
  Jonathan, 119
  Rachel, 194
  Samuel, 119
  Sarah, 119
  Stephen, 294
  Thomas, 294
Fordham, Benjamin, 149
  Catherine, 149
  Mary, 87
  Stephen, 219
Forken, John, 202
Forker, Adam, 202
Forkland, Mary, 315
Forman, Andrew, 153
  David, 239
  Elizabeth, 119
  Ezekiel, 89, 119
  George, 132
  Isaac, 119, 271
  Joseph, 20, 89, 119
  Joseph, Jr., 248, 249
  Lewis, 153, 239, 271
  Patience, 119
  Peter, 119
  Samuel, 239, 271
  Sarah, 119
  Thomas, 119
  Ursula, 77
Forrester, John, 188, 212
Forster, Mary, 147
  Richard, 143
Forsyth, John, 154

Fort, Jonathan, 266
  Marmaduke, 11, 46, 266
  Roger, 148
Fortimer, Daniel, 15, 69, 161
  Barsheba, 119
Foster, Alexander, 365
  Amariah, 78, 244, 257, 345
  Abner, 345
  Christopher, 235, 309, 310
  Ebenezer, 105, 187
  Edward, 144
  Hannah, 38
  Hannah, Jr., 90
  John, 143, 192, 309
  Joshua, 345
  Josiah, 13, 90
  Mary, 187, 235, 245
  Moses, 119
  Nathaniel, 22, 111, 142, 339, 350
  Reuben, 235
  Ruth, 297
  Thomas, 148, 202, 319, 345
  William, 38, 90, 119, 126, 137, 139, 221, 260, 286
Foter, William, 104
Foulke, Isaiah, 319
Fowler, Abigail, 120
  Deborah, 120
  Grace, 120
  Hannah, 120
  Jonathan, 93, 120, 204, 297
  Joseph, 367, 371
  Lydia, 120
  Marcy, 120
  Rebecca, 120
  Susannah, 120
  William, 39, 48, 120
Fox, Absolam, 120
  Ambrose, 120, 172
  Amos, 120
  Charles, 120
  Deborah, 120
  Ephraim, 120
  Esther, 120
  Gabriel, 120, 172
  Gatte, 120
  George, 120, 172
  James, 120
  John, 120
  Mary, 120
  Rachel, 120
  Thomas, 32, 94, 117, 210, 228, 358
  William, 120
Frances, Barnt, 322
  Richard, 198, 228, 270, 323, 349
Francisco, Livina, 334
Franklin, John, 263
  Jonathan, 199
  Gov. William, 106
Franks, David, 121
  Jacob, 121
Frazee, Abigail, 121
  Abraham, 121
  Edward, 84
  Eliphalet, 59, 121, 241, 274
  Ephraim, 122
  Esther, 121
  Francis, 184
  George, 84, 322
  Gershom, 121
  Henry, 85
  Humes, 84
  James, 122

Jeremiah, 122
Jonathan, 18, 19, 63, 84, 105, 122, 226, 228, 242, 312, 328
Joseph, 91, 122
Martha, 63
Mary, 91
Mathias, 121
Moses, 91, 121
Phebe, 84, 121
Rebecca, 84, 122
Shiphat, 84
Stephen, 121
Timothy, 121, 226, 242
Frazer, Elizabeth, 122
Hannah, 122
Freeland, Jacob, 182
Maritie, 182
Mollie, 182
(see Vreelandt)
Freeman, Benjamin, 16, 310
Esther, 91
Isaac, 95
Jedediah, 298
Jonathan, 212
Jonathan, Jr., 194
Mary, 122, 123
Samuel, 132, 194, 242
Samuel, Jr., 298
Sarah, 123
Freese, Jacob, 223, 326
Freinen, William, 148
Frelinghuysen, Dinah, 123
French, Anne, 123
Charles, 124, 138
Elizabeth, 123
Hannah, 123
James, 123
Jemima, 123
Jonas, 123
Jonathan, 168
Keziah, 123
Mary, 123, 124, 360
Philip, 207, 253
Robert, 123, 200, 221, 360
Susannah, 293
Thomas, 123
Uriah, 158
William, 55, 118, 164
Fretch, Daniel, 86
Frew, Catharine, 295
Frost, Abner, 278, 322
Samuel, 124
Susannah, 124
Fruhen, Thomas, 116
Fuchso, Frederick, 173
Fulford, Jeams, 173
Fulkerson (see Folkerson)
Fuller, Elkanah, 115
Fullerton, James, 124
Jane, 124
Fulse, Frederick, 124
Mary, 124
Funk, Charity, 152
Furman, Elizabeth, 277
Francis, 124
John, 32
Jonathan, 32, 124
Josiah, 22, 124, 260, 277
Moore, 41, 76, 95, 153, 210, 252, 362
Richard, 22
Samuel, 183
Samuel, Jr., 53
Sarah, 124

Furnis, Benjamin, 301, 371
Martha, 371
Fury, John, 83
Fyler, John, 112

G

Gach, Thomas, 33
Gade, Thomas, 173
Gage, Thomas, 184
Gagers, David, 337
Gail, Lydia, 194
Gaine, H., 257, 362
Gale, David, 148
Galleher, Charles, 125
John, 316
Susanna, 125
Gamble, Ann, 295
Burgess, 125
Henrietta, 295
Jacob, 301
Mary, 51
Olive, 125
Rebeckah, 125, 230
Samuel, 125
William, 7, 10
Gandy, Elias, 149
Mary, 330
Rebecca, 125
Gano, Catherine, 99
David, 99, 272
Elizabeth, 99, 125
John, 285, 363
Stephen, 99
William, 89
Gantt, Hannah, 31
Sarah, 31
Gaphin, Onrey, 310
Gard, Daniel, 238
Sarah, 125
Gardiner, Hannah, 125
Mary, 125
Richard, 72, 119
Robert, 274
Garner, Thomas, 21
Zeruah, 125
Garrabrants, Cornelius, 336
Garrabrant, Jr., 343
Jannatie, 336
Mercelius, 182
Myndent, 336
Garretson, Catherine, 188
Daniel, 19
Garret, Jr., 335
Jacob, 51, 131
Job, 19
Rem, 188
(see Gerretse)
Garrison, Abigail, 126
Alphias, 126
Anna, 126
Benjamin, 60
Catherine, 125
Cornelius, 126
Daniel, 126, 342
Elizabeth, 125, 126, 284
Ephraim, 126
Gamaliel, 126
Hannah, 126, 194
Hartshorn, 125
Isaac, 27
Jacob, 126
Jeremiah, 126, 140
Joel, 126
John, 73, 111, 125, 126, 183, 272

INDEX OF NAMES OF PERSONS 407

Joshua, 98, 263, 337
Mary, 125, 126
Matthew, 304
Phebe, 126
Samuel, 126
William, 126, 263
Garron, Abia, 251
Garthwait, Henry, 79
  Prudence, 259
  William, 259
Garwood, Alice, 45
  Charity, 103, 126, 139, 370
  Daniel, 126, 139
  Hope, 126
  Israel, 126
  John, 103, 126, 370
  Obed, 186
  Prisilla, 126
  Samuel, 36, 81, 186
  William, 126, 139, 314
Gaskill, Aaron, 130
  Ann, 127
  Benjamin, 176
  Charity, 126
  Edward, 201, 266
  Grace, 257
  Hope, 126
  Jacob, 44
  James, 311
  Jane, 126
  Joseph, 127, 257
  Joshua, 126
  Josiah, 126, 306
  Livina, 126
  Mary, 126, 306
  Moses, 127
  Nathan, 127
  Patience, 126
  Rachel, 126
  Samuel, 123
  Stephen, 130
  Zorobabel, 127
Gaston, James, 294
  John, 294
  Joseph, 186, 213
Gates, Noah, 84, 240
Gauch, Thomas, 82
Gauger, Charles, 166
  George, 166
Geiger, Adam, 127
  Henry, 127
  Simon, 127
  Susannah, 127
Gellvin, Jeremiah, 23
Genung, Jeremiah, 54, 102
  Thomas, 54
Gerbrants, Tunis, 336
Geren, Joseph, 82, 195
Gerhart, Jacob, Jr., 287
Gerrard, Elizabeth, 128
  Gwin, 128
  Hazel, 127
  Heckles, 128
  Jane, 128
  Margaret, 128
  Miles, 127
  Robert, 128
  Sarah, 128
  Tamzin, 127, 128
  Thomas, 127
  William, 127, 128, 139, 149, 263
Gerretse (Gerretsen), Abraham, 128, 335
  Anna, 129
  Cornelius, 128

Daniel, 235
Eyda, 129
Garret, 128, 339
Harsell, 362
Henry, 128
Margaret, 128
Marrete, 128
Mary, 129
Rem, 129
Samuel, 128, 129
  (see Garretson)
Gervis, Francis, 148
Gibbons (Gibbon), Grant, 108, 122, 129, 320
  Jonathan, 129
  Leonard, 40
  Mary, 129
  Nicholas, 108, 116
  Richard, 129
Gibbs, Benjamin, 12, 13, 31, 129
  Edward, 168
  Elizabeth, 15, 129
  Francis, 129
  Isaac, 129, 139
  Mary, 129
  Martha, 139
  Richard, 16, 129, 322
  William, 299
Giberson, James, 135
Giboney, Hugh, 131
Gibson, Elizabeth, 294
  Hannah, 130
  James, 276
  Joseph, Jr., 205, 236
  Levina, 129
  Luke, 61, 130
  Mary, 129, 130
  Rachel, 365
  Rebecca, 130
  Sarah, 129, 205
Giffing, John, 130
  Margaret, 130
  Martha, 130
  Rebecca, 130
Gifford, Ananiah, 175
  Ananiah, Jr., 9
  Hannah, 130
  John, 130
  Joseph, 254, 255, 366
  Joshua, 130, 174
  Mary, 32
  Phebe, 130
  Stephen, 130
  Zilphia, 130
Gilbert, Abraham, 130
  George, 252
  Mary, 130
  Patience, 130
  Sarah, 130
  Thomas, 130
Gildersleeve, John, 327
Giles, James, 277
Gill, Amy, 87
  Hannah, 158
  John, 119, 124, 176
  Matthew, 52, 74, 99, 124, 162, 205, 263, 276, 309, 331, 351
  Thomas, 110, 161, 175, 250, 298
Gilinan, John, 100, 130
Gillett, Elijah, 101
Gillilance, Matthew, 7
Gillingham, Ann, 170
Gilljohnson, Catherine, 306
  Henry, 70, 306

Gilman, David, 116
　John, 163
　Joseph, 131
　Sarah, 131
　William, 117
Gilmer, Alexander, 125
　David, 125
　Izabel, 125
Gilmore, Robert, 15
Ginkins, Ann, 96
　John, 96
Glanvill, Marius, 280
Glasset, Susannah, 157
Glenn, Gabriel, 120
　Ruth, 269
Glover, John, 47, 324
Goble, Robert, 363
Godfrey, James, 82, 283
Godley, Mary, 61
Goelet, Elizabeth, 112, 196
　Francis, 112, 196
　Isaac, 211
Goff, John, 207
　William, 80, 195, 207
Golder, Bethnia, 81
　Jacob, 81
Goldin (Golden), Abiah, 131
　Dorcas, 131
　Eleazer, 131
　Elias, 73
　Jacob, 131
　John, 131
　Nathan, 51
Golding, Joseph, 125, 235, 238
　William, 212
Goldy, John, 10, 11, 59, 107, 126, 131, 139, 157, 260, 328
　Joseph, 21, 25, 46, 157, 131
　Samuel, 266
Goodberlet, John, 175
Goodden, Cosiah, 131
　Samuel, 131
Goodfellow, Elizabeth, 131
　Thomas, 131
Goodin, John, 134
Gooding, Ezekiel, 157
Goodwin, Ezekiel, 233
　Hannah, 113
　John, 113
　Mary, 113
　Lewis, 113
　Sarah, 113
　Susanna, 113
　Thomas, 113, 152, 206, 320
　William, 95, 113, 181, 245
Gordon, David, 75
　Elizabeth, 77
　Jane, 132
　John, 77
　Joseph, 29, 213
　Lewis, 180
　Mary, 77
　Peter, 77, 151
Gosling, David, 89, 112
　Hannah, 311
　John, 104, 132
　John, Jr., 144, 150
　Sarah, 132
Gott, William, 69
Gould, Anne, 132
　James, 297
　Thomas, 90, 250
Goulden, Joseph, 173
Govett, Joseph, 279
Grace, Philip, 85

Grady, Daniel, 233
Graff, Henry, 186
Gragou, Elizabeth, 26
Graham, Ann, 132
　J., 22
　James, 132
　John, 132
　Mary, 132
　Peter, 132
　Sarah, 132
　William, 132
Graies, John, 81
Graisbury, James, 373
Grammon, Ichabod, 333
Grandin, Amos, 235
　Daniel, 58, 235, 325
　John, 235
　Mary, 235
　Patience, 235
　Phillip, 235
　Rachel, 235
　Samuel, 235
　Sarah, 235
Grant, Increase, 132
　John, 131, 132
　Phebe, 132
Graves, Eady, 133
　John, 133
　Prudence, 133
　Samuel, 331
　Thomas, 133
Gray, Agnes, 288
　Ann, 133, 149
　Benjamin, 44, 133
　Eunice, 133
　George, 148
　Jacob, 50, 213
　John, 181
　Jonathan, 133
　Joseph, 13, 122
　Martha, 133
　Mary, 133
　Dr. Patrick, 98, 99, 193
　Sarah, 133
　William, 26
Grazeillier, Elias, 157
Gready, John, 133
　James, 133
Green, Adam, 134
　Benjamin, 134
　Daniel, 134
　George, 134
　Hannah, 134
　Hezekiah, 134
　Jacob, 187, 238
　Jane, 311
　John, 36, 134, 148, 168, 311, 347
　Joseph, 124, 134, 197
　Mary, 134
　Rebecca, 134
　Richard, 120, 134, 178, 231, 260, 361
　Samuel, 134, 170
　Thomas, 39, 134
　William, 21, 134
Greenway, Jonas, 93
Gregory, Benona, 139
Griffe, Susannah, 134
Griffin, Edward, 299
　Sarah, 298
　William, 298
Griffing, Edward, 237
　William, 265
Griffith, John, 168
　Susanna, 372

INDEX OF NAMES OF PERSONS 409

Griggs, Ann, 111
  Barnet, 135
  Catlin, 135
  Daniel, 135, 136
  Jacomincha, 135
  Joachim, 89, 135
  John, 135
  Margaret, 135
  Mary, 135
  Samuel, 135
  Thomas, 111
Grigson, Thomas, 28
Grimes, Catherine, 23
  John, 31, 139, 262, 324
  Judith, 135
Griscom, Sarah, 87
  William, 164
Groenendyck, Johannis, 189
Grooms, Jean, 370
Groven, Joseph, 310
Grover, Dean, 287
  Hannah, 135
  James, 47, 135, 232, 357
  James, Jr., 288
  Capt. James, 37
  Rebecca, 135
  Silvanus, 135
Groves, Samuel, 196
Gudgeon, Stephen, 196, 197
Guest, Henry, 272
  John, 135
  William, 135, 290, 309, 337, 351
Guiberson, Elizabeth, 135
Guild, John, 48, 86, 147, 170, 242, 319, 326
Guinnot, Thomas, 139
Gulick, Alche, 136
  Autje, 136
  Catharine, 136
  Derrick, 136
  Fernandus, 136
  Gerrebradi, 136
  Hendrick, 136
  Jocham, 136
  Jochamyntia, 136
  John, 136
  Mary, 136
  Minnah, 136
  Peter, 136
  Rantsha, 136
  Samuel, 111, 136
Gunsalis, Jacob, 353
  Sarah, 353

H

Hackett, Hannah, 56
  John, 29, 295
  Richard, 256
Hackney, Agnes, 137
  Elizabeth, 136
  Joseph, 110, 136, 137
  Phebe, 94
  Thomas, 136, 201, 290, 347
Hadden, Elizabeth, 116
  Isabel, 116
  Margaret, 116
  Martha, 116
  Mary, 116
  Nathaniel, 116
  Joseph, 116
  Thomas, 82, 116, 136
Haddock, Francis, 148
  John, 136
  Margaret, 136

Hageman (see Hegeman)
Hagar, Johannes, 329
  John, 286
Hagewoudt, George, 55
  Isaac, 58
  John, 175
Haines, Abram, 136, 137, 138, 139, 254
  Amos, 38, 138, 139, 328
  Ann, 137
  Benjamin, 36, 136, 137, 138, 330
  Caleb, 81
  Daniel, 49, 138, 286
  David, 138
  Edmund, 136, 137, 286
  Elizabeth, 137, 138, 286
  Enoch, 9, 139, 156, 199
  Esther, 286
  George, 137, 138, 139
  Grace, 137
  Hannah, 261, 286
  Isaac, 136, 137, 286
  Isaiah, 137
  James, 199, 329
  Jane, 138
  Jeremiah, 138, 190
  Joab, 229
  Job, 139
  John, 127, 138
  Jonathan, 139, 229
  Joseph, 104, 139, 220
  Josiah, 137
  Levina, 137
  Margaret, 137
  Mary, 137, 138, 149
  Nathan, 136, 164, 328
  Nathaniel, 138, 149, 190
  Noah, 136, 137, 221, 227, 330, 357
  Patience, 139
  Rebecca, 137, 139
  Richard, 137
  Sarah, 137, 138, 200
  Simeon, 136
  Thomas, 136, 137, 138, 319
  William, 138
Hale, D., 139
Hall, Abigail, 139, 148, 243
  Anne, 140
  Blandina, 140
  Catharine, 62
  Charles, 141
  Clement, 56, 316
  Edward, 62, 140, 141, 366
  Elenor, 62
  Elisha, 81, 140
  Elizabeth, 140, 141
  Francis, 319
  George, 140, 141
  Gertrude, 141
  Hannah, 22, 139
  Henry, 139, 140
  Jacob, 148
  John, 34, 53, 88, 140, 141, 148, 179
  Joseph, 46, 278
  Mabel, 141
  Mary, 140, 141, 366
  Nathaniel, 366
  Neltia, 140
  Ootie, 140
  Polly, 139
  Rebecca, 140
  Richard, 140
  Samuel, 167
  Solomon, 84

Thomas, 23, 77, 139, 140, 141, 292, 243
Tobias, 140
William, 40, 56, 193, 268, 274, 313, 316, 366
Hallock, Sarah, 285
William, 285
Halsey, Benjamin, 363
Ezekiel, 39
Halstead (Halsted), Caleb, 20
Elizabeth, 353
John, 58, 254
Josiah, 29, 117, 254
Pearson, 10
Zilpha, 353
Halter, Francis, 249
Martin, 127
Ham, Fridrick, 151
Hambleton, David, 145
Hamilton, Andrew, 198
Archibald, 40
Charles, 40, 346
James, 216
John, 215
William, 40
Hammell, James, 5
John, Jr., 294, 307
Patrick, 242
William, 141
Hammer, Johann Peter, 37
Hammit, Aaron, 141
Ann, 141
Elias, 248
George, 141
Hannah, 141
John, 141
Prudence, 141
Sarah, 141, 158
Hammond, Joseph, 299
Hampton, Alice, 58
Andrew, 223
Edward, 257
John, 142
Jonathan, 122
Thomas, 148
William, 77, 141, 142, 148, 348
William, Jr., 148
Hanby, Hannah, 364
William, 364
Hance, Elizabeth, 142
Isaac, 36, 80
Hancock, Andrews, 13
Benjamin, 161
Edward, 364
Elizabeth, 53
Godfrey, 190
Hannah, 40
James, 235
John, 148, 201
Joseph, 142, 343
Nathaniel, 35, 364
Patience, 13
Rebecca, 142, 306
Samuel, 92
Susannah, 142
Thomas, 48, 53, 113, 154, 320
William, 370
William, Jr., 142
Hand, Anne, 269
Daniel, 104, 143, 258
David, 143, 144
Deborah, 143
Douesalah, 143
Eleazer, 80, 144
Elias, 143

Elihu, 142, 169
Elisha, 80, 82, 143, 144, 275, 318
Elijah, 144
Elizabeth, 144
Emily, 143
Experience, 142, 143
Ezekiel, 131, 144
George, 143, 169
Gideon, 144
Hannah, 142, 143, 144
Henry, 144
Hulda, 258
Isaiah, 109, 143, 144, 309
Jane, 143
Japheth, 143
Jeremiah, 19, 131, 143, 144, 179, 207, 237, 258, 299, 302, 308, 355
Jesse, 258
Johannah, 144
John, 143
Lois, 143
Lydia, 142, 143
Mary, 143, 269
Nathan, 143, 144
Neri, 144
Rachel, 143, 144
Recompense, 193
Rhoda, 143
Samuel, 176, 206
Sarah, 143
Shamgar, 299
Silas, 142
Stephen, 143
Susannah, 309
Thomas, 143, 144, 355
Timothy, 144, 315
Hankins, Mary, 109
William, 110, 309, 363
Hankinson, James, 40
Joseph, 212
Robert, 331
William, 363
Hanley, Christopher, 144, 154
Hanlon, Lydia, 162
Patrick, 185
Hanna, James, 40
John, 83
Hannah, 236
Hans, John, Jr., 40
Harbut, Thomas, 66
Harcourt, Richard, 194
Sarah, 165
William, 166
Harden, Edward, 115
Hannah, 115
(see Hardin)
Hardenbergh, Dinah, 123
Jacob Rutson, 123
Johannes, 341
Hardin, Ann, 145
Martin, 145, 178
Samuel, 145
Susannah, 145
Harding, Ezekiel, 347
Hargrove, Samuel, 319
Harker, Daniel, 145
Rachel, 145
Harlow, Isaac, 55
Harmon, Jonathan, 145
Lemuel, 145
Mary, 145
Thomas, 145
William, 145
Harned, Nathan, 180
Nathaniel, 33

INDEX OF NAMES OF PERSONS 411

Harp, Michael, 181
Harper, Leah, 85
Harperdink, Jan, 258
Harriman, David, 130
  John, 145
  William, 135
Harriot (see Herriot)
Harris, Abigail, 38, 146, 242, 313
  Abraham, 13
  Benjamin, 146, 206, 236, 348
  Daniel, 146
  David, 146
  Ellen, 146
  Elijah, 146
  Elizabeth, 146
  Emma, 146
  Ephraim, 105
  Ezekiel, 146
  George, 68, 341
  Hannah, 250
  Isaac, 146
  Jacob, 81, 146
  James, 146
  Jeremiah, 38
  John, 146, 334
  Mary, 146, 341
  Mersey, 146
  Noah, 112, 157, 314
  Peter, 85, 146
  Rachel, 81, 146
  Reuben, 38
  Ruth, 105
  Samuel, 146, 253, 287, 297, 319, 325
  Samuel, Jr., 348
  Sarah, 146
  Thomas, 30, 105, 115, 146, 177, 313
  Violetta, 85, 146
  William, 15, 130, 149
Harrison, Abigail, 324
  Amos, 346, 358
  Azubah, 147
  Caleb, 147, 317
  David, 20
  Dorcas, 69
  Francis, 342
  Ganennetta, 147
  Henry, 240
  Isaiah, 41
  J., 7, 158, 301
  Jane, 253
  John, 147, 284, 312
  Joseph, 8, 26, 65, 70, 74, 83, 128, 142, 158, 168, 237, 257, 305, 307, 317, 324
  Martha, 69
  Mary, 327
  Matthew, 147
  Nathaniel, 358
  Rebecah, 229
  Richard, 17
  Samuel, 8, 74, 128, 358
  Samuel, Jr., 104, 128, 324
  Sarah, 46
  Thomas, 182
  Timothy, 88, 209, 369
  William, 31, 74, 147, 168, 361
  William, Jr., 8, 74, 237, 324
Harrow, Isaac, 248
Harry, Mary, 57
  William, 57
Hart, Amos, 133, 242
  Constant, 115, 326
  Daniel, 109, 147, 283
  Edward, 319
  Elizabeth, 147
  Hannah, 320
  Jane, 229
  Joanna, 147
  John, 147, 165, 206, 227, 229, 285, 319, 320
  Jonathan, 122
  Joseph, 147, 226
  Lilya, 229
  Margaret, 133
  Mary, 147
  Moses, 269
  Richard, 133, 147
  Sarah, 133, 147
  William, 229, 320
Hartounge, Powlus, 241
Hartshorne, Hannah, 148, 149
  Hugh, 135, 154, 212, 268, 273
  John, 36
  Lucy, 36
  Phebe, 108
  Robert, 36, 126, 139, 148, 301
Harvey, Alexander, 273
  Elizabeth, 149
  Job, 149
  John, 149
  Mary, 149
  Peter, 149
  Rebecca, 149
  Sarah, 149
  William, 87, 212, 223, 256
Hatch, John, 139
Hathaway, Abel, 149
  Abner, 150
  Abraham, 150
  Benjamin, 150, 209
  Elizabeth, 150
  Jonathan, 150
  Meriam, 150
  Phebe, 150
  Philip, 150
  Sarah, 150
Hathorn, James, 51, 109, 173, 283
Hatkinson, John, 53
  (see Atkinson)
Hatter, Thomas, 98
Hatton, Elizabeth, 106
Hauck, Anna Barbara, 150
  Anna Margretha, 150
  Anna Maria, 150
  Catherine, 150
  David, 150
  Elizabeth, 150
  Johan George, 150
  Johannes, 150
  John Jacob, 150
  John Philip, 150
Hauschilt, Johannis, 372
Havens, Edward, 150
  Daniel, 117, 193
  George, 326
  John, 150
  William, 150
Haviland, Benjamin, 69
  Caleb, 33
  Joseph, 84
  Stephen, 74
Hawhey, William, 63
Hawk (Hawkes), Catherine, 36
  Joseph, 175, 213
Hawley, Ezra, 20
Hay, Andrew, 90
  Jane, 150

Haynes, Jane, 150
  Jonathan, 150
  Mary, 150
  Rebecca, 150
  Thomas, 256
Hays (Hayse), Abraham, 151
  Daniel, 151
  David, 151
  Freeman, 151
  Hannah, 151
  Henry, 151
  Isaac, 151
  Jacob, 7, 151
  John, 54, 151
  Joseph, 151
  Judah, 211
  Martha, 151
  Samuel, 151
  Thomas, 151
  William, 126, 151
Haywood, James, 149, 151
  William, 151
Hazard, Catherine, 151
  James, 27
  Nathaniel, 151
  Thomas, 27
  William, 12
Hazell, Samuel, 148
Hazleton, Ann, 149, 151
Headley, Samuel, 20
Heard, Agnes, 152
  Mary, 151
  Nathaniel, 34, 151, 152, 362
Heath, Andrew, 198
  Jonathan, 337
Hedden, Ebenezer, 306
  Jedidiah, 21
Hedding, Marcus, 44
Hedge, Hannah, 152, 366
  Joseph, 366
  Rebecca, 366
  Samuel, 366
Hedger, Deborah, 152
  John, 152
  Joseph, 65, 165, 180, 261
  Martha, 152
  Meribah, 152
Hedges, Gideon, 66, 348
  James, 80, 169, 275
  Joseph, 324
  Stephen, 265
Hegeman, Adrain, 152, 192, 342
  Barent, 152, 176, 177, 336
  Benjamin, 214
  Dennis, 152
  Dolleus, 152
  Jacobus, 152
  Joseph, Jr., 147
  Maria, 342
  Simon, 214, 255
Height, John, 136
Helebrant, Meheal, 282
Helm (Helms), David, 187
  Alice, 152
  Catherine, 351
  Elizabeth, 152, 351
  Israel, 162
  Jael, 152
  John, 54, 199, 206, 221, 231
  Okee, 162
  Rebecah, 235
  Robert, 211, 213
  Thomas, 77, 346
Hendershot, John, 34, 286, 287, 329

Henderson, John, 73, 243, 287, 351
Hendricks, Catherine, 241
  Daniel, 146, 175
  Gilbert, 153
  Helena, 241
  John, 153
  Phebe, 153
  Tunis, 241
  William, 153
Hendrickson, Daniel, 153
  Daniel, Jr., 153
  David, 153
  Elenor, 162
  Elizabeth, 153
  Henry, 15, 153, 203
  Hendrick, 302
  Hendrick, Jr., 323
  Johanna, 95
  Jonas, 153
  Nelly, 153
  Okenus, 153
  William, 95, 153, 187, 205, 243, 281, 324, 350
Hendry, Dinah Bard, 153
Henman, Elizabeth, 348
Hennion, Daniel, 146
  Johannes, 146
Henry, Arthur, 153
  Elizabeth, 153, 333
  Hannah, 153
  Isabel, 154
  Jane, 153
  John, 28, 90
  Marge, 372
  Micah, 153
  Michael, 153
  Nathaniel, 153
  Samuel, 22, 84, 269
  Sarah, 153
Hepard, Amy, 154
  Deborah, 154
  Hannah, 154
  Joseph, 154
  Mary, 154
  Thomas, 154
  William, 89, 154, 158, 305
Hepburn, James, 109, 110
  John, 60, 61, 98, 189, 195, 216, 257, 331, 333
Herbert, Deborah, 144, 145
  Edward, 145
  Felix, 154
  Francis, 154
  George, 14, 144, 145
  Hannah, 154
  Henry, 117, 240
  Isaac, 145, 223
  Jemime, 145
  John, 145, 154
  Levina, 145
  Obediah, 154
  Paul, 145
  Phebe, 145
  Peter, 145
  Rebecca, 145
  Richard, 74, 154
  Ruth, 154
  Thomas, 39
  Timothy, 145
  Walter, 145
  William, 154
Herd, Elsie, 154

INDEX OF NAMES OF PERSONS 413

John, 154
Samuel, 154
Heremise, Jans Jrh., 71
Heritage, Benjamin, 154
  Elizabeth, 155
  Ephraim, 154
  John, 154
  Joseph, 154, 155
  Rachel, 155
  Richard, 154
Hermitage, Reuben, 226
Hermon, Joseph, 219
  Stephen, 219
Herner, Malachi, 21
Herrick, Abigail, 249
  Anna, 249
  Cleopatra, 249
  Deborah, 249
Herriman, John, 220, 328
  Sarah, 328
Herrin, Abigail, 155
  Anne, 155
  Edmund, 155
  Isaac, 32, 155
  Martha, 155
  Mary, 155
  Penelope, 155
  Rachel, 155
  Rebecca, 155
Herriot (Harriot), David, 180
  Andrew, 155
  Ephraim, 155
  George, 18, 174
  John Forman, 155
  Mary, 18
  Ursulla, 155
Hertie, Jannetje, 96
  Michael, 96
Hesler, Martin, 221
Hess, Abram, 201
Hetfield, Aaron, 214
  Cornelius, 19, 26, 157, 228
  Deborah, 297
  Hannah, 222
  Helena, 155
  Jacob, 155
  Joseph, 157
  Mathias, 19, 21, 26, 214, 222, 228, 275
  Samuel, 155
Heulings (Hewlings), Abigail, 155
  Abraham, 57, 65, 155, 156, 188, 190, 262, 271, 273, 341, 350, 356, 359
  Agnes, 155, 156
  Andrew, 45
  Anne, 356
  Dorothy, 155, 156
  Esther, 356
  Hannah, 224
  Isaac, 57, 199, 216, 330, 350, 356
  Jacob, 11, 155, 156, 224
  Jacob, Jr., 11
  Joseph, 155, 156, 224, 356
  Rebecca, 155
  Samuel, 156
  Sarah, 155, 156
  Theodosia, 155, 156
  Thomas P., 356
  William, 11, 45, 49, 65, 81, 89, 113, 155, 156, 172, 283, 356
  William S., 356
  (see Hulings)
Hevil, Doctor, 139

Hewes, Aaron, 156
  Caleb, 104, 156
  Daniel, 156
  Hannah, 221
  Jacob, 221
  James, 156
  Jarvis, 221
  Joseph, 156
  Josiah, 156
  Mary, 156
  Providence, 156
  Rachel, 156
  Richard, 323
  Samuel, 252, 263
Hewett, Amy, 157
  Ann, 157
  Joseph, 299
  Joshua, 156
  Moses, 157
  Rebecca, 156
  Samuel, 166
  Sarah, 157, 353
  Susannah, 157
  Thomas, 144
  William, 157
Heyer, Abraham, 284
  Johannes, 332
Hibbits, Charles, 305
Hickman, Esther, 6
  John, 6
Hicks, Austin, 148
  Hannah, 158
  Samuel, 67
Hider, John, 159, 250, 330
Hierd, Elizabeth, 66
  Reuben, 66
Higbee, Joseph, 72, 85, 204, 216, 228
  Obediah, 196
  William, 345
Higgins, Abigail, 157
  Edward, 131, 147
  Hannah, 157
  Jemima, 348
  Joseph, 313
  Mary, 157
  Michael, 157
  Nathaniel, 157
  Sarah, 147
  Timothy, 214
  William, 157
Highter, Elizabeth, 140
Hildebrand, George, 5
Hill, Alexander, 157, 190
  Ann, 157, 373
  Bathsheba, 285
  Henry, 102, 373
  Jean, 157
  Moses, 39
  Robert, 59, 139, 190, 368, 369
  Samuel, 157, 301
  Thomas, 56
  William, 32
Hilldreth, David, 254
  Joseph, 371
  Joshua, 318
  Lydia, 177
  Manasseh, 219
  Phebe, 177
  Priscilla, 177
Hilliard, Abraham, 158
  Ann, 158
  Hannah, 158
  Joseph, 158

Hillier (Hiller), Edward, 360
  Isaac, 360
  John, 103, 131, 157, 224, 302
Hillman, Daniel, 69, 158, 236, 296
  Elizabeth, 158
  James, 96, 158
  Joab, 200, 201
  John, 46, 88, 158, 167, 180, 275, 304, 327
  Joseph, 158
  Josiah, 327
  Mary, 96
Hinchman, Elizabeth, 237
  James, 28, 43, 112, 158, 324
  John, 31, 99, 158, 266
  Kesiah, 158
  Talman, 158
  Thomas, 65, 127, 154, 158
  William, 168
Hinckley, Francis, 246
Hinderhit, John, 34
  (see Hendershot)
Hindesjun, Stephen, 79
Hindman, John, 176
Hinds (Hindes), Benjamin, 159
  James, 159, 219, 359, 360
  James, Jr., 219
  John, 159
  Jonathan, 159
  Joseph, 28, 176, 228, 328, 358
  Macy, 159
  Mary, 33, 159
  Samuel, 79
  Stephen, 209
Hinman, Elizabeth, 159
  Experience, 159
  Jemima, 159
  John, 159
  Mary, 159
  Naomi, 159
  Rebecca, 159
  Samuel, 159
Himrich, Catharina, 158
  Henry, 158
  Jacob, 158
  John, 158
  Margreth, 158
  Peter, 158
  William, 158
Hite, Abraham, 337
  Rebecca, 337
Hoagland, Abraham, 312
  Adrian, 175
  Cornelia, 312
  Derick, 22
  Dinah, 260
  Harmanus, 312
  Johanna, 312
  John, 260, 312, 356
  Martynus, 141, 372
  William, 141, 155, 365
Hockings, Sarah, 297
Hodge, Mary, 186
Hodghon, John, 334
Hodgkinson, Peteraris, 185
Hoel, Mary, 202
  Sarah, 298
Hoff, Burgon, 42, 99
  Charles, Jr., 8, 11, 61, 81, 95, 108, 153
  Francyntje, 99
  Isaac, 325
  John, 178, 325
  Lawrence, 62
  Mary, 178
  Richard, 326
Hoffman, Charles, 218
  David, 159
  Elizabeth, 159
  Frederick, 159
  James, 252
  John, 159
  Jonas, 159, 173
  Peter, 173
  (see Huffman)
Hoffmire, Elizabeth, 160
  Isaac, 160
  Josiah, 160
  Mary, 160
Hogbin, Nehemiah, 27
Hohenschilt, Johan Michel, 160
  (see Hosciel)
Holcombe, Richard, 89
Holcraft, William, 278
Holden, Hannah, 160
Holder, Francis, 298
  Hans Martin, 127
Holding, Daniel, 174
Holdsworth, John, 10, 244
  William, 160
Hole, Charles, 256, 333
  Elizabeth, 256
Hollinshead, Ann, 110, 161
  Edmund, 228
  Edward, 9, 181
  Francis, 18
  George, 161, 264
  Hugh, 50, 75, 110, 136, 347
  Jacob, 191
  James, 161
  Joseph, 52, 90, 110, 124, 132, 167, 180, 287, 339
  Mary, 50, 175, 228
  Robert, 156
  Samuel, 161
  Thomas, 110
  William, 161
Holloway, George, 253
  Isaac, 253
  James, 253
  John, 28, 253
  Margrate, 271
  Mary, 142
  Rebeccah, 253
Holly, Elnathan, 151
Holman, Elias, 161
  Francis, 211
Holme, Agnes, 161
  Benjamin, 104, 161, 323
  Benjamin, Jr., 323
  Ebenezer, 337
  Hannah, 161
  Hoppe, 161
  Jacob, 161
  James, 318
  John, 27, 94, 104, 161, 250, 267, 288
  Martha, 161
  Phebe, 161
  Samuel, 161
  William, 161
Holmes, Eleanor, 161
  Haunce, 161
  Huldah, 162
  James, 74, 75, 119, 161, 162
  John, 89, 161
  Jonathan, 75, 115, 316, 367
  Joseph, 162

INDEX OF NAMES OF PERSONS 415

Josiah, 135
Mary, 161
Obadiah, 161
Sarah, 161
Susannah, 161, 162, 296
William, 162
Holsten, Lawrence, 206
Holton, Bretta, 162
Christian, 162
Elizabeth, 105
Francis, 304
John, 156
Lawrance, 162
Mary, 162
Rachel, 116
Thomas, 97, 116, 269
Holts, Mary, 56
Homan, Jeptha, 309
Peter, 153
Homer, Samuel, 197
Honeywell, John, 163
Mary, 163
Hooker, Jacob, 148
Hooks, Mary, 163
Hooper, Anthony, 327
Margaret, 163
Robert Lettice, 76
Robert L., Jr., 245
Sarah, 341
William, 148
Hoose, Cornelia, 163
Harpert, 47
Janitye, 163
Hooten, Anne, 138
John, 110
Rachel, 163
Thomas, 220
William, 138
Hopewell, Daniel, 121, 138, 164, 266
Ebenezer, 65, 205
Hopkins, George, 164
Jonathan, 163
Sarah, 205
William, 265
Hopman, Peter, 178
Hoppe, Abraham, 373
Andris, 373
Cornelia, 37
Jacob, 373
Jannetie, 373
William, 6
Hopper, Antie, 6
John, 218, 317, 347, 348
Hoppock, Dennis, 91
Horess, George, 191
Horn, Elinor, 164
Stephen, 164
William, 118, 164, 168
Hornbeck, Jacobus, 164
Lenah, 164
Horner (Hornor), Amy, 165
Bartholomew, 203
Benjamin, 165
Content, 74
Isaac, 165
John, 139
Joseph, 88, 165
Joshua, 165
Samuel, 48, 165, 196
Sarah, 281
Hornett, Jonathan, 117
Horsfield, John, 165, 273
Horsman, Marmaduke, 273

Horton, Abigail, 364
David, 21
Jacob, 189
Joshua, 210, 256, 340
Mary, 189
Nicholas, 346
Phebe, 364, 365
Hose, Catherine, 166
Jacob, 166
Michael, 166
Hosiel, Adam, 160
Elizabeth, 160
George, 160
Henry, 160
Justin, 160
Louise, 160
Mary, 160
Michael, 160
Hoskins, John, 11, 121, 192, 264
Joseph, 264
Mary, 264
Ruth, 264
Houdin, Michael, 76
Hough, Elizabeth, 45
Jonathan, 14, 45, 264, 281, 361
Houghstedtre, Ann, 267
Houghton, Mary, 166, 181
Richard, 181
Houron, Samuel, 372
Housell, Johannis, 256
John, 372
Hovey, John, 159
How, Samuel, 235, 247, 290
Howard, Margaret, 166
Mary, 166
Robert, 100, 162, 139
Howell, Aaron, 166
Abraham, 166
Ann, 166
Arthur, 261, 283
Benjamin, 24, 166, 208
Caleb, 166
Charles, 166
Daniel, 213, 261
David, 261
Deborah, 166
Hannah, 69
Henry, 166
Hezekiah, 124, 321
George, 166
Isaac, 166
Jacob, 166
John, 166, 231
Joseph, 141, 236, 284
Joseph, Jr., 284
Josiah, 338
Lucy, 166
Lydia, 69
Margaret, 48
Mary, 69, 166, 260
Micah, 135
Moses, 166
Rachel, 166
Richard, 214
Samuel, 166, 167
Sarah, 318
Silas, 166
Howsell, Adam, 160, 167
Hubbard, Rachel, 368
Hubbell, Abijah, 225
Nathaniel, Jr., 12
Hubbert, James, 131
Hubbs, Lucy, 148
Huckings, Mercy, 167

Huddy, Daniel, 10, 17, 148, 217, 300
　Rachel, 298
Hudnut, Richard, 260
Hudson, Elizabeth, 167
　Joseph, 167
　Obed, 167
　Rachel, 167
　Samuel, 119
　Samuel, Jr., 64
Huestis, Dorrety, 168
　Hannah, 168
　John, 36, 168
　Joseph, 36, 168
　Mary, 168
　Moses, 168
　Sarah, 168
Huff, Elenah, 357
　Esther, 168
　Gershom, 168
　Richard, 197
Huffman, Catherine, 285, 293
　(see Hoffman)
Hugg, Barzillai, 25, 168
　Hannah, 168
　Hope, 25
　Isaac, 168
　Jacob, 25, 168, 200, 292, 361
　John, 168
　Joseph, 168
　Joseph, Jr., 128
　Leze, 168
　Samuel, 65, 49, 168
　Sarah, 168
　William, 148, 205
Hughes, Constant, 168
　David, 168
　Elias, 59, 65, 168, 169, 259
　Elijah, 142, 143, 144, 169, 275
　Elisha, 143
　Hannah, 168
　Humphrey, 169
　Jacob, 355
　Jesse, 168
　John, 143
　Memucan, 168
Hulett, Amy, 169
　Elizabeth, 169
　George, 169
　Hannah, 169
　Joseph, 202, 344
　Margaret, 169
　Mary, 169
　Michael, 169
　Sarah, 169
　Thomas, 169
　Timothy, 169
Hulick, Samuel, 135
Hulings, Abigail, 160, 345
　Jacob, 160
　Lorance, 160
　Sarah, 160
　(see Heulings)
Hull, Charity, 185
　Hopewell, 169
　Isaac, 169
　John, 111, 165, 169
　Joseph, 169, 198
　Moses, 169
　Robert, 186
　Ruth, 111
　Susannah, 307
Hulst, Richard, 363

Hummer, Harbart, 73
Humphries, Increase, 200, 201
　Joseph, 291
　Joshua, 110, 113, 123, 167, 200, 202, 271, 278, 290, 318
　Hannah, 296
　Mary, 170
　Richard, 170
　Thomas, 178
Hunloke, Thomas, 302
Hunn, Thomas, 153
Hunt, Abigail, 170
　Anglica, 170
　Anna, 170
　Azariah, 97, 109, 155, 260
　Benjamin, 170
　Daniel, 170
　Edward, 11, 12, 170, 214, 325, 326
　Elenor, 170
　Elizabeth, 69, 170
　James, 170
　Jean, 171
　Johanna, 170
　John, 78, 170, 229
　Mansfield, 81, 111
　Martha, 170
　Nathan, 155
　Nathaniel, 170
　Ralph, 170, 226
　Richard, 170
　Robert, 149, 328
　Samuel, 149, 170
　Sarah, 170
　Thomas, 157, 170, 171
　Wilson, 155, 241, 277, 282
Hunter, Andrew, 367
　Mary, 251
Huntington, Samuel, 78, 79, 219, 264
Huntzinger, Johannes, 229, 304
Hurd, Wallis, 352
Huse, Hannah, 56
Husk, Jane, 171
　John, 171
　Nicholas, 171
　Thomas, 171
Husted, David, 285, 355
Huston, George, 22
Hutch, Elizabeth, 139
Hutchin, John, 43, 130, 149
　Rebecca, 15
Hutchins, John Nathan, 27
Hutchinson, Ann, 248
　Elizabeth, 75, 248
　Isaac, 148
　Jean, 282
　John, 171, 225, 248
　Jonathan, 248
　Mary, 248
　Rachel, 248
　Richard, 315
　Robert, 199, 248, 357
　Sarah, 248
　Thomas, 210, 248
　William, 199
Hutton, Mary, 236
Hyder, Michael, 337
　Abraham, 171
　Abraham, Jr., 171
Hyers, Catharine, 171
Hyler, Adam, 296

INDEX OF NAMES OF PERSONS 417

I

Illey, John L., 318
Ilslee, Benjamin, 171, 225
  Elisha, 171
  Jean, 171
  John, 171
  Jonathan, 171, 173
  Rachel, 171
  Rebecca, 171
  (see Inslee)
Imlay, Alice, 171
  Elizabeth, 171, 371
  John, 114, 139, 148, 171, 319
  Margaret, 171
  Joseph, 149, 371
  Peter, 171
  Peter, Jr., 45
  William, 166, 171
Ingersul, Benjamin, 172
  Daniel, 172
  Ebenezer, 172
  Elizabeth, 172
  John, 172
  Joseph, 172, 230
Ingham, John, 172
  Jonas, 172
  Jonathan, 172
Inglis (Inglish), Benjamin, 174
  Mary, 151
  James, 151
  Thomas, 119, 131, 313, 323
Ingram, Benjamin, 174
Inloes, Joseph, 172
  Peter, 172
Inskeep, Benjamin, 172
  David, 172
  Isaac, 172, 290
  James, 172
  John, 42, 110, 172, 253
  Joseph, 172
  Mary, 172
  Sarah, 172
  William, 172, 194
Inslee, David, 7, 132
  Elisha, 173
  Elizabeth, 173
  John, 173
  Jonathan, 180
  Zachariah, 173
  (see Ilslee; Ensley)
Irannell, John, 148
Ireland, Amos, 173
  Ananias, 173
  Isaac, 173
  Isabella, 173
  Jacob, 173
  John, 39, 88
  Joseph, 289
  Mary, 173, 289
  Phebe, 289
  Sarah, 6
  Silas, 173, 289
  Titus, 39
Ireton, Obadiah, 50, 148
  Obadiah, Jr., 370
Irons, James, 9, 130, 145, 150, 204, 240
  James, Jr., 205
Irvine, Hannah, 245
Irwin, John, 94, 261
Isdell, Elizabeth, 214
  Sarah, 214
  Thomas, 214
Iselstine, Robert, 272

Iselton, Deborah, 173
  Jacob, 173
  Mathias, 173
  Robert, 173
  Samuel, 173
Iszard, Catharine, 173
  Gabriel, 251, 356
  Henry, 173
  Jane, 174
  John, 160
  Martha, 173
  Michael, 160, 173, 174
  Nicholas, 173
  Prisilla, 173
  Prudence, 173
  Reeves, 160
  Sarah, 173, 174
  Simeon, 160
Ivins, Abigail, 31, 174
  Isaac, 154
  Isaac, Jr., 174
  Moses, 319
  Solomon, 242

J

Jackaway, Reuben, 148, 347
Jackson, Amer, 166
  Benjamin, 84, 174
  Daniel, 315
  Elizabeth, 174
  Hugh, 174
  Isaac, 174
  James, 301
  Jane, 174
  John, 315, 370
  Joseph, 175
  Marcy, 174
  Mary, 116, 166, 174
  Peter, 174
  Sarah, 214
  William, 7, 174
Jacobson, Ann, 344
  Isaac, 344
  Mary, 344
Jacoon, Mr., 273
Jagger, Joseph, 88, 209
James, Anthony, 299
  David, 250
  Elizabeth, 84
Jamison, Rachel, 238
Janeway, George, 175
Janny, Abel, 102
Jansen, Albertie, 175
  Elizabeth, 175
  Garret, 175
  Isaac, 175
  Jan, 175
  Jannatie, 175
  Johannes, 175
  Sarah, 175
  (see Johnson)
Jaquat, Hance, 106, 175
  Hannah, 175
  Joseph, 283
  Rebecca, 175
  Sarah, 175
Jaques, John, 349
  Jonathan, 19
  Rebecca, 12
  Richard, 37, 84
  Samuel, 163, 311
  Sarah, 84
Jarman, John, 18
  Reuben, 60

Jarvis, Catharine, 175
Jeanes, Henry, 23, 245, 283
Jefferis, Caleb, 219
  Massey, 331
Jeffers, Mary, 328
  Thomas, 328
Jeffery, Daniel, 175
  Elisabeth, 175
  Francis, 56
  Jemima, 175
  Jeremiah, 175
  John, 56, 175
  Leady, 175
  Margaret, 175
  Mary, 175
  Mercy, 9
  Richard, 175
  Thomas, 9, 175
  Zilpah, 175
Jenkins, Abinidab, 176
  David, 348
  Esther, 176
  John, 219, 297
  Nathaniel, 80, 144, 177
  Nathaniel, Jr., 237, 299
  Ruth, 176
Jennings, Benjamin, 176
  Isaac, 214
  Jacob, 176
  Judith, 176
  William, 60, 105
Jerman, John, Jr., 226
Jess, David, 87, 112, 176
Jesse, Jonathan, 16
Jessup, Stephen, 238, 239
Jewell, Abigail, 176
  Althea, 176
  Cornelius, 176
  Elizabeth, 176
  Else, 176
  George, 176, 177
  Jean, 176
  John, 145, 155, 159, 176, 183, 240, 298
  Mary, 176
  Richard, 176, 339
  Sarah, 176
  William, 95, 176, 177
Jewet, Daniel, 157
  Mary, 329
Joan, John, 186
Jobs, Amy, 177
  George, 177
Joeling, Benjamin Christian, 126
Johe, Johann Adam, 59
Johnes, Timothy, 167, 265, 364
Johnson, Abigail, 178
  Abraham, 190
  Amos, 177, 179, 316, 318
  Andrew, 37, 181, 178
  Ann, 93, 190
  Anna, 92, 178, 242
  Benjamin, 177, 178, 243, 245
  Catherine, 177, 178
  Claud, 306
  Comfort, 178
  Cornelius, 178
  Daniel, 177
  David, 178
  David, Jr., 210
  Earick Gill, 106
  Ebenezer, 82, 104, 142, 144, 177, 192, 318
  Eleanor, 179
  Eliphalet, 178, 238
  Elizabeth, 37, 80, 178
  Else, 190
  Eunice, 178
  Ezekiel, 306, 327
  Garret, 217, 206
  Hannah, 177, 180
  Hannatche, 179
  Harman, 212
  Isaac, 50, 87, 256, 354
  Jabez, 178
  Jacob, 180, 357
  Jacobus, 178
  James, 84, 148, 179, 190, 263, 305
  Jannetie, 37
  Jemima, 178
  John, 94, 120, 177, 180, 190, 219, 224, 238, 240, 273, 333
  Joseph, 68, 178, 180, 190, 238, 273, 315, 335, 348, 359
  Katherine, 180
  Kezia, 178
  Kort, 282
  Martin, 177
  Mary, 178, 190, 273
  Martha, 178
  Mathias, 102, 194, 276, 339, 357
  Millicent, 177
  Mindred, 37
  Moses, 177
  Nathaniel, 52
  Nelly, 295
  Nicholas, 73, 98, 179, 252, 279, 324
  Othaniel, 30
  Ouke, 177, 179
  Peter, 135, 247
  Phebe, 178, 327
  Rachel, 179
  Ralph, 19
  Rebecca, 178
  Rhoda, 85
  Robert, 220, 246, 282, 298
  Ruelof, 190
  Samuel, 12, 177, 178, 180, 295
  Sarah, 178
  Temperance, 179
  Thomas, 89, 97, 143, 372
  Tunis, 255
  Uzal, 178, 210
  William, 177, 179, 298
  (see Jansen)
Johnston, Andrew, 80, 224, 303, 358
  Ann, 74
  Daniel, 115
  David, 9, 68, 83, 130, 175, 205
  Elizabeth, 179, 354
  Euphenia, 350
  Hannah, 147
  Hermon, 212
  James, 80, 166, 245
  John, 198, 199
  Lewis, 318
  Luke, 150
  Mary, 147
  Mathias, 88
  Michael, 259
  Rachel, 198
  William, 277
Joline, John, 59
Jolly, Ann, 180
  Charles, 180
  Deborah, 180
  Dinah, 180
  Elizabeth, 180

INDEX OF NAMES OF PERSONS 419

James, 273
John, 177
Mary, 180
William, 350
Jones, Aaron, 229
  Abraham, 85, 251, 287
  Alexander, 181
  Ambrose, 180
  Ann, 181
  Benjamin, 44, 49, 129, 148
  Christina, 181
  Daniel, 159, 363
  Daniel, Jr., 94, 121, 137, 157, 159, 213, 266, 328
  Elizabeth, 87, 182, 257, 345
  Evan, 257, 339
  Hannah, 170, 238
  Henry, 130, 345
  Hezekiah, 137, 319
  Hugh, 8
  Isaac, 52, 346, 350
  James, 159, 180
  Jane, 298, 345,
  Jean, 46
  John, 44, 61, 93, 155, 166, 190, 232, 233
  Jonas, 148
  Joseph, 181
  Joshua, 170
  Lydia, 181
  Mary, 44, 159, 181, 215
  Matthew, 8, 181
  Patrick, 189
  Rachel, 180, 181, 373
  Richard, 83, 148, 180
  Ruth, 180
  Samuel, 46, 180, 296, 371
  Sarah, 115, 180
  Sophia, 181
  Thomas, 71, 108, 234
  William, 53, 85, 152, 173, 201, 252, 257
Joralemon, Ariantje, 182
  Claus, 182
  Cornelia, 182
  Cornelius, 182, 322
  Daniel, 145
  Derrick, 182
  Elizabeth, 182
  Hannah, 182
  Hans, 182
  Hendrick, 182
  John, Jr., 182
  Peterje, 182
  Phebe, 182
  Teunis, 182
Jorden, Hannah, 268
  Samuel, 28
  William, 235
Joslane, (Joslin), Thomas, 24, 86, 320
Jouet, Cavalier, 182
Joyce, Henry, 115
  Thomas, 139, 327
Jubert, Mary, 99
  Susannah, 99
Juriansen, Abraham, 373
  Christoffel, 373
  Christyna, 373
  Frederick, 373
  Gerrebrant, 182
  Gerrit, 373
  Geurt, 373
  Isaac, 373
  Jacob, 373

Johannes, 373
Judith, 373
Juria, 182, 373
Margaret, 128
Marytje, 373
Neltie, 182
Sarah, 373
Thomas, 128, 373
Jurin, John, 120
Justeson, Andrew, 182
  Catheren, 182
  Elizabeth, 182
  Isaac, 182
  John, 182
  Juster, 182
  Nicholas, 182
Justice, John 63
  Nicholas, 83

K

Kaes, Ann Elizabeth, 183
  Catherine, 183
  Hendrick, 183
  Peter, 183
  Philip, 183
  Rachel, 183
  William, 183
  (see Case)
Kaighn, Abigail, 149
  Catharine, 50
  James, 307
  Dr. John, 345
  John, 56
  (see Cain)
Kallender, Katherine, 297
Kar, Martha, 164
Karmer, Dirck, 333
Kaull, Christian, 372
  (see Cool)
Kay, Elizabeth, 183
  Francis, 183
  Isaac, 25, 119, 149, 183
  John, 183
  Joseph, 13, 183
  Josiah, 56, 80, 113, 152, 181, 183, 217, 273, 298, 313, 320, 333, 335, 373
  Marian, 183
  Sarah, 183
Kearney, Thomas, 270
Keasbey, Bradway, 341
  Edward, 129, 159, 167, 185, 246, 263, 341
Keater, Jane, 353
Kee, John, 87
Keeffe, Arthur, 311
Keeler, Elizabeth, 187
Keely, Patrick, 241
Keen, (Keane), Daniel, 178
  James, 91
  Mounce, 212, 268
  Mounce, Jr., 171
Keiger, Matthias, 103
Keirstead, Samuel, 241
Kelch, Elizabeth, 183
Keldreth, Prisaler, 179
Kelly (Kelley), Abraham, 36
  Asa, 73, 184, 309
  Catherine, 78, 183
  Craig, 183
  Elizabeth, 95, 184
  George, 184
  James, 87, 184
  Jesse, 184

John, 82, 184
Margaret, 184
Mary, 184
Nugient, 12, 82, 116, 184, 217, 227
Patrick, 81
Richard, 184
Samuel, 95
Sarah, 66, 149
Susannah, 184, 217
Thomas, 9, 184
William, 73, 183, 304
Kelsey, Benjamin, 183, 184
  Daniel, 183, 184
  Jemima, 184
  John, 184
  Maney, 183
  Massa, 184
  Rachel, 184
  Ruth, 183, 184
  Robert, 96, 178, 316
Kemble, George, 15, 21, 104, 221
  Mary, 202
  Peter, Jr., 349
  Richard, 66
  Samuel, 31, 40, 200, 275
Kemple, Philipp, 372
Kempter, Mary, 184
Kempton, Jeams, 184
  John, 184
  Moses, 184
  William, 184
Kendall, Thomas, 148
Kennedy, Archibald, 8
  Katherine, 185
  Mary, 8
  Thomas, 76
Kennessen, Kennes, 338
Kenney, Charity, 185
  Elizabeth, 185
  John, 185
  Kathrine, 185
  Sarah, 184
  Simon, 185
  (see Kinney)
Kent, Ann, 162
  Daniel, 144
  Edmund, 56
  Ephraim, 360, 357
  Erasmus, 13, 56, 162, 220
  John, 366
  Lewis, 257
  Samuel, 257
  Sophia, 185
  William, 18, 33, 34, 84, 116, 174, 227
Kentin, Hannah, 96
  John, 96
Kep, Nickasie, 34
Ker, Joseph, 77, 305, 350
  Margaret, 77
  Nathan, 155
  Samuel, 77
  Walter, 77
  William, 155
Kerll, Uriah, 139
  (see Carll)
Kerstead, Sarah, 43
Kesley, Edward, 245
Kester, Anne, 185
Ketcham, Benjamin, 185, 226
  Elizabeth, 312
  Stephen, 312
Keteltas, Abraham, 263

Key, William, 162, 28
Keyser, John Garret, 192
Keyt, John, 182
Kiersteed, Jane, 185
Kilchrist, Mary, 341
Killey, Abraham, 290
  David, 254
  Elizabeth, 185
  Malachi, 366
  (see Kelley)
Killpatrick, Anne, 186
  Eliza, 186
  Francis, 186
  James, 186
  Mary, 185, 186
  Thomas, 186
Kimble, John, 148
  Samuel, 207
Kimsey, Jonathan, 53
  Mary, 331
  Thomas, 47, 347
  (see Kinsey)
King, Andrew, 148
  Bridget, 186
  Elizabeth, 186
  Francis, 294
  Frederick, 186
  Harmanus, 148, 370
  Jeremiah, 111
  John, 322
  John, Jr., 335
  Joseph, 81, 306
  Margaret, 43
  Mary, 63, 294
  Peter, 100
  Phebe, 78
Kingsland, Anna, 198
  Edmund, 182, 198
  Edmund Roger, 198
  Isaac, 341
  Nathaniel, 81
Kinnan, John, 211, 244
  Joseph, 230, 268
  Thomas, 299
  William, 74
Kinney, Adrian, 186
  David, 72, 186
  Elizabeth, 186
  Eve, 186
  Ida, 72
  John, 185
  Lydia, 186
  Michael, 186
  Peter, 186
  William, 186
  Yannetie, 72
  (see Kenney)
Kinsey, Annaple, 228
  Elizabeth, 228
  James, 228
  John, 228
  Jonathan, 117, 228
  Mootrey, 228
  (see Kimsey)
Kinter, Henry, 296
Kipp (Kip), Gertrude, 334
  Hendrick, 52, 182, 334
  Isaac, 334
  Jacob, 334
  John, Jr., 363
  Mary, 98
  Nicholas, 96
  Peter, 334

INDEX OF NAMES OF PERSONS 421

Kirby, Benjamin, 271
  Thomas, 175
Kirkbride, Hannah, 47, 192
  Duncan, 346
  John, 344
  Margery, 330
  Mary, 273
  Phebe, 344
Kirkpatrick, Alexander, 186
  Andrew, 186
  David, 186
  Elizabeth, 186
  Mary, 186
  John (see p. 186)
  William, 226
Kishan, Joshua, 125
Kitchel, Abigail, 187
  John, 69
  Joseph, 24, 187
  Ruth, 187
  Stephen, 187
  Uzal, 187
  Zenas, 187
Kitchen, Elizabeth, 124
  Thomas, 53, 272
Kite, Jonathan, 316
Kline (Klein), Christian, 187
  Isaac, 188
  William, 188
Knight, Isaac, 370
  Sarah, 154
Knihoff, John, 159
  Paul, 159
  Sarah, 159
Knipe, Jonathan, 262
  (see Nipe)
Knott, Abigail, 368
  Catherine, 368
  Catherine, Jr., 368
  David, 119, 344, 368
  Peter, 368
Knox, Jemima, 311
  Mary, 187
Koen, Matthias, 69
Kolb, John, 349
Kotts, Conrad, 14
Koul, Eva Marya, 183
  Paul, 183
  (see Cool)
Kouwenhoven, Catherine, 187
  Cornelius, 187
  Dominicus, 187
  Garret, 187
  Jacob, 187
  John, 187
  Mathias, 187
  Peter, 187
  Roleph, 187
  William, 45, 187
  Williamtie, 187
  (see Covenhoven; Conover)
Kreager, Katherine, 187
  Peter, 187
  Peth, 188
  William, 188
Kroesen, Catherine, 188
  Cornelius, 188
  Derick, 129
  John, 128
Krom, Mary, 188
Kuykendal, Leward, 214
  Pieter, 164

L

Labaw (Labagh), Francis, 265
  Ragul, 234
Lacey, Joseph, 102, 208
  Sarah, 188
Lack, Daniel, 189
  (see Lake)
Lacock, Elizabeth, 189
  Henry, 189
  John, 189
  Joseph, 188, 189
  Nathan, 189
  Sarah, 189
  William, 188, 189
Lacony, James, 189
  John, 189
  Katherine, 189
  Lecony, 189
  Mary, 189
  William, 108
Ladd, John, 15, 47, 102, 153, 266, 292, 318, 324
  Samuel, 15, 21, 87, 305
Lafetra, Edmond, 325
  Hannah, 9
  Mary, 9
Laffnard, Margaret, 73
  Peter, 73
Lafollet, John, 186
Lagrange (Legrange), Bernardus, 255, 306, 330, 340, 343
  Feytie, 332
  Jannetie, 332
  Johannes, 332
  John, 332
  Metie, 332
Laing, Benjamin, 189
  George, 97
  Hannah, 97
Laird, Alexander, 294
  Archibald, 294
  Susannah, 294
  William, 67, 123, 294
Lake, Andrew, 155
  Daniel, 39
  Elizabeth, 189
  Elsie, 189
  Garret, 185
  Guisbert, 189, 204
  Hannah, 189
  Jacobus, 152
  John, 179, 189, 204, 205
  Joseph, 189
  Martinah, 189
  Nellie, 189
  Rachel, 189
  Richard, 189
  Sarah, 189
  Thomas, 185
  (see Lack)
Lamb, Anne, 190
  Elizabeth, 190
  Jacob, 139, 190
  John, 37, 70, 190, 321, 322
  John D., 223
  Joseph, 129, 190, 277
  Lydia, 17
Lambert, Christian, 191
  Elizabeth, 190
  Joanna, 190
  Phebe, 190

Lambertson, Cornelius, 154
  Maycy, 190
    (see under John, p. 190)
Lamson (Lambson), Eunice, 191
  Daniel, 78, 346, 358
  Eleazer, 346
  Hance, 246, 306
  Mathias, 70, 106, 190, 246, 306
  Sarah, 70, 190
  Thomas, 190
Lance, Peter, 150
Landis, Henry, 256, 268
Landman, George, 13
Landon, Daniel, 168
Lane, Adrian, 107
  Barbara, 191
  Cornelius, 107, 188, 282, 372
  Garret, 243
  Guisbert, 212
  Harmen, 107, 339
  Hendrick, 343
  Isaac, 224
  William, 99
Langerfeldt, Christina, 191
Langlee, David, 172
  Margret, 191
Lanning, Anne, 191
  Daniel, 261, 231
  Isaac, 170, 243
  Robert, 111, 243
Lapton, Benjamin, 367
Laqueer, Ann, 191
  Hannah, 191
  John, 191
  Joseph, 191
  Mary, 191
Larew (Laroo), Abraham, 157, 198, 319, 332
  Aurey, 185
  Jacobus, 185
  Lambert, 185
Large, Ebenezer, 47
  Robert, 108
  Samuel, 108, 208
Larking, Patrick, 47
Larson (Larason), William, 287, 307
Latouch & Hanes, 192
  Isaac, 7
Lauer, Tobias, 35
Laughton, Benjamin, 309
  Elisabeth, 192
  William, 192
Lauree, Thomas, 67
Laux, Derrick, 192
  Mary, 192
Lavennor, John, 130
Lawrence, Abigail, 237, 238
  Anne, 45, 196
  Catherine, 368
  Daniel, 143, 174
  Elizabeth, 45, 192, 196
  Elizabeth, Jr., 192
  Elisha, 45, 57, 318
  Elisha, Jr., 45, 57
  George, 21, 156
  Jacob, 260, 318
  James, 83, 119, 158, 296
  John, 45, 88, 102, 148, 172, 192, 193, 195, 196, 268, 271, 273, 310
  Jonathan, 42, 46, 237, 238, 314, 355
  Joseph, 9, 75, 192, 324
  Lucy, 45
  Mary, 75, 192, 193, 367
  Nancy, 143
  Nathan, 289
  Rachel, 192
  Richard, 9, 160, 344, 368, 369
  Robert, 129, 192, 331
  Susannah, 204
  Thomas, 11, 17, 31, 40, 69, 127, 163, 192, 193, 230, 291, 294, 319, 361
  William, 66, 75, 114, 130, 139, 199, 272, 367
  William, Jr., 135
  (see Lorance)
Lawrie, Thomas, 110, 166, 271, 272, 367
Layer, John, 256
Layton, Ann, 277
  Hannah, 357
  John, 364
  John, Jr., 357
  Peter, 25, 100
  Samuel, 111
  Thomas, 55
  William, 131
Leaming, Aaron, 222
  Alice, 14
  Christopher, 160, 193
  Deborah, 193
  Jeremiah, 131
  John, 57
    (see Liming)
Leaycraft, Sarah, 342
Leberger, Adam, 103, 285
  Barbara, 193
Leboyteuix, Paul, 284
  Peter, 303
LeCount, Peter, 148
Lecouy, James, 61
Leddel, William, 333
Leddon, Elizabeth, 250
  Joanna, 250
  Margary, 250
  Mary, 250
  Perriman, 250
  Samuel, 250
  Susannah, 250
Lee, Abraham, 105, 193, 194, 329
  Agnes, 194
  Alice Ann, 207
  Ann, 208
  Daniel, 194
  Elizabeth, 194
  Gershom, 50
  Hannah, 194
  James, 193
  John, 7, 43, 90, 121, 194, 222, 224
  Joshua, 194
  Margaret, 194
  Mary, 193, 194
  Rachel, 193
  Robert, 43, 44
  Sarah, 25, 194
  William, 193
Leeds, Abraham, 14, 190
  Daniel, 194
  Felix, 194
  Hannah, 356
  Japhet, 194, 300
  Nehemiah, 302
  Philo, 148
  Philo, Jr., 360, 369
  Rebecca, 194
  Sarah, 172, 194

INDEX OF NAMES OF PERSONS 423

Vincent, 194, 222, 310, 360, 361, 369
Leek, Elizabeth, 59
  John, 102, 109, 144, 194, 232, 309
  Nathan, 46, 115
  Sarah, 194
Leet, Isaac, 39
Leets, William, 319
Lefferson, Aurt, 194
  Benjamin, 194
  Leffert, 95
  Margaret, 194
Lefferty, John, 309
Leforge, Abraham, 195
  David, 195
  David, Jr., 248
  Frances, 195
  Fremis, 195
  Isaac, 195
  Jane, 195
  John, 195, 257
  Mary, 195
  Nathaniel, 62, 195
  Nicholas, 118, 195
  Rachel, 257
  Temperance, 195
Legg, Samuel, 313
Leigh, Frances, 245
  Ichabod, 145, 183, 191, 268
Lemmon, Dinah, 199
  Henry, 199
  Mary, 199
  Sarah, 199
  Thomas, 199
Lenmire, Ann, 337
  Christopher, 337
Lennox, Marcy, 195
Leonard, Abigail, 196
  Ann, 196
  Caleb, 50
  Charity, 197
  Daniel, 196, 197
  Elizabeth, 195
  Capt. Henry, 75, 195, 196
  James, 196, 197
  John, 103, 195, 196, 222, 258, 302
  Lucy, 195, 197
  Mary, 195, 197, 235, 368
  Nathaniel, 68, 288, 364
  Pamelia, 197
  Ruth, 165
  Samuel, 196, 231
  Sarah, 196, 197
  Thomas, 148, 196, 197, 235, 368
  Thomas, Jr., 107
  Whitehead, 80, 196, 197
Lepper, Isabella, 271
  Thomas, 353
Leslie (Lesley), Edmund, 198
  Elizabeth, 147, 197
  George, 33
  George W., 198
  John, 198
  Margaret, 198
  William, 198
Lestorgen, Abigail, 167
Letts, Catrina, 147
  Elizabeth, 147
  Francis, 323
  John, 366
  William, 318
Levinor, John, 129
  Sarah, 129
Lewis, Abigail, 254
  Archelaus, 75

  Daniel, 357
  Elizabeth, 198, 368
  Francis, 25
  Hannah, 198
  Jacob, 198
  John, 8, 198
  Joseph, 139
  Lemuel, 368
  Martha, 198
  Mary, 198
  Paul, 198
  Philip, 357
  Rebecca, 198
  Samuel, 194, 231
  Squier, 185
  William, 98, 332
Leydecker, Abraham, 246
Lidden, Abraham, 199
  Alice C., 199
  Benjamin, 57, 282
  Elizabeth, 199
  Samuel, 199
  Susannah, 199
Lidenies, John A., 15, 127, 290
Liking, Michael, 199
Liming, De Wilda, 199
  Dinah, 199
  Henry, 199
  John, 59, 199
  Mary, 199
  Sarah, 199
  Thomas, 199
  William, 66, 75, 199, 357
  (see Leaming, Lemmon)
Limon, Abraham, 199
Linch, Samuel, 159, 181, 199, 231, 249, 337
Linde, Samuel, 186
Lines, William, 121
Lindley, H., 329
Lindsey, David, 273
  William, 217
Lindsley, Daniel, 119, 316, 363
  John, 167
Line, William, 225
Linmire, Alexander, 186
  Ann, 192
Lippincott, Aaron, 200, 201, 202, 286, 304
  Abel, 202
  Abigail, 202
  Abula, 202
  Ann, 110
  Anna, 201, 202
  Benjamin, 200, 201, 360
  Caleb, 200, 360
  Daniel, 139, 167, 200, 201, 202, 253, 254, 330
  David, 92, 200, 201
  Dinah, 201
  Elizabeth, 200, 201, 202, 286, 304
  Esther, 202
  Ezekiel, 200
  Freedom, 110, 125, 138, 172, 345
  Grace, 200
  Hannah, 192, 202, 360
  Hope, 360
  Increase, 201
  Isaac, 13, 202
  Jacob, 200, 201
  James, 56, 110, 141, 145, 200, 201, 202, 224, 233, 290, 319
  Jerusha, 201
  Job, 71, 148, 201

John, 167, 200, 201, 202
John, Jr., 9, 135, 344
Jonathan, 110, 200, 202
Joseph, 13, 200, 201, 344
Joshua, 200, 202, 345
Judith, 200, 202
Levi, 201
Lewis, 110
Lydia, 200, 201
Margaret, 200
Mary, 200, 201, 202
Mercy, 202
Meribeth, 202, 233
Moses, 200, 201
Nathaniel, 202
Obadiah, 55, 169, 200, 201
Phebe, 202
Rachel, 9, 201, 202
Rebecca, 278
Remembrance, 174, 201
Restore, 200, 205, 353
Robert, 174, 201
Samuel, 5, 54, 87, 99, 106, **127**, 130, 138, 167, 200, 201, **202**, 227, 364
Sarah, 38, 201, 202
Solomon, 77
Surviah, 203
Susannah, 201
Thomas, 200, 201, 202, 228, **345**
Thomas, Jr., 228
Uriah, 202
William, 10, 198, 200, 201, 202
Lister, James, 132
Litsinger, Peter, 67
Littell, Abraham, 203
  Amasa, 203
  Amos, 203
  Benjamin, 91
  Isaac, 203
  Jacob, 360
  John, 203, 322
  Joseph, 275
  Mary, 203
  Moses, 203
  Samuel, 360
  Sarah, 203
  Susannah, 203
Little, Benjamin, 328
  Hannah, 368
  John, 205
  Robert, 157
  Susannah, 328
  Thomas, 29
  Thomas, Jr., 29
Livingston, Mary, 8
  Neil, 96
  Patience, 203
  Peter Van Brugh, 8
  Robert, 299
  William, 9
Lloyd (Loyd), Bateman, 26, 106, 127, 193, 227, 337, 354, **365**
  Catherine, 77
  David, 28, 152, 206
  Elizabeth, 206
  Ephraim, 132
  John, 26, 77, 305, 364
  Joseph, 148
  Obadiah, 99
  Priscilla, 206
  Richard, 310
  Timothy, 65, 94, 190
  Thomas, 251

Lock, Andrew, 69, 105, 307
  Charles, 153, 203, 307
  Israel, 206
  Jasper, 203
  Jester, 153
  John, 292
  Jonas, 203
  Jussta, 351
  Lawrence, 15, 74, 93
  Peter, 203
  William, 120
Lockhart, Daniel Cox, 76
  Ephraim, 155
  James, 28
  Mary, 28
Lockoney, Katherine, 203
  William, 203
Lodge, Abraham, 258, 332
  Al., 8
  Benjamin, 43, 103, 115, 130, 148, 181, 213, 233, 263, 297, 302
  Matthew, 352, 364
Loftus, Jane, 204
Logan, John, 82, 186
Long, Abraham, 204
  Andrew, 38, 204, 336
  Ansell, 77, 204, 246
  David, 114, 204
  Deborah, 204
  Dorothy, 204
  Eleanor, 204
  Elizabeth, 204
  Grace, 204
  Hannah, 61
  John, 204, 257
  Joseph, 160
  Malachi, 204
  Margaret, 114
  Nathan, 204
  Paul, 204
  Peter, 49, 92, 115, 157, 204, 301
  Pleasant, 204
  Sarah, 204
  Shepard, 204
Longacre, Peter, 149
  Sarah, 149
Longfield, Henry, 192
Longhorn, Jeremiah, 198
Longman, Mary, 37
Longstaff, Samuel, 307
Longstreet, Aaron, 189, 240
  Abigail, 368
  Alice, 240
  Anne, 73, 205
  Catherine, 205, 240
  Christina, 204
  Derrick, 45
  Elizabeth, 204
  Garret, 189, 204
  Guisbert, 130, 145, 204, 205, 240
  Jane, 204, 205
  John, 190, 204
  Marcy, 205
  Moyca, 204
  Nelley, 204
  Onicha, 204
  Rachel, 204
  Sarah, 205
  Stoffel, 205, 224
Longworth, Mary, 317
  Thomas, 249
Looker, John, 54, 102
Loomis, Elijah, 80
  Margaret, 105
    (see Lummis)

INDEX OF NAMES OF PERSONS   425

Looshett, Christina, 188, 205
  John, 188
Lorance, Abigail, 85
  Jonathan, 38, 85, 146, 259, 313, 314
  Nathan, 85, 146
  (see Lawrence)
Lord, Abraham, 65, 205
  Ann, 205
  Elinor, 166
  Elizabeth, 205
  Eunice, 205
  Hannah, 200
  James, 267
  Joseph, 28, 182, 230, 251, 307
  Joshua, 38, 43, 96, 109, 114, 127, 139, 205, 267
  Joshua, Jr., 53, 77, 114, 138, 205, 266
Lore, Ann, 122, 205
  Daniel, 122
  David, 205
  Hezekiah, 159, 206
  John, 205
  Jonathan, 205, 287, 328
  Phebe, 122
  Richard, 269
  Seth, 122, 206
  William, 206
Loree, Samuel, 119
Lorsbach, Conrad, 150
Losee, Daniel, 167
Lott (Lot), Antie, 206
  Hannah, 206
  Hendrick, 206
  Isaac, 95
  Maria, 206
  Maurice, 206
  Peter, 84, 206, 283, 362
  Peter, Jr., 84, 273, 362
Lotton, Elizabeth, 307
Louden, John, 288
Louder, Jane, 83
Loutherback, Eliza, 206
Lovell, Beasy, 139
  Jonathan, 148
  Perkins, 186
Lovett, Jonathan, 206, 341
  Mary, 206
  Nathan, 279
  Samuel, 206
  Sarah, 206
Low, Abraham, 128, 312
  Benjamin, 141
  Cornelius, 62, 128, 206, 312, 343
  Court, Jr., 330
  Dirck, 107, 325
  Elizabeth, 206
  Helena, 206
  Isaac, 254
  Jane, 206
  John, 112, 128, 206, 224
  Joseph, 231
  Lawrence, 16
  Margaret, 206
  Mary, 161
  Nicholas, 206
  Peter, 206
  Rachel, 206
  Robert, 352
  Teunis, 295
Lowden, Samuel, 82
Lownes, Joseph, Jr., 168
Lucas, Francis, 282, 334
  Seth, 113

Luce, Benjamin, 207, 222
  David, 125
  Joseph, 207
Luckens, Herman, 351
Ludlam, Abigail, 207
  Alathea, 207
  Anthony, 207
  Cornelius, 203, 215
  David, 39
  Esther, 207
  Hannah, 208
  Henry, 207
  Joseph, 193, 207, 237
  Phebe, 207
  Providence, 207
  Samuel, 16
  Samuel, Jr., 208
  Thomas, 207
Ludlow, Cary, 175
  Gabriel, 341
  Henry, 8
  John J., 346
Lum, Anna, 208
  Daniel, 24
  David, 208
  Eunice, 208
  Israel, 208
  John, 208
  Martha, 208
  Mary, 208
  Matthew, 167, 208, 331
  Nancy, 208
  Samuel, 208
  Sarah, 208
  Shuah, 208
  Squire, 208
Lumley, John, 6
Lummis, Daniel, 180
  Edward, 115
  Joseph, 24
  Samuel, 116
  (see Loomis)
Lundy, Anne, 208
  Jacob, 208
  Joseph, 208
  Richard, 208
  Samuel, 208
  Thomas, 208
Luneberg, Nicholas, 158
Lupardus, Christianus, 340
  Ram, 340
Lupton, Christopher, 120
  Samuel, 24
Lurting, John, 174
Luse, Benjamin, 207
  David, 125, 207, 265, 285, 316
Luts, John, 291
Lutz, Jacob, 361
Luyster, Johannes, 27
Lycans, Andrew, 148
Lyde, Byfield, 26
  Mary Belcher, 26
  Sarah, 26
Lyell, Mary, 147
Lyle, John, 268
Lynch, Patrick, 160
Lyne, Ann, 140
  James, 140
  William, 176
Lynes, Captain William, 122
Lyon, Abraham, 209
  Ann, 209
  Benjamin, 209
  Daniel, 209, 210
  David, 209

Elizabeth, 210
Ezekiel, 50
Fanny, 209
Hannah, 364, 365
Henry, 333, 364, 365
Isaac, 21, 26, 249, 317, 335
James, 364, 365
Jonathan, 210
Joseph, 35, 259, 333, 364
Joseph, Jr., 364
Josiah, 209
Martha, 209
Mary, 209, 364
Mathias, 209
Moses, 259
Phebe, 209
Rebecah, 209, 249
Samuel, 209
Sarah, 159

M

McAllister, Archibald, 211
  Hugh, 170
  Joanna, 170
McCain, Bryan, 210
  Catherine, 210
  Charles, 210
  Daniel, 210
  Hugh, 210
  James, 210
  John, 210
  Mary, 210
  Nelly, 210
  Richard, 210
  William, 210
McCarter, John, 242
  Mary, 242
McCarthy, Elizabeth, 274
  James, 274
  Matthew, 148
McCarty, Ann, 268
McCaye, Jean, 210
McClane, Charles, 362
McClelche, James, 266
McClellan, William, 55, 124, 186
McColloch, Benjamin, 153
  Hannah, 153
  John, 172, 276
  Sarah, 172
McCollum, Hugh, 109, 212
  Jacob, 100
  John, 213
McColster, Archibald, 308
McComb, John, 15
McConnell, John, 162
  Susanna, 210
  Thomas, 210
McConnely, Eleanor, 315
  Neil, 315
McCoun, (McKoun), Jane, 212
  John, 86, 245
McCoy, Ann, Jr., 235
  Esebel, 297
McCreery, William, 66
McCue, Thomas, 266
McDaniel, John, 271
  William, 51, 60
McDowell, Ephraim, 6
  John, 83
  Peter, 83
McElhage, James, 40
MacElrath, James, 73
  Samuel, 7
  Sarah, 73

McEowen, Daniel, 132
  Mary, 211
  Robert, 211
  William, 213
  (see McEwen, McCoun, McQuown)
McEvers, Catherine, 211
  Charles, 211
  James, 211
  John, 211
  Mary, 211
  William, 211
McEwen, Alexander, 186
  Duncan, 186
  (see McEowen)
McFarrin, Hugh, 294
  Robert, 294
Macfell, William, 26
McFerrar, Margaret, 294
McGallird, Andrew, 73
  John, 24
McGinnis, John, 317
McGlaughlin, Elizabeth, 264
  William, 264
McHenry, William, 101
McIlhenny, Ann, 212, 213
  James, 210, 212, 213
  John, 196, 244
  Mary, 212
  William, 170, 213
McIlvaine, William, 273
McIntosh, Daniel, 61
McKearson, John, 179
McKenzie, Joseph, 99
McKim, Mary, 212
McKinley, James, 102
McKinney (McKenney), Abraham, 212
  Ann, 212
  Daniel, 66, 72, 212
  David, 212
  George, 321
  Jacob, 212
  John, 212
  Mary, 212
  Mordecai, 212
  William, 212, 320
McKittre, John, 212
McKnight, William, 131, 210, 267, 287
McKown (see McCoun, McEowen)
Macleese, Cornelius, 212
  Gisbert, 212
  John, 212
  Johnston, 212
  Margaret, 212
  Peter, 212
  Rachel, 212
  James, 239
McMasters, Lydia, 284
McMekin, Charles, 273
McMuelin, Elche, 213
  Ellenor, 213
  John, 213
McMurtry, Ann, 243
McNichol, George, 138
McPherson, James, 204
McQuown, William, 77, 243
  (see McEowen)
McVicker, James, 210
McWilliams, David, 213, 239
  Susannah, 213
Mackey, Elizabeth, 169
  John, 207, 357

INDEX OF NAMES OF PERSONS 427

Maers, John, 269
Maffet, Archibald, 263
  James, 213, 346
  Robert, 148, 199
  Samuel, 148, 149, 213
  (see Moffet)
Magee, James, 45
  John, 123
  Joseph, 275
  Thomas, 46
  (see Megie)
Mahurin, Ebenezer, 213
Mall, Mikan, 213
Mallison, Henry, 195
Mallock, Patience, 327
Man, David, 155, 214, 228
  Elizabeth, 214
  Joseph, 255
  Mary, 214
  Thomas, 214
Manderfield, Lao, 43
Mandeville, Hendrick, 343
Mandle, Andrew, 192
Manley, Charity, 214
  Elizabeth, 214
  John Adrian, 214
  Mary, 214
  Richard, 214
  Thomas, 214
Manners, John, 111
  John, Jr., 111
Manning, Benjamin, 28
  Catherine, 60, 214
  Clarkson, 60, 214
  Ephraim, 32
  Isaac, 60, 214
  James, 97, 189, 214, 218
  Jeremiah, 97, 214
  John, 60, 214
  Nathaniel, 146, 163
  Trustrum, 97, 295
Mapes, William, 230
Maple, Benjamin, 196, 315
  Benjamin, Jr., 315
Mares, James, 269
Margin, Hugh, 221
Marinus, Rev. David, 346, 373
Marlett, Abraham, 257
  Dirck, 107, 188, 282
  George, 98, 152, 257, 276, 277
  John, Jr., 339
Marner, Alexander, 214
  Christian, 214
  William, 214
Marple, George, 139
Marriage, Peter, 94, 148
Marriot, Abraham, 129, 130
  Isaac, 157
  Philip, 319
  Will, 243
  (see Merriot)
Marsh, Abraham, 215
  Catherine, 340
  Charles, 131
  Christopher, 215
  Damaris, 236
  Daniel, 215
  David, 215, 256
  Ephraim Markes, 215
  Esther, 84
  Henry, 215
  Jesse, 215
  Johannah, 215
  John, 215, 236
  Jonathan, Jr., 67
  Joshua, 78
  Mary, 215
  Mephibosheth, 215, 256
  Noah, 215
  Phebe, 215
  Rhoda, 215
  Rolfe, 215
  Samuel, 116, 225, 241, 274
  Sarah, 215
  William, 55, 215
Marshall, Catherine, 216, 351
  George, 207, 208
  James, 171, 278, 285, 292, 301
  Jane, 34
  John, 39, 83, 106, 190, 246, 254, 306, 351, 370
  Mary, 207, 208
  Moses, 161
Mart, Mathias, 158
Martin, Athanasius, 216
  Benjamin, 216, 217
  David, 150
  Elizabeth, 215
  Gershom, 217
  Henry, 228
  Jacob, 216
  James, 216
  Jeremiah, 216
  John, 171, 216, 282, 358
  Jonathan, 216
  Joseph, 216, 217
  Luther, 216
  Merrit, 216
  Mulford, 217
  Nathaniel, 216
  Peter, 216, 217, 292
  Philerato, 216
  Priscilla, 217
  Reuben, 216
  Robert, 217
  Sarah, 217
  Samuel, 216, 217
  Thomas, 217
  Valentine, 216, 217
  William, 51, 216, 350
  Zephaniah, 216
Maskell, Thomas, 232
Mason, Ann, 235
  Cornelius, 148
  Francis, 82
  Hannah, 80
  James, 23, 90, 95, 150, 236
  Martha, 217
  Mary, 217, 235, 366
  Samuel, 40, 56, 300
  Sarah, 217, 321
Matex, Samuel, 26
Mathews, David, 336
  John, 47
  Mary, 177, 179
  Samuel, 179
  Temperance, 177
  William, 174
Mathis, James, 97, 98
  Robert, 218
Matlack (Matlach), Elizabeth, 218
  George, 110, 136, 327, 347
  Isaac, 161
  Jane, 57
  Jeremiah, 181
  John, 123, 202
  Mary, 183, 275
  Rebecca, 136

Richard, 69, 158, 183
William, 330
Matson, Andrew, 15
  Elizabeth, 15
  Elenor, 15
  Jude, 15
  Marcy, 15
  Peter, 15
Mattheries, Marcy, 292
Mattison, Jacob, 16, 50, 135, 359
Matton, Elenor, 93
Maxfield, Abigail, 88
  Ann, 218
  David, 218
  Elizabeth, 223
  John, 218
  William, 88, 154
Maxwell, Ann, 218
  Esther, 371
  Gertrude, 218
  James, 371
  John, 15, 149, 183, 275
  Samuel, 218
  William, 25, 218, 261
May, Bowes, 212
  George, 298, 308
  John, 263, 367
Mayhew, John, 265, 274, 300
  Thomas, 8, 274, 300
Mayson, James, 90
Meadlis, Hannah, 219
  Samuel, 219
Mecum, John, 132, 241
Meeker, Abigail, 219
  Abraham, 219
  Charity, 219
  Daniel, 219, 220
  Edward, 316
  Gabriel, 219
  Hannah, 219, 220, 298
  Isaac, 298
  James, 80
  John, 67, 219, 220
  Mary, 219
  Mary Ann, 220
  Michael, 219
  Moses, 219, 220
  Nathaniel, 219, 220
  Obadiah, 364
  Phebe, 219
  Rachel, 219, 220
  Susannah, 219, 220
  Stephen, 259, 333
Megie, John, 159, 219
  Phebe, 219
  Safety, 273
  (see Magee)
Megrey, Edward, 163
Meldrum, George, 365
Meller, Jost, 80, 81, 217, 260
Melvin, William, 46
Menns, Gershom, 265
Mercer, William, 261, 262
Merrick, Roger, 245
Merrien, Merriam, 308
Merriot, Derick, 280
  Philip, 139
  Yanika, 280
  (see Marriot)
Merry, Major John, 106
  John, Jr., 106
  Mary, 220
Merselius, Catherine, 220
  Hannah, 220

John, 160, 220
Peter, 220
Mershon, Henry, 38, 40, 299
Messenger, William, 63
Messhow, Elizabeth, 220
Mestayer, Daniel, 71, 148, 213, 229, 294, 308, 366
  Henry D., 308
  Mary, 221, 294
Metseler, Abraham, 128
  Lodewych, 136
Mickle, Archibald, 32, 229
  Benjamin, W., 38
  Hannah, 221
  Isaac, 32, 97, 104, 221, 298, 301, 308
  John, 7, 8, 128, 136, 168, 324
  Joseph, 221
  Mary, 10
  Prudence, 221
  Rachel, 221
  Ruth, 221
  Samuel, 266
  Sarah, 221
  William, 38, 162, 338
Middagh, Angletie, 140
  Dirck, 140
  Maudlen, 62
  Peter, 16, 372
  Tunis, 95, 140, 280, 325
Middleton, Bulia, 221
  Hester, 221
  Hudson, 139, 164, 167
  Jane, 330
  Mary, 167, 221
  Nathaniel, 164, 167, 221, 229
  Rebecca, 202
  Sarah, 36
  Thomas, 110, 167, 240, 328
  William, 221
Miers, Ann, 73
  Anna, 223
  George, 13, 173
  Jane, 103
  John, 103
  Mary P., 260
  Michael, 73
  (see Myer)
Mifflin, G., 139
Miles, Francis, 29, 70, 106, 132, 342
  John, 72, 223
Miller, Aaron, 222
  Andrew, 222, 227, 297
  Barbara, 28
  Benjamin, 222
  Christopher, 257
  David, 121
  Ebenezer, 41, 299, 316
  Ebenezer, Jr., 41, 116
  Elizabeth, 199, 222, 228, 242
  Hannah, 222
  Hester, 146
  Jacob, 208
  James, 209, 230, 275
  John, 17, 59, 146, 209, 222, 232, 237
  Josiah, 49, 54
  Jost, 167, 337
  Michael, 175, 223, 234
  Moses, 219, 222
  Paul, 60
  Richard, 222
  Samuel, 19, 179, 215, 259, 279, 367

INDEX OF NAMES OF PERSONS 429

Samuel, Jr., 79
Susannah, 222
William, 14, 151, 222, 228, 259
Millican, John, 222
  Thomas, 368, 369
  (see Mollegin)
Mills, David, 51
  Elizabeth, 222
  Ephraim, 52
  Isaac, 115, 222, 232
  Isaac, Jr., 51
  James, 222
  Joanna, 222
  John, 222
  Martha, 115
  Mary, 177, 222
  Phebe, 222
  Samuel, 222
  Timothy, 167
  William, 222
  Mr., 346
Milnor, Martha, 148
Milton, Ann, 223
  Timothy, 223
Minary, Mary, 185, 186
Mingus, Jerome, 281
Minicomb, Rachel, 202
Mink, Andrew, 223
  John, 223
  Martin, 254
  Sarah, 223
  Susannah, 223
Minneer, Christian, 358
Minthorn, Richard, 54, 103
  William, 88
Mireover, Abraham, 13
Miseroll, Elizabeth, 258
  John, 258
  Peter, 356
Mitchel, Daniel, 68, 223
  Elizabeth, 150, 223
  Isaac, 68, 223
  Jacob, 329
  James, 85, 223
  John, 223
  Joseph, 195
  Lewis, 150
  Margaret, 85, 223
Mitchell, Nathaniel, 222
  Patrick, 173
Moelich, Johannes, 5
Moffat, Anne, 116
  Samuel, 116
Molate, Derick, 212
Mollegin, John, 212
  Moses, 212
  Robin, 212
  (see Millican)
Monday, Benjamin, 248
Monee, Abraham, 223
  Abraham, Jr., 223
  Elizabeth, 223
Monfort, John, 280
  Peter, 282
  Peter, Jr., 280
Monigle, William, 46
Monrow, John, 44
Montgomery, Alexander, 224
  Burnet, 224
  James, 224
  Mary, 223, 224
  Robert, 224, 325, 371
  William, 148, 224
Mood, William, 69
Moodey, Ruth, 224
Moon, Alice, 224
  Edward, 148
  Margaret, 121, 237
Mooney, Nicholas, 237
Moore, Aaron, 226
  Abigail, 110, 226, 227
  Alexander, 148, 172, 319, 355, 365
  Anabel, 228
  Ann, 36, 224, 227, 354
  Benjamin, 206, 224, 225, 226, 227, 357
  Christian, 134
  Cornelius, 227
  Daniel, 224, 225, 228
  Eber, 227
  Edward, 227
  Eliza, 134
  Elizabeth, 224, 225, 226
  Ely Moses, 134
  Enoch, 116, 224, 225, 227, 232
  Ephraim, 134
  Esther, 227
  Frances, 225
  Ganne, 225
  Gershom, 225
  Grace, 225
  Hannah, 224
  Helena, 225
  Henry, 227, 251
  Hope, 224, 225
  Isaac, 227
  Jacob, 18, 247, 291
  James, 225, 354
  Joanna, 226
  Job, 225
  John, 84, 122, 138, 134, 224, 225, 226, 227, 308, 311, 354
  Jonathan, 227
  Joseph, 30, 31, 33, 131, 224, 225, 226, 227, 319
  Kesiah, 226
  Martha, 226
  Mary, 84, 147, 225, 226, 227
  Michael, 122, 227
  Nancy, 227
  Nathan, 86, 170, 227
  Nathaniel, 226, 242, 299
  Patrick, 250
  Peter, 7
  Phebe, 225, 226
  Rachel, 52, 53, 94, 224, 225
  Rebecca, 134
  Richard, 55, 101, 134
  Robert, 59, 209, 227, 230
  Rosannah, 227
  Ruth, 225
  Samuel, 110, 133, 139, 224, 225, 226, 227, 325
  Sarah, 224, 227, 228
  Stephen, 225
  Susannah, 224
  Thomas, 20, 157, 167, 224, 225, 227, 228
  Valerian, 227
  William, 63, 66, 94, 134, 224, 225, 325
  (see More)
Moores, Daniel, 12, 236, 312, 349
  Experience, 227
  Marion, 228
  Mary, 227, 228
  Rachel, 228
Mootrey, Elizabeth, 228
Mordecai, Moses, 121

More, Jacob, 214
  Mary, 354
  (see Moore)
Morehouse, David, 228
  John, 228
  Mary, 228
  Stephen, 54, 103
  Susannah, 228
Moreland, Jacob, 299
  John, 228, 299
  Lydia, 299
Morford, Garret, 10, 232
  Jared, 325
  John, 201
Morgan, Abraham, 229
  Benjamin, 34, 228, 229, 237
  Daniel, 166, 302
  David, 229
  Evan, 149, 181
  George, 57, 155, 229
  George, Jr., 155
  Hannah, 228
  James, 333
  Jane, 229
  Jonathan, 229
  Joseph, 48, 198, 228, 229, 305, 358
  Lydia, 228, 229
  Martha, 229
  Mary, 229
  Morris, 148
  Patrick, 278
  Rachel, 228
  Randall, 229
  Rebecca, 217
  Sarah, 228
  Thomas, 148
  William, 154
Morland, John, 248
Morlaw, John, 82
Morris, Anthony, 55, 134
  Betty, 230
  Eleanor, 230
  Elizabeth, 9, 140
  Frederick, 140
  George, 350
  Jacob, 351
  John, 68, 130, 230
  John, Jr., 145, 174
  Joseph, 71
  Justus, 330
  Col. Lewis, 233
  Mary, 45, 230
  Richard, 234
  Ruth, 230
  Samuel, 229
  Sarah, 82, 220, 302
  Stephen, 46, 79, 330
  Susannah, 230
  Thomas, 230
  William, 44
  William, Jr., 297
Morrison, Agnes, 230
  David, 230
  Isaac, 230
  James, 230
  John, 230
  Margaret, 230
  Martha, 230
  Matthew, 118, 180, 249
  Mary, 230
  Sarah, 230
Morse, Amos, 215, 256
  Jacob, 15
  John, 15
  Joseph, 256, 328
  Joseph, Jr., 37, 256
  Magdalen, 15
  Mathias, 15
  Peter, 15
  Robert, 60, 86
Morton, Benjamin, 130
  Thomas, 16, 36, 123
  William, 145
Moshell, Esther, 230
Moslander, Abraham, 231
  Grace, 161
  Peter, 115, 251
Moss, William, 193
Mott, Asher, 163, 231, 317
  Gershom, 84, 231, 264, 355
  Gershom, Jr., 208
  James, 65, 125, 161, 162, 252
  John, 231
  Margaret, 231
  Sarah, 231
  Thomas, 231
  William, 261
Mounson, Ann, 231
  Eleanor, 231
Mount, Elsie, 340
  Ezekiel, 55
  Frances, 45
  George, 129, 231
  Hannah, 231
  Jemima, 231
  John, 231, 357
  John, Jr., 231, 325
  Joseph, 231, 340
  Mary, 231
  Mathias, 90, 232, 357
  Ordey, 231
  Samuel, 232
  Timothy, 232, 357
  Thomas, 129, 231, 232
  William, 259
Mountor, William, 165
Mourise, Frederick, 141
Muford, Jeremiah, 20
  Martha, 20
Muir, Robert, 253
Mulford, Aaron, 232
  Benjamin, 84, 232, 289
  Charity, 232
  Daniel, 232
  Elizabeth, 22, 67
  Ezekiel, 53, 143, 232, 244
  Jeremiah, 70
  Jonathan, 25, 53, 88
  John, 294
  Job, 322
  Joseph, 232
  Lewis, 60, 87, 219, 232, 237
  Mary, 232
  Moses, 232
  Rachel, 232
  Ruth, 315
  Stephen, 23, 85, 176, 232, 288, 294
  Thomas, 232
  William, 232
Mullica, Christian, 162
  Mary, 232
Mullin, (Mullen), Edward, 83, 130, 232, 290, 311
  Elizabeth, 233, 311
  John, 233
  Joseph, 17, 233
  Martha, 233
  Mary, 233, 311, 331

INDEX OF NAMES OF PERSONS 431

Patty, 311
Sally, 311
Mulliner, John, 62, 111
Mulloy, Dennis, 167
Mulock, James, 149, 183, 184, 373
Mun, John, 267
  Joseph, 78, 233
Mundin, Kittrell, 216
Mundy, Thomas, 217
Munroe, George, 139
  John, 266
Munson, Stephen, 363
  Tama, 348
Murfin, Mary, 241
  William, 44, 82, 233, 241, 248
Murgatroyd, James, 87
Murphy, Cornelius, 133
  Hardin (?), 233
  John, 135, 166
  Owen, 75
  Stephen, 369
  William, 82
Murray, Abram, 116
  Charles, 134
  James, 58
  Joseph, 75, 76
Murrel, Samuel, 164
Murrill, William, 369
Murrow, Joseph, 197
Myer (Myers), Abram, 234
  Cornelius, 234
  Isaac, 234
  Jacob, 234
  Jannetie, 234
  Johannes, 234
  Martin, 234
  Mary, 234
  (see Miers)

N

Nathermuch, Mathias, 128
Naylor, Benjamin, 357
  Esther, 357
Neaffey (Nevius), Lucas, 73
Nealson, Christianna, 234
  Margaret, 234
  Mathias, 249
Nefies, Catherine, 234
Negus, Levinah, 234
Neill, James, 130
Neilson, James, 18
  John, 82, 162
  Samuel, 39, 80, 274
Neisbet, James, 178
Nelinger, Elizabeth, 76
Nelson, Elizabeth, 102
  John, 102, 181
  Mary, 102
Neume, Brunt, 340
Nevius, David, 55, 295
  Peter, 55, 304, 312
Newbold, Barzillai, 292, 319
  Hannah, 235
  John, 142
  Joshua, 235
  Michael, 68, 130, 148, 292, 264, 281
  Rachel, 235
  Sarah, 234, 235
  Susannah, 281
  Thomas, 235
Newbrey, William, 117
Newby, Gabriel, 234

Newcomb, Joanne, 238
  Joseph, 142
  Silas, 115, 252, 267, 287
  William, 142, 239, 247, 289
Newell, Elizabeth, 45
  Hugh, 96
  James, 41, 89, 171, 210, 264, 272, 294, 323
  Mary, 235
  Robert, 273
Newman, Rachel, 105, 106
  Winchy, 178
Newton, Elizabeth, 118
  Hannah, 177
  Isaac, 235
  Joseph, 97, 313
  Mary, 118
  Nathan, 192
  Rachel, 235
  Samuel, 81, 118
  Susannah, 118
Niblet, Samuel, 7
Nickinson, Deborah, 235
Nickle, Daniel, 174
  William, 41, 69, 336
Nichols, Elizabeth, 143
  Humphrey, 79, 343
  Richard, 225
  Robert, 160, 204, 294, 358
  Simon, 60
  Theophilus, 20
  Dr., 235
Nicholson, Abel, 305
  Ann, 217
  Deborah, 131
  George, 344
  Isabel, 235
  John, 148, 235, 273, 282, 366
  Joseph, 236
  Nehemiah, 129, 130
  Rachel, 236
  Samuel, 56, 113, 148, 235, 305, 341
  Thomas, 345
  William, 235, 300
Nider, Mathias, 101
Nield, Judith, 349
Nightingale, Sarah, 94
Nilukirk, Abraham, 98
Nipe, Aaron, 248
  Daniel, 248
  Mary Q., 248
  Moses, 248
  Isaac, 248
  John, 248
  Robert, 248
  Thomas, 248
Nisbett, Jonathan, 198
Noble, Edward, 148
  Joseph, 47, 149, 302
  Robert, 149
Noe, Daniel, 236
  Isaac, 215, 236, 256
  John, 236
  Marsh, 147
  Peter, 236
Noland, Marmeduke, 164
Norbury, Jane, 52, 53
Norcross, Jane, 314
  Joshua, 314
  William, 148, 250
Nordike, Henry, 49
Norman, Edward, 12
Norris, Abigail, 256
  Frances, 237

Hannah, 237
Henry, 237
John, 236, 237
Joseph, 236
Martha, 237
Nathaniel, 237
Rebecca, 13
Richard, 357
Sarah, 236, 237
Thomas, 13, 236, 237
North, Zorobabel, 241
Norton, Daniel, 207
 Eunice, 143
 George, 143, 237
 Jonathan, 308
 Mary, 237
 Nathaniel, 237
 Phebe, 237
Norwood, Andrew, 209
 Anne, 333
Nox, Mary, 359
 Nancy, 359
Nutbold, Michael, 134
Nuton, Hannah, 179
Nutt, Levi, 292
Nuttman, Ephraim, 238
 Hannah, 237
 Isaac, 238
 James, 239, 330
 John, 238
 Phebe, 21, 238
 Samuel, 238
 Sarah, 238

O

Oakford, Hannah, 354
 Isaac, 316
 John, 229, 354
 Samuel, 125
 William, 27, 94, 316, 322, 323
Oblith, Elizabeth, 357
O'Brien, Daniel, 264
 Mary, 238
 William, 246
O'Conner, Timothy, 306
Odell, Temperance, 70
Ogborn, Caleb, 127, 137
 Margaret, 240
 Mary, 238
 (see Osborn)
Ogden, Abdon, 238
 Benjamin, 238
 Catherine, 238
 Daniel, 24, 86, 215, 239, 240, 299, 366
 Daniel, Jr., 240
 David, 24, 79, 90, 147, 237, 238, 239, 254, 279, 303, 348, 350, 355
 David, Jr., 267
 Edward, 239
 Elizabeth, 28, 239
 Elmer, 105, 238
 Ezekiel, 159
 Gabriel, 26, 230, 348
 Hannah, 237
 Hannah O., 239
 James, 239
 Jason, 105, 238
 Jedediah, 239
 Joel, 238
 John, 35, 81, 87, 105, 151, 155, 157, 159, 175, 209, 219, 230, 238, 240, 249, 298, 304, 310, 328, 359

John, Jr., 155, 159, 178, 267, 359
Jonathan, 238, 239
Joseph, 17, 24, 60, 86, 146, 220, 238, 259, 314, 329, 352
Josiah, 142, 238, 239, 348
Josiah, Jr., 348
Josiah (3rd), 220
Lewis, 25, 90, 91, 93, 149, 239, 243, 276, 277, 310, 347
Mary, 105, 222, 238
Moses, 219, 230
Nathaniel, 191, 238, 310
Rhoda, 239
Richard, 238
Robert, 20, 26, 56, 90, 122, 135, 151, 214, 215, 220, 222, 240, 259, 275, 322, 367
Samuel, 239, 314
Sarah, 277
Thomas, 17, 24, 38, 67, 86, 239, 278, 355
Uzal, 25, 26, 45, 52, 58, 78, 79, 81, 90, 92, 94, 128, 191, 234, 238, 239, 250, 264, 268, 272, 285, 298, 305, 306, 310, 315, 317, 335, 338, 339
Zephaniah, 238, 239
Ogley, Elizabeth, 92
O'Harrah, George, 239
 James, 6, 239
 Mary, 239
 Sarah, 239
Okeson, John, 254
Okhill, George, 245
 John, 245
Oldale, Ann, 151
 Lemuel, 151
 Solomon, 151
Olden, Benjamin, 239
 David, 239
 James, 239
 John, 239
 Joseph, 239
 Mary, 239
 Thomas, 239
 William, 67, 101, 146, 239, 333
Oliphant, David, 89
Oliver, David, 184
 Hannah, 183
 Jeremiah, 183
 Joseph, 328
 Mary, 183
 Samuel, 191, 363
 Sarah, 63, 256
 William, 63, 256, 329
O'Neill (O'Neale), Constantine, 8
 Daniel, 46, 149
 Dennis, 139
Ong, Jacob, 292
Opdike (Opdycke), Ann, 134
 Benjamin, 8, 240
 Catherine, 240
 Elizabeth, 240
 Frank, 240
 Hannah, 240
 John, 7, 91, 185, 192, 240
 Joshua, 240
 Margaret, 134
 Sarah, 240
 William, 240
 (see Updike)
Oppie, William, Jr., 240
Ord, John, 148
Orr, George, 101
 Sarah, 101

INDEX OF NAMES OF PERSONS

Osborn (Osborne), Abraham, 159
  Andria, 240
  Adonijah, 240
  Anna, 159
  Ananias, 223, 258
  Caleb, 64, 240
  Catherine, 223
  Cooper, 240
  David, 249
  Ebenezer, 327
  Jacob, 159
  James, 240
  Joanna, 241
  John, 240
  Jonathan, 182
  Lydia, 258
  Macy, 159
  Martha, 5
  Mary, 5, 159, 240
  Michael, 240
  Samuel, 9, 29, 145, 240, 241
  William, 193, 205, 240
  (see Ogborn)
Osgood, Catherine, 250
Osler, John, 305
  Joseph, 305
  Samuel, 305, 306
Ouke, Abraham, 33
  Antje, 33
  Jacob, 58, 111
  William, 58, 99, 111, 209, 284, 207, 338
Outgilt, Frederick, 58
Overton, Constantin, 241
Owens (Owen), Ann, 241
  Benjamin, 77
  Daniel, 279
  Hannah, 241, 279
  John, 220, 279
  Lewis, 39
  Mary, 241, 279, 295
  Rebecca, 279
  Robert, 245
  Rowland, 161
  Sarah, 279
  Thomas, 241
Oxford, Charles, 160, 220

P

Pack, Benjamin, 7, 194
  Job, 63, 66, 117, 241
Padgett (Pagett), David, 53, 116, 132, 242, 265, 297
  Dorothy, 232, 242
  John, 92, 242
  Martha, 52, 53
  Moses, 56, 92
  Sarah, 242
  Thomas, 242, 265
Page, Asa, 242
  Henry, 242
  John, 319, 169
  Joseph, 81, 82
  Priscilla, 142
  Sophia, 242
  William, 272
Pain (Paine), Abraham, 121, 242
  Alpheus, 242
  Elizabeth, 242
  Hannah, 242
  John, 242
  Jonathan, 242
  Mary, 242

  Peter, 242, 299
  Rachel, 242
  Samuel, 242
Painter, Stephen, 344
Pall, Marcy, 38
Palmer, Anne, 242
  Charity, 242
  George, 148
  Isaac, 254
  Jacob, 242
  James, 242
  Jemimah, 242
  Lewis, 242
  Priscilla, 242
  Samuel, 184, 361
  Thomas, 242
Pancoast, Ann, 243
  Fanny, 243
  Grace, 243
  John, 243
  Mary, 243
  Thomas, 243, 266
  Thomasin, 243
  William, 25, 77, 114, 295, 319
Pangborn, Mary, 63
  Samuel, 51, 105
  William, 63
Parcel, Nicholas, 210
Parent, Thomas, 119
Parke, Daniel, 126, 139
  David, 147, 243
  John, 70, 106, 306
  Jonah, 243
  Joseph, 243
  Marget, 243
  Richard, 126
  Thomas, 59
Parker, Abraham, 244
  Agnes, 244
  Andrew, 244
  Bristol, 8
  Catherine, 9, 243, 248
  Clarinda, 8
  Elisha, 84, 245
  Elizabeth, 243, 244, 248
  Isabel, 40
  Jacob, 202, 244
  James, 116, 244, 245
  Jane, 244
  John, 68, 244, 245, 248, 307, 312, 315
  Joanna, 195, 243
  Josiah, 36, 71, 200, 244
  Joseph, 10, 71, 244
  Lewis J., 245
  Mary, 244, 245
  Nathaniel, 248
  Peter, 130, 244
  Richard, 248
  Robert, 248
  Samuel, 36, 51, 63, 198, 243
  Surviah, 244
  Thomas, 12, 61, 110, 244
  William, 40, 244
Parkinson, Thomas, 286
Parmyter, Paroclus, 339
Parr, Hannah, 245
  Isaac, 126
  James, 245
  John, 245
  Mary, 245
  Samuel, 148, 245
  William, 245
Parrock, John, 305
Parrot & Ambler, 274

Parrot, Elizabeth, 245
  James R., 212
  Mary, 212, 245
  Rebeccah, 309
  Richard, 212, 245
  Samuel, 24
  William, 59, 179, 212, 245
Parry, Joseph, 326
Parsell, Richard, 95
Parsons, Mary, 284
  William, Jr., 25
Parvin, Benjamin, 115
  Jeremiah, 112, 308, 366
  Josiah, 101, 148, 214, 272, 316
  Matthew, 17, 355
  Sarah, 314
  Silas, 17, 67, 167, 365
  Silas, Jr., 178
Paschall, John, 13, 80, 320
Paslo, Stephen, 79
Paterson (Patterson), Alexander, 45, 330
  Ann, 149
  Elizabeth, 245, 246
  Henry, 7
  Jane, 245, 246
  John, 149, 245, 246, 288
  Joseph, 245, 246
  Josiah, 246
  Michael, 245
  Richard, 197
  Robert, 129, 131, 240
  Thomas, 245, 274
Patison, Elizabeth, 246
  James, 246
  John, 246
  Mary, 246
  Sarah, 266
Patmor, Henry, 35
Patrick, Mary, 226
  John, 226
Patton, James, 176, 186
Paul, David, 246
  Jeremiah, 246
  John, 246
  Joshua, 246
  Nathan, 246
  Samuel, 76, 128, 246
  Sarah, 127, 246
  Uriah, 246
Paullin (Pauling), David, 247
  Elias, 247
  Esther, 247
  Grace, 247, 289
  Hannah, 247
  Henry, 247
  Jacob, 246, 247
  John, 247
  Joseph, 87, 246, 247
  Marget, 247
  Rebecca, 67, 247
  Sarah, 247
  Whitlock, 247, 289
  William, 247, 289, 304
Paxson, Henry, 11, 27, 31, 94, 130, 139, 148, 201, 202, 266, 290, 291, 295, 321, 328, 352, 368
  Edward, 190
  Martha, 291
Pea, Ephraim, 124
Peace, Joseph, 57
Peacock, Abner, 247
  Adonijah, 247
  Alexander, 247
  Elizabeth, 247

  John, 247
  Melchizedeck, 247
Peairs, James, 176, 276, 339
  Jonathan, 65
  (see Pearse, Pierce)
Peake, Mary, 202
Pearsall, Jacob, 247
  John, 247
  Martha, 247
  Mary, 247
  Phebe, 247
Pearse, Anne, 360
  Benjamin, 360
  Daniel, 37
  Hannah, 360
  Mary, 360
  (see Peairs, Pierce, Peirce)
Pearson, Achsah, 248
  Azell, 167
  Catherine, 248
  Elizabeth, 248
  Henry, 46, 354, 355
  Isaac, 24, 248
  James, 13, 113
  John, 246, 248, 269
  Joseph, 148
  Mary, 248
  Rachel, 248
  Robert, 198, 248
  Samuel, 136
  Sarah, 248
  Theodosia, 248
  (see Pierson)
Peart, Samuel, 159, 287
Peat, Frances, 165
Peck, Harbert, 294
  Joseph, 239, 326
Pedit, Susannah, 223
  George, 223
Pedrick, Elizabeth, 249
  Hugh, 156
  Jacob, 249
  John, 249
  Mary, 249
  Michael, 106
  Thomas, 156
  William, 156
Pegg, Daniel, 108
Peir, Abraham, 43
Peirce, Catherine, 279
  John, 172
Pelston, Samuel, 262
Pemberton, Israel, 41
  Israel, Jr., 69
Penn, John, 148
  William, 245
Pennington, Edward, 134
  John, 108
  Thomas, 106
Pennistown, George, 198
Penquite, Jane, 58
Penton, Amos, 154, 246, 249
  Elizabeth, 59
  Elenor, 249
  Isaac, 249, 367
  Job, 250
  Joseph, 249
  Martha, 250
  Mary, 250
  Philip, 249
  Rebecca, 249
  Ruth, 250
  William, 249
Pepper, William, 121
Perce, John, 361

INDEX OF NAMES OF PERSONS 435

Perkeson, John, 267
Perkins, Abraham, 49, 113, 149
  David, 299
  John, 68
Perlee, Anne, 349
Perriman, Joane, 250
Perrine, Anthony, 250
  Daniel, 78, 134, 215, 222, 270
  Henry, 250, 276
  James, 27, 250
  John, 250, 276
  Joseph, 250
  Martha, 250
  Nancy, 250
  Peter, 37, 250, 261
  William, 250
Perry, Richard, 139, 140
  Sarah, 250
Person, Mary, 219
  Ruth, 47
Peters, Abraham, 250
  David, 250
  Elizabeth, 250
  Henry, 250
  John, 250
  Margaret, 250
  Mary, 250
  Philip, 250
Peterson, Aaron, 251
  Abraham, 251
  Andrew, 23
  Ann, 251
  Annatje, 284
  Antje, 254
  Britta, 252
  Christiana, 251
  Daniel, 85, 251
  Elizabeth, 254
  Frederick, 251
  Gertrude, 254
  Hance, 251
  Harpert, 284
  Isaac, 251
  Jeremiah, 338
  John, 251
  Klaesje, 254
  Lause, 162
  Lawrence, 159
  Mettje, 254
  Peter, 23, 249, 251, 254
  Rachel, 251, 254
  Ruth, 252
  Sarah, 251
  Thomas, 287, 356
  Vroutje, 254
  William, 87, 251
  Zacheriah, 252, 309
  (see Pieterse)
Pettinger, Hendrick, 95
  Johannis, 140
  Richard, 94
Pettit, Amos, 186
  Benjamin, 53, 252
  Benjamin, Jr., 252
  George, 170, 171
  Isaac, 170, 171
  John, 214
  Jonathan, 114, 134, 344, 350
  Joshua, 83
  Nathaniel, Jr., 369
  William, 139, 356
Petty, Israel, 166, 355
  Thomas, 41
Pew, James, 252
  Susannah, 252

Pharo, Amos, 253
  Ann, 253
  Elizabeth, 253
  James, 67, 231, 252
  Jarvis, 252
  Timothy, 253
Phelp, Deliverance, 270
Phillips, Abigail, 170
  Abner, 269
  John, 227, 253, 282, 349
  Josiah, 155
  Philip, 171, 226
  Richard, 227
  Samuel, 253
  Sarah, 170, 253
Phillpot, Catherine, 253
  John, 108, 253, 254
  Margaret, 67
  Nicholas, 23, 108, 172, 253
Pickel, Baltis, 5, 191, 280, 282
  John Nicklas, 334
Pidgeon, Ann, 279
  William, 76
Pierce, Catherine, 279
  Elizabeth, 103
  (see Peairs, Pearse)
Pierson (Peirson), Abigail, 270
  Abraham, 41, 254, 249
  Abraham, Jr., 41
  Anzel, 60, 204, 291
  Anzel, Jr., 204, 291
  Benjamin, 41, 254
  Daniel, 63, 83, 222, 239, 325, 343, 346
  David, 249
  Dorothy, 306
  Eunice, 249
  Frances, 249
  George, 204, 291
  Hannah, 254
  Henry, 314, 322
  Isaac, 41, 254
  Joannah, 249, 305, 283, 349
  John, 41, 219, 299
  Jonathan, 249
  Joseph, 306
  Mary, 69
  Nathaniel, 249
  Rebecca, 249
  Samuel, 78, 249
  Sarah, 249
  Surviah, 249
  Theophilus, 315
  Timothy, 254
  William, 213, 249, 301
Pieterse, Antie, 128
  Jurie, 128
  Matteys, 162
  Thomas, 73, 125
  (see Peterson)
Pigot, Edward, 26, 189
Pike, James, 151, 152
  John, 173
  Nathaniel, 33
  Timothy, 33
  Zebulon, 33, 84
Pimm, John, 167
  Mary, 167, 254
Pincock, John, Sr., 108
Pine, Benjamin, 141
Pintard, Abigail, 254
  Anthony, 254
  Florinda, 254
  John, 254
  Katherine, 254

Poncet S., 254
Samuel, 254
Pisher, Anne, 287
Pitcock, Sarah, 310
Pitman, Joshua, 238
  Robert, 162
Pitney, Jonathan, 316
Pitt, Jane, 233
  Thomas, 233
Pittenger, Richard, 95, 190
Plasket, William, 297
Platts (Platt), David, 52
  Hannah, 285
  Jonah, 226
  Jones, 255
  Lydia, 255
  Mary, 255
  Moses, 287
  Rebecca, 92, 93
  Rachel, 126
  Sarah, 92, 93
  Susannah, 92, 93
  Thomas, 49, 237
  Zephaniah, 285
Pledger, John, 115
Plum, Mary, 254
  Samuel, 233, 255
  Joanna, 327
Plume, John, 309
Plummer, John, 85, 105
Plumsted, Clement, 40, 198
  William, 101
Plunket, Mary, 94
Podmore, John, 41
Poland, Mathias, 189
  Samuel, 352
Pole, Anna, 301
  Edward, 301
  John, 301
  Rachel, 301
  Richard, 301
Polhemus, Cornelius, 338
  John, 172, 195
  Teunis, 107
  Theodore, Sr., 342
  Tobias, 35, 172
Poling, Cornelius, 255
  Sarah, 255
Pomyea, Dorcus, 255
  Elizabeth, 255
  Margaret, 255
  Mary, 255
  Peter, 255
  Sarah, 255
  Susannah, 255
Pond, Able, 263
  Robert, 263
Poole, John, 148
  Susannah, 255
Pope, Joseph, 279, 280
Popeloe, Peter, 150
Popeno, Abigail, 256
  James, 256
  Mary, 256
  Peter, 256, 265
Poppelsdorff, Albortus, 188, 205, 256
  William, 183
Porck, John, 61, 256
Porter, Phillip, 256
  Sarah, 77, 78
  William, 311, 329
Porterfield, John, 35
Post, Adrian, 128, 335, 338
  Hendrick, 254

Ida, 260
Janetie, 128
John, 54
Peter, 332, 334
Teunis, 123, 320
William, 260
Postgate, Thomas, 356
Potter, Daniel, 159, 256, 359, 360
  Capt. Daniel, 215
  David, 256
  Elizabeth, 61, 256
  Hannah, 256
  Isaac, 256
  Jemimah, 256
  John, 79, 92, 312
  Joseph, 10, 68, 117, 193, 203, 215, 218, 241, 252, 256
  Loes, 256
  Mary, 256, 312
  Nathaniel, 21, 238, 256
  Noadiah, 26, 256
  Phebe, 256
  Samuel, 256
  Sarah, 61, 256
Potts, John, 260
  Joshua, 257
  Nathaniel, 257
  Rebecca, 114, 257, 370
  Richard, 114, 165
  Stacey, 278
  Thomas, 77, 257, 370
  William, 25, 139, 141, 257
Pouelson, Andris, 141
Pound, Audrey, 257
  David, 277
  Elijah, 181, 152, 257, 276, 277
  Esther, 257
  Isaac, 257
  Johannah, 257
  John, 257
  Joseph, 96, 257
  Mary, 257
  Thomas, 135, 181, 257
Powell, Christopher, 257
  Daniel, 352
  Elizabeth, 217
  Grace, 257
  Howell, 18
  Isaac, 147, 244
  Jacob, 257
  James, 97, 257
  John, 106, 148, 257
  Joseph, 257
  Lena, 303
  Mary, 257
  Nicholas, 12
  Powel, 303
  Rachel, 257
  Rebecca, 12
  Richard, 313
  Robert, 64, 126, 161
  Ruth, 270
  Sarah, 257
Powers, John, 285, 293
Poyntsett, Peter, 49
Praa, Mary, 258
  Peter, 258
Prall, Abraham, 260, 359
  Isaac, 63, 227
  Peter, 22
  Peter, Jr., 359
Prance, Job, 297
  Sarah, 258
Prat, Joseph, 83

INDEX OF NAMES OF PERSONS 437

Praten, James, 258
  Thomas, 258
Predmore, John, 362
Preston, Elizabeth, 259
  Isaac, 259
  John, 259
  Joseph, 259
  Levi, 259
  Peter, 242
  Samuel, 34, 55, 66, 259, 289
  Sarah, 259
  William, 259
Price, Anna, 259
  Anthony, 259
  Benjamin, 259, 365
  Daniel, 33, 259
  Capt. Daniel, 79
  David, 145, 241, 260
  Ebenezer, 78, 203, 215, 222, 270, 279, 367
  Edith, 260
  Edward R., 90
  Eleanor, 259
  Elijah, 260
  Elizabeth, 221, 222, 259
  Ephraim, 124
  Ephraim, Jr., 146
  George, 259
  Hannah, 259
  Isaac, 294
  Jane, 260
  John, 148, 222, 240, 259, 260, 330
  Jonathan, 259
  Leticia, 260
  Margaret, 259
  Mary, 78, 259, 260, 353
  Moses, 35, 259
  Nathaniel, 66
  Philip, 145, 367
  Rebecca, 260
  Rece, 139
  Richard, 161, 183
  Robert Friend, 45, 57, 65, 102, 158, 164, 168, 221, 237, 259, 270
  Ruth, 66, 260
  Sarah, 79, 130, 170, 259, 260
Prickett, Elizabeth, 253
  Hannah, 260
  Hope, 260
  Jacob, 30, 31, 131, 137, 139, 247, 253, 260
  John, 137, 148, 314
  Richard, 260
  Sarah, 286
  William, 167, 213
  Zachariah, 139, 260
Priest, Robert, 88
Primrose, Henry, 149, 150, 184, 224, 269, 309
  Rebecca, 309
Prince, Sarah, 48
  Rev. Mr., 48
Pringal, Elizabeth, 262
Probasco, Christopher, 71, 260, 261, 338
  Dinah, 340
  Frederick, 260
  Helletie, 261
  Hendrick, 260
  Jacob, 260, 261
  John, 260, 261, 340
  Margaret, 260
Proctor, John, 73
Prosser, John, 148, 149

Prout, Elizabeth, 261
  Love, 261
Provost, John, 8
  Christiana, 258
Prudden, Joannah, 249
  Joseph, 64
  Peter, 249
Pryer, Amy, 284
Pryor, Andrew, 261, 284
  Johannis, 261
  Joseph, 191
  Nicholas, 261
  Samuel, 191
  Sarah, 261
  Thomas, 47, 191, 192
  Thomas, Jr., 47, 264
Purkins, Jane, 261
  John, 261
  Sarah, 261
  William, 261
Purviance, Samuel, 316
Purvine, David, 211
  Samuel, 211
Pyatt, Asa, 262
  James, 262, 307
  Martha, 262
  Ruth, 262
  Thomas, 163, 307

Q

Quest, Rebecca, 262
Quick, Cornelius, 81
  Petris, 332
  Willempe, 185
Quicksall, Ann, 262
  Daniel, 262
  Elizabeth, 271
  Jonathan, 262, 317, 323
  Joshua, 262
  Margrate, 271
  Mary, 262
  Rebeccah, 262
  Samuel, 262
  Sarah, 262
  Thomas, 262, 319
  William, 262
Quigg, Daniel, 266
Quigly, Bridget, 262
  Daniel, 262
  James, 262
  John, 262
  Mary, 248
  Neall, 262
  Phillip, 262
  Sarah, 262
  Susannah, 262
  Terrance, 262
  William, 262
Quimby, Martha, 69
Quinton, Temperance, 263

R

Radley, Elizabeth, 263
  John, 26, 218, 263
Rain, Samuel, 186
Raines, Robert, 300
Rambo, Benjamin, 263
  Gabriel, 51, 63, 127, 263, 331, 373
  John, 75, 76, 218, 263
  Madlena, 263
  Marta, 263
  Mary, 128

Mounce, 263
Peter, 144, 149, 154
Thomas, 25, 138, 218
John, 260, 275
Ramsden, Phebe, 260
Ramsted, Margaret, 291
Randall, Abel, 204, 337
  Alexander, 9, 38, 83, 120, 157, 162, 182, 204, 246, 263, 290, 292, 297, 302, 307, 336, 338
  Mary, 263
  Peter, 19
Randolph, Benjamin, 29
  Ephraim F., 218
  Johannah, 147
  Jonathan, 269
  Moses, 218
Rands, Simon, 369
Ranels, Gilbert, 166
Ranfeller, Margaret, 250
Ranshart, Christiana, 160
Raper, Abigail, 264
  Caleb, 273
  Joshua, 50, 62, 90, 215, 229, 311, 350
  Sarah, 264, 350
Rappleye, Catrina, 206
  Derrick, 340
  Jacob, 206
  Peter, 206
  Tunis, 261
Raris, Samuel, 149
Rattoone, Elizabeth, 264
  Mary, 147
Raworth, John, 134, 283
Rawsel, Zebulon, 126
Rawsor, William, 148
Ray, James, 177
Raymond, Christiana, 264
  Edward, 264
  Hannah, 264
  James, 264
  Peter, 264
  Rachel, 264
  Rebecca, 264
  Seth, 264
  Susannah, 264
Read, Alice, 90
  Ara., 90
  Charles, 76, 134, 201, 233
  Charles, Jr., 159
  Joseph, 253
  William, 74
Reader (Reeder), Elizabeth, 33
  Jacob, 48
  Jeremiah, 33
  John, 153
  Thomas, 185
Readey, William, 280
Reading, George, 64, 186, 241, 280, 293, 330
  John, 72, 233
  Rebecca, 330
  Richard, 326
Reagain, Anne, 161
  Benjamin, 264
  Gabriel, 264
  Lazerus, 264
  Margaret, 263
  Nebuchadnezer, 264
Reay, John, 247
  William, 247
Reckless, Anne, 367
  Joseph, 28, 57, 92, 153, 164, 242, 246, 253, 264, 318

Joseph, Jr., 164
Redford, Elizabeth, 14
  John, 123
  Samuel, 14, 44
  William, 80
Redman, Mercy, 87
  Thomas, 164, 270
Redmond, Mary, 307
Ree, Agnes, 265
  Elizabeth, 265
  James, 265
  John, 265
  Samuel, 265
  Sarah, 265
  Susannah, 265
  William, 265
Reed, Andrew, 85, 243, 248, 349
  Mrs. Andrew, 85
  Charles, 148
  Elizabeth, 248
  James, 84, 112, 119
  John, 261
  Jonathan, 265
  Joseph, 76, 170, 185, 187
  Joseph, Jr., 310
  Richard, 113
  Sarah, 248
  Thomas, 217
Rees, Aquila, 330
Reesel (see Russel)
Reeve, Ann, 265
  Berzila, 265
  Easter, 265
  Elizabeth, 41, 265
  Jesse, 265
  John, 265
  Jonathan, 265
  Joseph, 289
  Manassah, 265
  Mark, 122, 255, 289, 341
  Martha, 265
  Mary, 265
  Micajah, 265, 266
  Millicent, 122
  Nathan, 265
  Nathaniel, 207
  Puryer, 265
  Rachel, 265
  Rebecca, 148, 265
  Ruth, 265
  Samuel, 138, 265, 266
  Sarah, 265
  Walter, 265
  William, 265
Reeves, Abraham, 116, 174, 178, 179
  Anne, 231, 266
  Elizabeth, 231
  James, 231
  John, 59, 178, 231, 266
  Johnson, 178
  Joseph, 231, 289
  Lemuel, 178
  Mabel, 178
  Martha, 231
  Mary, 231, 338
  Micajah, 274
  Sarah, 126, 130, 230
  Thomas, 114, 173, 214, 266
  Walter, 266
Reid, Jean, 74
Reily, Charles, 157
  John, 53, 101, 317
Remer, John, 55

INDEX OF NAMES OF PERSONS 439

Remington, John, 85, 176, 204, 289
  Mark, 289
  Moses, 289
  Rachel, 289
Rennie, George, 130
Reul, Henrich, 211
Reutzel, Justus, 191
Reynolds, Ann, 151, 266, 267
  Elizabeth, 46
  Ereck, 152
  John, 74, 151, 153, 162, 189, 267
  Lydia, 266
  Mary, 266
  Patrick, 11, 27, 31, 112, 230, 266, 290
  Ruth, 266
  Thomas, 17, 266
  William, 267
Rhea, David, 362
  George, 309
Rhodes, Charles, 270, 271
Rice, Daniel, 115
  James, 232
  Rowland, 149
  Thomas, 206, 320
Richards, Rev. Aaron, 43
  Aaron, 267
  Abigail, 79
  Joseph, 139, 148, 319
  Mary, 267
  Mehetibel, 267
  Moses, 204
  Nathaniel, 267
  Thomas, 205, 267
Richardson, Amy, 267
  Anna, 267
  Edward, 267
  Jacob, 143
  Jesse, 267
  John, 116
  Joseph, 159
  Mary, 267
  Nathan, 319
  Richard, 18
  Tabitha, 267
  Thomas, 51
  William, 280
Richey, James, 70
Richman, Daniel, 108
  Jacob, 138, 166, 247, 250, 265
  John, 108, 131, 193, 240, 337
  Michael, 138, 181
  Sarah, 268, 337
Richmond, Ann, 253
  Jane, 268
  Rebecca, 253
Rickets, Caleb, 79
  Con'll, 79
  Elizabeth, 37
  William, 37, 77
Rickey, Ariantie, 268
  Brice, 28, 88, 211, 268, 333
  Hannah, 20
  John, 333
Riddel, William, 73, 147, 206, 257
Rider, John, 342
Ridgway, Isabel, 281
  James, 344
  Job, 243
  John, 344
  Joseph, 130
  Lot, 129, 130, 148, 368
  Richard, 151
  Robert, 344
  Timothy, 29, 68
Ridly, Thomas, 229
Riggs, Daniel, 268
  Elizabeth, 268
  Gideon, 363
  Joseph, 44, 330
  Joseph, Jr., 25, 268, 306
  Sarah, 268
  Samuel, 171
Right, James, 86
Ringo, Albartus, 268
  Catrina, 268
  Cornelius, 268
  Henry, 265, 268
  John, 268, 313
  Philip, 256, 268
Risdrell, John, 330
Risley, Samuel, 198
Ritchie, Ann, 268
  James, 70
  John, 268
Rite, Isaac, 269
Rittenhouse, Rebecca, 120
  Isaac, 120
Rivers, Joseph, 148
Riyel, Mary, 101
Robards, Samuel, 327
Roberson, Elizabeth, 269
  Esther, 6
  Phebe, 269
  Samuel, 87
  Sarah, 6
  William, 269
Roberts (Robarts), Abigail, 269
  Daniel, 270
  Elizabeth, 269, 270
  Enoch, 70, 110, 123, 138, 202, 278, 311, 327
  Ephraim, 270
  Ezra, 270
  Hannah, 154, 269, 270
  Jacob, 270
  John, 23, 110, 132, 269, 270, 366
  Jonathan, 205, 223
  Joseph, 269, 270
  Joshua, 311
  Keziah, 155, 270
  Moses, 159
  Nathan, 276
  Rebecca, 311
  Richard, 270
  Samuel, 16, 269
  Sarah, 269, 270
  Stephen, 269
  Thomas, 93, 124, 161, 163, 270, 271, 318, 331
  William, 223
Robertson, Duncan, 43, 109, 239, 270, 271
  John, 271
  Margaret, 270
  Mary, 271
  Patrick, 271
  William, 157, 271
Robeson, Edward, 107
  Ellinor, 107
  Jonathan, 111
Robins (Robbins), Aaron, 127, 271, 272
  Abigail, 272
  Amy, 272
  Andrew, 272
  Ann, 272
  Benjamin, 271
  Daniel, 109, 133, **134**, 271, **272**
  Elias, 18

Elisha, 252
Elizabeth, 271, 272
Ephraim, 271
James, 271
Jesse, 271
Job, 303
John, 60, 224, 269, 271
Jonathan, 171
Joseph, 66, 74, 75, 271
Judith, 269, 271
Lucia, 271
Lydia, 272
Marcy, 271
Margaret, 272
Martha, 272
Mary, 269, 272
Moses, 59, 109, 110, 133, 224, 271, 272, 294
Nathan, 271, 272
Nathaniel, 271, 294
Obadiah, 271, 341
Priscilla, 269
Rachel, 272
Randolph, 272
Richard, 120, 269, 271
Samuel, 271, 272
Sarah, 269
Sibbel, 269
Theodosia, 269
Vincent, 272
William, 271
Robinson, Abigail, 272
Andrew, 255, 272
Anne, 61
Dan, 24
Dearie, 272
Dinah, 195
Esther, 172
James, 172
John, 272
Margaret, 272
Mary, 272
Rebekah, 265
Thomas, 11, 134, 272, 370
Robson, Lambert, 60
Thomas, 87, 127, 139
Rock, Mary, 140
Thomas, 140
Rockefeller, Peter, Jr., 192
Rockett, James, 262
Rockhill, Abigail, 61
Achsah, 61
Amos, 202
Anne, 16, 61
Bridget, 61
David, 5, 16, 31, 241, 318
Edward, 329
Hannah, 61
Jerusha, 202
John, 29, 318, 329
Margaret, 61, 77
Mary, 61
Richard, 61
Robert, 319
Samuel, 77, 322
Sarah, 61
Rodgers, Dinah, 150
Elizabeth, 150
James, 229
Mary, 150
Sarah, 150
(see Rogers)
Rodman, Anna, 273
Elizabeth, 273
John, 273

Mary, 273
Samuel, 273
Scamon, 273
Thomas, 102, 139, 167, 229, 259, 273
William, 273
Roe, David, 152, 273
Elizabeth, 282
Henry, 149
John, 362
Roelofson, Herman, 273, 334, 335
Margaret, 335
Roelof, 273, 329
Rogers, Amos, 39
Ann, 273, 306
David, 79, 230
Elizabeth, 273
Esther, 285
Isaac, 83, 88, 135, 136, 175, 273, 311
John, 248, 273, 311
Joseph, 178
Martha, 273
Mary, 306
Mehetabel, 306
Nathaniel, 59
Othniel, 9, 160
Rebecca, 311
Robert, 39
Samuel, 20, 59, 88, 126, 273
Thomas, 273, 306
William, 49
(see Rodgers)
Rolfe (Rolph), Benjamin, 133
Elizabeth, 274
Hannah, 122, 274
Henry, 274
John, 7, 122, 274, 333
Jonathan, 274
Moses, 87
Samuel, 87, 88, 208
Sarah, 274
Roll, Feytie, 332
John, 332
Romine, James, 90
James, Jr., 90
Luke, 342
Romyne, Claes J., 373
Roosa, Catherine, 274
Dirck, 274
Isaac, 274
Jacob, 274
Marya, 274
Rebecca, 274
Rosaboome, Deborah, 342
Garret, 342
Hendrick, 342
Rose, Abraham, 274
Deborah, 261
Ebenezer, 261
Eliza, 261
Elizabeth, 98, 274
Ezekiel, 113
John, 150
Martha, 274
Mary, 113
Patience, 261
Phebe, 261
Stephen, 261
William, 69
Rosekrans, Johannis, 72
John, 333
Ross, Alexander, 201
Andrew, 21, 275
Catharine, 275

INDEX OF NAMES OF PERSONS 441

Christopher, 275
Daniel, Jr., 79, 132
David, 203, 275
Elizabeth, 275
George, 134
George (3rd), 37
Hannah, 275
Jacob, 275
Joanna, 215, 275
John, 21, 58, 79, 94, 134, 157, 215, 228, 275, 328, 355
John, Jr., 134
Joseph, 146
Joseph, Jr., 73
Lydia, 275
Marcy, 169, 275
Nathaniel, 275
Phebe, 21, 275
Robert, 51, 275
Ruth, 267
Samuel, 53
Sarah, 275
Thomas, 275
William, 275
Doctor, 130
Rossell, Ann, 133
Barzillia, 50
Briggs, 130
George, 38, 40
John, 38
Mary, 190
Peter, 133
Rebecca, 275
Stephen, 133
Thomas, 133, 148
Zachariah, 63, 74, 139, 144, 157, 190, 328, 363
Zachariah, Jr., 17, 121, 129, 157, 361, 363
Roteham, Christian, 281
Rounsavell, Richard, Jr., 319
Rouse, John, 53
John, Jr., 198
Row, Henry, 148
Rowand, Abigail, 275
Alexander, 275
Jacob, 275
James, 275
John, 275
Joseph, 275
Mary, 275
Sarah, 275
Rowe, Mary, 276
Rowland, Jonathan, 248
Rowlison, John, 78, 105
Mary, 78
Roy, John, 186, 209, 230, 268
Royal, Hannah, 314
Royse, John, 209
Rudderow, Abigail, 89, 305
Meribah, 202
William, 200
Rue, Ellenor, 276
James, 276
Jean, 276
John, Jr., 276
Joseph, 67, 276
Margaret, 276
Mathias, 276
Matthew, 305
Samuel, 276
William, 276
Rugg, Prudence, 366
Rumbah, Jacob, 198
Rumford, Elias, 276

John, 87, 162, 163, 336, 351
Jonathan, 163, 276
Thomas, 276
Runders, Richard, 169, 277
Runkle, Adam, 212
Runyon, Benjamin, 276, 277
Elizabeth, 152, 276
Joseph, 7, 276, 277
Martha, 277
Nathaniel, 197
Peter, 25, 152, 195, 276, 277
Peter, Jr., 257
Philip, 276
Providence, 276
Reune, 34, 51, 61, 97, 98, 146, 195, 216, 244, 257, 277, 307, 331
Rezia, 258
Thomas, 277
Vincent, 32, 277
Zirviah, 217
Rusco (Roscoe), Nathaniel, 34, 54, 119, 140, 180, 196, 197, 199, 218, 241, 323, 367
Russell, Catherine, 344
David, 284, 308
James, 149
John, 260
Rebecca, 260
Robert, 112
William, 18, 173
William, Jr., 101
Rutan, Abraham, 293, 339
Sarah, 179, 277
Peter, 293
Peter, Jr., 179
Rutherford, James, 321
Ryall, Henry, 211
Ryan, James, 245
Sarah, 86
Thomas, 319
Ryerse (Ryerson), George, 99, 108, 332
Martin, 64
Marytje, 99
Ryker, Catherine, 277
Ryley, David, 277
Elizabeth, 277
James, 277
Jonathan, 277
Levi, 277
Lornamy, 277
Mark, 320
Martha, 277
Nathan, 277

S

Saint, Daniel, 161
Elizabeth, 277
Thomas, 297
Sale, Edward, 94, 310
Salmon, Abner, 277
Hannah, 277
Nathaniel, 278
Salnave, Abigail, 278
Saltar, Richard, 68, 197
Thomas, 199
Sanderson, Anthony, 150
Sands, Mary, 90
Sanford, John, 178
Robert, 147
Sargent (see Sergeant)
Sarrin, Christian, 15
Sartor, Henry, 33
John, 23

Saruel, Laufet, 289
Satterthwaite, Elizabeth, 278
  Joshua, 278
  Mary, 278
  Richard, 318
  Samuel, 142, 154
  William, 278
Saul, Joseph, 307
Saunders, Edward, 143
  John, 11, 47, 350
  Philip, 160, 326
Savage, Jacob, 358
  James, 33
  Joseph, 115, 161, 207, 230, 251, 269, 345
  Martha, 161
  Robert, 43, 109, 186, 270, 349
Savery, Esther, 278
  Peter, 299
  William, 53
Sawyer, Hannah, 148
Say, Samuel, 245
  Thomas, 245
Sayre (Sayres), Abram, 115
  Ananias, 29, 30, 114, 115, 242, 279, 287, 302
  Benjamin, 115, 279, 365
  Daniel, 35, 222, 333
  David, 24, 238, 252, 277, 279, 288, 289, 355, 173
  Ephraim, 46, 51, 219
  Ichabod, 279
  James, 371
  Jedediah, 279
  John, 35, 279
  Jonathan, 17, 188, 237
  Martha, 279
  Mehetabel, 278
  Patience, 279
  Rebecca, 35, 179, 279
  Ruth, 348
  Samuel, 279
  Sarah, 238
  Thomas, 9, 52, 118, 132, 355, 264, 279, 314, 358, 364
Scat, Anne, 17
Scattergood, Elizabeth, 280
  Caleb, 37, 129, 280
  James, 321
  John, 279
  Joseph, 44, 112, 130, 139, 231, 259, 301
  Rebecca, 279
  Thomas, 112, 262, 279, 356, 371
Schaffer, Adam, 291
Schamp (Schomp), Aerian, 280
  Anne, 280
  Antia, 280, 282, 325
  George, 280, 282
  Hannah, 280
  Hendrick, 280
  Jost, 282
  Knearte, 280, 282
  Margaret, 280, 282
  Peter, 282
  Sarah, 282
  Seaby, 282
  Nicholas, 280
  Peter, 280
  Phebe, 280
  Sarah, 280
  Stonchy, 280
Scharfenstein, Johannes P., 329
Schellinks, Jane, 280
  Josena, 143

Schenck, Albert, 88, 180, 281
  Garret, 73, 153, 187, 191, 204, 281
  George, 281
  Hendrick, 342
  Jacob, 88
  Jannetie, 281
  John, 178, 179, 180, 210, 281
  Joseph, 179
  Koert, 204
  Lucas, 164, 176, 250, 336, 339
  Mary, 73, 342
  Nelly, 204
  Peter, 281, 342
  Philip, 281
  Roelof, 187, 281
  Sarah, 281
  William, 281
Schmidt, Adam, 187
Schmuck, Peter, 369, 370
  (see Snook)
Schneider, George, 150
Schooley, Avis, 253
  Frances, 281
  John, 148, 281, 349
  Joiada, 319
  Jonathan, 281
  Mary, 281
  Michael, 146
  Rachel, 107, 281, 349
  Samuel, 253
  Sarah, 44
  William, 64, 114, 150, 153, 216, 269, 271
Schoonover, Henry, 333
  Michloss (Michael), 333
Schorp, Mary, 282, 286
Schuffels, Martin, 135
Schureman, Jacobus, 71
Schuyler, Arent, 45, 151, 188
  Cornel P., 78
  Dirck, 140, 183
  Philip, 96, 146, 254
Schwart, Anna, 282
  Barbara, 282
  Catherine, 282
  Peter, 282
  Samuel, 282
  Sarah, 282
  (see Swart)
Scoby, John, 186
Scoggin, Ann, 282
Scott, Abigail, 282
  Alexander, 282
  Amy, 282
  Ann, 283
  Elizabeth, 282, 283
  Ellen, 329
  Hannah, 282
  Henry, 282
  Hester, 282
  John, 73, 101, 116, 282, 283, 311, 370
  Jonathan, 282
  Joseph, 283
  Mary, 283
  Moore, 282
  Patience, 282
  Robert, 283
  Ruth, 311
  Samuel, 283, 311, 353
  Sarah, 101
  Susanna, 283
  Temperance, 282
  Thomas, 145, 282, 353

INDEX OF NAMES OF PERSONS 443

Timothy, 282
William, 9, 283
Major, 165
Scram, David, 94
Scudder, Amos, 206, 283
  Corbett, 176
  Daniel, 206, 283
  Ephraim, 283
  Jacob, 88
  Jedediah, 283
  Jemima, 283
  John, 134, 270, 283
  Joseph, 170, 283
  Katurah, 283
  Nathaniel, 88
  Phebe, 283
  Prudence, 283
  Rebecca, 283
  Richard, 121
  Thomas, 84, 121, 122, 176, 241, 283
Scull, Abel, 112, 152, 194
  Abel, Jr., 112
  David, 298
  Elizabeth, 309
  Gideon, 94, 194, 230
  Hannah, 283
  John, 283
  Peter, 51
  Recompense, 283
Seagrave, Esther, 283
  Onesimus, 283, 337, 366
  Rebecca, 284
  Samuel, 284
  William, 284
Seal, John, 242
Search, Christopher, 272
  Lydia, 284
  William, 284
Searing, Affa, 284
  Daniel, 284
  Jacob, 284
  Jonathan, 284
  Nancy, 284
  Simon, 106
Searle, Thomas, 53
Sebring, Angenitje, 284
  Cornelius, 284, 340, 342
  Dirck, 284
  Folkert, 73, 93
  Johannes, 146
  John, 35, 284
  Joseph, 182
  Volkert, 284
Sedden, Mary, 284
Seely, Christopher, 264
  David, 256
  Enoch, 252
  Ephraim, 126
  Henry, 239
  Job, 285
  Joseph, 148
Seers, Jonathan, 335
Segler, Catherine, 285
  Henry, 285, 293
  James, 285, 293
  John, 285, 293
  Thomas, 285, 293
Seiler, Peter, 114
Selie, Ephraim, 174
Seley, David, 268
Sell, Jonathan, 364
Selove, Peter, 61
Sergeant, Daniel, 69
  Hannah, 69, 238

John, 69
Jonathan, 21, 43, 48, 178, 238, 249, 264, 269, 285, 317, 322, 348, 363
Mary, 285
Rachel, 112, 196
Samuel, 112, 196, 244, 311
Sarah, 69, 238
Thomas, 69, 79, 178
William, 115
Sevenar, John, 264
Severns, Joseph, 217
  Theodore, 72, 81, 163, 372
  Theophilus, 163, 216, 241
  Sarah, 134
Seward, Izabel, 285
Sexton, Charles, 285
  George, 285
  Japheth, 285
  Jared, 285
  Joseph, 285
  Nathaniel, 285
  Sarah, 285
Seymour, Ariantie, 342
Shaftner, Mary, 286
Shank (Schenck?), John, 246
Sharp, Amos, 139
  Ann, 314
  Anthony, 96
  Elizabeth, 137, 286, 298
  Hannah, 286, 298
  Hugh, 137, 286, 304, 314
  Isaac, 10, 99, 100, 105, 286, 298, 365, 87
  Jane, 286
  John, 139, 242, 265, 286, 304
  Joseph, 171, 206, 362
  Josiah, 286
  Mary, 96, 137, 286, 362
  Paul, 287
  Samuel, 286
  Sarah, 137
  Silvester, 200, 202
  Susannah, 286
  Thomas, 137
  William, 51, 64, 137, 139, 202, 265, 286, 304, 327
  Zeruiah, 242
Sharpenstine, Anna Gertrude, 280
  Anne, 286, 287
  Elsa, 287
  Johanas Ievry, 280
  (see Scharfenstein)
Shaver, Mary, 61
Shaw, Aaron, 287
  Abiel, 322
  Edmund, 206, 287
  Eleanor, 287
  Elishabe, 287
  Elizabeth, 239
  Elsie, 251
  Henry, 81, 268
  Icabod, 287
  Isaiah, 136
  Jeremiah, 287
  John, 65, 80, 237, 287, 324
  Joshua, 310
  Lucy, 287
  Nathan, 120, 287
  Patience, 120, 309
  Richard, 287
  Sarah, 287
  Temperance, 287
  Zachariah, 53
Sheldon, Joseph, 288

444 NEW JERSEY COLONIAL DOCUMENTS

Shepherd (Shepard), Abel, 341
  Abigail, 22, 49
  Abraham, 289
  Bilby, 125, 288
  Catherine, 288
  Cumberland, 288
  Daniel, 288
  David, 247, 288, 289, 304
  Deborah, 288
  Dickerson, 289
  Ebenezer, 288
  Eleanor, 204
  Elizabeth, 85
  Elnathan, 288
  Enoch, 176, 303, 304, 316
  Ephraim, 176, 288, 289
  Gibbons, 289
  Hannah, 286
  Job, 125, 180, 224, 262, 288, 289
  John, 70, 116, 255, 289, 321
  John, Jr., 277
  Jonadab, 81, 304
  Jonathan, 173, 288
  Joseph, 288, 289
  Kathrine, 288
  Keziah, 288
  Lovice, 289
  Martha, 288, 289, 316
  Mary, 288, 289
  Moses, 288, 289
  Nathan, 289
  Peter, 289
  Phebe, 288
  Philip, 86, 173, 288
  Rebecca, 288
  Ruth, 288, 289
  Samuel, 289
  Sarah, 288, 289
  Silvanus, 289, 313
  Stephen, 289
  Thomas, 288
  William, 148
Sherd, Anna, 289
  Frances, 289
  Lucy, 289
  Mary, 289
  William, 289
Sherin, Abram, 319
Sherman, Mary, 240
  Nathaniel, 238
Sherron, Griffin, 113
  Roger, 113, 122
Sherry, Samuel, 313, 337
Sherwin, Edith, 290
  George, 290
  Grace, 290
  James, 290
  Rebecca, 290, 347
  Sarah, 290
Shields, Robert, 29, 68, 213
  William, 321
Shimer Abraham, 353, 354
  Magdalin, 353
Shinkfield, Thomas, 315
Shinn, Abel, 138
  Aquilla, 291
  Caleb, 148, 316
  Earl, 40, 291
  Elizabeth, 291
  Francis, 17
  Gamaliel, 291
  George, 104, 266
  Jacob, 126, 130, 316
  Joseph, 290
  Levi, 57
  Mehetabel, 290
  Postrema, 291
  Ruth, 314
  Sarah, 290
  Solomon, 118
  Thomas, 69, 94, 144, 148, 167, 266, 286, 291, 314, 322
  Thomas, Jr., 200, 291
  William, 130, 266, 291, 292
Shipley, Jale, 113
  William, 113
Shipman, Jacob, 5
Shippen, William, 48
Shirm, Abram, 40
Shivers, John, 245
  Josiah, 105, 127, 154, 245, 270, 311
  Samuel, 124, 149, 364
Shophner, Redolph, 106
Shores, Samuel, 117
Shorp, William, Jr., 286
Shotwell, Abraham, 105, 174, 215, 256, 291
  Andrew, 239
  Anna, 291
  Benjamin, 291, 292
  Daniel, 105, 291
  Deborah, 291
  Hannah, 291
  Jacob, 225
  Jasper, 291
  John, 60, 64, 291
  John, Jr., 359
  Joseph, 12, 105, 174, 225, 274
  Joseph, Jr., 291
  Lydia, 291
  Mary, 291
  Rachel, 291
  Samuel, 330
Showet, Margaret, 342
Shreve, Abraham, 292
  Amos, 130
  Benjamin, 130, 292, 293
  Caleb, 33, 71, 235, 292, 293
  Israel, 292
  James, 22, 292
  John, 130, 292
  Jonathan, 130, 148
  Joseph, 292
  Joshua, 292
  Keziah, 292
  Rebecca, 292
  Samuel, 292
  Sarah, 292
  Thomas, 77, 292, 302
  William, 292
Shriner, Jane, 292, 293
Shuckburgh, Richard, 234
Shule, Atwood, 67
Shull, Jacob, 308
Shurts, Abraham, 293
  Anne, 293
  Elizabeth, 293
  Eve, 293
  George, 293
  Jane, 293
  John, 186, 293
  Margaret, 293
  Matthew, 293
  Michael, 293
  Rachel, 293
Shute, Joseph, 252
  Rebecca, 36
  Samuel, 36

INDEX OF NAMES OF PERSONS 445

Sarah, 252
William, Jr., 252
Sickelere, Catherine, 285
  (see Segler)
Sickels, Christian, 271
  Hendrick, 340
  Zackeriah, 43, 91, 340
Siddons, Achsach, 7
  Deborah, 294
  Edward, 294
  Elizabeth, 293, 294
  Ezekiel, 294
  Hannah, 294
  Henry, 286, 320
  Isaac, 294
  Joseph, 320
  Mary, 190, 294, 296, 320
  William, 170, 273, 294, 313, 320
Sidmond, John, 178
Sielden, Mary, 351
Siffin, Abel, 247
Sigler, Margaret, 178
  Thomas, 293
  (see Segler)
Sikes, John, 140
Siliman, Susan, 294
Sill, Mary, 123
Sillcock, Henry, 45, 165
Silver, Aaron, 87, 227
  Abel, 200
  Amos, 294
  Archibald, 14, 200, 205, 294
  David, 262, 294
  Gershom, 15, 294
  Hester, 294
  James, 294
  James, Jr., 135
  Job, 294
  John, 294
  Mary, 294
  Milicent, 15
  Rebecca, 294
  Samuel, 200
Silverthorn, Thomas, 243
Simcock, John, Sr., 62
Simkins, Abraham, 294
  Benjamin, 204
  Daniel, 49, 204
  David, 294
  Francis, 294
  Johanna, 294
  John, 294
  Joseph, 204
  Mercy, 294
  Rachel, 294
  William, 309, 318
Simons, Aaron, 294
  Appolonia, 294
  John, 139
  Sarah, 260
  Simon, 294
Simonson, Neeltje, 295
  (see Symonse)
Simpson, Alexander, 35, 162
  Ann, 162
  Arthur, 40
  Henry, 326
Sims, Abner, 159
  John, 264
  Joseph, 159
  Samuel, 262, 283
Singer, Johannis, 282
Sinnickson, Andrew, 39, 93, 125, 132, 145, 210, 241, 246, 253, 254, 306, 328, 370

Sip, Alche, 43
Sitlinton, Robert, 365
Sitter, Josach, 142
Skeeles, William, 130, 148, 293
Skeer, Martin, 29
Skelton, Joseph, 88, 95, 156, 165, 179, 210, 315
  Mary, 88
Skill, Samuel, 221
Skilleager, Cornelius, 120
Skillman, Jacob, 358
Skinner, Courtland, 58, 102, 150, 306, 360, 362
  Elizabeth, 262
  Gertrude, 245, 262
  Hannah, 31
  Richard, 131, 194
  Thomas, 89, 166
  Thomas, Jr., 255
  William, 150, 262
  William, Jr., 304
  Wright, 33
Skirm, Abraham, 38
Slayney, Edward, 295
Sleeper, Hannah, 295
  John, 295
  Jonathan, 295
  Leah, 295
Sleght, Johannis, 329
  Petrus, 209
Slingerlant, John, 295
Sloan, Andrew, 220, 236
  James, 221, 298, 308
Slocum, Athaliah, 296
  Elizabeth, 296
  Hannah, 296
  John, 296
  Jonathan, 296
  Katharine, 296
  Margaret, 296
  Peleg, 296
  Ruth, 296
  Susannah, 296
Small, John, 221
  Jonah, 221
  Mary, 221
Smalley, Anna D., 296
  Benjamin, 296
  Elisha, Jr., 51
  James, 296
  John, 181, 279
  Joshua, 296
  Mary, 296
  Sarah, 296
Smallwood, Ellinor, 45
  Jemima, 96
  John, 149
  Mary, 58
  William, 96, 148, 296
Smart, Catherine, 296
  Deborah, 296
  Isaac, 296
  Nathan, 86
Smedley, James, 16
Smick, Philip, 291
  William, 291
Smith, Aaron, 298
  Able, 297
  Abigail, 302
  Abner, 24
  Abraham, 18, 174, 277, 288, 300
  Alexander, 67, 297
  Andrew, Jr., 48, 113
  Anna, 301
  Ashbury, 242

Benjamin, 177, 299
Caleb, 70, 346
Carman, 299, 318
Casper, 148
Charity, 301
Christean, 300
Clark, 301
Cornell, 300
D. Jonathan, 139
Daniel, 9, 102, 130, 148, 266, 273, 297, 301, 309, 354, 360
Daniel, Jr., 264, 273, 354
David, 104, 143, 237, 298, 327
Dearie, 272
Ebenezer, 299
Eleanor, 297, 299, 301
Elias, 298
Eliezer, 24
Elihu, 144
Elijah, 298
Elisha, 298
Elizabeth, 47, 208, 300, 301
Esther, 67
Eve, 302
Experience, 301
Ezekiel, 224
Francis, 11
Gasper, 47
Gilbert, 139, 141, 301, 317
Grace, 246
Hannah, 143, 237, 301, 309
Henry, 15, 117, 298
Ichabod, 272
Jabez, 299
Jacob, 300
James, 121, 144, 151, 222, 297, 301, 302, 327, 360
Jane, 79, 298
Jasper, 39, 109
Jeremiah, 56, 300
Jesse, 297
Joannah, 298
Job, 297, 300, 302, 360
John, 18, 47, 80, 86, 102, 112, 139, 157, 182, 213, 215, 228, 297, 299, 300, 301, 327, 332, 346, 355, 371
Jonathan, 69, 268, 270, 287, 298, 301, 313, 318, 355
Joseph, 215, 298, 299, 300, 301, 302, 327
Joshua, 298
Joshua R., 264
Josiah, 271
Judith, 301
Kezia, 299
Leggit, 298, 299
Lodawick, 300
Lydia, 297
Margaret, 302
Mary, 174, 292, 297, 298, 300, 301, 327
Mathias, 178, 300
Moses, 359
Nathan, 297
Nathaniel, 300
Nehemiah, 152
Nicholas, 210
Noah, 94, 300
Patience, 260
Peter, 139
Phebe, 299, 300, 302
Philip, 102
Pile, 298
Priscilla, 298
Prudence, 117
Rachel, 45, 298, 300, 301
Ralph, 15, 28, 72, 185, 191
Richard, 19, 47, 174, 179, 192, 264, 301, 350, 354
Robert, 48, 149, 206, 266, 297, 301, 302
Robert, Jr., 264
Robert E., 67
Samuel, 11, 47, 56, 62, 148, 215, 265, 274, 301
Seth, 56, 185, 236
Susanna, 300
Sarah, 56, 151, 237, 264, 297, 298, 300, 301, 327
Sarah L., 302
Thomas, 15, 43, 139, 144, 164, 166, 207, 300
Timothy, 113, 206, 268, 277, 281, 326
Uriah, 299
Waters, 299
William, 44, 113, 151, 174, 187, 199, 213, 217, 224, 258, 298, 301, 308, 330, 362
William P., 48
Zeruiah, 298
(see Smyth)
Smithier, Joseph, 371
Smock, Abraham, 303
  Ann, 303
  Barns, 212, 303
  Catherine, 303
  Charles, 303
  Elizabeth, 303
  Garret, 303
  Ghertie, 303
  Hendrick, 303
  Jacob, 303
  Jacobus, 72
  Jane, 303
  Johannis, 212, 303
  John, 212, 261, 288, 303
  Leah, 303
  Margaret, 72
  Maria, 303
  Mathias, 261, 303
  Nelly, 303
  Peter, 208
  Rynier, 303
Smyth, Andrew, 58, 80, 92, 194, 196, 282, 362
  Benjamin, 88
  John, 53, 67, 69, 133, 136, 147, 151, 152, 194, 244, 245, 272, 279, 282, 284, 303, 323, 338, 362
  Margaret, 245, 303
  (see Smith)
Snetten, Elizabeth, 316
  Jeremiah, 316
  Joseph, 204
  Robert, 184
Snook, Catherine, 281
  John, 281
Snowden, James, 372
  John, 205, 248
  Margaret, 304
  Ruth, 267
  William, 305
Snyder, Elizabeth, 303
  William, 303
Sockwell, Elizabeth, 303
  Eve, 303
  Experience, 303

INDEX OF NAMES OF PERSONS 447

Jonadab, 303, 304
Lancit, 303
Leah, 303
Patience, 303
Phebe, 303
Rachel, 303
Soey, Nicholas, 172
Solmon, William, 285
Somers, Abigail, 6
  Hannah, 304
  James, 94, 283, 298
  James, Jr., 308
  Martha, 304
Sonmans, Peter, 192, 193
Soper, Richard, 216
Sorsby, William, 44, 148, 158
Sorter, Jacob, 304
  Johannes P., 304
South, Daniel, 304
  Dorothy, 304
  Joseph, 250, 304
Southard, Abraham, 7
Southwick, James, 112, 127, 130
  Josiah, 127
  Maim, 149
  Mayham, 304
  Rachel, 112
Southworth, William, 114
Sparks, Elizabeth, 351
  George, 305
  Henry, 141, 149, 216, 305, 314, 350, 354
  John, 49, 83, 120, 128, 266, 305, 329
  Mary, 305
  Richard, 14, 216, 218, 312, 317, 345, 351
  Robert, 305
  Simon, 128, 292, 305
  Thomas, 305, 351, 365
Spear, Tunis, 305
  Abraham, 63
  John, 63
Spence, Alexander, 305
  Hannah, 69
  Rachel, 305
Spencer, John, 131, 338
Sperling, Daniel, 80
  John, 356
  John M., 71, 342, 356
Spicer, Abigail, 305
  Deborah, 160
  Jacob, 9, 19, 131, 138, 142, 143, 160, 166, 169, 192, 193, 199, 207, 250, 290, 305, 309, 353
  Mary, 200
  Rebecca, 88, 89, 305
  Samuel, 61, 69, 89, 154, 183, 221, 228, 229, 270, 305
  Sarah, 160
  Sylvia, 160
  Thomas, 108, 154, 229, 270, 305
  Thomas, Jr., 161
Spier, Hendrick, 63
  Walter, 339
Spinning (Spining), Benjamin, 157, 214, 275
  Humphrey, 11, 329
  John, 190, 275
  Phebe, 190
Springer, Benjamin, 139
  Elizabeth, 37
  William, 191
Sproull, Robert, 89, 362
Squier, Jonathan, 68

Staats, Hendrick, 99
Stafford, John, 211
Stagg, Abraham, 351
  Nicholas, 334
Stalkop, Christian, 306
  Jane, 306
  John, 306
Stanberry, Jacob, 256
  Recompense, 59, 121, 275, 291
  Susannah, 256
Standfast, Elizabeth, 163
  John, 163
  Joseph, 163
  Margaret, 163
  Mary, 163
  Patience, 163
  William, 163
Standley (Stanly), Andrew, 71, 306
  Catherine, 306
  George, 347
  Mary, 110
Stannerd, Hannah, 151
  Lewis, 151
Staples, Martha, 306
  Mehetabel, 306
  Thomas, 322
  Thomas, Jr., 148
Stark, James, 189
Starkey, Nathan, 148
  Nathaniel, 148
Stathem, Jonathan, 116, 232, 297
  Susannah, 59
Steedam, John, Jr., 231
Steele, Isaac, 262
  James, 148
  John, 149, 304, 362
  Sarah, 178
Steelman, Alice, 306
  Charles, 162, 306
  Daniel, 306
  Haunce, 306
  James, 152, 306
  John, 94, 306
  Magdalen, 252
  Peter, 94
  Susannah, 94
Steenman, Catherine, 281
Stelle, Benjamin, 116, 296, 307
  Benjamin, Jr., 163
  Charity, 307
  Christian, 60
  Elizabeth, 307
  Experience, 307
  Isaac, 97, 98, 117, 181, 257, 296, 307
  John, 244, 307
  Lewis, 307
  Lydia, 307
  Phebe, 307
  Pontius, 76
  Rachel, 307
  Thomson, 307
Stellsts, Mary, 307
Stevens (Stephens), Benjamin, 12, 85, 240, 242
  Campbell, 147
  Elizabeth, 8
  Ezekiel, 308
  Henry, 93, 140, 141, 307, 308, 369
  Isaac, 43, 75, 97, 128, 263, 307
  James, 307
  John, 8, 100, 243, 307
  Jonathan, 308
  Mary, 126, 307, 308

Rachel, 307
Robert, 32, 97, 257, 260, 293, 307
Sarah, 307
Susannah, 307
Thomas, 299
Stevenson, Edward, 130
  Elizabeth, 84
  Elnathan, 306
  John, 248
  Samuel, 44
  Thomas, 297, 356
  William, 175, 356
Steward, Abraham, 308
  Charles, 213
  John, 10, 28, 35, 68, 92, 101, 102, 109, 255, 314, 326, 348, 349
  Joseph, 308, 371
  Josiah, 308
  Martha, 308
  Sarah, 308
Stewart, Andrew, 362
  Pricilla, 308
  William, 175, 229, 318
Steymets, Christopher, 327
Stiles, Ann, 229
  Ebenezer, 309
  Edward, 30
  Ephraim, 89, 309
  John, 309
  Jonathan, 309, 331
  Jonathan, Jr., 363
  Joseph, 309
  Stephen, 309
  Thomas, 309
Still, Hannah, 288
  Peter, 149
Stilley, Daniel, 309
  Eleanor, 309
  Jacob, 309
  Johannah, 309
  John, 309
Stillwell, Daniel, 235, 309
  Elias, 309
  Elijah, 309
  Elizabeth, 113, 309, 358
  Jeremiah, 74
  John, 309
  John, Jr., 238
  Joseph, 68, 246, 309
  Lydia, 309
  Margaret, 309
  Martha, 309
  Mary, 309
  Nathaniel, 119
  Nicholas, 48, 109, 194, 304, 309
  Obadiah, 309
  Permela, 272
  Phebe, 309
  Priscilla, 309
  Rebecca, 309
  Richard, 309, 358
  Sarah, 143, 288, 309
  Stites, 309
  Thomas, 136, 357
  William, 309
  Zerviah, 309
Stinson, James, 11
Stinyard, Joseph, 199, 250
Stippey, Richard, 197
Stites, Adonijah, 310
  Daniel, 310
  Esther, 310
  George, 310
  John, 91, 106, 203, 223, 284, 322
  John, Jr., 203

  Margaret, Jr., 203
  Nathan, 310
  Richard, 143, 309, 316
  Thomas, 144, 310
  William, 174, 310
Stitter, Herman, 192
Stoakham, Israel, 67
Stockman, Abigail, 310
Stockton, Ame, 310
  Daniel, 44, 81, 310
  Doughty, 310
  Elizabeth, 310
  Grace, 67
  Hannah, 310
  Jacob, 311
  Job, 20
  Mary, 310
  Philip, 310
  Rebecca, 310
  Richard, 48, 107, 178
  Samuel, 107, 310, 311
  Susannah, 310
  William, 102, 281, 310
Stogdel, John, 279
Stokes, Amy, 158
  Anne, 311
  Atlantica, 30
  Elizabeth, 311
  Jacob, 99, 104, 301, 373
  John, 221, 311, 360
  Joseph, 229, 234, 290, 311, 345, 370
  Joseph, Jr., 30
  Joshua, 141, 154, 202
  Mary, 311
  Samuel, 30, 50, 110, 136, 221, 229, 311, 346, 347, 370
  Thomas, 229
Stoll, John, 339
Stone, Jeremiah, 311
  Rhoda, 311
  William, 20, 89, 173, 306, 311
Stonebanks, Richard, 8, 247
  William, 181
Stoneman, Edward, 47
Stoothoff, Abraham, 312
  Albert, 312
  Anatje, 312
  Cornelius, 295, 312
  Garret, 135, 312
  Ida, 312
  Johanna, 312
  John, 312
  Margaret, 312
  Sarah, 312
  Wilhelmus, 214
  William, 312
Storm, Abraham, 6
Story, John, 312, 345
  Joseph, 312, 345
  Thomas, 312
Stott, Andres, 338
Stout, Beniaiah, 313
  Benjamin, 183, 227
  Benjamin, Jr., 95
  Daniel, 312
  David, 56, 97, 109, 232
  Elijah, 313
  Enelephe, 312
  Hannah, 178, 232, 357
  Harman, 211
  Helena, 362
  Hester, 357
  Hezekiah, 227
  Jacob, 109

INDEX OF NAMES OF PERSONS 449

James, 178, 183
Jemima, 312
John, 52, 56, 165, 184, 312, 313, 325, 344, 357
Jonathan, 48, 66, 165, 189, 325, 357
Joseph, 165
Leah, 357
Mabel, 285
Mary, 211, 313, 357
Rachel, 48
Richard, 357
Ruth, 165
Samuel, 319
Samuel, Jr., 319
Sarah, 313
Zebulon, 33, 52, 97, 184, 313
Stouten, Elizabeth, 313
  Joseph, 313
Stoutenburgh, Jacobus, 327
  John, 322
Stow, John, 144
  Thomas, 141
  William, 12
Strang, Daniel, 15
Stratton, Aaron, 314
  Abigail, 85, 259, 313
  Ann, 314
  Benjamin, 313
  Catherine, 314
  Daniel, 314
  David, 286, 314
  Elizabeth, 259, 313
  Emanuel, 139
  Enoch, 139, 314
  Ephraim, 314
  Fithian, 314
  Freelove, 259, 313
  Isaac, 313, 314
  James, 313
  John, 126, 313, 314
  Jonathan, 85, 115, 146, 259, 313, 314
  Levi 313
  Mary, 286, 314
  Phebe, 314
  Preston, 313
  Sarah, 156, 313
  Thomazine, 259, 313
  William, 226, 314, 366, 369
Straughan, David, 145
  John, 145
  Samuel, 145
Street, Aaron, 314
  Edward, 314
  Elizabeth, 314
  Lydia, 314
  Mary, 314
  William, 314
Streit, Leonard, 273
Stretch, Daniel, 204
  David, 226
  John, 213, 315, 369
  Joseph, 92, 118, 226, 255, 314
  Peter, 314
  William, 52, 314, 344
Strickland, Joseph, 57, 59
Sroy, Jacob, 61
Stryker, Barnt, 371
  Jacobus, 371
  John, 332
  Peter, 135, 371, 372
Stuard, David, Jr., 242
  Margaret, 271
  Mary, 271

Stuart, John, 269, 271
Stubbines, Henry, 170, 235, 236, 274, 294
Sturdevent, James, 83
Sturgis, Ebenezer, Jr., 269
  Phebe, 35
Stuyvesant, Peter, 336
Style, John, 315
  Rebecca, 315
Stylls, John, 278
Sullivan, Eleanor, 315
  Jacob, 36
  Masey, 269
  Owen, 315
Summeril, William, 54
Sutphen, Abraham, 72
  Arthur, 33, 313
  Catrine, 42
  Dirick, Jr., 73
  Guisbert, 304
  Isaac, 73, 204
  Jacob, 77
  James, 33
  John, 185, 190
  Margaret, 42
  Peter, 42
Sutter, Philipp, 337
Sutton, Amos, 279
  Benjamin, 250, 251
  Charles, 250
  Daniel Jackson, 174
  David, 35, 73
  Elizabeth, 315
  Henry, 66, 262
  Jane, 61, 315
  John Jackson, 174
  Mary, 315, 174
  Thomas, 359
Suydam, Antje, 340
  Charles, 34
  Cornelius, 34, 118
  Jacob, 340
Swaim, Abigail, 315
  Anne, 315
  Elizabeth, 315
  Hannah, 296
  Jane, 315
  Katherine, 315
  Saltye, 315
  Sarg, 315
Swain, Daniel, 315
  Jacob, 114, 262
  James, 315
  Lemuel, 104
  Mary, 114, 315
  Reuben, 315, 316
  Richard, 237
  Ruth, 315
  Silas, 177, 315
  Zebulon, 103, 104, 169, 174
Swallow, Jacob, 185, 198
Swan, Richard, 193
Swanson, Samuel, 132
Swartworth, Thomas, 333
Swayze, Barnabus, 316
  Caleb, 316
  Israel, 316
  Richard, 316
  Samuel, 316
  Susannah, 316
Sweetman, Jane, 351
  Michael, 287, 351
Swinney, Elisha, 316
  Jesse, 316
  Joseph, 18, 315

29

Martha, 316
Mary, 316
Rachel, 316
Ruth, 316
Sarah, 316
Valentine, 316
Swinter, Henry, 164
Sydenham, David, 317
  John, 317
  Martha, 317
  Sucke, 317
  Thomas, 317
  William, 317
Symonds, William, 48
Symonse, Antje, 295
  Arius, 295
  Deborah, 295
  Isaac, 295
  Jaques, 295
  Peter, 295
  Symon, 295
  William, 295
  (see Simonson)
Sykes, Anthony, 13, 31, 68, 139, 235, 281, 292, 349

T

Taber, Meribah, 296
Taft, William, 144
Tagart, Joshua, 317
  Mary, 317
Talmage, Daniel, 70
Talman, Benjamin, 5, 129, 322
  Hinchman, 317
  James, 136, 148, 158, 317
  James, Jr., 158
  Jeremiah, 10, 198
  Job, 129
  Joseph, 5, 43, 129, 317, 322
  Keziah, 158, 317
  Martha, 317
  Peter, 83, 175
  Sarah, 317
Tanner, John, 139
Tappen, Abraham, 116, 228
  Isaac, 84
Tapscott, William, 57, 59, 310, 318, 350
Tarry, Richard, 188
Tatum, Isaac, 162
  John, 347
  Joseph, 199, 317
  Samuel, 311
Tay, Edward, 304
  Elias, 328
  Gertrude, 328
  Marget, 328
  Mary, 196
  Rebecca, 328
  (see Toy)
Taylor, Abram, 13
  Anne, 13, 202, 318, 319
  Anthony, 318
  Benjamin, 319
  Catherine, 23, 318
  Charles, 139
  Daniel, 63
  Deborah, 318
  Deliverance, 271, 319
  Edward, 68, 232, 288, 303, 309, 324, 318, 319, 350, 357, 362
  Elias, 318
  Ephraim, 29
  Francis, 310, 315, 318
  George, 66, 149, 280, 316, 317, 319, 357
  George, Jr., 362
  Gilbert, 112
  Hannah, 318, 319
  Idaleasa, 318
  Isaac, 318
  Jacob, 13, 139
  James, 143, 318
  John, 25, 129, 151, 152, 160, 262, 271, 288, 316, 317, 318, 319, 324, 357, 362, 363
  John, Jr., 8
  Jonathan, 113, 130, 264
  Joseph, 165, 318, 363
  Judith, 316
  Lawrence, 318
  Lucretia, 318
  Lydia, 13
  Mary, 87, 310, 318
  Mehitable, 318
  Meribah, 202, 318
  Phebe, 151
  Rachel, 165
  Rebeccah, 319
  Richard, 51
  Robert, 318, 319
  Samuel, 32, 318, 319
  Samuel, Jr., 25, 61, 262
  Sarah, 61, 262, 318,
  Thomas, 202, 240, 318
  William, 184, 192, 198, 319
Temple, Abraham, 319
  Benjamin, 147, 226, 242, 319
  Elizabeth, 319
  Joanna, 226, 319
  John, 319
  Nathaniel, 319
  Rebecca, 319
  Return, 227, 319
  Sarah, 226, 319
  Timothy, 225, 319
Ten Brook, Eleanor, 319
  John, 320
  Wessel, 319
Ten Eyck, Anderies, 320
  Anetje, 320
  Conrad, 320, 339
  Conrad, Jr., 42
  Jacob, 320, 338
  Jacomintie, 338
  Janetje, 320
  Katrien, 320
  Mathius, 100
  Matthew, 320
  Peter, 320
  Samuel, 332
  Tobias, 335
Tennent, Gilbert, 263
  William, 305
Terhune, Abraham, 37
  Albartus, 6, 37
  Albert, 234
  Gerrit, 334
Terrill, Ephraim, 29, 151, 184
  Ephraim, Jr., 121
  Prudence, 239
Terry, John, 148
  Rebecca, 367, 371
  Richard, 173
Test, Daniel 320
  Edward, 13, 129, 144, 154, 181, 206, 298, 313, 320, 321
  Elisha, 320
  Elizabeth, 320

INDEX OF NAMES OF PERSONS 451

Francis, 9, 139, 225, 321
Grace, 321
Hannah, 320
John, 320, 358
Joseph, 320, 321
Joseph, Jr., 321
Priscilla, 321
Rebeccah, 321
Richard, 321
Samuel, 323
Sarah, 320, 321
Thomas, 235, 277
Walker, 321
William, 321
Thackery, Benjamin, 298
 Elenor, 204
 Hannah, 168
 Joseph, 168
Tharp, Benjamin, 66
 Job, 116
Thatcher, James, 19, 62
 Jeremiah, 39
Thickstun, Jonathan, 34, 66
Thomamont, Mr., 325
Thomas, Absalom, 139
 Anne, 230, 321
 Benoai, 256
 Edward, 321
 Elias, 163, 276
 Eva, 321
 James, 341
 Jarvis, 221
 John, 235, 321
 John, Jr., 70
 Jonathan, 35, 59, 129, 130, 131, 300, 319, 320, 361
 Lydia, 321
 Nancy, 139
 Nathaniel, 23, 24, 83, 90
 Rachel, 321
 Rebeccah, 321
 Sarah, 180, 321
 Timothy, 151
 William, 221
 Mrs., 329
Thomasee, Abraham, 322
 Aneltie, 322
 Aria, 322
 Cornelius, 322
 Johannis, 322
 Mary, 321, 322
 Rachel, 322
 Thomas, 322
Thomlinson, Daniel, 304
 Elenor, 286
 Isaac, 286, 304
 Lydia, 286, 304
 Mary, 286
 (see Tomlinson)
Thomson (Tomson), Alexander, 51, 77
 Andrew, 148, 323
 Anne, 323
 Benjamin, 184, 261, 267, 323, 330, 348
 Celib, 322
 Charity, 322
 Cornelius, 231
 Daniel, 298, 322
 Elizabeth, 6, 26, 184, 306, 323, 324, 348
 George, 145, 359
 Hannah, 322, 323
 Henry, 322
 Isaac, 323
 James, 116, 117, 307, 359
 John, 98, 136, 148, 169, 217, 219, 220, 231, 257, 302, 306, 322, 323, 357, 362, 365, 366
 John, Jr., 231, 294
 Jonathan, 79, 260
 Joseph, 267, 323
 Joshua, 86, 142, 235, 274, 296, 320, 326, 373
 Mary, 320, 322, 323
 Moses, 20, 218
 Nathaniel, 323
 Patience, 322
 Phebe, 322, 323
 Rachel, 306
 Rebecca, 306, 323
 Samuel, 20, 27, 317, 323, 343
 Sarah, 323
 Staples, 306, 322
 Thomas, 70, 129, 153, 162, 221, 223, 306, 307, 322, 333, 344, 360
 Uriah, 306, 322
 William, 139
 Zadok, 314, 322
Thorn (Thorne), Abraham, 225
 Abraham, Jr., 225
 Elizabeth, 324
 Hannah, 156
 Henry, 250, 324
 Henry, Jr., 324
 Isaac, 44
 Jacob, 291
 John, 111, 139, 317, 324
 Joseph, 19, 84, 96, 323
 Letitia, 324
 Mary, 154, 324
 Richard, 324
 Samuel, 130
 Sarah, 319
 Thomas, 148
 William, 198
 Zaccheus, 324
Thorp, Andrew, 42
 Benjamin, 311
 Eunice, 42
 Hannah, 325
 Norris, 299
 Thomas, 42, 325
Throckmorton, Alice, 325
 Ann, 325
 Catherine, 325
 Elizabeth, 235
 Hartness, 235
 James, 119
 Job, 74, 119, 235, 309, **325**
 John, 235, 251, 318, 325
 Joseph, 235
 Lewis, 235
 Lydia, 9
 Martille, 235
 Mary, 325, 353
 Patience, 325
 Rebecca, 325
 Samuel, 92, 235, 254
 Thomas, 235
 William, 189, 191, 235
Thurston, Israel, 51
Tice, Elizabeth, 36, 324
 Richard, 324
Tichenor, James, 325
 Jane, 325
 John, 21, 285
 Joseph, 325
 Mary, 285
Tielshofir, Christian, **325**

Elizabeth, 325
George, 325
Jacob, 325
John, 325
Margaret, 325
Martin, 325
Simon, 325
(see Titsilver)
Tietsort, Abraham, 325
  Catheline, 325
  Geertruy, 325
  Isaac, 325, 326
  Jacob, 33, 351
  John, 325
  Leonard, 326
  Margaret, 325
  Peter, 325
  Sarah, 321
  William, 325
Tiger, George, 114
Tilden, Richard, 175
Tiler, Benjamin, 255
Till, Demuras, 96
Tilton, John, 77, 312
  Joseph, 231
  Peter, 172
  Samuel, 66, 95, 126, 313, 357
  Thomas, 130
  Thomas, Jr., 68, 83, 193
Tindal, Amy, 36
  Esther, 326
  John, 82
  Joseph, 124, 147, 326
  Sarah, 196, 197
  Thomas, 82, 106, 248
Tingley, Ebenezer, 324
Tissa, Philip, 23
Titman, Lodwick, 358
Titsilver, Elizabeth, 326
  Martin, 326
  Michael, 326
  (see Tielshofir)
Titsworth, Hannah, 18
Titus, Dennis, 326
  Hannah, 326
  Jemima, 326
  John, 32
  John, Jr., 113
  Mary, 326
  Phebe, 320
  Philip, 240, 326
  Susannah, 326
  Timothy, 312, 326
Tobin, Thomas, 215, 263, 322, 328
Toers, Jacob, 351
Tolberd, John, 61
Tomkins, David, 327
  Esther, 327
  Eunice, 327
  Jonathan, 21
  Phebe, 25
Tomlins, Mary, 327
  Mathew, 157, 166, 327
Tomlinson, Ann, 327
  Catherine, 327
  Daniel, 286, 327
  Ebenezer, 148
  Eleanor, 304, 827
  Hannah. 327
  Isaac, 327
  Joseph, 327
  Mary, 304, 327
  Othniel, 159
  Samuel, 327
  (see Thomlinson)

Toms, Ann, 328
  Catherine, 328
  Charles, 228
  Elizabeth, 328
  Hannah, 327
  John, 328
  Jonathan, 328
  Rachel, 328
  Richard, 328
  Susannah, 328
Toner, Moses, 274
Tonkin, Charles, 185, 235
  Edward, 17, 145, 243
Tooker, Elizabeth, 328
  Joseph, 29, 328
  Joshua, 328
  Magdalene, 236
  Mary, 328
  Sarah, 328
Tool, Susannah, 44
Torse, Lourens, 91
Totten, James, 179
Toullard, Peter, 80, 275
Town, John, Jr., 298
  Morris, 367
Townby, Alus, 228
Townley, Abigail, 328
  Charles, 10
  Effingham, 328
  Elizabeth, 328
  Mary, 284, 328
  Rebecca, 328
  Richard, 11, 159, 328
Townsend, Amos, 206
  John, 169
  Martha, 328
  Mary, 315
  Richard, 22
  Sarah, 39, 328
Toy, Abigail, 328
  Daniel, 328
  Elias, 16, 189, 344
  James, 16, 36, 189, 344
  Mary, 36
  Nicholas, 17, 31, 45, 183
  Savory, 328
  Susannah, 328
  (see Tay)
Tracey, Daniel, 246
Tranbles, Ann, 329
  Daniel, 256
  Elizabeth, 329
  John, 329
  Margaret, 329
  Mary, 329
  Peter, 329
Trapnell, John, 90
  Rebecca, 90
Treadway, Henry, 329
  Sarah, 329
Treadwell, Jabez, 296
Tree, Ann, 134
Tremble, Daniel, 133
Trembly, Anne, 217
  Elizabeth, 217
  Hannah, 217
Tremer, Andrew, 205
Tremper, William, 187
Trenchard, Curtis, 308
  George, 9, 71, 86, 145, 181, 221, 256, 308, 321, 366
Trent, James, 297
Trimmer, Andrew, 188, 205
  Anthony, 329
  Antye, 108

INDEX OF NAMES OF PERSONS 453

Christian, 108
Elizabeth, 329
Elsye, 108
Johannis, 108
Judith, 108
Mary, 329
Mathias, 329
Nicholas, 108
Paul, 329
William, 108
Tromm, Philip, 150
Trons, James, 205
Trotter, Benjamin, 10, 79, 182, 329
  Elizabeth, 182, 329
  John C., 182, 329
  Katherine, 182, 329
  Sarah, 182
  William, 182, 324
Troup, John, 182, 329
Trout, Ann, 61
  George, 268, 359
Truesdell, Mary, 329
Tubman, John, 351
Tucker, Ann, 328
  Elizabeth, 130
  George, 56, 132, 233, 260
  John, 175
  Mary, 330
  Samuel, 226, 233, 241
  Samuel, Jr., 124, 132, 204, 226, 233, 253, 297, 319, 372
  Sarah, 224
Tuckniss, Ann, 330
  Harkness, 214
  James, 214, 330
  John, 330
  Mary, 330
  Phebe, 214
  Robert, 330
Tufte, William, 13, 346
Tullis, William, 93, 239
Tuly, Jonathan, 45
  Martha, 45
Tunison, Abigail, 330
  Abraham, 338
  Altje, 330
  Ann, 303
  Ariantje, 330
  Cornelius, 330
  Cornelius, Jr., 330
  Dennis, 35
  Geartje, 330
  Johannis, 330
  John, 303
  Philip, 330
  Sarah, 330
  Thomas, 259
  Tunis, 330, 338
Turner, Anne, 330
  Daniel, 330
  Hannah, 330
  John, 330
  Lillis, 330
  Lydia, 330
  Mary, 330
  Mehitabel, 330
  Peter, 148, 330
  Rachel, 330
  Temperance, 79
  William, 79, 330
Turnout, John, 148
Tussy, Joseph, 223
  Samuel, 223
Tust, William, 82
Tuthill, Sarah, 184
  Samuel, 150, 184, 367
Tuttle, Abigail, 238
  Abraham, 330
  Cissel, 330
  Daniel, 146, 208, 330, 331, 365
  David, 187
  Isaac, 330
  James, 238
  Joanna, 330
  Joseph, 238
  Joseph, Jr., 187
  Mary, 330
  Phebe, 238
  Samuel, 187, 220
  Stephen, 330
  Thomas, 330
  Timothy, 355, 365
Tylee, Elizabeth, 168
  John, 121, 331, 339
  Naomi, 331
Tyler, Benjamin, 92, 115, 364
  James, 185
  John, 331
  Samuel, 82, 144, 185, 373
Tyren, Thomas, 271
Tyrer, Thomas, 88
Tyson, Thomas, 155

U

Uenecomb, Zilpah, 107
Unander, Erick, 103, 227, 263
Updike, Ann, 178
  Samuel, 111
  Sarah, 259, 260
  William, 178
  (see Opdyck)
Urion, Hance, 232, 331
  James, 276
  John, 331
  Frederick, 232
Usher, Abram, 350
  Matthew, 350

V

Vail, Abraham, 291, 331
  Benjamin, 331
  Christian, 331
  Daniel, 331
  David, 331
  Isaac, 331
  Jacob, 331
  John, 225, 291, 331, 359
  John, Jr., 171, 359
  Joseph, 331
  Mary, 331
  Sarah, 291
  Steven, 331
Valentine, Adam, 30
  James, 27, 332
  Richard, 252, 344
Valleau, Ann, 332
  Fauconnier, 332
  John B., 332
  Peter, 332
  Susannah, 332
  Theodorus, 332
van Aken, Abraham, 353
Van Allen, Anderis, 332
  Hendrick, 332
  Jacob, 332
  Tryntie, 332
Van Allman, Autie, 295
  Cunrat, 295

Van Arsdalen, Abraham, 332
  Catherine, 332
  Cornelius, 110, 332
  Derrick, 135, 342
  Gerrit, 332
  Isaac, 332
  Jacobus, 332
  Johannis, 332
  Mary, 332
  Philip, 352
  Simon, 332
  William, 332
Van Blarcom, Altie, 6
Van Brakle, James, 162, 272
  John, 80, 332
  Sarah, 271, 332
Van Brunt, Hendrick, 281
Van Bryck, R., 140
Van Buren, Abraham, 303
  John, 181, 340
  Doctor, 209
van Buskirk, Abraham, 6, 225
  Cornelius, 332
  David, 336
  Feytie, 332
  John, 332, 372
  Luke, 212
Van Campen (Van Kampen, Van Camp), Abraham, 326
  Cornelius, 62, 141
  Giesbert, 333
  Gerrit, 296
  Gilbert, 333
  Isaac, 333
  Lowrance, 105
Vance, Alexander, 210, 333
  Alice, 333
  Edward, 333
  Esther, 333
  James, 333
  John, 333
  Patrick, 250
  Samuel, 333
  Thomas, 333
  William, 48, 333
Van Cleef (Van Cleave), John, 38, 40, 235, 260, 299
  Richard, 189
Van Cortlandt, Augustus, 234
  John, 206
Van Court, Elias, 73, 93, 101, 118, 146, 147, 175, 213, 236, 276, 308, 309
  John, 333
  Michael, 333
  Moses, 333
  Samuel, 279, 333
Van Culin, Jacobus, 200
Van de Grift, John, 134
Van de Mark, Benjamin, 333
  Elias, 333
  Elizabeth, 333
  James, 333
  Jeremiah, 333
  John, 333
  Leah, 333
  Peter, 333
  Samuel, 333
Vanderbeek, Paulus, 234
  Rem, 47
Vanderbilt, Cornelius, 95, 335
  Hendrick, 118
  Jacob, 12, 37, 295
  John, 153
Van der Cook, Anne, 333

Catherine, 333
Francis, 334
Henry, 333
John, 333
Michael, 333
Peter, 333
Sarah, 333
Van der Hoof, Johannes, 261
  John, 334
Vander Hovefman, Cornelius, 80
Vander Linde, Benjamin, 373
Vanderpool, Apphia, 272
  John, 272
Van Derspiegal, John, 258
Vanderveer, Cornelius, 288, 303
  Jacob, 132
  Johannes, 176, 255
  John, 363
  Joseph, 132
  Morritey, 303
  Tunis, 190
Van Deventer, Abraham, 334
  Elizabeth, 334
  Hannah, 368
  Isaac, 334
  Jacob, 334
  Jeremiah, 334
  Vinard, 295
  Wynand, 37
van die Grifth, Edith, 347
Van Dorn, Aaron, 218
  Abraham, 218
  Christian, 218, 261
  Isaac, 41
Van Drill, Deborah, 173
  William, 173
Van Duchren, Anna, 334
  Barbara, 334
  David, 334
  Dorithea, 334
  Elizabeth, 334
  Godfried, 334
  Johannes, 334
  Maria, 334
  Sarah, 334
Van Duyn (Van Dien), Albert, 334
  Denys, 340
  Derck, 334
  Gerret, 334
  Hendrick, 334
  Isaac, 130
  Janniette, 334
  Martin, 343
Van Dyke, Domenicus, 62
  Eleanor, 74
  Francis, 335
  Hannah, 335
  Jacobus, 43
  Johannis, 334
  John, 332
  Margaret, 62, 334
  Mathias, 95
  Nicholas, 335
  Peter, 334
  Thomas, 180, 193, 197, 315
  Thomas, Jr., 74
Van Emburgh, Peregrine, 270
  William S., 37
Van Eydersteyn, Thadeus, 341
Van Fleet, Frederick, 62
  Hannah, 280
  Jerome, 280
  (see Van Vliet, Vliet)

INDEX OF NAMES OF PERSONS 455

Van Gelder, Abraham, 295
  Elizabeth, 6
  John, 173
Van Giesen, Abraham, 335
  Andris, 335
  Anna M., 335
  Catherine, 335
  Dirkje, 335
  Hendrick, 335
  Isaac, 335
  Johannis, 335
  Madalene, 373
  Printie, 335
  Rynier, 6, 52, 91, 102, 182, 334, 335
Van Harlingen, Arnoldus, 343
  Ernestus, 27
  Johannes M., Jr., 343
Van Hook, Mary, 90
Van Horne (Van Horn), Abraham, 211, 280, 321, 335, 336
  Andrew, 211
  Annatye, 336
  Antia, 335
  Barrend, 334
  Catherine, 211
  Cornelius, 211, 253, 335
  David, 341
  Elsie, 336
  Gerret, 234
  Gritye, 336
  Jacob, 332
  James, 196
  Janitie, 332, 366
  John, 211, 301, 335
  Linah, 335
  Lucas, 91
  Marytye, 336
  Matthew, 335
  Neeltie, 335
  Phicha, 335
  Philip, 196
  Rachel, 336
  Samuel, 341
  Sietsye, 336
  Thomas, 75, 338
  William, 335, 336
Van Huys, Ann, 320, 366
  James, 336
  John, 336
  Ouke, 336
Vanicombe (see Venicomb)
van Keuren, Terck, 353
Van Kirk, Anna, 336
  Arthur, 177
  Elizabeth, 336
  Elsie, 336
  Henry, 98, 109
  Jennison, 336
  John, 107
  Mary, 336
  Sarah, 336
  William, 336
Van Leer, Bernard, 124
  Branson, 53, 122, 206
  George, 124
Van Liew, Frederick, 218, 261, 335, 342
  Henry, 261
  Preston, 139
Van Mater, Benjamin, 303, 336-7
  Catherine, 337
  Cyrenius, 288
  Daniel, 187
  David, 263, 336

  Elizabeth, 337
  Ephraim, 140, 336, 337
  Fetters, 336
  Garret, 157, 327
  Hannah, 337
  Hellita, 337
  Henry, 113, 263, 284, 337
  Jacob, 337
  John, 126, 140, 336
  Joseph, 140, 303, 313, 336, 337
  Mary, 113
  Rebecca, 337
  Richard, 241
  Sarah, 337
Van Middleswart, Abraham, 352
  Henry, 338
Vanneman, Andrew, 120, 162, 245
  Ann, 120
  Catherine, 337
  Christian, 186
  David, 159, 336
  Elizabeth, 337
  Gabriel, 159, 160, 267
  Garret, 38, 54, 157, 162, 181, 221, 246, 337
  Isaac, 336, 338
  Israel, 337
  Jacob, 341
  John, 40, 93, 249, 337
  Joseph, 336, 338
  Lawrence, 337
  Peter, 267, 268, 337
  Ruth, 336
  Samuel, 159
  Sarah, 337
  William, 157, 186
Van Neste, (Van Nest), Barnardus, 338
  Catherine, 42, 338
  Elizabeth, 337, 338
  Jacob, 338
  Jemima, 338
  Jeronimus, 42, 123
  John, 42, 62, 163, 320, 338
  Mary, 338
  Peter, 42, 163, 338
Van Noordstrand, Angenitie, 338
  Ann, 338
  Folkert, 27, 88, 338, 342
  Jacob, 182
  John, 338
Van Norden, John, 209, 338
  Tobias, 147, 175, 213, 236, 257
Van Note, Are, 141
Vannoy, Andrew, 97
Van Nuys (see Van Huys)
Van Ort, William, 352
Van Pelt, Chris., 271
  Margaret, 91
  Peter, 295
VanRiper, Abraham, 363
  Dirck, 338
  Isaac, 182
  Lena, 128
  Margaret, 338
  Thomas, 128
Van Rype (see p. 373)
van Rypen, Christoffel, 343
  Metye, 343
Van Schaick, John, 77
  Robert, 77
Van Schuiver, John, 339
  Walter, 7
Van Scyhawke, Aaron, 358

Van Sickle, Anne, 339
　Cornelius, 117
　Elizabeth, 293
　John, 339, 340
　Richard, 339
　Rynier, 339
　Sarah, 293, 339
Van Stay, Hendrick, 163
Van Tilburgh, William, 304
Van Tine, Jacob, 303
　Jaques, 37
　Neeltie, 37
van Tuyl, Abraham, 35, 73, 93
　John, 168
Van Veghten, Dirck, 123, 338
Van Vliet, Dirck, 188, 280, 333
　Frederick, 99
　Rebecca, 99
　William, Jr., 108
　(see Vliet, Van Fleet)
Van Voorhees, Albert L., 33
　George, 33
　Jacob, 6, 33
　Jan, 6
　Jannetie, 6
　Minne, 284, 338
　Sachyyos (Zaccheus), 332
　Sarah, 339
　Stephen, 164, 176, 260, 339
Van Vorst, Annatie, 336
　Cornelius, 336, 339
　Fytye, 339
　Gerrit, 339
　Janneke, 339
　Johannes, 339
　Maritie, 339
Van Wagenen, Cathallyne, 340
　Cathrine, 339
　Cornelius, 340
　Garret, 47
　Helmigh, 340
　Jacob, 340
　Johannes, 261, 340
Van Wert, Garret, 326
Van Wickle, Anne, 340
　Cornelia, 340
　Dinah, 340
　Elsie, 340
　Evert, 340
　Mattje, 340
　Mary, 340
　Nicholas, 340
　Seytje, 340
Van Winkle (Van Winckel),
　Abraham, 340
　Alexander, 340
　Daniel, 91
　Gesie, 128
　Leah, 340
　Magdalen, 340
　Marinus, 128, 340
　Marritie, 335
　Mary, 340
　Hannah, 340
　Jacob, 91, 340
　John, 256, 340
　Rachel, 340
　Sarah, 256
　Simon, 171
　Simeon, 340
　Tunis, 340
Van Wyck, Theodorus, 183
Van Wye, John, 333
　Magdalen, 333
Van Zandt, Garrit, 141

Johannes, 258
Madalena, 141
Peter P., 258
Varmes, Isaac, 277
Vastbinder, Jacob, 304
Vaughn (Vaughan), Azariah, 331
　Esther, 331
　James, 331
　John, 129
　Rachel, 129, 331
　Rebecca, 331
　Richard, 331
　Tabitha, 331
　William, 236, 237, 331
　Rev. Mr., 263
Vause, Margaret, 259
　Theodosia, 155, 156
Veghte, Nicholas, 135
Veiland, Mary, 262
Veiss, Philip, 282
Venable, Ester, 36
　Mary, 36
　Sarah, 345
Venicomb, Francis, 17, 30, 157,
　　201, 202, 261
　Rachel, 200, 201
　William, 157
Ver Bryck, Bernardus, 140
Vergerau, Susanna, 37
Verplanck, Anne, 341
　Mary, 341
　Samuel, 341
Verree, Isaac, 341
　James, 341
　Joseph, 341
　Rachel, 341
　Robert, 341
　Samuel, 341
　William, 341
Vickers, Hannah, 341
　Mary, 341
　Sarah, 341
　Thomas, 341
Vickery, Ann, 341
　Martha, 236
　Rebecca, 341
　Richard, 56, 235
　Sarah, 67, 341
　Thomas, 70, 341
Viele, Sarah, 342
Vierselius, George A., 16, 153, 188
Vince, Adam, 114
Vliet, Daniel, 64, 342
　Dirrickje, 342
　Geertje, 342
　John, 342
　Rebecca, 342
　Sarah, 342
　Simon, 342
　(see Van Vliet, Van Fleet)
Volbart, Elizabeth, 281
Volkertse, Derick, 258
　(see Falkerson)
Volschlaeger, Johannes, 267
Voorhees, Abraham, 95, 128
　Albert, 119
　Catlyna, 342
　Gerret, 27, 261, 342, 343
　Helena, 342
　Hendrick, 94, 190, 281
　Hendrick, Jr., 189
　Isaac, 73
　Janitie, 342
　Johanah, 342
　Johannis, 281, 342

INDEX OF NAMES OF PERSONS 457

John, 323
Lucas, 342
Maregrieta, 342
Mary, 342
Minnie V., 99
Roeloff, 342
(see Van Voorhees)
Veto. Paul I., 331
Vouck, Peter, 295
Vreeland, Claas, 343, 373
  Derrick, 343, 346
  Elias, 335, 343
  Elsie, 343
  George, 68, 338
  Hartman, 254, 343
  Hassel, 343
  Helmagh, 336
  Johannes, 254
  John, 341
  Joris, 261, 332
  Margaret, 346
  Marretye, 63
  Michael, 93, 343
  Nettie, 336
  Richard D., 346
  Simeon, 63
Vrian, Hance, 153
Vroom, Christian, 343
  Deborah, 295
  Hendrick, 343
  John, 343
  Peter, 343
  Sarah, 343

W

Wade, Abraham, 359
  Catharine, 284
  Daniel, 44, 343
  Deborah, 343
  Hannah, 159, 343
  John, Jr., 343
  Jothan, 343
  Mascey, 284
  Nathaniel, 26
  Rachel, 343
  Sarah, 284, 343
Wadington (Wodington), Ann, 343
  Elizabeth, 344, 364
  Isaac, 343
  Jane, 344
  Joan, 343
  Jonathan, 364
  Mary, 343
  Robert, 343, 364
  Sarah, 343
  William, 314, 344
Wady, Humphrey, 10, 344
  John, 344
  Sarah, 344
Wagner, Johan B., 191
Wainwright, Ann, 344
  Daniel, 234, 254, 358
  James, 344
  Jedediah, 368
  Jerushea, 368
  John, 344
  Lydia, 368
  Mary, 344
  Patience, 344
  Penelope, 344
  Rebecca, 344
  Susanna, 344
Waithman, Thomas, 343

Waldorff, Anthony, 307
Waldron, Leffert, 71
Walker, Benjamin, 191
  Daniel, 345
  David, 189, 203, 204
  Edward, 344
  Elizabeth, 344
  Hannah, 344
  Henry, 269
  John, 125, 138, 212, 298, 344
  Justus, 33
  Martha, 344
  Mary, 344
  Phebe, 344
  Ralph, 217
  Rebecca, 344
  Robert, 184, 224, 360
  Samuel, 344
  Sarah, 344
  William, 125, 224, 298
Wall, Abigail, 345
  Garret, 252
  Hannah, 345
  James, 345
  Jarratt, 125, 126
  John, 305, 357, 362
  John, Jr., 95
  Martha, 345
  Mary, 252
  Naomi, 345
  Rebecca, 345
  Walter, 312, 345
Wallace, Hope, 110, 345
  John, 161, 345, 358
  Mary, 36, 345
  Rebecca, 345
  Thomas, 16, 345
  William, 148
  (see Wallis)
Waller, Margret, 352
Walling, Elias, 174
  John, 174
  Thomas, 115, 174, 350
  William, 255
Wallis, John, 184
  Martha, 184
  Mary, 328
  Philip, 32, 138, 345
  Thomas, 110, 174, 348
  (see Wallace)
Walsh, Philip, 198
Walters, Thomas, 85
Walton, Gerard, 32
  Nathaniel, 28
Wanshaer, Johannis, 373
  John, 343, 346
  John, Jr., 346
Warburton, Mary, 245
Ward, Abigail, 347
  Abner, 178, 348
  Abraham, 348
  Amos, 346
  Benjamin, 58, 220, 347
  Daniel, 346
  David, 149, 178, 267
  Ebenezer, 348
  Elizabeth, 346, 347
  Esther, 346
  George, 347
  Hannah, 346
  Isaac, 346, 347
  Israel, 264
  Jabez, 348
  James, 347, 351
  Jehu, 347

Jemima, 346
John, 347, 348
Jonathan, 267, 347
Joseph, 347
Josiah, 346, 347
Lawrance, 322
Mary, 346, 347, 348
Mathias, 178, 367
Moses, 347
Nathaniel, 348
Nicholas, 347
Peter, 347
Phebe, 161
Rebecca, 346, 347
Richard, 347
Robert, 276
Ruth, 46, 347, 348
Samuel, 20, 149, 346, **347**
Sarah, 346, 347, 348
Stephen, 20
Susannah, 348
Timothy, 26
Uzal, 348
Walter, 14
William, 46, 208, 347
Zenas, 346
Wardell, John, 29, 195
Joseph, 288
Ware, Alexander, 318
Andrew, 154
Edith, 154
Elijah, 348
Elnathan, 232
Elizabeth, 348
Isabel, 164
Jacob, 116
Jane, 348
John, 19, 348, 370
Joseph, 321, 323, 348
Rebecca, 348
Sarah, 349
Solomon, 92
Warfle, George, 13
Warford, James, 39, 120
Sarah, 349
Waricote, Bartholomew, 200
Warl, Joseph, 314
Warmstal, Aryaentie, 341
Warne, Catherine, 349
Elizabeth, 349
Ezekiah, 349
James, 349
Job, 349
Joseph, 349
Joshua, 349
Mary, 349
Samuel, 349
Stephen, 110, 164, 169, 177, 231, 312, 336, 339, 345, 362
Thomas, 349
William, 349
Warner, George, 264
Nathaniel, 88
Simon, 56
Warrell, Grace, 349
John, 18
Joseph, 349
Warren, Achsah, **349**
Fellwell, 349
Gamaliel, 349
John, 111, 281, 349
Mary, 349
Rebecca, 349
Samuel, 349
Susannah, 111, **349**

Warrington, Joseph, 286
Warwick, John, 65
Rebecca, 46, 47
Waterhouse, Elizabeth, 172
John, 262
Joshua, 120, 172, 365
Sophia, 262
Waters, Catharina, 317
William, 285, 326, 363
Watkins, David, 256, 349
Elizabeth, 215
Mary, 349
Phebe, 105, 349
Solomon, 215
Watkinson, Elias, 349
Godfrey, 350
John, 44, 49, 341, 350
Mary, 350
Nathaniel, 349
Paul, 341, 350
Susanna, 350
Watson, Aaron, 165, 295
Abraham, 350
Elizabeth, 165, 350
Garven, 259, 267, 350
John, 150, 181
Margaret, 350
Marmaduke, 96, 295, 365
Marritye, 351
Nathan, 63, 112, 148, 167
Peter, 350
Richard, 37
Samuel, 351
Sarah, 350
Thomas, 31, 48, 114, 165, 197, 351
William, 351
Wayman, Henry, 31, 61
Wease, Jacob F., 230
Weatherby (Wetherby), Ann, 276, 351
Benjamin, 351
Daniel, 351
David, 351
Edmund, 23, 133, 175, 285, 263
Edmund, Jr., 133, 341
Edward, 351
Henry, 216, 351
Mary, 354
Weatherel, William, 295
Weavers, Mary, 269
Webb, Abraham, 98
Deborah, 351
Elizabeth, 351
Jane, 351
Jerusha, 351
Olive, 306
Oliver, 23, 254
Phebe, 351
Webley, Hannah, 352
Webster, Elizabeth, 291
Hannah, 168, 291
John, 195, 351
Joseph, 291
Lawrence, 14, 43, 168
Wedt, Lucas D., 195
Weed, George, 57, 110, 149, 156, 158, 183, 228, 275
Weeks, Miles, 112, 117
Richard, 47, 102, 168, 266, 270
Weiser, Jacob, 338
Weiss, Philip, 5
Welch, Elizabeth, 211
Henry, 296
Johan M., 329
Phillip, 248

INDEX OF NAMES OF PERSONS 459

Welden, Mary, 160
Welding, Hannah, 352
Welling, John, 225, 226
  William, 147
Wells, Henry, 66
  Lydia, 139
  James, 312
Wentzel, William, 267
West, Abigail, 353
  Andria, 368
  Asher, 353
  Bartholomew, 294
  Catherine, 353
  Daniel, 353
  Deborah, 353
  Elizabeth, 353
  Eunice, 353
  Israel, 353
  John, 94, 130, 145, 202, 353
  Joseph, 353, 368
  Mary, 139, 352
  Mercy, 353
  Rebecca, 353
  Richard, 128, 353
  Sarah, 368
  Stephen, 368
  Susanna, 353
  Thomas, 353
  Uriah, 9, 353
  Webley, 353, 368
  William, 75, 129, 169, 352, 353
Westbroek, Abraham, 353
  Aeltie, 353, 354
  Anthony, 274, 353, 354
  Benjamin, 72
  Cornelis, 353
  Elizabeth, 353
  Esther, 354
  Gideon, 353, 354
  Jacob, 353, 354
  Janneke, 353, 354
  Johannis, 353, 354
  Joseph, 353
  Lewis, 354
  Lydia, 353
  Marya, 353
  Soloman, 353, 354
  Susanna, 353
  Tereck VanKeuren, 72
Westcot (Westcott, Wescote),
  Abigail, 122, 288, 355
  Amos, 352
  David, 24, 38, 146, 238, 259, 289, 313, 352
  Ezra, 352
  Henry, 85, 115, 289
  Joseph, 354
  Josh, 352
  Lewis, 352
  Richard, 352
  Sarah, 352
Westervelt, Abraham, 34
  Cornelius, 234
  Roelof, 6, 37, 373
Westfall, Jurian, 164
Weston, Hannah, 354
  Samuel, 175, 223
Westvael, Jennetie, 353
  Johannis, 72, 354
  Jurrian, 72
  Maria, 353
  Simon, 353
Wetherill, Ann, 354
  Christopher, 354
  Daniel, 356

  George, 356
  John, 166
  Joseph, 354
  Samuel, 354
  Thomas, 298, 350, 354
  Thomas, Jr., 273
Wethman, Elizabeth, 358
Weygand, Albert, 334
  John Albert, 282
Wheat, Richard, 11
Wheatcraft, Edward, 352
Wheaten, Isaac, 41, 176
  Noah, 85
  Peter, 355
  Samuel, Jr., 355
  William, 285, 293
Wheeler, Caleb, 279, 348
  Charity, 355
  David, 355
  Elizabeth, 355
  Jehiel, 355
  John, 355
  Josiah, 258
  Mary, 172, 355
  Nathaniel, 285
  Phebe, 355
  Rhoda, 355
  Sarah, 355
Whilldin, Isaac, 143, 144
  James, 80, 143, 144, 169, 232, 355
  Jane, 232
  Joseph, 144
Whitaker, Ambrose, 355
  Daniel, 355
  Elizabeth, 355
  Elnathan, 355
  Freelove, 352
  Hannah, 355
  John, 46, 252, 355
  Lawrana, 355
  Lemuel, 355
  Lewis, 289, 355
  Lydia, 355
  Nathaniel, 184, 297
  Reuben, 355
  Richard, 355
  Ruth, 355
  Sarah, 355
  Susanna, 355
  Thomas, 115
  Vashti, 355
White, Abigail, 355
  Alexander, 153, 269
  Amos, 297, 357
  Andrew, 357
  Anne, 66, 202, 357
  Anthony, 18
  Britain, 71
  Daniel, 21
  Elizabeth, 31, 203, 231, 356
  James, 22, 44, 158, 264, 356
  Jemima, 232
  Joel, 297
  John, 167, 356
  Joseph, 356
  Josiah, 13, 40, 44, 112, 141, 202, 295, 352
  Leaming, 356
  Martha, 202
  Mary, 350, 356
  Meribah, 357
  Nancy, 198
  Peter, 169, 231
  Rebecca, 141, 355
  Samuel, 202, 232

460   NEW JERSEY COLONIAL DOCUMENTS

Sarah, 202
Thomas, 357
William, 5, 45, 356
Whiteall, James, 267
  John, 25, 113, 144, 246, 288
  Sarah, 236
  William, 113
Whitefield, Mary, 167
Whitehead, Daniel, 20
  Elisha, 61, 195
  John, 367
  Joseph, 87
  Samuel, 195
  Timothy, 20, 21, 70, 132, 159, 218, 249, 343, 360
Whitehorne, Christianna, 73
  Samuel, 71, 73, 106, 108, 175, 223, 234, 249, 283, 365
Whitlock, William, 259, 305
Whiton, Isaac, 116
  Joseph, 116
  Noah, 116
  Uriah, 116
Whitson, Elizabeth, 48
Whitte, Ann, 205
  James, 205
Whittemore, Samuel, 63
Whoman, Nicholas, 107
Wick, Jean, 119
Wickward, Samuel, 148
Wiggins, Hannah, 38, 284
Wigings, James, 38, 113, 284
  Stephen, 363
  Susannah, 45
  Thomas, 45
Wilcocks, Elizabeth, 358
Wilcockson, Isaac, 167
Wiley, John, 75
  William, 75
Wilgus, William, 372
Wilhelm, Margaret, 358
Wilkes, Edward, Jr., 19
Wilkins, Amos, 357
  Elizabeth, 357
  James, 347
  Joanna, 127
  John, 278, 329, 347, 364
  John, Jr., 347
  Lydia, 357
  Rachel, 14
  Sarah, 347
  Thomas, 28, 152, 162, 278, 357
  Thomas, Jr., 152
  William, 14, 28, 75, 114, 128, 139, 307, 347, 357, 364
  William, Jr., 307
Wilkinson, Edward, 355
  Edward, Jr., 224
  John, 203, 204
  Joseph, 23, 162, 351
  Richard, 12, 30, 230
  Sarah, 38
Willard, Thomas, 237
Willets (Willits), Amos, 358
  John, 109, 235, 252, 304
  Jonathan, 134
  Joseph, 169
  Michael, 358
  Richard, 36, 180, 241, 286, 358
  Richard, Jr., 36
  Sarah, 241, 358
  Solomon, Jr., 134
  Thomas, 346
  Timothy, Jr., 29
Williams, Abraham, 359

Amos, 344
Ann, 234, 344
Bathsheba, 282
Benjamin, 238, 358
Charles, 234
Daniel, 220, 296
David, 359
Ebenezer, 34, 358
Edward, 27, 57, 180, 276, 332
Elihu, 10, 198, 344
Enoch, 358
George, 251, 344
Gershom, 20
Grace, 234
Hannah, 69, 220
Humphrey, 344
Isaac, 302, 346
Israel, 149, 331, 358
James, 233, 358
Joanna, 282, 358, 359
John, 129, 203, 210, 344, 353, 369
Jonathan, 190, 358
Joseph, 30
Mary, 237, 238, 302, 344, 358
Mindwell, 358
Nathaniel, 238, 358
Rachel, 358
Reese, 13, 264
Samuel, 78, 219, 236, 237
Sarah, 238, 344, 358
Tatum, 57
Thomas, 219, 267, 358
Timothy, 358
William, 230
Williamson, Aaron, 359
  Aeltje, 73
  Benjamin, 359
  Catherine, 359
  Daniel, 359
  David, 150, 187
  Elbert, 187
  Elizabeth, 359
  Gerard, 37, 145, 188, 192, 205, 260, 272
  Hannah, 368
  Jacob, 359
  Jacobus, 342
  James, 218
  Jane, 73, 359
  John, 191, 368
  Margaret, 91, 359
  Mary, 359
  Mathias, 58, 321
  Peter, 73, 101, 123
  Rachel, 359, 361
  Robert, 359
  Sarah, 359
  William, 34, 55, 101, 185, 195, 203, 359
Willing, John, 194
Willis, Benjamin, 360
  David, 359, 360
  Elizabeth, 360
  Hannah, 223, 360
  Isaac, 215, 360
  John, 358
  Joseph, 360
  Mary, 360
  Micaja, 361
  Patience, 359
  Robert, 64
  Samuel, 67, 91, 359
  Stephen, 250, 360
  Thomas, 222
  Timothy, 223

INDEX OF NAMES OF PERSONS 461

William, 56
Willocks, George, 198, 268
Wills, Aaron, 360
  Abigail, 361
  Daniel, 134, 202, 360
  Daniel, Jr., 130
  David, 137
  Elizabeth, 361
  Hannah, 25
  Jacob, 107
  James, 36, 41, 138, 190, 368, 369
  John, 113, 253
  Jonathan, 50
  Keziah, 361
  Margaret, 103, 361
  Mary, 107, 202, 361
  Meribah, 345
  Micajah, 137, 156, 167, 172, 199, 201, 253, 357
  Moses, 360
  Noah, 361
  Rebecca, 155, 156, 253
  Robert, 140
  Thomas, 107, 361
  William, 361
Wilmot, Edward, 64, 186, 280, 287, 335, 338
Wilson (Willson), Abraham, 167
  Adam, 362
  Andrew, 362, 363
  Benjamin, 45, 362
  Christian, 17, 362
  Elizabeth, 362
  Euphemia, 361
  Frederick, 32
  Gabriel, 241
  Hannah, 312, 362, 363
  James, 94, 95, 108, 241, 257, 362
  Jane, 244, 362
  John, 217, 241, 362
  John, Jr., 54
  Joseph, 312
  Joseph, Jr., 315
  Margaret, 362
  Martha, 361, 362
  Mary, 362
  Peter, 300, 362
  Rachell, 361
  Robert, 241
  Samuel, 208, 241, 369, 370
  Samuel, Jr., 370
  Sarah, 230, 347, 353
  Sevill, 230, 346
Wimmer, Vankey, 295
Winans, Elydia, 183
  Isaac, 269
  Josiah, 278, 285, 292
  William, 19, 21, 155, 275
Winder, Elizabeth, 236
  John, 297
Windsor, George, 266
Wines, Zerviah, 363
Wingfield, Mary, 363
Winne, Abraham, 363
  Catherine, 363
  John, 363
  Leah, 363
  Margaret, 363
  Marte, 363
Winter Andrew, 288
  Ann, 363
  Catherine, 363
  Deborah, 363
  Frona Catharina, 183
  Hannah, 363
  Henry, 183
  James, 363
  Jonas, 348
  Mary, 363
  Moses, 363
  Thomas, 348
Wintermute, Philip, 353
Winterstine, Antye, 108
Wirt, Peter, 188, 205
Wishart, William, 103
Wistar, Caspar, 184
  Richard, 283, 293
Wogelom, John, 88
Wolcutt, Benjamin, 174
Wombock,, Ann, 281
Wood (Woods), Aaron, 365
  Abijah, 367
  Ann, 91, 344, 347
  Christopher, 209, 333, 365, 366, 367
  Daniel, 344
  David, 364, 371
  Deborah, 364
  Elias, 364, 365
  Elizabeth, 344
  Elnathan, 365
  Fortunatus, 321
  Francis, 28
  Gabriel, 217
  George, 183
  Hannah, 365, 367
  Henry, 20, 43, 61, 89, 114, 154, 161, 205, 220, 305, 347, 358
  Hopestill, 367
  James, 28, 128, 347, 364, 365
  Jean, 365
  Jacob, 364
  Jechonias, 173, 364
  Jehu, 364
  Jeremiah, 26, 193, 364
  Job, 365
  John, 184, 215, 301, 331, 344, 364
  Joseph, 125, 127, 183, 217, 278, 309
  Joshua, 221
  Mary, 344, 347, 364, 365
  Margaret, 365
  Matthew, 365
  Phebe, 183, 364, 365, 367
  Rachel, 221
  Rebecca, 14, 365, 367
  Richard, 19, 116, 367
  Ruth, 364
  Samuel, 22, 344, 358, 365, 369
  Sarah, 367
  Tabitha, 365
  Thomas, 237
  William, 13, 14, 58, 77, 221, 236, 267, 304, 318, 347, 364, 365
Woodbridge, Mary, 366
Woodcock, Elizabeth, 207, 208
  Richard, 207
Wooden, James, 149
  Peter, 214
Woodhouse, Anthony, 40
Woodmansee, David, 72
  Gabriel, 72
Woodnut, James Mason, 56
  Elizabeth, 366
  Henry, 56, 366
  Jonathan, 40, 56, 217, 366
  Richard, 23, 40, 56, 133, 152, 366
  Sarah, 56, 104

Woodrow, Henry, 119, 139
  Susanna, 119
Woodruff, Abigail, 367
  Abraham, 260
  Abner, 219, 220, 367
  Benjamin, 222, 366
  Catura, 366
  Cooper, 275, 367
  David, 366
  Ebenezer, 366
  Elihu, 219
  Elizabeth, 367
  Enos, 116
  Esther, 366
  Hannah, 366, 367
  Isaac, 284, 340, 366
  James, 54, 366
  Jesse, 366
  John, 203, 259, 366, 367
  Jonathan, 367
  Josiah, 260
  Lydia, 366
  Mary, 366
  Mathias, 367
  Merriam, 366
  Michael, 219
  Nathaniel, 35
  Phebe, 314, 366
  Rachel, 220, 366, 367
  Samuel, 26, 93, 122, 126, 135, 239, 365, 367
  Stephen, 222
  Thomas, 66, 67, 78, 190, 222
  Thomas, Jr., 325
  Timothy, 366
Woodward, Anthony, 310, 367
  Anthony, Jr., 9, 74, 240
  Apollo, 367
  Elizabeth, 65
  Hannah 367
  Henry, 300, 302
  John, 149
  Joseph, 28, 65, 367
  Ralph, 370
  Samuel, 102, 181
  Thomas, 270, 367
Woolard, Benjamin, 358
  (see Willard)
Woolcox, Joseph, 23
Woolley, Benjamin, 175
  Benjamin, Jr., 297
  Daniel, 175
  Edmund, 371
  George, 200
  James, 297
  Sarah, 371
  William, 175
Woolman, Asher, 50, 134, 360
  John, 13, 17, 30, 36, 40, 90, 123, 137, 138, 141, 233, 244, 288, 291, 298, 352, 360, 369
Woolsey, Henry, 86, 285, 326, 338
  Jeremiah, 48, 133
  Rachel, 40
Woolston, Ann, 361, 368, 369
  Barzillai, 368, 369
  Cornwell, 368
  Epicarius, 368
  Hance, 180, 365
  Hannah, 47, 192, 368
  Jacob, 244, 368
  John, 369
  Joseph, 369
  Joshua, 361, 369
  Lettice, 368, 369
  Melentus, 368
  Michael, 368, 369
  Newbold, 368
  Prudence, 368
  Ruth, 361, 368
  Samuel, 138, 361
  Sarah, 368, 369
  William, 233
Woolverton, Abigail 155
  Charles, 284
  Isaac, 155
  Mary, 369
  Roger, 277
  Thomas, 252, 326
Worford, John, 120
Worrell, Gibson, 251
  Jacob, 28
  Joseph, 148
Worth, Samuel, 156, 240
  Sarah, 145
  William, 92, 96, 156, 165, 178
Worthington, Ephraim, 40
  Henry, 148
  John, 40
  Sarah, 369
Worthley, Lydia, 369
Wortman, Bout, 108
  John, 42, 108
  Lodawick, 331
  Margaret, 41, 42
  Peter, 41, 42, 100
  William, 101
Worton, Benjamin, 238, 287, 337
  Sarah, 238, 369
Wouterse, Franscoys, 63
  Johannes, 335
  Sauke, 43
Wrag, Capt. 215
Wray, Bowes, 40, 93
Wren, Ann, 225
Wright, Abednego, 370
  Abner, 63
  Alyday, 370
  Amos, 31, 32, 237
  Ann, 31, 116, 370, 371
  David, 349, 370, 371
  Elizabeth, 103, 137, 370
  Eve, 370
  Frettwell, 126, 356
  George, 371
  Hannah, 75
  Isaac, 112
  Jeremiah, 60, 187, 291
  John, 371
  Jonathan, 23, 148, 279, 370, 371
  Joseph, 23, 29, 35, 39, 67, 124, 140, 190, 249, 270, 278, 371
  Lititia, 370
  Lydia, 371
  Mahlon, 370, 371
  Margaret, 63
  Mary, 370, 371
  Nathan, 370
  Prudence, 370
  Rebecca, 281
  Richard, 341, 371
  Robert, 370
  Samuel, 87, 108, 137, 270, 277
  Samuel, Jr., 49, 102, 215, 292
  Sarah, 371
  Susannah, 370
  Thomasin, 370
  William, 301, 370
Wuchman, Nicolaus, 107
Wulker, Charles, 273

INDEX OF NAMES OF PERSONS

Wyatt, Bartholomew, Jr., 298, 366
Wyckoff (Wikoff), Adriaentie, 372
  Cornelius, 16, 110, 206, 372
  Garret, 65, 190, 194, 195
  Geertye, 342
  Jacob, 218, 261, 335
  John, 239
  Maddelenti, 371
  Martin, 12, 371
  Mary, 372
  Nicholas, 12, 255
  Nicholas, Jr., 255
  Peter, 128, 129, 187, 218, 261, 325, 371
  Samuel, 37, 255
  Simon, 342
  Simon, Jr., 334
  Willentie, 371
Wynants, Josiah, 155
Wynkoop, Benjamin, 16, 206
  Cornelius C., 8

Y

Yager, John, 372
  John Peter, 372
  Peter, 372
  Philip, 372
  William, 372
Yapp, Thomas, 369
Yard, Ann, 85, 248
  Benjamin, 100, 372
  Isaac, 64
  James, 248
  John, 100, 179, 248
  Joseph, 85, 100, 103, 190, 197, 248, 333, 371
  Margaret, 372
  William, 290
Yardly, Mary, 114
  Thomas, 114
Yates, Benjamin, 285, 293
  James, 32
  Joseph, 101
  Rachel, 309
  William, 372
Yearling, Leonard, 107

Yoger, Philip, 7
Yohe, Adam, 111
Young, David, 348
  Elizabeth, 79
  Henry, 104, 143, 169, 174, 192, 207, 357
  James, 284, 313
  Job, 143
  Johanna, 79
  John, 49, 263, 364
  Mary, 143
  Millicent, 179
  Peter, 183, 343
  Sarah, 217
  Timothy, 263
  Tunis, 73
  William, 263
Younglove, Isaiah, 125
  Harme, 182
Yuriansen (see Juriansen)

Z

Zabriski, Albert, 373
  Albert C., 6
  Andries, 373
  Antie, 373
  Fitie, 373
  Henritie, 373
  Jacob, 373
  John, 373
  Peter, 351
  Steven, 373
Zane, Isaac, 373
  Jonathan, 24
  Joseph, 148, 274, 333
  Mary, 142, 158, 373
  Rebecca, 373
  Rhoda, 373
  Robert, 292
  Thomas, 373
Zeale, Daniel, 118, 316
Zeans, Joseph, 274
Zutphen, Aurt, 204
  Dirck, Jr., 204
  (see Sutphen)

Index of Place-Names

NOTE.—This Index has the modern spellings as a rule. Names of counties in New Jersey are omitted.

A

Absecom, 172
Acquackenonk, 128, 182, 243, 335, 338, 343, 346, 373
Alamatunk river, 198, 243
Albany county, N. Y., 341
Allentown, 88, 109, 133, 135, 185, 271
Alloways creek, 9, 10, 13, 27, 52, 92, 94, 109, 118, 125, 139, 167, 184, 223, 224, 225, 226, 245, 249, 262, 267, 284, 286, 300, 314, 315, 316, 322, 323, 326, 333, 341, 349, 360, 364, 365, 366, 369, 371
Alloways Creek township, 35, 255, 282, 343, 344, 348, 358
Amboy, 117, 198, 250, 313, 324 (see Perth Amboy)
Amwell township, 7, 19, 21, 36, 50, 53, 72, 81, 83, 89, 91, 135, 141, 145, 157, 178, 179, 183, 185, 186, 188, 189, 191, 192, 196, 198, 205, 213, 233, 256, 260, 265, 268, 272, 281, 284, 287, 297, 300, 303, 311, 313, 319, 326, 349, 354, 359, 362, 372
Annekey's creek, 303
Assanpink creek, 39, 169
Assisconk creek, 356
Attapunck Hana, 354

B

Back creek (Va.), 136
Barleborough, (Eng.), 207
Barnegat, 72
Basking Ridge, 180, 185, 186, 209, 210, 230, 268
Bedminster township, 28, 83, 124, 132, 155
Beef Point, 178
Belleville, 349
Bergen township, 91, 261, 297
Bermuda island, 344
Bernards township, 213
Bethlehem township, 8, 11, 19, 29, 61, 64, 68, 70, 82, 120, 170, 171, 273, 295, 300, 301
Big Timber creek, 172
Black Stake creek, 26
Block island (R. I.), 273
Blue Anchor, 368
Boiling Spring 178
Bordentown, 180, 262, 295, 317, 323, 352, 370
Boston (Mass.), 48
Bound Brook, 72, 146, 209, 212, 303, 334, 355, 362

Bradley's creek, 84
Bricks county (Pa.), 26
Bridgetown, 11, 17, 27, 31, 40, 45, 54, 63, 64, 121, 201, 213, 244, 290, 295, 300
Bridgewater township, 34, 35, 62, 73, 146, 147, 236, 308, 325, 338
Bridgewater (Eng.), 50
Bristol (Pa.), 54, 180, 185, 234, 370
Bristow township (Pa.), 262
Bull Skin (Va.), 136
Burlington, 11, 13, 28, 39, 45, 47, 50, 52, 56, 59, 62, 64, 65, 76, 81, 89, 90, 102, 121, 124, 129, 131, 132, 134, 137, 141, 142, 148, 151, 153, 159, 180, 181, 185, 188, 191, 199, 206, 213, 214, 216, 224, 229, 235, 259, 262, 264, 273, 279, 283, 287, 290, 295 297, 301, 306, 321, 330, 339, 341, 349, 350, 354, 356, 359, 361, 371
Burlington island, 90, 371
Burnt swamp, 371
Bushwick (L. I.), 258

C

Cape Fear river, 196
Cape island, 143
Cape May, 104, 144, 169, 193, 195, 222, 223, 235, 258, 308, 360
Carletown, 40
Carroway, 187
Cedar brook, 92, 247
Cedar swamp, 136
Chester township (Burl. Co.), 13, 16, 35, 36, 46, 105, 123, 136, 154, 161, 181, 189, 191, 198, 200, 202, 203, 218, 221, 229, 245, 278, 290, 311, 344, 345, 347, 348, 370
Chesterfield township, 6, 8, 25, 28, 31, 44, 61, 66, 96, 102, 111, 114, 117, 129, 154, 164, 165, 174, 198, 233, 242, 246, 252, 262, 292, 318, 319, 365, 370
Christian Bridge (Pa.), 181
Cleeter (Eng.), 7
Clenmell creek, 336
Cocxing, 311
Cohansey, 24, 40, 49, 76, 85, 173, 176, 277, 288, 289, 299, 313, 341
Cold brook, 197
Cold spring, 143
Cooper's creek, 183, 305
Cranbury, 150, 176, 211, 231, 250, 276
Crosswicks creek, 114, 262, 273
Curtis' mill, 114

D

Dead creek, 273
Deep Run, 196
Deerfield township, 17, 24, 27, 46, 67, 85, 112, 115, 126, 180, 203, 223, 226, 238, 239, 258, 299, 308, 313, 314, 320, 325, 326, 331, 354, 365, 366, 369
Delaware Falls, 198, 342
Delaware river, 162, 228, 248
Deptford township, 13, 14, 15, 21, 23, 25, 43, 47, 49, 53, 58, 75, 76, 94, 96, 97, 114, 127, 128, 130, 152, 155, 199, 205, 213, 216, 218, 220, 221, 229, 248, 261, 266, 267, 278, 296, 307, 317, 329, 331, 346, 347, 350, 351, 361, 364, 372
Derby (Eng.), 207
Devil's brook, 88
Dividing creek, 120, 121, 269, 328
Domine's Hook, 258
Dublin (Ire.), 233
Duke Creek hundred (Del), 241
Dutchess county (N. Y.), 341

E

Egg Harbor, 60, 67, 74, 86, 90, 129, 194, 198, 283, 300, 345, 352
Elizabeth (Borough, Township, etc.), 10, 19, 20, 21, 25, 26, 29, 34, 35, 37, 53, 54, 56, 58, 59, 60, 64, 66, 67, 70, 77, 78, 79, 87, 90, 91, 94, 97, 106, 121, 122, 132, 133, 134, 135, 151, 155, 157, 159, 171, 176, 182, 183, 184, 189, 190, 193, 195, 203, 209, 214, 215, 218, 219, 220, 222, 223, 225, 228, 237, 239, 240, 241, 249, 256, 259, 260, 263, 269, 274, 275, 278, 279, 283, 284, 285, 292, 293, 298, 308, 315, 317, 321, 322, 328, 329, 331, 334, 340, 343, 358, 359, 360, 367
Elsinborough township, 48, 86, 95, 100, 140, 171, 229, 235, 236, 296, 341
Evesham township, 9, 11, 13, 14, 23, 30, 35, 36 37, 89, 102, 104, 110, 125, 126, 131, 132, 136, 137, 138, 139, 155, 156, 161, 164, 167, 168, 172, 186, 199, 201, 202, 218, 221, 224, 227, 247, 250, 253, 254, 273, 286, 311, 314, 330, 345, 357

F

Fairfield township, 17, 18, 22, 24, 27, 38, 42, 46, 51, 60, 67, 81, 85, 86, 115 122, 142, 146, 166, 173, 177, 180, 238, 239, 247, 251, 258, 267, 278, 285, 287, 289, 303, 313, 314, 322, 328, 352, 354, 355
Fairfield (Conn.), 16
Fishing creek, 355
Five-Mile beach, 143
Five-Mile run, 39
Flatbush (L. I.), 218
Flybrook, 196
Freehold, 27, 41, 64, 67, 73, 74, 77, 80, 90, 93, 123, 161, 162, 187, 189, 190, 204, 210, 243, 248, 259, 294, 299, 305, 309, 325, 350, 363
Fulling brook, 135

G

Gales bay, 172
Gloucester, 128, 136, 141, 305, 317
Gloucester township, 25, 27, 45, 57, 58, 61, 70, 74, 87, 99, 104, 142, 152, 158, 168, 172, 176, 180, 203, 250, 261, 273, 276, 282, 286, 296, 304, 324, 327, 330, 331, 348, 358
Goodluckin, 92
Goshen township (N. Y.), 138
Granage, 271
Gravelly Run creek, 299
Gravesend (L. I.), 107, 189
Gravitz run, 144
Great Egg Harbor, 6, 70, 94, 130, 172, 194, 198, 230, 298, 302, 304, 308, 329
Great Egg Harbor river, 131
Great Flat, 207
Great Neck, 348
Great Pond, 76
Great Swamp brook, 259
Great Timber creek, 158, 168
Green brook, 359
Greenwich township, 9, 14, 15, 19, 28, 29, 30, 38, 43, 44, 49, 51, 53, 57, 59, 62, 63, 64, 69, 76, 83, 87, 93, 103, 112, 114, 115, 116, 120, 124, 127, 128, 132, 138, 150, 152, 153, 156, 157, 162, 163, 166, 171, 181, 182, 184, 193, 199, 200, 203, 204, 205, 213, 217, 221, 227, 229, 232, 242, 243, 246, 250, 252, 254, 255, 263, 269, 276, 278, 297, 299, 302, 305, 306, 309, 317, 318, 324, 325, 327, 331, 336, 338, 341, 351, 353, 364, 365, 397

H

Hackensack, 33, 91, 225, 332, 336
Hackensack river, 102
Haddonfield, 15, 70, 158
Haines Mills, 136
Hancock township, 11
Hanover township, 24, 36, 39, 49, 54, 68, 69, 101, 102, 119, 125, 130, 187, 208, 220, 238, 256, 281, 290, 292, 297, 330, 349, 355, 363
Hardwick township, 134, 168, 170, 188, 189, 208, 369, 370
Hazelwood Neck, 19
Hell Neck, 85
Homan's creek, 76
Homan's Neck, 90
Hope, 56
Hopewell township, 17, 18, 22, 30, 32, 41, 48, 51, 52, 67, 75, 84, 86, 95, 96, 97, 98, 109, 113, 133, 147, 155, 170, 173, 178, 179, 184, 185, 188, 204, 213, 217, 225, 226, 227, 228, 232, 241, 242, 247, 258, 265, 270, 277, 279, 282, 287, 289, 299, 300, 311, 316, 319, 326, 338, 349, 366

INDEX OF PLACE-NAMES 467

Horessimese, 339
Horse Neck, 277, 305
House Lot creek, 84

I
Indian run, 272

J
Jamaica (W. I.), 182, 329
Jarret's Gut, 207
Jumping brook, 135

K
Kensington, 236
Kent county (Del), 12
Kingston, 196, 197, 358
Kingwood township, 39, 62, 81, 107, 111, 120, 141, 153, 172, 187, 198, 365
Kopopon creek, 158

L
Landing, 197
Lebanon township, 22, 34, 39, 81, 117, 147, 158, 188, 191, 212, 242, 282, 287, 339
Lesliesland, 187
Lewistown (Del.), 103
Little Egg Harbor, 42, 60, 67, 72, 194, 344
Little Silver Neck, 169
Lockheart's Hill, 84
London (Eng.), 295
Long Bridge, 192
Long Hill, 88, 178
Long Island, 86, 95, 301
Lowland creek, 336
Lower Penn's Neck, 38
Lyons Farms, 364

M
Maidenhead township, 12, 38, 39, 85, 106, 157, 170, 178, 241, 240, 242, 259, 292, 299, 310
Manalapon, 276
Manasquan, 9, 83, 117, 223 (see Squan)
Mannington township, 10, 23, 40, 56, 80, 86, 94, 133, 150, 152, 180, 212, 217, 223, 225, 229, 236, 256, 263, 266, 274, 298, 300, 302, 354, 366
Mansfield township, 5, 16, 24, 25, 31, 37, 44, 77, 114, 129, 139, 141, 149, 165, 174, 177, 234, 243, 257, 262, 279, 280, 292, 293, 300, 315, 322, 329, 370
Man's Grove, 197
Mantua creek, 263
Maple Island creek, 348
Marble Mountain, 90
Marple township, 124
Martain's Neck, 217
Matshepeconck, 354
Maurice river township, 53, 85, 159, 160, 161, 231, 251, 269, 287, 345, 352, 356, 367
Mechepotuxing, 50
Mendham township, 17, 28, 50, 68, 88, 189, 195, 208, 209, 211, 242, 316
Merriman's Hole, 169

Mespets Kill (N. Y.), 258
Metetienunk, 196
Metuchen, 34, 84
Middlebrook, 236
Middlebush, 128, 218, 260, 261, **334**
Middletown, 37, 41, 47, 65, 66, **68**, 70, 73, 95, 129, 135, 153, 160, 175, 187, 204, 212, 231, 238, 246, 252, 270, 271, 281, 288, 303, 309, 312, 324, 325, 332, 350, 357, 362, 363
Middletown Point, 77, 249, 271, 323
Mill creek, 50, 134
Mill pond creek, 44
Millstone, 371
Millstone river, 76, 197, 211, 260, 342
Minachquay, 332
Minnisink, 72, 274, 353
Monantico creek, 173
Montague township, 353, 354
Moorestown, 74
Moorland township (Pa.), 361
Morristown, 16, 41, 54, 64, 66, 102, 124, 149, 150, 166, 167, 171, 208, 209, 224, 255, 265, 269, 310, 325, 363, 367
Morris township, 179, 243, 316
Mount Carmel, 76, 135
Mount Gulian (N. Y.), 341
Mount Holly, 40, 74, 80, 123, 141, 260, 368
Mullica river, 90
Musconetcong river, 137, 153, 191
Musquenica, 368

N
Namenock, 353
Nassau island (N. Y.), 27, 258
Neshanic, 280
Newark, 11, 16, 20, 21, 25, 26, 42, 44, 45, 48, 51, 52, 63, 69, 78, 79, 81, 83, 90, 94, 112, 147, 151, 159, 164, 178, 191, 209, 210, 219, 220, 226, 230, 233, 238, 239, 243, 249, 254, 264, 267, 268, 269, 272, 276, 279, 285, 293, 298, 310, 315, 317, 321, 327, 330, 333, 335, 343, 346, 347, 348, 358, 359, 363, 355
New Barbadoes township, 351
New Barbadoes Neck, 182
New Brittain, 275
New Brunswick, 16, 22, 27, 48, 58, 88, 95, 97, 111, 121, 135, 150, 169, 171, 189, 192, 197, 207, 209, 241, 246, 262, 268, 272, 274, 304, 307, 312, 338, 342, 355, 359, 361
Newcastle county (Pa.), 12
New Hanover township, 12, 46, 49, 90, 101, 102, 119, 181, 195, 215, 235, 237, 247, 270, 271, 277, 291
New Hurley (N. Y.), 333
Newport (R. I.), 299
New Providence township, 88, 293
New Stafford, 68, 251
Newton township (Burl. co.), 7, 8, 12, 32, 45, 54, 55, 57, 65, 69, 70, 96, 97, 99, 102, 104, 108, 114, 119, 124, 127, 149, 154, 156, 158, 164, 168, 169, 183, 186, 189, 221, 229, 234, 237, 252, 257, 258, 263, 266, 270, 293, 297, 301, 307, 326, 330, 373

Newton (Sussex co.), 369
Newton creek, 8
New Utrecht (L. I.), 107
Newry (Ire.), 171
Newtown (N. Y.), 27
New Windsor township, 179, 282, 294, 315
New York City, 8, 32, 48, 58, 151, 171, 182, 183, 192, 206, 211, 233, 234, 246, 258, 270, 297, 301, 310, 326, 329, 332, 341, 342, 346, 353, 357, 366
Northampton river, 167
Northampton township, 13, 16, 17, 27, 30, 31, 40, 41, 45, 46, 54, 69, 78, 81, 83, 107, 112, 125, 127, 131, 137, 138, 141, 144, 157, 163, 190, 194, 200, 201, 202, 222, 230, 234, 239, 257, 260, 265, 266, 275, 288, 291, 295, 298, 300, 328, 352, 360, 361, 363, 368, 369
North Branch river, 42, 99, 265, 266
Nottingham township, 14, 44, 82, 96, 114, 165, 198, 233, 241, 248, 260, 262, 271, 307
Nova Scotia, 26
Numies, 142

O

Oldman's creek, 87, 103, 317
Oxford township, 11, 150, 214
Oyster creek, 157

P

Padget's Point, 289
Paramus, 6, 37, 295, 373
Passaic river, 25, 373
Paxton (Pa.), 193
Penn's Neck township, 23, 29, 54, 55, 67, 70, 71, 73, 93, 99, 100, 101, 106, 108, 124, 132, 145, 156, 159, 162, 171, 172, 175, 181, 186, 190, 197, 199, 203, 206, 210, 213, 231, 234, 240, 245, 246, 249, 253, 278, 283, 300, 306, 328, 337, 341, 359
Pennington, 226
Pensaukin creek, 228, 345
Pequannock township, 10, 145, 213, 309, 333, 343
Perth Amboy, 39, 41, 46, 58, 89, 92, 94, 98, 112, 119, 131, 133, 147, 150, 154, 164, 166, 171, 173, 176, 177, 194, 196, 197, 213, 224, 235, 243, 244, 245, 254, 261, 262, 264, 268, 271, 272, 278, 282, 302, 303, 304, 305, 306, 311, 323, 336, 339, 358, 360, 368 (see Amboy)
Pexcroft (Eng.), 207
Philadelphia, 33, 39, 44, 48, 53, 54, 58, 64, 67, 87, 101, 103, 104, 121, 127, 128, 133, 147, 151, 156, 159, 180, 192, 204, 218, 219, 221, 233, 245, 252, 263, 293, 298, 307, 317, 331, 350
Phillipsburg, 358
Pike's brook, 84
Piles creek, 275
Piles Grove township, 5, 20, 21, 26, 53, 54, 65, 87, 92, 93, 98, 99, 103, 105, 106, 127, 131, 135, 138, 140, 162, 166, 167, 171, 181, 186, 193, 205, 206, 211, 212, 227, 246, 247, 263, 274, 278, 283, 298, 300, 313, 336, 337, 354, 364
Piscataway township, 34, 47, 51, 61, 66, 85, 97, 98, 100, 101, 102, 116, 118, 146, 152, 153, 181, 195, 206, 216, 217, 218, 244, 247, 257, 262, 269, 275, 276, 277, 291, 296, 303, 307, 343, 349
Plum Point, 370
Plumstead township, 192
Pohatcong creek, 153
Pond creek, 144
Poplar's Branch, 263
Potomac river (Va.), 337
Prince Maurice river, 173
Princeton, 47, 48, 52, 88, 165, 196, 197, 253, 310

Q

Queen Anne county (Md.), 13
Queenstown, 226

R

Raccoon creek, 14, 104, 205
Ragged Point, 172
Rahway, 131, 224
Rahway meadows, 44, 78, 193
Rahway Neck, 329
Rahway river, 21, 79, 219, 240, 256, 329
Rancocas creek, 113, 167, 201, 265, 302, 345
Raritan, 47
Raritan Landing, 55, 99, 306
Raritan meadows, 60
Raritan river, 42, 140, 169, 197, 340, 362
Readington township, 12, 16, 37, 64, 72, 107, 108, 186, 187, 188, 191, 198, 241, 280, 282, 293, 294, 333, 339, 370
Recklesstown, 246
Rehoboth, 90
Rockaway, 208, 334, 367
Rocky Hill, 136, 147, 197, 211, 312, 349
Ross's brook, 329
Rotterton (Eng.), 7
Roxbury township, 5, 28, 125, 189, 191, 265, 286, 307, 329
Rumford (Eng.), 7

S

Saddle River township, 23, 185, 234, 332
St. Kitts, W. I., 190
Salem, 13, 17, 22, 39, 82, 100, 122, 129, 142, 147, 152, 154, 170, 187, 206, 217, 220, 229, 246, 274, 288, 294, 308, 313, 320, 321, 335, 341, 346, 366, 373
Salem creek, 249
Salem township, 320
Salford (Eng.), 245
Salisbury township (Pa.), 191
San Island (N. Y.), 218

INDEX OF PLACE-NAMES 469

Schraalenburgh, 91
Scotch Plains, 182
Secaucus, 102
Second River township, 43, 63, 182, 293, 335
Sheffield (Eng.), 207
Sherburn (Eng.), 69
Shrewsbury, 9, 10, 29, 35, 36, 40, 55, 71, 75, 83, 92, 117, 118, 123, 130, 145, 150, 160, 169, 175, 193, 195, 196, 198, 200, 201, 202, 203, 204, 234, 240, 243, 244, 254, 296, 297, 344, 352, 353, 367, 368, 369
Shrewsbury township, 68, 92, 174, 205, 309, 312
Sippock's Neck, 186
Six-Mile Run, 107, 342
Slooping creek, 79
Solebury (Pa.), 172
South Amboy, 249, 274, 349 (see Amboy)
South Branch river, 47, 62, 140, 280, 312
Southold (L. I.), 222
South river, 216
Sow and Pig's creek, 289, 304
Spotswood North brook, 77
Springfield township (Burl. Co), 10, 14, 16, 31, 33, 39, 45, 49, 54, 113, 118, 126, 129, 130, 144, 201, 245, 264, 281, 292, 345
Squan, 189 (see Manasquan)
Squan river, 196
Staten Island, 98, 198, 223, 237
Stockins hollow, 371
Stony brook, 88, 310
Stow Creek township, 40, 41, 49, 51, 85, 92, 101, 114, 115, 116, 132, 160, 167, 193, 204, 242, 247, 291, 294, 301, 302, 325
Stow Neck, 364
Strawberry hill, 84
Swanwick (Pa.), 12

T

Telpahakin, 90
Ten-Mile Run, 22, 293
Tewokhaw, 335
Tewksbury township, 15
Three-Mile Run, 71
Timber creek, 153, 370
Tindall's island, 40
Tipperary (Ire.), 133
Tohoconchung, 76
Toms river, 135
Trenton, 12, 14, 18, 22, 41, 44, 52, 68, 72, 75, 76, 89, 100, 130, 131, 133, 134, 153, 160, 179, 190, 197, 198, 204, 206, 210, 216, 217, 218, 219, 220, 226, 228, 231, 233, 238, 241, 252, 253, 260, 261, 269, 278, 283, 289, 297, 319, 325, 333, 349, 361, 370, 371, 372
Trenton township, 22, 121
Tuckaho, 51, 144, 235, 283
Turkey, 25, 53 (see New Providence)
Turkey Point, 328
Turkis Hill, 44
Two-Mile brook, 178

U

Ulster county (N. Y.), 341
Upper Freehold township, 35, 45, 55, 57, 58, 65, 66, 74, 75, 109, 119, 165, 171, 192, 194, 199, 224, 272, 273, 294, 308, 309, 318, 324, 331, 357, 367
Upper Penns Neck, 365

W

Wading river, 90
Walpack township, 333, 353
Walton (Eng.), 141
Wantage township, 362, 363
Warwick township (Pa.), 273
Waterford township, 15, 20, 36, 48, 61, 88, 89, 99, 104, 105, 110, 124, 141, 154, 158, 160, 161, 181, 183, 228, 236, 245, 270, 275, 305, 311, 324, 337, 345, 357
Weesel, 128
Westerleigh (Eng), 141
Westfield township, 132, 222, 259, 367
White Haven (Eng.), 7
Whitekill, 114
White Marsh township (Pa.), 229
Wiccacoe (Pa.), 304
Willingborough township, 49, 50, 75, 81, 112, 113, 134, 151, 165, 311, 359
Wilmington (Del.), 82, 156
Wiltshire (Eng.), 60
Windsor township, 14, 39, 82, 165, 179, 180, 210, 239, 250, 311, 315
Wistow (Eng.), 103
Woodbridge, 7, 12, 18, 19, 30, 31, 33, 34, 42, 43, 44, 47, 51, 60, 63, 66, 82, 84, 90, 95, 97, 100, 105, 112, 116, 117, 122, 123, 131, 132, 133, 150, 151, 152, 163, 171, 173, 174, 180, 184, 194, 212, 216, 217, 223, 224, 225, 226, 227, 228, 230, 236, 242, 258, 275, 283, 291, 298, 299, 308, 311, 323, 325, 328, 349, 351, 355, 366
Woodbridge township, 62
Woodbury, 346
Woodbury creek, 138, 205, 236, 347
Woodruff's creek, 275
Worcester county (Md.), 12

www.ingramcontent.com/pod-product-compliance
Lightning Source LLC
Chambersburg PA
CBHW050829230426
43667CB00012B/1933

www.ingramcontent.com/pod-product-compliance
Lightning Source LLC
Chambersburg PA
CBHW050829230426
43667CB00012B/1933